For All University & Competitive Examinations in India

A Practical Guide to English Grammar

K P Thakur
MA, MEd, PhD, PGCTE (CIEFL, Hyderabad)
Former Principal, RDS College, Muzaffarpur

Bharati Bhawan
PUBLISHERS & DISTRIBUTORS

Published by
BHARATI BHAWAN (Publishers & Distributors)
www.bharatibhawan.in email: editorial@bbpd.in

4271/3 Ansari Road, Daryaganj, NEW DELHI 110 002, Phone: 23286557
A-61 B/2 Sector 63, NOIDA 201 307, Phone: 4757400
Thakurbari Road, PATNA 800 003, Phone: 2670325
10 Raja Subodh Mallick Square, KOLKATA 700 013, Phone: 22250651
No. 98 Sirsi Circle, Mysore Road, BENGALURU 560 018, Phone: 26740560

First edition 1982
Ninth edition 2002
2022 print

A Practical Guide to English Grammar
Printed at B B Printers, Patna-800 006

PREFACE

This book is meant for college students who have come through ten years of schooling. Some of its important features are as follows:

- It includes almost all the grammatical items necessary for an average student.
- In order to give the learner a real feel of the language, the book follows the descriptive approach, i.e., examples are given first followed by rules.
- Discussions and elaborations of rules have been kept to a bare minimum to avoid unnecessary strain on the learner's mind.
- Some examples have been worked out in each chapter before giving exercises. The aim here is to present a consolidated picture of the whole chapter at one place, and also to allow the learners to revise and master the whole chapter.
- A good deal of graded exercises have been given for all types of learners. Elementary, intermediate and advanced exercises on each chapter provide plenty of opportunities for them to learn the grammatical items thoroughly and well.
- An effort has been made to give exercises not only in isolated sentences but also in contexts. Such exercises should enable students to drill and practise English in meaningful and life-like situations.

Any credit, I happily share with you, but I am alone responsible for any flaw that might have crept in. I would sincerely welcome the comments and suggestions of students and learned teachers in the light of which I may like to improve the next edition of the book.

K P Thakur

CONTENTS

CHAPTER		PAGES
By + Agent	...	233
Deletion of 'by + agent'	...	233
Passive Verb Forms	...	234
Verb in the Simple Present Tense	...	235
Verb in the Simple Past Tense	...	235
Verb in the Simple Future Tense	...	235
Verb in the Present Continuous Tense	...	236
Verb in the Past Continuous Tense	...	236
Verb in the Present Perfect Tense	...	237
Verb in the Past Perfect Tense	...	237
Modal Verbs	...	238
Verbs With Two Objects	...	238
Passive of Commands: Let, Please, Kindly…	...	239
Passive of Yes-No Questions	...	240
Passive of Questions with Modal Verbs	...	241
Passive of Wh-Questions	...	241
Passive of Infinitives	...	242
Passive of Verb 'to be'	...	242
Passive of the Verb 'to have'	...	242
Passive of Verb + Prepositions	...	243
Another Word in Place of 'by'	...	243
Dummy 'it'	...	244
Passive of Negative Sentences	...	245
Double Passives	...	245
Use of Passive Voice	...	246
Examples Worked Out	...	246
Exercises	...	251
9. Prepositions	...	**261–317**
Kinds of Prepositions	...	261
Positions of Prepositions	...	262
Use of Some Prepositions	...	263
At, In (For Places)	...	266
On, In, At, By (For Time)	...	266
Between, Among	...	267
In, Into	...	267
Since, For	...	268
From, Since	...	268
To, Till, Until	...	268
By, With	...	269
During, For	...	269

❑

1 BASIC FACTS OF ENGLISH GRAMMAR

छात्रों को English Grammar के basic facts की जानकारी होगी। फिर भी उनकी सुविधा तथा ready reference के उद्देश्य से यहाँ कुछ key terms के definitions दिए जा रहे हैं।

Alphabetical order में दिए गए grammatical terms के definitions सरल और संक्षेप में हैं ताकि छात्रों को इस पुस्तक के main text को पढ़ने में किसी प्रकार की कठिनाई नहीं हो।

Abstract Noun : ऐसे शब्द जिनसे ऐसी वस्तुओं का बोध हो जिनका हम केवल अपने मन में अनुभव कर सकते हैं, पर जिन्हें हम न देख और न स्पर्श कर सकते हैं abstract noun (भाववाचक संज्ञा) कहलाते हैं। जैसे : doubt, height, life, geography इत्यादि।

Active Voice : verb के जिस रूप से subject की प्रधानता व्यक्त होती है, उसे active verb form कहते हैं। The subject of an active verb is usually the person or thing that does the action, or is responsible for what happens जैसे : breaks, told, will help आदि *active verb forms* हैं; is broken, was told, will be helped *passive verb forms* हैं।

Adjective : adjective उस शब्द को कहते हैं जिससे noun/pronoun के गुण, संख्या, मात्रा, क्रम इत्यादि का बोध हो। जैसे : green, hungry, impossible; a *green* apple, the *first* boy, I am *hungry*.

Adjective Clause : शब्दों का समूह या उपवाक्य जिसमें एक subject और एक verb हो और जो किसी noun का गुण बताए उसे adjective clause कहते हैं। जैसे : a *hungry* boy में hungry *adjective* है, किंतु The baby *that wants to eat* is crying में that wants to eat *adjective clause* है।

Adjectival Participle Clause : किसी adjective जैसा काम करनेवाले participle clause को adjectival participle clause कहते हैं। जैसे : Anybody *wanting to eat* should help themselves now. इस वाक्य में wanting to eat *adjectival participle clause* है।

Adverb : adverb उस शब्द को कहते हैं, जो किसी verb, adjective या अन्य किसी adverb की विशेषता बताए अथवा यह बताए कि कोई काम कब, कहाँ और कैसे होता है। जैसे : tomorrow, once, badly, there इत्यादि adverbs हैं। It rained *heavily*. She is *very* beautiful में heavily तथा very *adverbs* हैं।

Adverb Clause : adverb clause (उपवाक्य) वाक्य में adverb का कार्य करता है और वह किसी adjective, adverb या verb को modify करता है। जैसे : I will see you *tomorrow* में tomorrow *adverb* है; किंतु I will see you *when you get back* में when you get back *adverb clause* है।

Adverb Particle : up, out या off जैसा शब्द जिसका प्रयोग phrasal verb के part के रूप में किया जाता है adverb particle कहलाता है। जैसे : tell *off,* sold *out,* clean *up* इत्यादि।

Adverb Phrase : शब्दों का एक छोटा समूह (a short group of words) जो वही काम करे जो एक adverb करता है, adverb phrase कहलाता है। जैसे : on Monday. in the bathroom इत्यादि *adverb phrases* हैं।

Adverbial : शब्दों का एक समूह जो adverb, adverb phrase या adverb clause जैसा काम करे adverbial कहलाता है।

Adverbial Participle Clause : participle से आरंभ adverb clause को adverbial participle clause कहते हैं। जैसे : *Not knowing what to do,* I telephoned Mr Bose. इस वाक्य में not knowing what to do *adverbial participle clause* है।

Affirmative Sentence : स्वीकारात्मक वाक्य को affirmative sentence कहते हैं। An affirmative sentence is one that is not negative. जैसे : I agree *(affirmative)*. I don't agree *(negative)*.

Affix : anti-American, anti-communist, postwar, postnatal, older, younger, greenish, mannish शब्दों में anti-, post-, -er तथा -ish *affixes* हैं। (Anti- तथा post- को prefixes तथा -er एवं -ish को suffixes कहा जाता है।)

Agent : passive sentence में जिसके द्वारा कार्य किया जाता है उसे agent कहते हैं। जैसे : The picture was painted by *Mr Arora.* यहाँ Mr Arora *agent* है।

Alphabet : the set of letters used in writing any language, especially when arranged in order; the ABCDEFG............

Anaphora : जब हम कहते हैं—I put the money back in my pocket, तो इस वाक्य में article *the* (*the money*) से मालूम होता है कि उस money की चर्चा पहले हुई है। This use of articles (and pronouns) to 'point backwards' is called anaphora, or anaphoric reference.

Antecedent : उस noun को जिससे कोई relative pronoun या relative clause संबंधित होता है antecedent कहते हैं। जैसे : There is the boy who broke my window में the boy *antecedent* है who (broke my window) का। Here is a *cheque* that came by post में cheque *antecedent* है that (pronoun) का।

Apposition : जब हम कहते हैं—Mr Sinha, my brother-in-law, is an army officer, तो इस वाक्य में अभिव्यक्ति my brother-in-law वाक्य के subject से किसी preposition या conjunction द्वारा जुटा हुआ नहीं है। अतः, यह descriptive expression *apposition* में है।

Article : a, an तथा the को articles कहा जाता है। A/an को indefinite article तथा the को definite article कहते हैं।

Aspect : अंगरेजी में verb forms का प्रयोग यह बतलाने के लिए किया जा सकता है कि कोई कार्य किसी खास समय जारी था या वह पूरा हो चुका था।

जैसे : It was raining. It had rained. The use of verb forms to show this kind of meaning is called aspect (e.g., progressive aspect, perfective aspect).

Assertive Sentence : ऐसे वाक्यों को जिनमें कुछ कथन हों assertive sentences कहते हैं। जैसे : Tom has some books. I have a red pen.

Attributive Adjective : adjective जब noun के पहले आता है तब उस adjective को attributive position में कहा जाता है। जैसे : a *green* shirt, my *noisy* friend, a *new* book इत्यादि। इनमें green, noisy तथा new *adjectives* हैं जो *attributive* position में हैं।

Auxiliary Verb : जो verb वाक्य के principal verb में मिलकर tense, mood, voice बनाने में सहायक होता है, उसे auxiliary verb (सहायक क्रिया) कहते हैं। जैसे : She *was* writing. Where *have* you put it ? ये हैं *auxiliary verbs*—be, am, is, was, were, has, have, had, do, does, did, shall, should, will. would, may, might, can, could, must, need, ought, dare, used to.

Bare Infinitive : जब infinitive का प्रयोग बिना to का किया जाता है तब उसे bare infinitive कहते हैं। जैसे : Let me *go*. इस वाक्य में go *bare infinitive* है।

Base Form : verb के simplest form को base form कहा जाता है। जैसे : go, run, play, remember इत्यादि।

Case : वाक्य में जो nouns तथा pronouns रहते हैं उनका अन्य शब्दों से संबंध रहता है और कभी-कभी इस संबंध को व्यक्त करने के लिए उनका रूप विकार भी होता है। इसी को अँगरेजी व्याकरण में case कहते हैं। Case is the use of different forms of nouns or pronouns to show their function in a sentence. जैसे : I तथा me, या who और whom या John तथा John's में जो अंतर है वह उनके case के कारण है।

Clause : शब्दों का ऐसा समूह जिसमें एक subject और एक verb रहे clause कहलाता है। जब वाक्य में एक से अधिक clauses होते हैं तब वे एक-दूसरे से किसी conjunction द्वारा जुटे रहते हैं। जैसे : *Mary said* that *she was tired.* इस वाक्य में दोनों clauses *that* से जुटे हुए हैं।

Cleft Sentence : वैसा वाक्य जिसमें it या what जैसा structure का प्रयोग कर वाक्य के किसी एक भाग—subject या object—को विशेष महत्त्व दिया जाए cleft sentence कहलाता है। A sentence in which special emphasis is given to one part (e.g., the subject or the object) by using a structure with *it* or *what* is called a cleft sentence. जैसे : What I need is a book. It was you that caused the accident.

Collective Noun : ऐसे noun को जिससे एक ही तरह के व्यक्तियों या वस्तुओं के समूह का बोध होता है collective noun कहते हैं। जैसे : family, team इत्यादि।

Colloquial : colloquial उस शब्द या अभिव्यक्ति को कहते हैं जिसका प्रयोग मुख्यतः अनौपचारिक (informal) बोलचाल में किया जाता है, औपचारिक, सुविचारित या साहित्यिक भाषा में नहीं। जैसे : How's life ? Where's the loo (= 'the toilet') ?

Common Noun : ऐसे नाम को जो किसी खास व्यक्ति या वस्तु का नाम नहीं होकर उस जाति के प्रत्येक व्यक्ति या वस्तु का नाम हो उसे common noun कहते हैं। जैसे : dog, cat, boy इत्यादि।

Comparative Degree : जब adjective/adverb से दो व्यक्तियों/वस्तुओं/क्रियाओं की तुलना करके यह बोध हो कि एक में कोई गुण दूसरे से अधिक/कम मात्रा में है तो adjective/adverb *comparative degree* में कहलाता है। जो adjective/adverb comparative degree में होगा उसके अंत में -er लगा रहेगा (*older; faster*); या उसके पहले more/less लगा रहेगा। जैसे : *more* useful, *less* intelligent इत्यादि।

Complement : वाक्य का वह भाग जो subject (be, seem तथा कुछ अन्य verbs के बाद) या object के विषय में कुछ अधिक जानकारी देता है complement कहलाता है। Complement is a part of a sentence that gives more information about the subject (after *be, seem* and some other verbs), or in some structures, about the object. जैसे : You seem *very kind.* You are *the right person to help.*

Compound Word : दो या दो से अधिक भागों (parts) से बने हुए शब्दों को compound noun, verb, adjective या preposition कहते हैं। जैसे : bus-driver, get on with, one-eyed, in spite of इत्यादि।

Compound Sentence : जो वाक्य दो या दो से अधिक main clauses से बना हो, compound sentence कहलाता है। जैसे : I shouted and he ran up. We knocked on the door, but no one answered.

Concord : कभी-कभी verb form वाक्य के subject के singular या plural के अनुसार बदलता है। जैसे : he says किंतु they say, या कभी-कभी subject के person (first, second तथा third) के अनुसार verb का रूप बदलता है। जैसे : I am, you are, he is. Subject तथा verb के इस agreement को concord कहा जाता है। Harmony—of person, number, or gender—between different parts of the sentence is called concord.

Concrete Noun : जिस शब्द से ऐसी वस्तु का बोध हो जिसका स्थूल रूप हो और जिसे हम ज्ञानेन्द्रियों द्वारा परख सकते हैं (अर्थात आँख से देख सकते हैं या हाथ से स्पर्श कर सकते हैं या नाक से सूँघ सकते हैं या जिह्वा द्वारा आस्वादन कर सकते हैं) उसे concrete noun कहा जाता है। जैसे : Tom, milk, dog, army, flower, petrol इत्यादि।

Conditional Verb Form : (i) verb का वह रूप जो would तथा should के साथ प्रयोग किया जाता है conditional verb form कहलाता है। जैसे : I *would run.* She *should dance.* I *should write.*

(ii) जिस clause या sentence में if लगा हुआ हो और conditional verb form भी हो वह conditional clause या sentence कहलाता है। ऐसे वाक्य if के अलावा कुछ दूसरे शब्दों से भी शुरू हो सकते हैं। जैसे *If you try,* you will understand. I should be surprised *if she knew.* What would you have done *if the bus had been late ?*

Conjunction : clauses या वाक्यों को जोड़नेवाला word या group of words (and, but, although, because, when, if, neither ... nor इत्यादि) को conjunction कहते हैं। जैसे : I rang *because* I wanted to speak to you. *Neither* Tom *nor* his father was there.

Connective : वह शब्द जिसका काम किसी दूसरे शब्द या group of words को जोड़ना हो connective कहलाता है। Conjunctions तथा prepositions *connectives* हैं। कभी-कभी adjectives, adverbs तथा pronouns भी connectives का काम करते हैं।

Consonant : वह sound जो मुँह की साँस को बिना पूरा या थोड़ा रोके नहीं निकाला जा सके consonant कहलाता है। Consonant बिना vowel की सहायता से नहीं बोला जा सकता। अंगरेजी में a, e, i, o तथा u, जो vowels हैं, को छोड़कर alphabet के अन्य letters (b, c, d, f, g, h.....) consonants के प्रतीक (symbol) हैं। किन्तु w तथा y कभी consonant होते हैं तो कभी vowel.

Continuous Verb Form : इसका दूसरा नाम progressive है। Verb का वह रूप जो be + ...ing से बनता है continuous कहलाता है। जैसे : *I am writing.* He *was playing.*

Contraction : जब कोई subject और auxiliary verb या कोई verb और not को जोड़ कर एक शब्द बनाया जाता है तब उस short form को contraction कहते हैं। जैसे : I'm; who'll; can't, won't इत्यादि।

Conversational Word : वह शब्द या अभिव्यक्ति जिसका प्रयोग मुख्यतः बोलचाल में किया जाता है उसे conversational word कहा जाता है।

Co-ordinate Clause : (co-ordinate = of equal rank) ऐसे clauses जो वाक्य में एक ही कार्य करते हों और जिनका वाक्य में समान स्थान हो co-ordinate clauses कहलाते हैं। अतः, main clause भी co-ordinate clause हो सकता है (किसी अन्य main clause के साथ) और subordinate clause भी co-ordinate हो सकता है (किसी अन्य subordinate clause के साथ)। जैसे : *Shall I come to your place* or *would you like to come to mine ? It's cooler today* and *there's a bit of a wind.*

Co-ordinating Conjunction : जो एक ही तरह के शब्दों, शब्द-समूहों या वाक्यों को जोड़ते हैं वे co-ordinating conjunctions कहलाते हैं। इनमें प्रमुख हैं—and, but, or, yet, still, as well as इत्यादि।

Copula or **Linking Verb :** मुख्यतः verb *to be* (am, is, are, was, were, being, been) को copula या linking verb कहा जाता है जिसका प्रयोग केवल subject को उसके complement से जोड़ने के लिए किया जाता है। Become, seem, appear, taste, grow इत्यादि भी copula/linking verb कहलाते हैं। जैसे : My friend *is* in Delhi. The night *grew* cold. He *became* a teacher. The cow *ran* dry.

Count Noun or **Countable Noun :** वह noun जिसके पहले indefinite article *a/an* लग सके या जिसकी गिनती हो सके या जिसका plural form बन सके count noun या countable noun कहलाता है। जैसे : car, dog, idea इत्यादि।

Dangling Participle : वह participle जिसका वाक्य में subject नहीं होता dangling participle कहलाता है। A participle which does not have a subject in the sentence in called a dangling participle. जैसे : *Looking out of the window,* the mountains seemed very close. (The construction is usually avoided, because of the possibility of misunderstanding.) Dangling participle को hanging participle भी कहा जाता है।

Declarative Sentence : वह वाक्य जिससे कोई statement व्यक्त हो, command, exclamation या question नहीं, declarative sentence कहलाता है। जैसे : It was something of a shock. The earth is round.

Declarative Question : वैसा question जिसका वही grammatical form होता है जो एक statement का, declarative question कहलाता है। जैसे : That's your girl-friend ?

Defective Verb : वैसा verb (can, ought, must इत्यादि) जिसके सभी रूप (यानी infinitive, participle या past tense) नही होते जैसा एक सामान्य verb का होता है, defective verb कहलाता है। जैसे : can का infinitive रूप या participle रूप नहीं होता; must तथा ought का infinitive, participle या past tense रूप नहीं होता। जितने भी modal auxiliary verbs हैं वे सब defective verbs हैं।

Definite Article : The शब्द को definite article कहा जाता है। जैसे : *the* book, *the* misfortune, *the* virtue, *the* walls इत्यादि।

Defining Relative Clause : वह relative clause जो उस noun से तादात्म्य स्थापित करे जिसका वह उल्लेख करता है defining relative clause कहलाता है। A defining relative clause is a relative clause which identifies the noun it refers to—that is to say, it tells us which person or thing is being talked about. जैसे : There is the girl *who tried to steal your cat. Who tried to steal your cat*—defining relative clause है जो उस खास लड़की को बताता है या किस लड़की की चर्चा है, उसका उल्लेख करता है। Defining relative clause का दूसरा नाम identifying relative clause भी है।

Degree : adjectives और adverbs के degrees of comparison होते हैं। Degrees of comparison तीन होते हैं : (i) positive, (ii) comparative तथा (iii) superlative. जैसे : good-better-best, slowly-more slowly-most slowly.

Demonstrative Adjectives/Pronouns : this/these तथा that/those को demonstrative adjectives/pronouns कहते हैं। जैसे : *This* is a boy *(demonstrative pronoun). This* boy is tall *(demonstrative adjective).*

Dependent Clause : जो clause स्वतः अर्थ की पूर्ण अभिव्यक्ति नहीं करता, बल्कि main clause पर आश्रित रहता है, dependent clause कहलाता है। जैसे : I thought *that you understood. What I need* is a drink.

Determiner : वह शब्द जिसका प्रयोग noun या noun phrase के पहले होता है, determiner कहलाता है। A determiner is one of a group of words that are normally used at the beginning of noun phrases. जैसे : a, an, the, my, this, each, either, several, more, both, all इत्यादि।

Direct Object : वाक्य के verb का प्रभाव जिस व्यक्ति या वस्तु पर पड़ता है, उसे direct object कहते हैं। The *direct object* refers to a person or thing affected by the action of the verb. जैसे : Take the *dog* for a walk. इस वाक्य में dog *direct object* है।

Direct Question : पूछनेवाले के words में ही जो प्रश्न पूछा जाए direct question कहलाता है। जैसे : Where is the soap ? He asked, *"Where is the soap ?"* किंतु जब पूछनेवाले के words को बदल देते हैं, तब वह indirect question कहलाता है। जैसे : He asked *where the soap was.*

Direct Speech : जब किसी के मूल कथन को या अपने ही मूल कथन को हम दूसरे से हू-ब-हू उन्हीं शब्दों में कहते हैं, उसे direct speech कहा जाता है। जैसे : He said, *"This is my money."*

Do Form : verb के do form में verb *do* (do, does, did) के साथ principal verb का infinitive form रहता है। *Do* form को कभी-कभी emphatic form भी कहा जाता है; क्योंकि वाक्य को emphatic बनाने के लिए इसका प्रयोग किया जाता है। किंतु Modern English में *do form* का प्रयोग अकसर question पूछने या वाक्य को negative बनाने के लिए किया जाता है। जैसे : I *do* like her. He *does* talk a lot. It *doesn't* matter. *Do* you feel like talking ?

Double Comparative : यदि वाक्य में adjective या adverb के comparison में more तथा -er दोनों का प्रयोग साथ-साथ किया जाए तो इसे double comparative कहते हैं। जैसे : more braver, more quicker, more nobler इत्यादि। किंतु double comparative या double superlative का प्रयोग गलत माना जाता है।

Double Genitive : ऐसा structure जिसमें 's (या genitive form of the pronoun) के साथ-साथ preposition *of* लगा रहे, double genitive कहलाता है। जैसे : a friend of Moti's, a habit of mine, an uncle of Reeta's. कुछ लोग double genitive को गलत मानते हैं किंतु Modern English में इसे शुद्ध माना जाता है।

Double Negative : एक ही वाक्य में दो negative words के प्रयोग को double negative कहते हैं। जैसे : I should*n't* be surprised if we did*n't* have some rain.

Double Question : जब एक ही वाक्य में दो प्रश्न पूछा जाए तब उसे double question कहते हैं। जैसे : Who killed whom ? Who sits where ?

Dynamic Verb : वैसे verbs जिनसे किसी कार्य के होने (action) की अभिव्यक्ति हो, अवस्था (state) की नहीं, dynamic verbs कहलाते हैं। ऐसे verbs का प्रयोग प्रायः progressive tenses में होता है। Dynamic verbs express actions, not states; they can usually be used in progressive tenses. जैसे : fly, plan, shout इत्यादि।

Ellipsis : (adjective *elliptic)* जब हम वाक्य में कुछ शब्दों को छोड़ देते हैं और उसका अर्थ संदर्भ (context) से समझा जा सकता है, उसे elliptic sentence कहते हैं। जैसे : (It's a) Nice day, isn't it ? He could hit harder than I could (= hit).

Elliptical Clause : वह adverb clause जिसमें से subject तथा verb या part of the verb को छोड़ दिया गया हो, elliptical clause कहलाता है। जैसे : *While* *in Delhi,* we visted Mr Sen every week. यहाँ while in Delhi में we were छिपा हुआ है— While (*we were*) in Delhi, we visited Mr Sen every week.

Emphasis : शब्द या वाक्य के किसी एक भाग को विशेष महत्त्व देना emphasis कहलाता है। यह अधिक जोर से उच्चारण कर, या capital letters से लिखकर, या affirmative clause में do का प्रयोग कर या special word order के द्वारा किया जाता है।

Emphatic Form : *do* form को अकसर emphatic form कहा जाता है। जैसे: I *do* go shopping every day. He *does* listen to the radio till 10 o'clock.

Emphatic Pronoun : noun या pronoun पर जोर देने के लिए जिस pronoun का प्रयोग किया जाता है उसे emphatic pronoun कहते हैं। जैसे : I will tell him *myself.* He did it *himself.* इन वाक्यों में myself, himself *emphatic pronouns* हैं।

Exclamatory Sentence : an exclamatory sentence is one that primarily expresses emotion. ऐसा वाक्य अकसर what या how से शुरू होता है। जैसे : What a fool I was ! How beautiful she sings !

Ending : grammatical suffix को ending कहा जाता है। जैसे : -er, -ing, -ed इत्यादि।

Finite Verb : जो verb अपने subject द्वारा अनुशासित होता है और जिसका रूप number, tense, mood, voice के कारण बदलता है, उसे finite verb कहते हैं। A finite verb form is one that can be used with a subject to make a verb tense. जैसे : breaks, broke, is singing, has been इत्यादि।

First Person : first person का प्रयोग वक्ता (speaker) के लिए या वक्ता के संबंध में होता है। I, we, me, us, mine, our तथा ours *first persons* हैं।

Foreign Plural : foreign nouns (खासकर Latin तथा Greek के) के plural form को foreign plural कहते हैं। ऐसे words में अंगरेजी के -s plural marker का प्रयोग नहीं किया जाता। जैसे : formulae, errata, theses (Latin), phenomena (Greek).

Formal Style : किसी खास अवसरों पर जब अनजान व्यक्तियों से विनम्रतापूर्वक बातें की जाती हैं तब उस शैली (style) को formal style कहते हैं। ऐसी शैली का प्रयोग साहित्यिक लेखन, व्यापारिक पत्रों इत्यादि में होता है। जैसे start की जगह जब हम commence का प्रयोग करते हैं तब commence को एक formal word माना जाएगा।

Frequency (Adverb) : adverbs of frequency से पता चलता है कि क्रिया कितनी बार repeated हुई या नहीं हुई। मुख्य adverbs of frequency हैं : always, never, generally, frequently, often, seldom, hardly, daily, occasionally इत्यादि।

Fronting : clause के एक भाग को विशेष महत्त्व देने के लिए शुरू में रखना fronting कहलाता है (moving a part of a clause to the beginning in order to give it special emphasis). जैसे : *Tom* I like, but *his wife* I can't stand.

Full Verb : principal verb का दूसरा नाम full verb है।

Future (or Future Simple) Tense : *shall/will* + present tense plural के संयोग से simple future tense बनता है। इस tense से पता चलता है कि क्रिया भविष्य में होगी। जैसे : I shall arrive. Will he go ?

Future Perfect Tense : *shall/will+have*+past participle के संयोग से future perfect tense बनता है। इस tense से यह व्यक्त होता है कि भविष्य में किसी निर्धारित समय पर अथवा अन्य किसी क्रिया के पूर्व क्रिया समाप्त हो चुकी रहेगी। जैसे : I *shall have finished* writing by lunch time.

Future Progressive : shall/will+be+......ing के संयोग से future progressive tense बनता है। इस tense से यह भाव व्यक्त होता है कि क्रिया पहले प्रारंभ होकर भविष्य में किसी निर्दिष्ट समय पर होती रहेगी। जैसे : I *will be needing* the car this evening.

Gender : masculine, feminine तथा neuter या human और non-human के भेद/अंतर बतलाने के लिए जिन विभिन्न grammatical forms of sex distinction का प्रयोग किया जाता है उसे gender कहते हैं। जैसे—he, she, it, who, which इत्यादि।

Genitive : noun का वह रूप (form) जो 's, s' या of से बनता है तथा जिससे आधिपत्य (possession) का बोध होता है genitive case कहलाता है। Genitive is a case of nouns, marked, in English, either by *'s* or by the form word *of* Elementary grammars में इसे possessive case भी कहा जाता है। जैसे : the *earth's* gravity; *birds'* nest.

Gerund : verb का *-ing* form जिसका प्रयोग noun की तरह वाक्य के subject के रूप में या preposition के बाद होता है, gerund कहलाता है। जैसे : *Smoking* is dangerous. You can't get there by *walking*.

Gradable Adjective : *pretty, hard* या *cold* gradable adjectives हैं; चीजें *more* or *less* pretty (सुंदर), hard या cold हो सकती हैं। Adverb of degree (जैसे—rather, very) का प्रयोग gradable words के साथ हो सकता है। *Perfect* तथा *dead* gradable words नहीं हैं क्योंकि हम किसी चीज के विषय में more या less perfect अथवा very dead नहीं कहते।

Grammar : वे नियम जो यह बतलाते हों कि words विभिन्न अर्थों को बताने के लिए कैसे बदलते (change) हैं तथा वे वाक्यों में किस प्रकार मिलते (combine) हैं, grammar कहलाते हैं।

(i) The rules that say how words change to show different meanings, and how they are combined into sentences are called grammar.

(ii) A body of generalizations describing a language is grammar.

Head : किसी noun phrase का head वह main noun होता है जिसे बाकी अन्य शब्द qualify करते हैं। जैसे: It is *the best sports car ever made* में car *head noun* है। उसी तरह verb phrase में head *main verb* होता है। जैसे : I *should have been invited* में invited *head verb* है।

Hypothetical : conditional वाक्यों में hypothetical स्थितियों की चर्चा रहती है, अर्थात वैसी परिस्थितियाँ जो उत्पन्न ही नहीं होंगी या जो वास्तविक नहीं हैं। जैसे : What would you do if you had three months free ?

Historical Present : कभी-कभी यह दिखाने के लिए कि अतीत की घटना इतनी स्पष्ट है कि मालूम पड़ता आँखों के सामने हो रही है, हम simple present का प्रयोग करते हैं। इसे historical present कहते हैं। जैसे: Portia *goes up* to the Duke, *introduces* herself as a lawyer....

Idiom : शब्दों का समूह जिसका एक विशेष अर्थ हो तथा जिसे शब्दों को अलग-अलग अर्थ कर नहीं समझा जा सके idiom कहलाता है। An idiom is a group of words with a special meaning, which cannot be understood by taking the meanings of the words one at a time. जैसे : get on with (मिलनसार/सामाजिक ढंग से रहना या जीना); off hand (बिना पूर्व तैयारी का)।

Imperative Sentence : verb का मूल रूप (base form) जिसका प्रयोग आज्ञा देने या सलाह देने के लिए किया जाता है, imperative sentence कहलाता है। जैसे : *Bring* me a book. *Have* a good holiday.

Impersonal It : impersonal *it* has no meaning; it simply satisfies our feeling that a verb in an assertive sentence should have a subject. ऐसे वाक्यों में it का कोई अर्थ नहीं होता। जैसे : *It* is raining. *It* is going to snow. *It's* a hot day. *It* was late afternoon.

Indefinite Article : a/an को indefinite article कहा जाता है। one का weakened form a/an होता है।

Indirect Object : वाक्य में transitive verb के बाद आनेवाला noun या pronoun *object* कहलाता है। कभी-कभी transitive verb के बाद दो objects आते हैं, उनमें से पहले को indirect तथा दूसरे को direct object कहते हैं। *Indirect object* transitive verb तथा direct object के बीच आता है। The indirect object usually refers to a person who receives the direct object. जैसे : Tom gave *me* a watch में me *indirect object* है तथा watch *direct object*. I told *him* a lie. Do *me* a favour. I never gave *the matter* a thought. He sent *you* a plan. इनमें him, me, the matter तथा you *indirect objects* हैं।

Indirect Speech : किसी के मूल कथन को या अपने ही मूल कथन को हम दूसरे से अप्रत्यक्ष रूप में, शब्दों में कुछ हेर-फेर कर किंतु आशय को अक्षुण्ण रखते हुए कह सकते हैं। इसे indirect या reported speech कहते हैं।

Ram said, "Mohan is ill."—direct speech.
Ram said *that* Mohan *was* ill.—indirect speech.

Indirect Question : जब किसी question को पूछनेवाले के original words में न पूछकर, उसमें कुछ अदल-बदल (rephrased) कर पूछते हैं, तब उसे indirect question कहा जाता है। जैसे : Where is it ?—*direct question.* He asked, "Where is it ?"—*direct question.* He asked (me) where it was. *—indirect question.*

Infinitive : verb के मूल रूप (base form) को infinitive कहते हैं; इसमें verb के पहले साधारणतः to लगा रहता है। Infinitive का प्रयोग किसी दूसरे verb के बाद, किसी adjective या noun के बाद या वाक्य के subject या object के रूप में किया जाता है। जैसे : They want *to go* home. It is easy *to sing*. I have a plan *to start* a business. *To err* is human, *to forgive* divine. Please try *to remember*.

Inflection : वह form जिसे किसी word में जोड़कर उसके number, case, gender, person, tense, voice, mood आदि में change किया जाए inflection कहलाता है। जैसे : inflection *-ed* जोड़कर बहुत सारे English verbs का past tense बनता है; walk, walk*ed;* inflection *'s* जोड़कर genitive case बनता है। जैसे : boy, boy'*s*.

Informal Style : वह शैली (style) जिसका प्रयोग हम साधारण बातचीत या व्यक्तिगत पत्रों आदि में करते हैं जहाँ विनम्रतापूर्वक या सावधानीपूर्वक बोलने या लिखने की कोई खास आवश्यकता नहीं होती—informal style कहलाता है। जैसे : start एक अधिक informal word है commence से, यद्यपि दोनों के एक ही अर्थ हैं—यानी 'शुरू होना या करना'।

-ing Form : verb का वह रूप जिसके अंत में -ing लगा रहता है -ing form कहलाता है; ऐसे verb form का प्रयोग विशेषतः noun के रूप में होता है। जैसे : finding, keeping, running, firing आदि।

Initial (Adverb) : कुछ adverbs हैं जिनका प्रयोग वाक्य के शुरू में (in initial position) होता है। जैसे : *Sometimes* I wish I had never been born. यहाँ sometimes वाक्य के *initial position* में है।

Intensifying : intensifying का अर्थ होता है अधिक stronger या अधिक emphatic (जोरदार) बनाना। जैसे : He was *very* tall. She was *terribly* shocked. इन वाक्यों में very तथा terribly *intensifying* adverbs हैं।

Interrogative Words : interrogative words तथा structures का प्रयोग प्रश्न पूछने के लिए किया जाता है। In an interrogative sentence, there is an auxiliary verb before the subject. जैसें : Can you swim ? What, who तथा where *interrogative words* हैं।

Interrogative Sentence : a sentence that asks a question is an interrogative sentence. ऐसा वाक्य statement, exclamation तथा command से भिन्न होता है। जैसे : Why did he turn it off ? What business is it of yours ?

Intransitive Verb : वह verb जिसके बाद कोई object नहीं आ सकता हो तथा जिसका प्रयोग passive voice में नहीं होता हो intransitive verb कहलाता है। An intransitive verb is one that cannot have an object or be used in the passive. जैसे : The baby *sleeps*. Dogs *bark* at night. They *were talking*.

Introductory Subject : जब किसी वाक्य का subject कोई infinitive या clause होता है, तब हम इसे अकसर वाक्य के अंत में रखते हैं और pronoun *it* से वाक्य शुरू करते हैं और इस it को introductory subject कहते हैं। इसे anticipatory या preparatory subject भी कहा जाता है। When the subject of a sentence is an infinitive or a clause, we usually put it towards the end of the sentence and use the pronoun *it* as an introductory subject (also called *anticipatory* or *preparatory* subject). जैसे : *It's* important to get enough sleep.

There से शुरू होनेवाले वाक्य में there का प्रयोग introductory subject के रूप में होता है। जैसे : *There* is a house.

Introductory Object : *it* का प्रयोग कुछ खास structures में introductory object के रूप में होता है। जैसे : He made *it* clear that he disagreed.

Inversion : वैसी वाक्य-बनावट (structure) जिसमें subject के पहले verb का प्रयोग किया जाता है, inversion कहलाता है। जैसे : *Have you* seen Tom ? Under no circumstances *are visitors* allowed to stay here.

Irregular Verb (Not following the normal rules) : Irregular verb के past tense अथवा/या past participle रूप के अंत में -ed नहीं होता। An irregular verb has a past tense and/or past participle that does not end in *-ed,* जैसे : swim-swam-swum; fall-fell-*fallen* आदि।

Lexical Verb : वह verb जो auxiliary verb नहीं होता lexical verb कहलाता है। A verb that is not an auxiliary verb is called a lexical verb. जैसे : look, overtake, disturb, किंतु will या can *lexical verbs* नहीं हैं।

Lexis : words; vocabulary (शब्दावली) को lexis कहा जाता है।

Main Clause : जो clause स्वतः पूर्ण होता है और बिना अन्य किसी clause के संयोग के भी अर्थ की पूरी अभिव्यक्ति कर सकता है, main clause कहलाता है। Main clause को Principal clause भी कहते हैं। जैसे : *I told you* that I didn't care. Wherever you go, *you will find coca-cola.* इन वाक्यों में I told you तथा you will find coca-cola *main clauses* हैं।

Main Verb : वह verb जो किसी वाक्य के main clause के आधार के रूप में प्रयुक्त होता है, main verb कहलाता है। The verb which is used as the basis for the main clause in a sentence is called the main verb. जैसे : Running into the room, she *started* to cry. इस वाक्य में started *main verb* है।

Manner (Adverb) : adverb of manner से पता चलता है कि कोई काम किस प्रकार होता है। An adverb of manner describes how something happens. जैसे : well, fast, suddenly आदि।

Mass Noun : जो noun ऐसी वस्तु का नाम है, जिसकी न गिनती हो सकती है, जिसके पहले a/an नहीं लगता तथा न plural बनता है, mass noun या uncountable noun कहलाता है। जैसे : petrol, ink, tea, sugar, rice आदि।

Mid-Position Adverb : जो adverb वाक्य में subject तथा main verb के बीच रहता है, mid-position adverb कहलाता है। If an adverb is in *mid-position* in a sentence, it is between the subject and the main verb. जैसे : I *definitely* agree with you. यहाँ definitely *mid-position adverb* है।

Modal Auxiliary Verb : can, could, may, might, must, will, shall, would, should, ought और need को modal auxiliary verbs कहते हैं। Dare, used to

तथा had better को भी कभी-कभी modal auxiliary verbs माना जाता है। An auxiliary verb used to add to the principal verb such an idea as necessity, obligation, permission, possibility etc. is called a modal auxiliary verb. It has no third person singular in *-s* and no participle form, and it is used with the simple infinitive form of the principal verb : *can do, could go, must be.*

Modification or **Qualification :** किसी चीज के अर्थ को बदलने का नाम modification या qualification है। Modification or qualification means changing the meaning of something. Adjectives are said to *modify* or *qualify* the noun they refer to; adverbs are said to *modify* or *qualify* verbs, adjectives, adverbs or whole sentences.

Mood : the attitude of the speaker towards the sentence is called mood.

Mutation Plural : mutation का अर्थ होता है change. किसी शब्द के vowel में change कर उसे plural बनाना, न कि उसके अंत में -s/es जोड़कर, mutation plural कहलाता है। जैसे : foot-feet; goose-geese; tooth-teeth; lause-lice; mouse-mice; man-men; woman-women.

Negative Sentence : जिस वाक्य में verb के साथ no, not, never का प्रयोग होता है उसे negative sentence कहते हैं। A negative sentence is one in which the word *no, not* or *never* is used with the verb. जैसे : I do *not* know. He has *no* book. I have *never* seen him.

Nominal Relative Clause : a relative clause (usually introduced by *what*) which acts as the subject, object or complement of a sentence is called a nominal relative clause. जैसे : I gave him *what he needed.*

Non-Assertive Form : some, somebody इत्यादि को assertive forms कहते हैं; any, anybody इत्यादि को non-assertive forms कहते हैं। *Some, somebody* etc are called *assertive forms; any, anybody* etc. are called *non-assertive forms.* Other non-assertive forms are *yet, ever.*

Non-Finite Verb : जो verb किसी subject पर tense formation के लिए आश्रित नहीं होता उसे non-finite verb कहते हैं। A verb form that cannot be used with a subject to make a tense is called a non-finite verb. जैसे : to break, breaking, broken, being broken आदि।

Non-Defining Relative Clause : non-defining relative clause तथा non-identifying relative clause दोनों एक ही चीज हैं।

Non-Identifying Relative Clause : वह relative clause जो उस noun को इंगित नहीं करता जिसका वह उल्लेख करता है (क्योंकि हम जानते हैं कि वह कौन व्यक्ति या वस्तु को इंगित करता है), non-identifying relative clause कहलाता है। The non-identifying relative clause is a relative clause which does not identify the noun it refers to (because we already know which person or thing is meant). जैसे : There is Kartik Oraon, *who tried to steal my dog.* (The relative clause, *who tried to steal my dog,* does not identify the person—he is already identified by the name Kartik Oraon).

Defining तथा Non-defining clause में भेद—

(i) "A defining or restrictive clause may be distinguished from a non-defining or continuative one by the fact that if the former is removed the antecedent is left without any meaning, or at best a wrong one; but the latter may always be detached from the antecedent without disturbing the meaning of the main sentence." (FOWLER)

(ii) "......... non-defining clauses need commas and defining clauses do not." (FOWLER)

जैसे : The man *who hesitates* is lost. (defining clause)

I saw the Headmaster, *who recognised me immediately*. (non-defining clause)

Non-Restrictive Relative Clause : the same as *non-identifying relative clause*.

Notional Passive : a word that is active in form but passive in meaning, telling not what the subject does but what is done to the subject. जैसे : Ice cream *sells* fast in summer. This material won't *wash*. The car certainly *rides* well.

Noun : वह शब्द जिससे किसी प्राणी, वस्तु, जगह या विचार के नाम का बोध हो noun कहलाता है। A Noun is the name of a person, thing, place or idea. जैसे : Jack, boy, cap, Patna, beauty आदि।

Noun Clause : वह clause जो वाक्य में subject, object या complement इत्यादि का कार्य करता है, noun clause कहलाता है। A clause which acts as the subject, object or complement etc. of a sentence is called a noun clause. जैसे : Sita told me *why she was worried*. I know *that you like sweets*. *Whether I do or not* depends chiefly on the weather. *Whatever is*, is right.

Noun Phrase : शब्दों का एक समूह (जैसे : article+adjective+noun) जो वाक्य में subject, object या complement का कार्य करता हो noun phrase कहलाता है। जैसे : the last train.

Number : grammar में जिस तरह से एकवचन और बहुवचन में अंतर बताया जाता है उसे number कहते हैं। The way in which differences between singular and plural are shown grammatically is called number. जैसे : house तथा houses, mouse तथा mice, this तथा these में जो अंतर है, वह number के कारण है।

Object : active voice के वाक्यों में transitive verb के बाद आनेवाला साधारणतः noun या pronoun *object* कहलाता है। A noun or pronoun that normally comes after the transitive verb in an active sentence is called an object. जैसे : He buys a *book*. She helps *me*. I saw *him*.

Of Genitive : 's के बदले of से बने हुए genitive को of genitive कहते हैं। जैसे : the father *of the boy* या *the boy's* father.

Participle : verb का वह रूप जिसके अंत में -ing/-ed/-en/-d/-t/-n लगा हो तथा जो modifier का कार्य करता हो, participle कहलाता है। जैसे : He jumped into a *running* car. A *burnt* child dreads the fire. The *setting* sun cast a *deepening* shadow.

Participle Clause : वह clause के जैसा structure जिसमें participle हो और finite verb नहीं हो participle clause कहता है। A clause-like structure which contains a participle, not a finite verb form is called a participle clause. जैसे : *Discouraged by his failure,* he resigned his job. *Having a couple of hours to spare,* I went to see a film.

Parts of Speech : the major categories into which the vocabulary of a language is divided are known as parts of speech. अंगरेजी में आठ parts of speech हैं : noun, pronoun, adjective, verb, adverb, preposition, conjunction तथा interjection.

Passive : verb के जिस रूप से object की प्रधानता व्यक्त हो उसे passive verb form कहते हैं। Passive verb form की बनावट be + past participle होता है। Is broken, was told, will be helped—*passive verb forms* हैं। किंतु breaks, told, will help—*active verb forms* हैं।

They sent Moti to prison for a year. —active
Moti was sent to prison for a year. —passive

Past Participle : verb का वह रूप जैसे—broken, gone, stopped जिसका प्रयोग perfect tenses और passives बनाने के लिए होता है या जिसका प्रयोग adjective की तरह किया जाए, past participle कहलाता है। A verb form like *broken, gone, stopped,* which can be used to form perfect tenses and passives, or as an adjective is called the past participle. (The meaning is not necessarily past, in spite of the name).

Past Perfect Tense : had + past participle of principal verb द्वारा past perfect tense बनता है। जैसे : I *had forgotten.* The children *had arrived.*

Past Perfect Progressive Tense : had been + present participle of principal verb के संयोग से बनता है। जैसे : It *had been raining.* I *had been working.*

Past Progressive Tense : was/were + ...-ing के मिलाने से verb का past progressive tense बनता है। इस tense का दूसरा नाम past continuous tense है। जैसे : I *was going.* They *were singing.*

Past Simple Tense : इस tense में verb के past tense form का प्रयोग बिना auxiliary verb के किया जाता है। In the simple past tense, a past verb form is used without an auxiliary verb. जैसे : I *saw.* You *heard.* We *stopped.*

Perfect Conditional : should/would have + past participle के संयोग से perfect conditional बनता है। जैसे : I *should/would have agreed.* He *would have known.*

Perfect Infinitive : to have + past participle के संयोग से perfect infinitive बनता है। जैसे : *to have arrived; to have gone.*

Perfective : In some grammars, a form like *I have arrived* or *he has been working* is not called a *perfect tense* (because the verb form is used not just to refer to time, but also to express an idea such as completion or result). These grammars prefer the term *perfective aspect.*

Person : जिस तरह से grammar में वक्ता (first person), सुननेवाला (second person) और व्यक्ति या वस्तु जिसके विषय में कहा जाए (third person) में अंतर बताया जाता है, उसे person कहते हैं। The way in which, in grammar, we show the difference between the person speaking (*first person*), the person spoken to (*second person*), and the people or things spoken about (*third person*) is called person. जैसे : am, are तथा is में जो अंतर है, वह person में अंतर के कारण है।

Personal Pronouns : I, me, you, he, him जैसे शब्दों को personal pronouns कहते हैं।

Phrase : जब दो या अधिक शब्द समूह में एक साथ कार्य करते हैं, तब उसे phrase कहा जाता है। Two or more words that function together as a group are called a phrase. जैसे : in the country; the silly old woman; would have been repaired आदि।

Phrasal Verb : verb के मूल रूप तथा adverb particle से बने verb को phrasal verb कहते हैं। The phrasal verb is a verb that is made up of two parts : a 'base' verb followed by an adverb particle. जैसे : take in; fill up; run over आदि।

Possessive : noun या pronoun का वह form जिसका प्रयोग आधिपत्य (possession) या इसी तरह की भावना व्यक्त करने के लिए किया जाता है, possessive कहलाता है। जैसे : Tom's; our, mine, yours आदि।

Possessive Pronoun : my, your, her; mine, yours, hers जैसे शब्द possessive pronouns कहलाते हैं। My, your, her इत्यादि को कभी-कभी possessive adjectives भी कहा जाता है।

Postmodifier : वह शब्द जो किसी शब्द के बाद आकर पहलेवाले शब्द का गुण बताता (modify) है, postmodifier कहलाता है। A word which comes after the word which it modifies is called the postmodifier. जैसे : The people *invited* all came late में invited *postmodifier* है।

Predicate : subject के बारे में जो कुछ कहा जाए अर्थात वाक्य में subject को छोड़कर शेष भाग predicate कहलाता है। What is said about the subject of a sentence—that is to say, all of a sentence except the subject is called the predicate. जैसे : Boys *play football*. He *gave me a pen*. इन वाक्यों में verb तथा उसके साथ आए सारे words *predicate* हैं।

Predicative Adjective : be, seem, look जैसे verb के बाद आनेवाले adjectives *predicative position* में कहलाते हैं। जैसे : He looks *happy*. The house is *enormous*.

Prefix : anti-American, anti-communist, co-operate, co-ownership में anti-, तथा co- जो elements हैं उन्हें prefixes कहा जाता है।

Premodifier : वह शब्द जो किसी noun के पहले आकर उस noun को modify करे premodifier कहलाता है। A word that comes before the noun it modifies is called the premodifier. जैसे : He spoke before an *invited* audience. इस वाक्य में invited *premodifier* है।

Preparatory Subject, Preparatory Object : यह *introductory subject, introductory object* का दूसरा नाम है। जैसे : *It's* important to get enough sleep (= introductory subject). He made *it* clear that he agreed. (= introductory object).

Preposition : On, off, of, into जैसा शब्द जिसके बाद साधारणतः कोई noun या pronoun आता है, *preposition* कहलाता है। A word like *on, off, of, into,* normally followed by a noun or pronoun is called a preposition.

Prepositional Phrase : preposition + object of the preposition से बना phrase *prepositional phrase* कहलाता है। जैसे : in stock, against the wall, along the counter, from his coat इत्यादि।

Prepositional Verb : वह verb जिसमें दो भाग हों—एक 'base' verb + एक preposition, *prepositional verb* कहलाता है। A verb that has two parts : a 'base' verb and a preposition is called a prepositional verb. जैसे : care for, insist on आदि।

Present Participle : verb-form का वह रूप जिसके अंत में -ing लगा हो present participle कहलाता है। जैसे : She was *running*. *Opening* his newspaper, he started to read. I hate the noise of *crying* babies.

The present participle is used to make verb tenses, or in adjectival or adverbial expressions. The meaning of the present participle is not necessarily present, in spite of the name.

Present Perfect Tense : वह verb form जो have या has + past participle के संयोग से बनता है, present perfect tense कहलाता है। जैसे : I *have done* it. The man *has arrived*.

Present Perfect Progressive Tense : वह verb form जो have/has been +.....-ing के संयोग से बनता है, present perfect progressive कहलाता है। जैसे : I *have been working* all day. It *has been raining* since 3 p. m.

Present Progressive Tense : वह verb form जो am/is/are + ...ing के

संयोग से बनता है, present pogressive tense कहलाता है। जैसे : I *am going*. You *are playing*. He *is reading*.

Present Simple Tense : verb का मूल रूप infinitive का है और यह to-विहीन रूप (bare infinitive), simple present, plural number का रूप है। इस plural रूप में -s या -es जोड़कर simple present, third person, singular number बनता है। In the present simple tense, a present verb form is made without an auxiliary verb. जैसे : I *like* chocolate. He *goes* there every day.

Preterite : past tense का दूसरा नाम preterite है।

Principal Verb : verb phrase का वह भाग जिससे मुख्य अर्थ व्यक्त होता है principal verb कहलाता है। Auxiliary verb तो केवल principal verb के अर्थ को modify करता है। Verb phrase में principal verb का रूप past या present participle या infinitive होता है। जैसे : They are *coming* late. He does *talk* a little too much. You should have *seen* her face. We were *given* the medal. She has been *crying*.

Pro-Form : a word with a general meaning, which can be used to stand for any word of a certain kind when the context makes it clear what is meant is called a pro-form. *Do* is a pro-form for verbs; *you, it, one* are pro-forms for names and nouns; *there* and *then* are pro-forms for adverbial expressions of place and time.

Progressive (or Continuous) : वह verb form जो *be* + ... *–ing* के संयोग से बनता है progressive या continuous कहलाता है। जैसे : *be going; am reading*. we *were wondering*.

Progressive Infinitive : to *be going;* to *be waiting* जैसे form को progressive infinitive कहते हैं।

Pronoun : वह शब्द जिसका प्रयोग noun या noun phrase के स्थान पर किया जाता है, pronoun कहलाता है। जैसे : it, yourself, their आदि।

Proper Noun : वह शब्द जो किसी व्यक्ति-विशेष, स्थान-विशेष या संस्थाविशेष का नाम हो, proper noun कहलाता है। Proper noun का पहला अक्षर सदा capital letter होता है तथा इसके पहले साधारणतः कोई article नहीं लगता। जैसे : Ramesh, India, Bharati Bhawan.

Qualify : qualify तथा modify एक ही चीज है। see *modification*.

Quantifier : a word or expression like *many, few, several, plenty, a lot,* which is used in a noun phrase to show how many or how much we are talking about is called a quantifier.

Question Tag : auxiliary verb + pronoun subject से बनी हुई अभिव्यक्ति (जैसे : isn't it ? या don't you ?) जिसे वाक्य के अंत में रखा जाता है, question tag कहलाता है। An expression like *isn't it* or *don't you* (consisting of auxiliary verb + pronoun subject) put on to the end of a sentence is called a question tag. जैसे : It's a nice day, *isn't it* ?

Reciprocal Pronouns : each other, one another को reciprocal pronouns कहा जाता है।

Reflexive Pronouns : *myself, yourself, himself* etc. (used as objects) are called reflexive pronouns. जैसे : I cut *myself* shaving this morning.

Regular Verb : वह verb जिसके अंत में d, t या ed जोड़कर past tense बनाया जाता है, regular verb कहलाता है। जैसे : walk/walked; please/pleased; work/worked.

Reinforcement Tag : a tag which repeats (and so reinforces, or strengthens) the meaning of the subject and verb is called a reinforcement tag. जैसे : You're a real idiot, *you are.*

Relative Clause : relative pronoun जैसे : who, whom या which से शुरू होनेवाला clause, relative clause कहलाता है। जैसे : The man *whom you invited* has come. The man *who hesitates* is lost.

Relative Pronoun : who, whom, whose, which तथा that (और कभी-कभी what, when, where तथा why) को relative pronouns कहते हैं। Relative pronouns are used to repeat the meaning of a previous noun (the antecedent); at the same time, they connect the relative clause to the rest of the sentence (so they act as conjunctions and pronouns at the same time). जैसे : Is this the child *that* was causing all that trouble ? यहाँ that *relative pronoun* है।

Reply Question : वह question (जिसका structure question tag के समान होता है) जो किसी statement के उत्तर के लिए पूछा जाता है, reply question कहलाता है। A question (similar in structure to a question tag) used to reply to a statement (for instance, to express interest) is called a reply question. जैसे : I have been invited to dinner today. *Have you, dear* ?

Reported Speech : किसी के मूल कथन को या अपने ही मूल कथन को हम दूसरे से अप्रत्यक्ष रूप में, शब्दों में कुछ हेर-फेर कर (tenses, word-order, pronouns और दूसरे शब्दों को अदल-बदलकर), किंतु आशय को अक्षुण्ण रखते हुए कहते हैं, उसे reported speech या indirect speech कहा जाता है। जैसे :

Tom said, "I am tall."—direct speech.

Tom said *that he was tall.*—reported speech.

Retained Object : an object that is kept in its object position following the verb when the verb is put into the passive voice is known as a retained object. जैसे :

I asked Tom *a question.* (= object)—active voice.

Tom was asked *a question* (= retained object)—passive voice.

Second Person : जिसे संबोधित किया जाए या जिससे बात की जाए second person कहलाता है। जैसे : you, yours.

Sentence : शब्दों के ऐसे समूह को जिससे statement, command, question या exclamation व्यक्त हो, sentence कहलाता है। A sentence is a group of words that expresses a statement, command, question or exclamation. एक वाक्य में एक clause या एक से अधिक clauses हो सकते हैं और उसमें कम-से-कम एक subject और एक finite verb रहता है। लिखने में वाक्य का पहला अक्षर capital letter होता है और वाक्य के अंत में full stop, question mark या exclamation mark दिया जाता है। जैसे : Boys play football. What is this ? What a pity !

Sentence Adverb : वह adverb जो पूरे वाक्य को modify करता है, sentence adverb कहलाता है। जैसे : *Frankly,* I think he is making a big mistake. He answered my question *frankly*. प्रथम वाक्य में frankly *sentence adverb* है, किंतु दूसरे वाक्य में 'frankly' verb *answered* को modify करता है।

'S Genitive : *Tom's,* the *earth's*, our *parents'* जैसे form को 's genitive कहते हैं।

Short Answer : जिस answer में subject और auxiliary verb रहता है, short answer कहलाता है। जैसे : 'Who is ready for more ?' —'*I am*'.

Simple Sentence : शब्दों का समूह जिसमें केवल एक main clause हो और कोई subordinate clause नहीं हो, simple sentence कहलाता है। जैसे : I just saw a dog. Tom fought for five minutes.

Simple Subject : modifiers को छोड़कर noun या noun-equivalent जो subject होता है उसे simple subject कहते हैं। जैसे : *Birds* twitter. The long *day* ended. The *man* on the road has called you. इनमें Birds, day तथा man *simple subjects* हैं।

Simple Tense : a tense that is not progressive. जैसे : I *went;* she *wants;* they *eat.*

Singular : वह grammatical form जिससे एक व्यक्ति, एक वस्तु इत्यादि का बोध हो या जिससे अगणनीय मात्रा सूचित हो, singular कहलाता है। जैसे: me, bus, water, is, much, this आदि।

Slang : बोलचाल या किसी समुदाय द्वारा बोलचाल में प्रयोग किए जानेवाले word, expression या special use of language को slang कहते हैं। A word, expression or special use of language found mainly in very informal speech, especially in the usage of particular groups of people is called slang. जैसे : *thick* (= 'stupid'); *lose one's cool* (= 'get upset').

Split Infinitive : वह structure जिसमें to तथा infinitive verb form के बीच adverb आता है, split infinitive कहलाता है। जैसे : to easily understand; to completely finish; to in some way explain. (ऐसा structure प्रायः गलत माना जाता है)।

Standard Language : शिक्षित मूल निवासी द्वारा बोली जानेवाली भाषा को standard form of language कहते हैं। A standard form of language, or a standard accent, is one that is usually used by the most educated or influential people in a country, and is, therefore, considered more 'correct' than other forms, and taught in schools. जैसे: I'm not का standard English माना जाता है; I ain't को non-standard या sub-standard.

Statement : ऐसा वाक्य जिसमें कोई कथन हो, statement कहा जाता है। A sentence which gives information is called a statement. जैसे: Moti stayed out all night. I am fine today.

Stative Verb : वह verb जिससे अवस्था (states) का बोध हो, actions का नहीं और जिसका प्रयोग प्रायः progressive tenses में नहीं होता हो, stative verb कहलता है। A stative verb is one that is not normally used in progressive tenses. Most stative verbs refer to states, not to actions or events. जैसे : know, remember, contain आदि।

Stress : जिस तरह से word, phrase या sentence के एक या एक से अधिक part को शेष part से अधिक जोर से बोला जाता है, stress कहलाता है। Stress is the way in which one or more parts of a word, phrase or sentence are made to sound more important than the rest (by using a louder voice and/or higher pitch). जैसे : ˈcamel में प्रथम syllable पर stress है; deˈvelop में second syllable पर stress है।

Strong Form : कुछ शब्दों का उच्चारण दो तरह से किया जाता है, धीरे-धीरे और सावधानीपूर्वक, इसे strong form कहते हैं या तेजी से जिसमें vowel /ə/ या /i/ का प्रयोग किया जाता है, इसे weak form कहते हैं। जैसे : can में /kæn/ strong form है; /kən/ weak form है; was में /wɔz/ strong form है; /wəz/ weak form है।

Strong Verb : वह verb जो अपने अंतर्गत vowel के परिवर्तन से ही अपना past tense तथा past participle रूप बना सके strong verb कहलाता है। जैसे : drive-drove-driven; sing-sang-sung; eat-ate-eaten; fall-fell-fallen.

Subject : वह noun या pronoun जो affirmative sentence में verb के पहले आता है, subject कहलाता है। जैसे : *Oil* floats on water. *Mohan* broke another glass today. *Lying* won't help. *Telling lies* won't help. *To believe that* isn't easy.

Subject-Tag : A tag which repeats or identifies the subject is called a subject-tag. जैसे : She is an idiot, *that girl.*

Subjunctive Mood : When a verb *supposes* an action, it is in the subjunctive mood. इस verb form का प्रयोग कुछ खास structure में किया जाता है। जैसे : If I *were* you, I would do it. It's important that he *be* informed immediately.

Subordinate Clause : जो clause स्वतः अर्थ की पूर्ण अभिव्यक्ति नहीं करता, बल्कि main clause पर आश्रित रहता है, subordinate clause कहलाता है। जैसे : I think *he is a good boy.* I will follow you *wherever you go.*

Subordinating Conjunction : जो conjunction subordinate clause को शेष main clause से जोड़ता है, subordinating conjunction कहलाता है। इनमें प्रमुख हैं : that, which, who, when, where, while, before, until, if, after, since, because, though, although, unless, as इत्यादि। He asked *what* I meant. यहाँ what भी subordinating conjunction है।

Sub-Standard language : जो standard language में नहीं हो। Sub-standard language को incorrect समझा जाता है। जैसे : I *ain't* ready. She don't agree. He already *done* it.

Suffix : eating, working, hopeful, beautiful में -ing और -ful को suffixes कहा जाता है।

Superlative Degree : adjective या adverb का वह रूप जिसके अंत में suffix *-est* लगा रहता है, superlative degree कहलाता है। जैसे : oldest, fastest आदि। कभी-कभी superlative में structure *most* + adjective/adverb का भी प्रयोग किया जाता है। जैसे : most intelligent, most politely आदि।

Syntax : जिन नियमों के अनुसार words तथा expressions से clauses तथा sentences बनते हैं (the rules for the way words and expressions are combined into clauses and sentences), syntax कहलाता है।

Tag : वह short phrase (auxiliary verb + pronoun subject) जो वाक्य के अंत में जुटा रहता है, tag कहलाता है। जैसे : She doesn't care, *does she ?*

Temporal Conjunction : connected with *time.* जैसे : when, while, until—*temporal conjunctions* हैं।

Tense : वह verb form जिससे किसी कार्य या घटना के होने का समय पता चले, tense कहलाता है। A verb form which shows the time of an action or event is called tense. जैसे : will go (future); is sitting (present); saw (past).

Third Person : जिस व्यक्ति या वस्तु के बारे में बात की जाए (the people or things spoken about) उसे third person कहते हैं। जैसे : he, she, it, his, him, her, them, they. साधारणतः nouns, *third person* के ही होते हैं।

To-Infinitive : वह infinitive जिसके पहले to लगा हो, to-infinitive कहलाता है। जैसे : a difficult car *to start.* यहाँ 'to start' *to-infinitive* है।

Transitive Verb : वह verb जिसके बाद कोई object लग सके, transitive verb कहलाता है। A transitive verb is one that can have an object. जैसे : eat (a meal); drive (a car); give (a present); sing (a song). यहाँ eat, drive, give, sing *transitive verbs* हैं।

Uncountable Noun (or, **Mass Noun**) **:** वह noun जिसका न plural form होता हो और न जिसके पहले साधारणतः a/an लगता हो, uncountable या mass noun कहलाता है। जैसे : oil, love, happiness इत्यादि।

Verb : वह शब्द जिसका past tense रूप बन सके verb कहलाता है। जैसे : ask, play, can, wake इत्यादि।

Verb Phrase : वह verb जिसके कई भाग (several parts) होते हैं, verb phrase कहलाता है। जैसे : would have been forgotten.

Verbless Sentence : शब्दों का एक समूह जिससे पूरा अर्थ निकले किंतु जिसमें finite verb नहीं हो, verbless sentence कहलाता है। जैसे : Another book, please. Oh, what a beautiful morning! Glad to have been of service. Delighted to hear it.

Voice : The form of the verb which indicates whether the subject is the doer of whatever the verb expresses ("John saw") or the receiver ("John was seen") is called voice. Active तथा passive strutures में जो अंतर होता है, वह voice के कारण होता है; voice का संबंध वाक्य के verb से होता है।

Vowel : वह sound जो मुँह से हवा निकलने के रास्ते में बिना किसी रुकावट के बोला जा सकता हो, vowel कहलाता है। A sound produced by the unrestricted passage of air through the mouth is a vowel sound. English vowels are indicated by the letters *a, e, i, o, u* and sometimes *w* and *y.*

Unchanged Plural : वह plural जिसका रूप singular जैसा हो, unchanged plural कहलाता है। जैसे : Seven *sheep* were there. Two *deer* are in the lawn.

Weak Verb : जिस verb का past tense तथा past participle *d,t* या *ed* जोड़ने से बनता है, weak verb कहलाता है। (सीमित अर्थ में weak verb को regular verb कह सकते हैं)। जैसे : walk-walked, hurry-hurried, teach-taught, sell-sold, send-sent.

Word Classes : Professor Jespersen ने जिस तरह शब्दों का वर्गीकरण किया उसे word classes कहा जाता है, जिसे दूसरे grammarians *parts of speech* कहते हैं। (the chief difference being that, in definition, Jespersen puts rather more emphasis on form).

Zero Plural : वह irregular plural form जो singular जैसा ही रहता है, zero plural कहलाता है। An irregular plural form which is the same as the singular is called zero plural. जैसे : sheep, aircraft.

□ □ □

2 ARTICLES

(A) ARTICLES : A, AN, THE

1. *Look at these sentences :*

This is *a* book. | *The* earth is round.
That is *an* orange. | Here is *the* ink I want.

(i) A, An तथा The को articles कहा जाता है। Modern English Grammar में Articles को determiners के अंतर्गत रखा गया है।

Articles are members of a group of words called *determiners,* that are used before nouns.

Articles के अलावा कुछ अन्य मुख्य determiners हैं : my, your, this, that, these, those, some, any इत्यादि।

(ii) Articles के दो भेद होते हैं :

Articles [Definite Article : The
Indefinite Article : A/An

2. *Look at these sentences :*

This is *a* boy. **(indefinite)**
It is *an* egg. **(indefinite)**
That is *the* pen I want. **(definite)**

A/An का शाब्दिक अर्थ : 'एक, कोई' होता है किंतु The का कोई शाब्दिक अर्थ नहीं होता। Article noun को definite या indefinite बनाने में मदद करता है।

3. *Look at these sentences :*

This is the /दॅ/ boy. | This is the /दि/ ant.
That is the /दॅ/ car. | That is the /दि/ ox.
It is the /दॅ/ pen. | It is the /दि/ egg.

(i) अगर consonant से शुरू होनेवाले शब्द के पहले the आता है तो उसे /दॅ/ पढ़ा जाता है।

(ii) किंतु vowel से शुरू होनेवाले शब्द के पहले जब the आता है तब the को /दि/ पढ़ा जाता है।

(iii) अगर the के बाद आनेवाले शब्द पर हम जोर देना चाहते हों तो the का उच्चारण /दि/ होता है, चाहे वह शब्द consonant से ही शुरू क्यों न हो। जैसे :

This is the /दि/ boy who broke my window.
The /दि/ (= the most important) social event of the year was ...

(B) POSITION OF ARTICLES

1. *Look at these sentences :*

Give me *a* book. That is *the* box.
Here is *an* umbrella. These are *the* boys.

Articles का प्रयोग noun के ठीक पहले होता है।

2. *Look at these sentences :*

This is *a* good *book*. That is *the* new *box*.
Here is *an* old *man*. *The* red *ball* is mine.

अगर noun के पहले कोई adjective (good, old, new, red) रहे तो article हमेशा adjective के पहले आता है।

3. *Look at these sentences :*

I have *a* very good *table*. He is *an* extremely kind *man*.
That is *a* very old *school*. She was *a* fairly tall *girl*.

अगर noun के पहले कोई adjective रहे और adjective के पहले कोई adverb, तो article उस adverb के पहले आता है तथा a या an का प्रयोग अपने से सबसे नजदीक आनेवाले शब्द के अनुसार होता है।

4. *Look at these sentences :*

All *the* boys are here. I want such *a* pen.
Both *the* friends have gone. Such *a* boy will not pass.
Give me double *the* amount. Please come in half *an* hour.

साधारणतः all, both, such, double, half के बाद article आता है।

5. *Look at these sentences :*

How fine *a* day ! How beautiful *a* night !
He is so fine *a* man. It is too good *an* attempt.

How, so, too के बाद जब adjective आता है तब article का प्रयोग उस adjective के बाद तथा noun के पहले होता है।

(C) USE OF ARTICLES

1. *Look at these sentences :*

A cat eats meat. It is *an elephant*.
She has *a hat*. He wants *the ink* I bought.
Where are *the pens* he gave me ? *The tiger* is beautiful.

(i) Article (a/an/the) का प्रयोग noun (जैसे—cat, hat, elephant, tiger, ink, pens) के पहले किया जाता है।

(ii) A/An का प्रयोग singular countable noun (जैसे—cat, hat, elephant) के पहले किया जाता है। वैसा noun जिसकी गिनती हो सके और जो एकवचन में हो singular countable noun कहलाता है।

(iii) The का प्रयोग countable singular (जैसे—tiger) तथा countable plural (जैसे—pens) एवं uncountable noun (जैसे—ink) के पहले होता है। वैसा noun जिसकी न गिनती हो सके और न जिसका plural बन सके, uncountable noun कहलाता है; जैसे—water, milk, oil, tea इत्यादि।

(D) USE OF '*A/AN*'

1. *Look at these sentences :*

A girl likes *a toy.*	*A lion* killed *a cow.*
A cat has *a tail.*	*An apple* grows on *a tree.*
A dog is *an animal.*	*A girl* is buying *an inkpot.*

(i) A/An का प्रयोग singular countable noun (girl, toy, cat, tail, dog, animal, lion, cow, apple, tree, inkpot इत्यादि) के पहले अवश्य होता है।

(ii) अगर singular countable noun किसी consonant (b, c, d, f, g इत्यादि) से शुरू हो तो उसके पहले a लगता है।

(iii) अगर singular countable noun किसी vowel (a, e, i, o, u) से शुरू हो तो उसके पहले an लगता है।

2. *Look at these words :*

the 'h' pronounced	*with a silent 'h'*
a horse	**an** hour
a hill	**an** heir
a hotel	**an** heiress
a helicopter	**an** honour
a husband	**an** honorarium
a human being	**an** honest man
a humorous writer	**an** honourable man
a historical event	**an** hourly report
a humble man	**an** honorary job

(i) जब कोई singular countable noun 'h' से शुरू हो और उस 'h' का उच्चारण हो तब उसके पहले a लगता है।

(ii) जब कोई singular countable noun 'h' से शुरू हो और उस 'h' का उच्चारण नहीं हो तब उसके पहले an लगता है।

3. *Look at these words :*

a ewe	(यू)	**a** year	(यि)
a union	(यू)	**a** yell	(ये)
a uniform	(यू)	**a** yard	(या)

a eulogy	(यू)	**a** youth	(यू)
a unit	(यू)	**a** young man	(य)
a useful book	(यू)	**a** yellow pen	(ये)
a useless car	(यू)	**a** unique thing	(यू)
a European	(यू)	**a** united team	(यू)
a one-rupee note	(व)	**a** usual feature	(यू)
a one-eyed giant	(व)	**a** universal appeal	(यू)
a one-legged man	(व)	**a** university professor	(यू)
a one-man committee	(व)	**a** one-way ticket	(व)
a U.S. ally	(यू)	**a** U. K. plane	(यू)
a U. N. spokesman	(यू)	**a** U. S. S. R. ship	(यू)

(i) 'य', 'या', 'यि', 'ये' अथवा 'यू' जैसा उच्चारण से शुरू होनेवाले शब्दों के पहले a लगता है।

(ii) 'व' जैसा उच्चारण से शुरू होनेवाले शब्द के पहले भी a लगता है।

4. *Look at these sentences :*

Mr Sinha is *an* M.P.
He is *an* M.A.
You are *an* N. C. C. officer.
This is *an* L. P. school.
He is *an* M. L. A.
She is *an* M. Sc.
Mr Prasad is *an* S.D.O.
There is *an* H. E. School.
Here is *an* X–ray plant.
It is *an* R. T. C. bus.
They filed *an* F. I. R.
He is *an* S. I.

M.P., M.A., N.C.C., L.P., M.L.A., M.Sc., S.D.O., H.E., X-ray, R.T.C., F.I.R. तथा S.I. शब्द लिखने में consonant letter से शुरू होते हैं, किंतु उच्चारण में ये vowel sound (जैसे—एम॰ पी॰, एम॰ ए॰, एन॰ सी॰ सी॰ आदि) से शुरू होते हैं। इसलिए इनके पहले an लगता है।

The commonest ways of pronouncing the 26 letters

A,	a	/ए/	J,	j	/जे/	S,	s	/एस/
B,	b	/बी/	K,	k	/के/	T,	t	/टी/
C,	c	/सी/	L,	l	/एल/	U,	u	/यू/
D,	d	/डी/	M,	m	/एम/	V,	v	/वी/
E,	e	/ई/	N,	n	/एन/	W,	w	/डब्लू/
F,	f	/एफ/	O,	o	/ओ/	X,	x	/एक्स/
G,	g	/जी/	P,	p	/पी/	Y,	y	/वाआइ/
H,	h	/एच/	Q,	q	/क्यू/	Z,	z	/जेड/
I,	i	(आइ/	R,	r	/आर/			

अब तो आप स्वयं देख सकते हैं कि अंगरेजी के कौन-कौन letters vowel sound से उच्चारित होते हैं और कौन-कौन consonant sound से।

A/An के प्रयोग में किसी शब्द का written form नहीं वरन् spoken form महत्त्वपूर्ण होता है। जैसे : *an* R. A. F. किंतु *a* Royal Air Force Officer.

> Whether *a* or *an* is used before initials depends on how the initial is pronounced. A, E, F, H, I, L, M, N, O, R, S and X all begin with a vowel sound: hence *an* LEA school, *an* M. A., *an* M. P. but *a* BBC production, *a* B. A., *a* Ph.D., etc.
>
> —F. T. WOOD : CURRENT ENGLISH USAGE

Some more uses of A/An

5. *Look at these sentences/phrases :*

There is a boy. He is *a* teacher. There was *a* dog.	एक (one) या कोई (any) के अर्थ में a/an का प्रयोग किया जाता है।
6. A cow is *an* animal. A man gave me *a* book. *An* elephant killed a boy.	जब किसी singular countable noun का प्रयोग वाक्य के शुरू में किया जाता है तब उसके पहले indefinite article (a/an) लगता है।
7. He is *a* teacher. She is *a* nurse. Mr Sinha is *a* doctor. I am *an* engineer.	पेशा के नाम (name of the profession) के पहले प्रायः a/an का प्रयोग किया जाता है।
8. He came with *a* bag. She ran without *an* umbrella.	अगर with या without के बाद कोई singular countable noun रहे तो उसके पहले a/an लगता है।
9. I have *a* hundred rupees. He has *a* dozen pens. She had *a* thousand books.	hundred, dozen, thousand, million जैसे गिनती-सूचक शब्दों के पहले a लगता है।
10. He earns Rs. 500/- *a* month. They come here once *a* week. We walk six kilometres *an* hour. Rice sells three rupees *a kilo*.	'प्रत्येक', 'की दर से', 'के हिसाब से' के अर्थ में a/an का प्रयोग singular countable nounके पहले किया जाता है।
11. What *a* dog ! What *a* foolish boy ! What *a* beautiful building !	Exclamation में what के बाद singular countable noun के पहले *a* का प्रयोग किया जाता है।
12. He is *a* Dara Singh. She is *a* Lata. He is *a* Hitler. You are *a* Shakespeare.	व्यक्ति नहीं, व्यक्ति की विशेषता के अर्थ में proper noun के पहले indefinite article लगता है। जैसे : He is a Dara Singh = दारा सिंह जैसा मजबूत।

13. as *a* rule
in *a* hurry
a short time ago
it is *a* pity
to have *a* knowledge
to give *an* answer
to have *a* good education
to make *a* good guess at
to have *a* pain/*a* cold/ *a* headache/*a* cough
on *an* average
to make *a* noise
to be in *a* temper
it is *a* shame
to give *a* warning
to take *an* interest in
to pay somebody *a* visit
to make *a* wrong use of
to have *a* bath/*a* drink/ *a* talk/*a* rest/*a* walk.

कुछ खास phrases में a/an का प्रयोग किया जाता है।

(E) NO *'A/AN'*

1. *Look at these sentences :*

Cows give milk.
Birds are flying.
Dogs are *animals.*
Boys like *story-books.*

Plural nouns (जैसे—cows, birds, dogs, animals, boys, story-books) इत्यादि) के पहले a/an कभी नहीं लगता।

2. *Look at these sentences :*

This is *Hari.*
We live in *India.*
Patna is in *Bihar.*
Delhi is a city.
Today is *Monday.*
She came in *March*

किसी व्यक्ति, देश, राज्य, शहर, दिन तथा महीना के नाम को proper noun कहा जाता है। Proper noun के पहले a/an नहीं लगाया जाता।

Note : किंतु a का प्रयोग Mr/Mrs/Miss+surname के पहले विशेष अर्थ में किया जा सकता है। जैसे : a Mr Sinha, a Mrs Sinha, a Miss Bose. 'A Mr Sinha' का अर्थ हुआ 'Mr Sinha नाम का व्यक्ति' जो वक्ता के लिए अनजान है। अगर Mr Sinha बिना a का रहेगा तो उसका अर्थ है कि वक्ता Mr Sinha को जानता है। उसी तरह—This letter is written by *a Ramesh* (रमेश नाम का कोई अनजान व्यक्ति)।

3. *Look at these sentences :*

Milk is good for us.
Money is *honey.*
Gold is yellow.
We like *tea* without *sugar.*

(i) Uncountable nouns (जैसे—milk, money, honey, gold, tea, coffee, sugar इत्यादि) के पहले a/an कभी नहीं लगता।

(ii) किंतु uncountable noun को single item बनाने के लिए हम 'a....of+uncountable noun का प्रयोग करते हैं। जैसे :

a cup of coffee
a glass of water
a bottle of ink
a bag of rice

(iii) knowledge शब्द uncountable है, किंतु जब इसका प्रयोग किसी विशेष अर्थ में किया जाता है तब article का प्रयोग करते हैं। जैसे :

A knowledge of language is always useful.
He has *a* good knowledge of mathematics.

4. *Look at these sentences :*

This is good *news.*
I have new *furniture.*
This is useful *information.*
You should take legal *advice.*

News, information, furniture, advice, baggage, dust तथा luggage *singular uncountable* nouns हैं। इनके पहले a/an का प्रयोग नहीं किया जाता। किंतु उनसे संख्या या मात्रा का बोध कराने के लिए उनके पहले some, any, a little, a piece of आदि का प्रयोग किया जाता है। जैसे :

	uncountable		**countable**	
(i)	armour	a	piece / suit	of armour
	bread	a	piece / loaf	of bread
	cake	a	piece / slice	of cake
	chalk	a	piece / stick	of chalk
	furniture	a	piece / an article	of furniture
	grass	a	bit / blade	of grass
	ice	a	piece / block	of ice
	land	a	piece / strip	of land
	meat	a	piece / roast	of meat
	paper	a	piece / sheet	of paper
	rice	a	bit / grain	of rice
	rubbish	a	pile / heap	of rubbish
	sugar	a	piece / lump	of sugar
(ii)	abuse (गाली)		a word	of abuse
	advice	a	piece / word	of advice

uncountable	countable	
business ('commerce')	an item / a bit	of business
information	a piece / an item	of information
interest (सूद)	a bit / an amount	of interest
news	a piece / an item	of news
work (काम)	a piece / bit	of work
evidence	a piece	of evidence
fever	an attack	of fever
passion	a fit	of passion
research	a piece	of research.

अत:, हम *a piece of* chalk/coal/advice,..... *a bit of* grass/trouble,....*an item of* information/news,....कहते हैं। उसी तरह से :

length (लंबाई)	:	a foot of (water) / a yard of (cloth) / a mile of (cable)
area (क्षेत्रफल)	:	an acre of (land)
volume (मात्रा)	:	a pint of (beer) / a gallon of (petrol)
weight (वजन)	:	an ounce of (tabacco) / a pound of (butter) / a ton of (coal)

5. *Look at these sentences :*

We write on *paper*. Windows are made of *glass*.
I have a yard of *cloth*. *Iron* is a metal.

Paper (कागज), wine (शराब), glass (शीशा), cloth (कपड़ा), तथा iron (लोहा), uncountable nouns हैं, इनके पहले a/an नहीं लगता। किंतु जब paper (= अखबार), glass (ग्लास), cloth (किसी खास काम के लिए कपड़े का टुकड़ा) तथा iron (इस्तरी) से एक खास चीज का बोध हो तब उनके पहले a/an लगता है। जैसे :

Have *a* glass of wine. It's *a* (news) paper.
I use *an* electric iron. He has *a* dish-cloth.

6. *Look at these sentences :*

He was pale with *fear*. *We* live in *hope*.
Beauty is only skin deep. *Death* comes to all.

Fear, beauty, hope, death, happiness को uncountable nouns माना जाता है और इनके पहले a/an नहीं लगता। किंतु विशेष अर्थ में इनमें से कुछ के पहले a/an लगता है। जैसे :

Isn't she *a* beauty (= beautiful girl/woman) ?
Some children suffer from *a* fear of the dark.

(F) USE OF *'THE'*

1. *Look at these sentences :*

Mohan bought *a* pen.	*The* pen is Japanese.
She has *a* bag.	*The* bag is new.
I have *an* umbrella.	*The* umbrella is very good.

अगर कोई singular countable noun वाक्य में पहली बार आता है तो उसके पहले a/an लगता है। अगर वही noun दूसरी या तीसरी बार आता है तो उसके पहले the लगता है। जैसे :

A man came up to *a policeman* and asked him *a question. The Policeman* didn't understand *the question,* so he asked *the man* to repeat it.

2. *Look at these sentences :*

The tiger / *A* tiger } is a dangerous animal.

The cow / *A* cow } is a useful animal.

Singular countable noun के पहले जिससे पूरी जाति (species) का बोध हो, a या the का प्रयोग किया जाता है। A का प्रयोग करें या the का—इससे वाक्य के अर्थ में कोई अंतर नहीं आता।

3. *Look at these sentences :*

Rajeev is *the* tallest boy in the class.
Mr Jha is *the* oldest man in the village.

Superlative degree के पहले *the* लगता है।

4. *Look at these sentences :*

The rich should help *the* poor.
There is a school for *the* deaf in the city.

जब the+adjective का प्रयोग plural noun की तरह किया जाए (the poor = the poor men) तब उसके पहले *the* लगता है; जैसे—the old, the young, the blind, the educated, the needy, the wicked, the dead इत्यादि।

5. *Look at these sentences :*

The boys of this class are good.

He likes the tea of India.
The people of Bihar are in trouble.
The water of this glass is fresh.

जब किसी वाक्य की बनावट noun+of+noun हो तो प्रथम noun के पहले the का प्रयोग अवश्य किया जाता है।

6. *Look at these sentences :*

Who invented *the* radio ?
The television is a gift of science.
I hate *the* telephone.
He received a message on *the* wireless.

किसी आविष्कार (invention) के पहले *the* लगता है।

Note : Articles are used in the expressions *listen to the radio, on the radio,* but not in *watch television, on television,* or *on T.V.*—MICHAEL SWAN.

7. *Look at these sentences :*

He was wounded in *the* leg.
They hit him on *the* head.
She caught him by *the* arm.
The brick hit him in *the* face.

Parts of the body (शरीर के भागों) के नाम के पहले *the* लगता है।

8. *Look at these sentences :*

He plays *the* tabla.
Hari played *the* harmonium.
Moti will play *the* violin.
Can you play *the* trumpet ?

Musical instruments (वाद्य-यंत्रों) के नाम के पहले *the* लगता है।

9. *Look at these sentences :*

This is *the* house I live in.
The boy in the corner is my brother.
The tall man is the Minister for Health.

जब किसी noun की व्यापकता किसी adjective या adjective phrase द्वारा सीमित कर दिया जाता है तब उस noun के पहले *the* लगता है।

10. *Look at these sentences :*

He is *the* cleverer of the two.
This is *the* better of the two books.

अगर किसी comparative degree से selection (चुनाव) या contrast (विरोध) का बोध हो तो उसके पहले *the* लगता है।

11. *Look at these sentences :*

The more he gets, *the* more he wants.
The sooner that work is done, *the* better.
The harder you get, *the* more you will be paid.
The more, the merrier.

कुछ खास idiomatic use में *the* का प्रयोग होता है।

12. *Look at these sentences :*

Eggs are sold by *the* dozen. Ghee is sold by *the* kilo.
Cloth is sold by *the* metre. Petrol is sold by *the* litre.

'के हिसाब से', 'की दर से' के अर्थ में singular countable noun के पहले *the* का प्रयोग होता है।

13. *Look at these sentences :*

I wanted to see *the* Principal. Where is *the* Headmaster ?
Come to *the* blackboard in the class.

The का प्रयोग उस noun के पहले होता है जिससे किसी निर्दिष्ट व्यक्ति या वस्तु का बोध हो।

14. *Look at these sentences :*

He is *the* Tagore of Hindi Poetry.
Viv Richards is *the* Bradman of today's cricket world.

The का प्रयोग proper noun के पहले होता है यदि किसी व्यक्ति से समान गुण या स्वभाववाले दूसरे व्यक्ति का बोध हो; जैसे—He is *the* Tagore of Hindi Poetry. = He is to Hindi Poetry what Tagore was to Bengali Poetry.

15. *Look at these sentences :*

I'll catch *the* next bus. They got *the* first taxi.
He missed *the* last train. Tom is *the* second son.

The का प्रयोग next, last, first, second इत्यादि के पहले होता है अगर इनके बाद कोई countable noun रहे। किंतु—

I will see you *next* Monday.
He went home *last* Sunday.

16. *Look at these sentences :*

Most
All
Many
Five
A half
One-third
A large number
The majority
} of *the* students have gone home.

Pronoun से शुरू होनेवाले इन phrases में *the* का प्रयोग होता है।

17. *Look at these sentences :*

You are *the* man for the post. That is *the* book I wanted.

यहाँ *the* का अर्थ 'same', 'very same' है तथा *the* का उच्चारण /दि/ होगा।

18. *Look at these sentences :*

The mother in her cried out. *The* brother in him was moved.

यहाँ the + countable noun से व्यक्ति के गुण का भाव व्यक्त होता है; जैसे—the mother = motherly feeling.

19. *Look at the following :*

the Hindus
the Muslims
the Sikhs
the Christians

धार्मिक समुदाय के पहले *the* लगता है।

20. *Look at the following :*

the Army
the Navy
the Air Force
the Police

Armed Forces तथा कानून लागू करनेवाले नामों के पहले *the* लगता है।

21. *Look at the following :*

the sun
the moon
the earth
the east
the west
the world

जो वस्तु दुनिया में केवल एक हो उसके पहले *the* लगता है।

22. *Look at the following :*

the Gita
the Ramayana
the Bible
the Koran
the Vedas
the Mahabharata

धार्मिक ग्रंथों के नाम के पहले *the* लगता है।

23. *Look at the following :*

the President of India
the Home Minister
the Director
the Chairman

जब किसी व्यक्ति को उसके title/ पद के द्वारा इंगित करना हो तब उसके पहले *the* लगता है।

24. *Look at the following :*

the Communist Party
the Congress Party
the Janata Party
the Labour Party
the Democratic Party
the Bhartiya Janata Party

राजनीतिक दल के नाम के पहले *the* लगता है।

25. *Look at the following :*

the Ganga
the Indian Ocean
the Godavari
the Pacific Ocean

the Gandak
the Red Sea
the Suez Canal.
the Bay of Bengal
the Brahmaputra
the Mahanadi.

नदी, नहर, समुद्र तथा महासमुद्र के नाम के पहले *the* लगता है।

26. *Look at the following :*

the top
the bottom
the back
the front
the side
the centre
the outside
the inside

Physical position के पहले *the* लगता है।

27. *Look at the following :*

the executive
the legislative
the judiciary
the judicial branch

सरकारी शाखाओं (names of the branches of the Government) के नाम के पहले *the* लगता है।

28. *Look at the following :*

the Roman Empire
the Gupta Dynasty
the Civil War
the Middle Ages
the French Revolution
(*but :* World War I)

साम्राज्य (empire), वंशज (dynasty), ऐतिहासिक काल तथा घटनाओं के पहले *the* लगता है।

29. *Look at the following :*

the Rotary Club
the Ford Foundation
the United Nations
the Minerva Club

Committee, club तथा foundation के नाम के पहले *the* लगता है।

30. *Look at the following :*

the Makalu (हवाई जहाज का नाम)
the Vikrant (समुद्री जहाज का नाम)
the Punjab Mail (रेलगाड़ी का नाम)

Aeroplane, ship तथा train के नाम के पहले *the* लगता है।

31. *Look at the following :*

the Indians
the Americans
the Pakistanis
the Russians
the English
the Chinese
the Africans
the Europeans
the French
the Japanese
the Italians
the Asians

Nationality words (नागरिकता/राष्ट्रीयता सूचित करनेवाले शब्दों) के पहले *the* लगता है।

32. *Look at the following :*

Delhi, *the* capital of India,... Nehru, *the* maker of India,....

यदि countable noun का प्रयोग किसी proper noun के apposition (addition of one word or group of words to another as an explanation) में हुआ हो तो उस countable noun के पहले *the* लगता है।

33. *Look at the following :*

Amar, *the* clerk
Mohan, *the* typist
Heera, *the* cook
Rahman, *the* bookseller
Mr Sinha, *the* Manager
Abdul, *the* grocer

Proper noun के बाद आनेवाला countable noun के पहले *the* लगता है, जब उस countable noun से पेशा, व्यवसाय आदि का बोध हो।

34. *Look at the following :*

the late Pandit Nehru
the beautiful Radha
the immortal Tulsi
the great Mahatma Gandhi

जब proper noun को कोई adjective qualify करता हो तब उसके आगे the का प्रयोग किया जाता है।

35. *Look at these sentences :*

He goes to *the* office at 10.
Do you often go to *the* cinema ?
He went to *the* circus.
They always go to *the* theatre.

Go to *the* cinema/theatre/opera/pictures/movies/circus/office आदि idioms हैं जिनमें *the* लगता है।

36. *Look at these sentences :*

What is *the* matter ?
What is *the* difficulty ?
What is the trouble ?
Speak to *the* point.
Keep to *the* left/*the* right.
He is in *the* right/*the* wrong.
I am in *the* know of it.
The air is thick with *the* rumour.

ऊपर *the* के कुछ मुहावरेदार प्रयोग हैं।

Some more nouns with and without 'the'

	Type of name	*Without 'the'*	*With 'the'*
1.	ऋतु के नाम	in spring, in summer, in winter, in autumn	in *the* spring season, in *the* summer season...
2.	यातायात के नाम	go / come / travel } by { car	sit in *the* car
		bus	be on *the* bus
		train	take *the* train
		boat	be on *the* boat
		plane	to be on *the* plane
		bicycle	sit on *the* bicycle

	Type of name	*Without 'the'*	*With 'the'*
3.	त्योहार एवं छुट्टियों के नाम	Holi, Deepawali, New Year, Christmas, Easter, Good Friday, Independence Day	*the* Deepawali holiday(s), *the* Christmas holidays
4.	Family relations	Father (Mummy, Mum) is here. How is Auntie ? Uncle will come soon. Brother, sister..... (जब इन शब्दों से speaker के father, mother का बोध हो तब इनको capital से लिखा जाता है और इनके पहले *the* नहीं लगता।)	*The* father was the tallest in the family.
5.	देशों के नाम (अगर इनके पहले कोई adjective भी रहे तो उसके पहले प्रायः *the* नहीं लगता।)	America, India, Russia, China, Japan, Afghanistan, Modern India, North China, Ancient India, South Korea.	*the* U. S. A. (the United States of America), *the* U.S.S.R., *the* People's Republic of China, *the* Netherlands, *the* Congo.
6.	राज्यों और शहरों के नाम (इनके पहले कोई adjective भी रहे तो प्रायः the नहीं लगता।)	London, Delhi, Bihar, Bombay, ancient Rome.	*the* city of London/Delhi. *the* State of Bihar.
7.	Universities के नाम	Bihar University, Patna University, Delhi University, Jawaharlal Nehru University, L.N. Mishra University.	*the* University of Bihar *the* University of Patna (*of* लगने पर *the* लगता है। किंतु अगर किसी व्यक्ति के नाम पर University हो तो उसको ऊपर बताए गए form (the....of....) में नहीं बदला जाता।)
8.	Newspapers के नाम के पहले	today's Times of India, our Indian Nation (genitive या possessive के बाद *the* हट जाता है। Life, Language आदि मैगजिनों के नाम के पहले *the* नहीं लगता।)	*the* Times of India *the* Indian Nation *the* Hindustan Times *the* New York Times

Type of name	Without 'the'	With 'the'
9. भोजन के नाम	have / before / at / after / stay for } { breakfast / lunch / tea / dinner / supper	*the* breakfast is good he liked *the* lunch prepare *(the)* dinner *the* dinner was well-cooked
10. बीमारी के नाम	cholera, diabetes, influenza, typhoid, malaria, tuberculosis	*(the)* plague *(the)* flu *(the)* measles *(the)* mumps
11. दिन-रात का समय (खासकर at, by, after, before के साथ)	at dawn/daybreak, at sunrise/sunset, at noon/ midnight, at/by night (by) day and night	during *the* day in *the* afternoon in *the* night in *the* day time in/during *the* morning in *the* evening *the* day before yesterday, at *the* moment, for *the* time being
12. पहाड़ के नाम	Mount Everest (पहाड़ की एक चोटी)	*the* Himalayas or *the* Himalayan Mountains, *the* Alps
13. झील के नाम	Silver Lake	*the* Suez Canal
14. द्वीप के नाम	Ceylon	*the* West Indies *the* Phillipines *the* Andamans
15. Uncountable noun	Gold is yellow.	*The* gold of this ring is pure.
	Water is fresh.	*The* water of this well is fresh.
	Life is hard.	*The* life we live is hard.
	Honesty is the best policy	*The* honesty of the boy cannot be doubted.
16. महीना तथा सप्ताह के नाम	January, March, Monday, Sunday I hate Mondays.	On *the* first Sunday. (दिन के नाम Plural हो सकते हैं तथा इनके नाम के पहले adjective रहने पर *the* लग सकता है।)
17. व्यक्तिगत नाम	Doctor Gupta	

Type of name	*Without 'the'*	*With 'the'*
	Principal Sen Professor Ahmad President Reddy	*the* Duke *the* Lord (God) *the* Emperor
18. Proper noun	Shakespeare	*the* Shakespeare (Shakespeare जैसा नाटककार)
	Newton	*the* Newton (Newton जैसा वैज्ञानिक)
19. Proper noun (With adjective)	in India	in *the* India of today (to denote part of a collective whole)
20. Adjective+ noun	Indian paper	*the* paper of India
	Chinese history	*the* history of China
	American literature	*the* literature of America
	Japanese cameras	*the* cameras from Japan
	Restoration comedy	*the* comedy of the Restoration
21. Name+ common noun (denoting building, streets, bridges, etc)	Park Lane Mokamah Bridge Oxford Street Palam Airport Patna College L. S. College	
	London Road	*the* London road (= the road leading to London)
22. सार्वजनिक संस्थान		
(i) Hotels, restaurants		*the* Ashoka (Hotel) *the* Maurya
(ii) Theatres, cinemas, clubs etc.		*the* Amar Talkies *the* Jawahar Picture Hall.
(iii) Museums, libraries के नाम		*the* British Museum *the* Patna Museum
(iv) Banks, Shops, तथा Railway	Goraul Station Turki Station Patna Junction	*the* State Bank *the* Central Bank *the* Tata Textiles

Type of name	*Without 'the'*	*With 'the'*
Stations के नाम		*the* Book Palace
(v) Parks, Gardens के नाम	Hyde Park Central Park	*the* Zoo *the* Botanical Garden
(vi) Streets तथा Roads के नाम	Abid Road Club Road	*the* National High Way *the* Lateral Road
(vii) संस्थाओं के नाम (at, in, to, इत्यादि के साथ be in/go to	bed (साने के लिए) prison (सजा काटने के लिए) hospital (इलाज के लिए) school (पढ़ने के लिए) college (,, ,, ,,) church (प्रार्थना ,, ,,) market (खरीद-बिक्री के लिए)	on *the* bed see *the* prison. build *the* hospital go beyond *the* school/college/church
	be at/go home be in/leave town go to walk (जब इनसे इनके मौलिक उद्देश्य का बोध हो तब इनके पहले *the* नहीं लगता।)	(जब इनसे place का बोध हो तब इनके पहले *the* लगता है।)
	go to walk in/leave town at/go home	go to *the* office approach *the* village
23. ईश्वर के नाम के पहले	God	*the* gods (देवता)
24. -ing form	English teaching	*The* teaching of English (*the* is used with the... *ing* form followed by *of*)
25. (i) तिथि लिखने में (ii) नाम	May 15th 25th July Henry V (लिखने में *the* नहीं लिखा जाता किंतु पढ़ने में *the* जोड़कर पढ़ा जाता है।)	*The* fifteenth of May *The* twentyfifth of July. Henry *the* fifth.
26. Parallel (समानान्तर) structures में	man to man, face to face. day by day, day and	keep to *the* right.

Type of name	Without 'the'	With 'the'
या double expressions with prepositions में	night. father and son, brother and sister husband and wife, arm in arm, from begining to end, from village to village, from right to left, from west to north, man and wife, mother and child, side by side, with hat and coat, from top to bottom, on land and sea, inch by inch, day after day	he lives in *the* north from *the* beginning of *the* day to *the* end of it

(G) NO ARTICLES

1. *Look at these sentences :*

He knows *English, Hindi, French, Russian* and *Chinese.*
We know *German, Sanskrit, Bengali, Urdu,* and *Tamil.*

भाषा के नाम के पहले article नहीं लगता।

2. *Look at these sentences :*

They play *football, hockey* and *cricket.*
We play *tennis, polo* and *volleyball.*

खेल के नाम के पहले article नहीं लगता।

3. *Look at these sentences :*

Wordsworth was a poet of *Nature.*
Science has changed our life.
Society will not permit us to do it.
Life is very hard here.

Nature, science, life, parliament, freedom, death इत्यादि का प्रयोग जब सामान्य अर्थ में हो तब इनके पहले article नहीं लगता।

4. *Look at these sentences :*

Man is mortal.
Woman is man's mate.
It is a crime against *humanity.*
The future of *mankind* is bright.

Man, woman, humanity तथा *mankind* का प्रयोग जब व्यापक अर्थ में हो तब उनके पहले article नहीं लगता।

5. *Look at these sentences :*

They *elected* him President.
He was *appointed* teacher.
We *declared* him Captain.
We *made* him Monitor.

Appoint, declare, elect तथा *made* के बाद आनेवाले noun के पहले प्रायः article नहीं लगता।

6. *Look at these sentences :*

John's coat is new.
India's problems are serious.
Hari's cow is there.
Sita's frock is there.

Articles are not normally used in genitive expressions when the first word is a proper name.

7. *Look at these sentences :*

Most birds can fly.
Most of the girls are here.
Most boys have come.
Most people like it.

Most के तुरत बाद कोई noun आए या of तो most के पहले the नहीं लगाया जाता।

8. *Look at these sentences :*

I want this *type of* gun.
We don't like this *sort of* boy.
He is a different *kind of* man.

Type of, kind of, sort of के बाद आनेवाले noun के पहले article नहीं लगता।

9. *Look at these sentences :*

Tea is hot.
Water is useful for us.
Boys will be *boys*.
Dogs bark and *asses* bray.

Uncountable noun (tea/water) तथा plural noun (boys, dogs, asses) का प्रयोग जब सामान्य अर्थ में हो तब उनके पहले article नहीं लगाया जाता।

10. *Look at these sentences :*

Ragho is promoted to *the rank of* Major.
He was given *the title of* Raja.

Rank तथा title शब्द के बाद आनेवाले noun के पहले article नहीं लगता।

11. *Look at these sentences :*

Tom lives in *London*.
India is a big country in *Asia*.
Hari came from *Japan*.
Poland is in *Europe*.

व्यक्ति, शहर, गाँव, राज्य, देश तथा महादेश के नाम के पहले article का प्रयोग प्रायः नहीं किया जाता।

12. *Look at these sentences :*

He came in *March*.
She left home on *Sunday*.

January is very cold. I was busy on *Monday*.

Names of the months (= January, February, March....) तथा days of the week (= Sunday, Monday, Tuesday...) के पहले article नहीं लगता है।

Note : (i) दिनों के नाम का plural भी होता है। जैसे: I hate *Mondays*. I am free on *Sundays*.

(ii) दिनों के नाम के पहले अगर कोई ऐसा adjective रहे जिससे point of time का बोध हो तो उसके पहले the लगता है। जैसे:
He will leave on *the* first Sunday of the next month.
(iii) जब दिन के नाम से किसी खास दिन का बोध नहीं हो तब उसके पहले a लगता है। यहाँ a का अर्थ any होता है। जैसे :
He left on *a* (= any) Sunday (without reference to a particular Sunday).

13. *Look at these sentences :*

He is a student of *geography*.
I am interested in ancient *history*.
She got good marks in *chemistry*.

विषयों के नाम *(history, geography, physics, mathematics etc.)* के पहले article नहीं लगता।

14. *Look at these sentences :*

Mr Sinha *turned* communist. A frustrated writer *turns* critic.

अगर turn का अर्थ become हो तो उसके बाद आनेवाले noun के पहले article नहीं लगता।

15. *Look at the following :*

Missing family of newsman safe	(Newspaper heading)
Wire reply immediately.	(Telegram)
College closed for summer vacation.	(Titles in notices, posters)
Open packet at other end.	(Instructions).

Headlines, telegrams, notices, lists, तथा *outlines* के पहले article का प्रयोग नहीं किया जाता।

16. *Look at these sentences :*

Give me *another* book. *Her* dog is black.
My uncle is here. *That* man is tall.

दो determiners का प्रयोग एक साथ साधारणतः नहीं किया जा सकता। Another में 'an' article है, अतः *an* another कहना गलत है, *the* other कह सकते हैं। उसी तरह *the* my uncle, *a* her dog या *the* that man कभी नहीं लिखा या बोला जाता है। (Two determiners cannot be usually used together).

Note : All तथा both के बाद कभी-कभी the का प्रयोग नहीं किया जाता। जैसे: *All (the)* eight students in the class passed the exam. *Both (the)* children are good at maths.

We can say—all year, all week, all day, all night, all summer, all winter, *but not* all hour or all century. जैसे: I have been waiting for you *all day.* He has been idle for *all week.*

17. निम्नलिखित expressions में articles का प्रयोग नहीं होता :

(i) at first	by heart	by messenger	in time
at last	by mistake	in public	in town
at work	by accident	in fact	in debt
at peace	by sea	in conclusion	in silence
at fault	by train/car/bus	in general	in favour of
at noon	by post	in front of	next April
at night	by day	in turn	last Monday
at sunset	by night	in trouble	by agreement
(ii) by land	by air	by plane	on sale/for sale
on foot	at school		at tea
at dinner	by hand	at times	on purpose
on duty	on strike	on watch	on half-pay
on demand	on death	in ink/pencil (but, write with *a* pen/*a* pencil)	(but on *a* scholarship)
all morning	all night		all day
get in trouble		all day and night	by hand
(iii) to school	in/to class	at lunch	to/at/from work
at school	to/at college	by road	in fact
from school	for leave	at noon	

Note : American English में in school, in college अधिक प्रचलित है at school, at college से।

(H) REPETITION OF THE ARTICLE

18. *Look at these sentences :*

(i) I shall read *the* first and *the* second chapter.
I shall read *the* first and second chapters.

(ii) We know *the* English and *the* German language.
We know *the* English and German languages.

अगर and द्वारा जुटे दो या दो से अधिक adjective एक ही व्यक्ति/वस्तु को qualify करे तो article प्रथम adjective के पहले ही लगेगा।

किंतु अगर वे भिन्न व्यक्ति/वस्तु को qualify करें तो उनमें प्रत्येक adjective के आगे article लगेगा।

a black and white cat (= एक ही बिल्ली जो काली और उजली है।)
a black and *a* white cat (= दो बिल्लियाँ—एक काली और दूसरी उजली हैं।)
a poet and thinker (= एक ही व्यक्ति जो कवि और विचारक है।)
a poet and a thinker (= दो व्यक्ति—एक कवि है और दूसरा विचारक है।)

(I) NATIONALITY WORDS AND ADJECTIVES AS HEAD

बहुत सारे nationality words (राष्ट्रीयतासूचक शब्द) हैं जिनके पहले *a/an/the* का प्रयोग किया जाता है। जैसे : *an* Englishman, several Englishmen, *the* English. कुछ और examples देखें :

वह **अमेरिका** में रहता है।	He lives in *America.*	(noun)
यह (एक) **अमेरिकन** गाड़ी है।	This is an *American* car.	(adjective)
मैंने एक **अमेरिकन** को देखा।	I saw *an American.*	(singular noun)
दो **अमेरिकन** आ रहे हैं।	Two *Americans* are coming.	(plural noun)
अमेरिकन (अमेरिका के लोग) धनी होते हैं।	*The Americans* are rich.	(plural noun)

अब आप इस Table को ध्यानपूर्वक पढ़ें और देखें कि articles कहाँ लगता है और कहाँ नहीं।

Name of country or continent (देश या महादेश का नाम)	*adjective* (विशेषण)	*singular* (एकवचन : एक व्यक्ति)	*plural* (बहुवचन : लोग)
China	Chinese	a Chinese	the Chinese
Japan	Japanese	a Japanese	the Japanese
Portugal	Portuguese	a Portuguese	the Portuguese
Switzerland	Swiss	a Swiss	the Swiss
Vietnam	Vietnamese	a Vietnamese	the Vietnamese
Israel	Israeli	an Israeli	the Israelis
Pakistan	Pakistani	a Pakistani	the Pakistanis
Germany	German	a German	the Germans
Greece	Greek	a Greek	the Greeks
Africa	African	an African	the Africans
America	American	an American	the Americans
India	Indian	an Indian	the Indians
Europe	European	a European	the Europeans
Asia	Asian	an Asian	the Asians

Name of country or continent (देश या महादेश का नाम)	adjective (विशेषण)	singular (एकवचन : एक व्यक्ति)	plural (बहुवचन : लोग)
Australia	Australian	an Australian	the Australians
Italy	Italian	an Italian	the Italians
Russia	Russian	a Russian	the Russians
Belgium	Belgian	a Belgian	the Belgians
Brazil	Brazilian	a Brazilian	the Brazilians
Hungry	Hungarian	a Hungarian	the Hungarians
Norway	Norwegian	a Norwegian	the Norwegians
Denmark	Danish	a Dane	the Danes
Finland	Finnish	a Finn	the Finns
Poland	Polish	a Pole	the Poles
Spain	Spanish	a Spaniard	the Spaniards
Sweden	Swedish	a Swede	the Swedes
Arabia	Arabic	an Arab	the Arabs
England	English	an Englishman	Englishmen the English
France	French	a Frenchman	Frenchmen the French
Holland, the Netherlands	Dutch	a Dutchman	Dutchmen the Dutch
Ireland	Irish	an Irishman	Irishmen the Irish
Wales	Welsh	a Welshman	Welshmen the Welsh
Britain	British	a Briton	the British (Britons)
Scotland	Scots Scottish (Scotch)	a Scotsman a Scot (a Scotchman)	Scotsmen the Scots (the Scotchmen, the Scotch)

Examples Worked Out

Put in a, an *or* the *wherever necessary. Don't use any article where it is not necessary :*

1. ....dog is....animal.	A dog is *an* animal.
2. He became...great man.	He became *a* great man.
3. She is....good girl.	She is *a* good girl.

4. Windows are made of...glass.	Windows are made of *glass*.
5. I was invited to...dinner.	*I* was invited to *dinner*.
6. We write on...paper.	We write on *paper*.
7. ....old and....young should live together.	*The* old and *the* young should live together.
8. The brick hit him in...face.	The brick hit him in *the* face.
9. He went....home.	He went *home*.
10. She is going to....cinema.	She is going to *the* cinema.
11. Mr Khan is coming from........? office.	Mr Khan is coming from *the* office.
12. Where is....pen I bought ?	Where is *the* pen I bought ?
13. Meena likes....music of France.	Meena likes *the* music of France.
14. He turned on...television.	He turned on *the* television.
15. ....mother is out today.	*Mother* is out today.
16. I want....today's *Indian Nation*.	I want *today's Indian Nation*.
17. .....principal is not.... town.	*The* principal is not in *town*.
18. Mukul goes to....school every day.	Mukul goes to *school* every day.
19. They are.....brother and....sister.	They are *brother* and *sister*.
20. He invited me to....tea.	He invited me to *tea*.
21. I am a student of....Bihar University.	I am a student of *Bihar University*.
22. He reads in....Patna College.	He reads in *Patna College*.
23. Sita has....headache.	Sita has *a* headache.
24. What is on....radio tonight ?	What is on *the* radio tonight ?
25. We like....history and..... physics.	We like *history* and *physics*.
26. He writes about....Nature.	He writes about *Nature*.
27. I shall be back in....hour.	I shall be back in *an* hour.
28. She is....typist.	She is *a* typist.
29. I have got...cold.	I have got *a* cold.
30. He is not....Shakespeare.	He is not *a* Shakespeare.
31. Please open....window.	Please open *the* window.
32. .....richest are not always ....happiest.	*The* richest are not always *the* happiest.
33. ....honest man gets his due.	*An* honest man gets his due.
34. That the earth is round is.... universal truth.	That the earth is round is *a* universal truth.
35. .....milk comes from....cow.	Milk comes from *the* cow.
36. There is....dirt on...plate.	There is dirt on *the* plate.
37. .....child ran across....street.	*A* child ran across *the* road.
38. Mr Kerketta is....M.Sc. from..... University of Ranchi.	Mr Kerketta is *an* M.Sc. from *the* University of Ranchi.

39.	Most of....students are good.	Most of *the* students are good.
40.	What is....matter ?	What is *the* matter ?
41.	He is....Kalidas of our times.	He is *the* Kalidas of our times.
42.	....Bengali is.....Indian language.	Bengali is *an* Indian language.
43.	We have so fine....day !	We have so fine *a* day !
44.	....tiger is....fierce animal.	*A* tiger is *a* fierce animal.
45.	....cat is not so faithful as....dog.	*A* cat is not so faithful as *a* dog.
46.	....honesty is....best policy.	Honesty is *the* best policy.
47.	....more one has, ...more one wants.	*The* more one has, *the* more one wants.
48.	....Bombay is....London of India.	*Bombay* is *the* London of India.
49.	I am fond of....milk and....tea.	I am fond of *milk* and *tea*.
50.	I wrote to....Father for....money.	I wrote to *Father* for *money*.
51.	In.....summer, he went to Bombay.	In *summer* he went to Bombay.
52.	He is....socialist, not....communist.	He is *a* socialist, not *a* communist.
53.	Mr Sinha is....M.A. in....English.	Mr Sinha is *an* M.A. in *English*.
54.	Hari is....Hindu; Abdul is.... Muslim.	Hari is *a* Hindu; Abdul is *a* Muslim.
55.	Ruby is....taller of the two girls.	Ruby is *the* taller of the two girls.
56.	I spent....Holi at home.	I spent *Holi* at home.
57.	This is....best book on the subject.	This is *the* best book on the subject.
58.	What type of...answer is this ?	What *type of* answer is this ?
59.	....sun rises in....east.	*The* sun rises in *the* east.
60.	Open....book and read....passage.	Open *the* book and read *the* passage.
61.	.....drowning man catches at ...straw.	*A* drowning man catches at *a* straw.
62.	He is....worst player.	He is *the* worst player.
63.	I found...book you were asking for.	I found *the* book you were asking for.
64.	This is....historic occasion.	This is *a* historic occasion.
65.	After....year or two, ...question can be considered.	After *a* year or two, *the* question can be considered.
66.	We want....help of....few volunteers.	We want *the* help of *a* few volunteers.
67.	....teaching of....English is difficult today.	*The* teaching of English is difficult today.
68.	Yesterday I saw....European riding on....elephant.	Yesterday I saw *a* European riding on *an* elephant.

69. ....English often fought ....French.	*The* English often fought *the* French.
70. ....ink is....useful article.	*Ink* is *a* useful article.
71. It was....unique sight.	It was *a* unique sight.
72. ....Ganga is....sacred river.	*The* Ganga is *a* sacred river.
73. His brother is....University Professor.	His brother is *a* University Professor.
74. Have you read....Ramayana ?	Have you read *the* Ramayana ?
75. He was struck by....arrow.	He was struck by *an* arrow.
76. He was....African by birth, not.... European.	He was *an* African by birth, not *a* European.
77. He drives....motor car at.... uniform speed.	He drives *the* motor car at *a* uniform speed.
78. Try to come....hour before the class starts.	Try to come *an* hour before the class starts.
79. Let us go and bathe in....river.	Let us go and bathe in *the* river.
80. ....few days later people made.... appeal against it.	*A* few days later people made *an* appeal against it.
81. She approached....table to put.... glass of water on it.	She approached *the* table to put *a* glass of water on it.

EXERCISE 1

Put a *or* an *before the following phrases :*

EXAMPLES : (i) ....happy man = *a* happy man (ii) ....unanimous decision = *a* unanimous decision.

1. ....happy man
2. .....interesting play
3. ....university teacher
4. ... aspirin tablet
5. ....English name
6. ....angry tiger
7. ....old woman
8. ....urgent message
9. ...unique opportunity
10. .....European language
11. ....H.E. School
12. ... Urdu teacher
13. ....honourable man
14. ....ex-M.P.
15. ....hour's delay
16. ....high wall
17. ....united team
18. ....young officer
19. ...Australian team
20. ....independent country
21. ....useless book.
22. ....B. B. C. report

EXERCISE 2

Use Articles wherever necessary :

EXAMPLES : (i) India is...very large country.
= India is *a* very large country.

(ii) He thinks he is....Napoleon.
= He thinks he is *a* Napoleon.

(याद रखें : *Singular countable noun* के पहले *a/an* लगता है; *uncountable* या *plural noun* के पहले नहीं।)

1. India is....large country.
2. Would you like....tea ?
3. This is....best I can do.
4. He is....senior teacher.
5. Shekhar is....honest boy.
6. Delhi is....city.
7. He has....big dog.
8. Shut....door, please.
9. This is....book I wanted.
10. He bought,......untensil.
11. She is....hour late.
12. Rana hit him on....head.
13. Mr Sinha is....M.A.
14. ....man is mortal.
15. He has....interesting book.
16. ....table has four legs.
17. We like....music very much.
18. Do you play....football ?
19. ....headmaster calls you.
20. What....opportunity you missed !

EXERCISE 3

Use Articles wherever necessary :

EXAMPLES : (i) I have....one-rupee note.
= I have *a* one-rupee note.
(ii) Mr Sen is...officer.
= Mr Sen is *an* officer.

1. I have....one-rupee note.
2. My brother is....officer.
3. Ramesh is....fool.
4. I saw....beggar.
5. He plays....harmonium.
6. They read.....*Times of India*.
7. ....owl is....bird.
8. They shot....bird.
9. There is....school in Patna.
10. He has an attack of....malaria.
11. That is....red apple.
12. He is....N.C.C. cadet.
13. We can't live without....air.
14. English is....easy language.
15. This is....lovely island.
16. Have you read....Bible ?
17. He has seen....Red Fort.
18. I hate such....fool.
19. He is....real Hitler.
20. That is....very old school.

EXERCISE 4

Use Articles wherever necessary :

EXAMPLES : (i) Don't be in such....hurry.
= Don't be in such *a* hurry.
(ii) This is...watch that I gave you.
= This is *the* watch that I gave you.

1. He is....European.
2. Once there was....king.
3. Call....man waiting outside.
4. This is....historic occasion.
5. ....Quoran is a holy book.
6. He is....humble man.
7. I hate....dishonest man.
8. I like....uniform colour.
9. There is....old elephant in my village.
10. We arrived on....fourth of July.
11. I lost....umbrella.
12. ....sun shines by day.
13. How fine....player he is !

14. ....minute you came, he ran off.
15. I saw....one-eyed man.
16. What....idiot he is !
17. She is....better singer than you.
18. ....King of Nepal came to India.
19. Dry these boots in...sun.
20. Man has conquered....moon.

EXERCISE 5

Use Articles wherever necessary :

EXAMPLES : (i) It is....L. P. School.
= It is *an* L. P. School.
(ii) He bought...X-ray plant.
= He bought *an* X-ray plant.

1. Give me....onion.
2. He bought....history book.
3. That is....apple.
4. There was....one-legged man.
5. Oranges are sold by....dozen.
6. He has....Alsatian dog.
7. ....university is a temple of learning.
8. She was wearing....straw hat.
9. Which is....taller—Asha or Meena ?
10. ....more they get,....more they want.
11. My friend is....tall man.
12. ....man has....nose.
13. We eat....rice.
14. This is....historical novel.
15. I bought....one-way ticket.
16. Tom earns six thousand....year.
17. ....window is made of glass.
18. We must have compassion for.... poor.
19. ....longest day has...shortest night.
20. ....Prime Minister will address.... nation today.

EXERCISE 6

Use Articles wherever necessary :

EXAMPLES : (i) ...truth about the matter is unknown.
= *The* truth about the matter is unknown.
(ii) He went to...United Kingdom with his wife.
= He went to *the* United Kingdom with his wife.

1. I want....book you borrowed.
2. He gave me....book to read.
3. Most of....students are good.
4. This is....best book on the subject.
5. He is better of....two boys.
6. He is....only child.
7. Please give me....mango I bought yesterday.
8. He has never known....mother's love.
9. He died without....heir.
10. He is....M.L.A.
11. India is....unique country.
12. I am going to....station to receive a friend.
13. He is....U.S. ambassador.
14. Let us try for....unanimous decision.
15. Ram is one of....best boys in his class.
16. He is....honourable man.
17. The poor boy is....orphan.
18. We went to....theatre yesterday.
19. She protested against having ....X-ray.
20. I sent it on....5th of July.

EXERCISE 7

Use Articles wherever necessary :

EXAMPLES : (i) That's ....ugly book.
= That's *an* ugly book.
(ii) On such...cold morning I do not go out.
= On such *a* cold morning I do not go out.

1. He wants to become....politician.
2. .....most of the people like it.
3. He has returned from....office.
4. Sports make....body strong.
5. I saw....Captain standing there.
6. Many great ships cross....Atlantic Ocean.
7. She plays....tennis very well.
8. By....united effort we may achieve success.
9. It is....absurd story.
10. ....U.S.S.R. is a great country.
11. This is....very good radio.
12. I want to go to....cinema.
13. She works in....morning.
14. One of....children is called Jim.
15. ....breakfast is at eight o'clock.
16. There is fish for....dinner today.
17. She thanked me for. ...present I gave her.
18. It was....great honour to me.
19. His ambition is to be.... engineer.
20. ....*Statesman* has wide circulation.

EXERCISE 8

Use Articles wherever necessary :

EXAMPLES : (i) Go up...stairs.
= Go up *the* stairs.
(ii) This is....one-act play.
= This is *a* one-act play.

1. Go up....stairs.
2. This is.....one-act play.
3. ....Ganga is a sacred river.
4. Put on....light.
5. He is now....old man.
6. ....stitch in time saves nine.
7. It is....hour's distance from here.
8. Two men were seen in....old car.
9. Why do you want....day's leave ?
10. ....sick dog died yesterday.
11. She is....B.A.
12. I am....tallest boy here.
13. I found....book you were asking for.
14. This is....one-sided game.
15. My brother is....S.D.O.
16. He is....union leader.
17. There is....H. E. School.
18. He wants me to play...cricket.
19. Write in....ink or with....pencil.
20. This is....better of....two books.
21. ....bird in hand is worth two in....bush.
22. ....Nature is beautiful in spring.
23. Newton was....great scientist.
24. ...sky is blue.

EXERCISE 9

Use Articles wherever necessary :

EXAMPLES : (i) Do not make....noise.
= Do not make *a* noise.

(ii) You do not know...Hindi.
= You do not know Hindi.

1. Do not make....noise.
2. How tall....man he is !
3. Ramesh is....best boy of this class.
4. Bombay is....very dear place to live in.
5. Mr Roy is appointed....Manager of the firm.
6. These pencils cost one rupee.... dozen.
7. Which is....first day of the week ?
8. What....beautiful picture it is !
9. ....flowers in my garden were stolen.
10. He became....successful doctor.
11. She is....wife of....famous artist.
12. You do not know....Maithili.
13. He is....extremely careful driver.
14. ....cow is...useful animal.
15. What kind of....bird have you seen ?
16. Akbar was....noblest king.
17. When he joined....army, he was very young.
18. He is....able student but not.... ablest.
19. Once....man had....strange goose.
20. Mary always wanted to be.... scientist.
21. My friend is not....minister, he is ....M. P.
22. It is a world where....rich hate.... poor.

EXERCISE 10

Use Articles wherever necessary :

EXAMPLES : (i) What....nice girl she is !
= What *a* nice girl she is !
(ii) ....life of....writer is difficult.
= *The* life of *a* writer is difficult.

1. Gold is....useful metal.
2. You are....fool to say that.
3. Can....blind see ?
4. He looks as stupid as....ass.
5. Turn to....left.
6. He can play....violin.
7. It is....unit of measurement.
8. He is....intelligent student.
9. Mr Sinha is.....M.Sc.
10. I shall be back in....hour.
11. English is....language of....people of England.
12. ....French is more difficult to learn than...English.
13. ....rich are getting richer.
14. Sri Lanka is to....south of....India.
15. June is....hottest month of...year.
16. ....fox is....clever animal.
17. I shall catch....next bus.
18. Please turn....radio on.
19. ....Englishmen speak .... English.
20. ....tiger kills...animal.
21. She hit him on....ear.
22. Man is....land animal.
23. I bought....horse,....ox and.... buffalo.
24. ....hunter...saw...bird in... tree.

EXERCISE 11

Use Articles wherever necessary :

EXAMPLES : (i) ....dog is...animal.
= A dog is *an* animal.

(ii)....cow gives....milk.
= *A* cow gives milk.

1. ....dog is....animal.
2. ....cow gives....milk.
3. ....orange grows on....tree.
4. Do you take....sugar in....tea ?
5. ....cat has....tail.
6. He writes....letter on....paper.
7. I wrote to....Father for....money.
8. ....ox is....useful animal.
9. ....lion is....dangerous animal.
10. Moti is....socialist, not....communist.
11. He teaches us....English, not....history.
12. Ram and Sita were....husband and....wife.
13. ....Principal is not in....town.
14. There is....school for....deaf in this town.
15. Mukul and Ruby are....brother and....sister.
16. I saw....child ....child was crying.
17. You are in....right; he is in....wrong.
18. In....spring we go to Delhi, in....winter to Bombay.
19. ....Himalayas lie to....north of India.
20. ....Mount Everest is....highest peak.

EXERCISE 12

Correct these sentences :

EXAMPLES : (i) I have a homework to do.
= I have homework to do.

(ii) I want a soap, please.
= I want *a piece of* soap, please.

(iii) Give me half dozen red pencils.
= Give me half *a* dozen red pencils.

1. I love the music, the poetry, the art.
2. This is an one-man band.
3. Alice is studying to be doctor.
4. A water is made of oxygen and hydrogen.
5. I have got the headache.
6. They are playing the chess.
7. He has no a hat.
8. Frog usually lives in cold, damp places.
9. I had lesson yesterday.
10. We enjoyed the beauty of the nature.
11. Do you often go to pictures ?
12. Can you play piano ?
13. This is an nice inkpot.
14. The most birds can fly.
15. We live in small house.
16. I am afraid of a spiders.
17. I have got good idea.
18. She was wearing blue frock.
19. The John's coat is blue.
20. I have received a news from abroad.
21. I must give answer to the question.
22. I often ride horse.
23. It was not a best model.
24. The Mr Smith's house is here.
25. He went to university.
26. Boxing makes arms strong.

EXERCISE 13

Use Articles wherever necessary :

EXAMPLE : Are you going to England by...sea or by...air ?
= Are you going to England by sea or by air ?

1. Are you going to England by....sea or by....air ?
2. ....India is a very large country in....Asia.
3. Let us have....game of cricket.
4. ....pages of....book are torn.
5. Give me....ink to write...letter.
6. Go and buy....half....kilo of sugar.
7. ....birds can fly very high in....sky.
8. ....honesty is....best policy.
9. ....car made....loud noise.
10. There is....road behind....house.
11. .....door of.....classroom is broken.
12. I want....glass of....milk.
13. .....telephone is....very important means of communication.
14. There are....beautiful roses in....park.
15. His father is....doctor and earns Rs. 5,000.....month.
16. ....umbrella is....useful thing.
17. It is pleasant to read.....book in....evening.
18. .....donkeys are....stupid animals.
19. Grass grows everywhere, but....grass in....valley is....best.
20. When....milkman comes, tell him that I want....extra bottle today.

EXERCISE 14

Use Articles wherever necessary :

EXAMPLE : ....science tries to discover...law of....Nature.
= Science tries to discover *the* law of Nature.

1. ....science tries to disover....law of....Nature.
2. I saw....nest of....owl on....tree.
3. .....cow likes....green grass in....summer.
4. I want....cup of....tea with....sugar in it.
5. ....postman has just put....letter under....door.
6. He took up....painting as....hobby....last year.
7. Mr Rao always smokes....cigarette with....cup of....coffee.
8. We had....lunch at....hotel....last night.
9. ....Everest is....highest peak in....world.
10. There is....broken chair in....corner of....room.
11. I prefer....going by....car to going on....bicycle.
12. ....teacher asked....student to leave.....room.
13. All....work and no....play makes....Jack a dull boy.
14. ....book about....philosophy is not good for....child.
15. ....shopkeeper opposite....library sells....good tea.
16. I can write....letter in....ink or with....pencil.

17. There is....dirt on this book and there are....dirty marks on....tablecloth.
18. ....chair made of....wood is better than....one made of....iron.
19. My uncle is....trader, but he does....little farming with....help of his two sons.
20. .....monkeys are intelligent animals. But they are not....most intelligent of all ...animals.

EXERCISE 15

Use Articles wherever necessary :

EXAMPLE : ....headmaster asked...boys to copy down...sentences written on...blackboard.
= *The* headmaster asked *the* boys to copy down *the* sentences written on *the* blackboard.

1. ....headmaster asked....boys to copy down....sentences written on.....blackboard.
2. King Ashoka was moved deeply when he saw....dead and....wounded on.... battlefield.
3. We live within....easy reach of....river, so we are fond of....fishing and.... swimming.
4. My friend has just been awarded....scholarship to....University in ....U.S.A. It was awarded by....oil company of Iraq.
5. ....eldest is at....college, but....younger ones are still at....school.
6. There is....public meeting in....city hall this evening....speaker has come from Delhi by....plane.
7. ....boy who stood first in....State in....Secondary Board Examination has been given....scholarship for college studies.
8. My younger brother is at.....school now. If you go to....school on....bicycle, you will be just in....time to meet him.
9. I met....Frenchman and....American last week. ....Frenchman was here on pleasure but....American was here on business.
10. We travelled by....plane at....night, flying high up in....sky, it was too pleasant.... experience to forget.
11. I have just written....letter to....bookseller in Bombay asking him to send me.... copy of....book that I saw in today's *Times of India.*
12. I got this book from....college library....librarian said that I could keep it only....week as....teacher of English also wanted it.
13. ....word may have more than one meaning. If we look up....word in ....dictionary, we can find....different meanings.
14. On....whole I agree that....health of....people in this country has shown ....marked improvement during....last few years.
15. There was....storm last night, so I stopped at....home and played....chess with my brother. He taught me....rules of this game.
16. When my friend came to stay with me, I took him for....tour of.... district. We went to....zoo and to....museum.
17. I have....dog and....cow....dog is black but....cow is white.
18. I have....red book and....green book on....table. Will you bring me.... green one, please ?
19. In reply to your advertisement in....*Indian Nation* of yesterday's date, I beg to offer myself as....candidate for....post of....clerk in your office. I passed.... Secondary School Examination of Bihar two years ago. I have appeared at....

Intermediate Examination this year. I am....Indian, 28 years old and of excellent physique. I am also attaching here-to....copy of each of my certificates.

20. ....Minister of Education is coming here next month to open....new technical college. It is....first of its kind in....country.
21. Can you tell me how to get to....station ? Yes, turn to....left when you see.... large red brick building. You will see....station in front of you.

EXERCISE 16

Put in a, an *or* the *or* leave the space empty to show that no article should be used.

EXAMPLE : ....Bihar University has....more students than.... University of....Ranchi.

= Bihar University has more students than *the* University of Ranchi.

1. ....Bihar University has....more students than....University of....Ranchi.
2. ....student at....back of....class is reading....newspaper.
3. ....moon moves round....earth and...earth moves round....sun.
4. Mahesh bought....horse....ox and....camel in....fair.
5. ....love of....money is....root of all....evil.
6. When....Police Inspector reached....scene of....accident, he looked at.... vehicles first.
7. ....idle man is....curse to....family and....country in which he is born.
8. ....good knowledge of....English is....useful thing for....student today.
9. ....January and....February are....coldest months in....West Indies.
10. ....Taj Mahal is....most beautiful monument in....world. It is....wonderful building.
11. Whenever I get....chance, I go down to....river with....friend, and we spend ....hour there.
12. There is....time for play and....time for study. .....good boy should not mix up ....two.
13. Tom is....only boy in....school to get....scholarship. I hope to get it in....near future.
14. I went to borrow....book from....library, but....librarian was on....leave.
15. ....half of....world cannot understand....pleasure of....other.
16. I saw....very bad street accident yesterday. .....man on....foot had been knocked down by....jeep.
17. I want....information about....latest developments in....field of....Indian politics.
18. There isn't....train to....place I want to go until this afternoon. I missed....8.20 train this morning. So, I will go by....bus now.
19. We went to....circus yesterday. We saw....elephant,....tiger, two lions and.... number of trained horses and camels.
20. ....first chapter of....book is very interesting but....statements given in.... second chapter are not wholly correct.

EXERCISE 17 (With Answer)

(A) *Choose the most appropriate answer :*

(i) They were grateful for....bread we gave them.

(a) the (b) some

(c) any (d) a

(ii) ....honour was conferred on him for his services to the country.

(a) a (b) an
(c) some (d) any

(iii) We decided to stay at...hotel in the centre of the town.

(a) a (b) an
(c) the (d) some

(iv) It is....pleasure to do business with such an efficient organisation.

(a) a (b) some
(c) the (d) any

(B) *Insert* a, an *or* the *if necessary :*

(i) There was....knock on....door. I opened it and found....small dark man in....check overcoat and....soft hat.

(ii) You can fool some of....people all....time, and all ....people some of....time; but you cannot fool all ....people all....time.

(iii) There'll always be a conflict between....old and ....young. .....young people want....change but.... old people want....things to stay....same.

(iv) ....most of....stories that....people tell about....Irish aren't true.

Ans. (A) (i) the; (ii) an; (iii) a; (iv) a

(B) (i) a, the, a, a, a (ii) the, the, the, the, the, the (iii) the, the, nil, nil, nil, nil, the (iv) nil, the, nil, the.

□ □ □

3. SYNTAX : SUBJECT-VERB AGREEMENT

SYNTAX

Syntax का अर्थ होता है—वाक्य-विचार अर्थात 'the rules for the way words and expressions are combined into clauses and sentences'. इससे हम सीखते हैं कि वाक्य की रचना कैसे की जाए, वाक्य के शब्दों को किस क्रम (order) में रखा जाए तथा उनमें आपस में कैसा संबंध रहना चाहिए।

Syntax के दो प्रमुख भाग हैं :

(i) Agreement या Concord (मेल) अर्थात वाक्य में एक शब्द के साथ दूसरे शब्द का मेल।

(ii) Order (क्रम, स्थान) अर्थात वाक्य में विभिन्न प्रकार के शब्दों का स्थान या क्रम।

Word order के विषय में हमलोग विभिन्न संबंधित chapters में पढ़ चुके हैं किंतु यहाँ हम subject-verb agreement पर विस्तार से चर्चा करेंगे।

SUBJECT-VERB AGREEMENT

अंगरेजी के प्रत्येक sentence को हम दो भागों में बाँट सकते हैं : subject तथा predicate. जैसे :

Subject	*Predicate*
Rajeev	plays.
He	is here.
The rich	are seldom happy.

(i) वाक्य का subject (कर्ता) प्रायः कोई noun या pronoun होता है तथा वह एक शब्द का हो सकता है या एक से अधिक शब्दों का।

(ii) Predicate भाग में verb अवश्य रहता है। Predicate भाग एक शब्द का हो सकता है या एक से अधिक शब्दों का। (जिस शब्द का past tense रूप बन सके उसे verb कहा जाता है।)

किसी वाक्य का verb उस वाक्य के subject (कर्ता) के number तथा person के अनुसार singular या plural होता है। Subject के number (= he *thinks* किंतु they *think*) तथा person (= I *am*, you *are*, he *is*) के अनुसार verb के चुनाव को concord या agreement कहा जाता है।

KINDS OF AGREEMENT/CONCORD

Concord दो प्रकार के होते हैं—एक को formal concord तथा दूसरे को notional concord कहा जाता है।

(i) Word harmony of person, number, or gender based on form is called formal concord. जैसे : Two boys were in the room. इस वाक्य का subject 'boys' है जो form तथा meaning दोनों प्रकार से plural है, अतः इसके साथ plural verb 'were' का प्रयोग किया गया है। इस प्रकार के subject-verb agreement को formal concord कहते हैं।

(ii) Word harmony of person, number, or gender based on meaning, as opposed to formal concord, is called notional concord. जैसे :

The news was good. इस वाक्य में news तथा was दोनों meaning के अनुसार singular हैं, किंतु news का form plural है और 'was' singular form में है, इस तरह के subject-verb agreement को notional concord कहते हैं। उसी तरह—None were left में subject (*none*) singular form में है किंतु अर्थ में plural है, अतः plural verb (*were*) का प्रयोग किया गया है। यहाँ subject-verb में notional concord है।

1. *Look at these sentences :*

A			B	
Singular Subject	*Singular Verb*		*Plural Subject*	*Plural Verb*
The *pen* The *girl* The *boy* *He*	*is* new. *has* gone. *was* tall. *does* not *play*.		The *pens* The *girls* The *boys* *They*	*are* new. *have* gone. *were* tall. *do* not *play*.

(A) अंगरेजी के वाक्यों में singular subject के साथ singular verb; तथा
(B) plural subject के साथ plural verb आता है। जैसे :

	Singular	*Plural*
I Person :	I *am/have/do/was...*	We *are/have/do/were...*
II Person :	You *are/have/do/were...*	You *are/have/do/were...*
III Person :	He, She, It *is/has/does/was...*	They *are/have/do/were..*

अतः, subject-verb agreement के मुख्य नियम हैं :

(i) A singular subject requires a singular verb.

(ii) A plural subject requires a plural verb.

2. *Look at these sentences :*

Singular Subject (A)	*Singular Verb* (A)	*Plural Subject* (B)	*Plural Verb* (B)
A *cow*	*eats* grass.	*Cows*	*eat* grass.
My *friend*	*likes* tea.	My *friends*	*like* tea.

Verb अपने असली रूप में plural number में रहता है और प्रत्येक verb का असली रूप present tense में माना जाता है। Eat, like, go, play, run, come इत्यादि verb present tense तथा plural number में हैं।

इनमें s/es जोड़कर singular बनाया जाता है।

(A) Third person singular subject के साथ simple present tense में verb के अंत में s या es लगता है।

(B) Plural subject के साथ verb में s/es नहीं लगता है।

3. *Look at these sentences :*

Singular Subject (A)	*Singular Verb* (A)	*Plural Subject* (B)	*Plural Verb* (B)
I	*can* go.	*We*	*can* go.
He	*will* run.	*They*	*will* run.
She	*may* come.	*They*	*may* come.
The *boy*	*must* study.	The *boys*	*must* study.

Can, will, may, must, shall, would, should तथा *ought* के रूप singular तथा plural subjects के साथ एक जैसा ही रहता है।

4. *Look at these sentences :*

Singular Subject (A)	*Singular Verb* (A)	*Plural Subject* (B)	*Plural Verb* (B)
I	*had* a car.	*We*	*had* a car.
He	*did* the work.	*They*	*did* the work.
She	*liked* music.	*They*	*liked* music.
The *girl*	*ate* sweets.	The *girls*	*ate* sweets.

Had, did, liked, ate इत्यादि past tense verbs के रूप singular तथा plural में एक जैसा ही रहते हैं।

5. *Look at these sentences :*

Tom and Mary *are* now ready.
Hari and Abdul *have* gone to Ranchi.
Rice, wheat and pulse *were* available there.

जब दो या दो से अधिक singular subjects *and* से जुटे हों तब verb plural होता है।

6. *Look at these sentences :*

Slow and steady wins the race.
It
Hammer and sickle was there.
It
Rice and curry is my favourite dish. (दाल-भात=एक ही वस्तु)
It
Bread and butter is cheap food.
It
A horse and carriage is ready for us.
It
The rise and fall is caused by the storm.
It
The crown and glory of life *is* character.
It
Whisky and soda was there on the table.
It
The tumult and the shouting dies.
It
All coming and going was forbidden.
It
Screaming and shouting was heard coming from the hall.
It

यदि and द्वारा जुटे singular nouns से एक ही वस्तु या एक ही भाव का बोध हो तो compound subject singular ही समझा जाता है और तदनुसार उसके लिए singular verb का प्रयोग किया जाता है।

7. *Look at these sentences :*

Tom or Mary *is* now ready.
Hari or Abdul *has* gone to Ranchi.
Mr Sen or Mr Ghose *was* to take the class.

जब दो singular subjects *or* से जुटे हों तब **verb singular** होता है।

8. *Look at these sentences :*

Many boys *are* present today.
Both the books *were* new. *Several* girls *have* passed in the first division.
A few women *are* good-natured.

Many, Both, Several, A few, These, Those के बाद plural subjects तथा plural verbs आते हैं।

Note : Many *a* के बाद singular countable noun तथा singular verb का प्रयोग किया जाता है। जैसे:

Many a man *wants* to get rich very quickly.

9. *Look at these sentences :*

Each man *has* a car. *Each* egg *was* bad.
Every house *is* beautiful. *Every* player *has* played well.

Each तथा *Every* के बाद singular countable noun तथा singular verb का प्रयोग किया जाता है।

10. *Look at these sentences :*

A	B
All horses *are* animals.	*All* the money *was* lost.
Some flowers *were* red.	*Some* sugar *is* needed.

(A) *All* तथा *Some* के बाद अगर countable noun रहे तो वह noun plural होता है तथा उसके बाद verb भी plural होता है।

(B) *All* तथा *Some* के बाद अगर uncountable noun रहे तो उसके साथ singular verb आता है।

Note—(a) *All* का अर्थ जब प्रत्येक चीज (everything) हो तब उसके साथ singular verb आता है। जैसे :

All *is* ready now.
I will tell you all that *was* discussed.

(b) *All* से जब व्यक्ति या वस्तु की संख्या का बोध हो तब उसके साथ plural verb आता है। जैसे :

I've just seen the players. *All are* here.
I've checked the tyres. *All are* o.k.

11. *Look at these sentences :*

Everyone is playing. *No one was* in the class.
Some one was there. *Each of* the girls *has* a watch.
Nobody has a book. *Either of* the books *is* good.
Everybody is happy. *Neither of* the pens *was* red.
Somebody was there.

(i) *Everyone, some one, nobody, everybody, somebody, no one* तथा *each one* के बाद singular verb आता है।

(ii) *Either of, Each of* तथा *Neither of* के बाद subject plural रहता है किंतु verb singular.

12. *Look at these sentences :*

Many of the girls *are* tall.
Six of the girls *were* ill.
Two of the boys *have* gone home.
Several of the pupils *were* ill.
A few of the eggs *are* bad.
The majority of the students *have* come here.

Many of, Several of, A few of, Two of तथा *The majority of* के बाद subject तथा verb दोनों plural होते हैं।

Note : अगर वाक्य का subject केवल 'The majority' है तो आप singular verb का प्रयोग करें या plural, दोनों correct माना जाता है। जैसे :

'The majority *were/was* in favour of the proposal.'
—ADVANCED LEARNER'S DICTIONARY OF CURRENT ENGLISH

13. *Look at these sentences :*

Half of the mangoes *are* good.
Half of the land *is* cultivated.
Half of the boys *are* here.
Half of the milk *was* there.

(i) *Half of* के बाद अगर countable noun रहे तो वह noun plural होता है तथा उसके साथ plural verb आता है।

(ii) *Half of* के बाद अगर uncountable noun रहे तो उसके बाद singular verb आता है।

14. *Look at these sentences :*

Every man and *every* woman *has* equal rights.
Each boy and *each* girl *is* ready now.
No friend and *no* relative *has* anything to offer.

अगर दो singular subjects *and* से जुटे हों तथा उनके पहले *every, each* या *no* रहे तो verb singular होता है।

15. *Look at these sentences :*

A	B
Most people *think* so.	*Most of* the time *is* lost.
Most of the teachers *are* busy.	*Most of* the money *is* spent.
Most of the boys *have* come.	*Most of* the sugar *was* dirty.

(A) *Most* या *Most of* के बाद अगर countable noun रहे तो वह plural होता है तथा उसके बाद plural verb आता है।

(B) *Most of* के बाद अगर uncountable noun रहे तो उसके बाद singular verb आता है।

16. *Look at these sentences :*

A	B
There *is* a boy.	There *are* boys.
There *was* a king.	There *were* kings.

जब वाक्य Dummy subject 'There' से शुरू हो तब verb अपने वास्तविक subject, जो verb (am, is, are, was, were, has, have इत्यादि) के बाद आता है, के अनुसार singular या plural होता है।

17. *Look at these sentences :*

All his *luggage is* lost.	Their *knowledge* of English *is* sound.
All my *furniture was* new.	All the *apparatus is* new.
All your *advice is* good.	Their *behaviour was* good.
My *information is* true.	The *scenery* of Kashmir *is* beautiful.
Our *food has* run short.	There *is* heavy *traffic* on the road.
All his *work is* done.	*Electricity runs* our trains.
All the *equipment is* old.	All this *fruit has* gone bad.

(i) अंगरेजी में कुछ शब्द हैं जो सदा singular होते हैं, जैसे : *luggage, furniture, advice, information, food, work, knowledge, equipment, fruit* (फल), *apparatus, behaviour, scenery, traffic, electricity, dust, music, progress, weather, nonsense* इत्यादि।

(ii) इन शब्दों के साथ singular verb आता है।

(iii) इनमें s/es लगाकर इनका plural नहीं बनता।

(iv) इनके पहले a/an का भी प्रयोग नहीं किया जाता।

Note : लेकिन इनमें कुछ ऐसे noun हैं जिन्हें countable या plural अर्थ में प्रयोग करने के लिए इनके पहले *a piece of/pieces of/an item of/items of/a kind of/kinds of; a branch of/branches of* लगाया जाता है। जैसे :

He gave me *a piece/pieces of* information.
I have *a piece/some pieces of* work at home.
She gave him *a piece/pieces of* advice.

18. *Look at these sentences :*

These *people are* sometimes complaining.
The *cattle were* grazing in the field.
The *police have* searched the thief.

(i) *People, folk, gentry, vermin, cattle* तथा *police* plural nouns हैं, इनके साथ plural verb आता है।

(ii) इनमें s/es लगाकर इनका पुनः plural नहीं बनाया जाता।

(iii) Police का singular रूप policeman होता है; policeman का plural policemen भी होता है।

(iv) Peoples का अर्थ राष्ट्र (nation) या जाति (tribe) होता है। जैसे :

The *peoples* of the world must learn to live together.

19. *Look at these sentences :*

No *news is* good news.

'The *wages* of sin *is* death'.—Bible

Patil's *innings* in the Melbourne Test *was* his best.

There *is* a *barracks.*

Measles is a dangerous disease.

Physics is an important subject.

Politics has no attraction for me.

The *United Nations is* our only hope.

The *United States has* a big army.

(i) *News, innings, barracks* singular nouns हैं, इनके साथ singular verb आता है। किंतु Modern English में wages को plural माना जाता है; जैसे :

His wages *are* Rs.15/- a day.

(ii) कुछ बीमारियों के नाम singular होते हैं, जैसे :

measles, German measles, rickets तथा *mumps.*

(iii) कुछ विषयों के नाम जिनके अंत में s लगा रहता है singular होते हैं; जैसे : *classics, linguistics, mathematics, physics, phonetics, ethics, athletics, politics, statistics* इत्यादि। इनके साथ singular verb आता है।

(iv) खेल का नाम जैसे *billiards, darts* singular होता है।

(v) कुछ proper nouns जिनके अंत में s लगा रहता है singular होते हैं। जैसेः *Naples, Algiers, Athens, Wales, The United States, The United Nations* तथा इनके साथ singular verbs आते हैं।

Note : किंतु subjects के नाम के पहले *His, The, Such* आदि शब्द रहें तो उनके गुणों (qualities) का बोध होता है। तब इनके साथ plural verb आता है। जैसे : His *mathematics* (गणितीय हिसाब) *are* weak.

The *economics* (आर्थिक तथ्य) of the situation *are* yet to be discussed.

20. *Look at these sentences :*

Two and two *is* four.

Two plus two *is* four.

Ten minus four *is* six.

Five times ten *is* fifty.

Arithmetic के हिसाब (sums) में singular verb आता है। किंतु Two and two *are* four को भी सही माना जाता है।

(i) Five and five *is* ten—right. But don't jump to the conclusion that '**Five** and five *are* ten' is wrong—both verbs are equally acceptable in this or any similar construction. —NORMAN LEWIS

(ii) When the subject is a proposition in arithmetic, the singular is rather more common, though the plural is sometimes used :

Two and two is four.
Two and two are four.
Two times three is six.
Five from ten is five.
Ten divided by five gives two.

—PAUL ROBERTS : UNDERSTANDING GRAMMAR

21. *Look at these sentences :*

None of the boys *are* here.	*None of* the bags *are* lost.
None of them *want* this.	*None of* the girls *were* present.

(i) *None of* के बाद plural subject तथा plural verb आता है। किंतु कुछ लोग *none of* के साथ singular verb लगाते हैं। जैसे :

None of the boys *is* here.
None of them *wants* this.

(ii) Pronoun के अर्थ में *none* singular तथा plural दोनों होता है। जैसे :

Uncountable : I've ordered the cement, but *none* (of it) *has* yet arrived.

Countable : I've ordered the books, but *none* (of them) *have* yet arrived.

अब either, neither तथा none के प्रयोग के संबंध में इन बातों का ध्यान रखें—

When there is a choice between two, we use *either* and *neither.* When the choice is among more than two, we use *none* for the negative. *Neither* is singular, but *none* can be treated either as a singular or as a plural, e.g., None of the dogs was/were there.

—L. A. HILL : A GUIDE TO CORRECT ENGLISH

In 'I've ordered the shrubs, but none (of them) have/has yet arrived', grammatical concord would suggest that *none* is singular; but notional concord (we might paraphrase as 'they have not arrived') invites a plural verb. *Has* is therefore more conventionally 'correct', but *have* is more idiomatic in speech.

—RANDOLPH QUIRK & SIDNEY GREENBAUM

22. *Look at these sentences :*

A	B
One player is still there.	*One of* the players *is* still there.
One teacher is too young.	*One of* the teachers *is* so young.
One boy has a bicycle.	*One of* the boys *has* a bicycle.

(A) इन वाक्यों में singular subject के साथ singular verb का प्रयोग किया गया है। (One + singular subject + singular verb).

(B) *One of* के बाद plural subject किंतु singular verb आता है क्योंकि वाक्य का subject *one* होता है। (One of + plural subject + singular verb)

23. *Look at these sentences :*

Much time *is* lost.	*Much of* the flour *is* bad.

Much तथा *much of* के बाद uncountable noun तथा singular verb आता है।

24. *Look at these sentences :*

A	B
A number of boys *are* there.	*The number of* boys *is* ten.
A number of girls *have* come.	*The number of* mangoes *is* fifty.

(A) *A number of* (बहुत) को plural माना जाता है। इसके साथ plural subject तथा plural verb आता है।

(B) *The number of* (संख्या) को singular माना जाता है। इसके बाद आनेवाला noun plural होता है, किंतु verb हमेशा singular रहता है।

25. *Look at these sentences :*

Social and political freedom *are* necessary.
(Social freedom is.... + political freedom is....)
Indian and Cuban sugar *have* a good sale.
(Indian sugar has... + Cuban sugar has....)
Good and bad taste *are* created by examples.
(Good taste is.... + bad taste is....)

जब दो या दो से अधिक adjective किसी singular noun के पहले आए तब उस noun को प्रायः plural माना जाता है; क्योंकि विभिन्न adjectives के प्रयोग से विभिन्न subjects का बोध होता है।

26. *Look at these sentences :*

A	B
A lot of boys *like* it.	*A lot of* tea *is* in the cup.
Lots of boys *like* it.	*Lots of* sugar *was* there.
A great deal of things *are* there.	*A great deal* of time *is* lost.
Plenty of apples *were* on the table.	There *is plenty of* water in the glass.

(A) *A lot of* (बहुत), *lots of* (बहुत), *a great deal of* (बहुत) तथा *plenty of* (बहुत) के बाद जब plural countable noun रहता है तब उसके साथ verb भी plural होता है।

(B) *A lot of, lots of, a great deal of* तथा *plenty of* के बाद अगर uncountable noun रहे तो verb singular होता है।

27. *Look at these sentences :*

A (or two) dozen pens *are* there.

A (or two) hundred boys *have* come.
A (or four) thousand people live in this village.

(i) *Dozen* (दर्जन), *hundred* (सौ), *thousand* (हजार), *million* (दस लाख), *billion* (एक अरब) अपने-आपमें plural हैं, इनके बाद plural noun तथा plural verb आता है।

(ii) *A, two, three, five, ten* dozen/hundred/thousand/million/billion लिखा जाता है, न कि a, two, three, five, ten *dozens/hundreds/thousands/millions/billions.*

(iii) जब *dozen, hundred, thousand, million/billion* में s लगता है तब इनका अर्थ बदल जाता है। जैसे :

Dozens (दर्जनों) of eggs *are* there.
Hundreds (सैकड़ों) of boys *have* failed.
Thousands (हजारों) of people *were* killed.

अब ऐसे कुछ प्रचलित शब्दों को देखें—

	Zero plurals	**Regular plurals**
two	dozen glasses dozen of these glasses	dozens of glasses
several	hundred books hundred of these books	hundreds of books
many	thousand insects	thousands of insects
five	million people million	millions of people
a few	billion stars	billions of stars
eight	ton of coal	eight tons of coal
several	head of cattle	
ten	yoke of oxen	
five	foot two (normal if (numeral follows)	five feet

28. *Look at these setences :*

A	B
No person of that name *has* come.	*No* persons of that name *have* come.
No book of that colour *is* here.	*No* books of that colour *are* here.
No money *has* been spent so far.	

(A) *No* के बाद singular countable, plural countable या uncountable noun आ सकता है।

(B) जब *no* के बाद singular countable noun रहे तब singular verb; तथा

(C) जब plural noun रहे तब plural verb आता है।

29. *Look at these sentences :*

More than fifty boys *have* signed the petition.

More than one boy *has* signed the petition.

(i) *More than* के बाद अगर plural subject रहे तो plural verb, और

(ii) अगर singular subject रहे तो singular verb आता है। किंतु *More boys than one have* broken the window. *More cars than one are* there on the road.

30. *Look at these sentences :*

One or two boys *are* playing.

One or two books *were* lost.

One or two के बाद plural subject तथा plural verb आता है।

31. *Look at these sentences :*

The typing of the letters *is* over.

The pages of this book *are* missing.

Houses of this type *have* two rooms.

The people of this village *are* hard-working.

जब वाक्य की बनावट *noun + of + noun* रहे तब वाक्य का असली subject of के पहलेवाला noun होता है और उसी के अनुसार verb singular या plural रहता है।

32. *Look at these sentences :*

India *have won* the series.

Australia *pile up* a huge total.

England *have lost* the match.

कभी-कभी अखबारों, radio तथा TV commentaries में ऐसे वाक्य मिलते हैं। इन वाक्यों में India, Australia, England *disguised collective nouns* हैं। समाचारपत्रों के headlines में स्थानाभाव के कारण जहाँ articles का भी प्रयोग करना निषिद्ध है वहाँ team का प्रयोग करना संभव नहीं होता, ऐसी ही बात radio/TV commentators के साथ भी है। इसके अलावा, singular verb के प्रयोग से India से लोग Indian team नहीं समझकर India देश समझ बैठते हैं। Australia से Australian team का बोध नहीं होकर Australia देश का बोध होता है। इसीलिए इनके साथ team शब्द का लोप कर plural verb का प्रयोग कर दिया जाता है। यह प्रयोग पूर्णतः journalistic है; साहित्यिक भाषा में इसे अभी मान्यता नहीं मिली है।

Note : जब team शब्द के पहले a, each, every, this, that रहे अथवा team से एक unit का बोध हो तब इसके साथ singular verb लगता है; किंतु जब team से व्यक्ति (individuals) का बोध हो तब team के साथ plural verb लगता है। (जब एक से अधिक team का बोध कराना हो तब team का plural *teams* होता है; जैसे—Six *teams are* participating in the tournament.)

Team was, team were: The use of 'was' or 'were' is determined by the sense, by the way in which 'team' is regarded. Regarded as a unit, 'team' should be given a singular verb, e.g., 'The *team was* given an ovation' and 'the *team has* won the cup.' Regarded as so many individuals, 'team' should be given a plural verb, e.g., 'The *team were* given medals for winning the cup' and 'The *team* agree among themselves.

—R. D. THOMSON & A. H. IRVINE : EVERYDAY ENGLISH USAGE

33. *Look at these sentences :*

There *are other* houses like ours. There *is another* house like ours.

(i) *Other* के साथ plural subject तथा plural verb, एवं

(ii) *Another* के साथ singular subject तथा singular verb आता है।

34. *Look at these sentences :*

A *group of* people *was* standing there.
A *crowd of* students *is* waiting outside.
A *team of* students *has* been selected.
A *set of* books *has* been bought.

इन वाक्यों की बनावट है : singular collective noun + of + plural noun. यदि of के पहले singular collective noun आए, तो singular verb का प्रयोग किया जाता है। कुछ मुख्य collective nouns हैं :

a series of, a bunch of, a chain of, a garland of, a bouquet of, a fleet of, a team of, a batch of, a class of, a galaxy of, a band of, a flock of, a herd of, a set of इत्यादि।

कुछ और उदाहरण देखें :

A bunch of keys *is* lying there.
A series of events *has* happened.
A set of pens *was* bought.
A fleet of ships *has* been there.
A flock of sheep *was* grazing in the field.

Note : Series तथा species का प्रयोग singular तथा plural में बिना इनके रूप बदले किया जा सकता है। जैसे : He gave *one series/two series* of lectures.

35. *Look at these sentences :*

The poor are happy.	*The guilty are* punished.
The rich are not always happy.	*The honest are* rewarded.
The Chinese have come to India.	*The old are* generally neglected.

(i) ***The poor, the rich, the Chinese, the old, the sick, the blind, the dumb, the honest, the guilty, the virtuous, the young, the French, the***

Japanese इत्यादि जब किसी वाक्य के subjects हों तब ये plural माने जाते हैं। The poor = the poor people; the rich = the rich people इत्यादि। किंतु the evil = that which is evil. इसे singular माना जाता है।)

(ii) इन शब्दों में s/es लगाकर इन्हें पुनः plural नहीं बनाया जाता; जैसे—the poors, the sicks लिखना गलत है।

(iii) इनके पहले a/an भी नहीं लगता (जब इनका प्रयोग noun के जैसा हो); जैसे—a poor, a rich लिखना अशुद्ध है।

36. *Look at these sentences :*

Crime and Punishment is written by Dostoyevsky.
Gulliver's Travels is an interesting book.
Lamb's *Tales From Sheakespeare* is a popular book.

अगर किसी पुस्तक, देश, घर, होटल या संस्था का नाम plural हो तो भी उसके साथ singular verb लगता है। इसको पहचानने में कोई दिक्कत नहीं होती; क्योंकि names तथा titles के सभी शब्द capital letters से लिखे जाते हैं।

37. *Look at these sentences :*

A	B
Give me a *book* which *is* new.	Give me *books* which *are* new.
Help the *boy* who *is* poor.	Help the *boys* who *are* poor.

Adjective clause में *who, which, that* के पहले आनेवाले noun के अनुसार verb singular या plural होता है।

38. *Look at these sentences :*

A	B
The *man* who was rich *has* become poor.	The *men* who were rich *have* become poor.
The *book* I gave you *is* interesting.	The *books* I gave you *are* interesting.
The *pen* that was here *is* lost.	*One* of the pens that were here *is* lost.

Principal clause का verb अपने subject के अनुसार singular या plural होता है।

Note : ऐसे वाक्यों में adjective clause का verb *who, which, that* के पहले आने वाले plural noun/pronoun के अनुसार ही plural होता है। जैसे :

He is one of *those* who *do* not accept the views.
It is one of the *words* that *are* likely to be mis-spelt.

39. *Look at these sentences :*

What he says is not right. *Where he goes is* difficult to say.

अगर वाक्य का subject कोई एक clause रहे तो verb singular होता है।

40. *Look at these sentences :*

Your problem and *mine are* similar.
(= Your problem is...and my problem is...)
What I say and *think are* no business of yours.
(= What I say is....and what I think is....)
When she will sing and *dance are* not known.
(= When she will sing is...and when she will dance is...)
What you say and *what you do are* your own affair.
(= What you say is...and what you do is...)

अगर वाक्य का subject दो clauses हों (चाहे वे पूर्ण हों या उनके लघु रूप) तो verb plural होता है।

41. *Look at these sentences :*

I wish I *were* a millionaire.
God *save* the king.
If I *were* a bird, I would fly.
Long *live* Democracy.
I wish it *were* possible.
He talks as if he *were* mad.

इन वाक्यों से ऐसी अभिलाषा (wish) या कल्पना (supposition) का भाव व्यक्त होता है जिसकी पूर्ति संभव नहीं। याद रखें कि ऐसे वाक्यों में live, save, bless जैसे plural verb का प्रयोग third person singular subject के साथ भी होता है तथा conditional sentences में if, as if या I wish..., we wish..., के बाद singular subject के साथ भी were का प्रयोग किया जाता है।

42. *Look at these sentences :*

Singular	Plural
A quarter of it *is* good.	A quarter of them *are* good.
Part of the book *is* printed.	Part of the charges *are* correct.
Two-thirds of the site *is* lovely.	Two-thirds of girls *are* present.
Three-fourths of the job *is* done.	Three-fourths of people *were* ill.
The rest of the book *is* complete.	The rest of the books *are* sold.
Forty per cent of the amount *is* spent.	Forty per *cent* of votes *were* polled.

ऐसे वाक्यों में of के बाद आनेवाले noun के अनुसार ही singular या plural verb का प्रयोग किया जाता है।

Note : यदि of के पहले 'percentage' (per cent नहीं) रहे, तो verb सदा singular होता है। जैसे :

What percentage of his income *is* paid in income tax ?
The percentage of failures *is* very high.
The percentage of good students *was* very small.

43. *Look at these sentences :*

To walk is healthy.
How to do it is a problem.
Walking is a healthy exercise.
That he is wicked is known to us.

इन वाक्यों में to walk एक infinitive है, walking एक gerund है, how to do it एक phrase है और that he is wicked एक clause है। ये सभी noun के समान वाक्य के subject हैं। अतः, इनके साथ singular verb का प्रयोग किया जाता है।

44. *Look at these sentences :*

Ship after ship is sailing by.

One hour after another (hour) has passed.

Letter after letter describes the beauty of the place.

इन वाक्यों में singular noun + preposition और फिर उसी noun को दुहराया गया है, जैसेः ship after ship, one hour after another hour, letter after letter. ऐसे expressions के साथ singular verb का प्रयोग किया जाता है।

45. *Look at these sentences :*

I, Sita, *am* a girl.

You, boy, *are* very wicked.

She, your daughter, *has* come.

He, my friend, *is* very tall.

इन वाक्यों में Sita, boy, your daughter, my friend 'apposition' पद पर हैं जिनको वाक्य के subject के अर्थ को स्पष्ट करने के लिए (इनकी व्याख्या के रूप) comma के बीच प्रयोग किया गया है। अतः, verb अपने subject (I, you, she, he) के अनुसार singular या plural होता है।

46. *Look at these sentences :*

The chief points are *as follows* (not *as follow).*

The description is *as follows* (not *as follow).*

अंगरेजी में as follows ही लिखा जाता है, as follow नहीं, चाहे इसके साथ singular noun रहे अथवा plural.

...*as follows.* This is an invariable idiomatic expression and does not change to 'as follow' even when it refers to a word (or words) in the plural, e.g., 'The main items of business were *a. follows'* (not 'as follow'). 'Follows' is impersonal here. —R. D. THOMSON & A. H. IRVINE

47. *Look at these sentences :*

The following *are* the new rates.

The following *is* the weather report.

The undersigned *requests* the pleasure of your company today at 10 a.m.
Sunil

The undersigned *request* the pleasure of your company today at 10 a.m.
Sunil & Sobha

अगर the following, the undersigned का प्रयोग singular noun के लिए हो, तो singular verb और अगर plural noun के लिए हो, तो plural verb का प्रयोग किया जाता है।

48. *Look at these sentences :*

His *glasses are* lost.
These *shoes are* dirty.
My *pants are* new.
Those *scissors were* small.

औजार (tools) तथा पोशाक (articles of dress) के नाम जिनमें दो भाग होते हैं, plural माने जाते हैं तथा उनके साथ plural verb का प्रयोग किया जाता है। जैसे : glasses, shoes, pants, scissors, binoculars, scales, shears, tongs, spectacles, flannels, pyjamas (pajamas), shorts, trousers इत्यादि।

49. *Look at these sentences :*

A *pair* of shoes *belongs* to me.
A *pair* of scissors *has* been lost.
A *pair* of pants *is* blue.
A *pair* of trousers *was* here.

A pair of के बाद अगर glasses, shoes, scissors, pants, trousers, binoculars, scales, shears, tongs, spectacles, flannels, pyjamas, shorts रहे तो इनके दोनों भाग को एक समझा जाता है तथा उनके साथ singular verb लगता है।

Tools and articles of dress consisting of two equal parts which are joined constitute summation plurals. Countability can be imposed by means of *a pair of: a pair of scissors, three pairs of trousers.*

—RANDOLPH QUIRK & SIDNEY GREENBAUM : UNIVERSITY GRAMMAR OF ENGLISH

50. *Look at these sentences :*

These *goods have* arrived.
My *thanks are* due to you.
Those *premises were* raided.
His *looks are* good.

अंगरेजी में कुछ nouns हैं जिनके अंत में -s लगा रहता है, उन्हें सदा plural माना जाता है और उनके साथ plural verb का प्रयोग किया जाता है। कुछ वैसे nouns हैं :

goods (a goods train)
thanks
looks (he has good looks)
savings (a savings bank)
bowels
premises ('building')
manners
riches ('wealth')
surroundings
amends (make every/all possible amends)

arrears
auspices
earings
letters (a man of letters)
means (a man of means)
outskirts
ashes (*but* tobacco ash)
customs (customs duty).
lodgings
odds (in betting).
pains (take pains)

particulars (note the particulars)
regards (*but* win his regard)
spirits ('mood')
quarters, headquarters
remains
stairs (a flight of stairs)

spirits ('alcohol'; but alcohol is a spirit)	troops (*but* a troop of scouts)
valuables	clothes (*but* cloth + s = cloths)
contents (*but* the silver content of the coin)	arms ('weapon', an arms depot)
the Middle Ages	funds (money, for lack of funds) *but* a relief fund (a sum of money for a particular purpose)
holidays (summer holidays, *but* he is on a holiday)	wages (*but* he earns a good wage)
fireworks (*but* he let off a fire work)	wits (she has her wits about her *but* he has a keen wit).

51. *Look at these sentences :*

It *is* I who called you.
It *is* he who saw you.
It *is* they who have done it.
It *is* these boys who wrote it.

इन वाक्यों का subject 'it' है, अतः it के साथ singular verb का प्रयोग किया जाता है।

52. *Look at these sentences :*

Nothing but water *is* seen.
Nothing but snow *was* there.
Nothing but boys *was* seen.
Nothing but trees *is* there.

इन वाक्यों का subject *nothing* है जो singular है। अतः ऐसे वाक्यों में singular verb का प्रयोग किया जाता है चाहे nothing but के बाद singular noun रहे अथवा plural.

53. *Look at these sentences :*

Is Hari or his friends to blame ?
Has Sita or her sisters come ?
Were you or he there ?
Were you or I rewarded ?

जब भिन्न-भिन्न numbers या persons के nouns या pronouns यदि or, nor, either...or या neither...nor के द्वारा अलग किए जाते हैं, तो verb अपने सबसे नजदीक आनेवाले noun या pronoun के अनुसार singular या plural होता है।

54. *Look at these sentences :*

Every means *has* not been tried.
This *is* a dangerous means.
All means *are* unpleasant.
Such means *are* pleasant.

जब means का अर्थ होता है 'उपाय' तब यह शब्द अपने पहले आनेवाले शब्द के अनुसार singular या plural होता है, किंतु जब इसका अर्थ 'रुपया-पैसा' होता है तब यह हमेशा plural माना जाता है। जैसे : My means *are* not enough.

When it (*means*) means "a way to an end" this word is used with either a singular or a plural verb according to the words before it. When it means "money or material possessions", *means* is always plural. Her *means* are small.

—LONGMAN DICTIONARY OF CONTEMPORARY ENGLISH

55. *Look at these sentences :*

A *sheep is* there.	Two sheep *are* there.
A *deer is* an animal.	Deer *are* animals.
A new *aircraft is* brought.	Five *aircraft were* there.

Sheep, deer, aircraft कुछ ऐसे English words हैं जिनका रूप singular तथा plural में एक जैसा ही रहता है। उनमें -s/es लगाकर plural नहीं बनाया जाता।

56. *Look at these sentences :*

A	B
My uncle and guardian *has* come.	My uncle and my guardian *have* come.
My friend and classmate, Deepak, *is* here.	My friend and my classmate *are* here.
The Principal and Secretary *was* there.	The Principal and the Secretary *were* there.
The poet and thinker *is* dead.	The poet and the thinker *are* dead.
The Magistrate and Collector *is* here.	The Magistrate and the Collector *are* here.

(A) अगर दो singular nouns *and* से जुड़े हों पर उनसे एक ही व्यक्ति का बोध हो तो verb singular होता है।

(B) किंतु जब उनके पहले articles या determiners (my, your, our) लगा हो तब उनसे दो अलग-अलग व्यक्तियों का बोध होता है तथा उनके साथ plural verb लगता है।

57. *Look at these sentences :*

Ten kilometres *is* not a long distance. (not *are)*
Twenty miles *is* a long way to walk. (not *are*)
Ten years *is* a long time. (not *are*)
Three months *is* not enough time. (not *are*)
Fifty rupees *is* a lot of money for me. (not *are*)
Where *is* that twenty rupees I lent you ? (not *are*)
Five rupees *doesn't* buy as much as *it* used to. (not *don't*)
A thousand rupees *was* not a small sum. (not *were*)
One thousand and five hundred rupees *is* his fee. (not *are*)
Sixty miles *is* not a great distance these days. (not *are*)
Two kilos of coffee *costs* about three hundred rupees. (not *cost*)

जब plural noun के पहले कोई निश्चित संख्यासूचक शब्द रहे और उस sentence में एक ऐसा शब्द हो जिससे एक निश्चित दूरी, एक निश्चित समय या एक निश्चित राशि का बोध हो तब उसे एक सामूहिक इकाई (collective unit) मानकर उसके साथ singular verb का प्रयोग किया जाता है।

When a plural number applies to distances, weights, heights or amounts of money, and represents a single figure or quantity, it is treated as a singular and takes a singular verb.

—F. T. WOOD : A REMEDIAL ENGLISH GRAMMAR FOR FOREIGN STUDENTS

Note : किंतु जब इनसे अलग-अलग units का बोध कराना हो या plurality का भाव प्रधान हो तब इनके साथ plural verb लगता है। (Sometimes the idea of plurality is dominant, and a plural verb is used.—PAUL ROBERTS). जैसे

Five months *have* passed.
Two hundred rupees *are* spent on it.
A thousand dollars *were* distributed among them.
There *were* twenty silver rupees in his pocket.
The first fifty years *are* the hardest.
Those three minutes *were* the worst I ever spent.

When the subject is a sum of money considered as a whole, the singular verb is used. When the subject is a sum of money and the reference is to the bills or coins considered separately, the plural verb is used. —DAVID GREEN

58. *Look at these sentences :*

The *bag,* together with the boxes, *is* new.
The *crow,* like other birds, *has* wings.
A *boy,* with his brother, *was* there.
The *chairman,* as well as the members, *has* come.
The *driver,* rather than the conductor, *is* responsible.
Raju's *parents,* rather than Raju, *are* ready for the marriage.
Six *questions,* in addition to question 2, *have* to be answered.
The *box,* with all my articles, *has* been stolen.

अगर subject के बाद *with, together with, accompanied by* जैसा कोई phrase हो तो verb ऐसे phrase के पहलेवाले subject के अनुसार singular या plural होता है।

59. *Look at these sentences :*

Either Sonu *or* Moti *has* done it.
Neither the boy *nor* the girl *was* there.
Rajeev *as well as* Mukul *is* intelligent.
What I say *or* what I think *is* no business of yours.

अगर दो singular subjects *either....or, neither...nor* या *as well as* से जुड़े हों तो verb singular होता है।

60. *Look at these sentences :*

My parents *as well as* I *were* present there.
He *as well as* you *is* tired of the whole affair.
The mother *as well as* her three children *was* taken to hospital.

यदि भिन्न-भिन्न number और person के दो subjects *as well as* से जुड़े हों तो verb उस वाक्य के पहले आए हुए subject के अनुसार singular या plural होता है।

61. *Look at these sentences :*

Not only Rekha *but also* Ruby *is* tall.
Not only Abdul *but also* his friends *were* there.
Not (only) one *but* all of us *are* hoping to be there.

अगर दो subjects *not (only)...but (also)* से जुटे हों तो verb अपने अंतिम subject के अनुसार singular या plural होता है।

62. *Look at these sentences :*

Neither the men *nor* the women *are* present today.
Either the strikers *or* the bosses *were* in the wrong.

जब दो plural subjects *either...or/neither...nor* से जुटे हों तब verb plural होता है।

63. *Look at these sentences :*

Neither you *nor* I *am* wrong.
Neither he *nor* you *are* wrong.

Either the teacher *or* the boys *are* right.
Either the boys *or* the teacher *is* right.

Neither the teacher *nor* the boys *are* pleased.
Neither the boys *nor* the teacher *is* pleased.

Either I *or* my friends *are* going there.
Either my friends *or* I *am* going there.

I *or* my wife *is* going to attend the wedding.
My wife *or* I *am* going to attend the wedding.

Neither you *nor* I *nor* he *is* going to leave this room.
Neither you *nor* he *nor* I *am* going to leave this room.

जब दो subjects *or, either...or, neither...nor* से जुटे हों तब verb अपने नजदीकवाले subject के अनुसार singular या plural होता है।

Note : किंतु ऊपर के वाक्यों में verb को अपने नजदीक के subject के अनुसार singular या plural रखने से कभी-कभी वाक्य भद्दे लगते हैं। इस भद्देपन को दूर करने के लिए *may, can, will, shall, would, could* इत्यादि का प्रयोग किया जाता है।
जैसे :

A	B
Either my wife *or* I *am* going.	*Either* my wife *or* I *will be* going.
Neither you, *nor* I, *nor* anyone else *knows* the answer.	*Neither* you, *nor* I, *nor* anyone else *will* know the answer.

ऐसे वाक्यों के संबंध में कुछ modern grammarians के विचार देखें :

When two noun phrases are joined by *or* or *either...or,* the general rule is that the number of the verb is determined by the number of the *last* noun phrase (PROXIMITY) :

Either *your brakes* or *your eyesight* IS at fault. [1]
Either *your eyesight* or *your brakes* ARE at fault. [2]

In [1] the proximity rule applies, but is felt to be awkward by some people. To avoid this awkwardness, it is usually possible to use an auxiliary verb which has the same form in the singular and the plural, for example :

Either *your brakes* or *your eyesight* MUST be at fault.

—GEOFFREY LEECH & JAN SVARTVIK : A COMMUNICATIVE GRAMMAR OF ENGLISH

64. *Look at these sentences :*

Her *hair is* grey but her eyes are blue.
Five *hairs* on his head *are* grey.

Hair का प्रयोग singular में होता है किंतु जब बालों की गिनती बतलानी हो तो *hairs* लिखा जाता है तथा इसके साथ plural verb का प्रयोग किया जाता है।

65. *Look at these sentences :*

A	B
The *team is* at the bottom of the third division.	The *team are* full of enthusiasm.
The *audience* today *was* huge.	The *audience were* getting bored.
My *family is* an old one.	My *family are* early risers.
The *public consists* of you and me.	The *public are* tired of strikes.
The *crowd has* been dispersed.	The *crowd were* fighting among themselves.
The *committee was* of one opinion.	The *committee were* divided on the issue.
The *government has* decided it.	The *government are* determined to do it.

(A) अगर *audience, family, public, crowd, committee, team, company, staff* तथा *government* से एक group का बोध हो तो verb singular होता है।

(B) किंतु जब इन शब्दों से अलग-अलग व्यक्तियों का बोध हो तब verb plural होता है।

ऐसे collective noun के विषय में यह विचार देखें :

Words like *committee, congregation, audience, staff, personnel, the public:* group collectives. Many of these have plural forms (*committees, audiences, congregations*), which of course take plural verbs and pronouns; but with most, the singular form can be treated as singular or plural according to circumstances.

Generally the singular is to be preferred, but it is not always possible...But whether we choose to use a singular or a plural, the important thing is that we must be consistent, at least throughout the same sentence.

—F. T. WOOD : CURRENT ENGLISH USAGE

अतः, हम कह सकते हैं :

The audience has already expressed its approval. किंतु— The audience is requested to be in its seat by 7.25 कहना गलत होगा। इस वाक्य में are requested तथा their seats कहना सही होगा।

66. *Look at these sentences :*

Affirmative	*Negative*
He *needs* to go there.	He *need not* do it.
He *dares* to say so.	She *dare not* say what she thinks.
We *dare* to speak like that.	They *dare not* come here.

Affirmative sentence में singular subject के साथ *dare/need* का singular form *dares/needs* का प्रयोग किया जाता है। किंतु need not तथा dare not का प्रयोग singular subject के साथ singular रूप में और plural subject के साथ plural रूप में होता है। He needs not या dares not do it कहना गलत है।

Dare के modern usage के संबंध में ध्यान दें :

In practice, *dare* is not a very common word in modern English. In an informal style (e.g., ordinary conversation), we usually use other expressions instead, like *not to be afraid,* or *not to have the courage to.* A sentence like *He dares to say what he thinks* is possible, but most people would say *He's not afraid to say what he thinks.*

—MICHAEL SWAN : PRACTICAL ENGLISH USAGE

OTHER TYPES OF AGREEMENT

67. *Look at these sentences :*

A	B
The *child* was an *angel.*	The *children* were *angels.*
Tom is a *boy.*	*Tom* and *Jack* are *boys.*
He was *a doctor.*	*They* were *doctors.*
This *woman* is a *nurse.*	These *women* are *nurses.*

(A) ऐसे वाक्यों में अगर subject singular हो तो complement (*angel, boy, doctor, nurse* etc.) भी singular होता है।

(B) जब subject plural हो तब complement भी plural होता है।

Note : किंतु इस नियम के कुछ अपवाद हैं; जैसे—

What we need most *is* books.
Those chairs are *reproduction.*
Good manners are *a* rarity these days.

Children can be { fun. / *a* nuisance. / good company. / *an* investment. }

68. *Look at these sentences :*

Everyone thinks *he* has the answer.
Every student has to make up *his* own mind.
Every *student* has to make up *his* or *her* own mind.

जिस subject का लिंग (sex) स्पष्ट नहीं हो उसके लिए *he/his* का प्रयोग किया जाता है। जब subject से male तथा female दोनों का बोध कराना हो तो उसके लिए pronoun *his or her* का प्रयोग किया जाता है।

69. *Look at these sentences :*

We will need *an extra* ten rupees.
I go to Delhi *every six weeks.*
I want to stay for *another three months.*
He had *an additional sixty rupees.*
She has been waiting for *a good twenty-five minutes.*

कभी-कभी plural noun phrase के पहले an extra, every, another, an additional, a good का प्रयोग किया जाता है तथा वैसे plural noun phrase से a single thing का बोध होता है।

70. *Look at these sentences :*

A	B
Adjectives	*Determiners*
He is an *old* man.	*Much* furniture is needed.
These are *old* books.	*Many* chairs are there.
This is *old* furniture.	There are *several* books on this table.

(A) Adjective तथा उसके बाद आनेवाले noun में किसी agreement का सवाल नहीं उठता। जैसे *old* का प्रयोग singular countable noun (*man*), plural countable noun (*books*) तथा uncountable noun (*furniture*) के पहले हुआ है।

(B) किंतु determiners (*much, many, several, this* इत्यादि) adjective के ही sub-class हैं, जिनका प्रयोग noun के पहले होता है। कुछ determiners (जैसे—*much*) uncountable noun (जैसे *furniture*) के पहले आते हैं; कुछ determiners (जैसे—*many, several*) plural countable noun (जैसे—*chairs, books*) के पहले आते हैं, तो कुछ determiners (जैसे—*this*) singular countable noun (जैसे—*table*) के पहले आते हैं।

अतः, determiners तथा उसके बाद आनेवाले nouns में भी agreement होता है अर्थात singular तथा plural noun के लिए अलग-अलग determiners प्रयुक्त होते हैं।

नीचे दिए chart को देखें कि किस noun के पहले कौन-सा determiner लगता है।

Determiners used before nouns	*Type of noun*	*Examples*
a/an, each, every, either, neither, one, another	*singular countable nouns* के पहले प्रयोग किया जाता है	*a* book, *an* egg, *each* girl, *every* boy, *either* pen, *neither* car, *one* book, *another* man
both, few, a few, many, several, various, these, those, two, three, four, a large number of, the majority of etc.	*plural countable nouns* के पहले प्रयोग किया जाता है	*both* boys, *few* nibs, *a few* shirts, *many* cups, *several* boxes, *various* things, *these* boys, *those* fans, *two* cows, *a large number of* girls, *the majority of* boys
little, a little, less, much, a good deal of, a great deal of	*uncountable nouns* के पहले प्रयोग किया जाता है	*little* milk, *a little* water, *less* money, *much* oil, *a good deal of* petrol, *a great deal of* sugar
this, that	*singular countable noun* तथा *uncountable noun* के पहले प्रयोग किया जाता है	*this* book/milk *that* pen/money
all, a lot of, lots of, enough, more, most, some, such, plenty of	*plural countable noun* तथा *uncountable nouns* के पहले प्रयोग किया जाता है	*all* books/money, *a lot of* apples/tea, *lots of* toys/petrol, *more* boys/sugar, *most* girls/salt, *some* caps/water, *such* boxes/food, *plenty of* hats/energy
no, any, only, other, own, some, same, the, my, your, his, her, our, its, their	*singular, plural* या *uncountable nouns* के पहले प्रयोग किया जाता है	*no* boy/boys/milk, *any* man/men/water *only* man/men/tea *other* pens, *the* child/children/ink *the same* toy/toys/coffee *my* coats/money etc.

Examples Worked Out

Fill in the blanks with suitable verbs choosing from the brackets.

1. What we need most....books. (*is/are*)	What we need most *is* books.
2. Each child...an ice-cream. (*has/have*)	Each child *has* an ice-cream.
3. Two plus two...four. (*is/are*)	Two plus two *is* four.
4. A child...sweets. (*like/likes*)	A child *likes* sweets.
5. Cows...us milk. (*give/gives*)	Cows *give* us milk.
6. The writing of the letter....over. (*is/are*)	The writing of the letter *is* over.
7. There...a bus at 10 a.m. (*is/are*)	There *is* a bus at 10 a.m.
8. There...ten girls in this class. (*is/are*)	There *are* ten girls in this class.
9. The people of this village...hard-working. (*is/are*)	The people of this village *are* hard-working
10. Does the boy...English ? (*know/knows*)	Does the boy *know* English ?
11. Do barking dogs... ? (*bite/bites*)	Do barking dogs *bite ?*
12. Both of them...good. (*is/are*)	Both of them *are* good.
13. Most of the boys...gone home. (*have/has*)	Most of the boys *have* gone home.
14. One of my friends...a car. (*have/has*)	One of my friends *has* a car.
15. What....the latest news ? (*is/are*)	What *is* the latest news ?
16. Half of the mangoes...rotten. (*is/are*)	Half of the mangoes *are* rotten.
17. Most of the traffic...by the main road. (*go/goes*)	Most of the traffic *goes* by the main road.
18. A number of boys...there. (*was/were*)	A number of boys *were* there.
19. More than sixty boys... passed in the first division. (*has/have*)	More than sixty boys *have* passed in the first division.
20. Mr and Mrs Thakur...in the garden. (*is/are*)	Mr and Mrs Thakur *are* in the garden.
21. All that glitters...not gold. (*is/are*)	All that glitters *is* not gold.
22. The pen that you gave me... lost. (*is/are*)	The pen that you gave me *is* lost.
23. All...mortal. (*is/are*)	All *are* mortal.
24. The Ganges...a holy river. (*is/are*)	The Ganges *is* a holy river.

25. *Gulliver's Travels*...a famous satire. (*is/are*)	*Gulliver's Travels* is a famous satire.
26. The books that you gave me...cheap. (*was/were*)	The books that you gave me *were* cheap.
27. A lot of food...lying there. (*was/were*)	A lot of food *was* lying there.
28. The police...arrested the thief. (*has/have*)	The police *have* arrested the thief.
29. Twenty rupees.....not a big sum. (*is/are*)	Twenty rupees *is* not a big sum.
30. Lots of people...still coming. (*is/are*)	Lots of people *are* still coming.
31. The number of people killed..... very large. (*was/were*)	The number of people killed *was* very large.
32. Half of the milk...been spoiled. (*has/have*)	Half of the milk *has* been spoiled.
33. The public...invited to the meeting. (*is/are*)	The public *are* invited to the meeting.
34. Five miles...not a long distance. (*is/are*)	Five miles *is* not a long distance.
35. The Himalayas...a range of mountains. (*is/are*)	The Himalayas *are* a range of mountains.
36. The United States... a rich country. (*is/are*)	The United States *is* a rich country.
37. Most of the money...lost. (*is/are*)	Most of the money *is* lost.
38. Ten times five...fifty. (*is/are*)	Ten times five *is* fifty.
39. American and Dutch beer...costly. (*is/are*)	American and Dutch beer *are* costly.
40. More than one person...opposed it. (*has/have*)	More than one person *has* opposed it.
41. Mathematics...a very interesting subject. (*is/are*)	Mathematics *is* a very interesting subject.
42. A large number of people... applied for the job. (*has/have*)	A large number of people *have* applied for the job.
43. What I say and do...easy to know. (*is/are*)	What I say and do *are* easy to know.
44. Neither he nor his wife... arrived. (*has/have*)	Neither he nor his wife *has* arrived.
45. The United Nations...our only hope. (*is/are*)	The United Nations *is* our only hope.
46. He and I....in Delhi together. (*was/were*)	He and I *were* in Delhi together.

47. Age and experience...wisdom to man. (*bring/brings*)	Age and experience *brings* wisdom to man.
48. Each man and each woman ...a vote. (*has/have*)	Each man and each woman *has* a vote.
49. Politics...a dirty game. (*is/are*)	Politics *is* a dirty game.
50. Each of the boys....given a book. (*was/were*)	Each of the boys *was* given a book.
51. Neither of the boys...able to win the race. (*is/are*)	Neither of the boys *is* able to win the race.
52. Oil and water...not mix. (*do/does*)	Out and water *do* not mix.
53. No prize or medal...given to the boy. (*was/were*)	No prize or medal *was* given to boy.
54. Either Rana or Raju...done this mischief. (*has/have*)	Either Rana or Raju *has* done this mischief.
55. Kapildev is one of the players who....been selected for the test. (*has/have*)	Kapildev is one of the players who *have* been selected for the test.
56. It is I who...to blame. (*is/am*)	It is I who *am* to blame.
57. Twenty-five years....a long time. (*is/are*)	Twenty-five years *is* a long time.
58. Nobody, not even the teachers,.... present. (*was/were*)	Nobody, not even the teachers *were* present.
59. Mohan, rather than others,..... guilty. (*is/are*)	Mohan, rather than others, *is* guilty.
60. What we now need...a good government. (*is/are*)	What we now need *is* a good government.
61. One of the boys in camp..... fallen ill. (*has/have*)	One of the boys in camp *has* fallen ill.
62. The villages of our country.... poor. (*is/are*)	The villages of our country *are* poor.
63. The examination of the boys...... finished. (*is/are*)	The examination of the boys *is* finished.
64. Houses of this type...three rooms. (*has/have*)	Houses of this type *have* three rooms.
65. Stories of animals...children. (*attracts/attract*)	Stories of animals *attract* children.
66. One of Mr Das's sons...a doctor. (*is/are*)	One of Mr Das's sons *is* a doctor.
67. Every man, woman and child ...given food. (*was/were*)	Every man, woman and child child *was* given food.
68. My friend, philosopher and guide...no more. (*is/are*)	My friend, philosopher and guide *is* no more.

69. Either the boys or the teacher ....in the wrong. (*is/are*)	Either the boys or the teacher *is* in the wrong.
70. His secretary and his typist... on leave today. (*is/are*)	His secretary and his typist *are* on leave today.
71. Every one of the boys...in the playground. (*was/were*)	Every one of the boys *was* in the playground.
72. There....an army barracks. (*is/are*)	There *is* an army barracks.
73. Sweet...the uses of adversity. (*is/are*)	Sweet *are* the uses of adversity.
74. A great variety of objects...... the mind. (*distract/distracts*)	A great *variety* of objects *distracts* the mind.
75. I wish I....a king. (*was/were*)	I wish I *were* a king.
76. I wish it...possible. (*was/were*)	I wish it *were* possible.
77. If I...you, I would do it.(*was/were*)	If I *were* you, I would do it.
78. Plenty of sugar....been bought. (*has/have*)	Plenty of sugar *has* been bought.
79. A team of students...selected. (*was/were*)	A team of students *was* selected.
80. A set of combs...been bought. (*has/have*)	A set of combs *has* been bought.
81. A group of scholars....come. (*has/have*)	A group of scholars *has* come.
82. A bunch of keys...lying here. (*is/are*)	A bunch of keys *is* lying here.
83. A parcel of books...been received. (*has/have*)	A parcel of books *has* been received.
84. Your trousers....very loose. (*is/are*)	Your trousers *are* very loose.
85. More than one man... invited. (*was/were*)	More than one man *was* invited.
86. More girls than one...present. (*was/were*)	More girls than one *were* present.
87. ....either of your sisters working ? (*is/are*)	*Is* either of your sisters working ?
88. The orator and the statesman ...no more. (*is/are*)	The orator and the stateman *are* no more.
89. Bread and butter....a wholesome food. (*is/are*)	Bread and butter *is* a wholesome food.
90. A flock of sheep....grazing in the field. (*was/were*)	A flock of sheep *was* grazing in the field.

91. Half of the apples...bad. (*was/were*)	Half of the apples *were* bad.
92. Half of the land....uncultivated. (*was/were*)	Half of the land *was* uncultivated.
93. Time and tide....for no man. (*wait/waits*)	Time and tide *wait* for no man.
94. It....a busy headquarters. (*is/are*)	It *is* a busy headquarters.
95. The headquarters....here. (*is/are*)	The headquarters *is/are* here.
96. His whereabouts.... unknown. (*is/are*)	His whereabouts *is/are* unknown.

EXERCISE I

Fill in the gaps with one of the two verbs given in the brackets :

EXAMPLE : My friend...swimming. (*like/likes*)
= My friend *likes* swimming.

1. My friend...swimming. (*like/likes*)
2. A bird...in the sky. (*fly/flies*)
3. A new car....a lot of money. (*costs/cost*)
4. John and Jack...gone home. (*has/have*)
5. Those boys...healthy (*look/looks*)
6. All the books .... to me. (*belongs/belong*)
7. About ten boys...there. (*was/were*)
8. Sita....not like to play. (*do/does*)
9. .....you know his name ? (*Do/Does*)
10. ....the boys crying at night ? (*Was/Were*)
11. That pen...been stolen. (*have/has*)
12. A few dogs....black. (*is/are*)
13. His father and mother....there. (*were/was*)
14. Every man....two eyes. (*has/have*)
15. We all....English. (*learns/learn*)
16. ....Mr sen or Mr Roy in the class ? (*Is/Are*)
17. ....his friend come here every day ? (*Do/Does*)
18. Where....he live now ? (*do/does*)
19. Each boy....a bicycle. (*have/has*)
20. Both the pens...red. (*was/were*)

EXERCISE 2

Fill in the gaps with one of the two verbs given in the brackets :

EXAMPLE : Some of the water....dirty. (*is/are*)
= Some of the water *is* dirty.

1. Some of the water....dirty. (*is/are*)

2. Some people....travelling. (*dislikes/dislike*)
3. All the students....present today. (*are/is*)
4. Her uncle and aunt....a car. (*has/have*)
5. Oil and water....not mix (*do/does*)
6. Many workers...been suspended. (*has/have*)
7. Each child...a glass of milk. (*get/gets*)
8. Several girls....passed this year. (*have/has*)
9. It....not matter much. (*do/does*)
10. None of the boys....there. (*was/were*)
11. One of the players....well. (*plays/play*)
12. There...a new pen on the table. (*is/are*)
13. There....a few boys in the class. (*is/are*)
14. There....nothing to worry about. (*is/are*)
15. All the furniture....new here. (*is/are*)
16. Everybody....that man. (*knows/know*)
17. One of them....gone home. (*has/have*)
18. How many of them...tea ? (*likes/like*)
19. Everybody....him. (*hate/hates*)
20. The traffic....at a standstill. (*is/are*)

EXERCISE 3

Fill in the gaps with one of the two verbs given in the brackets :

EXAMPLE : The wages of sin...death. (*is/are*)
= The wages of sin *is* death.

1. The wages of sin....death. (*is/are*)
2. Where....you at 10 a. m. ? (*was/were*)
3. Some one....standing at the door. (*is/are*)
4. Most of the boys....hard-working. (*is/are*)
5. Some of these mangoes..ripe. (*was/were*)
6. The police...arrested the thief. (*has/have*)
7. The majority of workers....very hard. (*works/work*)
8. Either coffee or tea....good for me. (*is/are*)
9. What....phonetics ? (*is/are*)
10. No money....been spent on this. (*has/have*)
11. No man of that name...here. (*lives/live*)
12. He and I....at school together. (*was/were*)
13. A number of questions...asked. (*was/were*)
14. John as well as Hari...football. (*plays/play*)
15. Either Sita or Gita....done it. (*has/have*)
16. No prize or medal....given to Reeta. (*was/were*)
17. A lot of people...coffee. (*likes/like*)
18. Most of the money...been lost. (*has/have*)
19. Ill news....fast. (*travels/travel*)
20. Physics....his weakest subject. (*is/are*)

EXERCISE 4

Fill in the gaps with one of the two verbs given in the brackets :

EXAMPLE : Lots of meat...there on the table. (*was/were*)
= Lots of meat *was* there on the table.

1. Lots of meat....there on the table. (*was/were*)
2. A lot of work....still to be done. (*has/have*)
3. Plenty of opportunities....there for us. (*is/are*)
4. Much of the land....under water. (*was/were*)
5. Most of the visitors...known to me. (*is/are*)
6. Neither coffee nor tea...good for him. (*was/were*)
7. A large number of students....failed. (*(has/have*)
8. Measles....a dangerous disease. (*is/are*)
9. The majority of them...Sikhs. (*was/were*)
10. All his luggage...arrived. (*has/have*)
11. Good advice...difficult to follow. (*is/are*)
12. There.....a hundred boys in the class. (*is/are*)
13. The number of girls here...sixty. (*is/are*)
14. Half of the players....off the field. (*was/were*)
15. Each of the boys....rewarded. (*is/are*)
16. Neither of the two boys....an umbrella. (*has/have*)
17. One of my friends....won the prize. (*has/have*)
18. Many a man....after wealth. (*runs/run*)
19. A few boys....running outside. (*is/are*)
20. How many days....there in a week ? (*is/are*)

EXERCISE 5

Fill in the blanks with one of the two verbs given in the brackets :

EXAMPLE : Each boy and each girl...punished. (*was/were*)
= Each boy and each girl *was* punished.

1. Each boy and each girl...punished. (*was/were*)
2. Here are two books. Either....good. (*is/are*)
3. Statistics....a difficult subject. (*is/are*)
4. A great number of people....come here. (*has/have*)
5. There....plenty of time before the train comes. (*is/are*)
6. Several of my friends...been to America. (*has/have*)
7. Not only Mr Sen but also Mr Bose...there. (*is/are*)
8. The weight of these books...heavy. (*is/are*)
9. The safety of the people....on many things. (*depends/depend*)
10. The colour of her eyes...black. (*was/were*)
11. The leader of the gangs...a criminal. (*is/are*)
12. One of the girls who have come...a dancer. (*is/are*)
13. The captain of the players....not come yet. (*has/have*)
14. The greatest problem of our country...yet to be solved. (*is/are*)
15. A pair of shoes....in that room. (*was/were*)
16. A group of students....standing there. (*is/are*)
17. Most of the candidates....passed. (*has/have*)

18. Much of what he says...true. (*is/are*)
19. Give me a book which...new. (*looks/look*)
20. The cause of both the accidents....the same. (*was/were*)

EXERCISE 6

Fill in the blanks with one of the two verbs given in the brackets :

EXAMPLE : Savings in the bank....a great profit. (*is/are*)
= Savings in the bank *are* a great profit.

1. Savings in the bank...a great profit. (*is/are*)
2. Neither of us....going to Calcutta. (*is/are*)
3. Bread and butter....my breakfast. (*is/are*)
4. Each of you....guilty. (*is/are*)
5. All this....troublesome. (*is/are*)
6. The poor....generally honest. (*is/are*)
7. A team of speakers....reached here. (*has/have*)
8. 'Gulliver's Travels'....an interesting book. (*is/are*)
9. He as well as I...going. (*is/am*)
10. All that glitters....not gold. (*is/are*)
11. Sweet....the uses of adversity. (*is/are*)
12. The scholar and the poet....dead. (*is/are*)
13. Truth and honesty....the best policy. (*is/are*)
14. Neither apples nor oranges....expensive. (*is/are*)
15. A parcel of books....been received. (*has/have*)
16. Neither of the candidates...able to impress me. (*is/are*)
17. Fifty rupees....too much for this article. (*is/are*)
18. The jury....divided in their opinion. (*was/were*)
19. Rice and curry....his favourite food. (*is/are*)
20. The house with all its belongings...sold. (*was/were*)

EXERCISE 7

Fill in the blanks with one of the two verbs given in the brackets :

EXAMPLE : He ordered as if he....my master. (*was/were*)
= He ordered as if he *were* my master.

1. He ordered as if he...my master. (*was/were*)
2. Time and tide....for no man. (*wait/waits*)
3. A number of cattle...grazing. (*is/are*)
4. Neither he nor Sita...to go. (*is/are*)
5. The Magistrate and Collector...present there. (*was/were*)
6. Either you or I...to blame. (*am/are*)
7. Neither Ram nor his friends...hurt. (*was/were*)
8. He as well as you....going. (*is/are*)
9. Not only Ram but also his brothers...there. (*are/is*)
10. A large number of candidates...come. (*has/have*)
11. What we need most...books. (*is/are*)
12. Ram as well as his sons...arrested. (*was/were*)
13. Either Raman or his brother....done it. (*has/have*)
14. He as well as his friends....hard-working. (*is/are*)

15. Neither you nor he...guilty. (*is/are*)
16. The Principal and the Secretary...coming today. (*is/are*)
17. This is one of the finest houses which.... been built in this town. (*has/have*)
18. Of the four prisoners everyone...escaped. (*has/have*)
19. Neither of the two men....very strong. (*was/were*)
20. Many a man...applied for this job. (*has/have*)

EXERCISE 8

Fill in the blanks with one of the two verbs given in the brackets :

EXAMPLE : Acknowledging services....required of a polite man. (*is/are*)
= Acknowledging services *is* required of a polite man.

1. Both the train and the bus...unsafe these days. (*is/are*)
2. The fleet of ships...anchored in the docks. (*is/are*)
3. The bouquet of flowers....faded. (*have/has*)
4. The law in most lands....not prescribe that we should be impolite. (*do/does*)
5. The horse and carriage...at the door. (*is/are*)
6. The colour of these shirts....blue. (*is/are*)
7. Either of these roads...unsafe these days. (*is/are*)
8. The poet and the philosopher....dead. (*is/are*)
9. What I have to say....this. (*is/are*)
10. There....many objections to this plan. (*is/are*)
11. Neither his father nor his mother...alive. (*is/are*)
12. The public....requested not to walk on the grass. (*is/are*)
13. The accountant and the cashier....absconding. (*is/are*)
14. To take pay and then not to work....dishonest. (*is/are*)
15. The notorious dacoit with his followers....escaped. (*has/have*)
16. The whole herd of cattle...to be sold. (*is/are*)
17. His trousers....covered with mud. (*is/are*)
18. A pair of trousers....hanging over the chair. (*is/are*)
19. A pair of spectacles....lying on the table. (*is/are*)
20. A large crowd...expected at the football match. (*is/are*)

EXERCISE 9

Fill in the blanks with one of the two verbs given in the brackets :

EXAMPLE : More than ten boys...signed the petition. (*has/have*)
= More than ten boys *have* signed the petition.

1. More than ten boys...signed the petition. (*has/have*)
2. Neither the boys nor the girls...new books. (*has/have*)
3. Either you or I...mistaken. (*am/are*)
4. Mohan, rather than others,...guilty. (*is/are*)
5. What we now need...mental peace. (*is/are*)
6. Fifty years...half a century. (*is/are*)
7. Of the thirty girls, ten...fever. (*has/have*)
8. Mother, as well as others in the family,...it. (*wants/want*)
9. Father, with his sons and daughters, ...to Delhi. (*goes/go*)

10. Rajeev, like his father,....very tall. (*is/are*)
11. All his money....been wasted. (*has/have*)
12. Slow and steady ....the race. (*wins/win*)
13. Either the teacher or the boys...right. (*is/are*)
14. His secretary and his typist...present today. (*is/are*)
15. The workers as well as their leader...absent. (*is/are*)
16. Neither the men nor the women in the car... injured. (*was/were*)
17. A friend and colleague of mine...getting married. (*is/are*)
18. The United States....a rich country. (*is/are*)
19. The audience in the meeting...small. (*was/were*)
20. Thirty kilos....too heavy a weight for me to carry. (*is/are*)

EXERCISE 10

Fill in the blanks with one of the two verbs given in the brackets :

EXAMPLE : What you do here....no importance. (*has/have*)
= What you do here *has* no importance.

1. What you do here...no importance. (*has/have*)
2. When....the minister want to see you ? (*does/do*)
3. The United Nations...our only hope. (*is/are*)
4. Much of what they say...not true. (*is/are*)
5. There....been a big rise in prices. (*has/have*)
6. Where....the rest of the milk gone ? (*has/have*)
7. The rules of cricket....easy to understand. (*is/are*)
8. Most of his furniture....old-fashioned. (*is/are*)
9. The rich...not always happy. (*is/are*)
10. The West Indies...produced great cricketers. (*has/have*)
11. Reading and writing...two different skills. (*is/are*)
12. Where....the rest of the boys ? (*is/are*)
13. In villages there....a lack of facilities for people. (*is/are*)
14. Here....a list of the names of teachers to be invited. (*is/are*)
15. His hair...to be getting thinner each year. (*seems/seem*)
16. Most of the land in Bihar...fertile. (*is/are*)
17. Either your brakes or your eyesight...at fault. (*is/are*)
18. Either your eyesight or your brakes...at fault. (*is/are*)
19. The sharp rise in the prices of good grains...partly due to the flood. (*is/are*)
20. The wild ambitions which flow through his mind... a source of trouble to him. (*was/were*)

EXERCISE 11

Fill in the blanks with one of the two verbs given in the brackets :

EXAMPLES : (i) A variety of pleasing objects....the eye. (*charm/charms*)
= A variety of pleasing objects *charms* the eye.

(ii) Two-thirds of the work...left undone. (*was/were*)
= Two-thirds of the work *was* left undone.

1.	A variety of objects...the eye.	*(charm/charms)*
2.	Two-thirds of the work...left undone.	*(was/were)*
3.	Each of my brothers...made a good start in life.	*(has/have)*
4.	You, who....my friend, should guide me.	*(is/are)*
5.	His choice of words...excellent.	*(is/are)*
6.	Good news...come today.	*(has/have)*
7.	Neither of the sisters....very much liked.	*(was/were)*
8.	Every man and every horse....urgently needed.	*(was/were)*
9.	Neither reward nor punishment...to be expected from him.	*(are/is)*
10.	A large number of cattle...grazing in the field.	*(is/are)*
11.	The ideas of my teacher...from mine.	*(differ/differs)*
12.	The cost of paper and printing...too high.	*(is/are)*
13.	How he escaped...still a mystery.	*(is/are)*
14.	You are the man who...killed a lion.	*(has/have)*
15.	It is you who...done this.	*(has/have)*
16.	It is one of the best books that...been written.	*(has/have)*
17.	Mr John, with his wife and children, ...present at the show.	*(was/were)*
18.	Nothing but funny stories...him.	*(delight/delights)*
19.	The causes of his unpopularity...not far to seek.	*(is/are)*
20.	The sum and substance of the matter ...that he was wrong.	*(is/are)*

EXERCISE 12

Complete these sentences with one of the two verbs given in the brackets :

1. Good health (*depend/depends*) on a number of factors. An active mind (*is/are*) as necessary to health as a strong body. In Europe, very few people (*suffers/suffer*) from physical disease. But mental patients (*is/are*) not uncommon.

2. The word 'discipline' (*come/comes*) from the word *disciple.* A disciple (*is/are*) a learner. Discipline (*mean/means*) learning to obey rules. A child (*needs/need*) discipline at school.

3. Most of the sentences in this book (*has/have*) an Indian background or (*is/are*) related to Indian life and letters. Each of the sentences (*is/are*) idiomatic. It (*has/have*) been graded, too.

4. Astronomers, those people who (*study/studies*) the stars, (*tell/tells*) us that long long ago the earth and all the planets (*was/were*) parts of the earth. The sun (*was/were*) then a mass of flaming matter.

5. Malaria fever (*is/are*) probably the commonest of all tropical diseases. The discovery of its cause and the insect which (*carry/carries*) it (*provide/provides*) a good example of the scientific methods used by very clever men. Malaria (*has/have*) been known as a particular fever.

6. You (*know/knows*) that the earth (*go/goes*) round the sun and the moon (*go/goes*) round the earth. People (*know/knows*) also perhaps that there (*is/are*) several other bodies which (*go/goes*) round the sun. All these, including our earth, (*is/are*) called planets of the sun. The moon (*is/are*) called a satellite of the earth because it (*hang/hangs*) on to it.

7. If a man (*take/takes*) interest in work, (*spend/spends*) his time well, (*has/have*) good relations with friends and neighbours and (*care/cares*) for the needs and wishes of other people, he (*is/are*) free from worry. He (*has/have*) a healthy mind and if the mind (*is/are*) healthy, the body (*is/are*) healthy.

8. We (*say/says*) that a person (*has/have*) good manners if he or she (*behave/behaves*) politely and (*is/are*) kind and helpful to others. Everyone (*like/likes*) a person with good manners but no one (*like/likes*) a person with bad manners. But you may (*ask/asks*), "What (*are/is* good manners ?"

9. There (*is/are*) a hotel. People (*stay/stays*) at the hotel. There (*is/are*) some waiters. The waiters (*stand/stands*). It (*is/are*) a fine day. The sun (*is/are*) shining. Some of the men (*is/are*) drinking coffee. One of the women (*is/are*) drinking a cup of tea.

10. We (*get/gets*) rain in India in all seasons. Some parts of the country (*get/gets*) rain in some months. The other parts (*get/gets*) rain in other months. When (*do/does*) this part of the country get rains ? Here the rains (*start/starts*) in June. The monsoon (*come/comes*) in June. What (*is/are*) the monsoon ? What (*do/does*) it do ? The monsoons are winds which (*bring/brings*) rains.

EXERCISE 13 (With Answer)

Choose the correct word to fill in the blank space :

1. (a) One of my teachers....next door to my aunt.
   (i) live (ii) lives
   (b) All the books on that shelf...to me.
   (i) belong (ii) belongs
   (c) The tallest of the three boys...next door to me.
   (i) live (ii) lives
   (d) Mumps ...a serious illness for grown-up people.
   (i) is (ii) are.
   (e) What I say and what I think...my own affair.
   (i) is (ii) are
2. (a) An epidemic of measles...broken out in the district.
   (i) has (ii) have
   (b) Most of the time...spent looking round the shops.
   (i) was (ii) were
   (c) All his earnings...lost in a day.
   (i) was (ii) were
   (d) His looks...good.
   (i) is (ii) are
3. (a) Good manners....a rarity these days.
   (i) is (ii) are
   (b) The committee....divided on the question.
   (i) was (ii) were
   (c) Neither of us...willing to give in.
   (i) is (ii) are
   (d) A hundred dollars a month...rather high rent.
   (i) is (ii) are

(e) Sixty people...a huge party.
 (i) mean (ii) means

4. (a) Athletics...ruining American colleges.
 (i) is (ii) are
 (b) You, my friend,...going to get a surprise.
 (i) is (ii) are
 (c) No people of that name...here.
 (i) live (ii) lives
 (d) Not one, but all of us...hoping to be there.
 (i) is (ii) are
 (e) Billiards....my favourite game.
 (i) was (ii) were

5. (a) After the meeting...the time to speak.
 (i) is (ii) are
 (b) How you got there....not concern me.
 (i) do (ii) does
 (c) To treat them as hostages.....criminal.
 (i) is (ii) are
 (d) Ninety rupees...a lot of money.
 (i) is (ii) are
 (e) No one except his own supporters...with him.
 (i) agree (ii) agrees.

Ans. : 1. (a) lives; (b) belong; (c) lives; (d) is; (e) are.
2. (a) has; (b) was; (c) were; (d) are.
3. (a) are; (b) was; (c) is; (d) is; (e) means.
4. (a) is; (b) are; (c) live; (d) are; (e) was.
5. (a) is; (b) does; (c) is; (d) is; (e) agrees.

□ □ □

4. TIME AND TENSE

(A) TIME AND TENSE

1. *Look at these sentences :*

Kapil *plays* cricket.
Kapil *played* cricket.
Kapil *will play* cricket.

इन वाक्यों में *plays, played* तथा *will play* verbs हैं।

(i) *plays* present tense है तथा इससे present time का बोध होता है।

(ii) *played* past tense है तथा इससे past time का बोध होता है।

(iii) *will play* future tense है (किंतु modern grammarians इसे present tense कहते हैं) तथा इससे future time का बोध होता है।

इन वाक्यों से पता चलता है कि present, past तथा future tense क्रमशः present, past तथा future time का बोध कराते हैं।

By Tense we understand the correspondence between the form of the verb and our concept of time (past, present and future).

किंतु Time और Tense दोनों एक नहीं है। Time एक universal concept है, किंतु Tense का संबंध verb से होता है।

Time is a universal, non-linguistic concept with three divisions : past, present, and future; by *tense* we understand the correspondence between the form of the verb and our concept of time.

—Randolph Quirk & Sidney Greenbaum : UNIVERSITY GRAMMAR OF ENGLISH

Time को हम तीन भागों में बाँटते हैं :

Past Time   Present Time   Future Time

अब time और tense के संबंध को देखें :

2. *Look at these sentences :*

Could you help me ?
Would you do me a favour ?
I *wanted* to talk to you.
Did you want to see me ?
It *is going* to rain.
Milk *is* white.

(i) इन वाक्यों में *could, would, wanted* तथा *did* past tense में हैं किंतु इनसे present time का बोध होता है। *I wanted to talk to you* का अर्थ यह नहीं हुआ कि मैं आपसे बातें करना चाहता था और अब नहीं चाहता हूँ। Polite request (विनम्र आग्रह) में present time के लिए past tense का प्रयोग होता है।

(ii) अंतिम दो वाक्यों में *is* तथा *is going* present tense में है।

(a) It *is going* to rain से future time का बोध होता है क्योंकि 'वर्षा होनेवाली है', हो नहीं रही है यद्यपि *is going* present tense में है।

(b) Milk *is* white से past, present तथा future तीनों time का बोध होता है क्योंकि milk उजला था, है और रहेगा। लेकिन *is* present tense में है।

अतः, कोई जरूरी नहीं है कि verb अगर present tense में है तो present time का बोध हो, और अगर past tense में है तो past time का।

अब कुछ और उदाहरण देखें जिनसे यह पता चल सके कि time और tense दोनों एक चीज नहीं है और न इन दोनों में बिलकुल एक जैसा संबंध (one to one correspondence) हमेशा रहता है।

I hope the train *isn't* late.	(present tense, future time)
Tomorrow *is* Saturday.	(present tense, future time)
The match *takes place* on Monday.	(present tense, future time)
Mr Sinha *retires* next month.	(present tense, future time)
The Chairman *is about to resign*.	(present tense, future time)
You *have ruined* my dress.	(present tense, past time)
We *are moving* next week.	(present tense, future time)
He *may leave* tomorrow.	(present tense, future time)
Could I smoke in here ?	(past tense, present time)
Would you excuse me ?	(past tense, present time)
Could you do me a favour ?	(past tense, present time)
The sun *rises* in the east.	(present tense, present, past and future time).

3. *Look at these sentences :*

He *is* well today.	(Present Tense)
He *will be* quite well tomorrow.	(Present Tense)
Yesterday he *was* unwell.	(Past Tense)

Modern grammarians के अनुसार अंगरेजी में दो Tense होते हैं : PRESENT TENSE तथा PAST TENSE. इन दो tense forms से ही present, past तथा future time का बोध होता है।

English has two tenses : PRESENT TENSE and PAST TENSE. As the names imply, the present tense normally refers to present time and past tense to past time :

She *is* quite well today.
Yesterday she *was* sick.

—RANDOLPH QUIRK & OTHERS : A GRAMMAR OF CONTEMPORARY ENGLISH

अतः, English में future time का बोध कराने के लिए Future tense नहीं होता। Future time की अभिव्यक्ति modal auxiliaries (जैसे : shall, will, can, may इत्यादि) या simple present forms या progressive forms द्वारा होती है।

किंतु Traditional grammarians के अनुसार अँगरेजी में तीन Tense होते हैं : (I) Present Tense, (II) Past Tense तथा (III) Future Tense.

इस पुस्तक में मुख्यतः हम Traditional Grammar के अनुसार ही Tense की चर्चा करेंगे।

(B) KINDS OF TENSES

	Tense		*Example*	*Form*
I.	(a) Simple Present	:	I *play*.	V (= Verb)
			He *plays*.	V-s
			She *goes*.	V-es
	(b) Present Continuous	:	I *am playing*.	am+V-ing
			He *is playing*.	is+V-ing
			They *are playing*.	are+V-ing
	(c) Present Perfect	:	I *have played*.	have+V-en
			He *has played*.	has+V-en
	(d) Present Perfect Continuous	:	I *have been playing*.	have+been+V-ing
			He *has been playing*.	has+been+V-ing
II.	(a) Simple Past	:	I *played*.	*V-ed*
			He played.	
	(b) Past Continuous	:	I *was playing*.	was+V-ing.
			They *were playing*.	were+V-ing
	(c) Past Perfect	:	I *had played*.	had+V-en
			They *had played*.	
	(d) Past Perfect Continuous	:	I *had been playing*.	had+been+V-ing
			They *had been playing*.	
III.	(a) Simple Future	:	I *shall play*.	shall+V
			He *will play*.	will+V
	(b) Future Continuous	:	I *shall be playing*.	shall+be+V-ing
			He *will be playing*.	will+be+V-ing
	(c) Future Perfect	:	I *shall have played*.	shall+have+V-en
			He *will have played*.	will+have+V-en
	(d) Future Perfect Continuous	:	I *shall have been playing*.	shall+have+been +V-ing
			He *will have been playing*.	will+have+been +V-ing

(C) VERB FORMS

English Grammar में Verb का असली रूप present tense तथा plural number माना जाता है। Verb के पाँच रूप होते हैं :

	Verb forms	*Examples*
V^1=	Verb का प्रथम रूप (base form) present tense तथा plural number में होता है :	go, come play, run
V^2=	Verb का दूसरा रूप (past tense form या -ed form) जिसे past tense के singular तथा plural दोनों में प्रयोग करते है :	went, came played, ran
V^3=	Verb का तीसरा रूप यानी -en form :	gone, come played, run
V^4=	Verb का चौथा रूप यानी -ing form :	going, coming playing, running
V^5=	Verb का पाँचवाँ रूप यानी -s/es form जिसका प्रयोग present tense के third person, singular में होता है :	goes, comes plays, runs

List of Some Commonly Known Verbs

Present Tense (V^1= *plain form*)	*Past Tense* (V^2= *-ed form*)	*Past Participle* (V^3= *-en form*)
am (हूँ)	was	been
are (हैं)	were	been
arise (उठना)	arose	arisen
awake (जगना, जगाना)	awoke	awoke/awaked
bear (जन्म देना)	bore	born
bear (ढोना, सहना)	bore	borne
beat (पीटना)	beat	beaten
become (होना)	became	become
begin (शुरू करना)	began	begun
bend (झुकना, झुकाना)	bent	bent
bereave (वंचित करना)	bereaved/bereft	bereaved/bereft
bet (दाँव या बाजी लगाना)	bet/betted	bet/betted
bid (आज्ञा देना)	bade	bidden
bind (बाँधना)	bound	bound
bite (काटना)	bit	bitten
bleed (खून बहना, या बहाना)	bled	bled
blow (बहना)	blew	blown
break (तोड़ना)	broke	broken
bring (लाना)	brought	brought
broadcast (समाचार आदि प्रसारित करना)	broadcast	broadcast
build (बनाना)	built	built
burn (जलना, जलाना)	burned/burnt	burned/burnt
burst (फट जाना)	burst	burst
buy (खरीदना)	bought	bought

Present Tense (V^1= *plain form*)	*Past Tense* (V^2= *-ed form*)	*Past Participle* (V^3= *-en form*)
cast (फेंकना)	cast	cast
catch (पकड़ना)	caught	caught
chide (धमकाना, डाँटना)	chided/chid	chided/chid
choose (चुनना)	chose	chosen
climb (चढ़ना)	climbed	climbed
cling (चिकना)	clung	clung
come (आना)	came	come
cost (दाम लगना)	cost	cost
creep (रेंगना)	crept	crept
cut (काटना)	cut	cut
deal (बर्ताव करना, बेचना)	dealt	dealt
dig (खोदना)	dug	dug
do (करना)	did	done
draw (खींचना)	drew	drawn
dream (सपना देखना)	dreamed/dreamt	dreamed/dreamt
drink (पीना)	drank	drunk
drive (हाँकना)	drove	driven
dwell (रहना)	dwelt	dwelt
eat (खाना)	ate	eaten
fall (गिरना)	fell	fallen
feed (भोजन करना, भोजन देना)	fed	fed
feel (महसूस करना)	felt	felt
fight (लड़ना)	fought	fought
find (पाना)	found	found
flee (भाग जाना)	fled	fled
fling (फेंकना)	flung	flung
fly (उड़ना, उड़ाना)	flew	flown
forbid (रोकना)	forbade	forbidden
forget (भूलना)	forgot	forgotten
forgive (माफ करना)	forgave	forgiven
forsake (छोड़ना)	forsook	forsaken
freeze (जमना)	froze	frozen
get (पाना)	got	got
give (देना)	gave	given
go (जाना)	went	gone
grind (पीसना)	ground	ground
grow (उपजना, उपजाना)	grew	grown
hang (फाँसी देना)	hanged	hanged
hang (लटकाना)	hung	hung

Present Tense (V^1= *plain form*)	*Past Tense* (V^2= *-ed form*)	*Past Participle* (V^3= *-en form*)
have (होना)	had	had
hear (सुनना)	heard	heard
hide (छिपाना)	hid	hid/hidden
hit (मारना)	hit	hit
hold (रखना)	held	held
hurt (चोट पहुँचाना)	hurt	hurt
keep (रखना)	kept	kept
kneel (घुटने टेकना)	knelt	knelt
knit (बुनना)	knit/knitted	knit
know (जानना)	knew	known
lay (लेटा देना)	laid	laid
lead (राह दिखाना)	led	led
lean (किसी ओर झुकना)	leaned/leant	leaned/leant
leap (कूदना)	leapt	leapt
learn (सीखना)	learned/learnt	learned/learnt
leave (छोड़ना)	left	left
lend (उधार देना)	lent	lent
let (देना)	let	let
lie (लेटना)	lay	lain
lie (झूठ बोलना)	lied	lied
light (प्रकाशित करना, जलाना)	lighted/lit	lighted/lit
lose (खो देना)	lost	lost
make (बनाना)	made	made
mean (अर्थ होना या देना)	meant	meant
meet (मिलना)	met	met
mislead (पथभ्रष्ट करना)	misled	misled
mistake (गलती करना)	mistook	mistaken
owe (ऋणी होना)	owed	owed
pay (चुकाना)	paid	paid
prove (साबित करना)	proved	proved
put (रखना)	put	put
quit (छोड़ना)	quitted/quit	quitted/quit
read (पढ़ना)	read	read
rid (छोड़ देना)	rid	rid
ride (सवारी करना)	rode	ridden
ring (बजना, बजाना)	rang	rung
rise (उठना)	rose	risen
run (दौड़ना)	ran	run
saw (आरे से लकड़ी चीरना)	sawed	sawed
say (कहना)	said	said

Present Tense (V^1 = *plain form*)	*Past Tense* (V^2 = *-ed form*)	*Past Participle* (V^3 = *-en form*)
see (देखना)	saw	seen
seek (खोजना)	sought	sought
sell (बेचना)	sold	sold
send (भेजना)	sent	sent
set (डूबना, व्यवस्थित करना)	set	set
sew (सिलाई करना)	sewed	sewn
shake (हिलाना, हिलना)	shook	shaken
shave (दाढ़ी बनाना)	shaved	shaved/shaven
shed (बहाना, खून बहाना)	shed	shed
shine (चमकना)	shone	shoned
shoot (गोली मारना)	shot	shot
show (दिखाना)	showed	shown
shrink (सिकुड़ना)	shrank	shrunk
shut (बन्द करना)	shut	shut
sing (गाना)	sang	sung
sink (डूबना)	sank	sunk
sit (बैठना)	sat	sat
slay (कत्ल करना)	slew	slain
sleep (सोना)	slept	slept
slide (फिसलना)	slid	slid
slink (चुपके से निकल जाना)	slunk	slunk
smell (गंध का अनुभव करना)	smelled/smelt	smelled/smelt
sow [बोना, (बीज) डालना]	sowed	sown
speak (बोलना)	spoke	spoken
speed (तेज जाना)	speeded/sped	speeded/sped
spell (हिज्जे करना)	spelled/spelt	spelled/spelt
spend (खर्च करना)	spent	spent
spill (तरल पदार्थ आदि का गिरना, बहना)	spilled/spilt	spilled/spilt
spin (कातना)	spun/span	spun
spit (थूकना)	spat	spat
split (खण्ड-खण्ड करना या फाड़ना)	split	split
spoil (खराब कर देना)	spoiled/spoilt	spoiled/spoilt
spread (फैलना, बढ़ाना)	spread	spread
spring (उछलना)	sprang	sprung
stand (खड़ा होना)	stood	stood
steal (चुराना)	stole	stolen
stick (चिपका रहना)	stuck	stuck
sting (डंक मारना)	stung	stung
stink (बदबू करना)	stank/stunk	stunk

Present Tense (V^1 = plain form)	Past Tense (V^2 = -ed form)	Past Participle (V^3 = -en form)
strew (छितराना)	strewed	strewn
strike (चोट करना)	struck	struck/stricken
string (फीता आदि से बाँधना)	strung	strung
strive (चेष्टा करना)	strove	striven
swear (शपथ लेना)	swore	sworn
sweep (बुहारना)	swept	swept
swell (फुलाना, फूल जाना)	swelled	swelled/swollen
swim (तैरना)	swam	swum
swing (झुलना, झुलाना)	swung	swung
take (लेना)	took	taken
teach (पढ़ाना)	taught	taught
tear (फाड़ना)	tore	torn
tell (कहना)	told	told
think (सोचना)	thought	thought
throw (फेंकना)	threw	thrown
thrust (भोंकना, धक्का देना)	thrust	thrust
tread (कुचलना, पाँव रखना)	trod	trod/trodden
understand (समझना)	understood	understood
wake (जागना, जगाना)	woke/waked	waken/woke
wear (पहनना)	wore	worn
weave (बुनना)	wove	woven
weep (रोना)	wept	wept
win (जीतना)	won	won
wind (ऐंठना)	wound	wound
withdraw (लौटा लेना)	withdrew	withdrawn
withhold (रोकना)	withheld	withheld
work (काम करना)	worked	worked
write (लिखना)	wrote	written

(D) USES OF TENSES

I (a). SIMPLE PRESENT

1. *Look at these sentences :*

The sun *rises* in the east. Oil *floats* on water.

Cows *eat* grass.

(i) इन वाक्यों में आए verbs *rises, floats* तथा *eat* simple present में हैं।

(ii) किसी स्थायी तथ्य या सत्य को व्यक्त करने के लिए simple present का प्रयोग किया जाता है।

2. *Look at these sentences :*

I always *get* up at 5 a.m.
We *cycle* to school everyday.
They *drink* hot coffee every morning.

(i) जो काम हम नित्य या स्वभावतः करते हैं उसे व्यक्त करने के लिए simple present tense का प्रयोग किया जाता है।

(ii) ऐसे वाक्यों में प्रायः *always, never, everyday, every week, every month, often, usually, generally, once, twice, sometimes, several times a week/month* इत्यादि का प्रयोग होता है।

3. *Look at these sentences :*

Tom *leaves* for Bombay tomorrow.
The rocket *lands* on the moon at 10 a.m.
The college *re-opens* in July.

निश्चित प्रोग्राम (planned future action) को सूचित करने के लिए simple present का प्रयोग किया जाता है।

4. *Look at these sentences :*

We shall not go out if it *rains.*
We shall start as soon as we *are* ready.
I will let you know when I *hear* from you.

If, as soon as, when, unless, after, before, till, until, even if, in case, as के बाद subordinate clause में आनेवाला verb अगर हिंदी के वाक्यों में future tense में भी हों तो अँगरेजी में उसे simple present में ही लिखा जाता है। जैसे :

If you *come,* I will help you. = अगर तुम आओगे, मैं तुम्हारी मदद करूँगा।

5. *Look at these sentences :*

Shakespeare *says,* "Frailty, thy name is woman."
Dung Dung *pushes* the ball to Virendra, Virendra *passes* it on to Ashok.
Gandhi and Nehru *are* two great men of India.

(i) किसी लेखक (author) की बातों को हम simple present में लिखते हैं।

(ii) Radio या TV commentary में simple present का प्रयोग होता है।

(iii) History की बातों को simple present में लिखा जा सकता है।

Form of the Verb

(i) *I, we, you, they* तथा अन्य *plural subjects* के साथ V^1 (plain form of verb) का प्रयोग होता है। जैसे :

I/We/You/They/Boys *play* tennis.

(ii) *He, she it* तथा अन्य *singular* subjects के साथ verb+s/es का प्रयोग होता है। जैसे :
He/She/It/Sita *runs* very fast.

Negatives and Questions

6. *Look at these sentences :*

We *play*.	*We do not (don't) play.*
She *writes*.	She *does not (doesn't) write.*
Boys *run*.	Boys *do not (don't) run.*

(i) *I, we, you, they* तथा अन्य *plural* subject के साथ negative में *do not+V^1* का प्रयोग होता है। Do not का short form *don't* होता है।

(ii) *He, she, it* तथा अन्य *singular* subjects के साथ *does not+V^1* का प्रयोग होता है। Does not का short form *doesn't* होता है।

7. *Look at these sentences :*

You *eat*.	*Do* you *eat* ?
They *sing*.	*Do* they *sing* ?
She *dances*.	*Does* she *dance* ? (न कि *dances*)

(i) Plural subject के साथ simple present के question में *Do+I/we/you/they/plural subjects+V^1....?* लगता है।

(ii) Singular subject के साथ *Does+he/she/it/singular subject+V^1....?* लगता है।

I (b). PRESENT CONTINUOUS

1. *Look at these sentences :*

We *are playing* cricket. Rekha *is writing* a letter.
I *am reading* a newspaper now.

(i) इन वाक्यों में आए verbs *are playing, is writing, am reading* present continuous tense में हैं।

(ii) इन वाक्यों से बोध होता है कि कोई कार्य इस क्षण हो रहा है और उसका अंत होगा।

(iii) Present continuous tense में just, at present, at the moment, now, इत्यादि का प्रयोग किया जाता है।

2. *Look at these sentences :*

I *am meeting* Mukul tomorrow.
He *is going* to write a book soon.
We *are leaving* for Delhi next week.

Present continuous के ऐसे वाक्यों से भविष्य में होनेवाले कार्य का बोध होता है।

3. *Look at these sentences :*

He *is always complaining* about the boy.
She *is always demanding* money.
They *are always disturbing* me.

किसी कार्य से झल्लाहट व्यक्त करने के लिए present continuous का प्रयोग always, continually, often इत्यादि के साथ होता है।

4. *Look at these sentences :*

Incorrect	*Correct.*
I *am believing* it.	I *believe* it.
The book *is belonging* to me.	The book *belongs* to me.
I *am forgetting* his name.	I *forget* his name.
John *is having* a car.	John *has* a car.
He *is owning* a jeep.	He *owns* a jeep.
I *am understanding* it.	I *understand* it.
She *is requiring* a book.	She *requires* a book.
We *are hearing* the bell.	We *hear* the bell.
He *is knowing* it.	He *knows* it.

नीचे दिए गए verbs का प्रयोग साधारणतः present continuous में नहीं होता :

(i) Verbs of perception : *see, hear, smell, notice, feel, taste, please, prefer, recall.*

(ii) Verbs used to express feelings or state of mind : *want, desire, wish, refuse, forgive, care, hate, adore, like, dislike, admire, believe, doubt, hope, imagine, love.*

(iii) Verbs involving the process of thinking : *think, feel, know, mean, suppose, remember, realise, recollect, forget, recall, mind, understand.*

(iv) Verbs denoting possession : *own, belong to, possess.*

(v) Verbs such as : *contain, consist, keep, cost, seem, look, resemble, matter, require, suffice.*

Form of the Verb

Present continuous में verb का रूप होता है :

am
is } **+ verb+ing**
are

Negatives and Questions

5. *Look at these sentences :*

Affirmative	*Negative*
I *am playing.*	*I am not* playing.
You *are writing.*	You *are not* writing.
He *is working.*	He *is not* working.

Present continuous के negative sentence में *am/are/is* के बाद *not* लगाया जाता है। Is not तथा are not के short forms क्रमशः *isn't* तथा *aren't* होते हैं।

6. *Look at these sentences :*

Statement	*Question*
I *am running.*	*Am* I running ?
You *are reading.*	*Are* you reading ?
Sita *is cooking.*	*Is* Sita cooking ?

Present continuous के question form में subject के पहले *am/is/are* लगता है।

I(c). PRESENT PERFECT

1. *Look at these sentences :*

I *have lost* my exercise book.
He *has* just *arrived* here.
We *have written* a letter.

(i) इन वाक्यों के verbs *have lost, has arrived* तथा *have written* present perfect tense में है।

(ii) जो काम अभी समाप्त हुआ हो उसे व्यक्त करने के लिए present perfect का प्रयोग किया जाता है।

2. *Look at these sentences :*

I *have met* him before.
The guests *have left.*
She *has passed* the examination.

अगर काम पूरा हो गया हो किंतु काम के आरंभ तथा पूरा होने का समय निश्चित नहीं हो तो उसे व्यक्त करने के लिए present perfect का प्रयोग किया जाता है।

3. *Look at these sentences :*

We *have been* here *since* 10 o'clock.
She *has been* in the office *for* ten years.
They *have lived* here { *since* March. / *for* two months. }

(i) जो कार्य past में शुरू हुआ और अब भी जारी है—उसे व्यक्त करने के लिए *have been/has been+since/for* का प्रयोग किया जाता है।

(ii) Since का प्रयोग definite time, day, month, year या घटना के पहले आता है। जैसे :

since 10 o'clock since Monday
since January since 1980
since my childhood since World War II

(iii) for का प्रयोग period of time के पहले होता है। जैसे :

for two hours for six months
for five weeks for two years

(iv) for/since का प्रयोग present perfect tense में होता है।

4. *Look at these sentences :*

The bus has left *already.* The train has not arrived *yet.*
I have *just* finished the job.

Present perfect में साधारणतः *already, yet, since, just, so far, till now, up to the present* इत्यादि का प्रयोग होता है। कुछ और उदाहरण देखें :

I *haven't seen* him { since Tuesday/last week.
since I met you.
so far/up to now.
lately.

Form of the Verb

Present perfect tense में verb का रूप होता है :

has/have+V^3 (यानी Verb का तीसरा रूप)

(i) I, we, you, they तथा plural subject के साथ have+V^3 लगता है। जैसे :
I/You/We/They/Boys *have done* this work.

(ii) He, she, it तथा अन्य singular subject के साथ has+V^3 लगता है। जैसे :
He/She/It/Moti *has drunk* the milk.

Negatives and Questions

5. *Look at these sentences :*

Affirmative	*Negative*
Reeta *has answered.*	Reeta *has not* (hasn't) *answered.*
They *have heard* it.	They *have not* (haven't) *heard* it.

Negative sentence में has/have के बाद *not* लगता है। Has not तथा have not के short forms क्रमशः *hasn't* तथा *haven't* होते हैं।

6. *Look at these sentences :*

Statement	*Question*
You *have done* it.	*Have* you *done* it ?
She *has made* tea.	*Has* she *made* tea ?
Ruby *has gone.*	*Has* Ruby *gone ?*

Question form में Has/Have को Subject के पहले रखते हैं।

I(d). PRESENT PERFECT CONTINUOUS

1. *Look at these sentences :*

I *have been living* in this house since 1972.
He *has been sitting* here for two hours.
How long *have* you *been waiting* for the bus ?

(i) इन वाक्यों में आए verbs *have been living*, *has been sitting* तथा *have been waiting* present perfect continuous tense में हैं।

(ii) इनसे पता चलता है कि कोई कार्य भूतकाल में शुरू हुआ, अभी चल रहा है तथा भविष्य में भी जारी रहेगा।

(iii) साधारणत: present perfect continuous में *for/since* का प्रयोग किया जाता है।

2. *Look at these sentences :*

I *have been running* too fast.
He *has been working* in the garden.
They *have been drinking* a lot.

इन वाक्यों के present perfect continuous tense से पता चलता है कि कोई कार्य अभी हाल तक चलता रहा है जिसका प्रभाव अभी भी है।

3. *Look at these sentences :*

I have studied here *for five hours.* (Present Perfect)
I have been studying here *for five hours.* (Present Perfect Continuous)

We have lived in this town *since 1978.* (Present Perfect)
We have been living in this town *since 1978.* (Present Perfect Continuous)

(i) Since/for का प्रयोग present perfect tense या present perfect continuous tense में होता है।

(ii) ऊपर के pair of sentences (युगल वाक्यों) के अर्थ में कोई अंतर नहीं है।

Form of the Verb

Present perfect continuous tense में verb का रूप होता है :

has/have+been+V-ing

Negatives and Questions

4. *Look at these sentences :*

I have *not* been working here for five days.
He has *not* been studying here since morning.
Have you *been waiting* here for two hours ?
Has she *been cooking* since 10 o'clock ?

(i) Present perfect continuous tense में have/has के बाद *not* लगाकर negative बनता है।

(ii) इस tense में जब Have/Has को subject के पहले रखते हैं तब यह question बनता है।

II(a). SIMPLE PAST

1. *Look at these sentences :*

He *lost* his book yesterday.
I *saw* a film yesterday evening.
Pandit Nehru *died* in 1964.

(i) इन वाक्यों में आए verbs *lost, saw* तथा *died* simple past tense में हैं।

(ii) भूतकाल में समाप्त हुए किसी कार्य का बोध कराने के लिए simple past tense का प्रयोग किया जाता है।

(iii) Simple past tense में कभी-कभी yesterday, ago, yesterday evening, last week, last month, last year जैसा कोई भूतकालसूचक शब्द रह सकता है। इन शब्दों का प्रयोग present perfect tense में नहीं किया जाता। कुछ और उदाहरण देखें :

I	*saw*	him	yesterday (evening). a week ago. earlier this week. last Monday. the other uay. at four o'clock. in the morning. on Tuesday. last night. in June. in 1986.

2. *Look at these sentences :*

Could you give me your pen, please ?
Would you pass on the salt, please ?
I *wanted* to talk to you for a minute.

Polite request वाले वाक्यों में simple past का प्रयोग किया जाता है यद्यपि ऐसे वाक्य अर्थ के दृष्टिकोण से present tense के होते हैं। जैसे :

I *wanted* a ticket, please.=I *want* a ticket, please.

3. *Look at these sentences :*

Tom said, "He *is* tall."=Tom said that he *was* tall.

Rani said, "She *works* hard."=Rani said that she *worked* hard.

Direct speech से indirect speech में बदलने पर simple present tense की जगह simple past tense का प्रयोग किया जाता है।

4. *Look at these sentences :*

He speaks as if he *were* my boss. (जो वह नहीं है।)

I wish I *were* the Prime Minister. (यह सत्य नहीं है।)

It is (high) time we *started* for the station. (यह हुआ नहीं है।)

(i) शर्त या अनुमानसूचक वाक्यों में if, as if, I wish, it is (high) time इत्यादि के बाद simple past tense आता है।

(ii) किंतु simple past tense के इन वाक्यों से present time या future time का बोध होता है।

5. *Look at these sentences :*

I	*saw* *have seen*	him	today. this month/week/year. for an hour. recently.

जिस वाक्य में today, this month, this week, this year, for an hour, recently लगा रहे उस वाक्य का verb simple past में हो सकता है या present perfect में। दोनों ही correct माना जाता है।

Form of the Verb

Simple past tense में verb का form होता है :

V^2 (past tense form) जिसका प्रयोग किसी भी subject के साथ होता है। जैसे :

I/You/We/They/He/She/Tom *played* cricket yesterday.

Negatives and Questions

5. *Look at these sentences :*

Affirmative

I He They	*played.*

Negative

I He They	*did not*	**play.** (not, **played**).

Simpe past tense के negative sentence में subject के बाद did not+V^1 (verb का असली रूप) लगता है।

6. *Look at these sentences :*

Statement

I We She	*walked.*

Question

Did	I we she	*walk ?* (not, *walked*)

Simple past tense के question में Did+subject+V^1... ? रहता है।

II(b). PAST CONTINUOUS

1. *Look at these sentences :*

It *was raining* all day yesterday.
We *were playing* all this morning.
John *was writing* letters yesterday evening.

(i) इन वाक्यों के verbs *was raining, were playing* तथा *was writing* past continuous tense में हैं।

(ii) Past continuous tense से भूतकाल में शुरू और समाप्त हुए किसी कार्य का बोध होता है।

2. *Look at these sentences :*

I saw him when he *was running.*
As I *was going* to market, it started to rain.
While Ruby *was walking,* the postman came.
While I *was writing,* the phone rang.

(i) Past continuous tense से यह बोध होता है कि जिस समय एक कार्य जारी था कोई दूसरा कार्य जो उससे अधिक महत्त्वपूर्ण था, घटित हुआ।

(ii) ऐसे वाक्यों में जारी कार्य के लिए past continuous तथा प्रधान कार्य जो उस समय हुआ उसके लिए simple past tense का प्रयोग किया जाता है।

3. *Look at these sentences :*

Tom *was reading,* Abdul *was writing.*
While Rekha *was singing,* Radha *was dancing.*
While Mother *was cooking,* Father *was writing* a letter.

अगर भूतकाल में दो कार्य साथ-साथ चल रहे हों तो दोनों के लिए past continuous tense का प्रयोग किया जाता है।

4. *Look at these sentences :*

Direct : He said, "I *am doing* nothing."

Indirect : He said that he *was doing* nothing.
Direct : The teacher said, "The students *are always complaining.*"
Indirect : The teacher said that the students *were always complaining*.

Indirect speech में अगर reporting verb past tense में हो तो present continuous के स्थान पर past continuous हो जाता है।

Form of the Verb

Past continuous में verb का रूप होता है :
was/were+V+ing

Negatives and Questions

5. *Look at these sentences :*

Affirmative	*Negative*
I *was working*	I *was not (wasn't) working.*
He *was running.*	He *was not (wasn't) running.*
Boys *were singing.*	Boys *were not (weren't) singing.*

Past continuous में was/were के बाद *not* लगाकर negative बनाया जाता है। Was not तथा were not के short forms क्रमशः *wasn't* तथा *weren't* होते हैं।

6. *Look at these sentences :*

Statement	*Question*
I *was waiting.*	*Was* I *waiting ?*
You *were teaching.*	*Were* you *teaching ?*
Tom *was reading.*	*Was* Tom *reading ?*

Past continuous के question form में was/were को subject के पहले रखा जाता है।

II(c). PAST PERFECT

1. *Look at these sentences :*

He *had come* to my house before I got up.
The bell *had rung* when we entered the class.
He *had left* {before / when} I arrived.

(i) इन वाक्यों में आए verbs *had come, had rung* तथा *had left* past perfect tense में हैं। The past perfect has the meaning of past-in-the past.

(ii) कभी-कभी complex sentence में दो क्रियाएँ रहती हैं जो भूतकाल में समाप्त हो चुकी रहती हैं। दो क्रियाओं में जो क्रिया पहले समाप्त हुई रहती है उसको

past perfect tense में तथा जो क्रिया बाद में समाप्त हुई रहती है उसको simple past tense में रखा जाता है। कुछ और उदोहरण देखें :

When she *had sung* her song, she sat down.
He *had stayed* in his father's firm till his father died.
When I *had learnt* the work of one department, I left.
I *had seen* him twice before he left for Delhi.
Sita *had* not *finished* cooking when the visitors came.
Amar *had left* before Mohan arrived.
The goalkeeper *had injured* his leg, and couldn't play.
John *had lived* in London for ten years when I met him.

2. *Look at these sentences :*

We *had hoped* that you would come here.
I *had meant* (intended) to see you, but I couldn't do it.
She *had thought* of helping me but the weather did not change.
I *hadn't expected* that.
That was something I *had* not *expected.*
They *had wanted* to help but couldn't get here in time.

Past perfect tense का प्रयोग *hope, expect, think, intend, mean* (= intend), *suppose* तथा *want* verb के साथ भूतकालिक hope, expectation, intention, desire इत्यादि को व्यक्त करने के लिए होता है, जिसकी पूर्ति नहीं हुई हो।

The Past Perfect Tense is used with such verbs as *hope, expect, think, intend, mean* (= intend), *suppose* and *want* to indicate that a past hope, expectation, intention, desire, etc., was not realized.

—A. S. Hornby : A GUIDE TO PATTERNS AND USAGE IN ENGLISH

3. *Look ai tnese sentences :*

I ate my lunch after my wife *came* home from shopping.
I ate my lunch after my wife *had come* home from shopping.

After the teacher *left* the room, the children started talking.
After the teacher *had left* the room, the children started talking.

When the teacher *left* the room, the boys made a noise.
When the teacher *had left* the room, the boys made a noise.

कभी-कभी ऐसे वाक्यों में past perfect की जगह simple past का प्रयोग किया जा सकता है क्योंकि after तथा when से स्पष्ट हो जाता है कि कौन घटना पहले घटी।

When describing one event following another in the past, we can show their relation by using the past perfect for the earlier event, or else we can use the past tense for both, and rely on the conjunction (*e.g., after, when*) to show which event took place earlier. —Geoffrey Leech & Jan Svartvik : A COMMUNICATIVE GRAMMAR OF ENGLISH

4. *Look at these sentences :*

Direct : He said, "I *have sent* the book." (*present perfect*)

Indirect : He said that he *had sent* the book. (*past perfect*)
Direct : Rana said, "I *took* the pen." (*simple past*)
Indirect : Rana said that he *had taken* the pen. (*past perfect*)

Direct से Indirect speech में जो वाक्य present perfect या simple past में रहते हैं, past perfect बन जाते हैं।

5. *Look at these sentences :*

If I *had met,* I would have spoken to him.
If you *had asked* for help, I would have helped you.
I wish I *had passed* in the first division.

शर्त सूचक (conditional) वाक्यों में जिनसे यह झलकता हो कि शर्त या अनुमान पूरा नहीं हुआ past perfect का प्रयोग किया जाता है।

Form of the Verb

Past perfect tense में verb का रूप होता है :

had+V^3 (—en form of the verb)

इस tense का negative तथा question ठीक उसी तरह बनता है जिस तरह present perfect tense का। जैसे :

I had hated him all my life. (*Affirmative*)
I had *not* hated him all my life. (*Negative*)
The plane had left at nine o'clock. (*Statement*)
Had the plane left at nine o'clock ? (*Question*)

II(d). PAST PERFECT CONTINUOUS

1. *Look at these sentences :*

Tom stopped for a rest after he *had been playing* for two hours.
Hari *had been standing* for ten minutes before the door was opened.

(i) इन वाक्यों में आए verbs *had been playing* तथा *had been standing* past perfect continuous tense में हैं।
(ii) इनसे बोध होता है कि कोई कार्य भूतकाल में एक निश्चित समय तक जारी था।

2. *Look at these sentences :*

Direct : He said, "I *have been living* here for six months."
(*present perfect continuous*)
Indirect : He said that he *had been living* here for six months.
(*past perfect continuous*)

Direct speech में जब present perfect tense और reporting verb past tense में रहे तब indirect speech में past perfect continuous का प्रयोग किया जाता है।

Form of the verb

इस tense में verb का रूप होता है :

had+been+V+ing

III(a). SIMPLE FUTURE

1. *Look at these sentences :*

I *shall go* to Delhi on Monday.
They *will do* it next week.
We *shall play* hockey tomorrow.

(i) इन वाक्यों में आए verbs *shall go, will do, shall play* simple future tense में हैं।

(ii) इस tense से बोध होता है कि कोई कार्य भविष्य में होगा।

(iii) I, we के साथ प्रायः shall का, तथा अन्य subjects के साथ will का प्रयोग किया जाता है।

(iv) Shall/will के बाद V^1 (verb का असली रूप) आता है।

2. *Look at these sentences :*

We *are going to* buy a new car.
I *am going to* vote for Madan.
She *is going to* do it now.

(i) इन वाक्यों में *going to* से वक्ता का intention (इरादा) व्यक्त होता है।

(ii) इनसे पता चलता है कि भविष्य में कार्य होनेवाला है।

(iii) ऐसे वाक्यों में *am/is/are+going to+*V^1 का प्रयोग होता है।

3. *Look at these sentences :*

The meeting *starts* at half past four.
The wedding *is* on Monday next.
The Prime Minister *visits* Patna tomorrow.

(i) इन वाक्यों के verbs *starts, is,* तथा *visits* simple present में हैं किंतु इनसे future time का बोध होता है।

(ii) इन वाक्यों के actions पूर्व निर्धारित हैं।

(iii) ऐसे वाक्यों में future meaning के शब्द लगे रहते हैं। जैसे :

soon, shortly, tonight, tomorrow
next week (month, year)
in a few minutes (days, weeks, months)
by next week (tomorrow, two o'clock)

4. *Look at these sentences :*

We *are meeting* the Principal tomorrow.

They *are taking* their examination next month.
They *are playing* the final match on 5th.

(i) इन वाक्यों के verbs present continuous tense में हैं किंतु इनसे future time का बोध होता है।

(ii) ऐसे वाक्यों में next week, tomorrow इत्यादि लगा रहता है।

(iii) परंतु come/go के साथ time expression न भी रह सकता है। जैसे

They are *going* for a walk. Is he *coming* with me ?

5. *Look at these sentences :*

The bus *is about to start.*
The meeting *is about to begin.*
The bell *is about to ring.*

Be *(is/am/are)*+about to+V^1 से कोई शीघ्र होनेवाले कार्य का बोध होता है। ऐसे वाक्यों से future time व्यक्त होता है।

6. *Look at these sentences :*

I *am to finish* this book soon.
He *is to go* there tomorrow.
They *are to come* here next week.

इन वाक्यों में am/is/are+to+V^1 के प्रयोग से भविष्य में किसी निश्चित ढंग से होनेवाले कार्य का बोध होता है।

Negatives and Questions with *'Shall'* and *'Will'*

7. *Look at these sentences :*

Affirmative	*Negative*
I *shall do* it.	I *shall not do* it.
You *will buy* it.	You *will not buy* it.
They *will run* now.	They *will not run* now.

Simple future के negative sentence में *shall/will* के बाद not लगाया जाता है।

8. *Look at these sentences :*

Statement	*Question*
I *will play.*	*Will* I *play ?*
You *will go.*	*Will* you *go ?*
Rani *will sleep.*	*Will* Rani *sleep ?*

(i) Simple future tense के question form में *shall/will* को subject के पहले रखा जाता है।

(ii) Question form में तीनों persons (I, you, he...) के साथ *will* का प्रयोग किया जा सकता है।

III(b). FUTURE CONTINUOUS

1. *Look at these sentences :*

At 10 o'clock I *shall be reading.* It *will be raining* all morning.

They *will be playing* ludo this afternoon.

(i) इन वाक्यों में आए verbs *shall be reading, will be raining* तथा *will be playing* future continuous tense में हैं।

(ii) इस tense से यह भाव व्यक्त होता है कि सामान्य ढंग से भविष्य में कोई कार्य होता रहेगा।

2. *Look at these sentences :*

Mr Sinha *will be staying* with you.

He *will be marrying* Rekha next Sunday.

I *shall be going* to Bombay tomorrow.

Future continuous से व्यक्त होता है कि कोई काम भविष्य में वक्ता के किसी पूर्व निर्धारित योजना के अनुसार होगा।

Form of the Verb

Future continuous में verb का रूप होता है :

shall/will+be+V+ing

Negatives and Questions

3. *Look at these sentences :*

Affirmative	*Negative*
I shall be sleeping.	I shall *not* be sleeping.
He will be talking.	He will *not* be talking.
We shall be walking.	We shall *not* be walking.

Future continuous के negative sentence में *shall/will* के बाद *not* लगता है।

4. *Look at these sentences :*

Statement	*Question*
He will be watching TV.	*Will* he be watching TV ?
You will be finishing the book.	*Will* you be finishing the book ?
I shall be swimming.	*Shall* I be swimming ?

Future continuous tense के question form में subject के पहले *shall/will* लगाया जाता है।

III(c). FUTURE PERFECT

1. *Look at these sentences :*

I *shall have written* all the letters by 5 p.m.

You *will have finished* this work by the end of next month.
They *will have cleaned* all the rooms before John arrives.

(i) इन वाक्यों में आए verbs *shall have written, will have finished* तथा *will have cleaned* future perfect tense में हैं।

(ii) इस tense से यह सूचित होता है कि future में किसी निश्चित समय पर काम समाप्त हो चुका रहेगा। इस प्रयोग में साधारणतः by, before, by the time का प्रयोग किया जाता है।

2. *Look at these sentences :*

You *will have heard* about Bhagat Singh.
You *will have read* about our plans for the building.
They *will have heard* about Mahatma Gandhi.

ऐसे वाक्यों में future perfect tense के प्रयोग से future व्यक्त नहीं होता है, वरन् व्यक्त होता है—the speaker's belief that something has taken place.

Form of the Verb

Future perfect में verb का रूप होता है :

shall/will+have+V^3

III(d). FUTURE PERFECT CONTINUOUS

1. *Look at these sentences :*

By six o'clock I *will have been reading* for six hours.
By 15th April we *will have been working* here for ten years.
By the end of this month I *shall have been teaching* in this school for twenty years.

(i) इन वाक्यों में आए verbs *will have been reading, will have been working* तथा *shall have been teaching* future perfect continuous tense में है।

(ii) इस tense से पता चलता है कि भविष्य में किसी निश्चित समय तक कार्य चलता रहेगा।

Form of the Verb

Future perfect continuous में verb का रूप होता है :
shall/will+have+been+V+ing

PRACTICAL HINTS ON TENSES

1. जब verb present tense, third person तथा singular number में रहे तब उसके अंत में s या es अवश्य लगाया जाता है। जैसे: He runs. She goes.

2. Can, could, may, might, must, shall, should, will तथा would के बाद आनेवाला verb present tense plural number में होता है तथा third person subject के साथ भी verb में s/es नहीं लगता। जैसे :

He *can* go.	They *may* come.
Hari *will* run.	Tom *must* study hard.
He *could* play.	Moti *would* sing.

3. If, when, before, as soon as, until, unless से शुरू होनेवाले subordinate clause से कोई future time या condition का बोध हो तो उसमें *shall/will* नहीं लगता, वरन् verb simple present tense में होता है। जैसे :

If you *come* (अगर तुम आओगे), I shall go.
If he *studies* (अगर वह पढ़ेगा), he will get high marks.
He will do it if you *pay* (अगर तुम पैसे दोगे) him.
I shall let you know as soon as I *hear* (जैसे ही मैं सुनूँगा) from him.
When he *comes* (जब वह आएगा), I will tell him everything.

4. To के बाद आनेवाला verb अपने plain form में रहता है अर्थात उसमें -s/es, ing या d/ed कभी नहीं लगता। जैसे :

He is *to go* (not, *goes*).
She came here *to post* (not, *posting*) a letter.

5. किंतु *by, of, on, in, for, after, before, about* इत्यादि prepositions के बाद आनेवाले verb में -ing लगता है। जैसे :

What is the use *of shouting ?*
Think well *before writing.*

6. किसी उपन्यास, नाटक, फिल्म की कहानी कहने में, ऐतिहासिक घटनाओं के वर्णन में तथा अखबार के headlines में simple present tense का प्रयोग किया जाता है। जैसे :

The story *is* about a man who *jumps* into the river and *dies.*
Ashoka *decides* to conquer Kalinga. He *leads* a large army to attack. His army *suffers* a great loss.
Armed men *loot train, beat up* passengers.

7. Past perfect tense का प्रयोग अकेले में प्रायः नहीं किया जाता, उसकी जगह हम simple past का प्रयोग कर सकते हैं। जैसे :

× I *had gone.*	I *went.*
× She *had slept.*	She *slept.*

8. अपने writing में विभिन्न tenses को mix up नहीं करना चाहिए तथा sequence of tenses का हमेशा ध्यान रखना चाहिए, अर्थात main verb अगर past tense में रहे तो subordinate clause का verb भी past tense में होगा। जैसे :

Wrong	*Right*
He *said* that Reeta *takes* it.	He *said* that Reeta *took* it.
She *asked* what he *wants.*	She *asked* what he *wanted.*

9. *It's time* या *It's high time* के बाद कोई infinitive आ सकता है। जैसे :

It's time to buy a new car. *It's time* for you *to go* to bed.

When we want to say that 'it's time' for somebody else to do something, we very often use the structure. *It's time+subject+past-tense verb*. (The meaning is present or future, not past).

10. *It's time, It's high time, I wish, if-clause* (to talk about 'unreal' or improbable present and future situations) के बाद verb past tense में रहता है, यद्यपि इसका अर्थ present या future time से संबंधित होता है, past से नहीं। जैसे :

It's time we *started.*	(प्रस्थान करते/प्रस्थान करेंगे)
It's time she *washed* that dress.	(धोती/धोएगी)
It's high time we *went* home.	(जाते/जाएँगे)
I wish I *were* the Prime Minister.	(होता)
I wish the situation *were* a little clearer.	(होती)
If I *got rich,* I would travel round the world.	(धनी होता/धनी होऊँगा)
If I *had* a car, things would be fine.	(होती/होगी)
If I *knew* her name, I would tell you.	(जानता/जानूँगा)
If I *were* you, I would start packing now.	(होता/होऊँगा)
If my nose *were* a little shorter, I would *be* quite happy.	(होती)
If I *had* another Rs. 500/-, I could buy a car.	(होता)
If you *asked* me nicely, I might help you.	(कहते)

11. किंतु if I got तथा if I get, या if I had और if I have के अंतर को देखें। इन दोनों structures से present या future का बोध होता है, किंतु जब verb past tense में रहता है तब उससे पता चलता है कि उस परिस्थिति की कम संभावना है या वह असंभव या काल्पनिक परिस्थिति है। जैसे :

If I become president, *I will...*	(said by a candidate in an election)
If I became president, *I would....*	(said by a school boy)
If I win this race....	(said by an athlete)
If I won first prize...	(said by somebody who has bought a lottery ticket)

Both structures can refer to the present or the future : the past verb-form suggests that the situation is less probable, or impossible, or imaginary.

MICHAEL SWAN : PRACTICAL ENGLISH USAGE

Examples Worked Out

Fill in the blanks with the suitable forms of the verbs given in brackets :

1.	The sun (*shine*) by day.	The sun *shines* by day.
2.	Two and two (*make*) four.	Two and two *make/makes* four.
3.	I (*see*) him last Monday.	I *saw* him last Monday.
4.	He will do it if you (*pay*) him.	He will do it if you *pay* him.
5.	She (*be*)[1] born in 1965.	She *was* born in 1965.
6.	I (*live*) here since 1980.	I *have been living* here since 1980.
7.	Tom (*arrive*) last night.	Tom *arrived* last night.
8.	Since when (*you know*) him ?	Since when *have* you *known* him ?
9.	I never (*see*) the Taj.	I *have* never *seen* the Taj.
10.	The earth (*move*) round the sun.	The earth *moves* round the sun.
11.	He (*write*) a letter now.	He *is writing* a letter now.
12.	Did you (*sleep*) well ?	Did you *sleep* well ?
13.	I (*pass*) the exam. in 1980.	I *passed* the exam. in 1980.
14.	Honesty (*be*) the best policy.	Honesty *is* the best policy.
15.	Onions (*smell*).	Onions *smell.*
16.	We (*see*) him the other day.	We *saw* him the other day.
17.	I (*not see*) him so far.	I *haven't seen* him so far.
18.	She (*read*) a book at present.	She *is reading* a book at present.
19.	He (*go*) out an hour ago.	He *went* out an hour ago.
20.	Horses (*be*) animals.	Horses *are* animals.
21.	Moti (*come*) to see me yesterday.	Moti *came* to see me yesterday.
22.	How did you (*come*) here ?	How did you *come* here ?
23.	I (*read*) a book when he came.	I *was reading* a book when he came.
24.	He (*write*) to me last week.	He *wrote* to me last week.
25.	He'll help you if you (*ask*) him nicely.	He'll help you if you *ask* him nicely.
26.	Keep quiet, we (*listen*) to the radio.	Keep quiet, we *are listening* to the radio.
27.	Who (*build*) the Taj Mahal ?	Who *built* the Taj Mahal ?
28.	I (*not see*) him since we left school.	I *have not seen* him since we left school.
29.	We shall not go out if it (*rain*).	We shall not go out if it *rains.*
30.	He (*study*) in this school for five years.	He *has been studying* in this school for five years.
31.	The First World War (*begin*) in 1914.	The First World War *began* in 1914.

1. Verb *to be* के छह forms होते हैं : is, am, are, was, were, be.

32. It (*rain*) when I came.	It *was raining* when I came.
33. I (*not finish*) the work even now.	I *haven't finished* the work even now.
34. We (*study*) English for six years.	We *have been studying* English for six years.
35. I (*see*) that film already.	I *have seen* that film already.
36. We (*hope*) that he would visit us.	We *had hoped* that he would visit us.
37. He (*come*) tomorrow.	He *will come* tomorrow.
38. I (*see*) her yesterday in the college.	I *saw* her yesterday in the college.
39. It is not wise to (*fall*) out with friends.	It is not wise to *fall* out with friends.
40. The picture (*hang*) on the wall.	The picture *was hung* on the wall.
41. Examinations (*hold*) next month.	Examinations *will be held* next month.
42. He (*give up*) after a short struggle.	He *gave up* after a short struggle.
43. I (*receive*) a letter from my brother yesterday.	I *received* a letter from my brother yesterday.
44. It is time he (*go*) there.	It is time he *went* there.
45. It is high time we (*return*) home.	It is high time we *returned* home.
46. I wish I (*be*) a minister.	I wish I *were* a minister.
47. I thanked him for what he (*do*).	I thanked him for what he *had done*.
48. My father (*not come*) home everyday.	My father *does not come* home everyday.
49. He generally (*play*) very well but today he (*play*) very badly.	He generally *plays* very well but today he is *playing* very badly.
50. Water (*change*) into ice when the temperature (*drop*) below 32°F.	Water *changes* into ice when the temperature *drops* below 32°F.
51. It (*not snow*) in summer.	It *does not snow* in summer.
52. Electricity (*light*) our houses and (*drive*) our machinery.	Electricity *lights* our houses and *drives* our machinery.
53. My mother (*read*) a book last night when she (*hear*) a noise in the garden.	My mother *was reading* a book last night when she *heard* a noise in the garden.
54. I (*not see*) you for a long time ? What (*do*) you all these days ?	I *have not seen* you for a long time. What *have* you *been doing* all these days ?
55. We (*see*) with our eyes, (*hear*)	We *see* with our eyes, *hear* with

with our ears and (*smell*) with our nose.	our ears and *smell* with our nose.
56. I (*lose*) my purse near here and (*want*) to find it out before it (*get*) dark. I (*drop*) it when I (*go*) to school this morning.	I *had lost* my purse near here and *wanted* to find out before it *got* dark. I *had dropped* it when I *went* to school this morning.

EXERCISE I

Name the tense of the verb in each of the following sentences given below :

EXAMPLES : (i) Ruby always *works* hard. Simple Present
(ii) I *will buy* a car next year.—Simple Future

1. I *get* up at six o'clock.
2. He *ate* from twelve to one.
3. They *are doing* some work.
4. I *will come* again next Friday.
5. The headmaster *wants* to speak to you.
6. This man *has* already *seen* the Taj.
7. I *know* the man he *is talking* to.
8. They *had lived* in Delhi for five years.
9. We *shall be travelling* at night.
10. I *will meet* my friend at the station.
11. *Were* you at home yesterday ?
12. I *was* just *going* to ask him the time.
13. He *has worked* here since March.
14. They *had known* each other for six years.
15. Tom *will have finished* the work by next week.
16. I *have been learning* English for five years.
17. Last night from 8 to 9 p.m. I *was listening* to the radio.
18. He *had been waiting* for the bus for two hours.
19. Sita *has been living* here since 1975.
20. By this time next year Rajeev *will have taken* his final examination.

EXERCISE 2

Re-write the following sentences as instructed :

EXAMPLE : (i) Birds fly high.
= Birds *do not* fly high. (*negative*)
(ii) He teaches English.
= *Does* he *teach* English ? (*question*)
(iii) He has lost money.
= *Has* he *not lost* money ? (*negative question*)
(*Hasn't* he *lost* money) ?

1. Birds fly high. (*negative*)
2. He teaches English. (*question*)
3. He has lost money. (*negative question*)

4. She goes home for lunch. (*negative*)
5. Many buses arrive late. (*question*)
6. You will find him here now. (*negative*)
7. Reeta takes the kettle. (*negative question*)
8. They will go to the cinema. (*question*)
9. Rana will be happy. (*negative question*)
10. The bus starts at 7 p.m. (*negative*)
11. The train leaves at 6 a.m. (*question*)
12. We are going to Patna soon. (*question*)
13. He has eaten a mango. (*question*)
14. Dogs are barking. (*question*)
15. John is bringing toys. (*negative question*)
16. They have taken my pen. (*negative*)
17. I have been here since morning. (*question*)
18. My friends speak good English. (*negative*)
19. All of us want a lot of money. (*question*)
20. They have been reading for two hours. (*negative*)

EXERCISE 3

Re-write the following sentences as instructed :

EXAMPLES : (i) I forgot his name. (*negative*)
= I *did not forget* his name.
(ii) We invited him to lunch. (*question*)
= *Did* we *invite* him to lunch ?
(iii) Rani *will sing* a song. (*negative question*)
= Will Rani *not sing* a song ?
(*Won't* Rani *sing* a song ?)

1. I forgot his name. (*negative*)
2. We invited him to lunch. (*question*)
3. Rani will sing a song. (*negative question*)
4. They missed the train by five minutes. (*negative*)
5. We studied hard last week. (*neg. question*)
6. Boys did not support him. (*question*)
7. They will like the film very much. (*question*)
8. Suman won the first prize. (*negative*)
9. I was reading a story then. (*question*)
10. She prefers tea to coffee. (*neg. question*)
11. He is putting it on the table. (*question*)
12. They were crying there. (*neg. question*)
13. You helped me then. (*negative*)
14. Mukul will be successful. (*neg. question*)
15. Tom drove the scooter fast. (*question*)
16. The sun rises in the east. (*neg. question*)
17. Why are you playing ? (*negative*)
18. I have been reading since 8 a.m. (*negative*)
19. He is going to have his hair cut. (*neg. question*)
20. We shall drink coffee soon. (*question*)

EXERCISE 4

Re-write the following sentences in the tenses indicated in brackets :

EXAMPLES : (i) He *comes* very early. (*into simple past*)
= He *came* very early.
(ii) You *ride* a bicycle. (*into simple future*)
You *will ride* a bicycle.

1. He comes very early. (*into simple past*)
2. You ride a bicycle. (*into simple future*)
3. He will say 'no'. (*into simple present*)
4. It begins to rain. (*into present perfect*)
5. Soma made tea. (*into future continuous*)
6. We heard his speech. (*into present perfect*)
7. They go to the cinema. (*into present continuous*)
8. Boys play cricket here. (*into present perfect continuous*)
9. She comes here on Sundays. (*into simple future*)
10. I am going to have a bath. (*into past continuous*)
11. Did he like tea ? (*into simple present*)
12. Moti has thrown the ball. (*into past perfect*)
13. He writes a long letter. (*into present continuous*)
14. They drove a car. (*into simple future*)
15. I thank him for his help. (*into future continuous*)
16. We waited here for long. (*into present perfect continuous*)
17. Mr Sinha teaches us Hindi. (*into simple past*)
18. She has a sweet voice. (*into simple future*)
19. He does his work honestly. (*into present perfect*)
20. He gave me red flowers. (*into past continuous*)

EXERCISE 5

Write questions to which the italicized words in the following sentences are answers. Start with the question word given in brackets :

EXAMPLE : He wants *more money. (what)*
= *What does he want ?*

1. He wants *more money.* (*what*)
2. She will come here *at 4 p.m.* (*when*)
3. We go *to school* everyday. (*where*)
4. Tom comes home *by train.* (*how*)
5. Teachers like *good students.* (*whom*)
6. These men live *in Madras.* (*where*)
7. They need *a book* right now. (*what*)
8. I take tea *in the morning.* (*when*)
9. You will help him *by being kind.* (*how*)
10. He is unhappy *because he lost his pen.* (*why*)
11. She buys *a new bag.* (*what*)
12. I shall go to college *in the evening.* (*when*)
13. He came late *because he is ill.* (*why*)
14. Reeta has eaten *a mango.* (*what*)

15. They will go to London *by air*. (*how*)
16. *Mr Prasad* taught us history. (*who*)
17. Reena wakes *at 4 a.m.* (*when*)
18. I am going *to the garden*. (*where*)
19. She has got a prize by *working hard*. (*how*)
20. You want to see *your friends*. (*whom*)

EXERCISE 6

Write questions to which the italicized words in the following sentences are answers. Start with the question word given in brackets :

EXAMPLE : You will help him *because he is your friend*. (*why*)
= Why will you help him ?

1. You will help him *because he is your friend*. (*why*)
2. His father lives *in Calcutta*. (*where*)
3. I always hate *lazy students*. (*whom*)
4. India got independence *in 1947*. (*when*)
5. He met me *at the station*. (*where*)
6. People love him *because he is honest*. (*why*)
7. Mukul can stand first *by working very hard*. (*how*)
8. A man should make a friend *by being a friend*. (*how*)
9. These boys like *good books*. (*which books*)
10. We buy *ten pens*. (*how many*)
11. I want to sell *my old bicycle*. (*which bicycle*)
12. We like *Dinkar's poems* most. (*whose poems*)
13. You eat *two eggs* everyday. (*how many*)
14. She wanted *lots of money*. (*how much*)
15. There are *seven days* in a week. (*how many*)
16. This wall is *ten feet high*. (*how high*)
17. That river is *twenty feet deep* (*how deep*)
18. That room was *twelve feet wide*. (*how wide*)
19. Your brother is *180 centimetres tall*. (*how tall*)
20. Suri has taken *his sister's pen*. (*whose pen*)

EXERCISE 7

Fill in the blanks with suitable forms of the verbs given in brackets :

EXAMPLE : The sun (*rise*) in the east.
= The sun *rises* in the east,

1. The sun (*rise*) in the east.
2. Most buses (*not run*) on time.
3. She (*come*) here yesterday.
4. Tom (*buy*) a new pen next week.
5. The earth (*move*) round the sun.
6. Hard work (*bring*) success.
7. The meeting (*just begin*).
8. Patna (*stand*) on the bank of the Ganga.
9. Most Indians (*not speak*) English.
10. My brother (*be*) ten last Monday.
11. Shakespeare (*live*) from 1564 to 1616.
12. Mukul (*go*) to school last month.
13. I (*read*) a newspaper now.
14. Oil (*float*) on water.
15. Death (*come*) to every man.
16. They (*live*) here since May.

17. We (*have*) a letter last week.
18. They (*not go*) to school tomorrow.
19. When you last (*see*) your brother ?
20. Water (*freeze*) at 0 degree centigrade.

EXERCISE 8

Fill in the blanks with suitable forms of the verbs given in brackets :

EXAMPLE : Keep quiet, we (*listen*) to the radio.
= Keep quiet, we *are listening* to the radio.

1. Keep quiet, we (*listen*) to the radio.
2. I am fond of (*play*) tennis.
3. I have been (*read*) hard.
4. Sita has just (*go*) out.
5. Ram (*go*) to Ranchi yesterday.
6. He (*tear*) the letter a minute ago.
7. I have (*sit*) long here.
8. The man was (*bite*) by a dog.
9. He has (*take*) my pen.
10. He (*hide*) himself in a bush.
11. He (*come*) here last night.
12. Have you (*see*) him ?
13. The dog is (*bark*) at me.
14. I have (*get*) a prize.
15. He (*go*) to Kashmir last year.
16. She habitually (*come*) late.
17. He (*see*) this film yesterday.
18. Peter (*buy*) a car next year.
19. I (*finish*) the work just now.
20. He usually (*write*) in green ink.

EXERCISE 9

Fill in the blanks with suitable forms of the verbs given in brackets :

EXAMPLE : If I were a bird, I (*fly*) to the clouds.
= If I were a bird, I *would fly* to the clouds.

1. I (*go*) to college yesterday.
2. I wish I (*be*) a film actor.
3. He (*sing*) here last month.
4. He (*go*) to Delhi tomorrow.
5. It (*rain*) for three hours.
6. Did you (*see*) that ?
7. I (*meet*) him on Monday last.
8. This boy never (*see*) the sea.
9. He (*go*) to Patna last week.
10. He came oftener than we (*expect*).
11. Mohan (*go*) to school daily.
12. I (*meet*) him yesterday.
13. He talks as if he (*know*) everything.
14. He would succeed if he (*try*)
15. They (*come*) here a month ago.
16. He (*come*) tomorrow.
17. She (*go*) to the cinema everyday.
18. He speaks as one who (*know*).
19. I (*know*) him since 1961.
20. The village girl never (*see*) a train.

EXERCISE 10

Fill in the blanks with suitable forms of the verbs given in brackets :

EXAMPLE : We (*live*) in France when the war began.
= We *were living* in France when the war began.

1. He thought of (*do*) my work.
2. After you (*go*), I went to bed.
3. He (*work*) very hard for the examination.
4. She (*read*) books when I am away.
5. I do not (*like*) loud music.
6. We (*see*) the film yesterday.
7. They (*live*) here since Monday.

8. He (*meet*) me at the station everyday.
9. I (*read*) a book when he came in.
10. When I last (*see*), he was living in London.
11. He was (*dance*) with Mohan.
12. We (*study*) English for six years.
13. The fire (*spread*) to several places.
14. The minister (*deliver*) a long speech.
15. Mr Prasad (*teach*) in a school since 1968.
16. Prof. Sinha (*write*) a book on the novels of Dickens.
17. They (*not find*) him day before yesterday.
18. I (*leave*) the place when he came.
19. I wish he (*was*) the leader of the party.
20. If I were a nightingale, I (*sing*) day and night.

EXERCISE 11

Fill in the blanks with suitable forms of the verbs given in brackets .

EXAMPLE : I (*find*) this ring as I (*dig*) in the garden.
= I *found* this ring as I *was digging* in the garden.

1. Don't worry, I (*lend*) you Rs. 1,500/-.
2. He (*go*) to the cinema every Sunday.
3. She (*miss*) the train an hour ago.
4. He has (*grow*) old in my service.
5. I (*walk*) in the field when the storm broke.
6. I met him when he (*cross*) the street.
7. The teacher will help you if you (*go*) to him.
8. I (*visit*) him at the hospital last week.
9. No, he is not here. He just (*go*) to the office.
10. I saw him when he (*come*) home.
11. He ran away because he (*be*) afraid.
12. Newton (*discover*) the laws of gravitation.
13. When it rained, she (*carry*) an umbrella.
14. He (*not speak*) to me for over five weeks.
15. We (*not see*) the boy since yesterday morning.
16. He felt that he (*cheat*) by a shopkeeper.
17. I (*leave*) this place before he comes.
18. I (*live*) in Bombay for the last ten years.
19. (*Break*) the door if the key is lost.
20. He (*see*) many foreign cities before he returned home.

EXERCISE 12

Fill in the blanks with the suitable forms of the verbs given in brackets :

EXAMPLE : Whenever I (*go*) to see him, he was out.
= Whenever I *went* to see him, he was out.

1. Whenever I (*go*) to see him, he was out.
2. Sita (*comes*) to my house whenever she needs books.
3. It (*stop*) raining after a few hours.
4. These boys (*work*) very hard since December.

5. Sima (*come*) to see me every week last month.
6. She already (*ring*) the bell once.
7. They (*get back*) very late last night.
8. They (*not visit*) us after we had quarrelled.
9. A vegetarian is a person who never (*eat*) meat.
10. My grandmother was sixty years old when she (*die*).
11. We (*see*) that film the other day.
12. No one (*hear*) from him for the past five months.
13. The postman (*not come*) yet ?
14. My sister (*go*) to school for the past two years.
15. You will not succeed unless you (*work*) hard.
16. Think carefully before you (*answer*).
17. When Mukul (*be*) twelve, Rajeev will be fifteen.
18. I (*write*) my composition exercises now.
19. His friend (*not helped*) me.
20. My father (*not permitted*) me to go to the cinema.

EXERCISE 13

Fill in the blanks with the suitable forms of verbs given in brackets :

EXAMPLE : When evening (*come*), it (*get*) dark.
= When evening *comes,* it *gets* dark.

1. When evening (*come*), it (*get*) dark.
2. We (*come*) to this town in 1975 and (*live*) here ever since.
3. When I (*be*) a boy, I (*live*) with my parents.
4. Mr Jha (*go*) out at 8 o'clock and (*not return*) yet.
5. If water (*freeze*), it (*turn*) to ice.
6. She (*not write*) to me since last Holi.
7. Newspapers (*tell*) us about events that (*happen*) in all parts of the world.
8. The use of the present continuous tense (*tell*) us that an action (*be*) incomplete.
9. Electricity (*light*) our house and (*drive*) our machinery.
10. Somebody (*steal*) my purse yesterday. Fortunately, there (*not be*) much money in it.
11. I (*wash*) my hand when the bell (*ring*).
12. Yesterday I (*get*) up at 5 a.m. and (*study*) for five hours.
13. This year Mukul (*start*) to learn Sanskrit. Rajeev (*start*) last year.
14. We (*sit*) at the table yesterday evening when the children (*come*) home.
15. She (*not understand*) what you (*mean*).
16. Reena (*take*) the exam. four times and (*fail*) every time.
17. I just (*hear*) that my mother (*be*) taken ill suddenly.
18. If you (*go*) to the doctor, you must (*pay*).
19. My father sometimes (*go*) to the market but my mother (*not go*).
20. What you (*do*) when the light (*go*) out half an hour ago.

EXERCISE 14

Fill in the blanks with the suitable forms of the verbs given in brackets :

EXAMPLE : Reeta (*go*) to the cinema every Sunday. I (*talk*) to her last night and she (*tell*) me that she (*go*) to the cinema every Sunday for the last two years.

= Reeta *goes* to the cinema every Sunday. I *talked* to her last night and she *told* me that she *had been going* to the cinema every Sunday for the last two years.

1. Reeta (*go*) to the cinema every Sunday. I (*talk*) to her last night and she (*tell*) me that she (*go*) to the cinema every Sunday for the last two years.
2. The sun (*come*) up in the east and (*go*) down in the west. When the sun (*rise*), it is morning. When the sun (*set*), it is evening.
3. Mr Sen always (*talk*) to me in English but when he (*talk*) to his servant he (*use*) Bengali. He (*talk*) to an American now.
4. Yesterday I (*get up*) at six o'clock and (*study*) for two hours. I (*eat*) my breakfast before Mr Sharma (*come*) to see me.
5. While I (*sit*) in my drawing-room yesterday evening, I suddenly (*hear*) a noise. I (*look*) round and (*see*) a rat.
6. Mr Bose (*teach*) in this college since 1942. Before he (*come*) here, he (*live*) in Calcutta. Now he (*live*) in Patna and comes to college everyday.
7. Ramesh (*get*) up at half past five every morning. He (*go*) to the bathroom. He (*wash*) his face and (*clean*) his teeth.
8. The sun (*shine*) by day. It (*not shine*) at night. The moon and the stars (*shine*) at night. They (*not shine*) by day.
9. The moon (*move*) round the earth. The earth (*not move*) round the moon. It (*move*) round the sun. The sun (*not move*) round the earth.
10. Last Sunday I (*want*) to take the baby's photograph but he (*sleep*). When I (*get*) my camera out, his mother (*refuse*) to wake him.
11. I (*sit*) in the garden yesterday when my brother (*come*) and (*tell*) me that a visitor (*wait*) for me at the gate.
12. Yesterday while I (*read*) in the library, Hari (*come*) in and (*ask*) me to give him some money. "I want to take a cup of tea," he (*say*).
13. When you (*arrive*) two hours *ago,* I (*do*) most of my work. I (*write*) several letters and my mother (*make*) a lot of sweets.
14. In 1812, Napoleon (*decide*) to march on Moscow. For many years before that he (*be*) at war with several countries and he (*win*) and (*lose*) many important battles.
15. When I (*get*) to the station, I (*learn*) that the train that I (*expect*) to get (*leave*) five minutes before.
16. Before Columbus (*leave*) Spain, he (*study*) the geography of the world as it (*be*) then known and (*convince*) himself of the existence of land beyond the ocean.
17. In summer the sun (*rise*) at about five o'clock and (*set*) at about half-past six. In winter the sun (*rise*) at about half-past six and (set) at about five o'clock.
18. My brother (*read*) nearly all of Dinkar's poems by now. Last year he (*read*) the essays and this year he (*read*) his other works.
19. When the earth (*come*) between the sun and the moon, its shadow (*fall*) on the moon and there (*be*) an eclipse of the moon. Eclipse of the sun often (*frighten*) birds and animals.
20. Ramesh (*leave*) India in 1975 and (*go*) to England. He (*live*) in England for about six years now and he (*be*) very happy there.

EXERCISE 15

Fill in the blanks with the suitable forms of the verbs given below each sentence :

EXAMPLE : (i) I was born in 1974. I first....to school in 1980.

A. will go C. went
B. have gone D. had gone
= I was born in 1974. I first *went* to school in 1980.

1. I was born in 1974. I first...to school in 1980.
   A. will go C. went
   B. have gone D. had gone
2. He wants to know what you...... last week.
   A. will do C. have been doing
   B. have done D. did
3. Mukul always plays cricket but today he...football.
   A. play C. played
   B. is playing D. was playing
4. I...all day but I haven't finished my task yet.
   A. am working C. was working
   B. will be working D. have been working
5. We don't know how we....without a servant tomorrow.
   A. have managed C. managed
   B. shall manage D. are managing
6. I am sorry you can't see him. He...still.
   A. is sleeping C. has slept
   B. will be sleeping D. was sleeping
7. Mr Gupta....in Bombay for five years. Then he came to Patna.
   A. has lived C. is living
   B. lived D. will live
8. Please give him this report as soon as you...him.
   A. will see C. see
   B. have seen D. saw
9. Since 1975 Jack.....in this office and he is still here now.
   A. works C. has been working
   B. is working D. has worked
10. Amar says he....English lessons everyday.
    A. takes C. has taken
    B. is taking D. has been taking
11. Mohan, who...hard all his life, is now sick.
    A. works C. has worked
    B. is working D. was working
12. Sri Sinha often....to Delhi on business trips.
    A. is going C. goes
    B. has gone D. has been going
13. The sun....in the west everyday.
    A. is setting C. has been setting
    B. sets D. has set

14. Ruby....her English lessons yesterday when her father came in.
A. studied
B. is studying
C. has studied
D. was studying

15. When I....my little brother, I shouted his name with joy.
A. saw
B. was seeing
C. have seen
D. had been seeing

16. I asked my sister if she...the toys.
A. has found
B. found
C. finds
D. is finding

17. Rana....here since Holi. I don't know where he is.
A. is not seen
B. was not seen
C. has not been seen
D. had not been seen

18. I....working as a teacher for two years. Then I became a lecturer.
A. have been
B. am
C. had been
D. was

19. Nobody....to see us since we started living in this house.
A. will come
B. had come
C. has come
D. comes

20. These boys....to each other since they quarrelled.
A. do not speak
B. have not spoken
C. did not speak
D. will not speak

EXERCISE 16 (With Answer)

1. *Write only the correct form of the verbs given in brackets in each of the sentences below. Do not reproduce the sentences*

(a) I (*work*) in this office for the past six years. (b) You should (*complete*) the job by now. (c) If you (*help*) him tomorrow, you (*support*) by his friends in the coming election. (d) If you (*stay*) there for two days more last year, the manager (*impress*) with your patience. (e) Yesterday, when Mohan (*enter*) the room he was surprised to find that the students (*disappear*) already. (f) It (*be*) high time that we (*move*) out of this house. Make haste.

2. *Fill in the blanks in the following sentences with appropriate tense form of the verb given in brackets at the end of each :*

(a) An honest man always...the truth, (*tell*). (b) My mother's health....greatly since she....to live in the village. (*improve, go*). (c) My grandfather was seventy-six years old when he....(*die*). (d) I....that film last week. (*see*). (e) I....so many interruptions this morning that I....scarcely any work. (*have, do*) (f) I....letters since nine o'clock this morning (*write*).

3. *Write only the correct forms of the verbs given in brackets in each of the sentences below. Do not reproduce the sentences :*

(a) Renuka....(*leave*) by the time her friend came home. (b) Science....(*teach*) us many wonderful things. (c) I....(*stay*) here till Sunday as my work...(*be*) not over. (d) For the last two years clothes....(*be*) very expensive and the cost....(*increase*) day by day. (e) It....(*say*) to be bad mannered if one...(*talk*) loudly in public. (f) It....(*rain*) when we....(*go*) out.

4. *Rewrite the following with the verbs in the correct form :*

(a) I (*not see*) you for a long time.(b) I (*ring*) the bell for the last twenty minutes. (c) Old Gupta (*not be*) here for years. (d) He (*go*) abroad last week.

5. *Each of the following sentences has one or two verbs in brackets. Write the correct form of the verbs :*

(a) I will let you (*know*) as soon as I (*have*) any information.
(b) When I (*meet*) her last year, she (*marry*) for three years.
(c) Normally we get a lot of sun as our house (*face*) East, but now that circus tent (*cause*) some obstruction.
(d) You (*realise*) your mistake when you come of age.
(e) When she (*arrive*), I was rather fed up because I (*wait*) since eight o'clock.
(f) I certainly (*help*) him if it had been possible.
(g) He (*eat*) his lunch and (*be*) ready to go out now.

6. *Complete the following sentences with the correct forms of the verbs given within brackets :*

(a) We shall set out as soon as the weather...(*improve*). (b) Sheila could not help....(*tell*) her friend how unhappy she was. (c) If only I....(*know*) earlier, I would have met you at the station. (d) The lights...(*go out*) when the family was having dinner. (e) I....(*know*) him for the last ten years. (f) Were you asleep ? I....(*ring*) the bell for the last twenty minutes.

Ans. 1. (a) have been working. (b) have completed. (c) help, will be supported. (d) had stayed, might/would have been impressed. (e) entered, had disappeared. (f) is, moved.

2. (a) tells; (b) has improved, went; (c) died; (d) saw; (e) had, did; (f) have been writing.

3. (a) had left; (b) teaches; (c) stayed, was; (d) were, increased; (e) is said, talks; (f) was raining, went.

4. (a) have not seen; (b) have been ringing; (c) had not been; (d) went.

5. (a) know, have; (b) met, had been married; (c) faces, has caused (or, is causing); (d) will realise; (e) arrived, had been waiting; (f) would have helped; (g) has eaten, is.

6. (a) improves; (b) tell; (c) had known; (d) went out; (e) have known; (f) have been ringing.

□ □ □

5. AUXILIARY VERBS

(a) Primary (b) Modal (c) Marginal

1. Verb

1. *Look at these sentences:*

A	B
I *go*.	I *went*.
We *help* you.	We *helped* you.
He *writes* it.	He has *written* it.

(i) इन वाक्यों में *go* और *help* Present Tense हैं और इन शब्दों के Past Tense क्रमशः *went* और *helped* है।

(ii) उसी तरह से *writes* Present Tense है उसका Past Participle है *written.* ये सारे शब्द verbs हैं।

जिस शब्द का Past Tense या Past Participle रूप बनता है वह verb होता है।

2. Kinds of Verbs

Verbs के दो भेद होते हैं :

(i) Full verb तथा

(ii) Auxiliary verb

Full verbs को Main verbs या Principal verb कहा जाता है और Auxiliary verbs का अर्थ है Helping या Supporting verbs.

2. *Look at these sentences:*

A	B
He *is* a player.	He *is playing.*
I *am* a man.	I *am coming.*
I *have* a car.	I *have driven* my car.
You *do* it.	You *do not read.*
She *did* it.	*Did* you *know* the answer?

(i) A में प्रयुक्त वाक्यों में *is, am, have, do, did,* Full verbs हैं।

जब वाक्य में एक ही verb हो तब उसे Full Verb या Principal Verb कहा जाता है।

(ii) B में प्रयुक्त verbs—*is, am, have, do, did* Full verbs नहीं हैं। वे Helping verbs हैं। वे Full verbs (*play, come, drive, read, know*) को help करते हैं—(a) tense formation में (*is+playing* = Present Continuous Tense), (b) negative sentence बनाने में (*do+not+read*), (c) question बनाने में (*Did+you+know*...?).

जो verb वाक्य में Full verb से मिलकर Tense, Question, Negative या Passive Voice बनाने में सहायक होता है, उसे Auxiliary या Helping verb कहा जाता है।

3. Kinds of Auxiliary Verbs

Auxiliary verbs के तीन भेद होते हैं :

Anxiliaries

- Primary Auxiliaries
  - Full verbs: verb *to be*, *do*, *have*
  - Helping verbs: *to be* (*am, is, are, was, were*), *do* (*does, did*), *have* (*has, had*)
- Modal Auxiliaries
  - *can, could, may, might, shall, should, will, would, must, ought to*
- Marginal Auxiliaries
  - Full verbs: *need*, *used to*, *dare*
  - Helping verbs: *need*, *used to*, *dare*

1. Primary Auxiliaries: Verb *to be, do, have* को Primary auxiliaries कहते हैं। इनका प्रयोग Full verb और Helping verb दोनों में होता है।

इन्हें Primary auxiliaries इसलिए कहते हैं कि इनसे बहुत-सारे grammatical construction बनाने में सहायता मिलती है। जैसे : (i) question (ii) tense (iii) passive voice और (iv) इनके रूप भी subject के number और person के अनुसार बदलते रहते हैं।

2. Modal Auxiliaries: *can, could, may, might, shall should, will, would, must, ought* को modal auxiliaries कहते हैं।

Modal Auxiliaries की तीन विशिष्टताएँ होती है :

(i) Modal auxiliaries का प्रयोग अकेले में कभी नहीं होता, उनके साथ Principal verb का रहना अत्यंत आवश्यक है। Principal verb या तो स्पष्ट रह सकता है या वह समाविष्ट (implied) रह सकता है। जैसे :

I *can go*.

Will you go? Yes, I *will.*

(ii) Modal auxiliaries का, Present Tense किसी भी Person में, एक-सा ही रूप रहता है। जैसे :

I *may* pass. You *may* pass. He *may* pass.

(iii) Modal auxiliaries में Infinitive या Participle forms नहीं होता। जैसे :

to will; *to* must; may*ing*; shall*ing* इत्यादि हम कभी नहीं कहते हैं।

3. Marginal Modal Auxiliaries: *need, used to, dare* को Marginal modal auxiliaries या Semi-modal auxiliaries कहते हैं। इनका प्रयोग कभी Principal/Full verb की तरह और कभी Modal Auxiliary Verb की तरह होता है।

1. Use of the Primary Auxiliaries: Be, Have, Do

Be

Verb *to be* के मुख्य रूप हैं : *am, is are, was, were, be.*

(i) *Am, is, was* singular रूप हैं और *are, were* plural.

(ii) *Am, is, are, was, were, be* का प्रयोग Principal verb और Auxiliary verb दोनों में होता है।

(A) **Am, is, are, was, were, be, as Principal verb**

Sentence with Primary auxiliary: *am, is, are* etc.	Use
1. What *is* your height? I *am* 1.60 metres. What *is* your weight? I *am* 70 kilos. This city *is* ten miles long?	(i) *Am/is/are/was/were* का प्रयोग height, weight और size व्यक्त करने के लिए होता है।
2. What *is* the date? It *is* August 26. What *is* the time? It *is* 6 o'clock. It *is* hot/cold.	(i) *Am/is/are/was/were* का प्रयोग : तारीख और समय व्यक्त करने के लिए और (ii) मौसम (weather) के विषय में साधारण कथन के लिए होता है।
3. How old *are* you? I am nine/I *am* nine years old. How old *is* this house? It *is* 100 years old.	(i) *Am/is/are/was/were* का प्रयोग उम्र (age) बताने के लिए होता है। (ii) किसी व्यक्ति या वस्तु की उम्र बताने के लिए *year (s) old* कहना आवश्यक है। I am nine years कहना गलत है; इसकी जगह I am nine years old कहना शुद्ध हैं।
4. He *is* happy/angry. She *was* calm/excited.	(i) *Am/is/are/was/were* से विभिन्न शारीरिक या मानसिक अवस्थाएँ व्यक्त होतीं हैं।
5. He *is* a teacher. I *am* a shopkeeper. Gold *is* a metal. Sri Lanka *is* an island.	(i) *Am/is/are/was/were* का प्रयोग साधारणतः existence (अस्तित्व) बताने के लिए या किसी व्यक्ति या वस्तु के विषय में जानकारी देने के लिए होता है।
6. Be quiet. *Be* bold. Be a good boy. *Be* nice to him.	(i) Command या request व्यक्त करने के लिए Verb *to be* का प्रयोग होता है।

(B) **Am, is, are, was, were as Auxiliary verb**

1. She *is making* tea. I *am singing* a song. He *was working* here.	(i) *Am/is/are/was/were*+Present participle के सहारे Present Continuous Tense अथवा Continuous Tense बनाए जाते हैं।

2. He *is known* to me. She *was elected* President. We *were invited* to the party. — (ii) *Am/is/are/was/were* + Past participle के सहारे passive voice बनाया जाता है।

3. He *is to leave* for Delhi tomorrow. They *are to arrive* this morinig? She *is to address* a meeting here. — (i) *Am/is/are/was/were* + infinitive के प्रयोग से किसी योजना (plan) का भाव व्यक्त करते हैं।

4. He *is to write* his name here. You *are to stay* here till I return. You *are to see* (=*must see*) me in the office tomorrow. — *Am/is/are/was/were* + infinitive के द्वारा
   (i) किसी आदेश (order/instruction) का भाव व्यक्त होता है।
   (ii) इसका वही अर्थ होता है जो must या has/have to का अर्थ होता है।

5. He *was to go* to Ranchi today. They *were to arrive* this morning. The minister *was to make* a statement today. — (i) अगर *was/were* के बाद infinitive का प्रयोग हो तो उससे यह भाव निकलता है कि क्रिया का भूतकाल में होना तय हुआ था, लेकिन वह क्रिया या तो हुई या नहीं उसके विषय में वक्ता को कोई निश्चित जानकारी नहीं है।

6. I *am about to go.* They *are about to start.* She *is about to dance.* — (i) Verb *to be* + about + infinitive के प्रयोग से यह बोध होना है कि कोई कार्य निकट भविष्य (immediate future) में होना तय हुआ है।

Have, has, had

Have के रूप हैं : *have, has had, having*

(i) *Have* present tense और plural number है। इसका प्रयोग I, we, you, they आदि के साथ होता है।

(ii) *Has* have का singular form और present tense है। इसका प्रयोग he, she, it आदि के साथ होता है।

(iii) *Had* का प्रयोग past tense तथा सभी persons (I, you, we, he, they आदि) के साथ होता है।

(iv) *Have, has, had* का प्रयोग principal verb और auxiliary verb दोनों में होता है।

(A) **Have, has, had, as Principal verb**

Sentence with primary auxiliary: *have, has, had*	*Use*
1. I *have* a new car. (*possession*) He *has* two sisters. (*relationship*)	(i) *have, has, had* का अर्थ होता है : possess (का स्वामी होना),

She had a bad cold. (*illness*) You *have* a pleasant trip. (*experience*) He *had* a letter from his boss. (*receive*)	relatiohship (रिश्तेदारी), illness (बीमारी) experience (का अनुभव करना), receive (प्राप्त करना)।
2. I *have got* a new car. He *has got* his ticket. She *has got* a big nose. You *have got* a bad cold. *Have* you *got* any brothers or sisters?	(i) बोलचाल की भाषा में खासकर Britain में, *have/has* के साथ *got* का भी प्रयोग किया जाता है। (ii) लेकिन ऐसे वाक्यों में got का अपना कोई स्वतंत्र अर्थ नहीं होता। I *have* a car और *I have got* a car का एक ही अर्थ होता है।
3. We *have* lunch at one. (*eat*) What will you *have*—tea or coffee? (*drink*) I will *have* a bath (*do*) You will *have* a good time (*enjoy*)	(i) यहाँ have का अर्थ होता है : eat, drink, do, enjoy, take, experience. (ii) *have* breakfast/lunch/dinner/a meal/a drink/coffee/tea (iii) *have* a bath/a sleep/a dream (iv) *have* a holiday/ a good time (v) *have* a talk/a quarrel/a fight (vi) *have* a walk
4. He is *having* a bath. We are *having* a holiday. They are *having* a party tomorrow.	(i) *have* का Progressive (=Continuous) Tense मे भी प्रयोग होता है।
5. I *have been* to London. *Have* you ever *been* to see him?	(i) यहाँ *have been* का अर्थ होता है : '*to go*' या '*to visit*'.

(B) Have, has, had as Auxiliary verb

1. I *have eaten.* He *has worked.* *Has* she *gone* out?	(i) *have/has* का प्रयोग कर Principal verb का Present Perfect Tense बनता है।
2. I *had worked.* You *had gone* by that time. I *had eaten* before you came.	(i) had का प्रयोग कर Principal verb का Past Perfect Tense बनता है।
3. I *shall have eaten.* I *will have got married* by the end of June.	(i) have का प्रयोग कर Principal verb का Future Perfect Tense बनता है।

4. I *have had* my tea. (Present Perfect) I *had had* my tea. (Past Perfect) I *shall have had* my tea. (Future Perfect)	(i) *have* auxiliary verb के साथ have, principal verb का भी Perfect Tense बनता है। इस have का अर्थ होता है : drink.
5. I *had my hair cut.* (मैंने बाल कटवाया) I *had him sent to school.* (मैने उसको स्कूल भिजवाया) I *had my car cleaned.* He *had his eyes tested.*	(i) *have*+object+past participle द्वारा हम यह भाव व्यक्त करते हैं कि काम स्वयं नहीं किया बल्कि किसी और से कराया गया। (ii) इन वाक्यों में *had* का जगह *got* का भी प्रयोग हो सकता है (= I *got my hair cut.*)
6. I *have to go* now. You *have to guard* the house. He *has to write* the answer.	(i) *have to* + Infinitive से obligation (बाध्यता) का बोध होता है। (ii) *have to* का वही अर्थ होता है जो *must* का।
7. *Had* I (= *If I had*) known it, I would have informed you.	(i) *had* का *if* के अर्थ में प्रयोग होता है।

Do, does, did

Do के parts हैं : *do, does, did, done, doing*

(i) *Do* present tense और plural number में है। इसका प्रयोग first person (I, we), second person (you) तथा third person, plural number (they etc) में होता है।

(ii) *Do* का singular form *does* होता है। इसका प्रयोग, present tense, third person, singular number (he, Ram, etc) में होता है।

(iii) *Do* का past tense *did* होता है जिसका प्रयोग सभी persons (I, we, you, he, they etc) में होता है।

(iv) *Do, does, did* का प्रयोग Principal verb और Auxiliary verb दोनों में होता है।

एक ही वाक्य में Auxiliary और Prinicipal verb में *do, does, did* का प्रयोग हो सकता है। जैसे :

I *did* not *do* it.

इसमें *did* Auxiliary verb है और *do* Principal verb है।

(A) **Do, does, did as Principal verb**

Sentence with primary auxiliary: *do, does, did*	*Use*
1. I *do* it. He *does* it. We *did* it. Electricity has *done* wonders.	(i) *Do/does/did* का अर्थ होता है : करना (perform), काम करना, आदि।

2. I *do not do* it. He *does not do* it. She *did not do* it.	(i) *do/does/did* का प्रयोग negative वाक्यों में होता है।
3. *Do* you *do* it? *Does* he *do* it? *Did* she *do* it?	(i) *do/does/did* का प्रयोग interrogative वाक्यों में होता है।
4. What are you *doing* now? I am *doing* my homework. What are you *doing* tomorrow?	(i) *do* का प्रयोग continuous forms में भी होता है।

(B) Do does, did, as Auxiliary verb

1. I *like* football. =I *do not like* football. He *sells* newspapers. =He *does not sell* newspaper. We *played* well today. =We *did not play* well today.	(i) *do/does/did* की सहायता से simple Present Tense और Simple Past Tense के verb का negative sentence बनाया जाता है।
2. You *like* football. Do you *like* football? He *sings* beautifully. Does he *sing* beautifully? We *wanted* it. Did we *want* it?	(i) *do/does/did* की सहायता से simple Present Tense और Simple Past Tense के verb का interrogative sentence बनाया जाता है।
3. You *go* there. = You *do go* there. He *plays* well. = He *does play* well. I *saw* him. = I *did see* him.	(i) Affirmative sentence के verb को जोरदार बनाने के लिए (to give emphasis) *do/does/did* का प्रयोग किया जाता है।
4. *Come* with us. = *Do come* with us. *Help* me, please. = *Do help* me, please. *Stop* that noise. = *Do stop* that noise.	(i) do के प्रयोग से request या invitation को ज्यादा स्वीकार करानेवाला (more persuasive) बनाया जाता है।
5. You take tea, *don't* you? She loves him, *doesn't* she? They didn't come, *did* they? He lived here, *didn't* he?	(i) *do/does/did* के प्रयोग से question tags बनाए जाते हैं।

6. Raju likes cricket and *Munu likes cricket*, too. = Raju likes cricket and *Munu does* too/*so does Munu*. Mohan never goes to cinema, *neither does* his brother.	(i) Short answer में main verb की पुनरावृत्ति रोकने लिए *(do/does/did* का प्रयोग होता है। (ii) ऐसे वाक्यों में *so/neither/either/nor* + *do/does/did* + subject का प्रयोग होता है।
7. *Do* you sing?. Yes, I *do* (=*sing*). *Did* you talk to him? Yes, I *did* (=*talked* to him).	(i) Short answer के उत्तर में प्रश्नकर्त्ता से सहमति (agreement) व्यक्त करने के लिए Main verb की जगह *do/does/did* का प्रयोग किया जाता है।
8. *Do* you smoke? No, I *don't* (=don't *smoke*). *Did* he see you? No, he *didn't* (=didn't *see* me).	(i) Short answer के उत्तर में प्रश्नकर्त्ता से असहमति (disagreement) व्यक्त करने के लिए Main verb की जगह *do/does/did* का प्रयोग किया जाता है।

2. Modal Auxiliaries

Can

(i) Form

Modal auxiliary : *Can*	*Use*
1. You *can* go *now.* I *can* see you *tomorrow.* We *can* take a day off whenever we want.	(i) *Can* एक Modal Auxiliary verb है। (ii) *Can* का प्रयोग Present Tense में होता है। कभी-कभी इससे future time का भी बोध होता है।
2. He *can* read English. She *can* swim very well. (NOT: She *cans*.......)	(i) *Can* में Present Tense, Third Person singular में—*s* नहीं लगता।
3. I *can* hear music. We *can* see the moon. (NOT: We can *to see* ....)	(i) *Can* के बाद मूल रूप verb का प्रयोग किया जाता है। (ii) *Can* के बाद Infinitive का चिह्न *to* लुप्त रहता है। (iii) *Can* में—ing form नहीं लगता।
4. Can you run? (NOT: *Do* you *can*......) I *cannot* come. (NOT: I *do not can*........)	(i) Questions तथा Negatives बिना *do* के बनता है। *Cannot* एक शब्द होना है। *Can not* लिखना भयंकर भूल है।

(ii) Use

1.(a) Birds *can* fly. I *can* write French. *Can* you lift this box? She *can* sing and dance.	(i) *Can* से ability, power, capacity (शक्ति, सामर्थ्य, क्षमता) का बोध होता है।
(b) He *cannot* see you now. (= He is very busy now.) The blind *cannot* see. (= That is his permanent dis-ability.)	(i) जब *can* में *not* लग जाता है तब इससे यह बोध होता है कि काम करने की शक्ति और सामर्थ्य का अभाव (absence of power and ability) है।
2.(a) You *can* go home now. He *can* take the car. Can I come in, Sir? Yes, you *can*. *Can* I speak for a minute?	(i) बोलचाल की भाषा में, Permission (अनुमति) माँगनें या देने के लिए, *may* के स्थान पर आजकल *can* का ही प्रयोग होता है। (ii) फिर भी, Permission के लिए may का प्रयोग अधिक सही माना जाता है।
(b) Passengers *cannot* smoke inside the plane. You *cannot* travel first class with a second class ticket.	(i) *Cannot* से Prohibitition (निषेध, मनाही) का बोध होता है।
3. *Can* you pass the salt? *Can* you spare me some time tomorrow? *Can* you put the children to bed?	(i) *Can* से request करने का भाव व्यक्त होता है।
4. *Can* I carry your bags? *Can* I make tea for you?	(i) *Can* से किसी व्यक्ति के लिए कोई कार्य करने के प्रस्ताव (offer) का बोध होता है।
5. When you have finished cooking, you *can* clean the kitchen.	(i) *Can* से order का बोध होता है।
6. Accidents *can* happen to any one. Measles *can* be quite dangerous.	(i) *Can* से possibility (संभावना) का बोध होता है।
7. *Can* this be true? (It *can't* be true.) How *can* you be so unkind? *Can* a leopard change its spots? (It is impossible.)	(i) कुछ (Interrogative sentences) में can का प्रयोग होता है और उसका अर्थ होता है : *cannot (can't)*. (ii) ऐसे *can* वाले वाक्य देखने में affirmative लगते हैं, पर अर्थ होता है negative अर्थात 'यह बात संभव नहीं'।
8. { I *can* speak French. { = I *am able to* speak French.	(i) *Can* के बदले Present Tense में be + able to प्रयोग किया जा सकता है।

Can you type this letter?
= *Are* you *able to* type this letter?

9. He *can have* heard the news. (It is possible but not certain that he heard the news.) She *can have* overheard that conversation. (It is possible but not certain that she overheard that conversation.)	(i) *Can have* + past participle से past tense का बोध होता है। (ii) *Can have* से भूतकाल में किए गए कार्य के संबंध में possibility (संभावना) और uncertainty (अनिश्चितता) का भाव व्यक्त होता है।

Could

(i) Form

Modal auxiliary: *Could*	*Use*
1. He said, "I *can* speak English." He said (that) he *could* speak English. She said to me, "*Can* you do this?" She asked me if I *could* do this.	(i) *Could* एक model auxiliary verb है। (ii) *Can* का simple past tense रूप could होता है। Indirect speech में Past Tense के reporting verb के बाद *can* को *could* में बदलना पड़ता है।
2. *Could* I use your pen? (क्या मैं आपकी कलम का इस्तेमाल कर सकता हूँ?) You *could* be right. *Could* I see you tomorrow morning?	(i) *Could* का सभी जगह Past Tense में प्रयोग नहीं किया जाता। (ii) इन वाक्यों में present या future time बताने के लिए भी *could* का प्रयोग किया गया है।

(ii) Use

1. When he was young, he *could* sing very well. She *could* recite the *Ramayan* when she was five. He *could* read without glasses until six months ago.	(i) *Could* + Infinitive से किसी व्यक्ति में ability, power, capacity (शक्ति, सामर्थ्य, क्षमता) होने का बोध होता है।
2. That *could* be my car. She *could* be in the library.	(i) *Could* से possibility (संभावना) का बोध होता है।

3. *Could* I rest here for an hour?
Could I go home now?
Could I borrow the book for two days?
He asked if he *could* attend the meeting.

(i) *Could* से permission (अनुमति) माँगने का बोध होता है।

4. *Could* you show me the way?
Could you pass the salt?
Could you tell me the time?
Could you put out your cigarette, please?

(i) आजकल बोलचाल की भाषा में *could* का प्रयोग polite request (अत्यंत नम्र निवेदन) के अर्थ में होता है।
(ii) *Can* की अपेक्षा *could* से अधिक नम्रता का भाव व्यक्त होता है।

5.(a) You *could have told* me about it. (But you didn't.)
He *could have bought* it yesterday. (But he didn't.)
We *could have worked* much harder. (But we didn't.)

(b) The car is not in the garage. Mukul *could have taken* it out. (Perhaps Mukul took it out.)

Could have + past participle के दो अर्थ होते हैं :
(i) ऐसे वाक्यों से यह बोध होता है कि काम करने की शक्ति, क्षमता और सामर्थ्य होने पर भी भूतकाल में कोई कार्य पूरा नहीं हो सका।
(ii) ऐसे वाक्यों से यह बोध होता है कि कार्य हुआ या न हुआ इसकी सही जानकारी मुझे नहीं है।

6. She *could* recite the *Ramayana* when she was five.
= She *was able to* recite the *Ramayana* when she was five.
I *could/was able to* see him through the window.
They *were able to* complete the work.

(i) *Could* और *was/were able to* का प्रयोग past tense में ability (शक्ति) का बोध कराने के लिए होता है।

May

(i) Form

Modal auxiliary: *May*

Use

1. I *may* go there *now.*
You *may* play *today.*
He *may* come *tomorrow.*

(i) *May* एक modal auxiliary verb है।
(ii) Present tense और future time में इसका प्रयोग होता है।
(iii) सभी Persons (पुरुष) के साथ may का प्रयोग होता है।

2. He *may* be here soon.
(NOT: He *mays* ....)
She *may* be late for school.

(i) *May* में Third Person, Singular Number में कभी -s नहीं लगता।

3. You *may* be right.
I *may* help you.
(NOT: I *may to* help you)

(i) *May* के बाद Infinitive यानी मूल रूप verb का प्रयोग किया जाता है।
(ii) *May* के बाद Infinitive का चिह्न *to* लुप्त रहता है।

4. *May* I use your bicycle?
(NOT: Do I may.......)
You *may not* go today.

(i) *May* का questions और negatives बिना *do* लगाए बनाया जाता है।

(ii) Use

1.(a) *May* I come in?
May I go home now?
May I use your car?

(i) *May* से permission (अनुमति) माँगने का बोध होता है।

(b)(i) You *may* come in.
You *may* go home now.

(i) *May* से permission देने का भी बोध होता है।

(ii) *Can/May* I come in, Sir?

(ii) Permission माँगने या देने के लिए आजकल *may* की जगह *can* का भी प्रयोग होने लगा है।

2. *May* I play here?
No, you *can't/mustn't*.
May I use your pen?
No, you *can't/mustn't*.

(i) Permission के denial (अस्वीकृति) पर *may not* या *mayn't* का प्रयोग बहुत कम किया जाता है।
(ii) उसकी जगह *cannot* (*can't*) या *must not* (*mustn't*) का अकसर प्रयोग होता है।

3.(a) He *may* buy a scooter.
It *may* rain tonight.
The match *may* be postponed.
She *may* be in the library.

(i) *May* से possibility (संभावना) और uncertainty (अनिश्चितता) व्यक्त की जाती है।

(b) He *may not* succeed.
The report *may not* be true.

(ii) *May not* से यह बोध होता है कि कार्य होने की संभावना बहुत कम unlikely) है।

4. *May* God bless you!
May you live long!
May you have the best of luck!

(i) May से प्रबल इच्छा, आशीर्वाद, मनोकामना इत्यादि का बोध होता है।

5. He *may have gone*.
She *may have told* me about this.
He may *have missed* the train.
(उसकी गाड़ी छूट गई होगी।)

May have + past participle का संबंध Past Tense से होता है।
(i) ऐसे वाक्यों से यह बोध होता है कि भूतकाल में किए गए कार्य के होने की possibility (संभावना) अधिक थी, पर पता नहीं कार्य पूरा हुआ या नहीं।

6. She works hard (so) that she *may* pass the exam.
You should go by car (so) that you *may* not miss the train.
(i) *May* का प्रयोग adverbial clause of purpose में भी होता है और तब इसका अर्थ होता है : 'ताकि'।

Might

(i) Form

Modal auxiliary: *Might*	*Use*
1. He said, "I *may* run." He said that he *might* run. He said he *might* hire a car. (indirect speech)	(i) *Might* एक modal auxiliary verb है। (ii) *May* का Simple Past Tense रूप *Might* होता है। (iii) Indirect speech में Past Tense के reporting verb के बाद *may* को *might* में बदला जाता है।
2. You *might* go home *now.* He *might* come *tomorrow.*	(i) *Might* का प्रयोग सदा Past Tense में नहीं होता। (ii) इसका प्रयोग Present और Future time बताने के लिए भी होता है।
3. I *might* go. You *might* come. She *might* know his address. (NOT: She *mights*)	(i) *Might* का प्रयोग सभी persons के साथ होता है। (ii) Present Tense, Third Person, Singular में कभी -s नहीं लगता।
4. He *might* help me. (NOT: He might *to* help.......)	(i) *Might* के बाद Infinitive यानी मूल रूप verb का प्रयोग किया जाता है। (ii) लेकिन Infinitive का चिह्न *to* हमेशा लुप्त रहता है।
5. *Might* I go home? You *might not* play. *Might* I get a job soon? (NOT: *Do* I *might*.....?)	(i) Qustions में *might* को subject के पहले रख दिया जाता है। (ii) Negatives में *might* के बाद *not* का प्रयोग किया जाता है। (iii) Questions और negatives में *do* का प्रयोग नहीं किया जाता।

(ii) Use

1. *Might* I use your pen? *Might* I see your book? *Might* I say a word?	(i) *Might* से permission (अनुमति) माँगने का बोध होता है। (ii) *May* की जगह *might* के प्रयोग से अधिक नम्रता व्यक्त होती है।

(iii) इन वाक्यों में *might* से present/future time का बोध होता है।

2. The train *might* be late.
She *might* be ill.
He *might* be in the class.

(i) *Might* से possibility (संभावना) का बोध होता है।

3. It *may* rain. (50% chance)
It *might* rain (30% chance)
He *may* come. (50% chance)
He *might* come. (30% chance)

(i) यदि काम होने की possibility (संभावना) की मात्रा कम हो और doubtful possibility (संदेह) या अनिश्चितता की मात्रा बहुत अधिक हो तो *might* का प्रयोग होता है।

4.(a) He *might have missed* the train.
(Perhaps he missed the train.)
He *might have gone* there.
(Perhaps he went/has gone there.)

Might have + past participle से दो अर्थ व्यक्त होता है :

(i) ऐसे वाक्यों से यह बोध होता है कि भूतकाल में कार्य हुआ या न हुआ इसका सही जानकारी नहीं है।

(b) You *might have broken* your legs. (But you didn't.)

(ii) भूतकाल में किए गए कार्य के होने की संभावना अधिक थी, पर कार्य पूरा न हो सका।

5. He died (so) that others *might* live.
She worked hard (so) that she *might* finish the work in time.

(i) *Might* का प्रयोग adverbial clause of purpose में भी होता है।
(ii) तब इसका अर्थ होता है: 'ताकि'।

6. You *might* talk a little less loudly.
You *might* do me a favour tomorrow.

(i) *Might* + *Infinitive* से suggestion (सुझाव) या request का बोध होता है।

Shall

(i) Form

Modal auxiliary: *Shall* — *Use*

1. I *shall* work.
We *shall* go there.

(i) *Shall* एक modal auxiliary verb है। I/We/ + shall के प्रयोग से बोध होता है कि कोई काम आनेवाले समय (future) में होगा।

2. He *shall* pay the fine.
(NOT: He *shalls*...........)

(i) *Shall* के साथ Third Person Singular में कभी -s नहीं लगता।

3. I *shall* write a letter.
(NOT: I shall *to* write.......)

(i) *Shall* के बाद Infinitive यानी मूल रूप verb का प्रयोग किया जाता है।
(ii) लेकिन Infinitive का चिह्न *to* लुप्त रहता है।

4. *Shall I* work? We *shall not* play tomorrow.	(i) Questions में *shall* को subject के पहले रख दिया जाता है। (ii) Negatives में *shall not* का प्रयोग करते हैं। (iii) Questions और negatives में *do* का प्रयोग नहीं किया जाता।
5. *I'll* (= I shall) see you tomorrow. *I shan't* (= shall not) be late.	*Shall* का contracted form इस प्रकार होता है : (i) 'll = shall; will (ii) Shan't = shall not

(ii) Use

1. I *shall* be forty tomorrow. We *shall* arrive tomorrow. I *shall* do it next week.	(i) *I/We + shall* से व्यक्त होता है कि कार्य सामान्य रूप से भविष्यत् काल (future tense) में होगा। ऐसे वाक्यों में वक्ता की इच्छा या प्रवृत्ति का बोध नहीं होता।
2. *We shall* fight and we shall win. *We shall* defend our country whatever cost may be.	(i) *Shall* का प्रयोग first person के साथ determination (संकल्प) व्यक्त करने के लिए भी कभी-कभी होता है।
3. *Shall I* open the door? Shall we take a taxi? Shall I make a cup of tea for you?	(i) Interrogative sentence में *shall I, shall we* के प्रयोग से offer (प्रस्ताव), request या suggestion (सुझाव) का भाव व्यक्त होता है।
4. *You shall* go at once. *He shall* carry out my instructions.	(i) Second Person (*you*) और Third Person (*he, she, it, they* आदि) में *shall* से command (आदेश) का बोध होता है।
5. *You shall* get your salary. He *shall* be given a reward for this act of bravery.	(i) *You/He/She/It/They/Mohan+shall* से promise (प्रतिज्ञा) का भाव व्यक्त होता है।
6. Do it or *you shall* be fined. *He shall* be dismissed for his conduct.	(i) Second Person और Third Person में *shall* के प्रयोग से threat (धमकी) का भाव व्यक्त होता है।

Note: *Look at these sentences:*

I will do it. *He will* go next week.

You will play tomorrow. *Munu will* see you again.

(i) आजकल अमेरिका में सभी persons के साथ *will* का प्रयोग होता है।

(ii) ऐसी प्रवृत्ति अब ब्रिटेन में भी देखने को मिलती है।

(iii) लेकिन first person में formal English (औपचारिक अँग्रेजी) में अभी *shall* का प्रयोग ही accepted है। जैसे : I *shall* be 20 next week.

(iv) बोलचाल में first person में *will* का प्रयोग भी होने लगा है। जैसे : I *will* be 20 next week.

इस संबंध में इन मतों पर विचार करें :

1. "American English uses *will* for all persons. This is also beginning to appear in the English of Great Britain, but for the first person it is not yet accepted."

—F. T. Wood : A REMEDIAL ENGLISH GRAMMAR FOR FOREIGN STUDENTS

2. "**Shall** is still found in formal English, but it is no longer common in conversation."

—A. J. Thomson & A. V. Martinet: A PRACTICAL ENGLISH GRAMMAR

Should

Should *shall* का Past Tense रूप है। इसके अलावा यह एक स्वतंत्र verb भी है और इनके बहुत-से ऐसे प्रयोग हैं जिनका *shall* से कोई संबंध नहीं हैं।

(i) Form

Modal auxiliary: *Should*	*Use*
1. I *should* be perfectly happy. You *should* send the reply tomorrow. They decided that the house *should* be repaired.	(i) Should एक modal auxiliary verb है। (ii) इसका रूप Present, Future तथा Past Tense में एक-सा ही रहता है।
2. I *should* go there soon. He *should* play tennis. (NOT: He *shoulds*............)	(i) *Should* का रूप सभी Persons में एक-सा ही रहता है। (ii) Third Person Singular में *-s* नहीं लगाया जाता।
3. You *should* paint the door. We *should* go. (NOT: We should *to go*.)	(i) *Should* के बाद verb का मूलरूप प्रयोग किया जाता है। *Should* के बाद Infinitive का चिह्न *to* लुप्त रहता है।
4. *Should* we tell him? (NOT: *Do* we should........) You *should not* waste your time.	(i) *Should* से questions और negatives बिना *do* लगाए बनता है।
5. *Direct speech:* I said, "*I shall* read it" *Indirect speech*: I said that *I should* read it.	(i) *Shall* का Past Tense *should* होता है। (ii) First Person में subject रहने पर Indirect speech में *shall* के past form में *should* होता है।
6. *Direct speech*: He said, "*I shall* post the letter."	(i) अगर Indirect speech में subject Second या Third Person में रहे तो

Indirect speech: He said that *he would* post the letter
Direct speech: You said, "*I shall* come."
Indirect speech: You said that *you would* come.

shall को प्रायः *would* में बदल दिया जाता है।
(ii) यहाँ *shall/will* का Past Tense *would* होता है।

(ii) Use

1. You *should* do as he says.
We *should* respect our parents.
People *should* not tell lies.
You *should* keep your promise.

(i) *Should* से duty या moral obligation (नैतिक आभार) का बोध होता है।

2. You *should* take regular exercise.
I suggest that Madan *should* go.
He *should* not jump out of a running train.

(i) *Should* से advice देने का भाव व्यक्त होता है।
(ii) किंतु *should* में must या have की तरह compulsion (मजबूरी) का भाव नहीं रहता।

3. India *should* win the match.
He *should* be here by now—he left home at nine.
This is a costly watch; it *should* give correct time.

(i) *Should* से किसी काम की संभावना (possibility/probability) व्यक्त होती है।

4. If I were you, I *should* accept the post.
I *should* not worry, if I were you.
If I were you, I *should* get that car serviced.

(i) Should से unreal या imaginary conditions का बोध होता है।

5. I *should* give you the money if I had it.
If it *should* rain, we will not play the match.
If you *should* change your mind, please let us know.

(i) *Should* से conditional clauses में possibility (संभावना), supposition (अनुमान) आदि का भाव व्यक्त होता है।

6. I *shall* be happy to meet Mukul.
I *should* be happy to meet Mukul.

(i) *Shall* से किसी बात की अधिक संभावना और *should* से कम संभावना (possibility) का बोध होता है।

7. You *should have gone* by taxi. (But you didn't go by taxi.)

(i) *Should + have + past participle* से बोध होता है कि कोई उचित कार्य

I *should have phoned* mother this morning, but I forgot. If you had asked me for the loan yesterday, I *should have given* it to you. (But you didn't, so I couldn't give it to you.)	भूतकाल में पूरा नहीं हुआ या नहीं हो सका।
8. Work hard, *lest* you *should* fail. I was afraid *lest* she *should* be offended. Work hard, (so) that you may/*should* pass.	(i) *Lest* के बाद सदा और (*so*) *that* के बाद साधारणत: *should* का प्रयोग होता है।

Will

(i) Form

Modal auxiliary: *Will*	*Use*
1. He *will* work. I *will* write tomorrow.	(i) *Will* एक modal auxiliary verb है। *Will* का प्रयोग future tense में होता है।
2. She will help you soon. (NOT: She *wills*.......)	(i) *Will* के साथ Third Person Singular में कभी -s नहीं लगता।
3. He *will* arrive tomorrow. (NOT: He will *to* arrive.........)	(i) *Will* के बाद Infinitive यानी मूल रूप verb का प्रयोग किया जाता है। (ii) लेकिन Infinitive का चिह्न *to* सदा लुप्त रहता है।
4. *Will* the train be on time? I *will not* go tomorrow.	(i) Questions में *will* को subject के पहले रख दिया जाता है। (ii) Negatives में *will not* का प्रयोग करते हैं। (iii) Questions और negatives में *do* का प्रयोग नहीं किया जाता।
5. *He'll* (= *He will*) come back soon. I'll (= *will/shall*) be back in a minute. I *won't* (= *will not*) do that. He *won't* (= *will not*) help me.	*Will* का contracted form (लघुरूप) इस प्रकार होता है। (i) *'ll* = *will;* shall. (ii) *Won't* = will not.

(ii) Use

1. *I will* certainly attend the meeting. *(promise)* From Delhi *we will* go to Kashmir. *(intention)* All right, *I will* come with you. *(willingness)* *We will* teach you a lesson. *(threat)*	(i) *I/We* + *will* से promise (वादा), intention (इरादा), willingness (इच्छा), threat (धमकी) इत्यादि का भाव व्यक्त होता है।
2. *You will* go there tomorrow. *He will* arrive tonight. The *wedding will* take place in July. The *holidays will* begin soon.	(i) Second/Third Person + *will* से यह बोध होता है कि कार्य सामान्य रूप से भविष्यत (Simple futurity) में होगा।
3. *Will you* close the window, please? *Will you* have some more tea? *Will you* type this letter for me?	(i) *Will you*? से polite request (नम्र अनुरोध) या invitation (निमंत्रण) का भाव व्यक्त होता है।
4. *Accidents will* happen. *Boys will* be boys. *Oil will* float on water.	(i) Third Person + *will* से यह बोध होता है कि कोई कार्य स्वाभाविक या अवश्यंभावी है।
5. The silly *dog will* chase all cyclists. (यह उसकी आदत है।) A good *teacher will* never send his students away.	(i) Present habit अर्थात् वर्तमान काल में किसी कार्य के करने की आदत व्यक्त करने के लिए Third Person के साथ *will* का प्रयोग होता है।
6. If you step on a snake, *it will* bite you. The *game will* be finished by tomorrow. *That will* be the postman at the door now.	(i) Probability (संभावना) व्यक्त करने के लिए सभी Persons के subjects के साथ *will* का व्यवहार होता है।
7. He *will have posted* the letter. (Probably he posted the letter.) They *will have done* the work (Probably they did the work.)	(i) *Will have + past participle* से Past Tense (भूतकाल) के कार्य के संबंध में संभावना (likelihood) व्यक्त की जाती है।

Would

Would *will* का Past Tense रूप तो है ही, यह एक स्वतंत्र verb भी है जिसका प्रयोग Present Tense में भी होता है।

(i) Form

Modal auxiliary: *Would*	*Use*
1. I *would* go today. He *would* meet me at 10.30. (NOT: He woulds........)	(i) *Would* एक modal auxiliary verb है। *Would* का रूप सभी persons में एक-सा रहता है। Third Person Singular में -s नहीं लगाया जाता।
2. I *would* work. They *would* sing a song. (NOT: They would *to sing*.....	(i) *Would* के बाद verb का मूल रूप प्रयोग किया जाता है। Would के बाद Infinitive का चिह्न *to* लुप्त रहता है।
3. *Would* you work? (NOT: *Do* you *would* work?) He *would not* do it.	(i) *Would* से question और negatives बिना *do* लगाए बनता है।
4. *Would* you open the door, please? We said we *would* help them. *Would* you come this way?	(i) *Would* का Present Tense तथा Past Tense में एक ही रूप (form) रहता है।
5. *Direct speech*: He said, "I *shall* help him." *Indirect speech*: He said he *would* help him. *Direct speech:* She said, "I *will* be in Bombay on Monday." *Indirect speech*: She said she *would* be in Bombay on Monday.	(i) Second या Third Person में subject रहने पर Indirect speech में *Shall* और *will* के past form में *would* का प्रयोग होता है।

(ii) Use

1. *Would you* please *lend* me your bicycle? *Would you like* a cup of tea? *Would you mind* closing the window? (Please close the window.)	(i) *Would you, would you like, would you mind* का प्रयोग polite request/polite invitation में होता है। इनका अर्थ होता है : "*Please*....."
2. *Will you* come this way? (*firm request*) *Would you* come this way? (*softer request*)	(i) *Will you* से firm request का बोध होता है। (ii) *Would you* से less definite, softer और more polite request का बोध होता है।

Will you open the door, please? (*firm request*) *Would you* open the door, please? (*softer request*)	(iii) *Would you* is more polite than *will you.*
3. What is her age? She *would* be sixteen. That *would* be his mother.	(i) *Would* से अनुमान (guess) या संभावना (probability) का बोध होता है।
4. Every morning he *would* go for a long walk. On many days he *would* come home tired.	(i) *Would* से यह बोध होता है कि कोई कार्य भूतकाल में हमेशा या कभी-कभी (occasionally) होता था।
5. He *would* have her own way. (*determination*) I *would* try my best to help him. (*willingness*)	(i) Determination या willingness का बोध कराने के लिए *would* का प्रयोग होता है।
6. I *would like to* ask you something. He says he *would like to* go with you. I *should like to* know what they are doing.	(i) *Would like to/should like to* से wish (इच्छा) का बोध होता है।
7. He *would rather* start now. I *would rather* read than talk. I *would rather* not say what I think.	(i) *Would rather* से प्राथमिकता (preference) का भाव व्यक्त होता है। (ii) *Would rather* के बाद Infinitive का चिह्न *to* लुप्त रहता है। would rather + Infinitive without *to*
8. I *wish* you *would* write to me more often. I *wish* you *would* leave me alone. I *wish* they *would* settle the issue soon.	(i) *Wish* के बाद *would* का प्रयोग होता है, *will* का नहीं। (ii) इस *would* से strong desire का बोध होता है।
9. If a tiger came into the room, what *would* you do? If I were a king, I *would* make you my queen. I *would* build a hospital if I won a lottery.	(i) Conditional वाक्यों में *would* का प्रयोग साधारणत: main clause में होता है, और subordinate clause में अवास्तविक (unreal/impossible) परिस्थिति (condition) की अभिव्यक्ति होती है।
10. If he had written to me, I *would have helped* him. (But he didn't and so I couldn't help him.)	(i) *Would have + past participle* के प्रयोग से यह बोध होता है कि कार्य भूतकाल में नहीं हुआ, क्योंकि शर्त पूरी नहीं हुई।

If I had gone to Agra, I *would have seen* the Taj Mahal. (But I didn't go, so I couldn't see the Taj Mahal.)

Must

(i) Form

Modal auxiliary: *Must*	*Use*
1. He *must* go home. (NOT: He *musts*........) She *must* leave at once.	(i) *Must* एक modal auxiliary verb है। (ii) Present Tense Third Person Singular में *must* के साथ -s का प्रयोग नहीं होता।
2. *Must* you come? (NOT: *Do* you *must*..........) You *mustn't* worry. (NOT: You *don't must*......)	(i) *Must* का question और negative बिना *do* लगाए बनता है।
3. You *must* play. (NOT: You *must to*........) You *must* read this.	(i) *Must* के बाद Infinitive यानी मूलरूप verb का प्रयोग होता है। (ii) इसके बाद Infinitive का चिह्न *to* लुप्त रहता है। (iii) *Must* में *-ing* form नहीं लगता।
4. I *must* see him *now*. (*Present*) He *must* see him *tomorrow*. (*Future*)	(i) *Must* का प्रयोग Present और Future Tense में होता है। (ii) सभी Persons में *must* का एक-सा रूप रहता है।
5. I *must* do it. I *had to* do it *yesterday*.	(i) *Must* का Past Tense नहीं होता। Past Tense में *must* की जगह *had to* का प्रयोग करते हैं।
6. Yesterday you said he *must/had to* be back by night. He said that the boys *must/had to* go to school. He said he *must* go.	Reported speech में (i) *Must* को *must* ही छोड़ दे सकते हैं, या (ii) *had to* में बदल दे सकते हैं।

(ii) Use

1. I *must* do my duty. You *must* help the needy. You *must* obey your parents.	(i) *Must* से duty/obligation (कर्त्तव्य) का बोध होता है।
2. Candidates *must* answer all the questions.	(i) *Must* से instruction (निर्देश), strong advice या order का बोध होता है।

Staff *must* be at their desk by 9.00.
Passengers *must* use the overbridge.

3. It is raining; so I *must* go in.
The train is due in ten minutes; so I *must* be leaving now.

(i) *Must* से compulsion (बाध्यता) का भाव व्यक्त होता है।

4. I *must* finish the work today.
We *must* do as we are told.

(i) *Must* से necessity (आवश्यकता) का भाव व्यक्त होता है।

5. He *must be* mad to do that.
He *must be* an idiot.
There *must be* fifty people there.

(i) *Must be* से probability or likelihood (संभावना) का भाव व्यक्त होता है।
(ii) Must = जरूर ही; अवश्य ही।

6. You *must not* tell a lie. (निषेधात्मक)
You *must not* drive fast. (निषेधात्मक)
You *must not* miss the film. (जोरदार सलाह)

(i) जब निषेधात्मक भाव (prohibition) या जोरदार सलाह (emphatic advice) व्यक्त करना हो तो must का negative *must not* (*mustn't*) होता है।

7. *Must* I go with you?
Yes, you *must*./No, you *needn't*.
Must I go?
Yes, you *must*./No, you *needn't*.

Must से सवाल पूछा जाए तो उसके उत्तर में—
(i) Affirmative में *must* और
(ii) Negative में *need not* (*needn't*) का प्रयोग होता है, *must not* का नहीं।

8. Rajeev *must have passed*.
He had worked very hard.
I *must have dropped* my pencil somewhere.
I can't find it in my bag.
You *must have* seen him.
(= if you were there.)

(i) *Must* का Past tense *must have* होता है।
(ii) *Must have + past participle* से भूतकाल में किए गए कार्य के संबंध में अनुमान (deduction) का भाव व्यक्त होता है।

9. I *must* buy a dictionary.
= I *have to/have got to* buy a dictionary.
I *must* stop smoking.
= I *will have to* stop smoking.

(i) Present Tense में *must* की जगह obligation (बाध्यता) व्यक्त करने के लिए *has to/have to, has got to/have got to* का प्रयोग कर सकते हैं।
(ii) उसी तरह Future Tense में *must* की जगह obligation व्यक्त करने के लिए *shall/will have to* का प्रयोग कर सकते हैं।

Ought

(i) Form

Modal auxiliary: *Ought*	*Use*
1. I *ought* to write to him *today.* I *ought* to go home *tomorrow.* I *said* he *ought* to come here.	(i) *Ought* एक modal auxiliary verb है। (ii) *Ought* का रूप Present, Future और Past Tense में एक-सा ही रहता है।
2. You *ought to do* it. You *ought to see* a doctor.	(i) *Ought* के बाद Infinitive यानी मूल रूप verb का प्रयोग होता है। (ii) *Ought* के बाद Infinitive का चिह्न *to* का प्रयोग अनिवार्य है।
3. He *ought* to understand. (NOT: He *oughts*.......)	(i) *Ought* के Present Tense Third Person, Singular में -s नहीं लगता।
4. *Ought* we *to* go now? (NOT: *Do* we ought......) It *ought not to* rain today.	(i) *Ought* से questions और negative sentences बिना *do* लगाए बनता है। (ii) *Ought* + *subject* + *to* + *verb* = question sentence. (iii) *Subject* + *ought* + *not* + *to* + *verb...* = negative sentence.

(ii) Use

1. We *ought* to help the poor. You *ought* to respect your teacher.	(i) *Ought* से moral or social obligation (नैतिक या सामाजिक बंधन) या duty का बोध होता है।
2. We *ought* to walk every morning. The medicine *ought* to be taken in time. Coffee *ought* to be drunk while it is hot.	(i) *Ought* से advice (राय) का भाव व्यक्त होता है।
3. Rana *ought* to be here now. He *ought* to return soon—he left home early.	(i) *Ought* से probability (संभावना) या guess (अनुमान) का बोध होता है।
4. I said, "They *ought* to see the Principal." = I said (that) they *ought* to see the Principal.	(i) Indirect speech में Past Tense के verb के बाद ought के रूप में कोई परिवर्त्तन नहीं हाता।
5. He *ought not* to watch TV for so long. You *ought not* to talk to your teacher like that.	(i) कोई चीज सामाजिक् या नैतिक नियम के अनुसार अनुचित हो तो *ought* के negative रूप, *ought not*, का प्रयोग होता है।

6. He *ought to have invited* him.
(But he didn't.)
I *ought to have helped* Rajeev.
(But I didn't.)

(i) *Ought to + have + past participle* से बोध होता है कि कोई उचित कार्य sensible action) भूतकाल में पूरा नहीं हुआ या नहीं हो सका।

7. You *ought not to have* missed this lecture.
(तुम्हारा यह काम मुझे पसंद नहीं आया।)

(i) *Ought not to + have + past participle* द्वारा यह भाव व्यक्त किया जाता है कि भूतकाल में किए गए कार्य को पसंद नहीं किया गया।

8. I *ought* to see him.
I *should* see him.
I *ought to/should* go slowly here.

(i) *Ought* और *should* का अर्थ एक ही है।
(ii) *Ought* की जगह *should* और *should* की जगह *ought* का प्रयोग हो सकता है।
(iii) पर *ought should* से अधिक जोरदार (emphatic) है।

9. You *ought* to do it.
(यह अच्छी बात है।)
You *must* do it.
(यह उसका आदेश है।)

(i) *Ought* और *must* के प्रयोग में अंतर होता है।
(ii) *Must* से order (आदेश) का भाव व्यक्त होता है। *Ought* से मात्र duty/obligation का बोध होता है।

3. Marginal Modal Auxiliary

Need

(i) *Need* का प्रयोग कभी Principal Verb की तरह तो कभी Modal Auxiliary Verb की तरह होता है।

(ii) ऐसे verb को Marginal Modal Auxiliary या Semi-modal Verb कहा जाता है।

(i) Form and Use: As a Principal Verb

Marginal modal auxiliary: *Need*	*Use*
1. I *need* your help. You *need* a bicycle. Children *need* milk. He *needs* some rest.	(i) *Need* एक marginal modal auxiliary verb है। (ii) *Need* का प्रयोग Subject के Number/Person के अनुसार होता है। (iii) Third Person Singular में -s लगाया जाता है। (iv) *Need* का अर्थ होता है require (जरूरत होना)।
2. I *need* the book today. He *needed* some money yesterday. You *need* the bicycle tomorrow.	(i) *Need* को Present, Past और Future Tense में प्रयोग होता है। (ii) इसके सभी साधारण रूप होते हैं : need, needs, needed, needing.
3. I *need to see* him. He *needs to study* hard.	(i) *Need* के बाद Infinitive का चिह्न *to* का प्रयोग किया जाता है।

4. Do you *need* any money? Does he *need* any help? No, he *does not need* any?	(i) Question और negative sentences में *do/does/did* का प्रयोग होता है।

(ii) Form and Use: As a Modal Auxiliary Verb

1. *Need* I see you? I *need not* (*needn't*) wait. We *needn't* do all the exercises.	(i) Marginal modal auxiliary में *need* का रूप *need, need not* या *needn't* होता है। (ii) *Must* की तरह *need* का भी एक रूप होता है : *need.* (iii) इस *need* का अर्थ होता है : *have to.*
2. *Need* we go soon? No, we *need't* *Need* he come again? No, he *needn't.* *Need* she go to hospital today? No, she *needn't.*	(i) *Need, need not* या *needn't* का सभी Persons में एक-सा रूप (form) रहता है। (ii) Third Person Singular में -s का प्रयोग नहीं होता।
3. *Need* he *study* now? *I needn't pay* the fine. He *needn't come* every day.	(i) *Need* जब marginal modal auxiliary होता है तब Infinitive का चिह्न *to* सदा लुप्त रहता है।
4. *Need* I tell him? *Need* you go to school today? He *needn't* wear a coat. You *needn't* send me the cheque.	(i) *Need* जब marginal modal auxiliary होता है तब इसका प्रयोग साधारणतः question और negative sentences में होता है।
5. I *hardly need* say how much grateful I am to you. I *scarcely need* any introduction to him.	(i) Affirmative sentences में भी *need* का प्रयोग हो सकता है, अगर उन वाक्यों में *hardly, scarcely, only* इत्यादि नकारात्मक (negative) शब्दों का प्रयोग हुआ हो।
6. *Need I* go to college today? You *needn't* go there tomorrow. We *need not have* come. *Need* I *have* gone to the meeting?	(i) *Need* का प्रयोग Present और Future Tense में होता है। (ii) *Need* का marginal modal auxiliary verb के रूप में Past Tense में प्रयोग नहीं होता। (iii) *Need* का marginal modal auxiliary में past form में *need have* या *need not have* का प्रयोग किया जाता है।
7. I *must* go there. (*compulsion*) I *must not* go there. (*prohibition*) I *need* not go there. (*no compulsion*)	(i) *Must* से बाध्यता (compulsion) और *must not* से अनौचित्य (prohibition) का बोध होता है। (ii) *Need not* से बाध्यता का अभाव और कभी-कभी कार्य के अनावश्यक (unnecessary) होने का बोध होता है।

You *mustn't* leave his house.
(prohibition)

You *needn't* leave his house.
(no compulsion)

You *mustn't* travel first.
You *needn't* travel first.

8. He *needn't have stood* in a queue. (= But he did it.)
You *needn't have bought* this expensive car. (= But you have bought it.)
You *needn't have given* him my name. (= But you gave it to him.)

(i) *Needn't + have + past participle* से बोध होता है कि भूतकाल में जो कार्य हुआ वह अनावश्यक या अनुचित था, अर्थात् इस कार्य के करने से समय की बरबादी हुई।

सारांश :

Modal Auxiliary Verb	Principal Verb
Positive:	He *needs* to go now.
Negative: He *needn't* go now.	He *doesn't need* to go now.
Interrogative: *Need* he go now?	*Does* he *need* to go now?
Negative interrogative: *Need*n't he go now?	*Doesn't* he *need* to go now?

Modal auxiliaries के रूप में Modern English में *Need* और *Dare* का प्रयोग बहुत कम होता है।

'DARE and NEED as auxiliaries are probably rarer in American English than in British English'

—R. QUIRK, S. GREENBAUM, G. LEECH, J. SVARTVIK: A GRAMMAR OF CONTEMPORARY ENGLISH

Used to

जो verb कभी Principal Verb और कभी Modal Auxiliary की तरह प्रयोग में आए वैसे verb को Marginal Modal या Semi-modal Auxiliary Verb कहा जाता है।

(i) Form

Marginal modal auxiliary: *Used to* — *Use*

1.(a) I *used to* live in this house.
We *used to* play cricket at college.

(i) *Used to* एक marginal modal auxiliary verb है।

(b) You *used* the money to buy a car. I *used* a red pencil.	(ii) *Used* (*to*) का उच्चारण होता है 'यूस्ट'/'ju:st तथा used का उच्चारण होता है : 'यूजड्'/'ju:zd. (iii) *Used to* का use (= प्रयोग, प्रयोग करना), *used to* (=accustomed to, अभ्यस्त) से कोई संबंध नहीं है।
2. I *used to* live here. You *used to* live here. He *used to* live here.	(i) *Used to* का प्रयोग सभी Persons के साथ होता है। (ii) इसका सदा Past Tense में ही प्रयोग होता है। (iii) *Used to* (= accustomed to, अभ्यस्त) का use (= प्रयोग, प्रयोग करना) से कोई संबंध नहीं है।
3. I *used not to* make that mistake. I *did not use to* make that mistake. He *used not to* like films. He *did not use to* like films.	(i) *Used to* का negative form *used not to* होता है। (ii) किंतु आजकल *used to* के negative form में did का प्रयोग अधिक किया जाता है, अर्थात् *Used not to = did not use to*
4. He *used to* play cricket at college. *Used* he *to* play cricket at college?	(i) *Used* के question form में used को subject के पहले रख देते हैं, फिर, (ii) *to + verb* का प्रयोग करते हैं : **Used + subject + to + verb**
5. He *used to* play cricket at college. *Did* he *use to* play cricket at college?	(i) आजकल *used to* के question form में did का भी प्रयोग किया जाता है : **Did + subject + use to + verb**

(ii) Use

1.(a) I *used to* play cricket, now I don't. He *used to* live in Bombay when he was a boy. While at college, I *used to* smoke. (= But I don't smoke now.)	(i) *Used to* + verb से यह बोध होता है कि कोई कार्य भूतकाल में हुआ करता था। (ii) इसका प्रयोग केवल भूतकाल की ऐसी आदत या व्यवहार का बोध कराने के लिए होता है, जो अब नहीं है।[1]

1. "—to contrast past and present, to express something that existed or was done in the past (generally a repeated action), but no longer exists or is done now."

(b) I *play* cricket. He *lives* in Bombay. I *smoke* at college.	(i) अगर कोई कार्य, आदत या व्यवहार वर्त्तमान समय में हो तो उसे व्यक्त करने के लिए Active Voice में केवल Principal verb के Simple Present Tense का प्रयोग करते हैं, इसके पूर्व *use to* नहीं लगाते हैं।
2.(a) I am *used to* the noise. He is *used to* hard life. They are *used to* spicy food.	(i) जब *used to* का अर्थ होता है accustomed to (आदी/अभ्यस्त होना) तब *used to* का दो तरह से प्रयोग होता है। एक pattern है :
(b) I am *used to* working hard. He is *used to* driving in Delhi. You will soon get *used to* living in the village.	(ii) *to be/get/become + used to + noun* दूसरा pattern है : *to be/get/become + used to + ...ing.*

Dare

(i) Dare का प्रयोग कभी Principal verb और कभी Modal Auxiliary verb की तरह होता है।

(ii) ऐसे verb को Marginal Modal Auxiliary या Semi-modal verb कहा जाता है।

(i) Form and Use: As a Principal Verb

Marginal modal auxiliary: *Dare*	*Use*
1. We *dare* to swim across the river. I *dare* to oppose my employee.	(i) *Dare* एक marginal/modal auxiliary verb है। (ii) *Dare* का अर्थ होता है : to challenge (चुनौती देना), to defy या to venture (दुस्साहस करना).
2. I *dare* to call him a liar. I *dared* to challenge him. He *did* not *dare* to visit me.	(i) *Dare* का Principal verb के रूप में Present और Past Tense में प्रयोग होता है।
3. He does not *dare* to face me. He *dares* to slap her. She *dares* to say what she thinks.	(i) Third Person, Singular में -s लगाया जाता है, अर्थात Subject के Number/ Person के अनुसार *dare/dares* का प्रयोग होता है।
4. They *dare to do* it. He *dares to go* there at night.	(i) *Dare* के बाद Infinitive के चिह्न *to* का प्रयोग किया जाता है।
5. *Do* you *dare* to say that? *Does* he *dare* to criticise me. He *does not dare* to face me. She *did not dare* to speak to me.	(i) Question तथा negative sentences में *do/does/did* का प्रयोग होता है।

6. I *dare*say you are right. I *dare*say that is wrong. I *dare*say she will agree to the proposal. I *dare*say it will rain tomorrow.	(i) *Daresay* का प्रयोग केवल I के साथ होता है। (ii) I *daresay* का अर्थ होता है : Perhaps, it is probable, it is likely, I think, I expect. (iii) *Dare* और *say* अलग-अलग भी लिखा जाता है जैसे—I *dare say* she will agree to the proposal.

(ii) Form and Use: As a Modal Auxiliary Verb

1. He *dare not* say so. She *dare not* oppose me. *Dare* they say such things?	(i) *Dare* जब marginal modal auxiliary verb होता है जब इसका प्रयोग negative और question sentences में होता है।
Dare he go and speak to her? *Dare* he disobey his teacher?	(ii) *Dare* जब marginal modal auxilary हो तब Third Person singular में -s नहीं लगाया जाता।
2. *Dare* he *oppose* me? *Dare* she *speak* to the Principal? I *dare not (daren't) move.* We *dare not take* such risks.	(i) *Dare* जब marginal modal auxiliary होता है तब Infinitive का चिह्न *to* सदा लुप्त रहता है।
3. *How dare* he complain? *How dare* you do such things?	(i) How से शुरू होनेवाले questions में *dare* का प्रयोग कर हम अपना सदमा (shock) और क्रोध व्यक्त करते हैं।
4. Nobody *dare* (to) speak.	(i) Nobody, anybody इत्यादि के बाद Infinitive का चिह्न *to* का प्रयोग हो सकता है या छोड़ भी दे सकते हैं।
5. He *dare* not do it again. She *daredn't* leave without permission.	(i) इस *dare* का अर्थ होता है : दुस्साहस करना (to be courageous (rude) enough (to do something unpleasant).

Note: Modern English में *dare* का प्रयोग Principal verb के रूप में अधिक होता है, खासकर negative sentences में, जैसे : He *does not dare to* go out at night.

Examples Worked Out

Fill in the blanks with suitable verbs from brackets:

1. People .... drive carefully. (*may/must*)	People *must* drive carefully.
2. He ....not have done it. (*can/may*)	He *may* not have done it.
3. ....I swim? (*Could/May*)	*May* I swim?

4. You .... do your best? (*should/need*)	You *should* do your best.
5. .... you shut the door? (*Ought/Would*)	*Would* you shut the door?
6. I .... stop drinking. (*must/may*)	I *must* stop drinking.
7. .... God bless her! (*Can/May*)	*May* God bless her!
8. .... I borrow your pen? (*Must/Can*)	*Can* I borrow your pen?
9. He said he .... go. (*need/must*)	He said he *must* go.
10. He eats that he ...... live. (*may/will*)	He eats that he *may* live.
11. You .... do your duty. (*must/can*)	You *must* do your duty.
12. "Give me a lift." "Why ...... I?" (*would/should*)	"Give me a lift." "Why *should* I?"
13. He .... to be here now? (*can/ought*)	He *ought* to be here now.
14. We .... be punctual. (*ought/must*)	We *must* be punctual.
15. You .... be rude to your parents. (*need not/must not*)	You *must not* be rude to your parents.
16. You .... respect your elders. (*ought to/used to*)	You *ought to* respect your elders.
17. An accident .... easily happen. (*should/could*)	An accident *could* easily happen.
18. You .... start at once. (*ought to/used to*)	You *ought to* start at once.
19. You .... to go to him. (*dare/need*)	You *need* to go to him.
20. We .... have arrived. (*needn't/usedn't*)	We *needn't* have arrived.
21. I knew that he .... come. (*would/dared*)	I knew that he *would* come.
22. Anybody .... make mistakes. (*will/can*)	Anybody *can* make mistakes.
23. You .... help your brother. (*should/must*)	You *must* help your brother.
24. .... I use your phone? (*May/Can*)	*May* I use your phone?

25. .... I have a word with you? (*Should/Could*)	*Could* I have a word with you?
26. I .... to know the exact size. (*need/would*)	I *need* to know the exact size.
27. You .... ask a woman her age. (*need not/must not*)	You *must not* ask a woman her age.
28. You .... give up smoking. (*may/must*)	You *must* give up smoking.
29. Work hard lest you .... fail. (*would/should*)	Work hard lest you *should* fail.
30. You .... touch this live wire. (*need not/must not*)	You *must not* touch this live wire.
31. It...... rain tonight. (*must/might*)	It *might* rain tonight.
32. She ...... not do it. (*used/dare*)	She *dare* not do it.
33. We .... keep our promise. (*may/must*)	We *must* keep our promise.
34. I wish you .... get well soon. (*should/would*)	I wish you *would* get well soon.
35. His behaviour .... make us laugh. (*ought/can*)	His behaviour *can* make us laugh.
36. You have walked all the way. You.......be tired. (*should/must*)	You have walked all the way. You *must* be tired.
37. If you do this, you .... be dismissed. (*should/shall*)	If you do this, you *shall* be dismissed.
38. .... I do the work myself? Yes, you may. (*Can/Should*)	*Should* I do the work myself? Yes, you may.
39. Visitors .... tease the animals in this zoo. (*must not/need not*)	Visitors *must not* tease the animals in this zoo.
40. You may like the house but your mother....... (*cannot/may not*)	You may like the house but your mother *may not*.
41. Rakhi .... some problems in this office. (*must have/used to have*)	Rakhi *must have* some problems in this office.
42. Who have done the homework? We all .... (*have/do*)	Who have *done* the homework? We all *have*.
43. If I had worked hard, I .... have passed. (*could/would*)	If I had worked hard, I *would* have passed.
44. Who knows the next lesson? Mukul .... (*has/does*)	Who knows the next lesson? Mukul *does*.
45. He ....to live there when I was a boy. (*dare/used*)	He *used* to live there when I was a boy.
46. Must I leave tomorrow?	Must I leave tomorrow?

Yes, you .... (*must, need*)	Yes, you *must*.
No, you .... (*needn't/mustn't*)	No, you *needn't*.
47. Have you seen Mary?	Have you seen Mary?
No, I .... (*don't/haven't*)	No, I *haven't*.
48. If I were a king, I .... make you my queen. (*should/would*)	If I were a king, I *would* make you my queen.
49. He .... not come before me. (*used/dare*)	He *dare* not come before me.
50. Walk fast lest you .... be late. (*should/would*)	Walk fast lest you *should* be late.
51. He .... to go there regularly. (*dared/used*)	He *used* to go there regularly.

EXERCISE 1

Fill in the blanks with suitable forms of **be** *(am, is, are, was, were):*

EXAMPLE: A dog .... an animal.
= A dog *is* an animai.

1. Ants .... insects.
2. I .... going home now.
3. Bananas .... good to eat.
4. You .... absent yesterday.
5. A potato .... a vegetable.
6. Roses .... beautiful flowers.
7. They .... naughty boys.
8. He .... lucky, isn't he?
9. They .... brilliant, aren't they?
10. They .... little children, then.
11. .... the train likely to be late?
12. When .... you going to arrive?

EXERCISE 2

Fill in the blanks with suitable forms of **have** *(has, had) or* **do** *(does, did):*

EXAMPLES: (i) Mrs Sinha .... no children.
= Mrs Sinha *has* no children.
(ii) What .... he do in the evening?
= What *does* he do in the evening?

1. I .... three sisters. (*have*)
2. .... not come here. (*Do*)
3. ...... you any brothers? (*Have*)
4. She often .... a cold. (*has*)
5. .... you go there? (*Do*)
6. He .... not any sisters. (*have*)
7. I .... taken my pen. (*have*)
8. What .... you do yesterday? (*do*)
9. ..... you ever been there? (*Have*)
10. .... she sing Hindi songs? (*Do*)
11. We .... our lunch an hour ago. (*have*)
12. He ...... not been there before. (*have*)
13. I .... my homework. (*do*)
14. I .... been here all the time. (*have*)
15. I .... not meet him before. (*do*)
16. He ..... a lot of friends now. (*have*)

EXERCISE 3 (with answer)

Fill in the blanks with ***shall*** *or* ***will:***

EXAMPLES: (i) When .... we see you again?
= When *shall* we see you again?
(ii) He .... talk about nothing but films.
= He *will* talk about nothing but films.

1. Tomorrow .... be Sunday.
2. .... you have tea?
3. When .... you be twenty?
4. We .... discuss this later.
5. You .... regret this decision.
6. I .... not be insulted.
7. .... I fetch a doctor?
8. The engine .... not start.
9. .... we dance?
10. .... you keep quiet?
11. .... I close the door?
12. When .... the goods arrive there?
13. Which pen .... I buy?
14. That .... be the postman.
15. .... you lend me your scooter?
16. I .... be sixteen on my next birthday.

EXERCISE 4 (with answer)

Fill in the blanks with ***may, might, can*** *or* ***could.***

EXAMPLES: (i) .... you solve this sum?
= *Can* you solve this sum?
(ii) .... I use your dictionary?
= *May* I use your dictionary?

1. .... I swim?
2. .... you lift this box?
3. I .... be at home.
4. It .... not be true.
5. I .... bowl well.
6. It .... rain tomorrow.
7. .... you wait till tomorrow.
8. He ......, not have done it.
9. I thought he .... be in Patna.
10. .... you help me, please?
11. .... you type the letter?
12. He .... have missed the train.
13. .... I use your phone?
14. .... you be happy!
15. I .... swim across the river.
16. He .... not pay you today.
17. .... I have that book?
18. You .... go home now.
19. We .... go out whenever we wanted.
20. He said he .... hire a car.

EXERCISE 5 (with answer)

Fill in the blanks with ***may, might, can*** *or* ***could.***

EXAMPLE: I ..... swim well when I was young.
= I *could* swim well when I was young.

1. Measles ..... be quite dangerous. *(may, can)*
7. A visit to a museum .... be interesting. *(may, can)*

2. ....you spare a few minutes for me (*Could, Might*)

3. We .... hold another meeting tomorrow. (*may, can*)

4. I didn't know you .... play the piano. (*might, could*)

5. I .... speak French, but I can't write it. (*may, can*)

6. Don't touch a wire, it .... be dangerous. (*might, could*)

8. He wondered whether it...... be true. (*might, could*)

9. I .... not believe your story. (*can, may*)

10. I .... run a long way when I was younger. (*might, could*)

11. She .... recite the Gita when she was six. (*could, might*)

12. He said that she .... have missed the train. (*might, could*)

EXERCISE 6 (with answer)

*Fill in the blanks with **must** or **need:***

EXAMPLE: You ......come immediately.
= You *must* come immediately.

1. All men ....die.
2. You .... not go on a diet.
3. We .... obey the laws.
4. He...... be seventy now.
5. Your hair ...... to be cut.
6. Tom .... be older than Mary.
7. He .... be a very rich man.
8. I .... to know the exact size.
9. If you have told a lie, you .... be punished.
10. What you say .... be true.
11. He .... have lived here.
12. The village .... have water.
13. We .... pay our debts.
14. We....... work or starve.
15. How much money do you ....?
16. Do you .... to go now?
17. He .... have passed years ago.
18. Staff .... be at their table by 10.

EXERCISE 7 (with answer)

*Fill in the blanks with **must not** or **need not:***

EXAMPLE: You ...... hurry, there is plenty of time.
= You *need not* hurry, there is plenty of time.

1. We .... disobey our teachers.
2. Passengers .... walk on the railway lines.
3. You .... smoke in the office.
4. You .... drink this: it is poison.
5. Police notice: Cars....... be parked here.
6. You ....have given him my name.
7. You .... have bought me a present.
8. Candidates .... bring books in the exam. hall.
9. You .... turn on the light; I can see quite well.
10. He .... eat so much; it makes him fat.

EXERCISE 8 (with answer)

*Fill in the blanks with **should** or **would**:*

EXAMPLE: .... you like another cup of tea?

= *Would* you like another cup of tea?

1. I .... do this.
2. We .... obey the laws.
3. You .... keep your promise.
4. .... you mind opening the door?
5. I .... like to leave early.
6. They .... be more careful.
7. He .... know the address.
8. He .... prefer to have coffee.
9. They .... be here by now.
10. He .... have finished it by now.
11. .... you excuse me?
12. If he offered me money I .... refuse.
13. We .... have a party.
14. You .... paint your door.
15. You ..... have told me last week.
16. He worked hard lest he...... fail.
17. She said she......carry my books.
18. ..... you rather have tea or coffee?

EXERCISE 9

*Fill in the blanks with suitable auxiliary verbs (**is, are, has, have, can, will, did, should**):*

EXAMPLE: Everyone ...... looking at him now.

= Everyone *is* looking at him now.

1. Everyone...... looking at him now.
2. I .... lost my pocket knife.
3. He .... leave tomorrow.
4. She .... just asked a question.
5. He ...... not meet us last evening.
6. Children .... obey their parents.
7. We .... to be married next month.
8. He....to be there by five o'clock.
9. I .... swim across the river.
10. She .... see that he is right.

EXERCISE 10 (with answer)

*Fill in the blanks with **dare, ought** or **used to:***

EXAMPLE: I........ live there when I was a boy.

= I *used to* live there when I was a boy.

1. He .... not take such a step.
2. She said she .... to write.
3. How .... you contradict me?
4. You .... to do this.
5. He .... not come before me.
6. We .... to help him.
7. A large house .... stand on this spot.
8. He.....play football in his youth.
9. He .... not do it.
10. You .... to love your parents.
11. We .... to help the poor.
12. There .... be a house there.
13. He .... to have worked hard.
14. He .... not face his accusers.
15. He .... not do it.
16. I knew I ....to write to him.

EXERCISE 11 (with answer)

Fill in the blanks with appropriate words from the list given below each sentence.

EXAMPLE: You .... buy a new pen: this one is broken.

(A) can't (B) ought
(C) should (D) used to

= You should buy a new pen: this one is broken.

1. He......... have stood in a queue.
(A) shall (B) will not
(C) may not (D) shouldn't

2. Priya may be late but I am sure Ruby......... .
(A) would be (B) won't be
(C) is not (D) can't be

3. We .... live in a big house when I was a boy.
(A) could (B) had to
(C) used to (D) would

4. .... I use your pen for a minute, please?
(A) Should (B) Could
(C) Shall (D) Would

5. You .... drive fast; there is speed limit here.
(A) ought not (B) must not
(C) need not (D) used not

6. Make haste, lest you .... miss the train.
(A) might (B) shall
(C) should (D) would

7. If you invite me, I ...... certainly come.
(A) could (B) might
(C) would (D) would have

8. .... you stand on your head?
(A) Need (B) Shall
(C) May (D) Can

9. How many lessons ...... a month?
(A) do he have (B) do he has
(C) will he has (D) does he have

10. If he knew our address he .... see us.
(A) may (B) can
(C) might (D) will

11. The buses were all full; I .... get a taxi.

(A) may not (B) will not

(C) cannot (D) had to

12. If I bought a lottery ticket, I ...... win Rs 1,00000.

(A) might (B) can

(C) may (D) could

13. You ...... write to him for he will be coming here tomorrow.

(A) will not (B) may not

(C) shall not (D) need not

14. We ...... to buy some furniture.

(A) must (B) ought

(C) used (D) should

15. He ....be elected President of the club.

(A) may (B) can

(C) might (D) will

EXERCISE 12 (with answer)

Fill in the blanks with appropriate words from the list given below each sentence.

EXAMPLE: I don't have a piece of chalk, so I......... write on the blackboard.

(A) don't (B) won't

(C) can't (D) may not

= I don't have a piece of chalk, so I *can't* write on the blackboard.

1. He ...... to play cricket before his marriage.

(A) is used (B) was used

(C) used (D) should

2. They .... have received our letter by now.

(A) did (B) should

(C) shall (D) will

3. Birds can fly but dogs ..... .

(A) will not (B) shouldn't

(C) may not (D) can't

4. You .... take anything out of a shop without paying for it.

(A) need not (B) should not

(C) must not (D) would not

5. If I could fly like a bird, I...... be with you now.

(A) should (B) could

(C) must (D) would

6. You ought to buy now; prices ..... go up.

(A) can (B) shall
(C) may (D) will

7. I had no key so I ....lock the door.

(A) shouldn't (B) didn't
(C) wouldn't (D) couldn't

8. When I was young I ...... read without glasses.

(A) should (B) might
(C) would (D) could

9. If you .... change your mind, please let us know.

(A) shall (B) will
(C) should (D) can

10. I wish you ......not ask so many questions.

(A) should (B) would
(C) could (D) dared

EXERCISE 13: Final Test

Fill in the blanks with suitable verbs from brackets:

1. You .... learn to remain calm. *(ought, need, can)*
2. We .... never know the truth. *(can, may, must)*
3. You really .... be scared. *(daren't, needn't)*
4. She .... understand their feelings. *(can, used to)*
5. These birds .... be in a cage. *(shouldn't, couldn't)*
6. A picnic .... be any fun without you. *(must, will, wouldn't)*
7. Someone .... to turn that tap off. *(ought, used, may)*
8. I .... get angry in a moment. *(would, have to, shall)*
9. Perhaps this time it .... rain. *(won't, must, ought)*
10. Any bank .... do it for you. *(dare, need, will)*
11. Anybody .... become a qualified teacher. *(will, can, shall)*
12. These tablets .... cause sleepiness. *(may, used to, need)*
13. As a matter of fact it .... arrive tomorrow. *(dare, could, shall)*
14. Your family and children .... always come first. *(must, may, need)*
15. You .... a minimum deposit of Rs 1000/. *(ought, need, must)*
16. Somebody .... to do something about it. *(should, ought, used)*
17. I .... to live in this street. *(dared, used, needed)*
18. Shall I speak to Mr Pathak or .... you? *(shall, will, should)*
19. We .... plant a few trees in this garden. *(need, can, used to)*
20. There is no doubt that you .... glasses. *(must, need, may)*
21. Inflation is rising and .... continue to rise. *(used to, shall, will)*
22. I felt confident that everything .... be all right. *(would, ought, shall)*
23. That's the kind of job I .... be doing. *(can't, dare, should)*

24. If you do that I .... be very pleased. (*may, can, shall*)
25. It was difficult to find a house that we .... afford. (*shouldn't, ought to, could*)
26. It .... not be forgotten that we do all make mistakes. (*dare, need, must*)
27. .... a doctor tell a patient he is going to die? (*Need, May, Should*)
28. Some men would do more for a dog than they .... for a wife. (*would, can, should*)

ANSWERS

3. 1. will 2. will 3. will 4. shall 5. will 6. shall 7. shall 8. will 9. shall 10. will 11. shall 12. will 13. shall 14. will 15. will 16. shall

4. 1. may 2. can 3. may 4. can 5. can 6. might 7. can 8. may/might 9. might 10. may 11. can 12. may 13. may 14. may 15. can 16. can 17 may 18. can 19. could 20. might

5. 1. can 2. could 3. may 4. could 5. can 6. could 7. can 8. might 9. may 10. could 11. could 12. might

6. 1. must 2. need 3. must 4. must 5. needs 6. must 7. must 8. need 9. must 10. must 11. must 12. must 13. must 14. must 15. need 16. need 17. must 18. must

7. 1. must not 2. must not 3. must not 4. must not 5. must not 6. need not 7. need not 8. must not 9. need not 10. must not

8. 1. should 2. should 3. should 4. would 5. should 6. should 7. should 8.would 9. should 10. should 11. would 12. should 13. should 14. should 15. should 16. should 17. would 18. would.

10. 1. dare 2. ought 3. dare 4. ought 5. dare 6. ought 7. used to 8. used to 9. dare 10. ought 11. ought 12. used to 13. ought 14. dare 15. dare 16. ought.

11. 1. shouldn't 2. won't be 3. used to 4. could 5. must not 6. should 7. would 8. can 9. does he have 10. might 11. had to 12. might 13. need not 14. ought 15. may

12. 1. used 2. should 3. can't 4. must not 5. would 6. may 7. couldn't 8. could 9. should 10. would.

□□□

6. NON-FINITE VERBS

(a) Infinitives (b) Gerunds (c) Participles

सभी Verbs को हम दो श्रेणियों में बाँट सकते हैं :

(i) Finite (ii) Non-Finite

FINITE AND NON-FINITIVE

1. *Look at these sentences:*

A boy *plays* cricket. (*singular subject + singular verb*)

Boys *play* cricket. (*plural subject + plural verb*)

(i) पहले वाक्य में *A boy* वाक्य का subject (कर्त्ता) है, वह third person, singular number में है। उसके साथ प्रयुक्त verb *plays* भी third person singular number में है। यह verb अपने subject द्वारा अनुशासित होता है।

(ii) दूसरे वाक्य में *Boys* वाक्य का subject है। यह third person, plural number में है। उसके साथ प्रयुक्त verb *play* भी third person, plural number में है। यह verb अपने subject द्वारा अनुशासित होता है।

(iii) इन वाक्यों में finite verbs है : plays और play.

जो verb अपने subject के number और person द्वारा अनुशासित होता है, उसे finite verb कहते हैं।

2. *Look at these sentences:*

A boy likes *to play* cricket. Boys like *to play* cricket.

(i) इन वाक्यों में *to play* verb है, लेकिन इसका रूप अविकल (unchanged) है। पहले वाक्य में subject *A boy* है जो singular number में है और दूसरे वाक्य में subject *Boys* plural number में है।

(ii) फिर भी दोनों वाक्यों में *to play* का एक ही रूप है।

(iii) अत: *to play* non-finite verb है।

जो verb अपने subject के number और person से अनुशासित या नियंत्रित नहीं होता है, उसे non-finite verb कहते हैं,

Kinds of Non-Finites

Non-finites के तीन भेद होते हैं :

(i) Infinitive

(ii) Gerund

(iii) Participle

Infinitive
(Form and Use)

(A) Form

Verb के base form (मूलरूप) को infinitive कहते हैं। इसमें verb के पहले कभी *to* लगा रहता है और कभी नहीं भी। जैसे :

I want *to go*. Let him *go*.

(B) Infinitive के भेद :

1. (i) Present infinitive: (to + infinitive) to go, to do

   (ii) Negative infinitive: (not + infinitive) not to go, not to do
2. Present Continuous infinitive: (to be + ...ing) to be going, to be doing
3. Perfect infinitive: (to have + past participle) to have gone, to have done
4. Perfect Continuous infinitive: (to have been + ...ing) to have been going, to have been doing
5. Present infinitive passive: (to be + past participle) to be gone, to be done

(C) Full infinitive and bare infinitive

1. *Look at these sentences:*

It is easy *to sing*. (to + verb)

They want *to go* home. (to + verb)

Full infinitive में दो शब्द होते हैं : **to** + verb अर्थात *to* sing, *to* go आदि full infinitive के उदाहरण हैं।

2. *Look at these sentences:*

Let me *tell* you a story. We saw him *break* the lock.

(i) Tell या break भी infinitive हैं। इनके पहले *to* नहीं लगा हुआ है।

(ii) कभी-कभी *to* का लोप हो जाता है और तब *to* विहीन infinitive को bare या plain infinitive कहते हैं।

(iii) Bare infinitive में केवल verb रह जाता है। जैसे : come, go, do इत्यादि।

(D) Uses of the infinitive

(i) Infinitive with to

Infinitive with **to** का प्रयोग इन परिस्थितियों में होता है :

(a) Infinitive as subject to the verb

1. *Look at these sentences:*

To advise is easy. *To steal* is wrong.

To err is human. *To act* like that is childish.

यहाँ infinitive (*to advise, to err, to steal, to act*) का प्रयोग वाक्य के subject के रूप में हुआ है।

Note: (i) ऐसे वाक्यों को हम Introductory *It* से शुरू कर वाक्य के अंत में infinitive का प्रयोग कर सकते हैं। जैसे :

To advise is easy. = *It* is easy *to advise.*
To steal is wrong. = *It* is wrong *to steal.*

(ii) Infinitive तथा *-ing* form verbs को subjects के रूप में प्रयोग किए जा सकते हैं। जैसे :

To advise is easy. = *Advising* is easy.
To steal is wrong. = *Stealing* is wrong.
To learn Chinese is not easy. = *Learning* Chinese is not easy.

(b) Infinitive as object to the verb

2. *Look at these sentences:*

We *hope to start* tomorrow. She *forgot to write* to Ravi.
He *promised to marry* her. They *decided to see* the Prinicipal.

(i) ऊपर के वाक्यो में verb—*hope, promised, forgot, decided* के बाद infinitive with *to* यानी *to start, to marry, to write, to see* का प्रयोग हुआ है।

(ii) कुछ महत्त्वपूर्ण verbs जिनके बाद infinitive with *to* का प्रयोग किया जाता है :

agree	*attempt*	*care*	*fail*	*hope*	*like*	*plan*	*remember*
afford	*arrange*	*decide*	*forget*	*learn*	*manage*	*prepare*	*seem*
aim	*choose*	*demand*	*happen*	*long*	*neglect*	*promise*	*try*
appear	*claim*	*determine*	*hesitate*	*love*	*offer*	*refuse*	*want*

(c) Verb + how/what/when/where/which/why + infinitive

3. *Look at these sentences:*

I wonder *who to invite*. Tell me *when to pay.*
Show me *what to do.* We don't know *where to stay.*
I know *how to swim.* Do you know *how to do it?*

(i) कुछ verbs के बाद question-word *how/when* आदि + *to* infinitive का प्रयोग किया जाता है।

(ii) इस श्रेणी में कुछ अन्य महत्त्वपूर्ण verbs हैं :

discover *decide* *find* *learn* *know* *remember* *show* *think*

(d) Verb + object + infinitive

4. *Look at these sentences:*

I *told him to wait.* She *allowed him to go.*
He *requested her to sing.* He *advised her to work* hard.

(i) ऊपर दिए गंए वाक्यों में verbs—*told, requested, allowed, advised* के बाद object + infinitive with *to* का प्रयोग किया गया है।

(ii) कुछ अन्य महत्त्वपूर्ण verbs जिनमें object + *to* infinitive का प्रयोग किया जाता है :

advise	*encourage*	*instruct*	*order*	*remind*	*tell*	*warn*
allow	*force*	*invite*	*permit*	*request*	*tempt*	
compel	*forbid*	*oblige*	*persuade*	*teach*	*urge*	

(e) Verb + infinitive/verb + object + infinitive

5. *Look at thse sentences:*

Verb + infinitive	*Verb + object + infinitive*
I *asked to leave.*	I *asked him to leave.*
I *want to go* home.	I *want you to go* home.
He *likes to eat* well.	He *likes him to eat* well.

(i) कुछ verbs के दो patterns हो सकते हैं :

(a) verb + infinitive (b) verb + object + infinitive

(ii) कुछ महत्त्वपूर्ण verbs जिनके उक्त दोनों patterns का प्रयोग होता है :

ask	*expect*	*help*	*love*	*mean*	*wish*
beg	*hate*	*intend*	*like*	*prefer*	*want*

(f) Verb + object + to be

6. *Look at these sentences:*

We *know him to be* honest.

I *consider him to be* the best teacher.

He *thought her to be* the best singer.

(i) कुछ verbs के बाद object + to be का प्रयोग होता है।

(ii) वैसे कुछ अन्य verbs हैं :

assume *believe* *feel* *suppose* *understand*

(g) Infinitive after certain adjectives

7. *Look at these sentences:*

She was *anxious to go.*	I am *sorry to disturb* you.
I was *glad to see* him.	I am *pleased to see* you.

(i) ऊपर के वाक्यों में adjectives (anxious, glad, sorry, pleased) के बाद infinitive with *to* का प्रयोग किया गया है।

(ii) कुछ अन्य adjectives जिनके बाद infinitive with *to* का प्रयोग किया जाता है :

angry	*eager*	*fortunate*	*happy*	*keen*	*lucky*	*pleased*	*sorry*
difficult	*easy*	*glad*	*inclined*	*likely*	*nice*	*ready*	*surprised*

(h) Infinitives after certain nouns

8. *Look at these sentences:*

I have no *wish to change.*	She has a *plan to go* abroad.
He made an *attempt to stand up.*	I told her about my *decision to leave.*

(i) कुछ nouns के बाद infinitive with *to* लगता है।

(ii) वैसे कुछ nouns हैं :

attempt *decision* *demand* *desire* *effort* *failure* *promise* *request*

(i) Infinitive of purpose

9. *Look at these sentences:*

We eat *to live* (जीने के लिए), not live *to eat* (खाने के लिए).

I go there *to see* (देखने के लिए), not *to praise* (प्रशंसा करने के लिए) her.

(i) Infinitive with *to* के प्रयोग से 'के लिए' (purpose) का भाव व्यक्त होता है।

(ii) विद्यार्थी अकसर infinitive with purpose के स्थान पर गलती से for + gerund का प्रयोग कर देते हैं :

Correct	Incorrect
I came *to see* you.	I came *for seeing* you.
Give me a book *to read.*	Give me a book *for reading.*
We should eat *to live.*	We should eat *for living.*
He went there *to buy* a pen.	He went there *for buying* a pen.

(j) Infinitive after too and enough

10. *Look at these sentences:*

The box is *too* heavy *to lift.* He was strong *enough to pull* the box.

The shirt is *too* dirty *to wear.* She is intelligent *enough to solve* the problem.

Too तथा enough के बाद adjective/adverb + infinitive with *to* का प्रयोग होता है।

(ii) Infinitive without to

Infinitive without *to* का प्रयोग इन परिस्थितियों में होता है :

(a) Modal auxiliary verbs

1. *Look at these sentences:*

I *can speak* English. I *may go* home.

We *shall meet* him. It *might rain* tonight.

I *will help* you. We *must* go now.

(i) ऊपर दिए गए वाक्यों में *can, shall, will, may, might* तथा *must* modal auxiliary verbs हैं।

(ii) इनके बाद infinitive का चिह्न *to* लुप्त रहता है।

(iii) ये हैं modal auxiliary verbs जिनके बाद infinitive का चिह्न *to* लुप्त रहता है :

can	*may*	*shall*	*will*	*must*	*dare*
could	*might*	*should*	*would*	*need*	

Note: (i) *Dare* तथा *need* के बाद bare infinitive साधारणतः negative और interrogative वाक्यों में ही लगता है। जैसे :

I *daren't go.* I *needn't wait.*

Note: यदि *dare* का Principal verb की तरह प्रयोग हो तो उसके बाद भी infinitive with *to* का प्रयोग होता है। जैसे :

He *dares to go* there. He *dared to defy* me.

I don't *dare to do* so. He *dared to oppose* her.

(ii) *Ought* तथा *used* के बाद infinitive with *to* का ही प्रयोग होता है। जैसे :

We *ought to obey* our teachers.

I *used to play* football at school.

(b) Let, make, hear, feel etc

2. *Look at these sentences:*

Let us *go* now.	I *saw* him *come.*
What *makes* you *laugh*?	I *felt* him *touch* me.
She *heard* him *cry.*	We *watched* him *jump.*
I *observed* him *go* out.	He didn't *notice* you *speak.*

(i) ऊपर दिए गए verbs के बाद objects तथा infinitive without *to* का प्रयोग होता है।

(ii) ऐसे कुछ महत्त्वपूर्ण verbs हैं :

feel	*know*	*make*	*please*	*overhear*	*watch*
hear	*let*	*notice*	*observe*	*see*	

3. *Look at these sentences:*

Active	*Passive*
I *made* him *sing.*	He *was made to sing.*
We *saw* him *leave.*	He *was seen to leave.*
I *helped* him *climb* the tree.	He *was helped to climb* the tree.

Passive Voice में ऊपर दिए verbs के साथ infinitive with *to* का प्रयोग होता है।

(c) Had better, would rather, sooner than etc

4. *Look at these sentences:*

You *had better stop.*	They *had sooner run than walk.*
I *would rather starve than beg.*	*Better get* some *sleep* while you can.

इन शब्दों के बाद bare infinitive का ही प्रयोग होता है :

Better	*had rather*	*would sooner*	*cannot but*
had better	*had sooner*	*would rather*	*need hardly*

(d) Help, know

5. *Look at these sentences:*

Infinitive without *to*	**Infinitive with *to***
I *helped* him *mend* his bicycle.	I *helped* him *to mend* his bicycle.
I have never *known* him *lose* his temper.	I have never *known* him *to lose* his temper.

(i) आजकल *help* तथा *know* के बाद infinitive with *to* का प्रयोग कभी होता है या कभी नहीं भी होता है।

(ii) किंतु अकसर infinitive with *to* का प्रयोग करना ही बेहतर माना जाता है।

"It is perhaps best for the foreign students always to use the form with *to* since that is never incorrect."

F T WOOD: A REMEDIAL ENGLISH GRAMMAR FOR FOREIGN STUDENTS

(e) And, or, except, but, than

6. *Look at these sentences:*

There is nothing to do *but wait.*

She did no more *than weep.*
I want you to stand beside me *and hold* the torch.
Do you want to eat now *or wait* till evening?
I had nothing to do *except look* at the garden.

जब हम दो infinitives को *and, or, except, but, save, than* से जोड़ते हैं, तब दूसरेवाले infinitive में *to* का प्रयोग प्रायः लुप्त रहता है।

Note: कुछ वाक्यों में infinitive का चिह्न *to* का प्रयोग कभी हो भी सकता है और कभी नहीं भी/यह लिखनेवाले की इच्छा पर निर्भर है। जैसे :
All we can do is *(to) write* to him.

(f) Why, why not

7. *Look at these sentences:*

Why hire a taxi? *Why not write* to him?
Why worry about this? *Why not ask* him to help you?

(i) Why + infinitive without *to* का प्रयोग प्रश्न पूछने के लिए किया जाता है। ("The point of the question is usually to suggest that it is stupid or pointless to do something.")

(ii) Why not + infinitive without *to* से सुझाव एवं सलाह का भाव व्यक्त होता है।

8. *Look at these sentences:*

Incorrect	**Correct**
What *to do*?	What *shall we* do?
Who *to pay*?	Who *should I* pay?
How *to tell* her?	How *shall I* tell her?

Direct question: What to..... ? Who to ......? How to ....? इत्यादि से शुरू नहीं किया जाता, इसकी जगह *shall* या *should* + infinitive without *to* का प्रयोग किया जाता है।

(iii) The infinitive represented by its *to*

9. *Look at these sentences:*

Will you buy a scooter? Yes, I *want to* (=buy a scooter.)
Do you smoke? No, but I *used to* (smoke.)
Can the boys go home? Yes, if they *wish to* (= go home.)
Have you fed the dog? No, but I'm just *going to* (= feed the dog.)

(i) ऊपर के वाक्यों में पुनरावृत्ति (repetition) से बचने के लिए infinitive के स्थान पर केवल 'to' का प्रयोग किया जाता है और verb को लुप्त रखा जाता है। इसे anaphoric 'to' भी कहा जाता है।

(ii) इस तरह के वाक्यों में *to* का प्रयोग इन शब्दों के बाद किया जाता है :

(a) *Verbs:* *hate* *hope* *intend* *mean* *make* (passive)
play *try* *want* *would* *like/love*

(b) *Auxiliaries*: *be able to* *be going to* *have need* *ought to* *used to*

(iv) Split infinitive

10. *Look at these sentences:*

It is difficult *to easily understand* it.

It would take ages *to really master* this subject.

It is time *to immediately put* the work in hand.

(i) ऊपर के वाक्यों में adverbs—*easily, really, immediately* का प्रयोग *to* तथा infinitive अर्थात verb के बीच में हुआ है। इसे split infinitive कहते हैं।

(ii) साधारणतः infinitive, जब वह अपने चिह्न *to* के साथ रहता है तब *to* के बाद infinitive यानी verb का प्रयोग किया जाता है। जैसे : *to* understand, *to* master, *to* put

(iii) इन वाक्यों को इस प्रकार लिख सकते हैं :

It is difficult *to understand* it easily.

It would take ages really *to master* this subject.

It is time *to put* the work in hand immediately.

(iv) पुराने grammarians, split infinitive के प्रयोग को गलत मानते थे, लेकिन अब धीरे-धीरे modern grammarians की धारणा बदलती जा रही है।

(v) Introductory infinite phrases

11. *Look at these sentences:*

To be honest, I just don't like her.

To be frank, I have done my duty.

To *tell you the truth*, I don't have any money.

(i) ऊपर दिए गए infinitive phrases पूरे वाक्य को modify करते हैं। इसे introductory infinitive phrases कहते हैं।

(ii) कुछ और common phrases हैं :

to speak strictly	*to be fair (to him)*	*to use the correct expression*
to be honest	*to take a simple example*	*to cut a long story short*

(vi) Negative infinitive

12. *Look at these sentences:*

Try *not to be* late.	I want *not to do* this work.
He decided *not to study* medicine.	She wishes *not to speak* to him.

Not के बाद *to* लगाकर negative infinitive बनता है।

(vii) The continuous infinitive

Form: *to be + present participle:*

He *can be siting* there.	He *seems to be following* us.
He *must be coming* by car.	He *appeared to be listening*.

(viii) The perfect infinitive

Form: *to have* + past participle:

He should *have helped* her. (but he didn't)

She would *have gone* there. (but she didn't)

You might/could *have told* me. (but you couldn't)

(ix) The passive infinitive

Form: *to be* + past participle:

He ought *to be told* about it. This door must *be repaired* today.

I didn't expect *to be invited.* There is a lot of work *to be done.*

Gerund
(Form and Use)

(A) Form

Verb के अंत में जब *-ing* लगा रहे और वह noun का काम करे, तब उसे gerund कहते हैं। जैसे : *speaking, running, working.*

Gerund तथा Present participle का रूप एकसमान होता है, लेकिन इन दोनों में अंतर है।

(B) Gerund and participle

1. *Look at these sentences:*

Swimming is a good exercise. (*gerund*)

We went to the *swimming* pool. (*participle*)

(i) *Verb + ing* = gerund; *verb + ing* = present participle

(ii) प्रथम वाक्य में *swimming* gerund है जो noun का काम करता है।

(iii) लेकिन दूसरे वाक्य में *swimming* present participle है जो adjective का काम करता है।

(C) Uses of gerund (-ing form)

(a) Gerund (*-ing* form) as subject

2. *Look at these sentences:*

Singing is her hobby. *Reading* is a good habit.

Smoking is dangerous. *Sleeping* is necessary to life.

(i) ऊपर दिए गए वाक्यों में *singing, smoking, reading* तथा *sleeping* gerunds हैं।

(ii) यहाँ gerund का प्रयोग verb के subject के रूप में हुआ है।

(b) Gerund (*-ing* form) as complement

3. *Look at these sentences:*

Seeing is *believing.* My favourite activity is *reading.*

The best kind of rest is *sleeping*. What I most detest is *smoking.*

(i) ऊपर दिए गए वाक्यों में *believing, sleeping, reading* तथा *smoking* gerunds हैं।

(ii) यहाँ gerund का प्रयोग verb के complement के रूप में हुआ है।

(c) Gerund (*-ing* form) after certain verbs

4. *Look at these sentences:*

I like *swimming.* She loves *driving.*

We hate *smoking.* He enjoys *travelling.*

(i) ऊपर दिए गए वाक्यों में *swimming, smoking, driving* तथा *travelling* gerunds हैं।

(ii) कुछ खास verbs जिनके बाद gerund (*-ing* form) का प्रयोग किया जाता है :

admit	*defer*	*dislike*	*finish*	*miss*	*recollect*	*risk*
Appreciate	*delay*	*enjoy*	*forgive*	*postpone*	*remember*	*stop*
avoid	*deny*	*escape*	*involve*	*prevent*	*resent*	*suggest*
consider	*detest*	*excuse*	*mind*	*propose*	*resist*	*understand*

Examples of verb + gerund (-ing form) sentences

Let us *go swimming.* I could not *help laughing.*

We *stopped advising* others. Do you *enjoy teaching*?

I *love driving* a car fast . He wants to *avoid meeting* me.

He *kept compldining.* Do you *mind closing* the door?

We *missed seeing* the test matches. I *finish writing* that letter.

He *practised singing* every day. Children *like watching* football matches.

5. *Look at these sentences:*

This book is *worth buying.*

We could *not help being* late.

It is *no good learning* essays by heart.

कुछ शब्दों के बाद-*ing* form लगता है। जैसे :

It is worth	*It's no good*	*Did'nt help*	*Can't help*
It's no use	*What's the point of*	*Can't bear*	*There's no point in*

6. *Look at these sentences:*

You hair *needs cutting.* (=.......needs *to be cut.*)

Your suit *requires pressing.* (.......needs *to be pressed.*)

The scooter *wants servicing.* (=........ needs *to be serviced.*)

Passive अर्थ में *need, require* तथा *want* के बाद-*ing* form का प्रयोग होता है।

(d) Gerund (*-ing* form) after preposition

7. *Look at these sentences:*

He began *by going* there. You can't live *without eating.*

She is fond *of dancing.* They were punished *for coming* late.

Preposition (जैसे : *by, of, without, for, at, from, on, in, off, up, before* आदि) के बाद gerund (*-ing* form) का प्रयोग होता है।

8. *Look at these sentences:*

He *prefers reading to writing.*

I *look forward to hearing* from you.

I am not *used to getting* up early.

to का दो अर्थों में प्रयोग किया जाता है :

(i) पहले अर्थ में *to* infinitive का चिह्न है इसके बाद कोई verb आता है : जैसे : I want *to go*.

(ii) दूसरे अर्थ में *to* एक preposition है जिसके बाद noun/pronoun या verb का प्रयोग होता है। जैसे : Mr Sinha went *to* Delhi/him.

Preposition के अर्थ में अगर *to* के बाद कोई verb रहे तो इसमें *-ing* form लगाया जाता है। जैसे : I object *to working* on Sundays.

(e) Infinitive and gerund constructions

9. *Look at these sentences:*

Infinitive	**Gerund**
They *began to work.*	They *began working*.
We *prefer to go* by air.	We *prefer going* by air.
I *propose to leave* soon.	I *propose leaving* soon.
I *like to climb* mountains.	I *like climbing* mountains.

(i) ऊपर दिए गए verbs के बाद infinitives (*to* + verbs) तथा gerunds (*-ing* forms) का प्रयोग हुआ है।

(ii) इन verbs के बाद infinitive (*to* + verb) या gerund (*-ing* form) का प्रयोग होता है :

advise	*begin*	*dislike*	*intend*	*mean*	*permit*	*start*
allow	*bear*	*fear*	*love*	*need*	*prefer*	*stop*
agree	*continue*	*forget*	*like*	*neglect*	*regret*	*try*
require	*cease*	*hate*	*learn*	*propose*	*remember*	*want*

Some more examples:

Infinitive	**Gerund**
She *learnt to dance.*	She *learnt dancing.*
He *started to run.*	He *started running.*
She *hates to do it.*	She *hates doing it.*
We *fear to go* there.	We *fear going* there.
She *forgot to write* to him.	She *forgot writing* to him.
They *continue to live* there.	They *continue living* there.
He *stopped to watch* TV.	He *stopped watching* TV.

10. *Look at these sentences:*

Infinitive	**Gerund**
To gamble is a vice.	*Gambling* is a vice.
To smoke is forbidden.	*Smoking* is forbidden.
To see is to believe.	*Seeing* is beliving.
Can you teach me *to paint*?	Can you teach me *painting*?

(i) Infinitive तथा gerund दोनों noun का कार्य करते हैं और verb का भी।

(ii) अतः, बहुत वाक्यों में infinitive के स्थान पर gerund का, या gerund के स्थान पर infinitive का प्रयोग आसानी सें हो सकता है।

(f) Gerund with possessive adjective or 's

11. *Look at these sentences:*

I don't like *your boasting*. Please excuse *my leaving* early.

I insist on *his being* present. We don't approve of *Ram's going* there.

(i) ऊपर के वाक्यों में *boasting, being, leaving* तथा *going* gerunds हैं, अर्थात ये nouns हैं।

(ii) Gerund (*-ing* form) के पहले कोई pronoun (जैसे : *I, we, you, he, she, they, it* आदि) आए तो वह possessive adjective (*my, our, his, her, their, its* आदि) के रूप में रहता है।

(iii) Gerund के पहले कोई noun (जैसे : *Ram, John* आदि) रहे तो वह भी possessive case (*Ram's, John's*) आदि के रूप में रहता है।

12. *Look at these sentences:*

I don't *mind walking*. I don't *mind your walking*.

He *disliked working* late. He *disliked my working* late.

(i) ऊपर के वाक्यों के दो patterns हैं :

(a) verb + gerund (*-ing* form) और दूसरा

(b) verb + possessive adjective/pronoun object + gerund.

(ii) कुछ verb जिनके दो patterns होते हैं :

like, dislike, stop, mind, resent, object to आदि।

Participle
(Form and use)

Form:

ऐसे शब्द जिनमें verb और adjective दोनों के लक्षण होते हैं, participle कहलाते हैं। जैसे : *playing, working, talking.*

Verb + adjective = participle

1. *Look at these sentences:*

He told me an *interesting* story. He jumped into a *running* car.

(i) ऊपर के वाक्यों में *interesting* तथा *running* क्रमशः verbs, *interest* और *run* से बने हुए हैं।

(ii) *interesting* और *running* के बाद क्रमशः story और car आए हैं जो nouns हैं। अतः *interesting* और *running* adjective का काम करते हैं।

(iii) यहाँ *interesting* और *running* participles हैं।

Kinds of participles

Participles तीन प्रकार के होते हैं :

(A) Present Participle: (infinitive + *ing*)

(B) Perfect Participle: (*having* + past participle)

(C) Past Participle: (infinitive + *d/-ed/-t/-en/-n*)

(A) Present Participle

(i) **Form**: infinitive + ing जैसे : *going, sitting, making.*

Present participle से पता चलता है कि कार्य पूरा नहीं हुआ है।

(B) Uses of present participle

Present participle के निम्नलिखित uses हैं :

(a) To form continuous tenses

2. *Look at these sentences:*

He is *working.*	She was *reading.*
He is *going.*	I shall be *writing.*

Present participle की सहायता से present continuous, past continuous तथा Future continuous tenses बनाए जाते हैं।

(b) Present participles used as adjectives

3. *Look at these sentences:*

It was a *tiring* exercise.	The exercise was *tiring.*
It is an *interesting* film.	The film is *interesting.*

(i) ऊपर के वाक्यों में *tiring* और *interesting* present participles हैं। इनका प्रयोग adjective की तरह हुआ है।

(ii) प्रथम दोनों वाक्यों में अपने बाद आए nouns (*exercise/films*) को qualify करते हैं : *adjective + noun.*

(iii) दूसरे दोनों वाक्यों में present participle का प्रयोग adjective (complement of the verb) की तरह हुआ है, अर्थात *noun + adjective.*

(c) Present participles used after some verbs

4. *Look at these sentences:*

She *is busy packing.*	We *heard* the dogs *barking.*
I *left* him *talking* to Munu.	I *found* him *standing* there.

कुछ verbs के बाद present participles का प्रयोग होता है। जैसे :

(i) *See/hear/feel/smell* + object + present participle

(ii) *catch/find/leave* + object + present participle

(iii) *be busy* + present participle

(d) Present participle can combine main sentences

5. *Look at these sentences:*

He came out of the office.	He was smiling.

= He came out of the office *smiling.*

They went into the class-room.	They were laughing.

= They went into the class-room *laughing.*

(i) ऊपर दिए गए वाक्यों में दो-दो main/principal clauses हैं।

(ii) जब एक ही subject द्वारा एक से अधिक कार्य एक ही समय किए जाएँ तो उनमें से एक कार्य के स्थान पर present particple का प्रयोग होता है।

6. *Look at these sentences:*

He opened the box. He took out his shirt.

= *Opening* the box, he took out his shirt.

I looked out of the window. I saw a beggar.

= *Looking* out of the window, I saw a beggar.

जब दो कार्य एक ही व्यक्ति द्वारा किया जाएँ, तो पहले किए गए कार्य को present participle के रूप में व्यक्त किया जाता है।

(e) A present participle can replace a subordinate clause

7. *Look at these sentences:*

As he knew that he was early, he went to the bookshop.

= *Knowing* that he was early, he went to the bookshop.

Because/As/Since he was a player, he was interested in games.

= *Being* a player, he was interested in games.

(i) *As/Because/Since + subject + verb* से subordinate clause शुरू होता है।

(ii) ऐसे subordinate clause के स्थान पर present participle (जैसे : *Knowing, Being*) का प्रयोग करते हैं।

(iii) इस प्रकार subordinate clause को present participle द्वारा replace कर सकते हैं।

8. *Look at these sentences:*

The pen *which is lying* on the table is mine.

=The pen *lying* on the table is mine.

(i) ऊपर दिए गए वाक्य में *which is lying* subordinate clause हैं।

(ii) Subordinate clause के स्थान पर हम present participle (जैसे : *lying*) का प्रयोग कर सकते हैं।

(B) Perfect Participle

(Form and use)

(i) **Form:** having + past participle

जैसे : *having written, having done, having seen*—इसका प्रयोग सदा ऐसी क्रिया के लिए होता है जो पूर्व में समाप्त हो चुकी रहती है।

(ii) **Uses of perfect participle**

Perfect participle के निम्नलिखित uses हैं :

(a) Active voice में : having + past participle जैसे : *having done*

(b) Passive voice में : having been + past participle जैसे : *having been done*

(a) Perfect participles help to combine sentences

1. *Look at these sentences:*

Ramu has failed three times. He doesn't want to try again.

= *Having failed* three times, Ramu doesn't want to try again.

Suresh has passed the S.S.C. He wants to join college.

= *Having passed* the S.S.C., Suresh wants to join college.

(i) जब एक ही subject (कर्त्ता) एक कार्य के शीघ्र बाद दूसरा कार्य करे तब हम perfect participle का प्रयोग करते हैं।

(ii) उदाहरण के लिए : Ramu has failed three times पहला कार्य है, उसके बाद Ramu doesn't want to try again दूसरा कार्य है। अतः, पहले कार्य—Ramu has failed three times को हम Perfect participle के रूप में *Having failed three times* लिखते हैं।

(iii) इस प्रकार Perfect participles का प्रयोग कर हम sentences को जोड़ सकते हैं।

2. *Look at these sentences:*

The task was done. Then the boy went home.

= The task *having been done*, the boy went home.

The boy was expelled. Then he left the class-room.

=*Having been expelled,* the boy left the class-room.

यहाँ perfect participle का passive voice में प्रयोग हुआ है।

(b) Past participle
(Form and use)

(A) Form

Form: *Infinitive + -d/-ed/-t/-en/-n*

जैसे : *worked, burnt, stolen, broken, made, drunk* Past participles से पता चलता है कि कार्य भूतकाल में ही पूरा हो चुका था और अब वर्तमान में यह नहीं चल रहा है।

(B) Use of past participle

Past participle के निम्नलिखित uses है :

(a) Past participle to form perfect tenses

1. *Look at these sentences:*

He *has arrived.* I *had forgotten.*

He *has stolen* my watch. They *have completed* the work.

Past participle की सहायता से perfect tenses बनाए जाते हैं।

(b) Past participle as an adjective

2. *Look at these sentences:*

We gave a *written* complaint. There were some *fallen* trees.

यहाँ past participle का प्रयोग adjective की तरह से हुआ है : *adjective + noun.*

3. *Look at these sentences:*

The workers were *tired.* The hut was *burnt.*

The man looked *worried.* He bacame *discouraged.*

यहाँ past participle का प्रयोग adjective की तरह हुआ है; अर्थात *noun + adjective.*

(c) Past participles help to combine sentences

4. *Look at these sentences:*

He enters. *He is accompanied* by his friend.

= He enters, *accompanied* by his friend.

The doctor was appointed to treat the patient. He started working hard.

=*Appointed* to treat the patient, the doctor started working hard.

(i) ऊपर दिए गए वाक्यों में past participles (जैसे : *accompanied, appointed*) का प्रयोग subject + passive verb (जैसे : *He is accompanied, The doctor was appointed*) के स्थान पर किया गया है।

(ii) इस तरह Past participle का प्रयोग करके वाक्यों को जोड़ा जा सकता है।

Dangling or Unrelated participle

(i) जिस noun/pronoun को participle qualify करता हो उसका लोप नहीं होना चाहिए, बल्कि स्पष्ट उल्लेख होना चाहिए, और वह भी Finite verb के subject के रूप में।

(ii) वह participle जिसका वाक्य में subject नहीं होता *dangling participle/unrelated participle/misrelated participle* कहा जाता है। ऐसे वाक्य गलत होते हैं :

Waiting for a bus, a brick fell on my head.

Feeling sleepy, the book fell from his hands.

ऐसे वाक्यों को इस प्रकार लिखना चाहिए :

As I was waiting for a bus, a brick fell on my head.

As he was feling sleepy, the book fell from his hands.

Use of participle

Participle का प्रयोग कहाँ करना चाहिए और कहाँ नहीं करना चाहिए, इसके लिए इन बातों पर विचार करें।

1. *Look at this sentence:*

Walking along the street, Sonu gave me a book.

इस वाक्य में दो भाग (clauses) हैं :

(i) पहला भाग : Sonu was walking along the street. इसका संक्षिप्त रूप है : Walking along the street.

(ii) दूसरा भाग (clause) : Sonu gave me a book.

(iii) दोनों clauses का subject एक ही है, यानी Sonu.

(iv) जब वाक्य के दोनों भागों (clauses) का subject एक ही हो, तब पहले भाग (clause) के बदले participle का प्रयोग होता है, अर्थात :

Same subject in both clauses = Participle + Principal clause

2. *Look at this sentence:*

While going to college, a dog jumped at Sonu.

इस वाक्य में दो भाग (clauses) हैं :

(i) पहला भाग Sonu was going to college और दूसरा भाग a dog jumped at Sonu.

(ii) यहाँ Sonu was going to college का संक्षिप्त रूप है : While going to college.

(iii) इन दोनों भागों में Sonu और dog *subjects* हैं।

इसलिए यहाँ participle के प्रयोग से unattached participle का दोष आ गया है।

(iv) इस दोष को दूर करने के लिए participle के बदले पूरे clause का प्रयोग इस प्रकार करना चाहिए : *While Sonu was going to college*, a dog jumped at him.

(v) जब दोनों भागों (clauses) के subjects भिन्न हों, तब participle का प्रयोग नहीं करना चाहिए। वैसे वाक्यों में पूरे clause (*While + subject + verb*) का प्रयोग करना चाहिए। यदि वैसे वाक्यों में clause के स्थान पर participle का प्रयोग हो जाए, तो उसे ही unattached participle कहा जाता है। अर्थात :

Different subjects in both parts = Adv cl. (While) + p.c.

3. अब और उदाहरण लें :

Ploughing his field, Moti saw a big snake.

Ploughing his field, a scorpian stung him.

(i) पहले वाक्य के दोनों भागों का subject है—Moti. अतः इसमें participle उपयुक्त subject से attached (जुड़ा हुआ) है; यहाँ participle का प्रयोग उचित है।

(ii) दूसरे वाक्य की बनावट भिन्न है। यहाँ एक भाग का subject है *he* और दूसरे भाग का *scorpian.* इस प्रकार यहाँ participle उपयुक्त subject से जुड़ा हुआ नहीं है, दूसरे शब्दों में कहें यह unattached participle है। इसका correct form यह होना चाहिए :

While he was ploughing his field, a scorpian stung him.

Change of the voice

Look at these sentences:

Incorrect	**Correct**
Going round the corner, *a horrible sight was seen.*	Going round the corner, *I saw a horrible sight.*
Walking along the road, *a tower can be seen.*	Walking along the road, *one can see a tower.*

(i) कभी-कभी voice को ही बदल देने से wrongly attached participle का दोष मिट जाता है।

(ii) ऊपर के वाक्यों में passive voice को active voice में बदला गया है।

Examples worked out

Fill in the blanks with correct form of the verb (the Infinitive, the Gerund or the Participle) given in brackets.

1. He made me *(listen).* He made me *listen.*

2. You had better (*go*).	You had better *go*.
3. (*Find*) fault is easy.	*To find* fault is easy.
4. He played a (*lose*) game.	He played a *losing* game.
5. She wears a (*worry*) look.	She wears a *worried* look.
6. Stop (*play*).	Stop *playing*.
7. There is nothing (*say*).	There is nothing *to say.*
8. (*Read*) gives me a headache.	*Reading* gives me a headache.
9. He was punished for (*cheat*).	He was punished for *cheating*.
10. It is not worth (*read*).	It is not worth *reading*.
11. (*Speak*) is easier than writing.	*Speaking* is easier than writing.
12. He agreed (*wait*).	He agreed *to wait.*
13. He denied (*use*)the force.	He denied *using* the force.
14. He ran away (*whistle*).	He ran away *whistling*.
15. We felt (*bore*).	We felt *bored*.
16. I got a shirt (*make*).	I got a shirt *made*.
17. That is something (*remember*).	That is something *to remember.*
18. Let us (*go*) for a walk.	Let us *go* for a walk.
19. That parcel is heavy (*carry*).	That parcel is heavy *to carry.*
20. We must go on (*try*).	We must go on *trying*.
21. Don't make me (*laugh*).	Don't make me *laugh.*
22. I remember (*see*) him.	I remember *seeing* him.
23. I hate (*lie*) and (*cheat*).	I hate *lying* and *cheating*.
24. You had better (*say*) nothing.	You had better *say* nothing.
25. The tenants refused (*leave*).	The tenants refused *to leave.*
26. She could not think what (*say*).	She could not think what *to say.*
27. He told me (*go*).	He told me *to go.*
28. I don't mind (*walk*).	I don't mind *walking*.
29. The grass wants (*cut*).	The grass wants *cutting.*
30. He was busy (*pack*).	He was busy *packing*.
31. We found the child (*cry*).	We found the child *crying.*
32. I saw the snake (*kill*).	I saw the snake *killed.*
33. He told me what (*do*).	He told me what *to do.*
34. She didn't know where (*go*).	She didn't know where *to go.*
35. (*Run*) is a good exercise.	*Running* is a good exercise.
36. He avoided (*see*) me.	He avoided *seeing* me.
37. He wanted (*study*) medicine.	He wanted *to study* medicine.
38. He was heard (*go*).	He was heard *to go.*
39. He let me (*speak*).	He let me *speak.*
40. I saw her (*come*) in.	I saw her *come* in.
41. Please excuse my (*interrupt*) you.	Please excuse my *interrupting* you.

42. We watched him (*go*) and (*come*).	We watched him *go* and *come*.
43. (*Sleep*) is necessary to life.	*Sleeping* is necessary to life.
44. I had sooner (*run*) than (*walk*).	I had sooner *run* than *walk*.
45. I will not let you (*go*).	I will not let you *go*.
46. I heard him (*cry*).	I heard him *cry*.
47. You had better (*ask*) permission.	You had better *ask* permission.
48. Her greatest pleasure is (*sing*).	Her greatest pleasure is *to sing*.
49. He is too ill (*do*) any work.	He is too ill *to do* any work.
50. This house is (*let*).	This house is *to let*.
51. I have an aversion (*fish*).	I have an aversion *to fishing*.
52. The box is light enough (*lift*).	The box is light enough *to lift*.
53. It is wrong (*tell*) a lie.	It is wrong *to tell* a lie.
54. He disliked (*see*) the films.	He disliked *seeing* the films.
55. They became (*tire*).	They became *tired*.
56. I have given up (*smoke*).	I have given up *smoking*.
57. I saw/watched him (*drive*) off.	I saw/watched him *drive* off.
58. He helped us (*push*) it.	He helped us (*to*) *push* it.
59. The light is too weak (*read*) by.	The light is too weak *to read* by.
60. He is good at (*teach*).	He is good at *teaching*.
61. Would you mind (*wait*) a moment?	Would you mind *waiting* a moment?
62. (*Open*) the drawer he took out a pen.	*Opening* the drawer he took out a pen.
63. His words left me (*think*).	His words left me *thinking*.
64. Children like (*play*) games.	Children like *playing* games.
65. (*Smoke*) inside buses is prohibited.	*Smoking* inside buses is prohibited.
66. I had rather (*starve*) than (*beg*).	I had rather *starve* than *beg*.
67. A good man does not fear (*die*).	A good man does not fear *to die*.
68. I made him (*run*).	I made him *run*.
69. He is a man (*admire*).	He is a man *to be admired*.
70. I would prefer (*stay*) at home.	I would prefer *to stay* at home.
71. Most boys like (*play*) games.	Most boys like *playing* games.
72. This room needs (*clean*).	This room needs *cleaning*.
73. He enjoys (*smoke*).	He enjoys *smoking*.
74. She hopes (*succeed*).	She hopes *to succeed*.
75. Show me how (*do*) the exercise.	Show me how *to do* the exercise.
76. She does nothing but (*complain*).	She does nothing but *complain*.
77. You are too young (*understand*).	You are too young *to understand*.
78. I am looking forward (*see*) him.	I am looking forward *to seeing* him.

79. I wish (*buy*) a TV set.	I wish *to buy* a TV set.
80. I have known him (*laugh*) for nothing.	I have known him *laugh* for nothing.
81. (*Teach*) English is a difficult task.	*Teaching* English is a difficult task.
82. He stopped (*advise*) others.	He stopped *advising* others.
83. We found all the windows (*damage*).	We found all the windows *damaged.*
84. That was a sight (*see*).	That was a sight *to see.*
85. We must prevent their (*come*).	We must prevent their *coming.*
86. These shoes are fit (*wear*).	These shoes are fit *to wear.*
87. They began (*talk*).	They began *to talk/talking.*
88. I heard him (*lock*) the gate.	I heard him *lock* the gate.
89. I hate (*wait)* at the bus stop.	I hate *waiting* at the bus stop.
90. (*Climb*) mountains is a sport.	*Climbing* mountains is a sport.
91. Do you object to our (*smoke*)?	Do you object to our *smoking*?
92. Children like (*play*) more than (*study*).	Children like playing more than *studying.*
93. I need hardly (*tell*) you it is so.	I need hardly *tell* you it is so.
94. Would you mind (*I, come*) too?	Would you mind *my coming* too?
95. They liked (*see*) (*we, play*) together.	They liked *seeing our playing* together.

EXERCISE 1

Point out the infinitives in these sentences:

EXAMPLE: Children like to play. *To play:* infinitive

1. Children like to play.
2. Let him come here.
3. He made me run.
4. I told him to go.
5. She agreed to wait.
6. To forgive is divine.
7. They played to win.
8. I heard her sing.
9. I have come to see you.
10. To tell lies is wrong.
11. Birds love to sing.
12. Did you feel the earth shake?

EXERCISE 2

Point out the participles in these sentences:

EXAMPLE: Barking dogs seldom bite. *Barking*: participle

1. Barking dogs seldom bite.
2. We found him sleeping.
3. They play a losing game.
4. She had a worried look.
5. He kept me waiting.
6. She found the study boring.
7. It is an interesting story.
8. This is a rotten mango.
9. The man was pleased.
10. A lost opportunity never returns.
11. Seeing me, he ran away.
12. Having reached home, I had tea.

EXERCISE 3

*Point out the **gerunds** in these sentences:*

EXAMPLE: It has stopped raining. *Raining:* gerund

1. It has stopped raining.
2. I love eating mangoes.
3. We hate fighting.
4. He is fond of swimming.
5. Teach me singing.
6. I am tired of waiting.
7. Reading is his hobby.
8. Stop talking.
9. He enjoyed reading poetry.
10. We can't live without eating.
11. I began reading a novel.
12. Start doing the exercise now.

EXERCISE 4

*Point out the **infinitive**, the **gerund** or the **participle** in these sentences:*

EXAMPLES: (i) I want to go home. *To go*: infinitive

(ii) He is fond of driving. *Driving*: gerund

(iii) He is a walking dictionary. *Walking*: participle

1. This is difficult to understand.
2. The examiner caught him copying.
3. Parking is prohibited on this road.
4. There are broken toys in the room.
5. I don't know what to do.
6. He had a surprised look.
7. That was an interesting film.
8. I suggest leaving now.
9. Walking is a fine exercise.
10. He wants to learn painting.
11. The exercise was tiring.
12. He is a retired man.
13. Reading the book, I learnt much.
14. He is to be a great scholar.
15. I found him drinking tea.
16. Having finished all my work, I went out.

EXERCISE 5

Fill in the blanks, using the verbs within brackets with or without to.

EXAMPLE: She wants us ...... for her. (*to wait*)

= She wants us *to wait* for her.

1. She wants us ..... for her. (*to wait*)
2. He made his sister ..... she was sorry. (*to say*)
3. He let him ...... the family car. (*to drive*)
4. Ask your friend ..... me. (*to telephone*)
9. I heard her ..... so. (*to say*)
10. He is too dull .... (*to understand*)
11. .... a mistake is easy. (*To make*)
12. You are slow ..... . (*to move*)

5. We requested him ... (our) view. (*to consider*)
6. They try .... fault with me. (*to find*)
7. He refused .... the orders. (*to obey*)
8. My desire is .... you again (*to see*)
13. I do not mean ..... now. (*to work*)
14. We hear her ...... in the room. (*to sing*)
15. Everybody wishes ...... life. (*to enjoy*)
16. They watched him .... (*to leave*)

EXERCISE 6

*Insert **to** where necessary before the infinitives in brackets.*

EXAMPLE: We saw him (*come*) in.

= We saw him *come* in.

A1. We saw him (*come*) in.
2. May I (*use*) your phone?
3. He let me (*speak*).
4. You ought to (*go*) now.
5. We heard him (*cry*).
6. I am (*blame*).
7. He dare not (*go*).
8. They had been made (*work*).
9. They began (*speak*).
10. I made him (*run*).
11. We had better (*go*).
12. Need I (*come*)?
13. We decided (*start*) work.
14. I am pleased (*see*) you.
15. Tell me when (*pay*).
16. There is nothing to do but (*wait*).

B1. We need not (*go*) to day.
2. The tea is too hot (*drink*).
3. Sleeping is necessary (*life*).
4. Why not (ask) Moti (*help*) you?
5. It is not easy (*learn*) Chinese.
6. How dare you (*open*) the letters?
7. (*Learn*) Russian is not easy.
8. He can but (*say*) how sorry he is.
9. You must (*obey*) your parents.
10. She can (*dance*) quite well.
11. I don't want (*see*) you again.
12. You had better (*stop*).
13. I asked you (*come*).
14. She learnt how (*make*) tea.
15. You are asked (*not feed*) the animals.
16. I will not do anything but (*work*) on the farm.

EXERCISE 7

Replace the clause in italics with an infinitive.

EXAMPLE: I did not know what *I should do.*

= I did not know what *to do.*

1. I did not know what I *should do.*
2. He was the first man *who arrived.*
7. He was sorry *when he saw me* so ill.
8. He is not a man *who can be trusted.*

3. I have four letters *which I should write.*
4. We are happy *that we will help* you.
5. He hopes *that he will meet* you soon.
6. That is not a matter *which should be ignored.*
9. There was no place *where we could sit.*
10. I was sorry *when I heard* you were angry.
11. He has a brother *whom he should look after.*
12. We have not anything *which we must do.*

EXERCISE 8

*Combine each of the following pairs of sentences using **too** followed by an infinitive.*

EXAMPLE: She is very young. She can't get married now.

= She is *too* young *to get* married now.

1. This house is very small. We can't live here.
2. He is very honest. He can't tell any lies.
3. The mangoes were very sour. We couldn't eat them.
4. The tea is very hot. I can't drink it.
5. It is very cold. We can't go out.
6. It is very difficult. I can't understand it.
7. She is very proud. She can't talk to us.
8. It is very far. We can't walk.
9. This news is very good. It can't be true.
10. This problem is very difficult. You can't do it.
11. It is very heavy. We can't lift it.
12. He was very angry. He couldn't speak to me.

EXERCISE 9

*Rewrite the sentences below, using **it** with the dummy subject.*

EXAMPLE: To move with the times is easy.

= *It* is easy to move with times.

1. To compromise appears advisable.
2. To write a good book is no easy task.
3. To preach is easy.
4. To play with fire is dangerous.
5. To save money is impossible.
6. To live in these villages is a great experience.
7. To tell lies is a shame.
8. To answer this question is difficult for me.
9. To cut down our forests is a great mistake.
10. To blame others for our failures is a human tendency.
11. To lean out of the window is dangerous.

12. To read without glasses is difficult for him.
13. To move with the times is easy.

EXERCISE 10

Combine each of the following pairs of sentences into one sentence by using infinitives.

EXAMPLE: Every cricket team has a captain. He directs the other players.

= Every cricket team has a captain *to direct* the other players.

1. He works very hard. He has to feed his family.
2. I am saving money. I want to buy a TV set.
3. He sent me to England. He wanted me to learn English.
4. He has five children. He must provide for them.
5. I am learning Sanskrit. I want to understand the *Gita.*
6. He stepped into the running bus. He wanted to reach office on time.
7. John was playing very softly. He didn't want to disturb anyone.
8. He is buying paint. He wants to paint his windows.
9. He took off his shoes. He didn't want to make any noise.
10. He labours hard. He wants to come first in his class.

EXERCISE 11

Put the verbs in brackets into the correct form (gerund or infinitive):

EXAMPLES: (i) I am sorry for (*be*) late.

= I am sorry for *being* late.

(ii) He promised (*wait*).

= He promised *to wait.*

1. I am sorry for (*be*) late.
2. He promised (*wait*).
3. Please go on (*write*).
4. He hates (*borrow*) money.
5. It is no use (*wait*).
6. He hopes (*succeed*).
7. He avoided (*see*) me.
8. Stop (*talk*).
9. Our house needs (*paint*).
10. He urged us (*work*) faster.
11. He practised (*sing*) every day.
12. I agreed (*pay*).
13. I enjoyed (*go*) to the town.
14. The enemy began (*fire*).
15. I am fond of (*read*) novels.
16. He keeps (*ask*) me the time.
17. Do you remember (*write*) to him?
18. I wanted (*study*) medicine.
19. She finished (*speak*) and sat down.
20. He denied (*use*) the force.

EXERCISE 12

Put the verbs in brackets into the correct form (gerund or infinitive):

EXAMPLES: (i) They had been made (*work*).

= They had been made *to work.*

(ii) I am looking forward to (*see*) you.

= I am looking forward to *seeing* you.

1. They had been made (*work*).
2. I am looking forward to (*see*) you.
3. He warned us (*not touch*) the wire.
4. We missed (*see*) the test match.
5. There is no point in (*wait*).
6. They could not stop (*laugh*).
7. You are right in (*think*) so.
8. Would you mind (*open*) the windows?
9. He dislikes (*go*) to the films.
10. I managed (*catch*) the bus.
11. We don't like you (*work*) so hard.
12. I wish (*see*) the manager.
13. We decided (*vote*) for Mr Bose.
14. He doesn't like (*write*) the letters.
15. She expects him (*come*) today.
16. You must practise (*read*) English aloud.
17. Is there anything here worth (*buy*)?
18. I have come (*learn*) English.
19. He gave up (*gamble*).
20. Most boys like (*play*) games.

EXERCISE 13

Join each of the following pairs of sentences, using either a present participle, e.g., knowing or a perfect participle, e.g., having known.

EXAMPLES: (i) The hunter took a careful aim. He shot the tiger.

= *Taking* a careful aim, the hunter shot the tiger.

(ii) She taught the students. Then she left the school.

= *Having taught* the students, she left the school.

1. He saw me. — He ran away.
2. She started early. — She arrived at noon.
3. He took his umbrella. — He went out.
4. We felt pity for the beggar. — We gave him some money.
5. I did my exercise in the morning. — I went to have my bath.
6. The thief took out a pistol. — He threatened us.
7. He switched off the lights. — Then he went to bed.
8. I ate the breakfast in the morning. — Then I went to hospital.
9. He has read the novel twice. — He does not want to read it again.
10. I knew that he was poor. — I offered to give him help.
11. She took out her identity card. — She went to the office.
12. Ram found no one at home. — He left the house without food.
13. They crossed a street. — They went to a shop.
14. I saw him running. — I went to see what was wrong.
15. We left the car on the road. — We walked into his house.

EXERCISE 14

Use the correct verb form (infinitive with or without to, participle, or gerund) in these sentences:

EXAMPLE: It has begun (*rain*).
= It has begun *raining*.

1. It has begun (*rain*).
2. It has stopped (*rain*).
3. Would you mind (*make*) less noise?
4. Please don't forget (*post*) my letters.
5. We can hear somebody (*talk*) in his room.
6. Would you like (*go*) to the cinema today?
7. Do you enjoy (*do*) these exercises now?
8. Did she remember (*post*) the letters?
9. Please let me (*help*) you (*put*) your coat on.
10. I heard Mr Bose (*say*) he would like (*sell*) his car.
11. We make students (*work*) very hard here.
12. He does not feel like (*go*) to the office to day.

EXERCISE 15 (with answer)

Put the verbs in brackets into the correct form (gerund, infinitive or participle):

1. Try (*avoid*) (*be*) late.
2. I had to ask the boys (*stop*) (*play*).
3. She hates (*be*) kept (*wait*)
4. I dont't want you (*mention*) my (*arrive*) late.
5. I prefer (*watch*) TV to (*read*) a book.
6. Before (*go*) on tour, he wanted (*neet*) you.
7. He let us (*watch*) the actors (*rehearse*)
8. He went on (*write*); I didn't mind (*wait*).
9. We hate (*see*) a child (*cry*).
10. Can you manage (*finish*) (*pack*) these parcels?
11. He prefers (*spend*) money to (*earn*) it.
12. Have you ever watched people (*try*) (*catch*) fish?
13. A child can't learn (*spell*) without (*be*) helped.
14. You would better (*go*) back and (*do*) it now.
15. I keep (*tell*) him (*buy*) himself a watch.
16. I want (*show*) you how (*operate*) the machine.
17. I tried (*explain*) but he refused (*listen*).
18. Don't (*talk*); I am trying (*finish*) a letter.
19. Try (*forget*) it; it isn't worth (*buy*).
20. After (*read*) this article, you will stop (*smoke*).

EXERCISE 16 (with answer)

Put the verbs in brackets into the correct form (gerund, infinitive or participle):

1. I should like him (*start*) (*take*) more Tamil lessons.
2. Don't forget (*lock*) the gate before (*go*) to bed.
3. Children like (*play*) games but hate (*do*) lessons.
4. He would love (*have*) an opportunity of (*meet*) you again.
5. I advise you (*start*) (*look*) for a house at once.
6. Would you mind (*show*) me how (*work*) the machine?
7. I heard someone (*sob*) but I failed (*see*) anyone.
8. I hate (*get up*) early and (*dress*) in the dark.
9. Don't keep me (*wait*) long before (*answer*) my question.
10. I am thinking of (*leave*) my job and (*go*) to America.
11. She wore dark glasses (*avoid*) (*be*) recognized.
12. It is not much use (*have*) a motor-cycle if you don't know how (ride) it.
13. He rushed out of the room without (*give*) me a chance (*explain*).
14. The police suspect him of (*try*) (*sell*) stolen goods.
15. Please excuse us (*come*) a little late without (*inform*) you beforehand.
16. She hates (*answer*) the phone, and very often just lets it (*ring*).
17. He did not know how (*get*) to her house so he stopped (*ask*) the way.

EXERCISE 17 (with answer)

Correct the following sentences:

1. I enjoy to travel.
2. Why to pay more at other shops?
3. I suggest her to go home.
4. Why not to take a holiday?
5. He did not want that I should go.
6. It is no good to talk to him.
7. I made them to give me the money back.
8. We look forward to hear from you.
9. I decided to not study medicine.
10. Check the oil before to start the car.
11. It is not worth to get angry with her.
12. I request you to kindly grant me leave.
13. He has finished to write the letter.
14. I went to Delhi for learning English.

EXERCISE 18 (with answer)

From the given alternatives choose the most appropriate one to fill in the blanks in each of the following sentences:

1. Mr Sinha was very busy .... letters.

   A. to write **B.** write **C.** writing **D.** written

2. We don't allow .... in the office.
   A. to smoke B. smoke C. smoking D. smoked
3. He was fined for .... without lights.
   A. drive B. driving C. driven D. to be driven
4. Do you object to .... on Sunday?
   A. work B. be worked C. working D. have worked
5. The peons were not prepared .... a low salary.
   A. accept B. accepting C. to accept D. accepted
6. I am looking forward .... you at Christmas.
   A. to see B. seeing C. to seeing D. see
7. Our teacher won't like our .... late to school.
   A. to come B. coming C. came D. have come
8. It isn't good for children .... too many sweets.
   A. to eat B. eat C. eating D. ate
9. I am not used .... in Bombay.
   A. driving B. to drive C. to driving D. drive
10. .... my friend I decided to accompany him to a party.
    A. To meet B. Meet C. Meeting D. On meeting
11. When she spoke, it was difficult for me .... what she was trying to say.
    A. understand B. understanding C. to understand D. to be understanding
12. You should stop .... , it is bad for you.
    A. to smoke B. smoke C. smoked D. smoking
13. I didn't enjoy the party because I was ....
    A. to bore B. boring C. bored D. bore
14. The questions .... are on page 42.
    A. answering B. answered C. answer D. to be answered
15. There is nothing to do but ....
    A. to wait B. wait C. waiting D. to be waiting
16. Try .... being late for school.
    A. avoid B. to avoid C. avoiding D. to avoiding

ANSWERS

EX. 15. 1. avoiding, being. 2. to stop, playing. 3. being, waiting, 4. to mention, arriving. 5. watching, reading. 6. going, to meet. 7. watch, rehearsing (rehearse). 8. writing, waiting. 9. seeing, cry. 10. to finish, packing. 11. spending, earning. 12. trying (try), to catch. 13. to spell (spelling), being. 14. go, do. 15. telling, to buy. 16. to show, to operate. 17. to explain, to listen. 18. talk, to finish. 19. to forget, buying. 20. reading, smoking.

EX. 16. 1. to start, taking 2. to lock, going. 3. playing, doing. 4. to have, meeting. 5. to start, looking. 6. showing, to work. 7. sob, to see. 8. getting up, dressing. 9. waiting, answering. 10. leaving, going. 11. to avoid, being. 12. having, to ride.

13. giving, to explain. 14. trying, to sell. 15. coming, informing. 16. answering, ring. 17. to get, to ask.

EX. 17. 1. I enjoy *travelling*. 2. Why *pay* more ....? 3. I suggest *that she* (should) go home. 4. Why not *take* .....? 5. He did not want *me to* go. 6. It is no good *talking* to him. 7. I made them *give* me........ . 8. .... to *hearing* .... 9. .... not *to study* .... 10. .... before *starting*. 11. .... worth *getting* angry........ . 12. ......, you kindly to *grant* ....../I request you to *grant* .... 13. finished *writing*...... . 14. Delhi *to learn* English.

EX. 18. 1. C. writing. 2. C. smoking. 3. B. driving. 4. C. working. 5. C. to accept 6. C. to seeing 7. B. coming 8. A. to eat. 9. C. to driving 10. D. on meeting 11. C. to understand 12. D. smoking 13. C. bored 14. D. to be answered 15. B. wait 16. B. to avoid.

□□□

7. KINDS OF SENTENCES

(i) KINDS OF SENTENCES

1. *Look at these sentences :*

The bus arrived late. (statement)
Shall I switch off the television ? (question)
Open the door. (command)
What beautiful hair she has ! (exclamation)

ऊपर चार तरह के वाक्य हैं।

(i) प्रथम वाक्य में कुछ कहा गया है। इसे statement या assertive sentence कहा जाता है।

STATEMENTS are sentences in which the subject is present and generally comes before the verb.

I will speak to the boss today.

(ii) दूसरे वाक्य में प्रश्न पूछा गया है। इसे question या interrogative sentence कहा जाता है।

QUESTIONS are sentences which are marked in one or more of these ways :

a. The verb is placed immediately before the subject :

Will you speak to the boss today ?

b. The sentence begins with an interrogative word :

Who will you speak to ?

c. The sentence has rising intonation in <spoken> English :

You'll speak to the *boss* today ?

In >written< English, questions end with a question mark (?)

(iii) तीसरे वाक्य में आदेश दिया गया है। इसे command या imperative sentence कहा जाता है।

COMMANDS are sentences with the verb in the imperative (i.e., the base form). Although they usually have no expressed subject, they sometimes take *you.*

(You) speak to the boss today.

Note that in <written> English, command sentences do not normally end with an exclamation mark, but with a full stop :

Come here.

(iv) चौथे वाक्य में आश्चर्य की तीव्र भावना व्यक्त की गई है। इसे exclamation या exclamatory sentence कहा जाता है।

EXCLAMATIONS are sentences which begin with *what* or *how,* without inversion of subject and verb :

What a noise they are making !

In <written> English exclamations usually end with an exclamation mark (!).

इस तरह English में sentence चार प्रकार के माने जाते हैं : (1) Statements, (2) Questions, (3) Commands तथा (4) Exclamations.

(ii) AFFIRMATIVE AND NEGATIVE SENTENCES

2. *Look at these sentences :*

Affirmative Sentences	*Negative Sentences*
Mr Sen is a teacher.	Mr Sen is *not* a teacher.
Is Mr Prasad a doctor ?	Is Mr Prasad *not* a doctor ? (or, Is*n't* Mr Prasad a doctor ?)
Close the window.	Do*n't* close the window.
How nice a day !	Is*n't* it a nice day !

Statements, Questions, Commands तथा Exclamations में अगर स्वीकारात्मक अभिव्यक्ति हों तो उन्हें affirmative sentences कहते हैं और अगर नकारात्मक अभिव्यक्ति हों तो उन्हें negative sentences कहते हैं।

अब हमलोग (a) *no/not* के प्रयोग, (b) *affirmative sentence* को *negative* में, (c) *statement* को *question* में तथा (d) *question* को *statement* में बदलना सीखेंगे।

(iii) USE OF *'NO/NOT'*

No तथा not के प्रयोग :

1. *Look at these sentences :*

Affirmative	*Negative*
Mr Sen has money.	Mr Sen has *no* money.
I have umbrellas.	I have *no* umbrellas.
Have you a cigarette ?	Have you *no* cigarette ?
He is a friend of mine.	He is *no* friend of mine.
Words can describe the scene.	*No* words can describe the scene.

No शब्द के प्रयोग से वाक्य नकारात्मक (negative) बन जाता है। 'No' adjective तथा adverb दोनों है।

(i) Adjective की तरह 'no' का प्रयोग किसी singular या plural noun (money, cigarette, umbrellas) के पहले किया जाता है। No का अर्थ होता है : *not a* या *not any.*

Not+a can become *no,* and so can *not+any. No* cannot be followed by *a* or *any.*
—L. A. HILL : A GUIDE TO CORRECT ENGLISH

अब कुछ और उदाहरण देखें :

He is *no fool.*
No teachers went on strike.
Sorry—there is *no time* to talk.
She had *no idea* what I meant.
I have got *no Fridays* free this month.
No cigarette is completely harmless.
No beer ? How do you expect me to sing without beer ?
No tourists came to Nalanda that summer.
I can't get there—there is *no bus.*
Sorry I can't stop—I have *no time.*
There were *no letters* for you this morning.

2. *Look at these sentences :*

Affirmative	*Negative*
You have *cheaper* pens than these.	You have *no cheaper* pens that these.
You look *older* than twenty.	You look *no older* than twenty.
He likes to get *fatter.*	He likes to get *no fatter.*
She is *taller* than I.	She is *no taller* than I.

Adverb के रूप में no का प्रयोग (not at all के अर्थ में) comparative adjective के पहले होता है। साथ ही,

(i) No का प्रयोग different के साथ भी होता है। जैसे : I hadn't seen him for ten years, but he was *no different.*

(ii) No का प्रयोग no good तथा no use जैसे expressions में भी होता है। जैसे :

I am *no good* at tennis.
It is *no use* crying over spilt milk.
It is *no good* doing it.

(iii) No का प्रयोग अकसर *-ing* form में होता है यह बताने के लिए कि कोई काम करने की अनुमति नहीं है (something is not allowed). इस structure का प्रयोग केवल notices में या there is के बाद होता है। जैसे :

No Smoking. No Parking. No Waiting.
Sorry— *there is no smoking* in the waiting-room.

(iv) No के बाद noun/adjective (positive/comparative) आता है। जैसे: He is *no* fool.
He is *no* older than I.
No words can describe the scene.
John is *no* friend of mine.
The task is *no* easy one.

3. *Look at these sentences :*

Affirmative	*Negative*
Hari is a student.	Hari is *not* a student.
A person can help us.	*Not* a person can help us.
He is a good boy.	He is *not* a good boy.
Sita is a taller girl in the class than Rani.	Sita is *not* a taller girl in the class than Rani.

No की तरह *not* के प्रयोग से भी वाक्य negative बन जाता है। *Not* शब्द adverb है। इसका प्रयोग :

(i) उस noun के पहले होता है जिसके पहले article *a/an* लगा हो। जैसे :
He is *not a teacher*.

(ii) उस adjective+noun के पहले होता है जिसके पहले article *a/an* लगा हो। जैसे : She is *not a good girl*.

(iii) Not का प्रयोग adverb के पहले होता है तथा उस adjective के पहले होता है जो noun के बाद आता है। (A *positive adverb, or an adjective used predicatively, cannot be modified by 'no', 'not' must be used.*)

Incorrect	*Correct*
That answer is *no* right.	That answer is *not* right.
She is *no* very well today.	She is *not* very well today.

याद रखें :
(i) ..*not*+a/an+noun: This is *not* a pen.
(ii) ..*not*+a/an+adjective+noun : This is *not* a new pen.
(iii) ..*not*+predicative adjective : The book is *not* new.
(iv) ..not+adverb+adjective : She is *not* very tall.
(v) ...not+verb : He is *not* going today.

(iv) USE OF *'NO/ANY'*

No तथा **Any** के प्रयोग :

(i) Uncountable noun के पहले होता है। जैसे :
I have *no* milk.
Have you *any* milk ?

(ii) Singular countable noun के पहले होता है। जैसे :
He has *no* book.
Has he *any* book ?

(iii) Plural countable noun के पहले होता है। जैसे :
We have *no* pens.
No two men think alike.
Have they *any* pens.

अब आप इस table के वाक्यों को देखें :

He	has no hasn't a	hat. coat. bicycle.
She	has no hasn't any	money. books.

'He has no a hat' गलत है। इसके बदले हम—*He has no hat* या *He hasn't a hat* कहते हैं।

(v) MAKING NEGATIVE SENTENCES

4. *Look at these sentences :*

Affirmative	*Nagative*
Amar is tall.	Amar is *not* tall.
You are happy.	You are *not* happy.
Tom was weak.	Tom was *not* weak.
Moti will help you.	Moti will *not* help you.
Sudha can do it.	Sudha *cannot* do it.
I have eaten a mango.	I have *not* eaten a mango.

(a) ऊपर के वाक्यों में *is, are, was, will, can* तथा *have* के बाद *not* लगाकर उन्हें negative sentence बनाया गया है। (*The negative sentence is made by placing the adverb* **not** *after the anomalous finite.*)

(b) अंगरेजी में 24 ऐसे verbs हैं जिन्हें anomalous finites कहते हैं।

Anomalous Verbs[1]

Present Tense	Past Tense	Present Tense	Past Tense
am, is, are	was, were	may	might
have, has	had	must	—
do, does	did	ought	—
shall	should	need	—
will	would	dare	—
can	could	—	used

1. इन्हें *auxiliary* या *helping verbs* भी कहा जाता है। जिस *verb* का प्रयोग *tense* के *formation* में हो उसे *auxiliary* या *helping verb* कहते हैं। जैसे : They *are* reading. They *were* reading. They *have* gone. He *has* left. Tomorrow *will* be Tuesday. I *shall* be forty-one next year.

इन वाक्यों में *are, were, have, has, will* तथा *shall* auxiliary या helping verbs हैं।

(c) अँगरेजी भाषा में ये 24 verbs काफी महत्त्वपूर्ण हैं क्योंकि वाक्य में इनके बाद *not* लगाकर negative sentence बनाते हैं तथा इन्हें subject के पहले रखकर interrogative sentence बनाते हैं।

5. *Look at these sentences :*

Affirmative	*Negative*
I *like* mangoes	I *do not like* mangoes.
He *comes* here everyday.	He *does not come* here everyday.
We *played* cricket.	We *did not play* cricket.

अगर वाक्य में पहले बताए गए 24 verbs में से कोई नहीं रहे; उसमें केवल full verb (जैसे like, comes, played इत्यादि) रहे तो उस वाक्य के tense of the verb के अनुसार do/does/did+not+V^1 (verb का मूल रूप) का प्रयोग कर उसे negative बनाया जाता है।

(i) *Do* का प्रयोग present tense में first person singular या plural (I, we), second person singular या plural (you) तथा third person plural (they...) के साथ होता है। जैसेः We *do* not *go*.

(ii) *Does* का प्रयोग present tense में third person singular (He, She, It, इत्यादि) के साथ होता है। *Does* के बाद आनेवाला verb अपने मूल रूप अर्थात बिना s/es के रहता है। जैसेः He *goes* home. He *does* not *go*.

(iii) *Did* का प्रयोग past tense में first, second तथा third person के साथ singular और plural दोनों में होता है। जैसे :

He did not play.
They did not play.

इन वाक्यों में *do/does/did* का कोई अर्थ नहीं है, इनका प्रयोग वाक्य को negative बनाने में मदद के लिए किया गया है।

6. *Look at these sentences :*

Affirmative (*Question*)	*Negative* (*Question*)
Do you know his name ?	Do you *not* know his name ? *Don't* you know his name ?
Have you seen him ?	Have you *not* seen him ? *Haven't* you seen him ?
Can you help him ?	Can you *not* help him ? *Can't* you help him ?
Why do you like it ?	Why *do* you *not* like it ? Why *don't* you like it ?

(i) Interrogative sentence में subject के ठीक बाद *not* लगाकर negative बनाया जाता है।

(ii) किंतु interrogative sentence को negative बनाने में अकसर *not* के short form *n't* का प्रयोग किया जाता है तथा *n't* को subject के पहले आए

हुए auxiliary verb के साथ जोड़ देते हैं—(Auxiliary verb+n't + subject...?)

7. *Look at these sentences :*

Affirmative (*Command*)	*Negative* (*command*)
Stand up.	*Don't* (Do not) stand up.
Do it again.	*Don't* (Do not) do it again.
Open the window.	*Don't* (Do not) open the window.
Please write to me.	Please *don't* (do not) write to me.
Let us go home.	Let us *not* go home.

(i) Command में verb के पहले *do not* का प्रयोग कर उसे negative बनाया जाता है। किंतु Spoken English या informal writing में *don't* का प्रयोग किया जाता है।

(ii) Command अगर Please या Let से शुरू हो तो Please या Let के बाद *don't* या *do not* का प्रयोग किया जाता है।

8. *Look at these sentences :*

Affirmative	*Negative*
She told me something.	She *didn't* tell me *anything*. She told me *nothing*.
Peter has some money.	Peter *hasn't any* money. Peter has *no* money.
I was speaking to somebody.	I *wasn't* speaking to *anybody*. I was speaking to *nobody*.
He has seen me somewhere.	He *hasn't* seen me *anywhere*. He has seen me *nowhere*.

ऊपर अँगरेजी के कुछ ऐसे वाक्य हैं जिन्हें दो तरह से negative बनाया गया है :

(i) *no/not* का प्रयोग कर;

(ii) किसी शब्द-विशेष को negative बनाकर।

Note : Infinitive को negative बनाने के लिए *not* को *to* के पहले रखा जाता है। जैसे :

Affirmative	*Negative*
He told me *to go.*	He told me *not to go.*
We tried *to laugh.*	We tried *not to laugh.*
She asked me *to sleep.*	She asked me *not to sleep.*

(vi) NEGATIVE CONTRACTION

Short forms का प्रयोग अकसर Spoken English या informal writing में किया जाता है : जैसे :

aren't—are not
can't—cannot
couldn't—could not
daren't—dare not
didn't—did not
doesn't—does not
don't—do not
hasn't—has not
haven't—have not
hadn't—had not
isn't—is not
mayn't—may not
mightn't—might not
mustn't—must not
needn't—need not
oughtn't—ought not
shan't—shall not
shouldn't—should not
wasn't—was not
weren't—were not
won't—will not
wouldn't—would not

OTHER CONTRACTIONS

(i) Personal pronoun + auxiliary verb

I'm—I am
I've—I have
I'll—I will; I shall
I'd—I would; I should; I had
you're—you are
you've—you have
you'll—you will
you'd—you would; you had
he's—he is; he has
he'll—he will
he'd—he would; he had
she's—she is; she has
she'll—she will
she'd—she would; she had
it's—it is; it has
it'll—it will
we're—we are
we've—we have
we'll—we will
we'd—we would; we had
they're—they are
they've—they have
they'll—they will
they'd—they would; they had

(ii) Some other common contractions

here's—here is
there's—there is
that's—that is
that'll—that will
how's—how is ?
what'll—what will ?
what's—what is ?
when's—when is ?
where's—where is ?
who's—who is ?
who'd—who would ?
who'll—who will ?

Note : (i) *cannot* एक साथ लिखा जाता है; किंतु *could not* अलग-अलग।

(ii) *mayn't* तथा *mightn't* का प्रयोग प्रायः नहीं किया जाता।

8. *Look at these sentences :*

(i) *They're* not boys.
They've not written it.
Sonu's not here.

(ii) They *aren't* boys.
They *haven't* written it.
Sonu *isn't* here.

(i) जब auxiliary verb का लघु रूप subject के साथ जुटा रहता है तब negative में *not* का पूरा रूप लिखा जाता है।

(ii) **जब** auxiliary verb **का पूरा रूप लिखा जाता है तब उसके साथ** *not* **का लघु रूप** *n't* **जोड़ दिया जाता है।**

Formal writing	*Spoken English or informal writing*	
A	*B*	*C*
1. I am not....	I'm not...	....
2. You are not....	You're not....	You aren't....
3. We are not...	We're not...	We aren't...
4. He is not...	He's not...	He isn't....
5. He was not....	....	He wasn't....
6. She is not...	She's not...	She isn't....
7. It is not....	It's not...	It isn't....
8. They are not...	They're not...	They aren't....
9. Raju is not...	....	Raju isn't....
10. This is not....	....	This isn't....
11. That is not....	That's not...	That isn't....
12. These are not....	.....	These aren't...
13. Those are not...	....	Those aren't....
14. There is not....	There's not...	There isn't.....
15. There are not....	......,	There aren't....

Note : (i) { There aren*'t any* boys in the classroom.
There are *no* boys in the classroom. }

{ There is*n't any* ink in the pen.
There is *no* ink in the pen. }

ऊपर के युगल वाक्यों के अर्थ में कोई अंतर नहीं है। ....*n't any* **या** *no* **का प्रयोग** negative sentences **में किया जा सकता है; इनके बाद आनेवाले** nouns countable (singular/plural) **या** uncountable **हो सकते हैं।**

(ii) *Have* **को हम कई तरह से** negative **बना सकते हैं :**

Sima *hasn't* a car.
Sima *hasn't got* a car.
Sima *doesn't have* a car.

(vii) KINDS OF INTERROGATIVE SENTENCES

Questions **मुख्यतः निम्नलिखित प्रकार के होते हैं :**

(i) Yes/No Questions
(ii) Wh-Questions
(iii) Alternative Questions
(iv) Rhetorical Questions
(v) Tag Questions
(vi) Short Questions

10. *Look at these sentences :*

Does it taste bitter ? { Yes, it does.
No, it doesn't. }

Did he remain happy ? { Yes, he did. / No, he didn't.

Did he become a good scholar ? { Yes, he did. / No, he didn't.

जिस question का answer *yes/no* में दिया जा सके उसे yes/no question कहते हैं।

11. *Look at these sentences :*

Who is Sonu ?	Sonu is *my brother.*
What is Mr Sharma ?	Mr Sharma is *a teacher.*
Where is Mr Bose ?	Mr Bose is *in his office.*

Who, whom, whose, which, where, why, when तथा why से पूछे जानेवाले प्रश्न wh-questions कहलाते हैं। इन्हें information questions भी कहा जाता है।

Note : कभी-कभी एक wh-question में दो wh-word रहते हैं। जैसे :

Who is bringing *what ?*
How and *when* did you arrive ?
Where did you go and *why ?*

12. *Look at these sentences :*

Are you eating or not ?
Is this a pen or a pencil ?
What are monkeys, animals or insects ?

वैसे questions जिनमें or लगा रहे alternative questions कहलाते हैं।

13. *Look at these sentences :*

Who can predict the future ?	(No one can.)
Who will do this dirty work ?	(No one will.)
Do you think no one will marry me ?	(Someone will, surely.)

ये सारे प्रश्न forceful statements हैं किंतु ये question form में हैं। इन्हें rhetorical questions कहते हैं। Positive rhetorical question से strong negative भाव व्यक्त होता है तथा negative rhetorical question से strong positive भाव व्यक्त होता है। ऊपर brackets में दिए गए वाक्यों को देखें।

14. *Look at these sentences :*

She isn't here, *is she ?*
I am a teacher, *aren't I ?*
Honey tastes sweet, *doesn't it ?*

किसी statement के अंत में लगे हुए question को tag question कहते हैं। इसका उद्देश्य सुननेवाले का ध्यान उस statement पर खींचना होता है।

15. *Look at these sentences :*

(A) The old lady is buying a house.
(B) When ?/Where ?/Why ?/Which house ?/What old lady ?

(A) I am going to write an adventure story.
(B) What for ?/Who for ?/With whom ?/

कभी-कभी किसी statement के उत्तर में जब सुननेवाला कुछ और अधिक information चाहता है तब वह एक word या दो words का question पूछता है तथा वैसा प्रश्न grammar में short question कहलाता है।

(viii) CHANGING ASSERTIVE INTO INTERROGATIVE

Grammar की भाषा में transformation तथा change में अंतर है। Transformation of the sentence का अर्थ होता है : बिना वाक्य के अर्थ को बदले उसके रूप (form) को बदल देना। जैसे:

Everyone would love his country. —Assertive
Who would not love his country ? —Interrogative

To transform a sentence is to change it from one grammatical form to another without altering its sense. —NESFIELD

किंतु जब assertive को interrogative में change करते हैं तब subject+verb की जगह verb+subject अर्थात पहले verb फिर subject का word order लगाते हैं और तब उस वाक्य का meaning भी बदल जाता है। जैसे :

He is tall — Assertive
Is he tall ? — Interrogative

आगे हम changing assertive sentences into interrogative की बात करेंगे, transformation की नहीं। आप जानते हैं—interrogative या question उस वाक्य को कहते हैं जिसमें कुछ प्रश्न निहित हो या जिसके द्वारा कोई सूचना माँगी जाए।

Questions are typical sentences by which someone asks his hearer to give information.

16. *Look at these sentences :*

Statements	*Questions*
I am right.	*Am* I right ?
They are tall.	*Are* they tall ?
Rana is a student.	*Is* Rana a student ?
Tom was writing.	*Was* Tom writing ?
She has a hat.	*Has* she a hat ?

(i) Statement में subject + verb (I am..) का शब्द-क्रम रहता है किंतु question में verb + subject (Am I...) का।

(ii) Modern English में केवल *24 anomalous verbs (am, is, are, was, were, have, has, had, do, does, did, shall, should, will, would, can, could, may, might, must, ought, need, dare, used*) को subject के पहले रखकर प्रश्नबोधक वाक्य (interrogative sentence) बनाते हैं।

(iii) Statement के अंत में full stop (.) लगता है किंतु question के अंत में question mark (?) लगाया जाता है।

Note : American English में जब *have* का प्रयोग full verb की तरह होता है तब उसे question बनाने में पहले *Do/Does/Did* का प्रयोग किया जाता है। जैसे :

Do they *have* a new car ?
Does he *have* enough money ?
Did they *have* a large house ?

17. *Look at these sentences :*

Statements	*Questions*
I know him.	*Do* I *know* him ?
Sima likes it.	*Does* Sima *like* it ?
They went home.	*Did* they *go* home ?

(i) अगर वाक्य में 24 anomalous verbs में से कोई न हो तो subject के पहले अपनी ओर से *Do/Does/Did* लगाकर उस वाक्य को interrogative बनाया जाता है।

(ii) Present tense में singular subject के साथ *does*, तथा plural subject के साथ *do* लगता है। I तथा you के साथ भी *do* लगता है; *does* नहीं।

(iii) Past tense में किसी भी subject के साथ did लगता है।

(iv) याद रखें : *Does/Did* के बाद verb हमेशा अपने मूल रूप में रहता है। जैसे :

He *goes. Does* he *go ? (goes* नहीं होगा।)
She *played. Did* she *play ? (played* नहीं होगा।)

18. *Look at these sentences :*

Statements	*Wh-Questions*
He is at home. (*Where*)	*Where* is he ?
Ram will go today. (*When*)	*When* will Ram go ?
You came for help. (*Why*)	*Why* did you come ?
Boys like sweets. (*What*)	*What* do boys like ?
Hari lives in a village. (*Where*)	*Where* does Hari live ?
She has come here by car. (*How*)	*How* has she come here ?

(i) *Who, whom, whose, what, where, when, which, why* तथा *how* से शुरू होनेवाले प्रश्न *wh-questions* या *information questions* कहलाते हैं।

(ii) *Wh-questions* का form इस प्रकार होता है;

Wh-word + anomalous verb + subject + main verb....
Why + has + he + come ?

(iii) अगर statement में anomalous verb नहीं रहे तो उसे *wh-question* बनाते समय उसमें अपनी ओर से *do/does/did* लगाते हैं, नहीं तो वाक्य अशुद्ध हो जाएगा। जैसे :

Statements	*Questions*	
	Right	*wrong*
Mukul plays here.	Where *does* Mukul play ?	Where Mukul plays ?
You live there.	Where *do* you live ?	Where you live ?
He said it.	What *did* he say ?	What he said ?

19. *Look at these sentences :*

Negative Statements	*Negative Questions*
It *isn't* your ball.	*Isn't* it your ball ?
They *aren't* playing.	*Aren't* they playing ?
Sita *didn't* eat.	*Didn't* Sita eat ?
You *don't* like tea.	*Don't* you like tea ?
I *am not* crying.	*Aren't* I crying ?
They *have not* a car.	*Haven't* they a car ?

(i) Negative statements को negative questions बनाने में auxiliary + n't को subject के पहले रखते हैं :

Aux. + n't + subject + main verb.... ?

Isn't + Abdul + reading ?

(ii) 'I am not' का interrogative रूप 'Aren't I' या 'Am I not' होता है।

20. *Look at these sentences :*

Negative Statements	*Negative questions*
This *is not* a book.	*Is* this *not* a book ?
	(*Isn't* this a book ?)
You *have not* a bicycle.	*Have* you *not* a bicycle ?
	(*Haven't* you a bicycle ?
I *cannot* do this.	*Can* I *not* do this ?
	(*Can't* I do this ?)

(i) अगर negative statement में *not* का full form रहे तो केवल auxiliary verb को subject के पहले रखने से वह interrogative बन जाता है।

(ii) अगर *not* को n't में बदलकर interrogative बनाना चाहें तो auxiliary + n't को subject के पहले रखते हैं।

(iii) Interrogative में *have/has/had+ not* का अकसर short form में ही प्रयोग होता है।

(vii) SOME TYPICAL MISTAKES IN MAKING QUESTIONS

Questions या Interrogative sentences बनाने में हम कभी-कभी कई तरह के mistakes करते हैं, जिनमें से कुछ मुख्य इस प्रकार हैं :

21. *Look at these sentences :*

Incorrect	*Correct*
He has done the work ?	*Has he* done the work ?
You have received my letter of June ?	*Have you* received my letter of June ?

Written English तथा अकसर Spoken English में भी Questions में subject के पहले auxiliary verb (जैसे: has, have) को रखा जाता है।

22. *Look at these sentences :*

Incorrect	*Correct*
Like you tea ?	*Do you like* tea ?
What *means* 'phonetics' ?	What *does* 'phonetics' *mean ?*

अगर वाक्य में auxiliary verb नहीं रहे तो इसके question form में अपनी ओर से auxiliary verb *do, does, did* का प्रयोग किया जाता है।

23. *Look at these sentences :*

Incorrect	*Correct*
Did you *went* there ?	*Did* you *go* there ?
Does he *runs* fast ?	*Does* he *run* fast ?

Do, did तथा does के बाद आनेवाला verb अपने मूल रूप (अर्थात infinitive without *to*) में रहता है।

24. *Look at these sentences :*

Incorrect	*Correct*
Do you can tell me the time ?	*Can you tell* me the time ?
Do you have seen Sima today ?	*Have you seen* Sima today ?

अगर वाक्य में कोई auxiliary verb अथवा modal auxiliary verb *can, could, may, might, will, would, shall, should, must, ought* रहे तो question form बनाने में do का प्रयोग नहीं किया जाता।

25. *Look at these sentences :*

Incorrect	*Correct*
Is coming your mother today ?	*Is* your mother *coming* today ?
When was built this house ?	*When was* this house *built ?*

Question form में केवल auxiliary verb को subject के पहले रखते हैं तथा rest of the verb phrase को subject के बाद रखते हैं।

26. *Look at these sentences :*

Incorrect	*Correct*
Why *you are laughing ?*	Why *are you laughing ?*
How much *it costs ?*	How much *does it cost ?*

अगर कोई question किसी question-word (जैसे : why, how, where, what, when इत्यादि) से शुरू हो तो auxiliary verb को subject के पहले और main verb को subject के बाद रखा जाता है।

27. *Look at these sentences :*

Incorrect	*Correct*
Tell me when *are you going ?*	Tell me when *you are going.*
I ask him which book *does she like.*	I ask him which book *she likes.*

Reported questions अर्थात Indirect narration में affirmative sentence का word-order होता है subject + verb; अर्थात पहले subject और उसके बाद verb आता है।

28. *Look at these sentences :*

Incorrect	*Correct*
Which *does cost* more ?	Which *costs* more ?
What *did happen ?*	What *happened ?*
Who *did leave* the door open ?	Who *left* the door open ?

अगर which, what तथा who वाक्य का subject हो तो इसे verb के ठीक पहले रखा जाता है तथा *do, does, did* का प्रयोग नहीं किया जाता।

Note : किंतु जब who, what तथा which वाक्य का object रहे तब सामान्य नियम के अनुसार question form में *do, does, did* का प्रयोग किया जाता है। जैसे :

What *do* you *think* ?
Who *do* you *want* to speak to ?

(viii) CHANGING INTERROGATIVE INTO ASSERTIVE

Interrogative sentence को assertive sentence में बदलने के लिए नीचे दिए गए नियमों की जानकारी आवश्यक है।

29. *Look at these sentences :*

Interrogative	*Assertive*
Is it a book ?	It *is* a book.
Are they ill ?	They *are* ill.
Was he playing ?	He *was* playing.
Can you do it ?	You *can* do it.

(i) अगर interrogative sentence में 24 anomalous verbs में से कोई हो, तो उसे subject के बाद रखकर वाक्य को assertive बनाया जाता है।

(ii) वाक्य के अंत में question mark (?) की जगह full stop (.) दिया जाता है।

30. *Look at these sentences :*

Interrogative	*Assertive*
Do you know him ? (Do + know = know)	You *know* him.
Does he smoke ? (Does + smoke = smokes)	He *smokes.*
Did they say this ? (Did + say = said)	They *said* this.

(i) अगर प्रश्नबोधक वाक्य *Do/Does/Did* से शुरू हों तो उसे कथनात्मक वाक्य बनाने के लिए *Do/Does/Did* को हटा दिया जाता है।

(ii) *Do* हटाने के बाद वाक्य में कोई दूसरा परिवर्तन नहीं करना पड़ता।

(iii) *Does* को हटा देने के बाद main verb में *s/es* लगाना पड़ता है।

(iv) *Did* को हटाने के बाद main verb को past tense में बदलना पड़ता है।

31. *Look at these sentences :*

Direct Questions	*Indirect Questions*
	I want to know
What *is his name ?*	what *his name is.*
Where *has he* gone ?	where *he has* gone.
When *will she* come ?	when *she will* come.

(i) Direct question में verb + subject...रहता है, किंतु indirect question में subject + verb का शब्द-क्रम रहता है।

(ii) Direct question के अंत में question mark (?) रहता है; indirect question के अंत में full stop (.) दिया जाता है।

32. *Look at these sentences :*

Direct Questions	*Indirect Questions*
	I want to know
What *do* you *want ?*	what you *want.*
How *does* he *come ?*	how he *comes.*
Where *did* he *go ?*	where he *went.*

Indirect question में *do/does/did* को हटा दिया जाता है तथा main verb में *do/does/did* के अनुसार कुछ परिवर्तन करते हैं (जैसे: do + want = want; does + come = comes; did + go = went.)

33. *Look at these sentences :*

Direct Questions	*Indirect Questions*
	I want to know
Who called me ?	who called me.
Which came here ?	which came here.
What happened to him ?	what happened to him.

अगर direct question में केवल एक finite verb[1] **रहे तो indirect question में उसका स्थान-परिवर्तन नहीं होता।**

Examples Worked Out

(i) *Change the following sentences into negative :*

	Affirmative	*Negative*
1.	The room is very warm.	The room *is not* (*isn't*) very warm.
2.	They are learning English.	They *are not* (*aren't*) learning English.
3.	Tom has a new book.	Tom *has not (hasn't)* a new book.
4.	We have seen him.	We *have not* (*haven't*) seen him.
5.	I can hear what you say.	I *cannot* (*can't*) hear what you say.
6.	Sita will pass the examination.	Sita *will not* (*won't*) pass the examination.
7.	You must do that.	You *must not* (*mustn't*) do that.
8.	They should speak Bengali.	They *should not* (*shouldn't*) speak Bengali.
9.	We need start now.	We *need not* (*needn't*) start now.
10.	The school was closed yesterday.	The school *was not* (*wasn't*) closed yesterday.
11.	The exercises were easy.	The exercises *were not* (*weren't*) easy.
12.	We shall go to the meeting.	We *shall not* (*shan't*) go to the meeting.
13.	Rani works very hard.	Rani *does not* (*doesn't*) work very hard.
14.	Moti went to Bombay.	Moti *did not* (*didn't*) go to Bombay.
15.	The boys play hockey.	The boys *do not* (*don't*) play hockey.
16.	They came here yesterday.	They *did not* (*didn't*) come here yesterday.
17.	You saw me.	You *did not* (*didn't*) see me.
18.	Will you do it ?	*Will* you *not* (*won't* you) do it ?
19.	Does he know my name ?	*Does* he *not* (*Doesn't* he) know my name ?
20.	Has he taken it ?	*Has* he *not* (*Hasn't* he) taken it ?

---

1. *A verb that agrees with its subject in number and in person is called a finite verb, e.g., I* **play.** *He* **plays.** *They* **play.**

	Affirmative	*Negative*
21.	Can you touch the fan ?	*Can* you *not* (*Can't* you) touch the fan ?
22.	Why did you do it ?	Why *did* you *not* (*didn't* you) do it ?
23.	Should I see you ?	*Should* I *not* (*Shouldn't* I) see you ?
24.	Who says so ?	Who *does not* (*doesn't*) say so ?
25.	Wait for him.	*Do not* (*Don't*) wait for him.
26.	Please do it.	Please *do not* (*don't*) do it.
27.	Do it now.	*Do not* (*Don't*) do it now.
28	Let us go home.	Let us *not* go home.
29.	May he prosper.	May he *not* prosper.
30.	Boys, stand up.	Boys, *do not* (*don't*) stand up.
31.	Ask him to see me.	*Do not* (*Don't*) ask him to see me.
32.	Rekha has some bags.	Rekha *has not* any bags. (Rekha *hasn't* any bags.)
33.	I gave you something.	I gave you *nothing*. (I *didn't* give you *anything*).
34.	Anybody can do it.	*Nobody* can do it.
35.	Her mother is coming, too.	Her mother *is not* (*isn't*) coming *either*.
36.	I was speaking to someone.	I was speaking to *no one*. I *wasn't* speaking to *anyone*.

(ii) *Change the following statements into questions :*

	Statements	*Questions*
1.	Peter is late today.	*Is* Peter late today ?
2.	You are certain.	*Are* you certain ?
3.	The iron is hot.	*Is* the iron hot ?
4	It will break soon.	*Will* it break soon ?
5.	Reeta has a toy.	*Has* Reeta a toy ?
6.	There was a snake.	*Was* there a snake ?
7.	The thieves were caught.	*Were* the thieves caught ?
8.	Ramu can speak English.	*Can* Ramu speak English ?
9.	The car is working well.	*Is* the car working well ?
10.	She should learn music.	*Should* she learn music ?
11.	You must work hard.	*Must* you work hard ?
12.	He writes well.	*Does* he write well ?
13.	We live in India.	*Do* we live in India ?
14.	Rajeev sent a letter.	*Did* Rajeev send a letter ?

Statements	*Questions*
15. You can't come with me.	*Can't* you come with me ?
16. She won't sing now.	*Won't* she sing now ?
17. They aren't very old.	*Aren't* they very old ?
18. He didn't ask you to wait.	*Didn't* he ask you to wait ?
19. You were not going to school.	*Were* you not going to (*Weren't* you going to school ?)
20. I am not very fat.	*Am* I not very fat ? (*Aren't* I very fat ?)
21. I told him not to go there.	*Did* I tell him not to go there ?
22. My friend knows you.	*Does* my friend know you ?
23. There is a school here.	*Is* there a school here ?
24. They are disturbing me.	*Are* they disturbing me ?
25. They are not disturbing me.	*Are* they not (*Aren't* they) disturbing me ?
26. I thanked him.	Did I thank him ?
27. I have appointed him.	*Have* I appointed him ?
28. I can do the work.	*Can* I do the work ?
29. It rained yesterday.	*Did* it rain yesterday ?
30. They mustn't go there.	*Mustn't* they go there ?
31. He has applied for this job.	*Has* he applied for this job ?
32. We must listen to his words.	*Must* we listen to his words ?
33. I saw someone in the house.	*Did* I see someone in the house ?
34. There is nothing wrong with me.	*Is* there nothing wrong with me ?
35. Nobody else would have done it.	*Would* nobody else have done it ?
36. The telegraph wires have been cut.	*Have* the telegraph wires been cut?
37. The Ethiopian cannot change his colour.	Can the Ethiopian not (*Can't* the Ethiopian) change his colour ?

(iii) *Frame questions with the question words given in brackets against each sentence :*

Statements	*Questions*
1. They want a book. (*What*)	*What do* they want ?
2. She lives in Madras. (*Where*)	*Where does* she live ?
3. Tom will come today. (*When*)	*When will* Tom come ?
4. They are crying for milk. (*Why*)	*Why are* they crying ?
5. This is Ruby's house. (*Whose*)	*Whose* house is this ?
6. That tall girl stood first. (*Which*)	*Which* girl stood first ?
7. Mr Bose is there. (*Who*)	*Who* is there ?
8. It costs three rupees. (*How much*)	*How much does* it cost ?

Statements	Questions
9. I want a pen to write with. (*What*)	*What do* you want to write with ?
10. He gave it to his friend. (*Who*)	*Who* did he give it to ?
11. He gave it to his friend. (*Whom*)	To *whom* did he give it ?

(iv) *Change the following interrogative sentences into assertive :*

Interrogative	Assertive
1. Can he walk ?	He *can walk*.
2. Has the train left ?	The train *has left*.
3. Should I answer the letter ?	I *should answer* the letter.
4. Must they call off the strike ?	They *must call off* the strike.
5. Will they come tomorrow ?	They *will come* tomorrow.
6. Do you like coffee ?	You *like* coffee.
7. Does he play tennis ?	He *plays* tennis.
8. Did the bus arrive on time ?	The bus *arrived* on time.
9. Isn't it your car ?	It *isn't* your car.
10. Weren't they hungry ?	They *weren't* hungry.
11. Will you not go there ?	You *will not go* there.
12. Don't you like tea ?	You *don't like* tea.
13. Haven't they any house ?	They *haven't* any house.

EXERCISE 1

Use **no** *or* **not** *in the blank spaces in the following sentences :*

EXAMPLES : (i) The poor boy had...money for books.
= The poor boy had *no* money for books.
(ii) .....a single person knew the answer.
Not a single person knew the answer.

Note : (a) 'No' adjective तथा adverb दोनों है। अतः, *no* का प्रयोग noun तथा adjective (positive या comparative degree) + noun के पहले होता है।

(b) 'Not' adverb है। इसका प्रयोग verb तथा adverb के पहले एवं उस adjective के पहले होता है जो noun के बाद आता है (before the predicative use of adjective).

1. The poor boy had.........money for books.
2. ....a single person knew the answer.
3. There was.........end to our trouble.
4. She is.........friend of mine.
5. The speech was.........very interesting.
6. The task is.........easy one.
7. Rana is.........a tall boy.
8. Miss Green is.........beauty.
9. Smoking is.........allowed.

10. There are.........boys.
11. We went.........farther than the bridge.
12. We did.........play cricket yesterday.
13. There was.........a sound to be heard in the room.
14. I have.........more money.
15. We have.........found better hotels anywhere.
16. You could make.........greater mistake than that.
17. There is.........a cleverer girl in the school than Reeta.
18. ....a star was to be seen in the sky yesterday.
19. There is.........the slightest truth in the story.
20. ....a word was said about the coming examination.

EXERCISE 2

Make the following sentences negative. Write both the short and the full forms. Put the short forms within brackets :

EXAMPLES : (i) He is ready. =He *is not* (*isn't*) ready.
(ii) They went to Patna. =They *did not* (*didn't*) go to Patna.

1. He is ready.
2. They went to Patna.
3. You are right.
4. The girl is tall.
5. Mr Sen can stay here.
6. Mintu has a new skirt.
7. I am late today.
8. We can read English.
9. She must do it now.
10. It was dark in the room.
11. There was a strong wind yesterday.
12. We had a nice time.
13. The class began at 10 o'clock.
14. Manju saw a thief yesterday.
15. The examination was very difficult.
16. We have a television set.
17. Your friend has arrived.
18. I found that book very interesting.
19. Miss Sinha arrived at eight o'clock.
20. Sohan spends his money wisely.

EXERCISE 3

Make the following sentences negative. Write both the full ~~and~~ short forms. Put the short forms within brackets :

EXAMPLES : (i) Close the door, please.
= *Do not* (*Don't*) close the door, please.

(ii) Why did you come here ?
= Why *did* you *not* (*didn't* you) come here ?

1. Close the door, please.
2. Why did you come here ?
3. Are you Mr Prasad ?
4. Tell him a story, father.
5. Shall I go with him ?
6. Does Reeta sing with you ?
7. Keep the gate closed.
8. Walk on the grass.
9. Stay a little longer.
10. Does he speak English well ?
11. Is that book very easy to read ?
12. Open the window, please.
13. Stand up in the class.
14. Do you like English grammar ?
15. Pass me the sugar, Rani.
16. Give me another chance.
17. Will you have another cup of coffee ?
18. Turn to page 50 in your grammar book.
19. Did her friend write a letter from Delhi ?
20. Let him have a look at your answer.

EXERCISE 4

Add suitable negatives. Use only short forms :

EXAMPLE : (i) Mr Sharma is a teacher, he...a doctor.
= Mr Sharma is a teacher, he *isn't* a doctor.

1. Mr Sharma is a teacher; he.....a doctor.
2. The dog is small but elephants.....small.
3. He has two brothers but he.....a sister.
4. We have played five matches but we.....lost any.
5. I can play tennis but I.....play hockey.
6. They have bought a bat but they.....like it.
7. Madan.....want anything; he just came to see you.
8. Sima looked at five frocks but she.....buy any.
9. He was tired but he.....ill.
10. I asked him a question but he.....answer it.
11. Mr Prasad is tall but he.....fat.
12. His face is familiar but I.....remember him.
13. John speaks English; he.....speak Russian.
14. I am an Indian; I.....a Japanese.
15. You should labour hard; you.....neglect your studies.
16. The hotels were generally open but they.....open yesterday.
17. I have taken my books; I.....taken yours.
18. Something must be wrong; we.....be nervous.
19. She is ill but she.....look weak.
20. Amar took the examination but he.....pass it.

EXERCISE 5

Make the following sentences questions :

EXAMPLES : (i) They are your friends.= Are they your friends ?
(ii) Rekha is not lucky.= *Is* Rekha *not* lucky ? *Isn't* Rekha lucky ?

1. They are your friends.
2. Rekha is not lucky.
3. I am very tall.
4. Abdul will sing a song.
5. The dog was greedy.
6. They are our teachers.
7. Meera is going to cook.
8. I can run as fast as you.
9. We shall finish the work today.
10. They have been to London.
11. You have not any money.
12. Boys have not gone home.
13. It is not half-past ten.
14. The radio has not to be repaired.
15. Amar was not in time today.
16. We had not an enjoyable holiday.
17. That car is not very beautiful.
18. I should improve my handwriting.
19. We will not go to the canteen now.
20. These boys were playing hockey yesterday.

EXERCISE 6

Make the following sentences questions :

EXAMPLES : (i) You eat meat. = *Do* you eat meat ?
(ii) I wanted a cup of tea. = *Did* I *want* a cup of tea ?

1. You eat meat.
2. I wanted a cup of tea.

3. We like our English teacher.
4. The peon rings the bell.
5. They made us laugh.
6. I sit in the library for hours.
7. He takes English lessons everyday.
8. She feels well today.
9. Mr Sinha lives in that house.
10. They often go to the pictures.
11. Her dress looks beautiful.
12. That girl won the first prize.
13. Madan ran very fast yesterday.
14. They try to understand English.
15. Mukul wants to be a scientist.
16. You write to them every week.
17. Doctors earn a lot of money.
18. The sun rises in the east.
19. He succeeded in solving the problem.
20. I congratulated him on his success.

EXERCISE 7

Make the following sentences questions :

EXAMPLES : (i) The price includes postage. = *Does* the price include postage ?

(ii) We must listen to his words. = *Must* we listen to his words ?

1. The price includes postage.
2. We must listen to his words.
3. She will help me.
4. I can do this work.
5. He does not like fish.
6. He did not honour the agreement.
7. Mary comes here daily.
8. No one likes to pay taxes.
9. A man cannot change his nature.
10. John is going to Calcutta tomorrow.
11. India is a noble country.
12. I turned him out of the class.
13. I don't want more than I deserve.
14. People don't like to stand in queues.
15. A doctor lives in the next house.
16. I gave him a book.
17. A man cannot live for ever.
18. You play football.
19. She does not sing.
20. I cried out for help.

EXERCISE 8

Make the following sentences questions :

EXAMPLES : (i) No man can pay respect to a bad man.
= *Can* no man pay respect to a bad man ?

(ii) Students do not tolerate injustice.
= *Do* students not tolerate injustice ?
Or, *Don't* students tolerate injustice ?

1. He went to Calcutta.
2. Ram eats fruit.
3. I shall help you.
4. She will come tomorrow.
5. You don't like tea.
6. They must call off the strike.
7. I asked him to wait.
8. It is a bad idea.
9. We should start in time.
10. Sheela can write a long letter.
11. He knows Spanish.
12. Sita cannot sing.
13. I wanted a good novel.
14. Ram is going to learn Sanskrit.
15. He pays attention to his work.
16. I cannot repay your kindness.
17. Everyone would love his country.
18. We can never forget this incident.
19. I can tell you what he expects.
20. You must be home by 10 o'clock.

EXERCISE 9

Make the following sentences questions :

EXAMPLE : (i) Fair words and promises are of no avail in the time of danger.
=*Are* fair words and promises of no avail in the time of danger ?

1. No one can bear an unprovoked insult.
2. I shall never forget those happy days.
3. Students do not tolerate injustice.
4. No man can pay respect to a wicked man.
5. There is nothing better than a busy life.
6. The beauty of Nature is beyond description
7. No one ever saw a brighter dawn than this.
8. That is not the way to answer a question.
9. Raja always speaks to the professor.
10. You would know him if you saw him.
11. Every man thinks himself intelligent.
12. There are some books on the table.
13. One cannot gather grapes from thistles.
14. You never hear of a happy millionaire.
15. Macbeth hoped to succeed Duncan.
16. There's no fool like an old fool.
17. Your father will give you a gift.
18. No man can live in the world for all time to come.
19. Fair words and promises are of no avail in the time of danger.
20. It is foolish to waste time in reading trash.

EXERCISE 10

Ask questions. Begin each question with the question word given within brackets Put a question mark at the end of each question :

EXAMPLES : (i) The bus is half an hour late. (How)
= *How* late is the bus ?

(ii) His name is Rajeev. (What)
= *What* is his name ?

1. The bus is half an hour late. (How)
2. His name is Rajeev. (What)
3. Tom is six feet tall. (How)
4. Moti was born in 1970. (When)
5. That is Mohan's school. (Whose)
6. Tagore wrote *Gitanjali.* (Who)
7. My brother is in New York. (Where)
8. He has come here for money. (Why)
9. That is Hari's dog. (Whose)
10. They will go tomorrow. (When)
11. She will come in the evening. (When)
12. His father is a farmer. (What)
13. The car was made in Japan. (Where)
14. The meeting will start now. (When)

15. **The radio is on the table.** **(Where)**
16. **You saw a thief last night.** **(Who)**
17. **Democracy is rule by the people.** **(What)**
18. **The lion is the strongest animal in the world.** **(Which)**
19. **Sunil Gavaskar was the captain of our cricket team.** **(Who)**
20. **Jack is absent from the class because of illness.** **(Why)**

EXERCISE 11

Ask questions using the question words given within brackets :

EXAMPLES : (i) Mukul came here for books. (Why)
= *Why* did Mukul come here ?

(ii) He reads in class X. (What)
= *What* class does he read in ?

(iii) You go home once a month. (How often)
= *How often* do you go home ?

1. Mukul came here for books. (Why)
2. He reads in class X. (What)
3. You go home once a month. (How often)
4. The poem describes Lucy. (What)
5. Children made noises for sweets. (Why)
6. I chose this for myself. (Which)
7. We go to see a film on Sundays. (When)
8. The Prime Minister lives in Delhi. (Where)
9. Mr Sen will teach us English. (What)
10. The minister came here last week. (When)
11. Sima bought five bangles yesterday. (How many)
12. The wall is ten feet high. (How high)
13. This boy is ten minutes late. (How late)
14. This pen costs five rupees. (How much)
15. The play lasted for two hours. (How long)
16. This girl is sixteen years old. (How old)
17. This river is ten metres deep here. (How deep)
18. There are five colleges in this town. (How many)
19. This car can run sixty kilometres an hour. (How fast)
20. Your village is forty kilometres from here. (How far)

EXERCISE 12

Change these questions into statements :

EXAMPLES : (i) Are you certain ? = You *are* certain.

(ii) Isn't it a pen ? = It *isn't* a pen.

1. Are you certain ?
2. Isn't it a pen ?
3. Is the radio on ?
4. Did they win ?
5. Is Mukul working ?
6. Hasn't he a car ?
7. Can I help you ?
8. Will you write to me ?
9. Was his answer right ?
10. Were they happy ?

11. Did the bus stop ?
12. Do you know Mr Roy ?
13. Did he ask me a question ?
14. Should he answer the letter ?
15. Would you do it for me ?
16. Won't you come to me tonight ?
17. Don't you like black coffee ?
18. Shall I close the window ?
19. Have you seen the Taj Mahal ?
20. Could I borrow your bicycle ?

EXERCISE 13

Put **I want to know** *in front of the questions below and change them into indirect questions :*

EXAMPLES : (i) What is it ? = *I want to know* what it *is.*

(ii) Where is my car ? = *I want to know* where my car *is.*

1. What is it ?
2. Where is my car ?
3. How is she today ?
4. When does he go ?
5. Whose house is it ?
6. Why are your shoes dirty ?
7. Which is his cup ?
8. How does it open ?
9. What is your name ?
10. Who are they ?
11. Why is John absent ?
12. What do you want ?
13. Where are the keys ?
14. When will you come ?
15. What is she doing ?
16. Where did he live ?
17. Who has broken the cup ?
18. Who called you here ?
19. Why do you shout in the class ?
20. How much will it cost ?

EXERCISE 14

Make the following sentences (a) negative, (b) questions and (c) negative questions. (Use short forms) :

EXAMPLE : Today is Sunday.
(a) Today *isn't* Sunday. —*Negative*
(b) Is today Sunday ? —*Question*
(c) *Isn't* today Sunday ? —*Negative Question*

1. Today is Sunday.
2. Mr Sinha is in the office.
3. You are a good student.
4. Sita will sing a song.
5. It sounds all right.
6. He became a doctor.
7. The prices have gone up.
8. The clerks are typing letters.
9. Dark clouds bring rain.
10. There were sixty people at the party.
11. The man would like to see you.
12. Stupid people have stupid faces.
13. He has two brothers and a sister.
14. We should spend more time on English.
15. Mohan can complete the task today.
16. My mother liked a red *sari.*
17. He bought a watch for his sister.
18. The peon has closed the gate.
19. He must tell me everything.
20. Rani was happy to see her friends.

□ □ □

8. ACTIVE AND PASSIVE VOICE

[*FORM AND USE*]

(i) FORM

1. ***Look at these sentences :***

A	**B**
Tom *kicks* the ball.	The ball *is kicked by* Tom.
Tom *kicked* the ball.	The ball *was kicked by* Tom.
Tom *will kick* the ball.	The ball *will be kicked by* Tom.

(i) स्तंभ A के नीचे दिए गए वाक्य *Active Voice* में हैं तथा स्तंभ *B* के नीचे दिए गए वाक्य *Passive Voice* में हैं।

(ii) Active sentences की बनावट एक तरह से है तथा passive sentences की बनावट दूसरी तरह से।

(iii) Active तथा passive sentences के अर्थ में अंतर नहीं होता।

CHANGING ACTIVE VOICE INTO PASSIVE

(a) Verb form

2. ***Look at these sentences :***

Active	*Passive*
Mukul *posts* the letter.	The letter is *posted* by Mukul.
The cats *drank* the milk.	The milk *was drunk* by the cats.
Sita *will buy* the book.	The book *will be bought* by Sita.

(i) Voice का संबंध वाक्य के verb से होता है। Verb का रूप active sentence में जैसा होता है वैसा passive sentence में नहीं होता।

(ii) Passive sentence में active sentence के verb को V^3 यानी *past participle* रूप में बदलते हैं। तथा :

(iii) उसके पहले उस verb के tense के अनुसार verb *to be* (*am, is, are, was, were, being, been*) का प्रयोग किया जाता है।

(iv) Passive subject के अनुसार ही verb का *number* भी बदलता है; जैसे :

Hari *helps* the boys. (Active)
The boys *are helped* by Hari. (Passive)

(b) Subject and Object

3. *Look at these sentences :*

Active	*Passive*
Rani writes *a story.*	*A story* is written by *Rani.*
Hari helped *Moti.*	*Moti* was helped by *Hari.*
Mr Jha will teach *English.*	*English* will be taught by *Mr Jha.*

(i) Active sentences में Rani, Hari तथा Mr Jha *subjects* (कर्ता) हैं तथा a story, Moti एवं English *objects* (कर्म) हैं।

(ii) Active sentence का **subject** passive sentence में **object** बन जाता है तथा active sentence का **object** passive sentence में **subject** बन जाता है।

(c) By + Agent

4. *Look at these sentences :*

Active	*Passive*
Ramesh sells radios.	Radios are sold *by Ramesh.*
Gopi broke the cup.	The cup was broken *by Gopi.*
Tagore wrote this poem.	This poem was written *by Tagore.*

(i) Passive sentence में verb के बाद *by + noun (agent)* लगाया गया है क्योंकि इसके बिना वाक्य का पूरा अर्थ समझ में नहीं आता है। जैसे : This poem was written में जब तक *by Tagore* नहीं कहें वाक्य अधूरा लगता है।

(ii) अतः, passive sentence में वाक्य के अर्थ को पूरा करने के लिए तथा कुछ आवश्यक जानकारी देने के लिए *by + agent* का प्रयोग किया जाता है।

(d) Deletion of 'by + agent'

5. *Look at these sentences :*

Active	*Passive*
Someone stole my pen.	*My pen* was stolen.
Robbers looted the bank.	*The bank* was looted.
The man will sell the house.	*The house* will be sold.
Somebody invited you to tea.	*You* were invited to tea.
People speak Hindi all over India.	*Hindi* is spoken all over India.

(i) जब वाक्य का अर्थ **by + agent** के बिना ही पूरा हो जाए तब **by + agent** का प्रयोग नहीं किया जाता। जैसे : People speak Hindi all over India

में हमारा मतलब 'the speaking of Hindi' से है न कि इस वाक्य के अस्पष्ट subject *people* से। अतः, passive sentence में by + people हटा दिया जाता है।[1]

(ii) *One, someone, nobody, people, a man, a person, a boy, somebody* इत्यादि active subjects को passive sentence में हटा दिया जाता है।

(iii) *I, we, you, they,* इत्यादि active subjects को भी passive sentence में प्रायः हटा दिया जाता है।

याद रखें : Active subject को passive sentence में तभी mention किया जाता है जब speaker के लिए वह महत्त्वपूर्ण है या वाक्य के अर्थ को स्पष्ट करने के लिए आवश्यक है।

संक्षेप में, active को passive में बदलने के लिए :

(a) Subject को object में बदल दें।
(b) Object को subject बना दें।
(c) Main Verb को V^3 (past participle) में बदलें, तथा—
(d) उसके पहले am, is, are, was, were, been, being का प्रयोग subject के number तथा verb के tense के अनुसार करें।
(e) Verb के बाद आवश्यकतानुसार by + agent लगावें।

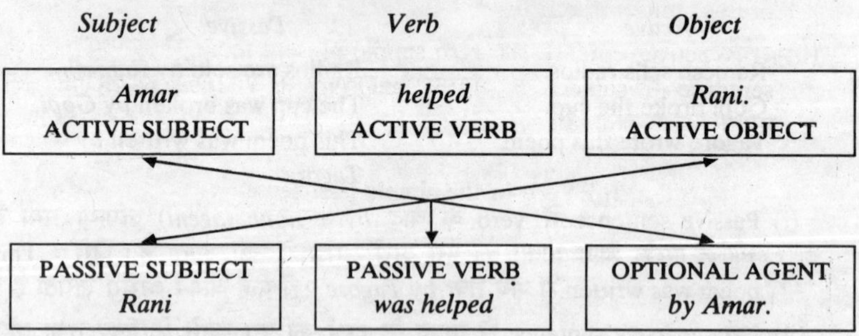

(e) Passive Verb-forms

Active को passive में बदलने पर verb हमेशा V^3 (past participle) रूप में रहता है तथा उसके पहले subject तथा tense के अनुसार verb *to be* (am, is, are, was, were, been, being) का प्रयोग किया जाता है। जैसे :

Tense	*Active Voice*	*Passive Voice*
Simple Present	help/helps	*am/is/are* helped
Simple Past	helped	*was/were* helped
Simple Future	shall/will help	shall/will *be* helped
Present Continuous	am/is/are helping	am/is/are *being* helped
Past Continuous	was/were helping	was/were *being* helped

1. *"In all passive voice exercises the use of 'by' with an agent must be rigorously suppressed, except in those examples where our interest in the predicate has led us to use the passive voice. We should omit the agent where the agent is vague or unknown."* —W. STANNARD ALLEN : LIVING ENGLISH STRUCTURE

Tense	*Active Voice*	*Passive Voice*
Present Perfect	has/have helped	has/have *been* helped
Past Perfect	had helped	had *been* helped
Modal Verb	may help	may *be* helped

अब हमलोग भिन्न-भिन्न Tenses में verb के active form तथा passive form को देखेंगे।

(a) Verb in the simple present tense

1. *Look at these sentences :*

Active	*Passive*
Rekha *helps* me.	I *am helped* by Rekha.
Sita *writes* a story.	A story *is written* by Sita.
Mr Prasad *teaches* the boys.	The boys *are taught* by Mr Prasad.

(i) ऊपर active sentences में आए verbs *helps, writes* तथा *teaches* simple present tense में हैं।

(ii) अगर active sentence का *verb* simple present tense में हो तो passive sentence में subject के अनुसार **am/is/are + V^3 (past participle)** का प्रयोग किया जाता है।

(b) Verb in the simple past tense

2. *Look at these sentences :*

Active	*Passive*
Tom *killed* the snake.	The snake *was killed* by Tom.
Ruby *bought* two bags.	Two bags *were bought* by Ruby.
Dinkar *wrote* this poem.	This poem *was written* by Dinkar.

(i) ऊपर active sentences में आए verbs *killed, bought* तथा *wrote* simple past tense में हैं।

(ii) अगर active sentence का *verb* simple past tense में रहे तो passive sentence में subject के number के अनुसार **was/were + V^3** का प्रयोग किया जाता है।

(c) Verb in the simple future tense

3. *Look at these sentences :*

Active	*Passive*
Mukul *will help* me.	I *shall be helped* by Mukul.

Active	*Passive*
The peon *will post* the letter.	The letter *will be posted* by the peon.
Mr Gupta *will solve* the problem.	The problem *will be solved* by Mr Gupta.

(i) ऊपर active sentences में आए verbs *will help, will post* तथा *will solve* simple future tense में हैं।

(ii) अगर active sentence का *verb* simple future tense में हो तो passive sentence में subject के अनुसार **shall/will + be + V^3 (past participle)** का प्रयोग किया जाता है।

(d) Verb in the present continuous tense

4. *Look at these sentences :*

Active	*Passive*
Mary *is answering* the question.	The question *is being answered* by Mary.
The Principal *is watching* the match.	The match *is being watched* by the Principal.
Mr Sinha *is drawing* the pictures.	The pictures *are being drawn* by Mr Sinha.

(i) ऊपर active sentences में आए verbs *is answering, is watching* तथा *is drawing* present continuous tense में हैं।

(ii) अगर active sentence का *verb* present continuous tense में हो तो passive tense में subject के अनुसार **am/is/are+ being + V^3 (past participle)** का प्रयोग किया जाता है।

(e) Verb in the past continuous tense

5. *Look at these sentences :*

Active	*Passive*
That woman *was cutting* the cloth.	The cloth *was being cut* by that woman.
The girls *were painting* the box.	The box *was being painted* by the girls.
Mr Ghosh *was eating* the mangoes.	The mangoes *were being* eaten by Mr Ghosh.

(i) ऊपर के active sentences में आए verbs *was cutting, were painting* तथा *was eating* past continuous tense में हैं।

(ii) अगर active sentence का *verb* past continuous tense में हो तो passive sentence में subject के अनुसार **was/were+ being+ V^3** का प्रयोग किया जाता है।

(f) Verb in the present perfect tense

6. *Look at these sentences :*

Active	*Passive*
Tom *has painted* the door.	The door *has been painted* by Tom.
Moti *has thrown* the balls.	The balls *have been thrown by* Moti.
The children *have made* the box.	The box *has been made* by the children.

(i) ऊपर के active sentences में आए verbs *has painted, has thrown* तथा *have made* present perfect tense में हैं।

(ii) अगर active sentence का *verb* present perfect tense में हो तो passive sentence में subject के अनुसार **has/have+been + V^3** का प्रयोग किया जाता है।

(g) Verb in the past perfect tense

7. *Look at these sentences :*

Active	*Passive*
Sima *had taken* the books.	The books *had been taken* by Sima.
Hari *had cleaned* the room.	The room *had been cleaned* by Hari.
Your sister *had bought* the nose pin.	The nose pin *had been bought* by your sister.

(i) ऊपर के active sentences में आए verbs *had taken, had cleaned* तथा *had bought* past perfect tense में है।

(ii) अगर active sentence का *verb* past perfect tense में हो तो passive sentence में subject के बाद **had + been+ V^3** का प्रयोग किया जाता है।

अब तक हमलोगों ने भिन्न-भिन्न tenses में verb के active तथा passive form को देखा है। अब उन्हें संक्षेप में दुहरा लें।

Tense	*Active Voice*	*Passive Voice*
Simple Present :	Raju *helps* Usha.	Usha *is helped by* Raju.
Simple Past :	Raju *helped* Usha.	Usha *was helped* By Raju.

Tense	*Active Voice*	*Passive Voice*
Simple Future :	Raju *will help* Usha.	Usha *will be helped* by Raju.
Present Continuous :	Raju *is helping Usha.*	Usha *is being helped by* Raju.
Past Continuous :	Raju *was helping* Usha.	Usha *was being helped* by Raju.
Present Perfect :	Raju *has helped* Usha.	Usha *has been helped* by Raju.
Past Perfect :	Raju *had helped* Usha.	Usha *had been helped* by Raju.
Future Perfect :	Raju *will have helped* Usha.	Usha *will have been helped by* Raju.

(h) Modal verbs

8. *Look at these sentences :*

Active	*Passive*
Rajeev *can win* the prize.	The prize *can be won* by Rajeev.
Madan *may drive* the car.	The car *may be driven* by Madan.
Amar *must send* a reply.	A reply *must be sent* by Amar.
A doctor *should examine* him.	He *should be examined* by a doctor.

(i) *Can, may, must, shall, will, should, would, could* तथा *might* को **modal verbs** कहा जाता है।

(ii) अगर active sentence में modal verb हो तो passive sentence में subject के बाद **modal verb+be+V^3** का प्रयोग किया जाता है।

(i) Verbs with two objects

9. *Look at these sentences :*

Active	*Passive*
Rana gave *me the letter.*	(a) *I* was given the letter by Rana. (b) *The letter* was given (to) me by Rana.
Mr Sen asked *him a question.*	(a) *He* was asked a question by Mr Sen. (b) *A question* was asked him by Mr Sen.
Mrs Gupta told *us stories.*	(a) *We* were told stories by Mrs Gupta. (b) *Stories* were told us by Mrs Gupta.
The headmaster offers *her a job.*	(a) *She* is offered a job by the headmaster. (b) *A job* is offered her by the headmaster.

(i) ऊपर के active sentences में verbs (gave, asked, told, offers) के बाद आए शब्द *me, the letter; him, a question; us, stories; her, a job objects* हैं।

(ii) वह शब्द जो verb के बाद किसी व्यक्ति के लिए आता है उसे indirect object कहते हैं तथा जो किसी वस्तु का नाम होता है उसे direct object कहते हैं।

ऊपर के active sentences में *me, him, us* तथा *her* indirect objects हैं, तथा *letter, question, stories* एवं *job* direct objects हैं।

(iii) दो objects वाले active sentence को passive में बदलते समय हम किसी भी object को subject बना सकते हैं। वह इस बात पर निर्भर करता है कि हम किसे प्रधानता देना चाहते हैं।

(iv) साधारणतः active sentence के प्राणिसूचक indirect object को ही passive sentence का subject बनाया जाता है।

(v) अँगरेजी में निम्नलिखित शब्दों के बाद दो *objects* आते हैं : give, tell, show, lend, get, write, pay, sell, buy, bring, make, fetch, promise, teach इत्यादि।

(j) Passive of commands : Let, Please, Kindly....

10. *Look at these sentences :*

Active	*Passive*
Open the box.	*Let* the box *be* opened.
Switch off the fan.	*Let* the fan *be* switched off.
Close the door at once.	*Let* the door *be closed* at once.
Inform the police of the accident.	*Let* the police *be* informed of the accident.

(i) ऊपर active sentences के वाक्यों से आदेश का भाव व्यक्त होता है; इन्हें *commands* या *imperative sentences* कहते हैं।

(ii) जिस *imperative sentence* से आदेश का भाव व्यक्त हो उसके passive form को **let** से शुरू किया जाता है तथा subject के बाद **be +** $\mathbf{V^3}$ का प्रयोग किया जाता है। अतः, verb form होगा : **let + be +** $\mathbf{V^3}$.

11. *Look at these sentences :*

Active	*Passive*
Help the poor.	The poor *should be helped.*
Love the children.	The children *should be loved.*
Hear him now.	He *should be heard* now.

अगर *imperative sentence* से सलाह (advice) का भाव व्यक्त हो तो उसके passive form को **let** से शुरू नहीं किया जाता, वरन् subject के बाद **should + be +** $\mathbf{V^3}$ का प्रयोग किया जाता है।

12. *Look at these sentences :*

Active	*Passive*
Take this chair, *please.*	*You are requested to* take this chair.
Kindly read this letter.	*You are requested to* read this letter.
Please give me a pen.	*You are requested to* give me a pen.

(i) ऊपर active sentences में *please* तथा *kindly* लगे हुए हैं तथा उनसे request का भाव झलकता है।

(ii) अगर active sentence में *please/kindly* हो तो passive sentence को **You are requested to** से शुरू किया जाता है। तथा

(iii) Passive sentence से *please/kindly* को हटा दिया जाता है।

(k) Passive of yes-no questions

13. *Look at these sentences :*

Active	*Passive*
Do machines *make* these buttons ?	*Are* these buttons *made* by machines ?
Does Sita *write* this story ?	*Is* this story *written* by Sita ?
Did you *see* him ?	*Was* he *seen* by you ?
Did Mukul *buy* the toys ?	*Were* the toys *bought* by Mukul ?

(i) ऊपर active sentences में yes-no questions हैं। *Do, does, did, am, are, is, was, were, have, has* तथा *had* से शुरू होनेवाले questions को *yes-no questions* कहते हैं।

(ii) अगर active sentence में कोई question *Do/Does/Did* से शुरू हो तो उसके passive sentence का verb form होगा: **am/is/are/was/were + V^3.**

14. *Look at these sentences :*

Active	*Passive*
Has Tom *invited* you ?	*Have* you *been invited* by Tom ?
Have the girls *asked* this question ?	*Has* this question *been asked* by the girls ?
Had Moti *done* the task ?	*Had* the task *been done* by Moti ?

(i) ऊपर active sentences के questions *present* तथा *past tenses* में हैं।

(ii) अगर active sentence में कोई question *has/have/had* से शुरू हो तो उसके passive sentence का verb form होगा : **has/have/had+been+V^3.**

(l) Passive of questions with modal verbs

15. *Look at these sentences :*

Active	*Passive*
Can we cut the tree ?	*Can* the tree *be cut ?*
Will they *sell* the house ?	*Will* the house *be sold ?*
Should the doctor *examine* him ?	*Should* he *be examined* by the doctor ?
Must we *send* the book by post ?	*Must* the book *be sent* by post ?

(i) ऊपर active sentences के questions *can, will, should* तथा *must* से शुरू होते हैं; इन्हें modal auxiliaries कहा जाता है। कुछ और modal auxiliaries हैं : *may, shall, would, could, might, ought* इत्यादि।

(ii) अगर कोई question active voice में *modal auxiliary* से शुरू हो तो उसके passive voice का verb form होता है : **modal auxiliary + be + V^3 (past participle.)**

(m) Passive of wh-questions

16. *Look at these sentences :*

Active	*Passive*
When do they send the letter ?	When *is* the letter *sent ?*
Why do they make a noise ?	Why *is* a noise *made ?*
How will he solve the sum ?	How *will* the sum *be solved ?*
Where did Sita buy the hat ?	Where *was* the hat *bought* by Sita ?
What did they do in the office ?	What *was done* by them in the office ?
Who wrote the Ramayana ?	*By whom was* the Ramayana *written ?* *Who was* the Ramayana *written* by ?
Which boy abused you ?	*By which* boy *were* you *abused ?*

(i) ऊपर active sentences के questions *wh-words* से शुरू होते हैं। *Who, which, whom, where, when, why, whose, whom* तथा *how* से शुरू होनेवाले प्रश्न *wh-questions* कहलाते हैं।

(ii) Wh-question को active voice से passive में बदलने में पहले उसे *yes-no question* जैसा बनाकर passive बना लें। पुनः *wh-word* को passive question के पहले लगा दें। जैसे :

Where did you find this book ? (Active)

Step I : *Did* you find *this book* ? (Active)
(*Where* हटा दें)
Step II : *Was this book* found ? (Passive)
Step III : *Where* was this book found ? (Passive)
(*Where* जोड़ दें)

(n) Passive of infinitives[1]

17. *Look at these sentences :*

Active	*Passive*
There is no time *to lose.*	There is no time *to be lost.*
We have nothing *to gain.*	Nothing is *to be gained.*
He is a man *to admire.*	He is a man *to be admired.*

ऊपर active sentences में *to lose, to gain* तथा *to admire* infinitives हैं जिनके passive forms *to be lost, to be gained, to be admired* होते हैं अर्थात **to** के बाद **be** $+\mathbf{V}^3$ लगाया जाता है।

(o) Passive of verb 'to be'

18. *Look at these sentences :*

Active	*Passive*
I *am to buy* a bat.	A bat *is to be bought* by me.
He *is to write* a letter.	A letter *is to be written* by him.
They *are to sell* the car.	The car *is to be sold* by them.
Abdul *was to do* this work.	This work *was to be done* by Abdul.
They *were to play* the match.	The match *was to be played* by them.

(i) ऊपर active sentences में verb form *am/is/are/was/were+to+verb*[1] है।
(ii) इन वाक्यों का passive बनाने में **am/is/are/was/were/to be**$+\mathbf{V}^3$ का प्रयोग किया जाता है।

(p) Passive of the verb 'to have'

19. *Look at these sentences :*

Active	*Passive*
Rekha *has to buy* a frock.	A frock *has to be bought* by Rekha.

---

1. *To play, to go, to run* इत्यादि infinitives (to+verb के मूल रूप) हैं। याद रखें *infinitive* के आगे प्रायः *to* लगा रहता है।

Active	*Passive*
Mr Sinha *has to plant* a tree.	**A tree *has to be planted* by Mr Sinha.**
The boys *have to write* letters.	**Letters *have to be written* by the boys.**
Hari *had to do* this work.	**This work *had to be done* by Hari.**

(i) ऊपर active sentences में verb forms *has/have/had+to+* **V**^{1} (मूल रूप) हैं।

(ii) इन वाक्यों को passive बनाने में **has/have/had+to be+V**^{3} का प्रयोग किया जाता है।

(q) Passive of verb+prepositions

20. *Look at these sentences :*

Active	*Passive*
The police enquired *into* the case.	The case was enquired *into*.
The children laughed *at* him.	He was laughed *at* by the children.
Your sister will look *after* you.	You will be looked *after* by your sister.
The govt. will arrive *at* the agreement.	The agreement will be arrived *at* by the govt.

(i) ऊपर active sentences में verbs के बाद *into, at, after* लगे हुए हैं जिन्हें हम prepositions कहते हैं।

(ii) अगर active sentences में *verb+preposition/adverb particle* हों तो उसके passive form में उस *preposition* या *adverb particle* को हटाया नहीं जाता[1]।

(r) Another word in place of 'by'

21. *Look at these sentences :*

Active	*Passive*
The news *pleased* him.	He was *pleased with* the news.
The result *surprises* me.	I am *surprised at* the result.
I *know* him.	He is *known to* me.

1. Verb+preposition (जैसे—*look after, find out* इत्यादि) के कई नाम हैं, जैसे : two-part verbs, composite verbs तथा phrasal verbs. कभी-कभी verb+preposition में preposition को prepositional adverb या adverb particle कहा जाता है।

Active	*Passive*
The *book interested* Mr Bose.	Mr Bose was *interested in* the book.
His progress *satisfied* me.	I was *satisfied with* his progress.

(i) ऊपर active sentences में *pleased, surprises, know, interested* तथा *satisfied* verbs हैं।

(ii) इनके passive sentences में *by* की जगह *with, at, to, in* का प्रयोग किया गया है। (*This is because these verbs express 'states' rather than 'actions' done by the 'agent'.*)

(iii) इसी तरह, *astonished, displeased, disinterested, disgusted, dissatisfied* के बाद भी passive voice में *by* नहीं आता वरन् किसी दूसरे preposition का प्रयोग किया जाता है।

(s) Dummy 'it'

22. *Look at these sentences :*

Active	*Passive*
Years ago, people believed *that the earth was flat.*	(a) Years ago, *it was believed* that the earth was flat. (b) Years ago, the earth was believed *to be* flat.
People felt *that the officers were corrupt.*	(a) *It was felt* that the officers were corrupt. (b) The officers were felt *to be corrupt.*
They believed *that Mr Gupta was very rich.*	(a) *It was believed* that Mr Gupta was very rich. (b) Mr Gupta was believed *to be very rich.*
Everyone thought *that the govt. was strong.*	(a) *It was thought* that the govt. was strong. (b) The govt. was thought *to be strong.*
People say *that he is a spy.*	(a) *It is said* that he is a spy. (b) He *is said to be* a spy.
People say *that he was a spy.*	(a) *It is said* that he was a spy. (b) He is said *to have been* a spy.

People think/know/consider/believe/acknowledge/understand/find/say/claim/report.... के बाद that he is...' जैसे वाक्य का passive दो तरह से बनाया जाता है :

(i) वाक्य के शुरू में dummy subject *it* का प्रयोग कर। जैसे :
It was believed that....
It was felt that....
It was thought that...
It was hoped that....
It is agreed that....

(ii) Active sentence में आए noun clause के subject को passive voice के subject के रूप में लाया जाता है तथा *to* का प्रयोग किया जाता है। जैसे :
The earth was believed *to be* flat.

(iii) *People say* की जगह *It is said* का प्रयोग किया जाता है।

(t) Passive of negative sentences

23. *Look at these sentences :*

Active	*Passive*
We *can't take up* this work now.	This work *can't be taken* up now.
Some people *don't eat* onions.	Onions *aren't eaten* by some people.
Some students *did not attend* the class.	The class *was not attended* by some students.
They should *not ask* this question now.	This question *should not be* asked now.

(i) ऊपर active sentences में *not* या *n't* लगे हैं; इन्हें *negative sentences* कहा जाता है।

(ii) Negative sentence का passive form उसी तरह बनता है जिस तरह affirmative sentence का। Negative में *not* को auxiliary (*am, is, are, was, were,* etc.) तथा main verb के third form के बीच रखा जाता है।

(u) Double passives

24. *Look at these sentences :*

Active	*Passive*
They *looted* the house and *took away* the things.	The house *was looted* and the things *were taken away*.
She *wrote* the letter and *posted* it.	The letter *was written* and (it was) *posted* by her.
The police *arrested* the thief and *sent* him to jail.	The thief *was arrested* and (he was) *sent* to jail.

(i) ऊपर active sentences में दो clauses है, एक को principal clause तथा दूसरे को co-ordinate clause कहा जाता है।

(ii) अगर active sentence में principal+co-ordinate clause हों और प्रत्येक clause में transitive verb रहे तो प्रत्येक clause का passive form इन उदाहरणों में बताए गए तरीकों के अनुसार होता है।

(ii) USE OF PASSIVE VOICE

Passive voice का अकसर प्रयोग निम्नलिखित परिस्थितियों में किया जाता है :

(i) जब यह नहीं मालूम हो कि कोई कार्य किसने किया अर्थात जब subject अज्ञात हो तब passive voice का प्रयोग किया जाता है। जैसे :

The child *was lost* in the fair.
The temple *was built* years ago.
The glass *was broken* yesterday.
A bomb *was exploded* there.

(ii) वाक्य के object को महत्त्वपूर्ण बनाने के लिए passive voice का प्रयोग किया जाता है। जैसे :

The fearful lion was killed by me.
This letter was drafted by the principal.
A mistake was made in publishing the results.
(किसने गलती की यह महत्त्वपूर्ण नहीं है।)

(iii) कभी-कभी वाक्य को polite (विनम्र) बनाने के लिए passive voice का प्रयोग किया जाता है तथा *doer* को mention नहीं किया जाता। जैसे :

A lot of harm *has been done* to us.
It is hoped that he will stand first in the class.
It is said that the teacher will punish some boys.

(iv) जब करनेवाला (subject) लगभग सबको मालूम हो तब active sentence की जगह passive sentence का प्रयोग किया जाता है। जैसे :

America *was discovered* in 1492.
(= खोजनेवाले का नाम लगभग सबको मालूम है।)
Pension *will be increased* for the retiring people.
English *is spoken* all over the world.

(v) Scientific तथा technical writings में passive voice का प्रयोग किया जाता है क्योंकि उनमें *doer* महत्त्वपूर्ण नहीं होता है। जैसे :

Common salt *is got* from the sea.
The engine *is run* with electricity.
Water *is produced* when oxygen and hydrogen *are combined.*

Examples Worked Out

Put the sentences below into the passive voice :

	Active	*Passive*
1.	Tom *kills* a tiger.	A tiger *is killed* by Tom.

	Active	*Passive*
2.	The peon *opened* the gate.	The gate *was opened* by the peon.
3.	Sita *will write* a letter.	A letter *will be written* by Sita.
4.	They *are repairing* the house.	The house *is being repaired* by them.
5.	Abdul was *cleaning* the car.	The car *was being cleaned* by Abdul.
6.	Moti *has broken* the window.	The window *has been broken* by Moti.
7.	Sita *had made* tea.	Tea *had been made* by Sita.
8.	She *can win* the prize.	The prize *can be won* by her.
9.	A doctor *should see* him.	He *should be seen* by a doctor.
10.	Our team *could win* the match.	The match *could be won* by our team.
11.	They *must send* a reply.	A reply *must be sent* by them.
12.	We *may finish* the work soon.	The work *may be finished* soon.
13.	China *attached* India in 1962.	India *was attacked* by China in 1962.
14.	John *kisses* Mary.	Mary *is kissed* by John.
15.	The mason *is building* the house.	The house *is being built* by the mason.
16.	Rekha *was writing* a story.	A story *was being written* by Rekha.
17.	The boy *will kick* the ball.	The ball *will be kicked* by the boy.
18.	The postman *has brought* a telegram.	A telegram *has been brought* by the postman.
19.	*People* speak Hindi in Bihar.	Hindi *is spoken* in Bihar.
20.	*Someone* stole my watch this morning.	My watch *was stolen* this morning.
21.	*No one* told me about it.	I *was not told* about it.
22.	*They called* him a fool.	He *was called* a fool.
23.	You *can take* it away.	It *can be taken* away by you.
24.	Switch on the fan.	*Let* the fan *be switched* on.
25.	Inform the police.	*Let* the police *be informed.*
26.	Let him *do* the work.	Let the work *be done* by him.
27.	*Please* help the poor girl.	*You are requested to* help the poor girl.
28.	*Kindly* close the door.	*You are requested to* close the door.
29.	*Take* this medicine in time.	This medicine *should be taken* in time.
30.	*Love* the children.	The children *should be loved.*

	Active	*Passive*
31.	*Has* anyone *asked* this question ?	*Has* this question *been asked* by anyone.
32.	*Did* Rajeev *help* him ?	*Was* he *helped* by Rajeev ?
33.	*Does* he *like* this pen ?	*Is* this pen *liked* by him ?
34.	*Do* the boys *buy* the books ?	*Are* the books *bought* by the boys ?
35.	*Will* she *do* this work ?	*Will* this work *be done* by her ?
36.	*Are* you *writing* this story ?	*Is* this story *being written* by you ?
37.	*Who did* this ?	*By whom was* this *done ?*
38.	*Who sent* this parcel ?	*By whom was* this parcel *sent ?*
39.	*Where did* you *buy* this bag ?	*Where was* this bag *bought* by you ?
40.	*When do* you *post* the letter ?	*When is* the letter *posted* by you ?
41.	*What did* they *learn* in the class ?	*What was learnt* by them in the class ?
42.	*How* do they *make* coffee ?	*How is* coffee *made ?*
43.	*Why* did Sita *write* such an essay ?	*Why was* such an essay *written* by Sita ?
44.	I *am to sing* a song.	A song *is to be sung* by me.
45.	He *is to send* a book.	A book *is to be sent* by him.
46.	He *has to sell* the house.	The house *has to be sold* by him.
47.	I *have to teach* English.	English *has to be taught* by me.
48.	There was no time *to lose.*	There was no time *to be lost.*
49.	There is a lot of work *to do.*	There is a lot of work *to be done.*
50.	We *must write to* him.	He *must be written to* (by us).
51.	You *can rely upon* his word.	His word *can be relied upon.*
52.	All the boys *laughed at* him.	He *was laughed at* by all the boys.
53.	He *found* a house *for him.*	A house *was found for him.*
54.	This news *pleased me.*	*I was pleased with* the news.
55.	We *know* Mr Prasad.	Mr Prasad *is known to us.*
56.	His work *satisfied me.*	*I was satisfied with* his work.
57.	The results *surprised him.*	*He was surprised at* the results.
58.	You *must look after* the boy.	The boy *must be looked after.*
59.	He *should take care of* his brother.	His brother *should be taken care of.*
60.	*Nobody has slept in* the bed for two days.	The bed *has not been slept in* for two days.
61.	Readers *must not read* that book.	That book *must not be read.*
62.	Some members *did not attend* the meeting.	The meeting *was not attended* by some members.
63.	Gopal *gave me a book.*	(a) *I was given* a book by Gopal.

	Active	*Passive*
		(b) *A book* was given (to) me by Gopal.
64.	Mr Roy teaches *us history.*	(a) *We* are taught history by Mr Roy. (b) *History* is taught to us by Mr Roy.
65.	He *offered him a job.*	(a) *He* was offered a job. (b) *A job* was offered him.
66.	They awarded *him the Nobel Prize* in 1980.	(a) *He* was awarded the Nobel Prize in 1980. (b) *The Nobel Prize* was awarded him in 1980.
67.	*People say* that there may be another world war.	*It is said* that there may be another world war.
68.	*We hope* that they will call off the strike.	*It is hoped* that they will call off the strike.
69.	*They say* that there are living beings on Mars.	*It is said* that there are living being on Mars.
70.	Prepare yourself for the worst.	*Be prepared* for the worst.
71.	He *made* us work.	We were made *to* work.
72.	They *let us* go.	*We were let* go.
73.	We saw them go out.	They were seen *to* go out.
74.	*The police* arrested the thief.	The thief was arrested.
75.	Shah Jehan *built* the Taj Mahal.	The Taj Mahal *was built* by Shah Jehan.
76.	He taught *me* how to sing.	*I* was taught how to sing.
77.	The teacher permitted *the boy* to go and play.	*The boy* was permitted to go and play.
78.	Nobody *can do* it.	It *cannot be done.*
79.	A car *ran over* the dog.	The dog *was run over* by a car.
80.	*Give* the order.	Let the order *be given.*
81.	*Who* wrote 'Hamlet' ?	(a) *Who* was 'Hamlet' written *by ?* *(b) By whom* was 'Hamlet' written ?
82.	We *can play with* the dog.	The dog *can be played with.*
83.	You *must write to* the Principal.	The Principal *must be written to.*
84.	The police *enquired into* the *accident.*	The accident was *enquired into.*
85.	Animals *cannot* make *tools.*	*Tools cannot be* made by animals.
86.	We drove *him* out of the house.	*He* was driven out of the house by us.

	Active	*Passive*
87.	We *need* six *camels* for our work.	Six *cameis are needed* by us for our work.
88.	The shepherd *has lost* six sheep.	*Six sheep have been lost* by the shepherd.
89.	God *will bless good men.*	*Good men will be blessed* by God.
90.	Some boys *were flying kites.*	*Kites were being flown* by some boys.
91.	*Who broke* the window ?	*By whom was* the *window broken ?*
92.	*Have* you *shut* the door ?	*Has* the *door been shut* by you ?
93.	*Why* did your sister give such a rude reply ?	*Why was* such a rude reply *given* by your sister ?
94.	Who taught her French ?	(a) *By whom* was *French* taught *her ?* (b) *By whom* was *she* taught French ?
95.	One *should keep* one's promise.	Promises *should be kept.*
96.	*They told us* to walk on the left.	*We were told* to walk on the left.
97.	Give the order.	*Let* the order *be given.*
98.	Shut all the doors.	*Let* all the doors *be shut.*
99.	They *refused him* admission.	*He was refused* admission.
100.	Someone *has cut* the telegraph wires.	The telegraph wires *have been cut.*
101.	*Do* it now.	*Let* it *be done* now.
102.	Who *broke* the window ?	By whom *was* the window *broken ?*
103.	You *must shut* the doors.	The doors *must be* shut.
104.	*Did* you ever *hear* such a story ?	*Was* such a story ever *heard* by you ?
105.	*Listen* to me.	I *should be listened* to.
106.	Someone *has picked* my pocket.	My pocket *has been picked.*
107.	The people *elected* him Mayor.	He *was elected* Mayor.
108.	We *must write* to him.	He *must be written* to.
109.	What *caused* this crack ?	What *was* this crack *caused* by ?
110.	I remember my father *taking* me to the zoo.	I remember *being taken* to the zoo by my father.

EXERCISE 1

Underline the verbs in the following sentences and say whether they are in the Active or in the Passive voice :

EXAMPLES : (i) He *will finish* the work soon. (*Active voice*)

(ii) My pocket *has been picked.* (*Passive voice*)

1. He will finish the work soon.
2. My pocket has been picked.
3. The milkman is selling milk.
4. The bag may be stolen.
5. The field is ploughed.
6. We see a dark cloud.
7. The cat killed the rat.
8. Tom was beaten by the teacher.
9. The letter has just been posted.
10. He is writing a book.
11. You can play with these dolls.
12. The boys were well-looked after.
13. Let the chair be brought here.
14. Does he like this picture ?
15. Will this work be done tomorrow ?
16. This house was built in 1978.
17. The police have arrested the thief.
18. The window was broken yesterday.
19. It can be taken away.
20. I was taught how to drive.

EXERCISE 2

Fill in each of the blanks below by using the third form of the verb given in brackets :

EXAMPLE : Rice is....in Bihar (grow)
= Rice is *grown* in Bihar.

1. Rice is.....in Bihar. (grow)
2. The thief was.....by the police. (arrest)
3. Hindi is.....in many States. (speak)
4. We were.....by the teacher. (reward)
5. This book will be.....by Bharati Bhawan. (publish)
6. Now the road is being..... (build)
7. The tiger was.....by Mr Prasad. (kill)
8. He will be.....a reward. (give)
9. Wolves have been.....in the valley. (see)
10. A letter may be.....to him. (write)
11. The elders must be..... (respect)
12. The mad man was.....at. (laugh)
13. Mr Das was.....chairman. (elect)
14. The sugar may be.....by ants. (eat)
15. I was.....how to speak well. (teach)
16. A bat has to be.....by him. (buy)
17. Let this work be..... (do)
18. The boys were.....to go. (allow)
19. A picture can be.....by Ruby. (draw)
20. These cats may be.....with safely. (play)

EXERCISE 3

Put each of the sentences below into the passive voice :

EXAMPLES : (i) Sima *brings* the newspaper. (*Active*)
= The newspaper *is brought* by Sima. (*Passive*)

(ii) Gopi *broke* the mirror. (*Active*)
= The mirror *was broken* by Gopi. (*Passive*)

1. Sima brings the newspaper.
2. Gopi broke the mirror.
3. This boy sells toys.
4. Reeta writes the letter.
5. Mr Sinha shot a lion.
6. He ate all the biscuits.
7. They open the door.
8. Shakespeare wrote *Macbeth*.
9. Tom killed a snake.
10. Mrs Bose cooks rice.
11. The cat drank all the milk.
12. The teacher corrects my answer.
13. They stopped the bus yesterday.
14. Mukul drives the car.
15. Jack loves Mary.
16. The teacher asked the question.
17. The mechanic repaired the bicycle.
18. The doctor examined the patient.
19. Rekha paints the box.
20. Mr Roy raises this point.

EXERCISE 4

Put each of the sentences below into the passive voice :

EXAMPLES : (i) The boy *will bring* the coffee. (*Active*)
= The coffee *will be brought* by the boy. (*Passive*)
(ii) Moti *has kicked* the ball. (*Active*)
= The ball *has been kicked* by Moti. (*Passive*)

1. The boy will bring the coffee.
2. Moti has kicked the ball.
3. They will receive the money.
4. Miss Ghosh will visit you.
5. Hari has closed the gate.
6. John has answered the questions.
7. She will prepare tea.
8. We shall finish the task today.
9. The servant has cleaned the room.
10. The lion has attacked the travellers.
11. We shall solve the problem.
12. He will do this work.
13. They have seen the wolf.
14. Sohan will learn English.
15. Our team has won the match.
16. The boy will buy a coat.
17. I have sharpened the knives.
18. Mukul has revised the lessons.
19. The police will catch the thief.
20. This boy has broken the glass.

EXERCISE 5

Put each of the sentences below into the passive voice :

EXAMPLES : (i) Reeta *can do* it. (*Active*)
= It *can be done* by Reeta. (*Passive*)
(ii) Amar *must finish* this work. (*Active*)
= This work *must be finished* by Amar. (*Passive*)

1. Reeta can do it.
2. Amar must finish this work.
3. Peter may win the prize.
4. We might sell the bicycle.
5. They should call the doctor.
6. We can't open the window.
7. Jack may need a lot of money.
8. You must avoid the mistakes.
9. We could consider the points later.
10. Animals cannot make tools.
11. They should post the letters today.
12. My sister would serve the food.
13. They cannot arrest the criminals.
14. He might solve the mystery.
15. We shall repay the money.
16. They would start the project.
17. Students should follow the rules.
18. The teacher may not dictate the answers.
19. The police should stop the fight.
20. Everyone ought to obey the laws of the country.

EXERCISE 6

Put each of the sentences below into the passive voice :

EXAMPLES : (i) Reeta *is helping* Manju. (*Active*)
= Manju *is being helped* by Reeta. (*Passive*)
(ii) They *were repairing* the road. (*Active*)
= The road *was being repaired* by them. (*Passive*)

1. Reeta is helping Manju.
2. They were repairing the road.
3. John is eating the mangoes.
4. The teacher was calling the boys.
5. She was buying the vegetables.
6. Anmola is reading the story-book.
7. The servant is bringing the coffee.
8. Those men were cutting the tree.
9. I am learning new words.
10. You are teaching Moti.
11. Rani was making the noise.
12. Dr Sen is examining the patients.
13. The girl is catching the birds.
14. Peter was speaking English.
15. That man is pushing the cart.
16. Amar was selling the old books.
17. They are holding the meeting.
18. Manohar is ploughing the field.
19. That man was carrying the box.
20. Some boys were helping the old man.

EXERCISE 7

Put each of the sentences below into the passive voice :

EXAMPLES : (i) *Advertise* the post. (*Active*)
= *Let* the post *be advertised.* (*Passive*)
(ii) *Please* forgive him. (*Active*)
= *You are requested to* forgive him. (*Passive*)
(iii) Let him do it. (*Active*)
= Let it *be done* by him. (*Passive*)

1. Advertise the post.
2. Please forgive him.
3. Let him do it.
4. Send the child to school.
5. Help yourself, please.
6. Give the order.
7. Please keep to the left.
8. Come here, please.
9. Kindly do it tomorrow.
10. Shoot the tiger.
11. Write the answer soon.
12. Never cheat a friend.
13. Post these letters today.
14. Close the door at once.
15. Take this book, please.
16. Deposit the money in the bank.
17. Please love your children.
18. Give this pen to your teacher.
19. Type this letter before 4 p.m.
20. Send invitations to all the members.

EXERCISE 8

Put each of the sentences below into the passive voice. Use the word(s) in italics as the subject of the passive sentence :

EXAMPLES : (i) *Does* the noise disturb *you ?* (*Active*)
= *Are you* disturbed by the noise ? (*Passive*)
(ii) *How* did Sita write *it ?* (*Active*)
= *How* was *it* written by Sita ? (*Passive*)

(Note : *do/does* को *am/is/are* में तथा *did* को *was/were* में passive subject के अनुसार बदल दें।)

1. Does the noise disturb *you ?*
2. How did Sita write *it ?*
3. Do cats eat the *meat ?*
4. Where do they make *the toys ?*
5. Did Hari buy *the radio ?*
6. Why do they ask *this question ?*
7. Where can you get *good pictures ?*
8. When does she clean *the room ?*
9. Who has done *this work ?*
10. Who has insulted *you ?*
11. How do they paint *the pictures ?*
12. Who wrote *this poem ?*
13. Did they give you *enough sugar ?*
14. Will Mr Mehta tell me *the real story ?*
15. Why did they offer *him* a job ?
16. Who broke *the news ?*
17. Did they buy *a bat ?*
18. How do you record *the song ?*
19. Have you washed *all the plates ?*
20. Has anyone ever asked *you* a question ?

EXERCISE 9 (Revision)

Change the voices of the verbs in the following sentences :

EXAMPLE : We *must write* to him. (*Active*)
He *must be written* to by us. (*Passive*)

1. We refused them admission.
2. The principal promised us a holiday.
3. They kept us waiting.
4. We elected Kapil Dev captain.
5. Mr Sinha teaches us grammar.
6. We must listen to his words.
7. We expected good news.
8. Who wrote this letter to her ?
9. Give a paisa to the beggar.
10. Animals do not possess hands.
11. The king punished the thief.
12. They gave him a book.
13. The boys were playing football.
14. Do not leave waste paper on the grass.
15. The President appointed him governor.
16. When will you pay your fees ?
17. The policeman caught him asleep.
18. We will raise many objections.
19. He promised me a present.
20. Did your uncle pay your college fees ?

EXERCISE 10 (Revision)

Change the following sentences into the passive voice :

EXAMPLE : It is time *to take* tea. (*Active*)
= It is time for tea *to be taken.* (*Passive*)

1. They are doing the work.
2. He defended the boys.
3. Sohan loves Sharmila.
4. Who did this ?
5. Give the order.
6. Will he do this work ?
7. The car hit the man.
8. A car ran over the child.
9. It is time to take coffee.
10. I looked into the matter.
11. They laughed at him.
12. His conduct shocked me.
13. He satisfied everybody.
14. The news pleased me.
15. Mohan has killed a snake.
16. He did it.
17. He has drawn the picture.
18. The peon opened the gate.
19. She eats an apple.
20. Put out the light.

EXERCISE 11 (Revision)

Change the voice of the verbs in the following sentences:

EXAMPLE: I *had posted* the letter before I met him. (*Active*)
= The letter *had been posted* (by me) before I met him. (*Passive*)

1. Shut all the doors.
2. My friends will blame me.
3. Who rang the bell?
4. We saw you and him.
5. Please enter by this door.
6. We shall finish the task today.
7. Who can help me?
8. Sanjeev will eat an apple.
9. Hari purchased the land.
10. The cat killed the mouse.
11. We can do it.
12. She has done the work.
13. They elected him their leader.
14. You can win the prize.
15. There is no time to lose.
16. He turned down my request.
17. We were kept waiting by them.
18. Brutus accused Caesar of ambition.
19. It is time to open the shop.
20. I asked him to come on time.

EXERCISE 12 (Revision)

Change the voice of the verbs in the following sentences:

EXAMPLE: One *should keep* one's promise. (*Active*)
= One's promise *should be kept.* (*Passive*)

1. Shyam is reading a book.
2. The manager will give you tickets.
3. My brothers were taking me home.
4. It is now time to start the race.
5. By whom were you taught English?
6. The steam engine was invented by Watt.
7. People believe that he is a liar.
8. They found him guilty of murder.
9. Did you never hear that name?
10. Somebody has stolen my umbrella.
11. Mother told her to be quick.
12. Why did Radha help Reeta?
13. The children have painted the wall.
14. I saw him opening the box.
15. Do not insult the weak.
16. Why should anyone question you?
17. Someone has broken my vase.
18. Have you shut the door?
19. We keep the butter here.
20. You ought to open the windows.

EXERCISE 13

Change the following sentences into the passive voice:

EXAMPLES: (i) Tell him to leave the room at once. (*Active*)
= Let him *be told* to leave the room at once. (*Passive*)
(ii) You *can play* with these cubs quite safely. (*Active*)
= These cubs *can be played* with quite safely. (*Passive*)
(iii) It is her duty to do her homework every day. (*Active*)
= She *is supposed* to do her homework every day. (*Passive*)

1. Rash driving causes many accidents.
2. He looked after the children well.
3. You can play with the dog quite safely.
4. Ramu will clean the room in the morning.
5. He ordered the police to pursure the thief.
6. He invited me to his house yesterday.
7. Nobody has answered my questions properly.

8. Students should follow the rules of grammar.
9. The stone struck him in the right shoulder.
10. We drove him out of the house.
11. Why did your father write such a letter ?
12. Someone will wake you up at 6 o'clock.
13. He hurt his leg in an accident.
14. He doesn't like people laughing at him.
15. It is your duty to make tea at six o'clock. (use *suppose*)

EXERCISE 14

Put each of the sentences below into the passive voice. Use the word(s) in italics as the subject of the passive sentence :

EXAMPLES : (i) He gave *me* a book. (*Active*)
= *I* was given a book by him. (*Passive*)
(ii) The results surprised *me*. (*Active*)
= *I* was surprised *at* the results. (*Passive*)
(iii) We have spoken to *the officer*. (*Active*)
= *The officer* has been spoken to. (*Passive*)
(iv) *People believe* that he is an honest man. (*Active*)
= *It is believed* that he is an honest man. (*Passive*)

1. He gave *me* a book.
2. The results surprised *me*.
3. We have spoken to *the officer*.
4. *People believe* that he is an honest man.
5. She writes *him* a letter.
6. Social work interests *Mr Roy*.
7. Mr Sen advised *him* to give up smoking.
8. *People say* that Mr Prasad is a rich man. (*It is said....*)
9. Mr Sinha is teaching *me* chemistry.
10. The police enquired into *the matter*.
11. *Many people now think* that politics is a dirty game. (*It is now thought....*)
12. They promised *Sita* a new doll.
13. Someone can ask for *money*.
14. A bus ran *him* down.
15. *We understand* that he opposes our plan. (*It is understood....*)
16. A friend will tell *me* the story.
17. Our work pleased *the teacher*.
18. They appointed *him* manager.
19. He has written to *the minister*.
20. Years ago, *people believed* that the earth was flat. (*....it was believed....*)

EXERCISE 15

Put each of the sentences below into the passive voice. The words(s) in italics will be the subject of the new sentence. No 'by+ agent' is required in the following exercise :

EXAMPLE : People always praise *this man*. (*Active*)
= *This man* is always praised. (*Passive*)

1. People always praise *this man*.
2. Someone has broken *two of my cups*.

3. People speak *English* all over the world.
4. We shall discuss *the matter* next week.
5. They held *the party* in his honour.
6. Someone can easily repair *the door*.
7. The author will write *the book* in March.
8. Has somebody done *all the work* ?
9. He painted *the picture* beautifully.
10. Somebody has stolen *my money*.
11. They make *cotton goods* in Bombay.
12. Have you fed *the cows* yet ?
13. People speak *Bengali* in Bengal.
14. The authorities have published *the results*.
15. The police arrested *the thief*.
16. Nobody has picked *my pocket*.
17. Somebody built *the bridge* last year.
18. Did anyone ask *any question* about me ?
19. People mustn't take *these chairs* away.
20. One praises *a pupil* when he works hard.

EXERCISE 16

(A) *Complete the following sentences using the third form of the verb given in brackets :*

EXAMPLES : This shirt———of silk. (*make*)
= This shirt *is made* of silk.
Or, This shirt *was made* of silk.

1. This shirt.....of silk. (*make*)
2. The Taj Mahal.....hundreds of years ago. (*build*)
3. Our answers.....last week. (*correct*)
4. The letter.....yesterday. (*post*)
5. The door.....of wood. (*make*)
6. Last month the whole building.....by fire. (*destroy*)
7. A new book.....next month. (*publish*)
8. Rice.....in India in plenty. (*produce*)
9. He cheated me; so he...... (*punish*)
10. My shirt is clean; it.....yesterday. (*wash*)

(B) *Ask questions using the question words given in brackets :*

EXAMPLE : The house was built in 1972. (*When*)
= *When* was the house built ?

1. The house was built in 1972. (*When*)
2. The book was written in Delhi. (*Where*)
3. The building was destroyed by fire. (*How*)
4. The letters are delivered at 11 a.m. (*What time*)
5. The bridge will be constructed next year. (*When*)
6. The gate is closed at 10.15 a.m. (*What time*)
7. The telegram was sent yesterday. (*When*)
8. It was designed by an Indian scientist. (*By whom*)
9. The work was completed in August. (*In which month*)
10. The watch was stolen by the servant. (*By whom*)

EXERCISE 17

(A) *Fill in each blank with the correct form of verb, chosen from the alternative given in brackets :*

EXAMPLE : We heard the noise...in the class. (*producing/being produced*)
= We heard the noise *being produced* in the class.

1. We heard the noise.....in the class. (*producing/being produced*)
2. The boys are eager.....to the higher class. (*to promote/to be promoted*)
3. Gavaskar is willing.....Captain of the Indian cricket team. (*to make/to be made*)
4. We want.....to watch the football match. (*to permit/to be permitted*)
5. People expected Mr Gupta.....but he lost. (*to elect/to be elected*)
6. We saw the trees.....down. (*cutting/being cut*)
7. He does not like to.....a fool. (*call/be called*)
8. The children need to.....how to speak well. (*teach/be taught*)
9. We saw the thief.....to jail. (*being taken/taking*)
10. On.....of his success in the exam, Rajeev cried with joy. (*being told/telling*)

(B) *In each of the following passages, put in place of the brackets the appropriate passive forms of the verbs given in brackets :*

EXAMPLE :

One night some thieves came into my house. A lot of gold and clothes (*take*) away. Early in the morning this (*discover*) by my mother. She (*shock*) to see all that. The matter (*report*) to the police immediately.

Ans. One night some thieves came into my house. A lot of gold and clothes *were taken* away. Early in the morning this *was discovered* by my mother. She *was shocked* to see all that. The matter *was reported* to the police immediately.

1. One night some thieves came into my house. A lot of gold and clothes (*take*) away. Early in the morning this (*discover*) by my mother. She (*shock*) to see all that. The matter (*report*) to the police immediately.

2. Two finger-print experts (*send*) to my house yesterday. All the rooms (*check*) by them. A thorough enquiry (*promise*) by the police officer. We all (*satisfy*) with what had so far been done.

3. Last week the stolen property (*find*) out by the police and everything (*bring*) to my house. The thieves (*arrest*) and they (*send*) to jail.

4. For several years in the beginning of the 19th century, Europe (*dominate*) by Napoleon. Almost every European nation except England (*attack*) and it (*conquer*) by his armies, and it (*force*) to sign treaties of peace.

5. Boys like to switch electric lights on and off quickly; they like the noise which (*make*) when the switch (*move*) up and down. But the boys must (*tell*) that they should not play with such things. Electric lights should (*handle*) by them carefully.

6. If you have a bicycle, it is a good thing to keep it clean. Certainly, bicycles ought to (*keep*) clean. However, the moving parts have to (*oil*). If the oil (*remove*) from the moving parts, they move with difficulty. Sometimes water (*use*) for making a bicycle bright.

EXERCISE 18 (with Answer)

Change into the Active or Passive Voice as required :

1. (a) He was told by his uncle to give up the project. (b) I advised her to see the chairman regarding the matter. (c) The Principal informed the parents that the boy should give up studies.

2. (a) No one thinks of the prisoner as a human being. (b) He approached me for a loan. (c) Let all the doors be shut. (d) People helped Miss Evans to get back to the ship.

3. (a) No one told me to do the work. (b) Let this work be done. (c) Everybody laughed at his plan. (d) He was elected President by them.

4. (a) We use this room only on special occasions. (b) Someone switched on a light and opened the door. (c) They are pulling down the old theatre. (d) Why didn't they mend the roof before it fell in ?

5. (a) They gave her a clock. (b) He expected us to offer him the job. (c) The author has written a special edition for children. (d) What did he write it with ?

6. (a) Did the idea interest you ? (b) The lawyer gave him the details of his uncle's will. (c) The Prime Minister was to have opened the dry dock. (d) We will not admit children under sixteen.

7. (a) Boys of sixteen to eighteen are to man this training ship. (b) Children couldn't have done all this damage. (c) Everyone looked up to him. (d) He hasn't slept in his bed.

8. (a) Burglars broke into the house. (b) They frown on smoking here. (c) The crowd shouted him down. (d) People often take him for his brother.

9. (a) People say that he is a spy. (b) We saw them enter. (c) Don't touch this switch. (d) He likes people to call him 'sir'.

10. (a) We don't allow smoking. (b) Evening dress will be worn. (c) People know that he is armed. (d) Why don't you have your eyes tested ? (e) For a long time the earth was believed to be flat.

Ans. 1. (a) His uncle told him to give up the project. (b) She was advised by me to see the chairman regarding the matter. (c) The parents were informed by the Principal that the boy should give up studies.

2. (a) The prisoner is not thought of as a human being. (b) I was approached by him for a loan. (c) Shut all the doors. (d) Miss Evans was helped to get back to the ship.

3. (a) I was not told to do the work. (b) Do this work. (c) His plan was laughed at. (d) They elected him President.

4. (a) This room is used (by us) only on special occasions. (b) A light was switched on and the door opened. (c) The old theatre is being pulled down. (d) Why wasn't the roof mended before it fell ?

5. (a) She was given a clock. (b) He expected to be offered a job (by us). (c) A special edition for children has been written. (d) What was it written with ?

6. (a) Were you interested in the idea ? (b) He was given details of his uncle's will by the lawyer. (c) The dry dock was to have been opened by the Prime Minister. (d) Children under sixteen will not be admitted.

7. (a) This training ship is to be manned by boys of sixteen to eighteen. (b) All this damage couldn't have been done by children. (c) He was looked up to by everyone. (d) His bed hasn't been slept in.

8. (a) The house was broken into by the burglars. (b) Smoking is frowned on here. (c) He was shouted down by the crowd. (d) He is often taken for his brother.

9. (a) It is said that he is a spy./He is said to be a spy.(b) They were seen to enter.(c) This switch isn't to be/mustn't be touched. (d) He likes to be called 'sir'.

10. (a) Smoking is not allowed. (b) Guests will wear evening dress. (c) He is known to be armed. (d) Why don't you get an oculist to test your eyes ? (e) For a long time people believed that the earth was flat.

□ □ □

9. PREPOSITIONS

Look at these sentences :

Mr Rao is coming *by* train.
Cows were grazing *in* the field.
The teacher is pleased *with* you.

ऊपर के वाक्यों में आए शब्द *by, in* तथा *with* prepositions हैं। Preposition का प्रयोग noun या pronoun के पहले किया जाता है।

(A) KINDS OF PREPOSITIONS

(i) English में अधिकांश prepositions एक शब्द के होते हैं, उन्हें *single-word prepositions* कहा जाता है। जैसे :

after	before	beside	during	into
of	outside	plus	through	toward(s)
up	within	about	against	among
behind	besides	by	for	inside
off	over	round	under	throughout
upon	without	above	along	around
below	between	despite	from	minus
on	past	since	till	until
via	across	at	beneath	beyond
down	in	opposite	per	than
to	with	amid		

(ii) नीचे दिए गए शब्द देखने में verbs या adjectives की तरह लगते हैं किंतु इनका प्रयोग preposition जैसा होता है :

except	considering	pending	excepting	like
unlike	barring	including	worth	near
concerning	following	despite		

(iii) कुछ prepositions एक शब्द के होते हैं तो कुछ एक से अधिक शब्द के, जिन्हें *complex prepositions* कहा जाता है। जैसे :

up to	out of	owing to	due to	because of
as for	as to	along with	apart from	away from
such as	in view of	together with	in spite of	by means of
on account of	instead of	on to	in comparison with	in accordance with

(B) POSITIONS OF PREPOSITIONS

English sentences में preposition वाक्य के शुरू, मध्य या अंत में आ सकता है।

1. *Look at these sentences :*

This is a book *of* poems.
This train goes *to* Delhi.
School begins *at* ten o'clock.

ऊपर के वाक्यों में prepositions (*of, to, at*) का प्रयोग nouns (poems, Delhi, ten o'clock) के पहले किया गया है।

2. *Look at these sentences :*

What are you *afraid of ?*
She likes being *looked at.*
Mathematics is something I have a lot of *difficulty with.*

Afraid of, looked at, difficulty with कुछ ऐसे शब्द हैं जिनके साथ preposition clause के अंत में आते हैं।

3. *Look at these sentences :*

Who are you *thinking of ?*
What are you *looking at ?*
What are you so *angry about ?*
'I'm getting married.'—'*who to ?*'
Where has the bus *come from ?*

Wh-words या how से शुरू होनेवाले questions के अंत में preposition आता है।

4. *Look at these sentences :*

What a lot of *trouble* I am *in* !
His address—that's *what* I'm not *sure of*.

What से शुरू होनेवाले दूसरे clauses में भी preposition end-position में रहता है।

5. *Look at these sentences :*

There is the house *I told you about.*
You remember the boy *I was going out with.*
This is the song *that I am fond of.*
This is the boy (who) *I was referring to.*

Relative clauses में preposition अंत में आता है।

6. *Look at these sentences :*

I hate *being laughed at.*

The patient has already *been operated on.*

Passive clauses में preposition अंत में आता है।

7. *Look at these sentences :*

It's a boring place *to live in.*

I need something *to write with.*

Infinitive phrases के अंत में preposition आता है।

8. *Look at these sentences :*

Who is it *for* ?

What is she *like* ?

What was it *about* ?

अगर question में *am, is, are, was, were* main verb रहें तो preposition अंत में आता है।

9. *Look at these sentences :*

For whom was the warning intended ?

On which flight is the general travelling ?

The problem *about which* I consulted you has been solved.

Wh-questions तथा relative clauses में preposition को पहले भी रखा जा सकता है।

10. *Look at these sentences :*

Who do you intend to travel *with* ?

With whom do you intend to travel ? (Not: *With who*)

Who के पहले preposition नहीं आता है, किंतु whom के पहले आता है।

11. *Look at these sentences :*

There is the boy (*that*) I used to be in love *with*.

It was the boy *with whom* she used to be in love. (Not *with that....*)

Relative clauses में केवल whom या which के पहले preposition आ सकता है, that के पहले नहीं।

(C) USE OF SOME PREPOSITIONS

(i) Position in Time

निश्चित या अनिश्चित समय या अवधि का भाव व्यक्त करने के लिए भी हमें prepositions या prepositional phrases का प्रयोग करना पड़ता है। इनमें मुख्य prepositions हैं— at, on, during, from, since, between, before, after, around, about, throughout, by, over, past, till, until, to, under आदि।

About का प्रयोग 'लगभग' के अर्थ में होता है :

It is *about* ten o'clock.	It is *about* time to get up.
It is *about* lunch hour.	It is *about* time to play.

After का प्रयोग 'के बाद, के उपरांत' के अर्थ में निश्चित तिथि/समय/घटना के पूर्व होता है :

She came *after* Christmas.	She sang *after* his departure.
They play *after* 4 o'clock.	I saw him *after* appointment.

Around का भी प्रयोग about के ही अर्थ में होता है, लेकिन about six o'clock का साधारण अर्थ होता है 'लगभग छः बजे, लेकिन उससे अधिक नहीं'; around six o'clock का अर्थ होता है 'छः बजे के आस-पास, कुछ मिनट कम या बेशी'।

Tom came *around* ten o'clock.	We play *around* four o'clock.
He left *around* five o'clock.	They slept *around* midnight.

At का प्रयोग निश्चित समय (precise points of time) सूचित करने के लिए होता है :

I got up at 6 o'clock.	She danced *at* 10 o'clock.
You had tea *at* 4 o'clock.	We play *at* 4.30 p.m.

Note : *at* noon, *at* night में भी *at* का प्रयोग recognised divisions of the day के साथ होता है।

Between का प्रयोग 'दो points of time के बीच में' के अर्थ में होता है :

He went there *between* five and six.	Stay here *between* ten and twelve.
I came here *between* Sunday and Tuesday.	See me *between* one and two.

Before का प्रयोग 'के पहले,' 'के पूर्व' के अर्थ में निश्चित तिथि या समय या घटना के पूर्व होता है :

Do it *before* March.	See me *before* 6 o'clock.
Get it *before* Monday.	Tell him *before* his return.

By का प्रयोग 'तक' के अर्थ में निर्धारित समय/तिथि के प्रसंग में होता है :

He will return *by* 10 o'clock.	She may come *by* midnight.
They may do it *by* Monday next.	Tom will be in London *by* May.

During का प्रयोग 'के समय, में, के दौरान' के अर्थ में अवधि (period of time) सूचित करने के लिए होता है :

That man was killed *during* World War I.	Jack came in *during* the night.
They did it *during* my absence.	The sun gives us light *during* the day.
What will you do *during* Holi ?	He was happy *during* his childhood.

Note : जहाँ समय सूचित करने के लिए in का प्रयोग हो सकता है, वहाँ during भी प्रयोग हो सकता है।

For का प्रयोग definite period of time का बोध कराने के लिए होता है :

He stayed here *for* months. She was here *for* a day.
She lived there *for* a year. Please wait for me *for* ten hours.

From का प्रयोग निश्चित समय सूचित करने के लिए होता है, खासकर जब यह बोध हो कि क्रिया उस समय से शुरू होकर जारी रही या जारी रहेगी। From का प्रयोग सभी tenses में होता है :

The work will start *from* Monday next. He waited *from* 6 a.m.
Examinations begin *from* 7th May. Shops will be open *from* 8 o'clock.

In से period of time सूचित होता है। महीना, ऋतु तथा साल के नाम के पहले भी in का प्रयोग होता है :

We read *in* the morning. We play cricket *in* winter.
He did it *in* April. India became independent *in* August.

उसी तरह हम in the evening, in the daytime भी कहते हैं।

On का प्रयोग दिन तथा तिथि के नाम के पहले होता है :

He came here *on* Monday. Come here *on* 5th May.
Will you help me *on* Sunday ? Go there *on* 9th of this month.

Over का प्रयोग 'for the period of' (पर, के समय, में, तक) के अर्थ में होता है :

He has been invited *over* the week-end.
Can you stay here *over* Monday (i.e., until Monday) ?

Past का प्रयोग 'के बाद, के आगे, से अधिक' के अर्थ में होता है :

It was *past* midnight. (मध्यरात्रि से अधिक समय)
It is five minutes *past* five. (पाँच बजकर पाँच मिनट)

[लेकिन past Monday, past Holi, past Diwali के बदले last Monday, last Holi, last Diwali का ही प्रयोग होता है।]

Since का प्रयोग बीते हुए समय के किसी निश्चित point of time को सूचित करने के लिए होता है :

He has been here *since* Monday last.
She has been ill *since* the birth of her first child.
These boys have been playing *since* morning.
What have you been doing *since* 8 o'clock ?

Throughout का प्रयोग लगातार के अर्थ में होता है :

He worked *throughout* the night. (रातभर, सारी रात)

What will you do *throughout* winter ? (जाड़ेभर, जाड़े के शुरू से लेकर अंत तक)

I shall remember it *throughout* my life. (जीवनभर)

Till का प्रयोग 'तक' के अर्थ में होता है :

Wait *till* I come.

Stay here *till* 5 p.m.

He will return *till* next Monday.

Good-bye *till* tomorrow.

To का प्रयोग—Five minutes *to* ten = दस बजने में पाँच मिनट बाकी; *to* time = बिलकुल ठीक समय पर।

Under का अर्थ समय के प्रसंग में है 'less than' :

under two hours = less than two hours.
under a fortnight = in less than a fortnight.

Until का प्रयोग 'तक' के अर्थ में किसी निर्धारित समय/तिथि/घटना के पहले होता है :

Can I stay *until* Monday ?

He will stay there *until* Holi.

He is usually in his office *until* midday.

I will wait *until* I hear from you.

(ii) A Note on Some Prepositions

कभी-कभी एक ही अर्थ में एक से अधिक preposition का प्रयोग होता है। अब हम उनके सूक्ष्म अर्थ-विभेद को देखें :

(i) At, In (for places)

1. *Look at these sentences :*

He lives *in* Delhi.
She was born *at* Manpura *in* Bihar.
They live *at* Club Road, Muzaffarpur.

(i) *In* का प्रयोग महादेश, देश, राज्य तथा बड़े शहर के नाम के पहले होता है।

(ii) *At* का प्रयोग छोटे शहर, गाँव तथा पता (address) के पहले होता है।

A big city can also be treated as a point, when we speak of global distances; in that case, *at* is used, e.g., While flying to New York I had a brief stopover *at* London.

(ii) On, In, At, By (for time)

2. *Look at these sentences :*

I go to bed *at* 10 o'clock.

Days are hot *in* summer.

I always walk *in* the evening.

He came *on* Tuesday.

They were here *on* 10th May. Be here *by* 6 o' clock.

(i) At से निश्चित समय सूचित होता है।

(ii) In से period of time सूचित होता है। ऋतु, महीने तथा साल के नाम के पहले भी in का प्रयोग होता है। जैसे : *in* March, *in* 1985.

(iii) *On* का प्रयोग दिन तथा तिथि (on 15th August) के नाम के पहले होता है।

(iv) *By* का प्रयोग 'तक' के अर्थ में निर्धारित समय या तिथि के प्रसंग में होता है।

(iii) Between, Among

3. *Look at these sentences :*

Hari stands *between* Madan and Abdul.

Divide this mango *among* the four boys.

(i) *Between* का प्रयोग दो व्यक्तियों या वस्तुओं के बीच की बात को सूचित करने के लिए होता है।

(ii) *Among* का प्रयोग दो से अधिक व्यक्तियों या वस्तुओं 'के बीच/में' बताने के लिए किया जाता है।

Note : किंतु Modern English में between का प्रयोग दो से अधिक व्यक्तियों या वस्तुओं के बीच की बात को सूचित करने के लिए भी किया जाता है।

(i) इस संबंध में आप कुछ modern usage देखें—

(i) The rule, at one time insisted upon, that *between* is used of only two things or persons, and *among* of more than two is no longer strictly observed.

—F. T. Wood : CURRENT ENGLISH USAGE

कुछ उदाहरण देखें :

(a) We shall do the work more quickly if we share it *between us*. यहाँ between us से दो से अधिक व्यक्तियों का बोध होता है। उसी तरह between ourselves का अर्थ होता है : in confidence.

(b) The three children saved over a hundred pounds *between* them.

(ii) *Between* can relate more than two objects, if we have a definite number in mind.

—Geoffrey Leech & Jan Svartvik : A COMMUNICATIVE GRAMMAR OF ENGLISH

जैसे : Switzerland lies *between France, Germany, Italy and Austria.*

(iv) In, Into

4. *Look at these sentences :*

Mr Prasad is *in* the house. There is a coin *in* the box.

Mr Prasad went *into* the house. A boy jumped *into* the river.

(i) *In* का अर्थ होता है—अंदर, भीतर। इससे गति का बोध नहीं होता।

(ii) *Into* से अंदर जाने की गति का बोध होता है।

'In' denotes position or rest; 'into' denotes motion inward.

(v) Since, For

5. *Look at these sentences :*

He has been here *since* { six o'clock. / Monday. / April. / 1986. }

He has been here *for* { two hours. / five days. / three months. / six years. }

(i) *Since* से निश्चित समय (छह बजे से, सोमवार से, अप्रैल से, 1986 से) का बोध होता है तथा इसके पहले present perfect continuous tense या present perfect tense का प्रयोग किया जाता है।

(ii) *For* से समय की अवधि (दो-तीन महीने से, चार घंटे से, पाँच दिन से, छह साल से इत्यादि) सूचित होती है।

(vi) From, Since

6. *Look at these sentences :*

He waited *from* 6 till 6.30.
They went *from* Delhi to Bombay.
She has been here *since* Monday.

(i) *From* का प्रयोग समय तथा स्थान को बताने के लिए होता है। *From* का प्रयोग सभी tenses में होता है।

(ii) *Since* का प्रयोग point of time के साथ होता है। *Since* का प्रयोग future tense के साथ नहीं होता। जैसे :

He will be present here *since* Friday कहना गलत होगा, इसके बदले हम कहेंगे—He will be present here *from* Monday.

(vii) To, Till, Until

7. *Look at these sentences :*

We are going *to* Patna.
He works *from* 8 *to* 9.
They studied *till* 6 p.m.
Please stay here *until* next Monday.
She walked *to* the window.
How long is it *to/till* dinner ?
I did not see him *till* last week.

(i) *To* का प्रयोग place तथा time दोनों बताने के लिए होता है।

(ii) *Till* या *until* का प्रयोग केवल time बताने के लिए होता है। If there is no *from*, we put *till* (not *to*) before the final time. जैसे :

Let us work *till* 4 p.m.
We stayed *from* June *to* September.

(iii) जब किसी घटना के पहले का length of time को consider करते हैं (When considering the length of time before an event) तब to अथवा till का प्रयोग कर सकते हैं। जैसे :

It is an hour *to* dinner.
या It is an hour *till* dinner.

Note : Till तथा until के अर्थ में कोई अंतर नहीं है और एक की जगह दूसरे का प्रयोग किया जा सकता है। किंतु till का प्रयोग अकसर point of time के लिए तथा until का duration of time के लिए किया जाता है। जैसे :

We didn't get home *till* ten o'clock.
Don't do anything further *till* you hear from him.
She lived with an aunt *until* she married.
We shall have to stay here *until* help arrives.

Until का प्रयोग प्रायः वाक्य के शुरू में किया जाता है :

Until we know the facts, we can do nothing further.

(viii) By, With

8. *Look at these sentences :*

The tiger was killed *by* Amar (=the agent).
The letter was written *with* a pen. (=the instrument).
The snake was killed *by* Hari (=the agent) with (=the instrument) a stick.
This essay is written *by* me *with* a pen.

(i) *By* का प्रयोग किसी agent या doer (कर्ता) के पहले होता है।

(ii) *With* का प्रयोग किसी instrument (यंत्र/औजार) के पहले होता है। यों by तथा with का अर्थ 'से, द्वारा' होता है।

(ix) During, For

9. *Look at these sentences :*

He was away from home *during* the Pujahs.
The prices of things shoot up *during* the war.
They went to London *for* two months.

(i) During का एक अर्थ 'की अवधि तक' (throughout the duration) होता है, जैसा आप ऊपर प्रथम वाक्य में देखते हैं। During का दूसरा अर्थ 'के दौरान' (in course of) होता है। जैसे : during Holi, during summer, during his childhood, during the war इत्यादि।

(ii) *For* का प्रयोग definite period of time के लिए होता है। जैसे : for two years, for five months.

Note : "*During* answers the question, 'when ?' *For* answers the question 'How long ?' जैसे :

'When did you complete the work ?'—'*During* the vacation.'
'How long was the college closed ?'—'*For* two months.'

(x) Around, Throughout

10. *Look at these sentences :*

Mr Jha came here *around* 10 p.m.
He worked *throughout* the night.
I shall remember it *throughout* the life.

(i) *Around* का प्रयोग about के अर्थ में होता है, *around 10 p.m.* का अर्थ होता है 'दस बजे के आस-पास—कुछ मिनट कम या अधिक'।

(ii) *Throughout* का प्रयोग लगातार के अर्थ होता है। अतः, *throughout the night*=रातभर, सारी रात; *throughout the life*=जीवनभर।

(xi) In, Within

11. *Look at these sentences :*

I shall be back again *in* a year.
I shall be back again *within* a year.

(i) *In a year*=एक साल में अर्थात साल समाप्त होने पर, in a week=एक सप्ताह में अर्थात सप्ताह समाप्त होने पर।

(ii) *Within a year*=एक साल के अंदर, within a week=एक सप्ताह के अंदर।

(xii) Beside, Besides

12. *Look at these sentences :*

Go and sit *beside* (=by the side of) Hari.
Besides (=over and above) Mr Bose, five persons were there.

(i) Beside=by the side of, की बगल में, next to, उसके बाद।

(ii) Besides=in addition, के अलावा, over and above all, के अतिरिक्त।

(xiii) In, On, To

13. *Look at these sentences :*

Himachal Pradesh is *in* (=inside) the north of India.

The Himalaya is *on* (=on the frontier) the north of India.

Tibet is *to* (=outside) the north of India.

(i) In का अर्थ 'के भीतर, के अंदर' होता है; on का अर्थ 'सीमा पर' और to का अर्थ 'सीमा से बाहर' होता है।

(xiv) Before, within

14. *Look at these sentences :*

He came *before* ten o'clock.	Do it *within* an hour.
Please go there *before* Monday.	Finish it *within* two days.

(i) Before (=के पहले) का प्रयोग point of time को सूचित करना है।

(ii) Within (=में, के अंदर) से period of time का बोध होता है।

(xv) In, Among

15. *Look at these sentences :*

We found him *in* the crowd.	He was lost *among* groups of boys.
He spoke *in* Parliament.	They sat *among* the trees.

(i) In का प्रयोग singular collective nouns के पहले होता है।

(ii) Among का प्रयोग plural तथा plural collective nouns के पहले होता है।

(xvi) Among, Amongst

16. *Look at these sentences :*

He was sitting *among* her children.	He stood *amongst* elephants.
Among those present were my friends.	She is the best *amongst* us.

(i) Among तथा amongst का अर्थ होता है: में, में से, बीच में।

(ii) Among तथा amongst के प्रयोग में अंतर नहीं है। किंतु among का प्रयोग amongst से अधिक होता है।

(iii) Among तथा amongst का प्रयोग plural noun या pronoun अथवा collective noun—singular in form तथा plural in sense के पहले होता है।

(iv) Amongst का प्रयोग अकसर vowel से शुरू होनेवाले शब्द के पहले होता है।

(v) किंतु among या amongst के बाद यदि the आए, तो दोनों में किसी एक का प्रयोग कर सकते हैं : among *the* people, amongst *the* people.

इन दोनों शब्दों के प्रयोग के संबंध में एक modern grammarian का विचार देखें :

There is no difference of meaning, and no rule as to which should be used in particular circumstances, though some authorities suggest that *amongst* is more usual before a vowel. The deciding factors are really euphony and the rhythm of the sentence *Among* is more common. —F. T. WOOD : CURRENT ENGLISH USAGE

(xvii) of, off

17. *Look at these sentences :*

The box is made *of* wood.	Keep *off* the grass.
That is a real work *of* art.	Get this ring *off* your finger.

(i) Of का अर्थ—'का, के, की, से, के विषय में' होता है।

(ii) Off का अर्थ—'से दूर, से, से नीचे, से अलग' होता है।

(xviii) Among, Amid, Amidst

18. *Look at these sentences :*

The house stands *among* trees.
The house stands *amid* trees.
He was sitting *among/amid/amidst* his pupils.

(i) Among का अर्थ होता है—'में, बीच में तथा amid/amidst का भी अर्थ होता है—'में, बीच में' (in or in the middle of).

(ii) Among की तरह amid/amidst का भी प्रयोग indefinite number of objects (जैसे : trees, children, pupils) के पहले होता है।

(iii) किंतु amid/amidst का प्रयोग uncountable noun के पहले भी होता है, पर ऐसा प्रयोग among का नहीं होता। जैसे :

A child's doll was found *amid/amidst* the wreckage of the plane.

(xix) Underneath, Beneath

19. *Look at these sentences :*

She wore a fur coat with nothing *underneath.*	There is a village *beneath* the hills.
The letter was pushed *underneath* the door.	Everything looks bright *beneath* the moon.
The insect crept further *underneath.*	It is *beneath* (=not worthy of) you to complain.

(i) Underneath का अर्थ होता है—'के नीचे, के तले' तथा beneath का अर्थ होता है—'नीचे, तले, अयोग्य'।

(ii) Modern English में underneath तथा beneath की जगह under का प्रयोग किया जाता है, beneath का प्रयोग साहित्य या formal writing में किया जाता है।

(D) VARIOUS MEANINGS OF PREPOSITIONS

1. About से बोध होता है :

(i) विषय में—What do you know *about* him ?
What is he so angry *about* ?

(ii) के चारों ओर—He had a belt *about* (=around) *his waist.*

(iii) आसन्न—The train is *about* to leave. (=खुलने-खुलने को है)

(iv) लगभग—It is *about* ten o'clock.
They were *about* five in all.

(v) में लगा हुआ, में व्यस्त—What are you *about ?* (क्या कर रहे हो ?)

(vi) इधर-उधर—He can now move *about.*

2. Above से बोध होता है :

(i) से अधिक—It weighs *above* ten tons.

(ii) के बाहर, से फाजिल—He lives *above* (=beyond) his means.

(iii) ऊपर—You must have a roof *above* your head.

(iv) अपने से ऊपर—A soldier should value honour *above* life.
He married *above* (=in a higher family) himself.

(v) के परे—This book is *above* me (=too difficult for me).

3. After से बोध होता है :

(i) बाद में, के उपरांत (time के संदर्भ में)—He started *after* 2 o'clock.

(ii) के बावजूद—*After all* my care it was broken.

(iii) की खोज में, को पकड़ने के लिए—The policeman ran *after* the thief.

(iv) पीछे (क्रम के संदर्भ में)—He left first and his son left *after* him.

(v) मनपसंद—This car is *after* my heart.

(vi) के विषय में—He enquired *after* your health.

4. Against से बोध होता है :

(i) विरुद्ध में—Public opinion was *against* the Bill.

(ii) में सटाकर—The ladder was placed *against* the tree.
He was *leaning* against a post.

(iii) के वास्ते (in preparation for, in anticipation of)—Take precautions *against* fire. Save money *against* a rainy day.

(iv) की तुलना में—The pine-trees were black *against* the morning sky.

5. At से बोध होता है :

(i) निर्दिष्ट स्थान—He was *at* his office.

(ii) निर्दिष्ट समय—We went there *at* two o'clock.

(iii) की उम्र में—He left school *at* (the age of) 15.

(iv) क्रम (order)—*at* first, *at* last, *at* the second attempt etc.

(v) (कार्य) में रत (occupation, activity)—He is *at* work.
You are *at* play.

(vi) मात्रा (rate)—The car was *at* full speed.
I borrowed money from him *at* 6% interest.

(vii) की दर से (value, cost)—Buy it at Rs. 15/-. Don't sell it *at* a loss.
The property was valued *at* two lakhs.

(viii) की ओर—The bull ran furiously *at* the woman.

(ix) कारण (cause)—He has done this *at* my request.

(x) कुछ adjectives के बाद दक्षता या कमी—He is good *at* mathematics.
She is poor *at* languages.
I am good *at* translation.

(xi) कुछ superlatives के साथ—*at* least, *at* most, *at* the worst,
at its (his, their etc.) best.

(xii) कुछ और प्रयोग—*at* leisure, *at* war, *at* peace, *at* a gallop, finish something *at* a sitting.

6. Before से बोध होता है :

(i) के पूर्व—He came here the day *before* yesterday.
Do it *before* 8 o'clock.

(ii) के सामने—The accused was produced *before* the judge.

(iii) अधिक पसंद (in preference to)—Every Indian would choose death *before* dishonour.

7. Behind से बोध होता है :

(i) पीछे (क्रम में)—There is an orchard *behind* the house.

(ii) पीछे (समय में)—Your schooldays will soon be far *behind* you.

(iii) पीछे (छिपा हुआ)—The sun was *behind* (=hidden by) the clouds.

8. Beyond से बोध होता है :

(i) उस पार (on the farther side of)—Don't go *beyond* the town boundary.

(ii) के बाहर—He lives *beyond* his income.

(iii) बाद में (of time)—Don't stay out *beyond* (=after) 10 o'clock.

(iv) के ऊपर (surpassing)—Your work is *beyond* all praise.
(=so good that it cannot be praised enough).

9. By से बोध होता है :

(i) निकट (near)—Come and sit *by* me (=by my side).
My house is *by* the river.

(ii) तक (समय के प्रसंग में)—Can you finish the work *by* 10 o'clock/ *by* tomorrow ?

(iii) साधक (agent, agency or means)—The watch was stolen *by* the servant.
The streets were lighted *by* electricity.

(iv) के अनुसार (in accordance with)—What is the time *by* your watch ?
By my watch it is 2 o'clock.

(v) द्वारा—I will go *by* train, not *by* car.

(vi) मात्रा (to the extent of)—The bullet missed him *by* two inches.
It needs to be longer *by* two inches.

(vii) का नाम लेकर (in oaths)—I always swear *by* Almighty God. He swears *by* you all the time.

(viii) होकर गुजरना (pass)—I go *by* (=I pass) the post-office every morning.
I came *by* the fields not *by* the roads.

(ix) के हिसाब से—I hired a bicycle *by* the day (जैसे एक दिन के लिए पाँच रुपए).
I engaged a clerk *by* the month.
We pay a labourer *by* the day/*by* the hour.
He sells cloth *by* the yard, coal *by* the tons and eggs *by* the dozen.

(x) तरीका (manner)—I caught the thief *by* the hand.

10. For से बोध होता है :

(i) उद्देश्य, के वास्ते—I read *for* pleasure.
He goes *for* a walk.

(ii) के कारण—He will suffer *for* his evil habits.

(iii) के बावजूद—*For* all his learning, he proved a failure in life.
For all his wealth, he is unhappy.

(iv) के लिहाज से (in view of)—She is rather tall *for* her age.
It is quite warm *for* January.

(v) के पक्ष में (in support of, in favour of)—I will vote *for* you.

(vi) की अवधि तक/में/से (extent in time)—I have now studied English *for* several years.
I am going away *for* a few days.

(vii) के लिए (destination के अर्थ में)—Let us start *for* home.
The train is bound *for* Delhi.

(viii) की ओर से—We should fight *for* (=on behalf of) the weak and the poor.

(ix) के बदले में—He exchanged his book *for* another book.
The letters M.P. stand *for* Member of Parliament.

(x) कीमत—I bought this pen *for* five rupees.

(xi) उपयुक्त, अनुपयुक्त—Drinking is good/bad *for* health.
You are the man *for* the job.

(xii) की दूरी तक—We walked (*for*) three miles.
For miles and miles, there is not a house to be seen.

(xiii) जैसा—They left him on the battle-field *for* dead.
They chose him *for* (=as, to be) their leader.

11. From का अर्थ होता है 'से', लेकिन इस 'से' के कई अर्थ होते हैं :

(i) से (अलग होना, बच निकलना)—His absence *from the* class was soon noticed.
The mango fell *from* the tree.

(ii) दूर—The village is five miles (away) *from* the town.
It is only a few steps *from* here to the post office.

(iii) कारण (because of, as a result of)—She suffered *from* heart disease.
He died *from* loss of blood.

(iv) देखते हुए (judging by, considering)—*From* a practical point of view it is stupid.
From his appearance, he looks old.

(v) आरंभ (in place or time)—He is coming *from* home.
We have been working *from* morning to night.

(vi) के बाद—The shop will be open *from* half past 8.
It will be open *from* about 9 o'clock.

(vii) के द्वारा (based on, using, out of)—Bread is made *from* flour.
She played the music *from* memory.

(viii) के बदले में (instead of)—He needs a rest *from* work.

(ix) तुलना में (as being unlike)—He is different *from* his brother in character.

(x) सुरक्षा देना, रोकना—She saved the child *from* the fire.
A tree gave us shelter *from* the rain.

(xi) उत्पत्ति, स्रोत (source, origin)—Many evils flow *from* fear.
I knew *from* him all about you.

12. In का 'में' के अर्थ में प्रयोग होता है :

(i) के भीतर (within)—There are five men *in* this room.

(ii) स्थान संबंध में (position)—He is *in* London these days.
He was wounded *in* the leg.

(iii) पोशाक में (wearing)—He was dressed *in* silk.
I saw a girl *in* red/*in* a fur coat/*in* uniform.

(iv) के द्वारा (with or by means of)—Write it *in* pencil/*in* ink.
It was printed *in* red.

(v) समय के अर्थ में—He came here *in* January.
She was born *in* 1980.
He learnt English *in* 3 years.

(vi) के बाद, के अंत में—I will come *in* an hour.
The work will be finished *in* a month or so.

(vii) Showing division and arrangement—Pack them in 10's (=10 in each parcel).
Cut it in 2 (=into 2 halves).

(viii) अवस्था के अर्थ में—He was *in* difficulties/*in* danger/*in* good health/*in* a hurry/*in* ruins/*in* doubt/*in* tears.
We fall *in* love.

(xi) के बदले में (as, by way of)—She said nothing *in* reply.
What did you give him *in* return ?

(x) पेशा या कार्य (occupation or activity)—You are *in* politics.
He is *in* the army.

13. Into का भी अर्थ है 'में', किंतु इससे आगे की ओर गति (motion towards) का बोध होता है :

(i) के भीतर—They broke *into* his store.
He fell *into* the well.

(ii) उसमें होना (so as to be in)—He went *into* the law and then *into* business.

(iii) में बदल देना—Translate it *into* English. He turned the prince *into* a rabbit. Divide it *into* 5 parts. She developed *into* a beautiful woman.

(iv) एक अंक से दूसरे में भाग देने के अर्थ में—3 *into* 6 goes twice.

(v) समय के अर्थ—You should not work so late *into* the night.

14. Of का मूल अर्थ होता है 'का/के/की' या 'से', लेकिन इससे कई भाव व्यक्त होते हैं।

(i) रखना, होना, मालिक होना (belonging to, has)—The colour *of* her dress is red.
The roots *of* your hair are weak.
This is the house *of* my uncle.

(ii) बना होना (made from)—It is a dress *of* silk.
The house is made *of* brick.

(iii) में रखना (containing)—It is a bag *of* potatoes.

(iv) मात्रा (quantity)—Give me two kilos *of* sugar.
We crossed two miles *of* the bad road.

(v) तिथि के साथ—He came on the 27th *of* March.

(vi) Uncountable noun के साथ—I don't eat lots *of* sugar.
There isn't a blade *of* grass.

(vii) में से (from among)—The members *of* the team are here.
Two *of* us will do it.

(viii) से (origin)—She is a girl *of* a good family.

(ix) द्वारा (by)—The plays *of* Shakespeare are immortal.

(x) के विषय में—These are the stories *of* adventure.

(xi) कारण—He died *of* fever.

(xii) *of* के कुछ और प्रयोग देखें :

the older *of* the two, the most important *of* all, those blue eyes *of* hers, the love *of* God, the city *of* New York, at the page *of* 5, *of* one's free will, the king *of* Nepal, a lover *of* good music, a woman *of* no importance, die *of* hunger, cure someone *of* a disease, rob someone *of* his money, hard *of* hearing.

15. Off का प्रयोग 'से' के अर्थ में विच्छेद (separation) व्यक्त करने के लिए होता है :

(i) दूर होना (away from)—Get *off* my foot. Keep *off* the grass.
He jumped *off* the horse.

(ii) से अलग करना—Take the curtains *off* their hooks.
The child is eating *off* the plate.

(iii) से लेना—He borrowed two rupees *off* me.

(iv) किसी निर्धारित लक्ष्य से दूर होना—We are going *off* the subject.
We are a long way *off* understanding it yet.
The ship was blown *off* her course.

(v) सड़क पर घूम जाना (turning off a road)—He lives/drove/stayed 2 miles *off* the main road.

(vi) *off* के कुछ और प्रयोग देखें :

He is sleeping half-on and half-*off* the sofa.
The book slipped *off* the table.
The mango fell *off* the tree.
The house is just a little way *off* the playground.

16. On (upon) का 'पर' के अर्थ में प्रयोग होता है :

(i) पर (स्पर्श के अर्थ में)—The book is *on* the table.
The ring is *on* my finger.
He jumped *on/onto* the horse.

(ii) के बहुत नजदीक— Patna is *on* the river Ganga.
My village is *on* the border.

(iii) समय (during)—They arrived *on* Monday/*on* 9th July.

(iv) तुरत बाद— *On* thinking about the idea, I decided against it.
Send me a telegram *on* your arrival.

(v) के विषय में (about)—He wrote a book *on* India.

(vi) के जरिए (by means of)—They live *on* potatoes.
A car runs *on* petrol.

(vii) कुछ मशीन— He heard it *on* the radio.
They speak *on* the telephone.

(viii) कारण, परिणाम, से— He acted *on* the lawyer's advice.
On (=as a result of) a representation to the Govt., he was promoted.

(ix) की मदद से (support of money)—He went round the world *on* the money his aunt gave him.

(x) का सदस्य— He was *on* the committee.
She was *on* the jury.

(xi) के साथ (with)—Have you got any money *on* you ?

(xii) आधार— He has been sent there *on* transfer.

(xiii) *on, upon* के कुछ और प्रयोग देखें :

on my right, make an attack *on* the enemy, trees *on* (=along) both sides of the street, *on* my way to college, *on* his arrival, *on* the morning of 10th, *on* thinking about the idea, *on* foot, *on* horseback, *on* a ship, *on* the 9 o'clock train, *on* fire, *on* sale, *on* strike, *on* holiday, *on* the run, *on* offer, *on* purpose, *on* a journey, a tax *on* income, *on* credit, *on* good terms, interest *on* the loan.

17. Over का अर्थ होता है 'के ऊपर', किंतु इससे कई तरह के भाव व्यक्त होते हैं :

(i) के ऊपर (बिना स्पर्श के) — The lamp hung *over* the table.

(ii) दूसरी ओर जाना (पहले ऊपर फिर नीचे) — He jumped *over* the wall.

(iii) एक किनारे से दूसरे किनारे तक— There is a bridge *over* the river.
The car ran *over* a girl and killed her.

(iv) शासन करने के अर्थ में— He ruled *over* a large kingdom.

(v) अधिक (more than)—I have *over* thirty books.

(vi) के क्रम में, में (during, in the course)—We had two meetings *over* dinner.

(vii) दूर किनारे पर— They live *over* the street.

(viii) विभिन्न भागों से होकर—He travelled all *over* Europe.

(ix) अंत तक—Are you staying in Delhi *over* Christmas ?

(x) के द्वारा (heard or said by means of or using)—I don't want to say *over* the telephone.

(xi) के संबंध में, के विषय में—He had no difficulties *over* his income tax.

(xii) से ज्यादा (beyond)—He has been absent *over* a week.
He spent *over* five thousand rupees for this show.

(xiii) समाप्त—The match is *over* (adverbial use).

18. Than से सूचित होता है :

(i) तुलना के अर्थ में—More *than* fifty boys were there.

(ii) अंतर (difference)—Students other *than* those belonging to the scheduled castes need not apply for this post.

19. Through से सूचित होता है :

(i) से होकर—We had to march *through* the forest.
I have passed *through* many difficulties.

(ii) आर-पार, शुरु से लेकर अंत तक—I have gone *through* this book.
He ran a thorn *through* my finger.

(iii) के जरिए—It was *through* John that they found out.
I got this book *through* the library.

(iv) कारण, परिणामस्वरूप—The war was lost *through* bad organization.
It is *through* honest labour that you can hope to succeed.

(v) सफलतापूर्वक समाप्त करना—Did you get *through* your examinations ?

(vi) समाप्ति पर आना—Are you *through* your work yet ?

(vii) के बावजूद (a noise)—I could hear his voice *through* the crashing of the bombs.

20. To का प्रयोग भिन्न-भिन्न अर्थों में इस प्रकार होता है :

(i) की ओर (in a direction towards)—He has gone *to* Bombay.

(ii) तक (as far as)—The water came *to* our necks.

(iii) की अवस्था तक—The child was kicked *to* death by the wild horse.
Wait until the lights change *to* green.

(iv) स्पर्श की अवस्था में—The two lovers danced cheek *to* cheek.
The paper stuck firmly *to* the wall.

(v) आमने-सामने—They stood face *to* face/back *to* back.
I was sitting with my back *to* the engine.

(vi) तक (as far as, until and including)—Count from 10 *to* 20.
It is ten miles (from here) *to* Patna.
I am wet *to* the skin.

(vii) ध्यान या स्वामित्व के लिए—Have you told all your news *to* John ?
I want a present to give *to* my friend.

(viii) के लिए (for, of)—Have you got a key *to* this lock ?
He got a job as secretary *to* a doctor.

(ix) के अनुसार—Your dress isn't really *to* my liking.

(x) और (and)—Add two *to* four.

(xi) की इज्जत में (in honour of)—Let's drink *to* the health of our respected foreign guests.

(xii) पहले (time)—It is five minutes *to* four. How long is it *to* (till) dinner ?

(xiii) स्थान पर (in the position of)—Bangladesh is *to* the east of India.

(xiv) प्रति (per)—This car does 30 miles *to* the litre.

(xv) जहाँ तक मेरी बात है—*To* me this seemed silly.

(xvi) के संबंध में—What's your answer *to* that ?
It will do a lot of good *to* your chest.

(xvii) के बीच (between)—He was in ten *to* twelve feet of water.
She is 40 to 45.

(xviii) के प्रति—We should be kind *to* animals.

(xix) उद्देश्य—I invited him *to* dinner.

(xx) में (change of state)—When heated, ice turns *to* water.

(xxi) अनुपात (ratio, proportion)—Our chances of victory are ten *to* six. Six is *to* three as ten is *to* five.

21. Towards का अर्थ होता है 'की ओर' तथा इससे सूचित होता है :

(i) की ओर (direction)—He has gone *towards* the station.

(ii) के प्रति—We should be kind *towards* the poor.

(iii) के लिए—We must contribute *towards* the building of the nation.

(iv) के नजदीक (time)—*Towards* morning his temperature came down.

22. Under से सूचित होता है :

(i) से कम (less than)—You can't get it *under* twenty rupees.

(ii) ठीक नीचे—Tired and thirsty, we sat down *under* a tree.
The box is *under* the table.

(iii) अवस्था—The patient is *under* chloroform. The house is *under* repairs.

(iv) में—Enter this expenditure *under* the head 'Miscellaneous'.

(v) अधीनता—The department is *under* a class I officer.

(vi) के नीचे (beneath)—What are you wearing *under* your coat ?

(vii) में (in, during, because of)—*Under* present conditions no change is possible.

(viii) *under* के कुछ प्रयोग देखें—

under water, *under* orders, *under* the rules, *under* control, *under* the circumstances, *under* the impression, *under* the name of, *under* (the) threat, *under* great difficulties.

23. With से सूचित होता है :

(i) के साथ—I am staying *with* a friend. I am living *with* my children.

(ii) प्रदर्शित करते हुए—She came in *with* a smile.

(iii) के जरिए (by means of)—He is fighting *with* a sword.
We hear *with* our ears.
Cut it *with* a knife.
What will you buy *with* this money ?

(iv) In favour of—The whole country is *with* the Prime Minister.

(v) के विरुद्ध—Stop fighting *with* your brother. Have a race *with* me.

(vi) उसी दिशा में—He is sailing *with* the wind.

(vii) उसी अनुपात में—Her hair became grey *with* the passing of the years.

(viii) के बावजूद—With all your advantages, you are not a success.

(ix) कारण से—She was singing *with* joy. The grass was wet *with* rain. He is sick *with* fever.

(x) जवाबदेही—It rests *with* you to make or mar his career.

(xi) अलग करना—You will have to part *with* money.
We must break *with* the past.

(xii) के संबंध में—There is a difficulty *with* this time-table.

(xiii) *with* के कुछ और प्रयोग देखें—

to eat *with* a spoon, to kill *with* an arrow, cover *with* dirt, a cake made *with* eggs, at peace *with*, in love *with*, patient *with*, combine *with*, mix *with*, connect *with*.

(E) TRANSITIVE VERBS WITH AND WITHOUT PREPOSITIONS

कुछ ऐसे verbs हैं जिनका प्रयोग अगर बिना किसी preposition का हो तो एक अर्थ होता है और preposition के साथ प्रयुक्त होने पर अर्थ बदल जाता है।

Attend — *Attend* (=जाना) your classes regulary. You must *attend to* (=ध्यान देना) your studies.

Bear — We must *bear* (सहना, बर्दाश्त करना) sufferings patiently. We must *bear with* (=tolerate, सह्य करना) his fits of anger. [Bear with में concession (रियायत) का भाव छिपा रहता है।]

Call — I *called* (पुकारा, बुलाया) Hari and warned him. Mohan *called on* (के यहाँ जाना) us.

Count — Can you *count* (गिनना) from one to hundred ? I *count on* (निर्भर करना) your help.

Eat — We *eat* (खाना) so that we may live. The rats *ate up* (खा डाला) all the grains. Anxiety *eats into* (खा-खा कर खोखला बना देना) the health of a man.

Feel — The doctor *felt* (छू कर देखा) my pulse. He *felt for* (सहानुभूति हुई) me. In the darkness I tried to *feel for* (टटोलकर खोजना) the switch.

Guard — The dog *guards* (रखवाली करना) the house at night. You should *guard against* (होशियार रहना) theft.

Guess — Please *guess* (अटकल लगाकर पता लगाना) some important questions. I try to *guess at* (अटकल लगाना) the facts.

Search — The policeman *searched* (तलाशी ली) the house. They *searched for* (खोज की) the murderer.

See — A blind man cannot *see* (देखना). Please *see to* (=ख्याल रखना) it that my book is not lost.

Send — I *send* (=भेजना) him a letter every week. I have to *send for* (=बुलवाना) his father.

Taste — I *tasted* (स्वाद चखा) the pulse. It *tasted of* (=had the flavour of, इसमें स्वाद आ रहा था) lemon.

Touch — Don't *touch* (छूना) the wall. In your answer, *touch upon* (संक्षेप में जिक्र करना) all the points.

(F) SOME COMMON EXPRESSIONS

नीचे दिए गए expressions के अर्थ को समझें तथा मौखिक रूप से वाक्य में प्रयोग करना भी सीखें।

1. about (विषय में/लगभग/के चारों ओर)

about ten o'clock	quarrel *about* something
about two feet long	argue *about* something

2. on (पर)

on Monday	*on* sale	*on* fire
on the table	*on* the whole	*on* purpose
to live *on*	*on* guard	*on* the wall
on that day	*on* a cold day	*on* foot
on holidays	*on* leave	*on* loan
on the committee	*on* 15th March	*on* New Year's Day
on the radio	*on* T V	*on* the phone/ *on* the telephone

3. in (में)

in the bag	*in* pain	*in* winter
in India	*in* trouble	*in* reply
in hospital	*in* love	*in* common
in the world	*in* 1983	swim *in* the river
in old age	*in* (the) future	*in* past
in uniform	*in* poverty	*in* debt
in doubt	*in* joke	*in* politics
in March	fail *in* the exam.	

4. at (निर्दिष्ट समय, निर्दिष्ट स्थान, मात्रा, क्रम)

at 10 a.m.	*at* play	*at* full speed
at six o'clock	*at* work	*at* first
at school	*at* once	*at* last
good *at*	bad *at*	laugh *at*
at war	*at* any rate	*at* a distance
at leisure	*at* sunset	*at* (the page) 15
at the station	*at* times	*at* his best/worst

5. for (के लिए)

ready *for*	to be fit *for*	useful *for*
good *for* him	to pay *for*	a car *for* sale
prepare *for* an exam.	hope *for* the best	read *for* pleasure
preparation *for* an exam.	pray *for* peace	cry *for* help

6. by [पास में, तक (समय के प्रसंग में), के अनुसार, मात्रा द्वारा)]

done *by* Sita	learn *by* heart	*by* accident
made *by* hand	*by* day/night	*by* electricity
by one o'clock	little *by* little	*by* the way
go *by* bus/train/air/sea	*by* no means	to tell *by* looking at
by daylight	*by* tomorrow	*by* post
by mistake	*by* chance	*by* my watch
by the time	*by* evening	know somebody *by* name

7. to (तक, के प्रति, के लिए)

forced *to*	try to	go *to*
easy *to*	want *to*	kind *to*
hope *to*	like *to*	walk *to* school
fall *to* the ground	from Saturday *to* Monday	go *to* school
from beginning *to* end	from village *to* village	from morning *to* night

8. from (से)

away *from*	absent *from*	free *from*
different *from*	to suffer *from*	*from* memory
from time to time	*from* 18th May	draw water *from* a well
from this point of view	seen *from* above	quotation *from* Tagore

9. of (का/की, से)

full *of*	made *of*	sure *of*
think *of*	take care *of*	cured *of*
for fear *of*	built *of* brick	hard *of* hearing
the writing *of* a letter	the leg *of* the table	at the thirty years *of* age
a dress *of* silk	short *of* money	the first *of* june

10. out (दूर, बाहर, अलग)

to go *out*	*out* of town	*out* of stock
to find *out*	*out* of sight	*out* of reach
out of practice	*out* of fashion	he is *out*
out of control	*out* of order	*out* of danger

11. with (के साथ, के द्वारा)

with pleasure	argue *with*	quarrel *with*
play *with*	cut it *with* a knife	go *with* him
write *with* a pen	see *with* our eyes	*with* your help
at war *with*	*with* joy	tremble *with* fear
shake *with* cold	fight *with* courage	mix this *with* that

12. after (बाद में)

after dinner	*after* the game	*after* all
after breakfast	a week *after* that	*after* that
after two o'clock	soon *after*	the day *after* tomorrow
one *after* another	bus *after* bus	*after* dark

13. before (सामने, के पूर्व)

before the war	*before* the holi-days	the year *before* last
before 1980	two days *before* Holi	the problem *before* us

14. away (दूर, अलग)

to run *away*	a mile *away*	to throw *away*

15. Miscellaneous examples

to pay *back*	to hit *back*	to come *back*
see *below*	*beyond* my powers	write it *down*
rush *into* the house	divide *into* four parts	a *near* relative
get *into* difficulties	switch it *off*	*opposite* our school
the *opposite* sex	on the *opposite* side	The meeting is *over*.
over-age	*over* weight	*over* two kilometres
through the window	come *together*	work *together*
towards the evening	*under* the bridge	*under* the water
under the sun	*on* (the) earth	*under* fifteen
without doubt	*without* any money	see page 16 *above*
the *above* examples	*above* a hundred	to go *across* the road
vote *against*	walk *along* the road	to be *among* friends
all *around* us	to travel *around* the country	the electricity is *off*.
to pay *off* our debts		

(G) MISTAKEN USE OF PREPOSITION WHERE NONE IS REQUIRED

(i) Next, Last, Today, Tomorrow, Yesterday, This, That

1. *Look at these sentences :*

Incorrect	*Correct*
I saw him *on last Monday*.	I saw him *last Monday*.
I will tell him *at next time*.	I will tell him *next time*.
Mangoes are more plentiful *in this year*.	Mangoes are more plentiful *this year*.
He will come here *in the next month*.	He will come here *next month*.

(i) निम्नलिखित शब्दों के पहले preposition *at, in, on* का प्रयोग नहीं किया जाता :

last week	next week	every morning	this summer
last month	next month	every night	this morning
last year	next year	every evening	that winter
last Sunday	next Sunday	every week	this afternoon
	the next morning/ afternoon	this week	
		the next day/ evening	the day after tomorrow

(ii) किंतु अगर noun पहले और adjective बाद में आए तो preposition लगाया जाता है। जैसे :

on Saturday next   *in* January next

on Monday last	*in* March last

2. *Look at these sentences :*

Incorrect	*Correct*
I will telephone you *on tomorrow*.	I will telephone you *tomorrow*.
She saw me *on yesterday*.	She saw me *yesterday*.
He promised to come *on today*.	He promised to come *today*.

(i) *Tomorrow, yesterday* तथा *today* के पहले किसी preposition (जैसे—*at, on, in)* का प्रयोग नहीं किया जाता।

(ii) ठीक उसी तरह इन शब्दों के पहले भी preposition नहीं लगता :

yesterday evening	tomorrow morning
yesterday afternoon	a week ago

(iii) *Yesterday* तथा *tomorrow* के बाद morning, afternoon तथा evening लगता है, किंतु *today* के बाद नहीं।

Incorrect	*Correct*
today morning	this morning
today afternoon	this afternoon
today evening	this evening
last evening	yesterday evening

(iv) हमलोग *tomorrow night* कहते हैं किंतु *today night* के बदले *tonight*, *yesterday night* के बदले *last night*, तथा *last evening* के बदले *yesterday evening* कहा जाता है।

We almost always leave out the preposition before phrases beginning *last, next, this, that;* also before *today, yesterday, tomorrow* (The phrases *at this/that time, on this/that occasion* are however normal.)

GEOFFREY LEECH & JAN SVARTVIK

(ii) Home

3. *Look at these sentences :*

Incorrect	*Correct*
Father comes *at* (or *to*) *home* at five o'clock.	Father comes *home* at five o'clock.
We go *to home* every Saturday.	We go *home* every Saturday.

Come, go, arrive, get, send, take, bring के बाद अगर *home* रहे तो home के पहले कोई preposition नहीं लगता। यहाँ *home* adverb है।

4. *Look at these sentences :*

Incorrect	*Correct*
I shall go *his home*.	I shall go *to his home*.
He will come *my friend's home*.	He will come *to my friend's home*.

अगर *home* के पहले my, your, his, her, their, John's, brother's इत्यादि रहे तो home के पहले *to* लगता है।

5. *Look at these sentences :*

My father is *at home*.
If you are not well, stay *at home*.

अगर *home* का अर्थ उस स्थान से हो जहाँ कोई व्यक्ति रहता है या काम करता है तो *home* के पहले *at* लगता है।

(iii) Verbs

6. *Look at these sentences :*

Incorrect	*Correct*
I *asked to* him a question.	I *asked* him a question.
We *entered into* the room.	We *entered* the room.
Let us *discuss about* the problem.	Let us *discuss* the problem.
He *reached at* the office late.	He *reached* the office late.
China *attacked on* India.	China *attacked* India.
Please *describe about* the story.	Please *describe* the story.
She *answered to* my question.	She *answered* my question.

(i) *Ask, enter, discuss, reach, attack, describe, answer, approach, resemble* तथा *climb* जैसे verbs के बाद preposition का प्रयोग नहीं किया जाता।

Note : 1. *Enter into* का प्रयोग होता है—'भाग लेने' या 'शुरू करने' के अर्थ में। जैसे :

He *entered into* an agreement.
We *entered into* a discussion.

(iv) For, All

7. *Look at these sentences :*

We stayed there *(for) three weeks*.
They stayed here *all week*.

(i) Phrases of duration के पहले *for* का प्रयोग प्रायः नहीं होता।

(ii) All से शुरू होनेवाले phrases के पहले भी *for* का प्रयोग प्रायः नहीं किया जाता। जैसे: all day, all (the) week इत्यादि।

(H) MISTAKES IN OMITTING THE PREPOSITION

Look at these sentences :

We *go to* Madan every day.
I *write to* him every week.
He *listened to* me in full.

Could I please *speak to* the manager ?
We must *reply to* Hari.
He *talked to* me about the matter.
They *complained to* me about the food.
Please *explain to* me what this means.
Rekha *says to* Sita that Rani will sing a song.

(i) *Go, come, write, listen, speak, reply, talk, complain, explain* तथा *say* के बाद अगर किसी व्यक्ति को संबोधित किया गया हो तो इन verbs के बाद *to* लगता है।

(ii) किंतु *tell, order, invite, request, compel* तथा *allow* के बाद object+to लगता है। जैसे :

He *told me to* meet him there.	He *invited me to* dinner.
They *ordered me to* run fast.	Hari *allowed him to* go home.
She *requested her to* go soon.	You *compelled her to* resign.

(I) MISTAKES IN THE USE OF 'TO-FORM' AND 'ING-FORM' OF VERB

1. *Look at these sentences :*

Incorrect	*Correct*
I want *to goes* there.	I want *to go* there.
He asked me *to writing* a letter.	He asked me *to write* a letter.
Sita likes *to ate* a mango.	Sita likes *to eat* a mango.

To के बाद verb का पहला रूप (V^1) लगता है, *-s/es, -d/ed* या *-ing* forms नहीं।

2. *Look at these sentences :*

Incorrect	*Correct*
I buy a pen *for write* a letter.	I buy a pen *for writing* a letter.
He helps me *by give* money.	He helps him *by giving* money.
After read my lesson, I take rest.	*After reading* my lesson, I take rest.
We must finish our work *before go* home.	We must finish our work *before going* home.
You can't get a job *without pass* the test.	You can't get a job *without passing* the test.

For, by, after, before, without, in, on इत्यादि के बाद अगर कोई verb आए तो उस verb में *–ing* लगता है।

(J) NOUNS FOLLOWED BY PREPOSITIONS

ability *for* or *in* some work
abundance *of* food
access *to* a person or place
(in) accordance *with rule*
acquaintance *with* a person or a thing
advantage *over* a person of something
admission *into* a place
advice *on* some matter
affection *for* a person
agreement *with* someone
,, *on* something
alliance with a person
anxiety *about* someone
appetite *for* something e.g., knowledge
appreciation *for/of* something
approach *to* anything
arrival *at* a place
,, *in* a country
attention *to* something
attitude *toward(s)* something
authority *over* a person
,, *on* a subject
,, *for* saying or doing
aversion *to* something
bar *to* success
basis *for* something
candidate *for* election
capacity *for* something
care *for* his safety
care *of* his books
cause *for* anxiety
,, *of* trouble
chance *of* something, e.g., success
choice *of* one thing or another
,, *between* two or more things

command *of* army, subject, situation etc.
comparison *with* something
,, *between* two things.
,, *of* something *to* something.
competition *with* a person
,, *for* a thing
complaint *against* a person
,, *about* a thing
concern *about* a matter
,, *for* someone or something
,, *in* a business
confidence *in* someone
consequence *of* something
contact *with* something
contempt *for* a person or thing
contrast *between* two things, persons etc.
control *of* something
,, *over* someone, or a situation
correspondence *with* a person
,, *to* a thing
craving *for* something
cure *for* a disease
danger *of* something
demand *for* something
desire *for* something, food, wealth etc.
difference *between* two or more things
difficulty *in* doing something
disagreement *with* someone
,, *on/over* something
discussion *on/about* some subject
disgust *at* something
distaste *for* something
distrust *of* a person
doubt *about* something
duty *to* a person

enmity *with* a person,
in phrase *at enmity with*
,, *to/toward(s)* someone
exception *to* a rule
excuse *for* doing something
experience *in* doing something
,, *of* a thing
expert *in* something
exposure *to* something
expression *of* some thought
facility *for* something
failure *of* a plan
,, *of* a person *in* something
faith *in* a person or thing
,, (*in*) favour *of* a person
fear *of* something
feeling *toward(s)* someone
,, *about* something
fine *for* an offence
fondness *for* something
(has) a genius *for* mathematics
(is) a genius *in* mathematics
grasp *of* something
gratitude *to* a person
,, *for* something
guess *at* the *truth*
hope of/for something
hunger *for* something
impression *on* someone
,, *of* something or someone
improvement *in* something
,, *on* some other thing
influence *on/over* someone
information *about/on* something
interest *in* a subject
interest *with* a person
interference *in/with* something
invitation *to* a party
judge *of* something
knack *for* something
,, *of* doing something
knowledge *of* something, e.g., English

lack *of* something, e.g., money
liking *for* something
limit *to* something
look *of* a thing
love *for* something, e.g., music
lust *for* money
malice *against* a person
match *for* something or someone in some skill
method *of* doing something
motive *for* some action
necessity *for* something
need *of* something,
in phrase *in need of*
need for something, e.g., anxiety, a book
nomination *of* a person
,, *to* a post
objection *to* something
opinion *on/about* something
order *for/against* doing a thing
payment *for* something
penalty *for* an offence
pity *for* someone *on* someone
in phrase *take pity on*
preference *for* something or someone
prejudice *against* something or someone
preparation *for* something
prevention *against* something, e.g., a disease
proficiency *in* something, e.g., Sanskrit
progress *in* something, e.g., studies
proof *of* something
provision *for* something
punishment *for* a crime
pursuit *of* something, e.g., knowledge
qualification *for* office
quarrel *with* another person

quarrel *between* two persons
reaction *to* something
recovery *from* an illness
regard *for* someone
regret *for* something done
relation *with* a person
relief *from* some trouble
remedy *for* an illness etc.
reply *to* some person or a letter
request *for* a thing
resemblance *to* something or someone
,, *between* two things or persons
respect *for* a man or office
response *to* something
result *of* something that has taken place
revenge *on/upon* a person,
,, for something done, e.g., an insult
reward *for* something
search *for/after* wealth
(in) search *of* wealth
sin *against* God
skill *in* something
slur *on* his character
stranger *to* a place

substitute *for* something else
suggestion *for* some course of action
superiority *over* a person
surprise *at* something
sympathy *for* a person
talent *for* something
taste *for* hard work
thankful *to* a person
,, *for* something
thirst *for* something
tolerance *for* something
triumph *over* an opponent, a difficulty
trespass *against* the law
use *of* something
,, *for* something, in phrase *have no use for*
victim *of* a trick, circumstances
victory *over* his passions
want *of* money
warrant *for* his arrest
witness *to* something that happens
zeal *for* something
zest *for* something, e.g., sports

(K) ADJECTIVES FOLLOWED BY PREPOSITIONS

absorbed *in* work, thought
acceptable *to* a person
accomplished *in* music
accountable *to* a person
accountable *for* a thing
accused *of* a crime
accustomed *to* something
acquainted *with* a person, a subject

acquitted *of* a charge
addicted *to* a habit, etc.
affectionate *to* children etc.
afraid *of* something
alarmed *at* something
alive *to* a danger
allied *with* a country, party, etc.
,, *to* something

amazed *at* something
angry *with* a person
,, *at* something
annoyed *at* something
,, *with* a person *for* saying or doing something
answerable *to* a person
,, *for* something
anxious *for* something or someone
,, *about* something
applicable *to* a person or thing
appropriate *to* an occasion, etc.
ashamed *of* something
associated *with* a person or thing
astonished *at* something
averse *to* something, e.g., hard work
aware *of* something
bent *on* something
beset *with* difficulties, dangers etc.
blessed *with* good health
blind *to* one's own fault
,, *of* an eye
boastful *of* something
born *of* rich, poor parents
bound *for* a place
busy *with* something
capable *of* something
careful *of* one's health
,, *about* one's health, money, dress, etc.
,, *with* one's work, etc.
certain *of* something, e.g., success
,, *about* failure, etc.
charged *with* a crime
clear *of* blame
committed *to* a course of action
common *to* everyone
comparable *to* something
confident *of* success
concerned *about* something
,, *with* a person or place
conscious *of* something
contented *with* something
contrary *to* rule
convicted *of* a crime
convinced *of* a fact
deaf *to* advice, etc.
defective *in* workmanship, etc.
deficient *in* something
delighted *with* one's success etc.
,, *at* the news
deprived *of* one's right etc.
determined *on* doing something
devoid *of* something
different *from* something
disappointed *with* a person
,, *in* our hopes
,, *at* something
disgusted *with* a thing
,, *at/with* a person
displeased *with* a person
disqualified *for* a post
,, *from* competing
doubtful *of* success
,, *about* what to do, etc.
eligible *for* appointment
endowed *with* an ability
engaged *in* something
,, *to* a person
entitled *to* something
envious *of* someone, something
essential *to/for* happiness
equal *to* the occasion
exhausted *with* work
exposed *to* danger
faithful *to* a person

familiar *to* a person
,, *with* a language
famous *for* something
fascinated *by* something
favourable *to* a person
fit *for* a position
fond *of* music
full *of* something
foreign *to* something
gifted *with* an ability
glad *of/about* something
good *at* something, e.g., cricket
,, *for* nothing
grateful *to* a person
,, *for* something
greedy *for* something
guilty *of* a crime, etc.
harmful *to* something, e.g., health
honest *in* his dealings
honoured *with* something
hopeful *of* success, gain, etc.
identical *with* something
ignorant *of* something
ill *with* fever
impatient *with* someone
impatient *at* something happening
,, *of* something, e.g., waiting for a long time
indebted *to* a person
,, *for* some kindness
inclined *to* something
independent *of* something
indifferent *to* something
indispensable *to* some task or result
infested *with* something
informed *of* a fact
innocent *of* a charge
inspired *with* hope
intimate *with* a person
introduce *to* a person
,, *into* a place
irrelevant *to* something
jealous *of* a person or thing
lame *of* one leg
liable *for* something, e.g., debts
,, *to* a fine, illness, etc.
loyal *to* a person
mad *with* anger, pain, etc.
,, *about/at* something, e.g., missing the bus
,, *for* something
mistaken *for* a thing or a person
moved *to* tears
,, *with* pity
,, *at* the sight
,, *by* requests
negligent *in* work, etc.
,, *of* duties, etc.
notorious *for* something bad
obliged *to* a person
,, *for* something
occupied *with* some work
offended *with* a person
overwhelmed *with* grief, pity, gratitude, etc.
parallel *to* something
partial *to* someone
peculiar *to* a person or a place
polite *to* a person
,, *in* manners
preferable *to* something else
prepared *for* something
proficient *in* something, e.g., music, English
profitable *to* a person
proper *for* an occasion
proud *of* something
qualified *for* teaching music
quick *of* understanding
,, *at* mathematics

ready *for* something
,, *in* one's answers
reduced *to* poverty
reardless *of* something
related *to* a person
relevant *to* some matter or subject
repentant *of* one's mistakes
respectful *to* a person
responsible *to* a person
,, *for* something
restricted *to* place, person quantity, etc.
rich *in* something
rid *of* trouble
sacred *to* someone
satisfied *with* something
sensitive *to* something, e.g., criticism
serviceable *to* a person
shocked *at* your behaviour
shocking *to* everyone
short *of* something needed, e.g., money

silent *about* a matter, etc.
similar *to* something
skilful *in* doing something
slow *at* something, e.g., doing sums
,, *in* making up his mind
sorry *for* someone
,, *about* something
subject *to* rules, authority etc.
sufficient *for* a purpose
suitable *for* a purpose, e.g., a post
sure *of* success, winning, etc.
suspicious *of* someone
tired *of* doing something
true *to* his conviction
vexed *with* a person
,, *at* something, e.g., failures
void *of* meaning
wanting *in* something, e.g., commonsense
weak *in* spelling, the leg
worthy *of* praise, etc.

(L) VERBS FOLLOWED BY PREPOSITIONS

abide *by* a promise
abstain *from* wine
accede *to* a request
acquit (someone) *of* a charge
accuse (someone) *of* a crime
agree *with* a person
,, *to* a proposal
aim *at* something
apologise *to* a person
,, *for* rudeness
appeal *to* a person
,, *for* something, help etc.
,, *against* a sentence

apply *to* a person
apply *for* something, e.g., leave
appoint (a person) *to* a post.
approve *of* an action
argue *with* a person
,, *for/against* something
arrive *at* a place
,, *in* a country
ask *for* a thing
,, *of* a person
attend *to* a speaker
,, on a person
avail (oneself) *of* an opportunity

beg pardon *of* a person
,, ,, *for* something *from* someone
believe in something
belong *to* a person
bestow (something) *on* someone
beware of the dog
blame a person *for* something
boast *of* something
borrow *from* a person
break *into* a house
,, *with* a person
bring a thing *to* light
,, ,, ,, *under* notice
buy (something) *from* someone
call *on* a person
,, *at* a place, a house
,, *for* an explanation, report, etc.
care *for* a person or thing
catch up *with* someone
caution a person *against* a danger
charge (someone) *with* a theft etc.
clear a man *of* blame
coincide *with* one's opinion
compare (someone) *with* someone or something
compensate a person *for* his loss
compete *with* a person
,, *for* a prize
complain *to* a person
,, *of* a pain, etc.
,, *against* a person or thing
comply *with* a request, order etc.
concede *to* some demand
confide *in* a person
congratulate (someone) *on* something
consent *to* some proposal
consist *of* something
consult (*with*) a person
,, *on/about* something
contribute *to* a fund
convict (someone) *of* crime, etc.
convince a person *of* a fact
cut a thing *in* or *to* pieces
,, ,, ,, *in* half
deal *in* something
,, *with* a person or a subject
,, well or badly *by* a person
debar *from* doing something
depend *on* a person or a thing
deprive (someone) *of* something
die of a disease
,, *from* some cause, e.g., overwork, a wound
,, *by* violence
,, *for* one's country
,, *through* neglect
,, *in* battle
differ *with* a person
,, *from* someone or something
,, *on/about* something, e.g., a question
disagree *with* a person or thing
disapprove *of* anything
dispense *with* a man's services
dispose *of* property
dissuade (someone) *from* something
distinguish (something) *from* something
,, *between* two things
divide *in* half
,, *into* four parts

enter *upon* a career
,, *into* an agreement
entrust (something) *to* someone
,, (a person) *with* a thing
escape *from* jail
exempt a person *from* a rule
exchange (something) *for* something
fail *in* an attempt
fall *in* love *with* a person
,, *on* the enemy (attack)
,, *into* a mistake
feel *for* a person in his trouble
free *from* anything, e.g., debt
furnish (somebody) *with* something
get at the fact
,, *out* of debt
,, *through* an examination etc.
glance *at* an object, e.g., the clock
,, *over/through* a letter
grumble *at* something
guard *against* a danger, etc.
guess *at* something
hanker *after* wealth
hope *for* something
impress an idea *on* a person
impress a person *with* an idea
inform (a person) *of* something
inquire *into* an accident, etc.
,, *of* a person *about* something
insist *on* something
interfere *in* someone's affairs, etc.
,, *with* a person in some matter
introduce a person *to* someone
,, *into* a place or seat

invest money *in* some project
invite (someone) *to* lunch
laugh *at* a person or thing
listen *to* music
live *at* a place
,, *in* a city
,, *on* fruit, etc.
,, by honest labour
long *for* something
look *at* a person or thing
,, *after* some business
,, *into* (examine) an account
,, *for* something
meddle *with* something
merge *into* anything
object *to* something
overwhelm *with* kindness
part *with* a person or thing
persist *in* doing something
play *on* the guitar
plot *against* a person
plunge *into* a river
pray *for* pardon
prefer (something or someone) *to* something or someone
prepare *for* the worst
present (someone) *with* something
preside *over* a meeting
prevail *on* a person
prevent *from* going
prohibit *from* doing something
protect *from* harm
protest *against* injustice
provide *for* one's children
,, *against* the evil day
,, (oneself) *with* something
put up *with* somebody or something
quarrel *with* a person
,, *over* something
recover *from* illness, etc.

refer *to* a book, person, etc.
relieve *of* something
rely *on* a person or thing
remind a person *of* something
repent *of* an action
revolt *against*
run *after* a fashion
,, *into* debt
save a person or thing *from* harm
search *for* something
side *with* a person *in* a dispute
speak *to* a person
,, *about* something
,, *on* a subject
stand *by* someone
,, *against* (resist) an enemy
,, *to* one's opinion
stare *at* a person
,, a person *in* the face
stick *to* the point
submit *to* authority
succeed *in* something, e.g., exam.
supply a thing *to* a person
surrender *to* the enemy
suspect (someone) *of* something
sympathise *with* someone in his trouble
take revenge *on* a person
take *to* smoking
talk *to/with* a person
,, *about* an event
taste *of* salt
tell *about* an event
think *of* or *about* something
,, *over* a matter
throw a stone *at* someone
touch *upon* a subject
translate *into* English, etc.
trespass *against* rules
,, *in* a man's house
,, *on* a man's time
turn verse *into* prose
,, *to* a friend for help
wait *for* a person or thing
warn (someone) *of/against* something
wish for something
work *at* mathematics
yield *to* a temptation, a threat, etc.

Examples Worked Out

Fill in the blanks with suitable prepositions wherever necessary :

1. The lady was dressed....black. — The lady was dressed *in* black.
2. Cows live...grass. — Cows live *on* grass.
3. He is married...my sister. — He is married *to* my sister.
4. Sita writes....her left hand. — Sita writes *with* her left hand.
5. I asked....him a question. — I asked him a question.
6. She is very careful...her health. — She is very careful *of* her health.
7. He died....over-eating. — He died *from* over-eating.
8. This is different....the other. — This is different *from* the other.
9. Your suggestion is helpful....us. — Your suggestion is helpful *to* us.
10. His dress was made....silk. — His dress was made *of* silk.
11. We listen....the music. — We listen *to* the music.
12. This is the book that I told you.... — This is the book that I told you *about.*

13. He depended....his friend's word. — He depended *on* his friend's word.
14. He was greedy...money. — He was greedy *for* money.
15. Line *AB* is parallel...line *CD*. — Line *AB* is parallel *to* line *CD*.
16. I have no acquaintance....that man. — I have no acquaintance *with* that man.
17. His capacity....hard work seems unlimited. — His capacity *for* hard work seems unlimited.
18. He prevented me...speaking. — He prevented me *from* speaking.
19. What are you laughing... ? — What are you laughing *at* ?
20. Which class are you.... ? — Which class are you *in* ?
21. He is coming...plane. — He is coming *by* plane.
22. He has been absent....Monday last. — He has been absent *since* Monday last.
23. I stood....Hari and Sita. — I stood *between* Hari and Sita.
24. We shall start....15th April. — We shall start *on* 15th April.
25. I have been waiting here....two hours. — I have been waiting here *for* two hours.
26. His brother lives...Delhi. — His brother lives *in* Delhi.
27. He spoke....our holidays. — He spoke *about* our holidays.
28. We started....the morning of 24th. — We started *on* the morning of 24th.
29. He travelled....a bicycle. — He travelled *on* a bicycle.
30. She stayed....home yesterday. — She stayed *at* home yesterday.
31. We work from 6....8.. — We work from 6. *to* 8.
32. Who are you speaking.... ? — Who are you speaking *to* ?
33. This is the house he lived.... — This is the house he lived *in*.
34. The train comes...7 o'clock. — The train comes *at* 7 o'clock.
35. The prices of things go up...the war. — The prices of things go up *during* the war.
36. He was ill....Monday to Friday. — He was ill *from* Monday to Friday.
37. Rice sells...Rs.180/- a quintal. — Rice sells *at* Rs. 180/- a quintal.
38. Let us work....peace and prosperity. — Let us work *for* peace and prosperity.
39. He died....loss of blood. — He died *from* loss of blood.
40. The Bank is close....my house. — The Bank is close *to* my house.
41. Here is a girl...blue eyes. — Here is a girl *with* blue eyes.
42. I will come....Friday. — I will come *on* Friday.
43. She was born....August 15, 1970. — She was born *on* August 15, 1970.
44. I do not agree....what you say. — I do not agree *with* what you say.
45. I am willing to agree....your suggestion. — I am willing to agree *to* your suggestion.

46. You should apply...the post.	You should apply *for* the post.
47. The train will depart.....the other platform.	The train will depart *from* the other platform.
48. We hope....an easy examination.	We hope *for* an easy examination.
49. I rely....his help.	I rely *on* his help.
50. I must reply....his letter.	I must reply *to* his letter.
51. Do you object....my opening the window ?	Do you object *to* my opening the window ?
52. I wish to remind you....the promise you made.	I wish to remind you *of* the promise you made.
53. Could I please speak....the manager ?	Could I please speak *to* the manager ?
54. I hope you will succeed... your task.	I hope you will succeed *in* your task.
55. I will think....the matter.	I will think *about* the matter.
56. Every week I write....my friend.	Every week I write *to* my friend.
57. Where has the bus come... ?	Where has the bus come *from* ?
58. I was annoyed...his brother.	I was annoyed *with* his brother.
59. He entrusted me...the letter.	He entrusted me *with* the letter.
60. He dispensed....my services.	He dispensed *with* my services.
61. I cannot be confident.... success	I cannot be confident *of* success.
62. There is no cause...anxiety.	There is no cause *for* anxiety.
63. He has no control....his servants.	He has no control *over* his servants.
64 There is an exception....every rule.	There is an exception *to* every rule.
65. There is no alternative...this question.	There is no alternative *to* this question.
66. She is related...him.	She is related *to* him.
67. The teacher is pleased....him.	The teacher is pleased *with* him.
68. What is the time....your watch ?	What is the time *by* your watch ?
69. (a) He is busy....his work.	(a) He is busy *with* his work.
(b) I am busy...writing this letter.	(b) I am busy writing this letter.[1]
70. I was ill....fever.	I was ill *of/with* fever.
71. He repented....his action.	He repented *of* his action.
72. I was appointed....the post.	I was appointed *to* the post.
73. He differs...you.	He differs *with* you.
74. Some people are sensitive.... criticism.	Some people are sensitive *to* criticism.
75. I must be faithful....you.	I must be faithful *to* you.
76. Is it an answer....that question ?	Is it an answer *to* that question ?

1. *Busy* is followed by an-ing from of the verb, or by with+noun or pronoun.

77.	The teacher was popular....his students.	The teacher was popular *with* his students.
78.	Rekha is good...music.	Rekha is good *at* music.
79.	We have duty....our parents.	We have duty *to* our parents.
80.	Can you cure him...his disease ?	Can you cure him *of* his disease ?
81.	He dealt...his subject.... length.	He dealt *with* his subject *at* length.
82.	He soon got....his illness.	He soon got *over* his illness.
83.	I was horrified....the sight.	I was horrified *at* the sight.
84.	He did not die.....cholera.	He did not die *of* cholera.
85.	Will you entrust me...that letter ?	Will you entrust me *with* that letter ?
86.	Always be prepared....the worst.	Always be prepared *for* the worst.
87.	He touched....the subject of tides.	He touched *upon* the subject of tides.
88.	He once put me....an obligation.	He once put me *under* an obligation.
89.	He had a great affection...his parents.	He had a great affection *for* his parents.
90.	I disapprove...your way.... working.	I disapprove *of* your way *of* working.
91.	You will have to answer...me ....your misconduct.	You will have to answer *to* me *for* your misconduct.
92.	Forty students competed...one another....a single scholarship.	Forty students competed *with* one another *for* a single scholarship.
93.	I must consult...you...that matter.	I must consult *with* you *on* that matter.
94.	I inquired....him...that matter.	I inquired *of* him *into* that matter.
95.	Aim....doing your duty...all risks.	Aim *at* doing your duty *at* all all risks.
96.	I am vexed...him...what he has done.	I am vexed *with* him *at* what he has done.
97.	A young man should be...his guard....bad company.	A young man should be *on* his guard *against* bad company.
98.	Please fill....the form....ink.	Please fill *in* the form *in ink*.
99.	I feel....you but cannot relieve you....your want.	I feel *for* you but cannot relieve you *of* your want.
100.	I sympathised .... him .... his sorrow.	I sympathised *with* him *in* his sorrow.

101.	I shall talk .... him .... the question.	**I shall talk *to* him *on* (or *about*) the question.**
102.	We prefer milk....tea.	We prefer milk *to* tea.
103.	I congratulate you....your success...the exam.	I congratulate you *on* your success *in* the exam.
104.	I am familiar...the facts, but the man is not familiar ....me.	I am familiar *with* the facts, but the man is not familiar *to* me.
105.	He has been accused.... hitting a policeman....the head.	He has been accused *of* hitting a policeman *on* the head.
106.	This stick differs...that....length ...two inches.	The stick differs *from* that *in* length *by* two inches.
107.	The beggar was grateful....the rich lady...her kindness.	The beggar was grateful *to* the rich lady *for* her kindness.
108.	He lives....17, Boring Road .....Patna.	He lives *at* 17, Boring Road *in* Patna.
109.	He is sitting....a chair and looking....of the window.	He is sitting *on* a chair and looking *out* of the window.
110.	Take the book...your hand and open it...page 5.	Take the book *in* your hand and open it *at* page 5.
111.	You must apologize...him.... what you have done.	You must apologize *to* him *for* what you have done.
112.	I cannot agree...you in this matter, and therefore I do not agree...your proposal.	I cannot agree *with* you in this matter, and therefore I do not agree *to* your proposal.
113.	You will have to answer....your master....that mistake.	You will have to answer *to* your master *for* that mistake.
114.	You can appeal....a higher court and apply....a fresh trial.	You can appeal *to* a higher court and apply *for* a fresh trial.
115.	They brought a complaint....the magistrate...their neighbour.	They brought a complaint *to* the magistrate *against* their neighbour.
116.	The court sentenced him....six months' imprisonment....theft.	The court sentenced him *to* six months' imprisonment *for* theft.
117.	You cannot compete....a man who is superior...you...resources.	You cannot compete *with* a man who is superior *to* you *in* resources.
118.	He did not die....any disease but ....the after effects....over-work.	He did not die *of* any disease but *from* the after-effects *of* over-work.
119.	You should not conceal anything ....a friend but consult....him..... all matter.	You should not conceal anything *from* a friend but consult *with* him *on* all matters.

120. I am afraid he has fallen....love.... a girl who, although not devoid.... intelligence or deficient..... common sense, is certainly a bit weak....the head.	I am afraid he has fallen *in* love *with* a girl who, although not devoid *of* intelligence or deficient *in* common sense, is certainly a bit weak *in* the head.

EXERCISE 1

Fill in the blanks with suitable prepositions given in brackets :

EXAMPLE : We are going....England. (*in/at/to*)
= We are going *to* England.

1. We are going...England. (*in/at/to*)
2. He put the book....the table. (*from/upon/in*)
3. This fresh air is good....you. (*for/to/about*)
4. She carries a bag....her hand. (*from/in/by*)
5. I am thinking...you all the time. (*about/on/in*)
6. Did you come here....train ? (*in/on/by*)
7. He is the best boy....my class. (*at/in/for*)
8. She was born....the year 1970. (*on/at/in*)
9. He suffered...cold and hunger. (*about/from/over*)
10. I am....trouble now. (*at/on/in*)
11. This man went...door to door. (*from/before/down*)
12. What is the advantage...doing this ? (*in/at/of*)
13. I don't like to travel by car...night. (*in/at/into*)
14. We began this work....March. (*on/from/in*)
15. The train stops...all stations. (*at/in/on*)
16. Translate it from Hindi....English. (*in/for/into*)
17. Everyone was listening...Hari. (*at/to/for*)
18. What country do you come.... ? (*at/of/from*)
19. I bought this pen....Rs. 5. (*in/for/from*)
20. He has been writing....6 a.m. (*from/since/for*)

EXERCISE 2

Fill in the blanks with suitable prepositions given in brackets :

EXAMPLE : Sima is confident....her victory. (*at/in/of*)
= Sima is confident *of* her victory.

1. Sima is confident....her victory. (*at/in/of*)
2. I congratulate you....your success. (*on/at/for*)
3. Always depend....your own efforts. (*in/for/on*)
4. That man is not fit....this job. (*at/for/from*)
5. Don't laugh....the poor people. (*on/for/at*)
6. Soma is married....Pradeep. (*for/with/to*)
7. She seems to be proud...her beauty. (*at/of/for*)
8. You are not qualified.....this post. (*at/from/for*)
9. This book is useful...students. (*for/about/at*)

10. This school is suitable....my children. (*to/for/about*)
11. He is satisfied....my work. (*at/from/with*)
12. She has no capacity....hard work. (*to/for/in*)
13. Please pay attention....what he says. (*at/in/to*)
14. The train arrived....the platform. (*on/into/at*)
15. You are afraid...cats. (*to/of/from*)
16. Who is responsible...this mistake ? (*for/by/at*)
17. I am not able....pay you right now. (*by/to/for*)
18. They deal....foodgrains. (*at/for/in*)
19. I differ....you on that matter. (*to/with/about*)
20. The child did not ask....mangoes. (*to/at/for*)

EXERCISE 3

Fill in the blanks with suitable prepositions given in brackets :

EXAMPLE : That rule does not apply....you. (*for/at/to*)
= That rule does not apply *to* you.

1. That rule does not apply....you. (*for/at/to*)
2. Mr Sen died.....cancer. (*from/of/by*)
3. The book belongs...my brother. (*to/at/for*)
4. This pen differs....that in price. (*at/in/from*)
5. Have you any difficulty...English ? (*in/on/for*)
6. I have no desire....a new car now. (*at/for/about*)
7. The soldier died....the wounds. (*by/of/from*)
8. He was guilty....the murder. (*at/of/for*)
9. This book deals....life in Bombay. (*in/at/with*)
10. He filled the glass....water. (*in/with/for*)
11. This man has no control....his children. (*at/on/over*)
12. Life is full....surprises. (*at/of/from*)
13. We are glad....help you. (*to/for/in*)
14. Have you ever heard...Tagore ? (*of/on/after*)
15. She has great affection...all her children. (*on/to/for*)
16. They went to Calcutta....train. (*in/by/on*)
17. I got angry...Moti. (*at/from/with*)
18. Is that question clear....you ? (*for/to/off*)
19. We all hope....a better life. (*at/for/on*)
20. This medicine is good...malaria. (*at/on/for*)

EXERCISE 4

Fill in the blanks with suitable prepositions given in brackets :

EXAMPLE : You should be honest....business. (*at/in/on*)
= You should be honest *in* business.

1. You should be honest....business. (*at/in/on*)
2. I want a chance...go there. (*for/at/to*)
3. Suman is hopeful...winning a prize. (*of/for/in*)
4. She is careless...her dress. (*for/about/to*)
5. Please look....me when I speak to you. (*on/at/into*)
6. Please listen...what I am going to say. (*at/to/for*)

7. Mr Sinha is kind....all his students. (*for/on/to*)
8. Are you in need....some money ? (*of/for/about*)
9. He has some interest...cricket. (*of/for/in*)
10. Food is necessary....life. (*to/for/about*)
11. I have all the qualifications....the job. (*at/on/for*)
12. Are you related....Mr Bose ? (*with/to/from*)
13. I hope you will succeed...your plan. (*in/at/for*)
14. Are you proficient...English ? (*at/in/of*)
15. He is opposed....a sudden change. (*to/for/of*)
16. She has no regard...anyone else. (*about/for/to*)
17. Are you ready....the party ? (*for/at/to*)
18. Children should be obedient....their parents. (*for/to/by*)
19. Have you replied....your friend's letter ? (*to/for/on*)
20. He has been ill....fever. (*by/in/with*)

EXERCISE 5

Fill in the blanks with suitable prepositions given in brackets :

EXAMPLES : (i) I am a teacher...English. (*on/of/in*)
= I am a teacher *of* English.
(ii) She has oil...her hair. (*into/to/on*)
= She has oil *on* her hair.

1. I am a teacher...English. (*on/of/in*)
2. She has oil....her hair. (*into/to/on*)
3. We have great respect...our teacher. (*in/for/to*)
4. Is he satisfied...your work ? (*at/in/with*)
5. I am not sure....his age. (*to/about/on*)
6. Meena is qualified....this post. (*at/to/for*)
7. We always sympathise...you. (*on/with/for*)
8. He prevented me....going there. (*from/of/about*)
9. We were prepared....that kind of question. (*at/for/to*)
10. You must participate....games. (*at/for/in*)
11. I got angry....Moti's remarks. (*at/on/with*)
12. I was annoyed....him. (*on/with/for*)
13. The money was divided...five men. (*between/to/among*)
14. My father was displeased....my answer. (*at/with/from*)
15. You must be faithful....your friends. (*at/for/to*)
16. Could I borrow some money....you ? (*on/from/by*)
17. You have no cause....worries. (*for/in/into*)
18. I talked...this girl about it. (*at/of/to*)
19. I saw the President....television last night. (*with/on/in*)
20. We thank you....your advice. (*to/on/for*)

EXERCISE 6

Fill in the blanks with suitable prepositions :

EXAMPLE : Flour is made....wheat.
= Flour is made *from* wheat.

1. **Flour is made....wheat.**
2. **We disapprove....your action.**

3. **Soma was pleased....her new dress.**
4. **Let us sit....this seat for a while.**
5. We are very sorry....that person.
6. You should take care....your health.
7. The note was written....ink.
8. The box was full....papers.
9. We are not interested....your story.
10. I do not approve....your action.
11. He was quickly cured....his cold.
12. What is the best cure....a cold ?
13. There is an exception....every rule.
14. He has a taste....music.
15. They were accused....cheating him.
16. I am astonished....his failure.
17. He was deficient....energy.
18. His father turned him....of doors.
19. He purchased the book....Rs.10/- only.
20. The candidate was anxious....the result.

EXERCISE 7

Fill in the blanks with suitable prepositions :

EXAMPLES : (i) He did not turn...today.
= He did not turn *up* today.

(ii) I came....his request.
= I came *at* his request.

(iii) The band will play...request.
= The band will play *on* request.

1. He was down...fever.
2. Aim....doing your duty.
3. I differ...you entirely.
4. I will always stand....you.
5. The lights were turned....
6. Nobody is acquainted....him.
7. We pray....God for mercy.
8. Moti takes....his father.
9. This work is...his capacity.
10. I am sick....the whole business.
11. We have no control...fate.
12. He devoted himself...his studies.
13. I asked him...a favour.
14. He is....the top of his class.
15. She was here....time.
16. He rushed....the room.
17. They have settled...England.
18. He was invited...dinner.
19. Do not cry....spilt milk.
20. Let us hope....the best.

EXERCISE 8

Fill in the blanks with suitable prepositions :

EXAMPLE : We got....difficulties.
= We got *into* difficulties.

1. The house was...fire.
2. He jumped....the river.
3. I saw it...the newspaper.
4. My cousin is laid up....fever.
5. We go to college...foot.
6. Sugar is not...stock.
7. She was....the platform.
8. He told me something...the end.
9. Come and sit...me.
10. The book is written...Hari.
11. She is the apple...my eye.
12. We shall travel...train.
13. Keep....good work.
14. He has no house to live...
15. What are you looking... ?
16. Beware....mad dogs.
17. He is blind....his own faults.
18. He died....the loss of blood.
19. Let us prepare....our exam.
20. Boys were shouting...joy.

EXERCISE 9

Fill in the blanks with suitable prepositions :

EXAMPLES : (i) He deals...rice and other grains.
= He deals *in* rice and other grains.

(ii) He was left...dead on the battlefield.
= He was left *for* dead on the battlefield.

1. He has been missing...yesterday.
2. Tom is weak...mathematics.
3. I have great affection...her.
4. My efforts were crowned...success.
5. Will you entrust me...that money.
6. No, I will entrust nothing...you.
7. I am sensitive....such things.
8. He shot this bird...a gun.
9. The car was running...full speed.
10. Take care to be back...mid-day.
11. Divide this mango...four parts.
12. The book belongs...me.
13. Don't put the blame....others.
14. He is putting....weight.
15. Here is a present....you.
16. He has fallen...bad habits.
17. We can't do....money.
18. What brought....the quarrel ?
19. He is not aware...your intention.
20. There are signs...misery everywhere.

EXERCISE 10

Fill in the blanks with suitable prepositions :

EXAMPLE : My friend is learned...English.
= My friend is learned *in* English.

1. My friend is learned...English.
2. He agreed....my proposal.
3. She appealed...help.
4. I have been doing it...one year.
5. The work was done....haste.
6. We are fond....music.
7. My watch is not...order.
8. He is appointed....the post.
9. She is in search....a job.
10. I do not believe....the news.
11. He is blind...one eye.
12. She comes...a high family.
13. We do not hanker...wealth.
14. They were horrified...the sight.
15. Rajeev is clever...mathematics.
16. His sister is bad....geography.
17. He was sentenced...theft.
18. I have little faith....new doctors.
19. We must be faithful....our friends.
20. Do not complain....your hard lot.

EXERCISE 11

Fill in the blanks with suitable prepositions :

EXAMPLE : He is ashamed....his conduct.
= He is ashamed *of* his conduct.

1. He is ashamed.....his conduct.
2. The man is eager....promotion.
3. The prisoner escaped...the jail.
4. At last the secret was brought...light.
5. I insisted....having my say.
6. He is liable...his wife's debt.
7. Gandhiji had a great influence.... people.
8. I was engaged....some work.
9. I object....your statement.
10. Mr Sinha suspects you....theft.
11. We warned him....the danger.
12. They were in doubt...it.
13. They were not....breakfast.
14. A dog barked....them.

15. **He came in contact....me.**
16. **Hari is contented....his income.**
17. **He was dull....hearing.**
18. **They are spoiled.....bad education.**
19. **I was impressed...it.**
20. **He comes to college...foot.**

EXERCISE 12

Fill in the blanks with suitable prepositions :

EXAMPLE : Teaching...school hours is not too tiring.
= Teaching *during* school hours is not too tiring.

1. He was always short...money.
2. He fell....a window.
3. He comes to school...bicycle.
4. He comes to school....his bicycle.
5. I don't care....all this.
6. He asked me...some money.
7. I couldn't pay....this book.
8. What are the reasons...it ?
9. It is difficult...me.
10. I hope they get pleasure...it.
11. He was saved...death.
12. We got down....the train.
13. He is innocent...the crime.
14. He came here....12th August.
15. It is cold....winter.
16. ....my opinion you are right.
17. We can see two boys...the picture.
18. I was born....a small village.
19. We swam...the river.
20. A cork floats...water

EXERCISE 13

Fill in the blanks with suitable prepositions :

EXAMPLE : She had ribbon...her hair.
= She had ribbon *in* her hair.

1. She had ribbon...her hair
2. He takes interest....his work.
3. Are there any mistakes....the sentence ?
4. It reminds me...my dog.
5. It is covered....snow.
6. He fell....love with her.
7. What is your attitude....sport ?
8. He interferes....my work.
9. They were joking....each other.
10. He was trembling...fear.
11. The poet compared her face...the moon.
12. Compare this book....a good one.
13. We spent a lot of time...our lessons.
14. The workers were....strike.
15. Nobody saw him...the way.
16. Be careful....it.
17. I said goodbye....my aunt.
18. He wasn't here....the first day.
19. He left...a winter morning.
20. They have been teaching here.... 4 a.m.

EXERCISE 14

Fill in the blanks with suitable prepositions :

EXAMPLE : He introduced me....Mr Prasad.
= He introduced me *to* Mr Prasad.

1. He introduced me....Mr Prasad.
2. I prefer dogs...cats.
3. We came....college.
4. They tied their horse....a tree.
5. He could not cope...this work.
6. They are busy ...their work.
7. I know nothing...the affair.
8. It may result....trouble.

9. He gave correct answers....all my questions.
10. He teaches English....small boys.
11. I paid a visit....my friend.
12. I won't comment....what people say.
13. I was filled....joy as I watched him.
14. He gave a description....what he had seen.
15. I succeeded....the examination.
16. We are having a party....New Year's Day.
17. He has been absent....the class for two days.
18. This suggestion is acceptable...us.
19. He is anxious.....see his son in Delhi.
20. Regular walking is beneficial.... health.

EXERCISE 15

Fill in the blanks with suitable prepositions :

EXAMPLE : It was allotted......me.
= It was allotted *to* me.

1. It was allotted....me.
2. The news is not based...facts.
3. He takes pleasure...riding.
4. She is devoted...her parents.
5. I object....your saying so.
6. I was confined...bed for a month.
7. He was taken....surprise.
8. He is eligible...the post...lecturer.
9. He lives...Bombay...India.
10. She once put me....obligation.
11. You must conform...the rules.
12. Temperance is conducive...health.
13. Your talk is relevant...the subject.
14. Don't be intolerant...opposition.
15. It is compatible...public safety.
16. He is not amenable....discipline.
17. I am sensitive...criticism.
18. Many aspire....greatness.
19. She is entitled....all praise.
20. Aim...doing your duty...all risks.

EXERCISE 16

Complete the following sentences by using the suitable form of the verb given in brackets at the end, either with or without a preposition (whichever you think is correct) :

EXAMPLE : As I....him, he walked away. (*approach*)
= As I *approached* him, he walked away.

1. As I....him, he walked. (*approach*)
2. Two boys have...the classroom. (*enter*)
3. We shall....the point later. (*discuss*)
4. We shall....it. (*talk*)
5. They....the house. (*attack*)
6. They make an....the house. (*attack*)
7. The child....its father in looks. (*resemble*)
8. We found no one who could...our inquiries. (*answer*)
9. She addressed me so rudely that I refused to...her. (*answer*)
10. The policeman....the motorist to move his car. (*ask*)
11. The teacher....him a question in English. (*ask*)
12. Have you....his letter yet ? (*answer*)
13. John....Mary last year. (*marry*)
14. John was....Mary last year. (*marry*)
15. I cannot...this pen. (*write*)

16. He....home in the evening. (*comes*)
17. We...the station late. (*reach*)
18. He...his journey in detail. (*describe*)
19. They....the roof of the house. (*climb*)
20. The question was....the students. (*explain*)

EXERCISE 17

Fill in the blanks with suitable prepositions :

EXAMPLE : We don't go...school...Sundays.
= We don't go *to* school *on* Sundays.

1. We don't go....school...Sundays.
2. Wait....me...the bus-stop.
3. We arrived....Bombay exactly...six o'clock.
4. Come....5 p.m.....Friday morning.
5. We went....Patna...car.
6. I'll call....you....a more convenient time.
7. Read...line 5...line 15....page 8.
8. He spoke....me....his hands....his pockets.
9. Most children remain...school...the ages of six and sixteen.
10. We are staying....our friends not far...the station.
11. My school was founded....a business man....1960.
12. Do you want to speak....me...anything ?
13. Don't go out....the rain...an umbrella.
14. The cat is hiding...us...the table.
15. I must work very hard....history because I am not very good...it.
16. You can cut this mango....two...this knife.
17. Let us go....a walk....the garden....dinner.
18. I am taller than my sister...six inches.
19. He is dependent....me and I have to look....him.
20. He failed...want of help as his father failed....engage a teacher for him.

EXERCISE 18

Fill in the blanks with suitable prepositions :

EXAMPLE : My father goes...his office...bus and I go... college....my bicycle.
= My father goes *to* his office *by* bus and I go *to* college *on* my bicycle.

1. My father goes...his office...bus and I go...college...my bicycle.
2. I am a man...peace, I believe...peace. I am all...peace, but I do not want peace... any price.
3. Yesterday I was talking...my friend, Sohan. I'm very fond...him. But it seems to me that he worries too much...his health. He thinks that he suffers ...several diseases.
4. I am angry...you...your late coming. I will speak...my mind, for I am not afraid...the consequences.
5. If you want to live....happiness, live...your means, for those who live...their means, fall...debt.
6. The sun shines....day, but the moon and the stars shine...night. Sometimes there are clouds....the sky, and the sun goes...them.

7. The meeting started...5 p.m.....the Town Hall. The D.M. was in the chair. The function began...an opening song...some school girls.
8. How far is it....here...the nearest station ? Does this road lead...the station ? What time does the train start...Delhi ?
9. Cricket is played...ball and bat. A cricket match is played....two teams. Each team consists...eleven players. They play...the supervision of an umpire.
10. Could you do something...me ? I left my little red bag...the dressing table...my room....home.
11. I wrote....my brother yesterday, and said if you called...him he would give it... you, and you might bring it when you come...Delhi.
12. I have arranged a room....you quite close....my place. I shall be...the station to meet you. Please drop a card...the time you will be reaching here.
13. ....regard...that business, I don't want to do anything more, but I'll be ....touch ....you.
14. It was somewhere...five o'clock....the afternoon when he called...my house. He wanted some help...me.
15. The teacher has gone...the class. He has a chair to sit...., a piece of chalk to write...and a table to work...
16. Don't worry...finding your way....my house. I will write down the instructions ...full...you.
17. There was an acute shortage...food last year...account...the failure...the monsoon.
18. What shall I say...reply...his letter ? Shall I congratulate him...his unexpected success....the examination ?
19. My brother has gone...study...the U.S.A. He has promised...write ....us every week.
20. I shall be away....school tomorrow. My brother is coming back...Bangalore, so, we are going...the station...welcome him.
21. A man who confides...a friend will not conceal anything....him, but will confer ...him....all matters...real importance.
22. It is better to be blind...an eye than to be blind...one's own fault. As an exception...the usual rule, I hope, you will make an exception....my son's case, and show some forbearance...his inexperience.

EXERCISE 19

Fill in the blanks with appropriate words from the list given below each sentence. Put a cross mark (X) *in case 'no word' is to be used :*

EXAMPLES : (i) Which hand do you write... ?

(a) to (b) for
(c) with (d) no word
= Which hand do you write *with ?*

(ii) We signed...the agreement.

(a) to (b) at
(c) on (d) no word
= We signed (X) the agreement.
Or, We signed the agreement.

1. Which hand do you write.... ?

(a) to, (b) for,
(c) with, (d) no word.

2. We signed...the agreement.
   (a) to, (b) at,
   (c) on, (d) no word.

3. He blamed the cyclist...the accident.
   (a) in, (b) for,
   (c) upon, (d) no word.

4. There is another side...this question.
   (a) on, (b) into,
   (c) of, (d) no word.

5. I will inform....your brother about his mistake.
   (a) for, (b) to,
   (c) about (d) no word.

6. He has not replied...my letter yet.
   (a) on, (b) for,
   (c) to, (d) no word.

7. A blind man cannot distinguish light...darkness.
   (a) between. (b) to,
   (c) from, (d) no word.

8. My relations...him are now quite friendly.
   (a) to, (b) with,
   (c) about, (d) no word.

9. Do not complain...your lot.
   (a) about, (b) for,
   (c) with, (d) no word.

10. Did you beg pardon...your teacher ?
   (a) from, (b) of,
   (c) in, (d) no word.

11. He ordered...Tom's dismissal.
   (a) for, (b) about,
   (c) on, (d) no word.

12. You may be surprised...the news.
   (a) on, (b) at,
   (c) about, (d) no word.

13. No one has seen the old man...a long time.
   (a) for, (b) since,
   (c) from, (d) no word.

14. Mr and Mrs Sharma have been in Delhi...last August.
   (a) from, (b) for,
   (c) since, (d) no word.

15. He had to commit the entire passage...memory.
   (a) for, (b) to,
   (c) from, (d) no word.

16. We should feel sorry....the unfortunate victims.
   (a) at, (b) for,
   (c) about, (d) no word.

17. **What is the time...your watch ?**
    (a) in, (b) before,
    (c) by, (d) no word.

18. **This is the book I was telling you....**
    (a) about, (b) from,
    (c) with, (d) no word.

19. **I have nothing in common....him.**
    (a) at, (b) with,
    (c) about, (d) no word.

20. **This man was dismissed...his job...his idleness.**
    (a) from, (b) in,
    (c) for, (d) no word.

21. **I am not interested...modern art...all.**
    (a) at, (b) to,
    (c) in, (d) no word.

22. **Does the old lady object...my smoking...this room ?**
    (a) into, (b) in,
    (c) to, (d) no word.

23. **The success...our attempt will depend...our skill.**
    (a) on, (b) of,
    (c) from, (d) no word.

24. **Please answer....my questions...detail.**
    (a) for, (b) to,
    (c) in, (d) no word.

25. **I am looking forward...hearing...you soon.**
    (a) in, (b) from,
    (c) to, (d) no word.

EXERCISE 20 (with Answer)

1. *In the following sentences the blanks are numbered. Select the most appropriate word from the given list and write it against the numbered space.*

among, between, about, in, down, over, out, by, up, at, into, on, below, under, behind, upon, for.

(a) He was found lacking..[1]....self-confidence.
(b) I am laid..[2]....with fever.
(c) You cannot learn all the rules...[3]....heart.
(d) She burst..[4]....tears at the sight of her son after a long separation.
(e) The Principal felt.[5]...the teacher's proposal.
(f) Over-exercise tells...[6]...one's health.
(g) The soldiers always carry..[7]...the captain's order.
(h) The new secretary will take..[8]...the charge tomorrow.
(i) I could see..[9]...his cleverness easily.
(j) I have put.[10]...considerable weight recently.
(k) A hard-working man does not lag.[11]...others for long.
(l) There is no love lost.[12]....the two friends now.

2. *Choose suitable words from the list given below and complete the following sentences. Write against each serial number the appropriate words. Do not write the sentences.*

from, up, out, with, of, away, on, for, to, in, over, into.

EXAMPLE : The teacher asked the class to get...their work.

Ans. *on with.*

(a) It wasn't easy to put...her bad temper.
(b) They did....that law years ago.
(c) If she persists in her tricks she is...trouble.
(d) At the end of the two mile race, Gopal ran...breath.
(c) They decided to break...the party.

3. *Supply appropriate prepositions for the blanks in the following sentences . Do not write the sentences.*

(a) He killed two birds...one shot. (b) He has been here...nine o'clock. (c) Spencer, the great English poet, lived...the time of Queen Elizabeth. (d) Human sacrifices are still practised...some tribes. (e) She conducted me...her house.

4. *Use suitable prepositions below.*

EXAMPLE : Jaunpur is famous (*for*) its perfumes.

(a) The writer is enamoured...the subject. (b) A true gentleman is courteous...his inferiors. (c) The cat appears to have originated...Egypt. (d) It is better to abstain....food when angry. (e) He had to commit the entire passage...memory. (f) The people were angry...the king.

5. *Put in correct prepositions or adverbs. Write only the required word against the numbers given in the blanks. Do not rewrite the sentences.*

(a) He kept.[1]...telling me to give.[2] .....smoking. (b) Thanks.[3]...you that he was able to see his plans.[4].... (c) He shook me.[5]...the hand and helped me.[6]...my coat. (d) He is terribly absorbed.[1]...his work.[8]..bacteria. (e) He will accept no compromise.[9]...the enemy.[10]...any terms.

6. *Supply appropriate prepositions for the blanks in the following sentences. Do not rewrite the sentences.*

(a) We could not wish....better weather than this.
(b) He insisted...my attending the meeting.
(c) We all sympathise...the unfortunate person.
(d) I wish to remind you...the promise you made.
(e) He cannot compete...so experienced a player as Hanif.

7. *Fill in the blanks with suitable prepositions/adverb particles. Do not reproduce the sentences.*

(a) They wanted advice...how they could procure funds for their new business. (b) There is already active oppostion...the government industrial policy. (c) In an election those in power should be obliged to compete...their opponents on equal terms.

(d) Housewives can telephone a shop and send....goods. (e) I want a place where I can work quietly free...interruptions. (f) He is completely oblivious...his surroundings. (g) The lecturer went...to explain the most important point. (h) This house is very expensive to keep...(i) The work on this project has been seriously set...(j) He hung his head...shame.

8. *Insert appropriate prepositions in the following sentences.*

(a) I do not wish to intrude......you. (b) All ministers are responsible.......Lok Sabha. (c) He connived.......his subordinate's downfall. (d) High principles were instilled......him in youth. (e) He is not amenable......discipline. (f) Such conduct does admit...excuse.

9. *Use the correct prepositions in the following.*

(a) Put.......a *saree* which is suited.......the occasion. (b) She was reading.......bed when the jewels were stolen.......her neighbour's flat. (c) How long have you been.......Bombay, that you are so critical.......it ? (d) She was very keen.......meeting her parents.

10. *Choose the correct prepositions from the following list to fill in the blanks in the sentences below. Write the correct word against each letter; do not write out the whole sentence.*

with, for, on, in, of, at, about, from, along, off.

(a) She was overjoyed...the prospect of meeting him again. (b) I can't be angry...him now that he has apologized...what he has done. (c) That young man is very keen...cycling. (d) I am very reluctant...ask him to do this job. (e) He was charged...a whole series of crimes. (f) I hate sitting beside him; he always smells...garlic. (g) I had always thought...her as a plain girl; now I am amazed...her beauty. (h) He is certainly not devoid....intelligence. (i) He jumped...my suggestion that he should take charge...the arrangements.

11. *Fill in the blanks, in sentences below, with suitable prepositions.*

(a) He is senior.......me. (b) My father generally complies.......all my requests. (c) I wish to live.......New Delhi. (d) When I arrived.......the station, I nearly missed the train. (e) I do not approve.......your action. (f) We should feel sorry.......the unfortunate victims.

12. *Fill in the correct prepositions.*

(a) He told me he believed...love...first sight. (b) This medicine, which tastes...moth balls is a wonderful cure...insomnia. (c) She's homesick....her family, and pining....her native country. (d) She was bent...having that scooter; now she's disappointed...it. (c) Stop brooding...your trouble, or you'll end by dying...a broken heart.

13. *Fill in the blanks with appropriate prepositions. Write the prepositions only, when answering the questions.*

(a) He was charged....theft. (b) He is in the habit of quarrelling.......trifles. (c) I always count........your support. (d) He has dedicated his life.......the cause of village uplift.

14. *Correct the prepositions in the following sentences :*

(a) The boys threw stones on the frogs. (b) He is an asset in the institution. (c) I acquainted him about the facts of the case. (d) Let us go out on a walk. (e) He should refrain on harming others.

15. *Choose the appropriate word from among the words given in brackets at the end of each of the following sentences. Write the number of the sentence and the word you have chosen for it.*

(a) A storm suddenly blew....(over, up, out)
(b) The performance passed...quite successfully. (out, away, off)
(c) The circulars have all been sent....(in, out, away)
(d) When I visited her last evening, we talked the matter....(over, up, oft)
(e) It is mainly due to their lethargy that the plan fell....(off, out, through)
(f) He took....an insurance policy soon after his marriage. (in, up, out)
(g) She wrote....the notes that she had scribbled at the meeting. (up, on, down)
(h) The story developed....a thrilling climax. (up, out, into)
(i) It is not at all easy to put....an air of innocence. (in, on, up).
(j) He slept the day....(by, down, away)

16. *In each of the following cases select the most appropriate preposition from amongst the words given below the sentence to fill in the blank :*

(i) (a) His behaviour admits...no forgiveness.
(i) of (ii) for (iii) on (iv) about (v) with
(b) Dirt often brings...disease.
(i) into (ii) up (iii) for (iv) over (v) on
(c) Never deviate...the path of duty.
(i) at (ii) from (iii) to (iv) into (v) by
(d) He imputed his failure....his bad luck.
(i) with (ii) to (iii) on (iv) at (v) up
(e) The pick-pocket has made...with my purse.
(i) off (ii) away (iii) at (iv) out (v) up.

(ii) (a) This man has had a severe illness but is coming...again.
(i) up (ii) upon (iii) on (iv) round (v) over
(b) I confided...her and she has not betrayed me.
(i) in (ii) with (iii) on (iv) to (v) against
(c) The policeman made...the thief.
(i) with (ii) on (iii) after (iv) for (v) at
(d) He tried to pass...counterfeit coin.
(i) on (ii) away (iii) with (iv) off (v) over

Ans. 1. (1) *in.* (2) *down.* (3) *by.* (4) *into.* (5) *for.* (6) *upon.* (7) *out.* (8) *over.* (9) *through.* (10) *on.* (11) *behind.* (12) *between.*

2. (a) *up with.* (b) *away with.* (c) *in for.* (d) *out of.* (e) *away with.*

3. (a) *in.* (b) *since.* (c) *during.* (d) *by.* (e) *round.*

4. (a) *of.* (b) *to.* (c) *from.* (d) *from.* (e) *to.* (f) *with.*

5. 1. *on.* 2. *up.* 3. *to.* 4. *through.* 5. *by.* 6. *with.* 7. *in.* 8. *on.* 9. *with.* 10. *on.*

6. (a) *for*. (b) *on*. (c) *with*. (d) *of*. (e) *with*.

7. (a) *on*. (b) *to*. (c) *with*. (d) *for*. (e) *from*. (f) *of*. (g) *on*. (h) *up*. (i) *about*. (j) *in*.

8. (a) *upon*. (b) *to*. (c) *at*. (d) *into*. (e) *to* (f) *of*.

9. (a) *on, for* (or *to*). (b) *in, from*. (c) *in, of*. (d) *on*

10. (a) *at*. (b) *with, for*. (c) *on*. (d) *to*. (e) *with*. (f) *of*. (g) *of, at*. (h) *of*. (i) *at, of*.

11. (a) *to*. (b) *with*. (c) *in*. (d) *at*. (e) *of*. (f) *for*.

12. (a) *in, at*. (b) *of, for*. (c) *for, for*. (d) *upon, with*. (e) *over, with*.

13. (a) *with*. (b) *over*. (c) *on*. (d) *to*.

14. (a) *.....at the frogs*. (b) *....an asset to....* (c) *....with the fact....* (d) *....for a walk*. (e) *....refrain from harming*.

15. (a) *over*. (b) *off*. (c) *in*. (d) *over*. (e) *through*. (f) *up*. (g) *down*. (h) *into*. (i) *on*. (j) *away*.

16. (i) (a) *of*. (b) *on*. (c) *from*. (d) *to*. (e) *off*.

(ii) (a) *round*. (b) *in*. (c) *after*. (d) *off*.

□ □ □

10. COMMON ERRORS

वाक्य में grammar के नियमों के उल्लंघन से बहुधा विभिन्न प्रकार की भूलें हुआ करती हैं जिन्हें हम *common errors* कहते हैं। ऐसे errors साधारणतः article, tense, number, noun, pronoun, verb, adverb, adjective, preposition, conjunction इत्यादि के गलत प्रयोग के कारण होते हैं। जैसे :

	Incorrect	*Correct*	*Type of mistake*
1.	He is doctor.	He is *a* doctor.	*Article*
2.	I am going to home.	I am going *home.*	*Preposition*
3.	He didn't went there.	He *didn't go* there.	*Tense*
4.	He asked me what I am doing.	He *asked* me what I *was* doing.	*Sequence of tenses*
5.	She told, "I shall play now."	She *said,* "I shall play now."	*Verb*
6.	Today I have many works to do.	Today I have *a lot of work* to do.	*Number*
7.	They ran very fastly.	They ran very *fast.*	*Adverb*
8.	Rajeev is six feet high.	Rajeev is six feet *tall.*	*Adjective*
9.	What you have done ?	What *have you* done ?	*Word-order*
10.	The people of this village is poor.	The people of this village *are* poor.	*Subject-verb agreement*
11.	This boys will play cricket.	*These* boys will play cricket.	*Determiner[1]-noun agreement*
12.	Is he a fool.	Is he a fool ?	*Punctuation*
13.	This pen is beautifull.	This pen is *beautiful.*	*Spelling*
14.	We went to him, but he is not there.	We *went* to him, but he *was* not there.	*Consistency of tense*

अतः, common errors से बचने के लिए मुख्यतः article, singular तथा plural nouns, preposition, tense, punctuation, sequence of tense, spelling इत्यादि के सही प्रयोग पर ध्यान रखना होगा। साथ ही, आप जो कुछ भी लिखें उसे revise अवश्य कर लें।

आगे incorrect sentences तथा उनके correct forms भी दिए गए हैं। आप पहले स्वयं incorrect sentences को correct करने का प्रयास करें और उसके बाद दिए गए correct answers से मिला लें। ऐसा तब तक करते जाएँ जब तक आपके answers 100% सही नहीं हो जाते हैं।

---

1. The following are determiners : *this, that, these, those, any, no, some, both, the, all, a, an, each, either, one, my, your, his, her, its, our, their* etc.

1. CORRECT USAGE OF ARTICLES

निम्नलिखित वाक्यों में तिरछे अक्षरों में दिए गए शब्दों को ध्यानपूर्वक पढें और देखें कि Articles (*a, an* तथा *the*) का प्रयोग किस प्रकार के शब्द के पहले किया गया है अथवा छोड़ दिया गया है।

	Incorrect	*Correct*
1. (a)	I saw *an U.S.* plane yesterday.	I saw *a U.S.* plane yesterday.
(b)	It was *an unique* sight.	It was *a unique* sight.
(c)	He is *an European.*	He is *a European.*
(d)	This is *an useful* book.	This is *a useful* book.
(e)	He is *an university* professor.	He is *a university* professor.

Note : U.S., unique, European, useful तथा university/य/ध्वनि से शुरू होते हैं जो consonant sound है। अतः, इनके पहले a का प्रयोग होता है।

2. (a)	My boots were *in a good condition.*	My boots were *in good condition.*
(b)	My books were *in bad state.*	My books were in *a bad state.*

Note : In good/bad condition को idiom माना जाता है तथा इसके साथ a नहीं लगाया जाता। किंतु in a good/bad state कहा जाता है।

3. (a)	He is *in a good health.*	He is *in* good *health.*
(b)	I have *a homework* to do.	I have *homework* to do.
(c)	The accused asked for *a mercy.*	The accused asked for *mercy.*
(d)	I have received *a news* from abroad.	I have received *news* from abroad.
(e)	He gets *a* good *pay.*	He gets good *pay.* *Or,* He gets *a* good *salary*
(f)	We like to have *a* perfect *safety.*	We like to have perfect *safety.*
(g)	I want *a soap,* please.	I want (some) *soap,* please. *Or,* I want *a piece/cake of soap, please.*
(h)	*I like a* comfortable *travel.*	I like comfortable *travel.* *Or,* I like *a* comfortable *journey.*
(i)	It was *a* bad *weather.*	It was bad *weather.* *Or,* It was *a* bad *climate.*
(j)	Teachers' work is *a* useful *work.*	Teachers' work is useful *work.*
(k)	We write on *a paper.*	We write on *paper.*

Note : Health, homework, mercy, news, pay, safety, soap, travel, weather, work, paper (कागज)—uncountable nouns हैं, इनके पहले a नहीं लगाया जाता। किंतु salary, journey, climate तथा paper (=newspaper) countable nouns हैं, इनके पहले a लगता है।

4. (a) I must give *answer* to the question.	I must give *an answer* to the question.
(b) They got into *boat.*	They got into *a boat.*
(c) Everybody needs *holiday.*	Everybody needs *a holiday.*
(d) I often ride *horse.*	I often ride *a horse.*
(e) I had *lesson* yesterday.	I had *a lesson* yesterday.
(f) On such *cold morning,* I do not go out.	On such *a cold morning* I do not go out.
(g) He wants to become *politician.*	He wants to become *a politician.*
(h) I take *rest* for an hour.	I {take / have} *a rest* for an hour.
(i) Calcutta is *big city.*	Calcutta is *a big city.*

Note : Answer, boat, holiday, horse, lesson, morning, politician, rest तथा city *singular countable nouns* हैं, इनके पहले a/an का प्रयोग किया जाता है। लेकिन by boat/car/train/bus/plane इत्यादि idiom हैं, इनके साथ a नहीं लगाया जाता।

5. (a) He took *a habit* of smoking.	He took *the habit* of smoking.
(b) It is very important in *a life* of a person.	It is very important in *the life* of a person.
(c) I have a cat and *a cat* is black.	I have a cat and *the cat* is black.
(d) She hit him on *a nose.*	She hit him on *the nose.*
(e) *A sea* was rough.	*The sea* was rough.
(f) *Sky* is blue.	*The sky* is blue.

Note : अगर किसी noun से definite वस्तु का बोध हो तो उसके पहले the लगाया जाता है।

6. (a) I play *piano.*	I play *the piano.*
(b) She likes *harmonium.*	She likes *the harmonium.*
(c) He learns *a guitar.*	He learns *the guitar.*

Note : Play, learn तथा like *verbs* के बाद अगर कोई musical instrument का नाम हो तो उस musical instrument के पहले the लगाया जाता है।

7. (a) It was not *a best* model.	It was not *the best* model.
(b) This is *a smallest* TV set they make.	This is *the smallest* TV set they make.
(c) That is *biggest* gramophone we have.	That is *the biggest* gramophone we have.

Note : Superlative degree of adjective (=best, smallest, biggest आदि) के पहले the का प्रयोग किया जाता है।

8. (a) *A poor* always suffer.	*The poor* always suffer.
(b) *Rich* are seldom happy.	*The rich* are seldom happy.

(c) *An unemployed* is losing hope.	*The unemployed* are losing hope.
(d) He is collecting money for *blind*.	He is collecting money for *the blind*.

Note : कुछ adjectives हैं जिनके पहले सदा the का प्रयोग किया जाता है, उनमें कुछ मुख्य हैं :

the blind, the deaf, the sick, the mentally ill, the poor, the old, the dead, the rich, the unemployed, the handicapped.

इन शब्दों का plural meaning होता है, जैसे—the dead=the dead people या all dead people.

9. (a) All *the mankind* should be happy.	All *mankind* should be happy.
(b) We enjoyed the beauty of *the nature*.	We enjoyed the beauty *of nature*.
(c) We have to learn to live in *the society*.	We have to learn to live *in society*.
(d) *The man* is mortal.	*Man* is mortal.

Note : Mankind, nature, society तथा man का प्रयोग general अर्थ में हुआ है, तथा इनके पहले article नहीं लगाया जाता।

10. (a) *The most* people like it.	*Most* people like it.
(b) *The most* of the people like it.	*Most of* the people like it.

Note : अगर most या most of के ठीक बाद कोई noun आए तो most के पहले the नहीं लगाया जाता।

11. Our clock struck *the 7 o'clock*.	Our clock struck 7 *o'clock*.

Note : जब o'clock का प्रयोग noun की तरह हो तो उसके पहले the नहीं लगाया जाता।

12. (a) He was given the post of *the director*.	He was given *the post of director*.
(b) He accepted the job of *the headmaster*.	He accepted *the job of headmaster*.
(c) He had the rank of *a captain*.	He had *the rank of captain*.

Note : The post/job/rank/position of के बाद आनेवाले noun के पहले article नहीं लगाया जाता।

13. (a) I get up before *the sunrise*.	I get up before *sunrise*.
(b) He came here after *the sunset*.	He came here after *sunset*.

Note : हम Before/after/at sunrise या sunset कहते हैं तथा इसके साथ the नहीं लगाया जाता।

14. (a) I want to go to *cinema*.	I want to go to *the cinema*.

(b) Do you often go to *pictures* ?	Do you often go to *the pictures* ?
(c) He went to *theatre*.	He went to *the theatre*.
(d) She went to *movies*.	She went to *the movies*.
(e) He goes to *office* at ten.	He goes to *the office* at ten.

Note : Go to *the* cinema/theatre/pictures/movies/opera/office/circus कहा जाता है। He is *at the office* (but *at work*).

15. (a) *Nile* is a fine river.	*The Nile* is a fine river.
(b) *Ganga* is a holy river.	*The Ganga* is a holy river.

Note : नदियों के नाम के पहले the लगाया जाता है।

16. (a) Can you play *the tennis* ?	Can you play *tennis* ?
(b) Do you like *the cricket* ?	Do you like *cricket* ?
(c) Have you ever played *a football* ?	Have you ever played *football* ?

Note : Games के नाम (जैसे—tennis, cricket, football, hockey आदि) के पहले article नहीं लगाया जाता।

17. (a) Sports make *body* strong.	Sports make *the body* strong.
(b) Games make *arms* strong.	Games make *the arms* strong.
(c) Boxing makes *back* strong.	Boxing makes *the back* strong.

Note : Parts of the body (जैसे—body, arms, legs, back, muscles आदि) के पहले the लगता है।

18. (a) I saw *an one-act play*.	I saw *a one-act play*.
(b) He gave me *an one-rupee note*.	He gave me *a one-rupee note*.
(c) I bought *an one-way ticket*.	I bought *a one-way ticket*.

Note : One का उच्चारण /व/ से शुरू होता है जो consonant sound है। अतः, इसके पहले a लगता है, an नहीं।

19. (a) He speaks *the English*.	He speaks *English*.
(b) Don't you know *the Hindi* ?	Don't you know *Hindi* ?

Note : भाषा के नाम के पहले artcle नहीं लगाया जाता। किंतु, the English language, the Hindi language कहा जाता है।

20. (a) He came here at *the Christmas*.	He came here *at Christmas*.
(b) *The Holi* falls in March.	*Holi* falls in March.
(c) *The Diwali* is a happy festival.	*Dewali* is a happy festival.

Note : त्योहारों (festivals) के नाम के पहले the नहीं लगाया जाता।

21. (a) *The December* is the last month.	*December* is the last month.
(b) *The Sunday* is a day of prayer.	*Sunday* is a day of prayer.
(c) *The Everest* is the highest peak in the world.	*Everest* is the highest peak in the world.

Note : December, Sunday, तथा Everest **(खास चोटी का नाम)** proper nouns हैं, इनके पहले article नहीं लगता। किंतु the Himalayas कहते हैं क्योंकि Himalayas—range of mountains है।

22. (a) My friend is in *Army*. — My friend is in *the Army*
    (b) He joined *a Navy*. — He joined *the Navy*.
    (c) He retired from *Air Force*. — He retired from *the Air Force*.

Note : Armed forces के नाम के पहले the लगाया जाता है।

23. (a) I have *a x-ray* plant. — I have *an x-ray* plant.
    (b) He is *a N.C.C.* officer. — He is *an N.C.C.* officer.
    (c) My friend is *a M.P.* — My friend is *an M.P.*
    (d) She is *a M.A.* — She is *an M.A.*
    (e) He is *a M.L.A.* — He is *an M.L.A.*

Note : X-ray, N.C.C., M.P , M.A., तथा M.L.A का उच्चारण /ए/ ध्वनि से शुरू होता है जो vowel sound है। अतः, इनके पहले an लगाया जाता है।

24. (a) We reached *the home*. — We reached *home*.
    (b) He came from *the home*. — He came from *home*.

Note : Home के पहले article नहीं लगाया जाता।

25. (a) He is good at *the history*. — He is good *at history*.
    (b) She is bad at *the economics*. — She is bad *at economics*.
    (c) He failed in *the physics*. — He failed *in physics*.

Note : Subject के नाम के पहले article नहीं लगाया जाता।

26. (a) I go to *the school* every day. — I *go to school* every day.
    (b) He goes to *the college* every day. — He *goes to college* every day.

Note : जब हम पढ़ने या पढ़ाने के लिए school/college जाते हैं तब go to school/college कहा जाता है, इनके साथ article नहीं लगाया जाता।

27. (a) *The rice* is cheap this year. — *Rice* is cheap this year.
    (b) *The gold* is yellow. — *Gold* is yellow.
    (c) *Rice* that I bought is fine. — *The rice* that I bought is fine.

Note : Rice तथा gold *uncountable nouns* हैं, इनके पहले article नहीं लगता। किंतु अगर uncountable noun का किसी particular अर्थ में प्रयोग हो तो उसके पहले the लगाया जाता है।

28. (a) He came here *by the car*. — He came here *by car*.
    (b) Go there *by a train*. — Go there *by train*.

Note : By car/train/bus/plane/ship/air/water आदि idioms हैं, इनके साथ the या a नहीं लगता। किंतु हम in a car, in the train, in a boat आदि कहते हैं।

29. (a) I got *hundred* books. — I got *a hundred* books.
    (b) I have *thousand* rupees. — I have *a thousand* rupees.
    (c) He made *noise*. — He made *a noise*.

	Incorrect	Correct
(d)	He has *dozen* eggs.	He has *a dozen* eggs.

Note : A hundred, a thousand, a dozen तथा a noise कहा जाता है।

	Incorrect	Correct
30. (a)	We pray to *the God.*	We pray *to God.*
(b)	Durga is *goddess.*	Durga is *a goddess.*

Note : God के पहले article नहीं लगता, किंतु god/goddess (देवता/देवी) के पहले लगता है।

	Incorrect	Correct
31. (a)	*The cars* are made in India.	*Cars* are made in India.
(b)	*The boys* like sweets.	*Boys* like sweets.

Note : Plural nouns का प्रयोग general अर्थ में हो तो उसके पहले article नहीं लगता।

	Incorrect	Correct
32. (a)	*Books* that you gave me are very fine.	*The books* that you gave me are very fine.
(b)	*Combs* that you sell are black.	*The combs* that you sell are black.

Note : अगर plural nouns का प्रयोग किसी खास अर्थ (particular sense) में हो तो उसके पहले the लगता है।

	Incorrect	Correct
33. (a)	He invited me to *the lunch.*	He invited me *to lunch.*
(b)	We have *a breakfast* at eight.	We have *breakfast* at eight.
(i)	I was invited to *the dinner.*	I was invited *to dinner.*

Note : Names of meals के पहले article नहीं लगता। किंतु कोई special meal हो या name of the meal के पहले कोई adjective हो तो article का प्रयोग किया जाता है। जैसे : I was invited to *a dinner* given to welcome the minister. He gave us *a good breakfast.*

	Incorrect	Correct
34. (a)	I have never seen *a such pen.*	I have never seen *such a pen.*
(b)	*What* beautiful house he has !	*What a* beautiful house he has !

Note : Such तथा what के बाद कोई singular countable noun रहे तो such a/what a कहा जाता है।

	Incorrect	Correct
35. (a)	He tells *lie.*	He tells *a lie.*
(b)	You speak *truth.*	You speak *the truth.*

Note : a lie/the truth कहा जाता है।

	Incorrect	Correct
36. (a)	He went to *U.S.A.*	He went to *the U.S.A.*
(b)	She came from *U.K.*	She came from *the U.K.*
(c)	I returned from *U.S.S.R.*	I returned from *the U.S.S.R.*

Note : इन देशों के ऐसे नाम (U.S.A., U.K., U.S.S.R.) के पहले the लगता है, किंतु America, Britain, Russia के पहले the नहीं लगता।

	Incorrect	Correct
37. (a)	He talked to me by *a telephone.*	He talked to me *by telephone.*
(b)	We hear *radio* in the morning.	We hear *the radio* in the morning.

Incorrect	Correct
(c) Do you ever listen to *wireless ?*	*Do* you ever listen to *the wireless ?*

Note : यद्यपि telephone *countable noun* है, किंतु by telephone एक idiom है, इसके साथ a नहीं लगता। Radio तथा wireless (meaning the system of broadcasting) के पहले the लगता है।

Incorrect	Correct
38. (a) I work *in morning.*	I work *in the morning.*
(b) I rest *in afternoon.*	I rest *in the afternoon.*
(c) She plays *in evening.*	She plays *in the evening.*

Note : In the morning/afternoon/evening/night कहा जाता है।

Incorrect	Correct
39. (a) The sun shines *by the day,* and not *by the night.*	The sun shines *by day,* and not *by night.*
(b) He came here *on the foot.*	He came here *on foot.*
(c) She went there *at the night.*	She went there *at night.*

Note : By day, by night, on foot, at night कहा जाता है, इनके साथ article का प्रयोग नहीं होता।

Incorrect	Correct
40. (a) I am *B.A.*	I am *a B.A.*
(b) He is *S.D.O.*	He is *an* S.D.O.
(c) She came in *a hour.*	She came in *an hour.*

Note : B.A. /ब/ ध्वनि से शुरू होता है जो consonant sound है, इसके पहले a लगता है। किंतु S.D.O. /ए/ तथा hour /आ/ ध्वनि से शुरू होते हैं, जो vowel sound हैं, इनके पहले an लगता है।

Incorrect	Correct
41. (a) He is seeking *an employment.*	He is seeking *employment.*
(b) He is in search of *job.*	He is in searh of *a job.*

Note : 'रोजगार' के अर्थ में employment *uncountable noun* है, इसके पहले a नहीं लगता। किंतु job *countable noun* है, इसके पहले *a* लगता है।

Three Golden Rules : Articles

Articles के प्रयोग के संबंध में तीन बातों का हमेशा ध्यान रखना चाहिए जिनमें से किसी के उल्लंघन से अधिकांश mistakes होते हैं :

(i) Do not use *the* (with plural and uncountable nouns) to talk about things in general.
Life is hard. (Not : *The life* is hard.)

(ii) Do not use singular countable nouns without articles.
the car, a car (But not : *car*)

(iii) Use *a/an* to say what people's professions or jobs are.
He is *a bank manager.* (Not : He is *bank manager*).

2. CORRECT USAGE OF NOUNS

वाक्य में उपयुक्त noun का प्रयोग नहीं करने से वाक्य गलत हो जाता है। जैसे :

	Incorrect	*Correct*
1.	(a) I had no *rupees.*	I had no *money.*
	(b) He has *lots of rupees.*	He has *lots of money.*

Note : 'रुपए-पैसे' के अर्थ में money का प्रयोग किया जाता है। किंतु I have a rupee. He gave me two rupees आदि कहा जाता है।

2.	He enjoyed *the theatre.*	He enjoyed *the play.*

Note : Theatre का अर्थ होता है—a special building or place for performance of plays. अतः, हम play का आनंद लेते हैं, theatre का नहीं।

3.	(a) He got two *breads.*	He got two *loaves of bread.*
	(b) I eat a *bread.*	I eat *bread*/I eat *a loaf of bread.*

Note : Bread *uncountable noun* है। अगर इससे गिनती का बोध कराना हो तो a loaf of/a piece of या loaves of/pieces of का प्रयोग किया जाता है।

4.	(a) He applied for *teachery.*	He applied for *teachership.* *Or,* He applied for *the post of teacher.*
	(b) I work for the *upliftment* of my village.	I work for the *uplift* of my village.
	(c) He applied for *lecturership.*	He applied for *lectureship.*
	(d) I got a *freeship.*	I got a *freestudentship.*

Note : Teachery शब्द नहीं होता; uplift शब्द स्वयं noun है, uplift में ment जोड़कर upliftment शब्द नहीं बनाया जाता; lecturer स्वयं noun है, उसमें ship जोड़कर lecturership बनाना गलत है। उसी प्रकार freeship नहीं, वरन् freestudentship होता है।

5.	(a) It is a nice *poetry.*	It is a nice *poem.*
	(b) Quote the poem from *heart.*	Quote the poem from *memory.*
	(c) *Good night,* Sir, have a seat.	*Good evening,* Sir, have a seat.
	(d) There is no *place* for us in the car.	There is no *room* for us in the car.

Note : Poetry (=the art of a poet; poems in general) *uncountable noun* है, एक कविता के लिए a poem कहते हैं, get by heart (याद कर लेना)—idiom है, किंतु याद की हुई चीज को memory से दुहराते हैं, अतः quote from memory कहते हैं; good night किसी व्यक्ति से विदा लेने के समय कहते हैं, शाम में मिलने पर good evening कहा जाता है; place का अर्थ जगह, जैसे—Patna, Delhi, Bihar आदि, room का अर्थ 'कमरा' तथा 'जगह' (space) दोनों होता है।

6.	(a) He lost *a quantity* of books.	He lost *a number* of books.

	Incorrect	Correct
(b)	We had a large *number* of money.	We had a large *amount* of money.
(c)	Sorry, *Mr,* I can't come.	Sorry, *Mr Sen,* I can't come. Sorry, *Sir,* I can't come.
(d)	Do you like *his new dress* ?	Do you like *his new clothes* ? Do you like *his new suit* ? Do you like *her new dress* ? Do you like *her new clothes* ?

Note : Quantity/amount से मात्रा का बोध होता है, number से संख्या का; Mr/Mrs का प्रयोग अकेले में नहीं होता—Mr Kumar, Mrs Bose आदि के साथ होता है; dresses अकसर लड़कियाँ या औरतें पहनती हैं, clothes का अर्थ होता है—'garments such as trousers, dresses, shirts etc. worn on the body'.

	Incorrect	Correct
7.	This is the *cause* why I don't like it.	This is the *reason* why I don't like it. This is *why* I don't like it.

Note : Cause के बाद why का प्रयोग नहीं किया जाता। इसके बाद of लगता है। जैसे : What was the cause of the accidents ?

	Incorrect	Correct
8.	The *weather* of Ranchi suits me.	The *climate* of Ranchi suits me.

Note : Climate का अर्थ होता है—जलवायु; weather का अर्थ होता है—मौसम।

Climate denotes the general atmospheric conditions of a country; *weather,* the conditions at a particular time.—BRACKENBURY : STUDIES IN ENGLISH IDIOM.

	Incorrect	Correct
9. (a)	My *girl* is too young to marry.	My *daughter* is too young to to marry.
(b)	I saw a *daughter* on the road.	I saw a *girl* on the road.

Note : *Girl* (बालिका, बच्ची)—'a female child'; daughter (पुत्री, लड़की)—a female child in relation to her parents'.

	Incorrect	Correct
10. (a)	My husband is a very good *cooker.*	My husband is a very good *cook.*
(b)	I prefer gas *cooks* to electric ones.	I prefer gas *cookers* to electric ones.

Note : *Cook* उस व्यक्ति को कहा जाता है जो खाना पकाता है; *cooker* उस बरतन (apparatus) को कहते हैं जिसका उपयोग खाना पकाने के लिए होता है।

3. ERRORS OF NUMBER

(a) Plural for Singular

	Incorrect	*Correct*
1. (a)	He gave me good *advices.*	He gave me good *advice.*

	Incorrect	*Correct*
	(b) He gave me *many advices.*	He gave me *lots of advice.* He gave me many *pieces of advice.*
	(c) I sold my *furnitures.*	I sold my *furniture.*
	(d) He bought *some furnitures.*	He bought *some furniture.* He bought *some pieces of furniture.*
	(e) Please give me all *informations.*	Please give me all *information.*

Note : Advice (सलाह), furniture तथा information *uncountable nouns* हैं, इनका न तो plural होता है और न इनके पहले a/an लगता है।

2.	(a) I need some *cardboards for* this.	I need some *cardboard* for this. I need some *pieces of cardboard* for this.
	(b) Our children need some *educations.*	Our children need some *education.*
	(c) I need some new *equipments.*	I need some new *equipment.*
	(d) I took some *foods* to eat.	I took some *food* to eat.

Note : Cardboard, education, equipment तथा food *uncountable nouns* हैं। 'बहुत खाना/बहुत भोजन' के लिए हम a lot of food कहते हैं।

3.	(a) Did you buy *fruits* today ?	Did you buy *fruit* today ?
	(b) We went there *on horsebacks.*	We went there *on horseback.*
	(c) We heard some good *musics.*	We heard some good *music.*
	(d) The *news* are bad today.	The *news* is bad today. I heard some bad *pieces of news* today.

Note : Fruit (meaning apples, oranges, etc.) अकसर *uncountable* होता है, fruits का अर्थ 'reward' होता है, जैसे—to enjoy the fruits of all one's hard work; horseback सदा singular रूप में प्रयुक्त होता है; music *uncountable noun* है; news भी *singular* तथा *uncountable noun* है।

4.	Two *peoples* were in the garden.	Two *people* were in the garden.

Note : People (लोग) अपने आप plural है, किंतु जब इसका अर्थ राष्ट्र (nation) होता है तो इसे singular माना जाता है तथा इसमें -s लगाकर plural बनाया जाता है। जैसे : The peoples (=nations) of Europe.

5.	(a) The *sceneries* around here *are* beautiful.	The *scenery* around here *is* beautiful.
	(b) In their *free times,* they played tennis.	In their *free time,* they played tennis.

(c) We had to do several *works.*	We had to do several *pieces of work.*
(d) There were many *works* that I had to do.	There was *a lot of work* that I had to do.
(e) I don't like household *works.*	I don't like *household work.* I don't like *housework.*
(f) Do you have *many homeworks* ?	Do you have *much homework* ?

Note : Scenery सदा uncountable होता है, scene *countable* होता है; free time तथा lesson time *uncountable* होता है; work (काम) *uncountable* होता है, works का अर्थ—'कल-कारखाने' होता है, जैसे: iron and steel works.

6. (a) I met *a six-years-old girl.*	I met a *six-year-old girl.* She was *six years old.*
(b) He has *a six-months-old son.*	He has a *six-month-old son.* My son is *six months old.*

Note : (i) Five-year-old boy, six-month-old girl, three-week-old brother, two-day-old baby इत्यादि कहा जाता है, ऐसे constructions में year/month/week/day के साथ s नहीं लगता। लेकिन six years old, five weeks old कहा जाता है।

(ii) कुछ और उदाहरण देखें :

a ten-pound note	a six-cylinder car
a five-dollar bill	a five-yard space
a twelve-inch ruler	a sixty-acre farm
a four-foot ladder	a two-hour exam.
a six-mile walk	a ten-minute conversation

7. (a) They live in *another towns.*	They live in *another town.*
(b) Have you got *other letter ?*	Have you got *another letter* ? Have you got *other letters* ?

Note : Another *singular* है किंतु towns *plural* है, another के साथ singular noun आता है; other *plural* है, इसके साथ plural noun (letters) का प्रयोग होता है।

8. (a) *Each houses are* white.	*Each house is* white.
(b) They help *each others.*	They help *each other.*
(c) *Each* wanted a book for *themselves.*	Each wanted a book for *himself.* Each wanted a book for *herself.*

Note : Each (प्रत्येक) के बाद आनेवाला noun सदा singular होता है; each other *idiom* है, each others नहीं होता है; each के साथ आनेवाला pronoun (himself/herself) भी singular होता है।

9. (a) *Everything* are ready.	*Everything is* ready.
(b) *Everybody* were there.	*Everybody was* there.

	Incorrect	Correct
	(c) *Everyone* have a cap.	*Everyone has* a cap.

Note : Everything, everybody तथा everyone सदा singular होता है।

	Incorrect	Correct
10.	(a) He who plays and *take* part in sports is popular.	He who plays and *takes* part in sports is popular.
	(b) *Neither* he *nor* his sister *were* there.	*Neither* he *nor* his sister *was* there. (*Both* he and his sister *were* there.)
	(c) *Either* Moti *or* Madan *have gone*.	Either Moti *or* Madan *has* gone.
	(d) There was not *many food* to eat.	There was not *much food* to eat.

Note : He *singular* है अतः इसके साथ takes होगा, take नहीं; अगर दो singular subject *neither...nor, either...or* से जुटे हों तो verb singular होता है; many *plural noun* के साथ प्रयुक्त होता है; food *uncountable* है, इसके साथ much का प्रयोग होगा। जैसे—There *is* not *much food/water* there. There *are* not *many books/people* left.

	Incorrect	Correct
11.	(a) His *luggages* are at the station.	His *luggage* is at the station.
	(b) I bought three *dozens* eggs.	I bought three *dozen* eggs.
	(c) This town has fifty *thousands* people.	This town has fifty *thousand* people.
	(d) I have five *hundreds* rupees.	I have five *hundred* rupees.

Note : Luggage सदा singular होता है; dozen, thousand, hundred, million के पहले a रहे अथवा two, three, four रहे तो वह उसी form में रहता है, उसमें -s नहीं लगता। जैसे—एक दर्जन—a dozen, पाँच दर्जन—five dozen. किंतु dozens of pens (दर्जनों कलम), hundreds of boys (सैकड़ों लड़के), thousands of trees (हजारों पेड़) आदि का प्रयोग किया जाता है।

	Incorrect	Correct
12.	(a) Do you know the English *alphabets ?*	Do you know the English *alphabet ?*
	(b) They are using new *machineries*.	They are using new *machinery*.
	(c) Please help *the poors*.	Please help *the poor*.

Note : Alphabet (वर्णमाला) तथा machinery का प्रयोग plural में नहीं किया जाता; the poor (=the poor men), the poors का प्रयोग कभी नहीं होता।

	Incorrect	Correct
13.	(a) What *a nonsense* to have a picnic today !	What *nonsense* to have a picnic today !
	(b) It is *a* nice *weather*.	It is nice *weather*.
	(c) India is making *a progress* in the field of science.	India is making *progress* in the field of science.

Note : Nonsense, weather तथा progress *uncountable nouns* हैं, इनके पहले a/an का प्रयोग नहीं किया जाता। किंतु a piece of nonsense, a spell of weather कहा जाता है।

	Incorrect	Correct
14. (a)	**By means of books *knowledges* are spread.**	**By means of books *knowledge* is spread.**
(b)	I saw *a magic* yesterday.	I saw *magic* yesterday.

Note : Knowledge तथा magic *uncountable nouns* हैं, इनके पहले a का प्रयोग नहीं किया जाता और न इनका plural -s जोड़कर बनाया जाता है। किंतु knowledge के साथ कभी-कभी a लगता है। जैसे :

Knowledge is power (=Learning)
He has *a knowledge* of the truth (=information about).
He has *a good knowledge* (=information) of London.

(b) Singular for Plural

	Incorrect	Correct
1. (a)	I like *this three kinds* of sports.	I like *these three kinds* of sports. I like *these three* sports.
(b)	They gave us *three kind* of food.	They gave us *three kinds* of food.

Note : This तथा kind *singular* हैं, three तथा kinds *plural* हैं। अतः, this का प्रयोग three तथा kinds के पहले नहीं हो सकता और न three का प्रयोग kind के पहले हो सकता है।

	Incorrect	Correct
2.	Citizens have *all sorts of right*.	Citizens have *all sorts of rights*.

Note : All sorts/kinds/types+of के बाद plural countable noun का प्रयोग किया जाता है या uncountable noun का। जैसे—All sorts of bread, all kinds of milk, all types of food, all types of books आदि।

	Incorrect	Correct
3. (a)	He lived in *several part* of the country.	He lived in *several parts* of the country. He lived in *every part* of the country.
(b)	All *these sport* are amusing.	All *these sports* are amusing.

Note : Several *plural* है, उसके साथ *plural noun* parts का प्रयोग होना चाहिए, part का नहीं। उसी तरह these *plural* है, उसके साथ *plural noun* sports का प्रयोग सही होगा, sport का नहीं।

	Incorrect	Correct
4. (a)	I have seen her *lots of time*.	I have seen her *lots of times*. (I had *lots of time* before our train left.)
(b)	We have met him *lots of time*.	We have met him *lots of times*.

Note : जब time का अर्थ occasion होता है तब इसे countable noun माना जाता है, किंतु time से जब 'समय' का बोध होता है तब इसे uncountable माना जाता है। Lots of के बाद plural countable noun आ सकता है या singular uncountable.

	Incorrect	Correct
5.	(a) There *is a lot of people* here.	There *are a lot of people* here.
	(b) *A lot of books is* on the table.	*A lot of books are* on the table.
	(c) There *are a lot of money* here.	There *is a lot of money* here.
	(d) I have seen *a lot of film.*	I have seen *a lot of films.*

Note : *A lot of* के बाद plural countable noun आ सकता है या singular uncountable noun.

6.	(a) Teaching is *one of my task.*	Teaching is *one of my tasks.*
	(b) *One of my friend* is a pilot.	*One of my friends* is a pilot.
	(c) *One of the boy* was ill.	*One of the boys* was ill.
	(d) *One of my dog* has no tail.	*One of my dogs* has no tail.
	(e) One of our cats *have* disappeared.	One of our cats *has* disappeared.

Note : One of के बाद plural noun किंतु singular verb का प्रयोग किया जाता है, क्योंकि वाक्य का *subject* one है जो singular है।

7.	(a) I like *apple* more than *orange.*	I like *an apple* more than *an orange.*
	(b) Ripe *mango* is sweeter than ripe *guava.*	*A* ripe *mango* is sweeter than *a* ripe *guava.*

Note : फल का नाम countable noun होता है, उनके पहले a/an लगेगा अथवा उनका प्रयोग plural रूप में करना होगा। जैसे: I like *apples* more than *oranges.*

8.	(a) I got *the mark* for the examination.	I got *the marks* for the examination.
	(b) He gave me *full mark* in mathematics.	He gave me *full marks* in mathematics.

Note : Teacher परीक्षा में *marks* (plural) देते हैं, तथा *full marks* सही होता है, full mark नहीं।

9.	(a) They are called *optimist.*	They are called *optimists.*
	(b) They are good *doctor.*	They are good *doctors.*
	(c) We are *a student.*	We are *students.*

Note : *They are, We are* के बाद आनेवाला noun complement सदा plural होता है। कुछ और उदाहरण देखें :

These people are *players.* Those men were *hunters.*

10.	(a) *They* could become *a lawyer.*	*They* could become *lawyers.*
	(b) *We* were then *a schoolboy.*	*We* were then *schoolboys.*
	(c) *Children* must become *an honest man.*	*Children* must become *honest men.*

Note : They, we तथा children *plural* हैं, किंतु a lawyer, a schoolboy तथा an honest man *singular* हैं। अत:, अधिक व्यक्तियों का मिलकर एक व्यक्ति बन जाना असंभव है।

	Incorrect	Correct
11. (a)	*The rich is* **happier than the poor.**	*The rich are* happier than the poor.
(b)	It is kind to give something to *a poor.*	It is kind to give something to *the poor.*
(c)	*The sick lives* an unhappy life.	*The sick live* an unhappy life.

Note : Adjectives (जैसे—the rich, the poor, the sick, the young, the strong) का प्रयोग जब nouns की तरह हो तब वे सदा plural होते हैं।

12. (a)	They don't give *much benefits.*	They don't give *many benefits.*
(b)	He has *much children.*	He has *many children.*

Note : Much का प्रयोग uncountables (जैसे—not much water), तथा many का प्रयोग plural countables (जैसे—many boys) के साथ होता है।

13. (a)	He went to *the picture* to see 'Gandhi'.	He went to *the pictures* to see 'Gandhi.'
(b)	Our *surrounding* was pleasant.	Our *surroundings* were pleasant.
(c)	We were in *high spirit.*	We were in *high spirits.*

Note : Pictures का अर्थ जब cinema होता है तब वह हमेशा plural रहता है; surroundings भी सदा plural रहता है; high/low/good spirits हमेशा plural रूप में रहता है, यहाँ spirits का अर्थ 'mood' होता है।

14.	There are *some* who *calls* it a bore.	There are *some* who *call* it a bore.

Note : यहाँ some *plural* है, तथा who 'some' को refer करता है जो call का subject है, अतः *call* को भी plural बनाना होगा।

15. (a)	*Nowaday,* the towns are very crowded.	*Nowadays,* the towns are very crowded.
(b)	*Sometime* I had milk for breakfast.	*Sometimes* I had milk for breakfast.
(c)	His *whereabout* is still unknown.	His *whereabouts* is/are still unknown.

Note : Nowaday के साथ हमेशा -s लगा रहता है, अर्थात nowadays (आजकल) होता है; sometimes= कभी-कभी; some time= किसी समय (जैसे—See me *some time* tomorrow); whereabout के साथ हमेशा -s लगा रहता है, अतः शब्द whereabouts (पता-ठिकाना) होता है तथा इसके साथ आप is या are का प्रयोग कर सकते हैं।

16. (a)	*Two-third* of the work is done.	*Two-thirds* of the work is done.
(b)	They gave me *thank.*	They gave me *thanks.*
(c)	He placed the necessary *order.*	He placed the necessary *orders.*

Note : Two-thirds होता है, तथा thank (धन्यवाद के अर्थ में) सदा *plural Thanks* are due to him. होता है। जैसे : Order का अर्थ जब 'command given

with authority' होता है, तब उसका plural रूप orders का प्रयोग किया जाता है, । जैसे—Soldiers must obey *orders*. He gave *orders* for the work to be started soon.

17.

(a)	I gave *alm* to the beggar.	I gave *alms* to the beggar.
(b)	I can't read without *glass*.	I can't read without *glasses*.
(c)	His *asset* was seized.	His *assets* were seized.
(d)	I have no *scale* to weigh it.	I have no *scales* to weigh it.
(e)	Do you eat *vegetable* every day ?	Do you eat *vegetables* every day ?

Note : Alms (भीख), glasses (चश्मा), assets (संपत्ति), scales (तराजू), vegetables (साग-पात), measles (चेचक), eatables (खाने की चीजें), bowels (आँत), credentials (परिचय पत्र), pants, pyjamas, shorts, fetters (हथकड़ी), moveables, ashes (from the fire, but cigarette ash) सदा plural होते हैं। उनका 's' या '-es' हटाकर singular में प्रयोग उसी अर्थ में नहीं करना चाहिए। जैसे—asset का अर्थ जब गुण होता है तब इसका singular में भी प्रयोग होता है—Good health is a great *asset*. Beauty is her only *asset*.

(c) Nouns: Singular or Plural ? Some Special Cases

		Incorrect	*Correct*
1.	(a)	A *group* of people *were* there.	A *group* of people *was* there.
	(b)	A *crowd* of women *are* there.	A *crowd* of women *is* there.
	(c)	A *herd* of cattle *were* stolen.	A *herd* of cattle *was* stolen.
	(d)	A *flock* of sheep *are* grazing in the field.	A *flock* of sheep *is* grazing in the field.
	(e)	A *team* of players *have* arrived.	A *team* of players *has* arrived.
	(f)	A *regiment* of soldiers *are* there.	A *regiment* of soldiers *is* there.

Note : (i) Collective nouns जैसे—a group (of things), a crowd (of people), a herd (of cattle), a flock (of sheep), a regiment (of soldiers), a congregation (of worshippers) प्रायः singular माना जाता है। इनके बाद of + plural noun + singular verb का प्रयोग किया जाता है।

(ii) कुछ collective nouns हैं (जिन्हें modern grammar में group nouns कहा जाता है) जो grammar के अनुसार singular किंतु अर्थ के अनुसार plural होते हैं। उनके साथ उसी अनुसार singular या plural verb लगता है। जैसे :

The *public is/are* tired of demonstrations.
The *audience was/were* enjoying the show.
The *committee has/have* considered your request.
The vast *majority* of students *needs/need* financial support.

My *family is* very large. My family (=father, mother, brothers, sisters etc.) *are* all tall.

A new *government (=ministry) is* formed.

The *government (=the people who rule) have* decided to ease import licences.

The government {have / has} broken all {their / its} promisses.

जब group को a single undivided body के रूप में समझा जाता है तब उसके साथ singular verb का प्रयोग किया जाता है,

The *public consists* of you and me.

The *audience was* enormous.

My company *is* opening a new factory.

The plural verb after a group noun is more characteristic of British English than of American English. GEOFFREY LEECH & JAN SVARTVIK

2.	(a) The *goods was* sent.	The *goods were* sent.
	(b) This *premises looks* too big.	*These premises look* too big.

Note : Goods, premises, people, police, riches, scissors, shears, trousers आदि सदा plural माने जाते हैं।

3.	(a) That *pair of shoes are* mine.	That *pair* of shoes *is* mine.
	(b) This *pair of* scissors *belong* to me.	This *pair of* scissors *belongs* to me.

Note : *A pair of* shoes/shears/scissors/gloves/trousers को singular माना जाता है। किंतु जब a pair of नहीं रहे तो उसे plural माना जाता है। जैसे :

His shoes *were* dirty. His trousers *were* torn. Those scissors *belong* to me.

4.	(a) He has *plenty of opportunity*.	He has *plenty of opportunities*.
	(b) There are *plenty of* rice.	There *is plenty of* rice.
	(c) *Most of* the boy *is* ill.	*Most of* the boys *are* ill.
	(d) *Most of* the sugar *are* rotten.	*Most of* the sugar *is* rotten.

Note : अगर *a lot of, plenty of, a great deal of, most of* तथा *some of* के बाद uncountable noun आए तो इन्हें singular माना जाता है और अगर plural countable noun आए तो इन्हें *plural* माना जाता है।

5.	(a) *People does* not like to be kept waiting.	*People do* not like to be kept waiting.
	(b) The *cattle was* grazing in the field.	The *cattle were* grazing in the field.
	(c) He bought five *sheeps*.	He bought five *sheep*.

Note : *People, cattle* तथा *sheep* सदा plural होते हैं।

6.	(a) *Measles are* a serious disease.	*Measles is* a serious disease.

	Incorrect	Correct
(b)	*Physics are* a difficult subject.	*Physics is* a **difficult subject**.
(c)	*Mathematics are* easy to understand.	*Mathematics* **is easy** to understand.
(d)	*Politics have* no attraction for me.	*Politics has* no attraction for me.

Note : बीमारी का नाम जैसे measles, mumphs तथा diabetes को singular माना जाता है; mathematics, politics, physics, economics, ethics, dynamics, classics, phonetics, इत्यादि से जब किसी विषय के नाम का बोध हो तब उन्हें singular माना जाता है। लेकिन जब इनका प्रयोग plural अर्थ में इनके qualities का बोध कराने के लिए होता है तब इनके पहले प्रायः His, The, Such लगा रहता है।

...The rules that seem to emerge (i) singular for the name of a science strictly so used; (ii) plural for those same names more loosely used, e.g., for a manifestation of qualities, often recognisable by the presence of 'his', 'the' etc.

—FOWLER : MODERN ENGLISH USAGE

कुछ उदाहरण देखें :

A person's *politics are* his own affair.

The *economics* of the situation *have* yet to be improved.

(d) Compound Nouns

	Incorrect	Correct
1. (a)	He hates all *mother-in-laws*.	He hates all *mothers-in-law*.
(b)	I have five *brother-in-laws*.	I have five *brothers-in-law*.

Note : Mother-in-law, brother-in-law, father-in-law, passer-by का plural क्रमशः mothers-in-law, brothers-in-law, fathers-in-law, passers-by होता है।

	Incorrect	Correct
2. (a)	They are *woman-teachers*.	They are *women-teachers*.
(b)	We are *ladies-doctors*.	We are *lady-doctors*.
(c)	You all are *houses-maids*.	You all are *house-maids*.

Note : दो nouns से बने compound nouns का plural second noun को plural बनाकर किया जाता है। जैसे: boy-friend—boy-friends; fountain pen—fountain pens. किंतु अगर compound noun में first noun 'man' या 'woman' रहे तो दोनों noun को plural बनाया जाता है। जैसे—man-servant—*men-servants;* woman-servant—*women-servants;* woman-teacher—*women-teachers,* woman-doctor—*women-doctors.*

(e) Possessive Case of Nouns

	Incorrect	Correct
1. (a)	Her *house's number* was not known.	The *number of her house* was not known.

	Incorrect	*Correct*
(b)	The bell was at the *front-door's* side.	The bell was at the *side of the front door.*
(c)	It was a *walk of five minutes.*	It was *five minutes' walk.*
(d)	I spent a *holiday of a month.*	I spent *a month's holiday.*

Note : (i) 's का प्रयोग प्रायः सजीव के साथ होता है। जैसे :

cow's milk	a women's college	a men's lavatory
my father's car	the bull's horns	a child's toy
a butcher's shop	a children's story	my mother's headache
the dog's name	my father's name	mother's hat

(ii) किंतु 's का प्रयोग निर्जीव वस्तुओं के साथ खासकर time, distance तथा money से संबंधित expressions के साथ होता है :

a fortnight's holiday	a stone's throw	a rupee's worth
the sun's ray	a ship's doctor	in his mind's eye
yesterday's paper	today's news	tomorrow's programme
an hour's delay	a night's sleep	two days' journey
ten minutes' walk	the train's arrival	next week's arrangements
the government's decision	the volcano's eruption	to his heart's content
at my wit's end	at his fingers' ends	for conscience' sake
for God's sake	this year's sale	
for goodness' sake	a day's work	their money's worth

(iii) 's के कुछ अन्य प्रयोग देखें :

the government's policy	Europe's future	China's development
Delhi's water supply	the world's economy	the school's history
a country's population	television's future	the body's needs

2. (a)	Adam's and Eve's children.	Adam and Eve's children (single sense unit)
(b)	Shakespeare and Tennyson's poetry	Shakespeare's and Tennyson's poetry (separate)

Note : *Group Genitives.* When several words are in apposition be careful to form their possessive with the 's on the last word only if you are sure that they form a single sense unit and the result is free from ambiguity.

—MARGARET M. MAISON : EXAMINE YOUR ENGLISH.

3. (a)	The *rich's hobbies* are costly.	The *hobbies of the rich* are costly.

	(b) The *old's sufferings* cannot be fully described.	The *sufferings of the old* cannot be fully described.

Note : कुछ adjectives हैं जिनका प्रयोग nouns की तरह व्यक्ति का बोध कराने के लिए होता है किंतु उनमें 's लगाकर possessive नहीं बनाया जाता।

4.	(a) Six *B.A.s* are there.	Six *B.A.'s* are there.
	(b) Four M.A.s applied for the post.	Four *M.A.'s* applied for the post.
	(c) Add two *4s* and three *2s* to this figure.	Add two *4's* and three *2's* to this figure.

Note : Letters तथा arithmetical figures में Traditional grammarians के अनुसार 's लगाकर उनका plural बनाया जाता है। किन्तु modern grammarians इससे सहमत नहीं हैं :

It is wrong to form the plural adding 's to abbreviations : *M. P's, T. V's.* This may lead to confusion with the possessive.

The possessive of abbreviations is formed by adding *'s* or *s'* : *an M. Ps' speech,* both *J. P's qualifications.*

An apostrophe may also be used for the plurals of numbers when they are written as figures : *He makes his 8's like 3's; the 1970's,* but the modern tendency is to omit the apostrophe here : 8s like 3s; the 1970s.

—F. T. Wood : CURRENT ENGLISH USAGE

5.	(a) I am fond of *Keat's* poems.	I am fond of *Keats'* poems.
	(b) Do you like *Yeat's* poems ?	Do you like *Yeats'* poems ?

Note : Singular proper nouns जिनके अंत में *s* रहे उनमें या तो 's जोड़ा जाता है या केवल ' :

Keats's poems या *Keats'* poems; *Dickens's* novels या *Dickens'* novels; *Hercules's* labour या *Hercules'* labour, *Burns's* poems या *Burns'* poems; *Jones's* car या *Jones'* car.

याद रखें : एक ही वाक्य में कई बार *'s* के प्रयोग से वाक्य भद्दा तथा अर्थ अस्पष्ट हो जाता है, जैसे :

I am god-father's nephew's Headmaster's secretary.

ऐसा वाक्य लिखने से अच्छा है of का प्रयोग करना ताकि अर्थ स्पष्ट हो सके।

(f) Gender

	Incorrect	*Correct*
1.	(a) A *policeman* left *her* cap.	A *policeman* left *his* cap. A *police woman* left *her* cap.

Note : (i) अँगरेजी में कुछ nouns हैं जो masculine हैं तथा कुछ feminine जैसे— policeman/policewoman; postmaster/postmistress; mayor/mayoress;

author–authoress आदि। किंतु chairman के लिए feminine gender नहीं है, अतः Madam chairman कहा जाता है। Chairman के बदले आजकल chairperson कहा जाता है।

(ii) कुछ ऐसे nouns हैं जिनका प्रयोग male तथा female दोनों के लिए होता है, इन्हें dual gender कहा जाता है तथा इनकी संख्या दिनों-दिन बढ़ रही है। जैसे :

enemy	teacher	guest	artist	politician	minister
writer	speaker	friend	person	servant	neighbour

(iii) कुछ dual gender के nouns कई तरह से specific बनाया जाता है : जैसे

boy friend	girl friend	manservant	maidservant
man student	woman student	male guest	female guest.

(iv) Dual gender वाले noun के लिए general अर्थ में *he* pronoun का प्रयोग किया जाता है। जैसे :

A *politician* may try to be completely honest, but *he* always finds *he* has to compromise.

2. India has a Shakespeare of *his* own.	India has a Shakespeare of its/her own.

Note : देश को neuter gender या feminine gender माना जाता है तथा उसके लिए प्रयुक्त होनेवाला pronoun है *its* या *her*.

3. CORRECT USAGE OF PRONOUNS

Incorrect	*Correct*
1. (a) *One* should love *his* country.	*One* should love *one's* country.
(b) *One* must do *her* work.	*One* must do *one's* work.

Note : यदि one किसी वाक्य का subject रहे तो वाक्य में his, our, your, her का नहीं वरन् one का ही प्रयोग किया जाता है।

2. (a) He and *myself* went there.	He and *I* went there.
(b) *Myself* will do it.	*I* will do it. / *I myself* will do it.

Note : Relative pronouns (myself, yourself, itself इत्यादि) को subject की तरह प्रयोग नहीं करना चाहिए।

3. (a) *I* and *you* have done it.	*You* and *I* have done it.
(b) *He* and *you* went there.	*You* and *he* went there.
(c) *I* and *he* liked it.	*He* and *I* liked it.
(d) *Tom, I* and *you* ate sweets.	*You, Tom* and *I* ate sweets.

Note : Pronoun के प्रयोग के लिए आप '231 का नियम' याद रखें, अर्थात पहले second, third और फिर first person pronoun प्रयोग किया जाता है।

	Incorrect	Correct
4. (a)	You and I have done *your* duty.	You and I have done *our* duty.
(b)	John and you wanted *his* money.	You and John wanted *your* money.
(c)	He and I have learnt *his* lesson.	He and I have learnt *our* lesson.
(d)	Dick, you and I have lost *your* wealth.	You, Dick and I have lost *our* wealth.

Note : फिर '231 का नियम' याद रखें तथा ध्यान रखें कि—

'When a pronoun refers to more than one noun or pronoun of different persons, it must be of the first person plural in preference to the second, and of the second person plural in preference to the third.'

5. (a)	These two boys help *one another.*	These two boys help *each other.*
(b)	These three boys help *each other.*	These three boys help *one another.*

Note : *Each other* का प्रयोग दो व्यक्तियों या वस्तुओं को सूचित करने के लिए होता है; *one another* का प्रयोग तीन या तीन से अधिक व्यक्तियों या वस्तुओं का बोध कराने के लिए होता है।

6. (a)	*Any of* these two girls *is* your sister.	*Either of* these two girls *is* your sister.
(b)	*Either of* the five boys will do it.	*Any of* the five boys will do it.

Note : *Either of* दोनों में कोई एक) का प्रयोग दो व्यक्ति या वस्तु को सूचित करने के लिए किया जाता है; किंतु *any of* (कोई) का प्रयोग तीन या तीन से अधिक व्यक्तियों या वस्तुओं को सूचित करने के लिए किया जाता है।

7. (a)	*Neither of* the six can succeed.	*None of* the six can succeed.
(b)	*None of* the two girls is very tall.	*Neither of* the two girls is very tall.

Note : *Neither of* (दोनों में से कोई नहीं) का प्रयोग दो व्यक्तियों या वस्तुओं का बोध कराने के लिए होता है, किंतु *none of* (उनमें से कोई नहीं) का प्रयोग तीन या उससे अधिक व्यक्तियों या वस्तुओं का बोध कराने के लिए किया जाता है।

8. (a)	Let you and *I* try.	Let you and *me* try.
(b)	The Principal wants to see you and *I*.	The Principal wants to see you and *me*.

Note : *I* का objective case *me* होता है।

9. (a)	*Your's* truly.	*Yours* truly.
(b)	*Your's* is the best painting in the school.	*Yours* is the best painting in the school.

Note : *Your* में *'s* जोड़कर *your's* लिखना गलत है, उसकी जगह आप *yours* लिखें।

10. (a) The climate of India is hotter *than* England. — The *climate* of India is hotter than *that of* England. / The *climate* of India is hotter than the *climate* of England.

(b) The streets of Karachi are wider than Bombay. — The streets of Karachi are wider than *those of* Bombay.

Note : यहाँ India के climate की तुलना England से नहीं वरन् England के climate से है; उसी तरह Karachi के streets की तुलना Bombay से नहीं वरन् Bombay के streets से है।

11. (a) Your pen is better than *that of mine.* — Your pen is better than *mine.*

(b) My book is cheaper than that *of yours.* — My book is cheaper than *yours.*

Note : यहाँ mine से my pen तथा yours से your book का बोध होता है। अतः, that of mine/yours का प्रयोग नहीं किया जाता।

12. (a) Tom is *older than me.* — Tom is *older than I.*

(b) Sita is *taller than him.* — Sita is *taller than he.*

Note : पुराने grammarians *older than me/taller than him* को अशुद्ध मानते हैं तथा older than I/taller than he को शुद्ध। किंतु modern grammer में older than me/taller than him भी सही माना जाता है।

In informal English, we often use object pronouns (*me, him, her, us, them*) after *than.* In a more formal style subject pronouns (*I, He,* etc.) are considered more 'correct'.

She's *older than me.* (informal)
She's *older than I* (*am*). (formal)

When the pronoun is used with a verb, only subject pronouns are possible, of course.

Lucy found *more* mushrooms *than I did.* (Not,...*than me did.*)

—MICHAEL SWAN : PRACTICAL ENGLISH USAGE

4. CORRECT USAGE OF ADJECTIVES

	Incorrect	*Correct*
1.	(a) He dead.	He *died.* / He *has died.* / He *was dead.*

Note : *Dead* adjective है; *died* verb 'to die' का past simple या past participle रूप है।

2.	(a) I have a toothache, so I can't eat *something.*	I have a toothache, so I can't eat *anything.*

(b) I have *any* books.	I have *some* books.
(c) He hasn't *some* pens.	He hasn't *any* pens.
(d) Have you *some* sugar ?	Have you *any* sugar ?

Note : Some का प्रयोग अकसर affirmative sentences में तथा any का negative sentences तथा questions में होता है।

3. (a) I am *the younger* in the family.	I am *the youngest in* the family.
(b) Your accent is *worst than* mine.	Your accent is *worse than mine.*
(c) This one is *worst* than that one.	This one is *worse than* that one.
(d) Which is the *better* of the three methods ?	Which of the three methods is *the best ?*

Note : दो व्यक्तियों या वस्तुओं में तुलना के लिए comparative degree तथा तीन या उससे अधिक व्यक्तियों या वस्तुओं में सबसे अच्छा/बुरा का बोध कराने के लिए superlative degree का प्रयोग किया जाता है।

4. (a) The weather is *warmer as* last week.	The weather is *warmer than that of* last week.
(b) Rekha is *taller from* her sister.	Rekha is *taller than* her sister.

Note : Comparative degree में than का प्रयोग किया जाता है।

5. (a) My boy-friend is *very older* than me.	My boy-friend is *much older* than I am.
(b) You are *far much tolerant* than I am.	You are *far more tolerant* than I am.

Note : *Very* का प्रयोग comparatives में नहीं होता, उसके बदले *much* या *far* का प्रयोग किया जाता है। Very much, a lot, lots, any, no, rather, a little, a bit कुछ अन्य शब्द हैं जिनका प्रयोग comparatives में होता है :

very much nicer — a lot happier rather more quickly
a bit easier — a little less expensive
Things are *no better* than before.

6. (a) This is a *more safer* place.	This is a *safer* place.
(b) The *most busiest* hour is 10 o'clock.	The *busiest hour* is 10 o'clock.

Note : Double comparative (=more safer) या double superlative (=most busiest) का प्रयोग नहीं किया जाता।

7. (a) This photograph is *the best of* the two.	This photograph is *the better of* the two.
(b) Tom is *the tallest of* the two boys.	Tom is *the taller of* the two boys.

Note : जहाँ दो व्यक्ति/वस्तु का बोध कराना हो, comparative degree का प्रयोग किया जाता है।

	Incorrect	Correct
8.	This little girl is *better than clever.*	This little girl is *more good than clever.*

Note : यदि किसी एक ही व्यक्ति/वस्तु के दो गुणों की तुलना की जाती है तो *more* का प्रयोग किया जाता है।

	Incorrect	Correct
9. (a)	I saw a *most unique* sight.	I saw a *unique* sight.
(b)	Is there anything *more eternal ?*	Is there anything *eternal* ?
(c)	I found that dog *more dead.*	I found that dog *dead.*

Note : Unique, eternal, round, dead, triangular, golden, entire, chief, dumb, free, blind, universal, ideal, weekly, monthly आदि adjectives का प्रयोग comparatives या superlatives में नहीं किया जाता।

Adjectives like *unique, dead, blind, dumb,* which express an absolute idea of which there cannot be degrees, obviously cannot have a comparative. One thing cannot be more unique than another or one person more dead or more dumb than another.

—F. T. Wood : CURRENT ENGLISH USAGE

	Incorrect	Correct
10. (a)	He is *more inferior than* me.	He is *inferior to* me.
(b)	You are *the most superior* of all.	You are *superior to* all
(c)	I am *senior than* you.	I am *senior to* you.

Note : Inferior, superior, senior, junior, anterior, posterior के पहले more/most नहीं लगाया जाता और न उसके बाद than लगता है; than की जगह to का प्रयोग किया जाता है।

	Incorrect	Correct
11. (a)	My brother hasn't *much* book.	My brother hasn't *many* books.
(b)	Is there *many* sugar in the bottle ?	Is there *much* sugar in the bottle ?

Note : Much (बहुत) से मात्रा का बोध होता है; many (बहुत) से संख्या का।

	Incorrect	Correct
12. (a)	He is *the tallest* boy *of* the school.	He is *the tallest* boy *in* the school.
(b)	It is *the most expensive* car *of* the world.	It is *the most expensive* car *in* the world.

Note : After superlatives, we use *in* (or other prepositions) to show what place we are talking about.

It's *the most expensive* car *in* the world.
I'm *the happiest* girl *under* the sun.

of is not normally used, but it is possible after a superlative without a noun. :

She is *the most sensible of* the Smith Girls.

—Michael Swan : PRACTICAL ENGLISH USAGE

	Incorrect	Correct
13. (a)	It is *best* book I have ever read.	It is *the best* book I have ever read.
(b)	He is *fastest* runner here.	He is *the fastest* runner here.

Note : (i) Superlatives के पहले *the* अवश्य लगता है।

(ii) किंतु इसके कुछ अपवाद हैं :

That's *most* (=very) kind of you.
Which do you *like best* ?
I like that one *most*.
I buy the pen that costs *least*.

जब most का प्रयोग very के अर्थ में हो तब उसके पहले the को छोड़ दिया जाता है। Like best, cost least एक set phrase की तरह बन गया है, अतः इसमें the नहीं लगाया जाता।

(iii) कभी-कभी बिना nouns के भी superlative adjectives का प्रयोग किया जाता है :

I'm the *greatest*.
This one is *the fastest*.

(iv) Superlative adjective के बाद of-structure संभव है :

You are *the nicest of* the lot.

14. (a) It seems to me a *good* and *finest* job.	It seems to me a *good* and *fine* job.
(b) He is *taller* and *old* than my friend.	He is *taller* and *older* than my friend.
(c) I got the *sweetest* and charming thing.	I got the *sweetest* and *most charming* thing.

Note : यदि किसी वाक्य में दो या दो से अधिक adjectives विभिन्न degrees में हों तो पहले adjective के degree के अनुसार बाद वाले adjective का degree होता है।

15. (a) Health is *more preferable than* wealth.	Health is *preferable to* wealth.
(b) Knowledge is *even more preferable* than riches.	Knowledge is *preferable* even *to* riches.

Note : *Preferable* के बाद 'to' preposition लगता है तथा इसके पहले *more* या *most* नहीं लगता, क्योंकि *preferable* का अर्थ है : 'more desirable'.

(c) We prefer reading *than* writing.	We prefer reading *to* writing. We prefer to read *rather than* (*to*) write.

Note : यथासंभव prefer के बाद *to* preposition लगाएँ, किंतु जहाँ दो काम करने में preference का प्रश्न आता है वहाँ *rather than* भी प्रयुक्त किया जाता है।

16. (a) Patna is larger than *any* city in Bihar.	Patna is larger than *any other* city in Bihar.
(b) Bombay is richer than *any city* in India.	Bombay is richer than *any other* city in India.

(c) He is as clever as *any* boy in the class. — He is as clever as *any other* boy in the class.

Note : यदि किसी positive या comparative degree के बाद *any* हो तो उसके बाद *other* का प्रयोग करना चाहिए।

17. (a) He was the laziest of all *other* workmen. — He was the laziest of *all* workmen.
(b) She was the best of all *other* singers. — She was the best of *all* singers.

Note : Superlative degree of adjective के बाद other का प्रयोग नहीं करना चाहिए।

18. (a) Mahatma Gandhi was a *greater* leader of India. — Mahatma Gandhi was a *great* leader of India.
(b) He is *more intelligent* student of the class. — He is a *very* intelligent student of the class.

Note : यदि तुलना का स्पष्ट बोध नहीं हो तो comparative degree का प्रयोग नहीं किया जाता।

19. (a) This house is *elder* than that house. — This house is *older* than that house.
(b) Tom is *elder* than his friend. — Tom is *older* than his friend.
(c) My *older* brother is respected by all. — My *elder* brother is respected by all.

Note : Elder का प्रयोग एक ही परिवार के व्यक्ति के लिए होता है तथा इसके बाद than नहीं लगता। *Older* व्यक्ति तथा वस्तु दोनों के लिए प्रयुक्त होता है तथा इसके बाद *than* लगता है।

20. (a) America is ready to give us *farther* help. — America is ready to give us *further* help.
(b) Patna is *further* from Delhi than Lucknow. — Patna is *farther* from Delhi than Lucknow.

Note : Fore (अगला) का *comparative degree* further होता है और इसका अर्थ होता है : 'अगला, और, अधिक'। किंतु far (दूर) का *comparative degree* farther होता है जिसका अर्थ है : 'और दूर'।

21. (a) There is *not any* boy in the class. — There is *no* boy in the class.
(b) He has *no a* hat. — He has *no* hat. / He *hasn't* a hat.
(c) She has *no a* book. — She has *no* book. / She *hasn't a* book.
(d) There is *no any* man there. — There is *no* man there.

Note : Not+ a मिलकर no तथा not + any भी मिलकर no बनता है। अतः, not any, no any, no a की जगह हम no या -n't any का प्रयोग करते हैं।

22. (a) He is *one of the taller boys in* the class.	He is *one of the tallest* boys in the class.
(b) John is *one of the more intelligent* boys I know.	John is *one of the most intelligent* boys I know.

Note : *One of* के बाद आनेवाला adjective प्रायः superlative degree में रहता है।

23. (a) I am very fond of *these kind* of flowers.	I am very fond of *this kind* of flowers. I am very fond of flowers of *this kind.*
(b) I never like *those sort* of people.	I never like *that sort* of people. I never like people of *that sort.*

Note : This तथा that का plural क्रमशः these तथा those होता है। यदि noun singular हो तो उसके लिए singular adjective का प्रयोग किया जाता है। kind तथा sort *singular nouns* हैं, इनके पहले this या that का ही प्रयोग करें, these या those का नहीं।

24. (a) This box is three times *heavier* than the other.	This box is *three times as heavy as* the other.
(b) India is ten times *bigger* than Burma.	India is ten times *as big as* Burma.

Note : Since the comparative indicates merely superiority, and is not in itself confined to any definite limit, there cannot be multiples of it. It can be modified only by adverbs of degree, like *much, little, rather, scarcely, barely, far,* or by a statement of a definite amount, as *five kilos heavier, 50 pence dearer.*

—F. T. Wood : CURRENT ENGLISH USAGE

25. (a) *Many a men* hanker after wealth.	*Many a man* hankers after wealth.
(b) His illness was very *heavy.*	His illness was very *serious.*
(c) They had a *heavy* quarrel.	They had a *serious* quarrel.
(d) I know him very *good.*	I know him very *well.*

Note : Many a के बाद noun तथा verb दोनों singular होते हैं; heavy से वजन (weight) का बोध होता है किंतु serious का अर्थ होता है—'important because of possible danger', जैसे—a serious mistake, a serious crime.

26. (a) I am two years *smaller* than you.	I am two years *younger* than you.
(b) He is three years *bigger* than Sita.	He is three years *older* than Sita.

Note : Smaller तथा bigger से size का बोध होता है, किंतु younger तथा older से age का।

	Incorrect	Correct
27. (a)	He has grown into a *beautiful* youth.	He has grown into a *handsome* youth.
(b)	She has grown into a *handsome* young girl.	She has grown into a *beautiful* young girl.

Note : 'सुंदर' के अर्थ में beautiful का प्रयोग खासकर women के लिए तथा handsome का प्रयोग खासकर men के लिए किया जाता है।

	Incorrect	Correct
28. (a)	He acted *well* in comedies *than* in tragedies.	He acted *better* in comedies *than* in tragedies.
(b)	My *English knowledge* is sound.	My *knowledge of English* is sound.
(c)	He is my *family member.*	He is *a member of my family.*

Note : Comparative degree में well नहीं better का प्रयोग होता है; English knowledge के बदले knowledge of English तथा a family member के बदले a member of the family का प्रयोग किया जाता है।

	Incorrect	Correct
29. (a)	*Older* I get, *happier* I am.	*The older* I get, *the happier* I am.
(b)	*More* you work, *less* you learn.	*The more* you work, *the less* you learn.
(c)	*The more* it is *dangerous, the more* I like it.	*The more dangerous* it is, *the more* I like it.

Note : Comparatives के पहले the...the का प्रयोग special way में होता है—to say that two changes happen together. आप वाक्य (c) को देखें—In sentences like this, do not separate *more* from the adjective, adverb or noun.

	Incorrect	Correct
30.	The *two first* chapters of that book are interesting.	The *first two* chapters of that book are interesting.

Note : The two first की जगह the first two का प्रयोग करना चाहिए क्योंकि the two first एक meaningless expression है।

	Incorrect	Correct
31. (a)	He is a *greedy man for* money.	He is a *man greedy* for money.
(b)	All these are *worthy matters of attention.*	All these are *matters worthy of attention.*

Note : An adjective can be placed after a noun when the adjective is followed by a prepositional phrase.

	Incorrect	Correct
32. (a)	This book is more interesting than *any* book I have read.	This book is more interesting than any *other* book I have read.
(b)	He is more wicked than *any* living man.	He is more wicked than any *other* living man.

Note : Other का प्रयोग comparative degree के साथ होता है, superlative के साथ कभी नहीं। जब किसी व्यक्ति/वस्तु की तुलना दूसरे व्यक्ति/वस्तु से हो

जिसमें पहला व्यक्ति/वस्तु शामिल नहीं हो तब comparative में any के साथ other का प्रयोग किया जाता है।

	Incorrect	Correct
33. (a)	I saw *an asleep man.*	I saw a man *asleep.*
(b)	*An alone* lady might be in danger here.	A lady *alone* might be in danger here.
(c)	That is an *ill* man.	That man is *ill.*
(d)	These two are *alike* friends.	These two are friends *alike.*

Note : Asleep, alone, ill, afraid, akin, alike, awake, ashamed, averse कुछ ऐसे adjectives हैं जिनका प्रयोग प्रायः noun के बाद किया जाता है।

Twofold Comparisons

Latter, last तथा later, latest late से बने हैं।

(i) Latter (बादवाला) तथा last से order (क्रम) का बोध होता है, जैसे :

Of pigs and cows, the *latter* (=cows) are more valuable. (latter के साथ *than* नहीं लगता।)

He was the *last* to arrive.

(ii) Later तथा latest से time का बोध होता है। जैसे :

Hari came *later* (अधिक देर से) than Mohan.

Have you heard the *latest* (=the most recent) news ?

5. CORRECT USAGE OF ADVERBS

	Incorrect	*Correct*
1. (a)	Everybody *feels contentedly.*	Everybody *feels contented.*
(b)	He *seems happily.*	He *seems happy.*
(c)	She *looks sadly.*	She *looks sad.*
(d)	This food *tastes sweetly.*	This food *tastes sweet.*
(e)	That milk *smells sourly.*	That milk *smells sour.*
(f)	The music *sounds pleasantly.*	The music *sounds pleasant.*

Note : अगर subject के बाद feel, seem, look, appear, sound, taste या smell रहे तो उसके बाद आनेवाला शब्द adjective होता है, adverb नहीं। किंतु अन्य structures में adverb आ सकता है, जैसे :

He *looked* at us *sadly/happily/angrily.*

She *tasted/smelt* the food *carefully/quickly.*

They *sounded* the bell *loudly/noisily.*

2. (a)	I don't *hardly* know this girl.	I *hardly* know this girl.
(b)	He can't *scarcely* see in this light.	He can *scarcely* see in this light.

Note : Hardly तथा scarcely का अर्थ होता है 'शायद ही' तथा इनमें negative भाव छिपा रहता है। अतः, इनके साथ negative *no/not* का प्रयोग नहीं किया जाता।

	Incorrect	Correct
3.	(a) He came *always* late.	He *always* came late.
	(b) She did it *never.*	She *never* did it.
	(c) We went *often* there.	We *often* went there.
	(d) I visit him *frequently* while in Delhi.	I *frequently* visit him while in Delhi.

Note : Always, never, often, generally, sometimes, quite, hardly, nearly, frequently, almost, just, usually तथा scarcely—*subject* और *principal verb* के बीच में आते हैं।

	Incorrect	Correct
4.	(a) He *always* is early.	He is *always* early.
	(b) She *never* has been early.	She has *never* been early.
	(c) They *often* will go there.	They will *often* go there.

Note : Always, never, often, generally, sometimes, usually, already, almost, just, nearly, quite, hardly, scarcely का प्रयोग verb *to be* (am, is, are....) तथा auxiliaries के बाद किया जाता है।

	Incorrect	Correct
5.	(a) The water of this river is *too* pure.	The water of this river is *very* pure.
	(b) He is *very* blind *to* read small print.	He is *too* blind *to* read small print.
	(c) This house is *too much* small for me.	This house is *very* small for me. This house is *much too* small for me.

Note : Too का अर्थ होता है : आवश्यकता से अधिक, हद से ज्यादा; very का अर्थ होता है : अत्यंत, अधिक।

The adverb *too* means 'more than enough' and should not be used instead of *very* or *much.*

	Incorrect	Correct
6.	(a) I am *quite* sorry to hear it.	I am *very* sorry to hear it.
	(b) This climate is *quite* injurious to health.	This climate is *very* injurious to health.
	(c) He is *almost quite* well.	He is *quite* well.

Note : Quite का अर्थ होता है : पूर्णतया, पूर्णरूपेण (perfectly, completely); very का अर्थ होता है : बहुत। Quite के पहले किसी qualifying word (जैसे almost) का प्रयोग नहीं किया जाता।

	Incorrect	Correct
7.	(a) He is *very friendly enough* to help me.	He is *friendly enough* to help me.

Note : Enough का अर्थ होता है : पर्याप्त मात्रा में 'the proper limit or amount', अतः इसके पहले very या much का प्रयोग निरर्थक है।

	Incorrect	Correct
8.	(a) He *eagerly* wishes to do it.	He wishes *eagerly* to do it.
	(b) She sang last night *beautifully*.	She sang *beautifully* last night.

Note : Adverb को यथासंभव उस शब्द के बाद रखना चाहिए जिसको वह qualify करता है।

	Incorrect	Correct
9.	(a) No one saw us there *fortunately*.	*Fortunately*, no one saw us there.
	(b) He was *fortunately* not present there.	*Fortunately*, he was not present there

Note : अगर adverb पूरे वाक्य को qualify करे तो उसे वाक्य के प्रारंभ में रखा जाता है।

	Incorrect	Correct
10.	(a) He *quickly* ran.	He ran *quickly*.
	(b) They *immediately* disappeared.	They disappeared *immediately*.

Note : यदि adverb किसी intransitive verb को qualify करे तो वह adverb उस intransitive verb के बाद आता है।

	Incorrect	Correct
11.	(a) I *only* worked two sums.	I worked *only* two sums.
	(b) He *only* succeeded in the exam.	*Only* he succeeded in the exam.

Note : Only जिस word को qualify करे, उसे उस शब्द के ठीक पहले रखना चाहिए।

	Incorrect	Correct
12.	(a) *No* boy *other but* Hari has done it.	*No* boy *other than* Hari has done it.
	(b) It is nothing *else than* pride.	It is nothing *else but* pride.

Note : No other के बाद than आता है, किंतु else के बाद but प्रयुक्त होता है, than नहीं।

	Incorrect	Correct
13.	(a) I hit him *hardly*.	I hit him *hard*.
	(b) He was *hardly-hit* by his friend's death.	He was *hard-hit* by his friend's death.

Note : Hardly का अर्थ होता है : 'करीब-करीब नहीं', किंतु hard का अर्थ होता है : 'जोर से'।

	Incorrect	Correct
14.	(a) I have *not* got *no* paper for my exercise.	I have *not* got *any* paper for my exercise.
	(b) I *forbade* you *not* to enter this room.	I *forbade* you to enter this room.
	(c) That will *not* stop him; *nothing never* did.	That will *not* stop him; *nothing ever* did.
	(d) *Unless* you do *not* labour hard, you can't succeed.	*Unless* (=if not) you labour hard, you *can't* succeed.

Note : Double negative के प्रयोग से वाक्य affirmative बन जाता है। अतः, वाक्य को जोरदार बनाने के लिए double negative का प्रयोग नहीं करना चाहिए।

	Incorrect	Correct
15.	We returned *more quicker* than we expected.	We returned *more quickly* than we expected.

Note : Adverb की जगह adjective का प्रयोग नहीं करना चाहिए।

	Incorrect	Correct
16. (a)	I *seldom or ever* refuse a request.	I *seldom or never* refuse a request.
(b)	I *seldom or ever* find a mistake in this book.	I *seldom or never* find a mistake in this book.

Note : Seldom or never तथा seldom if ever शुद्ध है, किंतु seldom or ever अशुद्ध है।

	Incorrect	Correct
17. (a)	The air is *very* hotter today than yesterday.	The air is *much hotter* today than it was yesterday.
(b)	Tom is *very* better today.	Tom is *much* better today.
(c)	I am *much happy* to receive your letter.	I am *very happy* to receive your letter.

Note : यदि adjective comparative degree में रहे तो उसे much *qualify* करता है, किंतु जब वह positive degree में रहता है तब very का प्रयोग करना चाहिए।

	Incorrect	Correct
18. (a)	The news is *much* interesting.	The news is *very* interesting.
(b)	The result was *very much* surprising.	The result was *very* surprising.
(c)	The picture was *very* admired.	The picture was *much* admired.
(d)	The question has been *very* discussed.	The question has been *much* discussed.

Note : (i) Very *present participle* को modify करता है किंतु much *past participle* को।

(ii) लेकिन कुछ participles हैं जिनका प्रयोग adjectives की तरह होता है और उनके पहले very लगता है। ऐसे participial adjectives हैं : tired, pleased, satisfied, annoyed, concerned, surprised, disappointed, interested, worried, bored, limited, shocked, swollen, heated (=angry), excited. जैसे :

She felt *very* tired.

We are *very* pleased to hear of your success.

I am *very* satisfied with my new house.

	Incorrect	Correct
19. (a)	He ran very *fastly*.	He ran very *fast*.
(b)	I *last night* went to the cinema.	I went to the cinema *last night*.
(c)	He likes the cinema *too much*.	He likes the cinema *very much*.
(d)	The boy is *too* late.	The boy is *very* late.

Note : *Fastly* word नहीं है, आप उसकी जगह fast लिखें; last night, last year/month/week प्रायः वाक्य के अंत में आता है; वाक्य (c) तथा (d) में too की जगह very शुद्ध होगा।

	Incorrect	Correct
20.	(a) They came *always late* to school.	They always came *late* to school.
	(b) He will be *tomorrow here.*	He will be *here tomorrow.*
	(c) Come *at four o'clock* to my office.	Come *to my office at four o'clock.* (=place before time.)
	(d) I went *at once* there.	I went there *at once.* (=place before time.)

Note : सामान्यतः end-position adverbs का नियम है: adverbs of manner (how) + adverbs of place (where) + adverbs of time (when). जैसे :

She sang *perfectly/in the town hall/last night.* (= manner + place + time.)

	Incorrect	Correct
21.	(a) He *has thirty-five.*	He is *thirty-five.*
	(b) He is *thirty-five years.* He is *thirty-five old.*	He is *thirty-five years old.*

Note : (i) You can give your age either by just giving the number, or by giving the number plus the expression *years old.*

(ii) किसी की उम्र पूछने के लिए हम अकसर *How old are you ?* कहते हैं; *What is your age ?* बहुत कम ही कहा जाता है।

	Incorrect	Correct
22.	(a) I do not know *to dance.*	I do not know *how to dance.*
	(b) I do not know *to ride* a bicycle.	I do not know *how to ride* a bicycle.
	(c) I know *to make* omelettes.	I know *how to make* omelettes.

Note : Know के बाद कोई infinitive (=to dance, to ride, to make) नहीं आ सकता। इसके बदले हमलोग know how to का प्रयोग करते हैं।

	Incorrect	Correct
23.	He is *comparatively better* today.	He is *better* today. He is *comparatively good* to day.

Note : Double comparative का प्रयोग वाक्य में नहीं किया जाता।

6. CORRECT USAGE OF VERBS

	Incorrect	*Correct*
1.	(a) I did not *answer to* him.	I did not *answer* him.
	(b) They *attacked on* the house.	They *attacked* the house.
	(c) We shall *discuss about* it.	We shall *discuss* it.
	(d) He has *married with* Sita.	He *married* Sita.
	(e) Tom will *pass in* the exam.	Tom will *pass* the exam.
	(f) I *accept to* that offer.	I *accept* that offer.

	Incorrect	Correct
(g)	We are *approaching* to the bridge.	We are *approaching* the bridge.

Note : Answer, attack, discuss, marry, pass, accept तथा approach *transitive verbs* हैं, इनके बाद कोई object (noun/pronoun) आता है, preposition नहीं। किंतु marry के बाद passive voice में to लगता है :

Ram was *married to* Sita. (passive)
Ram *married* Sita. (active)

		Incorrect	Correct
2.	(a)	I *visited to* my friend.	I *visited* my friend.
	(b)	She *reached to* my house.	She *reached* my house.
	(c)	They *climbed in* the tree.	They *climbed* the tree. They *climbed up* the tree.
	(d)	They *confuse between* the noun and verb forms.	They *confuse* the noun and verb forms.
	(e)	He *described about* what he had seen.	He *described* what he had seen.

Note : Visit, reach, climb, confuse तथा describe *transitive verbs* हैं, इनके बाद कोई object आता है, preposition नहीं। किंतु climb a tree तथा climb up a tree दोनों शुद्ध हैं।

		Incorrect	Correct
3.	(a)	I *disbelieve in* it at all.	I *disbelieve* it completely. I don't *believe it* at all. I don't *believe in it* at all.
	(b)	I *enjoy in* doing it.	I *enjoy doing* it.
	(c)	I *enjoyed from* my freedom.	I *enjoyed* my freedom.
	(d)	I *entered in* the house.	I *entered* the house.
	(e)	He *greeted* to me.	He *greeted* me.

Note : Disbelieve, enjoy, enter तथा greet *transitive verbs* हैं, इनके बाद कोई object आता है, preposition नहीं। किंतु believe *transitive verb* के रूप में प्रयुक्त हो सकता है या in के साथ। Believe in का अर्थ होता है : have faith in.

		Incorrect	Correct
4.	(a)	He *gave to* me a pen.	He *gave me* a pen.
	(b)	He *takes to* it.	He *takes it.*
	(c)	She always *helps to* her mother.	She always *helps her* mother.
	(d)	He *joined to* them.	He *joined* them.
	(e)	They don't *like to* him.	They don't *like* him.

Note : Give, take, help, join तथा like, *transitive verbs* हैं, इनके बाद object आता है, preposition नहीं।

		Incorrect	Correct
5.	(a)	We *need to* good food.	We *need good food.*
	(b)	You should *obey to* your parents.	You should *obey your parents.*
	(c)	He *opposes against* us.	He *opposes* us.

(d) He *passed* from the park.	He *passed* the park. He *passed by* the park.
(e) You should *serve to* your country.	You should *serve* your country.

Note : Need, obey, oppose, pass तथा serve *transitive verbs* हैं, इनके बाद कोई object (noun/pronoun) आता है, preposition नहीं। Pass का अर्थ 'के पास से गुजरना' होगा तो pass या pass by कहते हैं, अगर 'के बीच होकर गुजरना' होगा तो pass through कहते हैं। जैसे :
He *passed through* the park.

6. (a) He *stopped with* reading.	He *stopped* reading.
(b) He wants to *stress on* some grammatical rule.	He wants to *stress* some grammatical rule.
(c) I *teach to* soldiers.	I *teach* soldiers.
(d) He *treated to* her badly.	He *treated* her badly.
(e) He *turned at* the knob.	He *turned* the knob.

Note : Stop, stress, teach, treat तथा turn *transitive verbs* हैं, इनके साथ object लगता है, preposition नहीं।

7. (a) I do not *trust to* him.	I do not *trust* him.
(b) I can do it without *using of* a knife.	I can do it without *using* a knife.

Note : Trust तथा use भी transitive verbs हैं, इनके बाद कोई object (noun/pronoun) का प्रयोग किया जाता है, preposition का नहीं।

8. (a) He *behaved* her badly.	He *behaved* badly *towards* her.
(b) I won't *comment* what people say.	I won't *comment on* what people say.
(c) He has *gone* Patna.	He has *gone to* Patna.
(d) Don't *interfere* their quarrel.	Don't *interfere in* their quarrel.
(e) *Listen* me now.	*Listen to* me now.

Note : Behave, comment, gone, interfere तथा listen *intransitive verbs* हैं, इनके बाद कोई preposition आता है, noun/pronoun नहीं।

9. (a) He was *looking* me.	He was *looking at* me.
(b) A teacher *profits* long holiday.	A teacher *profits from* long holiday.
(c) He didn't *reply* me.	He didn't *reply to* me.
(d) It may *result* trouble.	It may *result in* trouble.
(e) She *succeeded* her examination.	She *succeeded in* her examination.
(f) I am *waiting* you.	I am *waiting for* you.

Note : Look, profit, reply, result, succeed तथा wait *intransitive verbs* हैं, इनके बाद कोई noun/pronoun नहीं, वरन् कोई preposition आता है।

		Incorrect	Correct
10.	(a)	I will *ask it to* him.	I will *ask* him.
	(b)	He will *ask from* me a question.	He will *ask* me a question.
	(c)	I *asked* you *that* (you) tell him your story.	I *asked* you *to tell* him your story.
	(d)	I will *ask to* him some money.	I will *ask* him *for* some money.

Note : यदि हम किसी व्यक्ति से कुछ कहते हैं तो ask him/her/them इत्यादि कहते हैं; जब हम किसी से कुछ पूछते हैं तब ask him/her something (=ask him a question) कहते हैं; जब हम किसी से कुछ करने को कहते हैं तब—ask him/her to do something (=he asked me to go) कहते हैं; जब हम किसी व्यक्ति से कुछ माँगते हैं तब—ask him/her for something (=he asked me for money) कहते हैं।

		Incorrect	Correct
11.	(a)	Did you *avail* the opportunity ?	Did you *avail yourself of* the opportunity ?
	(b)	I *enjoyed* at the party.	I *enjoyed myself* at the party.
	(c)	I *enjoyed myself* the fresh air.	I *enjoyed* the fresh air.
	(d)	I *enjoyed* during the holidays.	I *enjoyed myself* during the holidays.

Note : *Avail* के साथ *myself, yourself, ourselves, themselves...+.of* का प्रयोग किया जाता है; किंतु *enjoy* something, *enjoy doing* something या *enjoy oneself doing* something कहते हैं। जैसे :

I *enjoyed* the party.
I *enjoyed* dancing with you.
I *enjoyed myself* at the party.

		Incorrect	Correct
12.	(a)	I *informed* that I had arrived.	I *informed you* that I had arrived.
	(b)	He *ordered* to follow him.	He *ordered us* to follow him. [We were *ordered* to follow him.]

Note : Inform तथा order के बाद कोई noun/pronoun का प्रयोग किया जाता है।

		Incorrect	Correct
13.	(a)	I *said* him goodbye.	I *said* goodbye *to* him.
	(b)	He *said* me to come in.	He *told me* to come in. He *said to me, "Come in."* He *said, "Come in."*
	(c)	She *said* me, 'No'.	She *said to me,* 'No'.

Note : You can *say* something (=He *says* goodbye); or say something *to* someone (=He said a few words *to* us); say के बाद to लगता है फिर उसके बाद कोई noun/pronoun आ सकता है।

		Incorrect	Correct
14.	(a)	He *told to me,* 'Yes'.	He *said to me,* 'Yes'.
	(b)	He *told to open* the door.	He *told someone* to open the door.

(c) He *told that* he was coming.	He *told me* that he was coming.

Note : Tell के बाद कोई noun/pronoun (=He tells me/you/Hari/Sita) कहते हैं, tell to, tell that अशुद्ध माना जाता है।

'*Tell* cannot be followed by a clause or an infinitive unless an object of person comes beween them.'

15. (a) The murderer was caught and *hung*.	The murderer was caught and *hanged*.
(b) He *hanged* the picture.	He *hung* the picture.

Note : Hang (फाँसी देना) का past tense *hanged* तथा past participle *hanged* होता है। Hang (लटकाना) का past tense रूप *hung* तथा past participle रूप भी *hung* ही होता है।

16. (a) America was *invented* by Columbus.	America was *discovered* by Columbus.
(b) Edison *discovered* the gramophone.	Edison *invented* the gramophone.
(c) He *gave* the examination.	He *appeared at* the examination. He *sat for* the examination.
(d) The man *gave* a speech.	The man *made* a speech.
(e) He *made* a lecture.	He *delivered/gave* a lecture.

Note : Invent का अर्थ होता है—'आविष्कार करना'; discover का अर्थ होता है—'खोज करना' अर्थात जो पहले से है ही किंतु मालूम नहीं उसे खोजा जाता है; जो चीज पहले से नहीं है, उसे आविष्कार किया जा सकता है; 'परीक्षा देने' के लिए—*appear at the exam.* या *sit for the exam.* कहते हैं; *make a speech* तथा *deliver* या *give a lecture* set expressions हैं।

17. (a) I *make* my homework.	I *do* my homework.
(b) The boy *denied* to take the money.	The boy *refused* to take the money.
(c) He *refused* that he was a thief.	He *denied* that he was a thief.

Note : *Do homework* कहा जाता है; deny का अर्थ होता है—'to say that something is false'; किंतु refuse का अर्थ होता है—'not to accept or do or give.' जैसे :

She *refused* his offer.

She *refused* him even a kiss.

Can you *deny* the truth of his statement ?

He *denied* it to be the case.

18. (a) He tried to *found* his last book.	He tried *to find* his lost book.
(b) He *said* me a thief.	He *called* me a thief.
(c) He *admitted* Sonu *into* a school.	He *got* Sonu *admitted into* a school.

(d) The river has *flown* over its banks. — The river has *flowed* over its banks.

Note : To के बाद verb का simple रूप लगता है (=to go, to play, to find, etc); say का अर्थ होता है 'कहना' किंतु जब हम किसी को कुछ कहकर/नाम देकर पुकारते हैं तब call कहा जाता है (=call him an idiot); नाम लिखवाना के लिए *get* someone *admitted to* या *into* कहा जाता है; *flow* (बहना) का past participle रूप *flowed* होता है।

19. (a) I *enjoy to learn* English. — I *enjoy learning* English.
(b) He *avoids to speak* to me. — He *avoids speaking* to me.
(c) He has *finished to study*. — He has *finished studying*.
(d) I don't *mind to open* the window. — I don't *mind opening* the window.

Note : (i) कुछ verbs हैं जिनके बाद अगर कोई दूसरा verb आता है तो उसमें -ing लगा रहता है। ऐसे common verbs हैं :

enjoy	avoid	finish	mind	can't bear
stop	risk	keep (continue)	delay	can't help
detest	imagine	practise	postpone	can't mind
admit	escape	mention	suggest	it wants (need)
deny	excuse	mind	resent	feel like
miss	dislike	appreciate	consider	give up

जैसे : *Excuse* my *interrupting*...
I really *appreciate having* time to relax.

(ii) The *-ing form* का प्रयोग निम्नलिखित cases में भी होता है :

to burst out crying/laughing	to go swimming/shopping
to spend money/waste time doing something	to keep (on) doing something

(iii) *Need, require* तथा *want* के बाद passive sense में -ing लगता है :

Your hair *needs cutting* (=to be cut).
Does your suit *require pressing*, sir ?
The car *wants servicing*.

20. (a) I *hope seeing* you soon. — I *hope to see* you soon.
(b) She *failed doing* it. — She *failed to do* it.
(c) He *promised helping* me. — He *promised to help* me.

Note : (i) कुछ verbs हैं जिनके बाद infinitive *to* का प्रयोग किया जाता है; -ing का नहीं। ऐसे common verbs हैं :

hope	fail	promise	afford	learn
offer	propose	swear	refuse	prefer
decide	beg	agree	appear	begin
prepare	regret	try	want	manage

expect	choose	arrange	seem	neglect
forget	consent	attempt		

(ii) किंतु कुछ ऐसे verbs हैं जिनके बाद to या -ing form आ सकता है:

begin	intend	like	continue	love
hate	prefer	remember	start	

जैसे : I *love lying/to lie* on my back.
I *hate working/to work* in the early morning.
I *prefer working/to work* in the morning.

(iii) *To* infinitive तथा preposition दोनों है। Infinitive *to* (चाहे व्यक्त हो या अव्यक्त) के बाद verb का simple रूप लगता है :

I want *to go* home. You *can go* home now.

To preposition के बाद कोई noun आ सकता है :

He has *gone to* Bombay.
I am *looking forward to* Diwali.
Do you *object to* Sunday work ?
I am not *used to* Delhi traffic.

किंतु यदि *to* preposition के बाद कोई verb आता है तो -ing form का प्रयोग किया जाता है :

I *prefer* riding *to walking.*
I am not *used to driving* in Bombay.
Do you *object to working* on Sunday ?
I am *looking forward to seeing* you at Dewali.

21. (a) Now she *orders that* I come. Now she *orders me to* come.
(b) My wife *wants that* I come home. My wife *wants me to* come home.
(c) I *ask that* you should pay for the meal. I *ask you to* pay for the meal.

Note : Order, want तथा ask के बाद object + infinitive आता है, *that*-clause नहीं। कुछ ऐसे common verbs (verb + object + infinitive structure वाले) इस प्रकार हैं :

ask	advise	invite	like	tempt
warn	wish	want	tell	teach
remind	request	permit	leave	instruct
press	persuade	expect	compel	encourage
cause	beg	allow	force	help

किंतु *suggest* verb को देखें :

I *suggested* her to go home. (incorrect)
I *suggested* that she should go home. (correct)
I *suggested to her* that she should go home (correct)

7. CORRECT USAGE OF TENSES

	Incorrect	*Correct*
(a)	I *have gone* there *yesterday*.	I *went* there *yesterday*.
(b)	She *has come* here two days *ago*.	She *came* here two days *ago*.
(c)	He *has done* it *last* June.	He *did* it *last* June.
(d)	You *have built* a house *last* year.	You *built* a house *last* year.

Note : जब वाक्य में yesterday, ago, last year/month/week, in 1985 आदि हों तब उस वाक्य का verb past indefinite में होता है। किंतु जब कार्य पूरा हो गया हो परंतु the period of time stated पूरा नहीं हुआ हो तब present perfect का प्रयोग हो सकता है। जैसे :

I *have read* four books this week. (week not yet finished.)
He *has seen* her this morning. (morning not yet finished.)

		Incorrect	*Correct*
2.	(a)	I *am* here *since* 1981.	I *have been* here *since* 1981.
	(b)	He *doesn't* write to you for a week.	He *hasn't written* to you *for* a week.
	(c)	You *are sitting* here *since* five o'clock.	You *have been sitting* here *since* five o'clock.
	(d)	We *study* here *for* the last five years.	We *have been studying* here *for* the last five years.
	(e)	This *was* my ideal *since* a long time ago.	This *has been* my ideal *for* a long time.

Note : यदि वाक्य में for या since रहे तो उस वाक्य का verb present perfect या present perfect continuous tense में होता है। Since से point of time का बोध होता है; for से period of time का।

जब इसी अर्थ में since किसी clause को govern करता है तब उस clause का verb simple past tense में ही रहेगा। जैसे :

I haven't eaten bananas *since I have been* a child. (incorrect)
I haven't eaten bananas *since I was a child*. (correct).
Tunu hasn't written to us *since he has left* home. (incorrect)
Tunu hasn't written to us *since he left* home. (correct)

		Incorrect	*Correct*
3.	(a)	I *didn't yet* see him.	I *haven't yet* seen him.
	(b)	She *finished* her work *now* and is satisfied.	She *has finished* her work *now* and is satisfied.
	(c)	He *already gave* me a book.	He *has already given* me a book.
	(d)	They *just came* here.	They *have just come* here.

Note : Yet, now, already, just, not yet *adverbials of present time* हैं, इनके साथ present perfect का प्रयोग किया जाता है। किंतु now/at this moment के साथ present progressive का भी प्रयोग होता है। जैसे :

I am writing *now*.

He is sleeping *at this moment.*

4.	(a) We *shall look* forward to seeing you.	We *look* forward to seeing you.
	(b) I *shall accept* your invitation with pleasure.	I *accept* your invitation with pleasure.

Note : Don't use a future tense when a present meaning is really intended.

5.	(a) He will come *when he will be* ready.	He will come *when he is* ready.
	(b) They will write *as soon as* they *will arrive* home.	They will write *as soon as* they *arrive* home.
	(c) She will do it *if she will have* time.	She will do it *if she has* time.

Note : When, as soon as, if, after, before, until, till *temporal conjuctions* हैं, इनके बाद future tense का प्रयोग नहीं करें।

6.	(a) *It's high time* that you *go* home.	*It's high time* that you *went* home.
	(b) *If only* he *can* swim!	*If only* he *could* swim!
	(c) *I wish* I *will be* the Prime Minister.	*I wish* I *were* the Prime Minister.

Note : (i) It's time (that), it's high time (that), suppose (that), if only, I wish (that) के बाद past simple का प्रयोग किया जाता है, future या present tense का नहीं। कभी-कभी if only के बाद past perfect का भी प्रयोग किया जाता है। जैसे :

If only I *had* a camera ! (Now)

If only I *had had* a camera ! (Yesterday)

7.	(a) Many people *are go* to Europe.	Many *people go* to Europe.
	(b) I *am* seldom *go* to the cinema.	I seldom *go* to the cinema.
	(c) I *shall went* home at 10.	I *shall go* home at 10.
	(d) He *did* not *believed* it.	He *did* not *believe* it.
	(e) *Does* the boy *writes* every day ?	*Does* the boy *write* every day ?
	(f) He *can speaks* English well.	He *can speak* English well,

Note : (i) Am/are/is + infinitive without *to* (=am go/are play/is sing) का प्रयोग नहीं किया जाता; (ii) shall, will, should, would, may, might, can, could, must के बाद verb का simple रूप आता है (=may come, will run, could see, must play आदि); (iii) *do, does* तथा *did* के बाद verb का simple रूप आता है (=do go, does run, did play).

8.	(a) He *swum* out.	He *swam* out.
	(b) He *run* and *climbed* the tree.	He *ran* and *climbed* the tree.

Note : Swim का *past tense* swam होता है, *past participle* रूप swum होता है; run *present tense* है, ran *past tense.*

9. (a) We *were changed* into another train.	We *changed* (in) to another train.
(b) Will you go to Patna *last month* ?	*Will* you go to Patna *next month ?* / *Did* you go to Patna *last month ?*

Note : We were changed into another train का अर्थ होता है—We became a train; *last month*—past tense है, *will go*—future, दोनों एक साथ प्रयुक्त नहीं हो सकते।

10. (a) Whom *do you like* to meet this afternoon ?	Whom *would you like* to meet this afternoon ?
(b) They *had gone* to Pune last summer.	They *went* to Pune last summer.

Note : Do you like के बाद अकसर -ing form लगता है (=Do you like swimming ?) तथा इससे habitual action का बोध होता है; Would you like के बाद *to*+infinitive लगता है तथा इससे future action का बोध होता है।

11. (a) I *am born* in India.	I *was born* in India.
(b) I *have been born* in a village.	I *was born* in a village.

Note : *Was born* idiomatic है, और इसी का प्रयोग होता है।

12. (a) I *have forgot* to bring the book.	I *have forgotten* to bring the book.
(b) I *had finished* the work yesterday.	I *finished* the work yesterday.
(c) I *shall went* home at 10.	I *shall go* home at 10.
(d) I *have* not *think* about it.	I *have* not *thought* about it.
(e) He *has arrange* a good programme.	He *has arranged* a good programme.

Note : Present perfect tense में has/have के बाद past participle लगता है (=has done, have finished); shall/will के बाद verb का simple रूप लगता है; yesterday/last year आदि के साथ verb simple past tense में रहता है।

13. (a) The earth *is moving* round the sun.	The earth *moves* round the sun.
(b) We *are playing* cricket *every day.*	We *play* cricket *every day.*

Note : जो कार्य नित्यदिन होता है, उसके लिए simple present tense का प्रयोग किया जाता है।

	Incorrect	Correct
14.	It is necessary that the weather *is* dry.	It is necessary that the weather *should be* dry. It is necessary for the weather *to be* dry.

Note : It is necessary that के बाद verb *should* का प्रयोग किया जाता है।

15.	(a) I am *hearing* a lot about England.	I *hear* a lot about England.
	(b) You must be *knowing* Mr Bose.	You must *know* Mr Bose.

Note : कुछ verbs हैं जिनका प्रयोग *-ing* के साथ (कुछ special cases छोड़कर) होता ही नहीं। उनमें कुछ मुख्य हैं :

see	hear	feel	seem	taste	smell
know	think	believe	forget	like	love
hate	hope	mean	need	prefer	want
recognize	remember	understand			

16.	(a) He speaks *as if* he *knows* the subject well.	He speaks *as if* he *knew* the subject well.
	(b) She walks *as though* she *is* going away.	She walks *as though* she *were* going away.
	(c) He looks *as if* he *is* mad.	He looks *as if* he *were* mad.
	(d) He talks as if he *is* my boss.	He talks as if he *were* my boss.

Note : (i) As if तथा as though के बाद past tense का प्रयोग किया जाता है, (will के बदले would, can के बदले could, does के बदले did, is/am के बदले were, has gone के बदले had gone, knows के बदले knew.)

(ii) As if तथा as though के अर्थ में कोई अंतर नहीं है। जब इनसे कोई imaginary case या unreal comparison व्यक्त करना हो तब इनके बाद आए subject के साथ past tense *were* का प्रयोग करते हैं ('We often use past tense with a present meaning to show that a comparison is *unreal.'*) जैसे :

He looks *as if* he *were* my boss. (किन्तु वास्तव में वह मेरा boss है नहीं।)
He looks *as if* he *is* my boss. (चाल-ढाल या देखने से मेरा boss जैसा मालूम पड़ता है—हो सकता है वह मेरा boss हो।)

He walks *as if* he *were* drunk. (implying 'but he is not')
He walks *as if* he *is* drunk. (meaning 'He is drunk judging from the way he walks.')

8. SEQUENCE OF TENSES

	Incorrect	Correct
1.	(a) She *asked* me what I *am* reading.	She *asked* me what I *was* reading.

	Incorrect	Correct
(b)	He *said* that he *will* come soon.	He *said* that he *would* come soon.
(c)	She *thought* that she *can* win the prize.	She *thought* that she *could* win the prize.
(d)	He *ran* outside to see what *is* happening.	He *ran* outside to see what *was* happening.
(e)	I *asked* him what he *has* done.	I *asked* him what he *had* done.
(f)	The lion *did* not eat her because he *is* a kind lion.	The lion *did* not eat her because he *was* a kind lion.

Note — (i) अगर principal clause का verb past tense में रहे तो subordinate clause का verb भी past tense में बदल दिया जाता है।

(ii) अगर principal clause का verb present या future tense में रहे तो subordinate clause का verb किसी tense (present, past या future) में रह सकता है। जैसे :

He *says* that Tom *is* tall.
She *says* that Sita *was* ill.
Jack *thinks* that Moti *will play* today.

	Incorrect	Correct
2. (a)	He *said* that the sun *rose* in the east.	He *said* that the sun *rises* in the east.
(b)	He *said* that the earth *was* round.	He *said* that the earth *is* round.

Note : अगर principal clause का verb past tense में रहे किंतु subordinate clause में कोई universal truth रहे तो subordinate clause का verb present tense में रहता है।

9. SUBJECT-VERB AGREEMENT

	Incorrect	Correct
1. (a)	The news of the train accident *are* shocking.	The *news* of the train accident *is* shocking.
(b)	Mathematics *are* not easy to learn.	Mathematics *is* not easy to learn.
(c)	All his money *are* kept in the bank.	All his money *is* kept in the bank.
(d)	Politics *are* a dirty game.	Politics *is* a dirty game.

Note : *News, mathematics, money* तथा *politics* singular nouns हैं, singular subject के साथ singular verb प्रयुक्त होता है।

	Incorrect	Correct
2. (a)	*The number of* pupils *are* increasing.	*The number of* pupils *is* increasing.
(b)	*A number of* boys *is* absent.	*A number of* boys *are* absent.

Note : The number (=संख्या) singular है, इसके साथ singular verb का प्रयोग किया जाता है; a number of (=बहुत) plural है, इसके साथ plural noun तथा plural verb का प्रयोग किया जाता है।

	Incorrect	Correct
3. (a)	*Each of* them *were* happy.	*Each of* them *was* happy.
(b)	*Everyone of* them *are* here.	*Everyone of* them *is* here.
(c)	*Neither of* the two boys *are* tall.	*Neither of* the two boys *is* tall.
(d)	*Either of* these girls *have* a book.	*Either of* these girls *has* a book.

Note : Each of, everyone of, neither of तथा either of से प्रारंभ वाक्य का verb singular होता है।

4. (a)	*Neither* the boy *nor* the girl *were* there.	*Neither* the boy *nor* the girl *was* there.
(b)	*Either* Hari *or* Moti *have* done it.	*Either* Hari *or* Moti *has* done it.

Note : अगर neither...nor या either...or से दो singular subject जुटे हों तो verb singular होता है।

5. (a)	*Every* boy and *every* girl *are* present today.	*Every* boy and *every* girl *is* present today.
(b)	*Each* man and *each* woman *have* a bag.	*Each* man and *each* woman *has* a bag.

Note : अगर दो singular subject *every* या *each* से modified हो तो verb singular होता है।

6. (a)	The bag, *together with* the books *are* lost.	The bag, *together with* the books, *is* lost.
(b)	A man, *besides* his sons, *were* there.	A man, *besides* his sons, *was* there.

Note : इन वाक्यों का subject क्रमशः The bag तथा A man है जो singular है, अतः इनके साथ verb भी singular होगा।

7. (a)	'Gulliver's Travels' *are* a good book.	'Gulliver's Travels' *is* a good book.
(b)	The United States *have* a big army.	The United States *has* a big army.

Note : किसी किताब का title या देश का नाम singular माना जाता है।

8. (a)	*Many a* things *are* used for show.	*Many a* thing *is* used for show.
(b)	*Many a* men *want* to be rich overnight.	*Many a* man *wants* to be rich overnight.

Note : Many a के बाद आनेवाले subject तथा verb दोनों ही singular रहते हैं।

9. (a)	Five miles *are* not a long distance.	Five miles *is* not a long distance.
(b)	Three years *are* a long time.	Three years *is* a long time.

	Incorrect	Correct
(c)	Two hundred rupees *are* not a big sum.	Two hundred rupees *is* not a big sum.

Note : इन वाक्यों में five miles, three years तथा two hundred rupees को एक single unit माना जाता है तथा उसके साथ singular verb का प्रयोग किया जाता है।

	Incorrect	Correct
10. (a)	*One of* the boys *have* done it.	*One of* the boys *has* done it.
(b)	*One of* the pens *are* lost.	*One of* the pens *is* lost.

Note : इन वाक्यों में *one of* subject है जो singular है, अतः इसके साथ प्रयुक्त होनेवाला verb भी singular होता है।

	Incorrect	Correct
11. (a)	He is one of those boys who *is* wicked.	He is one of those boys who *are* wicked.
(b)	I have lost one of the books which *was* costly.	I have lost one of the books which *were* costly.

Note : इन वाक्यों में who के पहले है *boys* तथा which के पहले है *books* जो दोनों plural हैं, अतः who/which के बाद आनेवाला verb भी plural होगा क्योंकि who/which के बाद आनेवाला verb who/which के पहले आए noun/pronoun के अनुसार ही singular या plural होता है।

10. WORD ORDER

अँगरजी के वाक्यों में प्रत्येक शब्द का एक निश्चित word order रहता है।

	Incorrect	*Correct*
1. (a)	What *you are* saying ?	What *are you* saying ?
(b)	Where *he is* going ?	Where *is he* going ?
(c)	Why *you can't* come ?	Why *can't you* come ?
(d)	Where *you went* ?	Where *did you* go ?
(c)	Why *she wants* to see him ?	Why *does she want* to see him ?

Note : Interrogative sentence का word order *verb+subject* का होता है।

	Incorrect	Correct
2. (a)	What *she wanted* to do ?	What *did she want* to do ?
(b)	Why *she did not like* it ?	Why *did she not like* it ?
(c)	*Are you know* him ?	*Do you know* him ?
(d)	When *do he came* ?	When *did he come* ?
(e)	What *does she had* ?	What *did she have* ?

Note : Interrogative sentence में verb+subject का word order उस वाक्य के tense का ध्यान रखकर किया जाता है।

	Incorrect	Correct
3. (a)	What *did* she *made* ?	What *did she make* ?
(b)	*Do* you ever *seen* him ?	*Have you ever seen* him ? / *Do you ever see* him ?
(c)	How she *was* ?	How *was she* ?

	Incorrect	Correct
(d)	*How* is that boat called ?	*What* is that boat called ?
(e)	*If* you *know* him ?	*Do you know* him ?

Note : Direct Question में हमेशा verb+subject का word order रहता है, tense of the verb (principal तथा auxiliary) भी ठीक होना चाहिए।

	Incorrect	Correct
4. (a)	Tell me *where is the post office.*	Tell me *where the post office is.*
(b)	Ask him *why does he want a pen.*	Ask him *why he wants a pen.*

Note : Indirect Question में subject+verb का word order रहता है।

	Incorrect	Correct
5. (a)	Do you know *where does he live* ?	Do you know *where he lives* ?
(b)	Does he ever think *why are they crying ?*	Does he ever think *why they are crying ?*

Note : वाक्य में double question (direct question + direct question) का प्रयोग नहीं किया जाता। ऐसे वाक्यों में पहला direct question (verb + subject) तथा दूसरा indirect question (subject + verb) रहता है।

	Incorrect	Correct
6. (a)	I *exactly* do not know.	I do not know *exactly*.
(b)	He speaks *very well* English.	He speaks English *very well.*
(c)	We want to go home *back.*	We want to go *back* home.

Note : वाक्य में adverb को उस शब्द के पास रखा जाता है जिसको वह adverb qualify करता है।

	Incorrect	Correct
7.	Please speak to the *concerned* clerk.	Please speak to the clerk *concerned.*

Note : *The concerned clerk* का अर्थ होता है : 'चिंतित किरानी; *the clerk concerned* का अर्थ होता है : 'संबंधित किरानी'।

	Incorrect	Correct
8. (a)	It was *a such* cold morning.	It was *such a* cold morning.
(b)	It was *so a* good pen.	It was *so* good *a* pen.

Note : *Such a, so good a* कहा जाता है।

	Incorrect	Correct
9.	Shakespeare is *for me* still very difficult.	Shakespeare is still very difficult *for me.*

11. CORRECT USAGE OF PREPOSITIONS

	Incorrect	*Correct*
1. (a)	He accused me *for* cheating him.	He *accused* me *of* cheating him.
(b)	The prisoner was accused *for* murder.	The prisoner was *accused of* murder.
2. (a)	My small sister is *afraid for* dogs.	My small sister is *afraid of* dogs.
(b)	She is *afraid for* being knocked down.	She is *afraid of* being knocked down.

Note : Afraid of **कहा आता है** किंतु जब afraid के बाद infinitive *to* आता है, तब afraid **के बाद किसी** preposition का प्रयोग नहीं किया जाता। जैसे :
She was *afraid to go* near the barking dog.

		Incorrect	Correct
3.	(a)	The father was *angry at* his son.	The father was *angry with* his son.
	(b)	I was *angry with* what he said.	I was *angry at* what he said.

Note : We are angry *with* a person, but *at* something he does or says. Angry *about* something :
I am angry *with* you for not telling me.
What are you angry *about* ?

		Incorrect	Correct
4.	(a)	I do not *approve* your action.	I do not *approve of* your action.
	(b)	We did not *approve for* smoking in the office.	We did not *approve of* smoking in the office.

Note : Approve के साथ *of* लगता है।

		Incorrect	Correct
5.	(a)	We *arrived to* school late.	We *arrived at* school late.
	(b)	I *arrived at* here early.	I *arrived* here early.

Note : Arrive के बाद at का छोटी जगह के लिए तथा in बड़ी जगह के लिए प्रयोग किया जाता है। किंतु arrive के बाद अगर here, there, somewhere, anywhere या nowhere रहे तो arrive के बाद कोई preposition नहीं लगता।

		Incorrect	Correct
6.	(a)	Has your father *arrived at home* yet ?	Has your father *arrived home* yet ?
	(b)	He is *going to home.*	He is *going home.*
	(c)	She *arrived her friend's home.*	She *arrived at her friend's home.*

Note : Home शब्द adverb है और उसके पहले preposition नहीं लगता, किंतु जब home के पहले कोई possessive adjective (my, your, his, her, their) या genitive (Tom's, my friend's) रहे तो *home* noun होता है और तब उसके पहले preposition लगता है।

		Incorrect	Correct
7.	(a)	A modest man does not *boast for* his success.	A modest man does not *boast of* his success.
	(b)	A proud man *boasts at* his achievement.	A proud man *boasts of* his achievement.

Note : *Boast of* कहा जाता है। *Boast about* भी correct माना जाता है।

		Incorrect	Correct
8.	(a)	She is very *careful for* her health.	She is very *careful of* her health.
	(b)	He is quite *careless for* the danger.	He is quite *careless of* the danger.

Note : Careful तथा careless के बाद of लगता है, किंतु जब careful के बाद infinitive *to* आता है तब careful के बाद कोई preposition नहीं लगता। जैसे :

Be *careful* not *to drive* fast.
He was *careful to* see that the door was locked up.

9. (a) The doctor will *cure* you *from* influenza.	The doctor will *cure* you *of* influenza.
(b) He was *cured for* his cold.	He was *cured of* his cold.
(c) What is the best *cure of* a cold ?	What is the best *cure for* a cold ?

Note : To cure के बाद of लगता है, किंतु जब cure (=a remedy) noun रहे तब उसके बाद *for* लगता है।

10. (a) Many people *die from* cancer.	Many people *die of* cancer.
(b) He *died from* malaria.	He *died of* malaria.
(c) He *died of* over-eating.	He *died from* over-eating.
(d) She *died of* the loss of blood.	She *died from* the loss of blood.

Note : जब कोई किसी बीमारी (disease or illness) से मरता है तब die of कहते हैं, लेकिन जब वह किसी अन्य कारण या कुछ दूसरा काम करने से मरता है तब die from कहा जाता है।

11. (a) This is *different than* the other.	This is *different from* the other.
(b) My pen is *different to* that.	My pen is *different from* that.

Note : Different के बाद from लगता है।

12. (a) How does this *differ than* the other ?	How does this *differ from* the other ?
(b) He *differs from* his brother on this issue.	He *differs with* his brother on this issue.

Note : Differ *with* a person, *from* a thing. जैसे :

Nylon differs *from* silk.
My friend differs *with* me about this matter.

13. (a) She was *dressed with* black.	She was *dressed in* black.
(b) The lady was *dressed with* bright colours.	The lady was *dressed in* bright colours.
(c) The box was *full with* papers.	The box was *full of* papers.
(d) The glass was *filled of* milk.	The glass was *filled with* milk.
(e) We were *glad for* a rest after our long journey.	We were *glad of* a rest after our long journey.

Note : किंतु glad के बाद अगर infinitive *to* आए तो उसके बाद कोई preposition नहीं लगता। जैसे :

We were *glad to be* home again.

14. (a) Your suggestions were very *helpful for* us.	Your suggestions were very *helpful to* us.

(b) She is very interested *with* my story.	She is very interested *in* my story.
(c) We are *proud for* our new car.	We are *proud of* our new car.

Note : Helpful to, interested in तथा proud of को सही माना जाता है।

15. (a) He cannot *live with* his small wages.	He cannot *live on* his small wages.
(b) Cows *live by* grass.	Cows *live on* grass.
(c) He earns scarcely enough to *live with.*	He earns scarcely enough to *live on.*

Note : Live के साथ on लगता है, किंतु जब live का अर्थ 'to earn a living' होता है, तब earning के तरीका को specify करने के लिए by का प्रयोग किया जाता है। जैसे :

He lived *by* cheating others.

16. (a) Flour is *made of* wheat.	Flour is *made from* wheat.
(b) Her dress is *made from* silk.	Her dress is *made of* silk.

Note : When one substance is changed into another, so that a new substance is produced, we use *from,* but when the original material is not actually changed, but is merely formed into some object, then we use *of.*

17. (a) He *married to* my sister.	He *married* my sister.
(b) He is *married with* Rani.	He is *married to* Rani.

Note : (i) Marry का प्रयोग जब active voice में किया जाता है तब उसके साथ कोई preposition नहीं लगता, किंतु passive voice में marry के साथ to लगता है।

(ii) जब marry शब्द के बाद कोई direct object नहीं रहे तब marry के बदले अकसर get married का प्रयोग किया जाता है। जैसे :

When are you going to *get married* ?
Lulu and Joe *got married* last week.

18. (a) The teacher is *pleased for* the boy's progress.	The teacher is *pleased with* the boy's progress.
(b) He is *pleased at* me.	He is *pleased with* me.

Note : Pleased with होता है, किंतु pleased के बाद infinitive *to* आए तो pleased के बाद कोई preposition नहीं लगता। जैसे :

We were *pleased to hear* that he had succeeded.

19. (a) I cannot *get rid from* my cold.	I cannot *get rid of* my cold.
(b) We should *take care for* our health.	We should *take care of* our health.

Note : किंतु जब take care के बाद infinitive *to* या clause आए तब take care के बाद कोई preposition नहीं लगता। जैसे :

Take care to lock everything up safely.
I'll *take care that* this does not happen again.

20. (a) The pupils were *sitting on* their desks.	The pupils were *sitting at* their desks.
(b) There is no chair for me to *sit at.*	There is no chair for me to *sit on.*
(c) Let us *sit in* this seat for a while.	Let us *sit on* this seat for a while.
(d) She was *sitting on* an armchair.	She was *sitting in* an armchair.
(e) Mrs Sen was *sitting on* the car.	Mrs Sen was *sitting in* the car.

Note : A person sits *at* a desk, *on* a chair or a seat (but *in* an armchair), *in* a car, *in* a room.

We sit *at* something that is placed before us, *on* something that is beneath us and *in* something that is around us or to some extent encloses us.

Sit *in* your places.
While we were sitting *at* dinner we heard a disturbance outside.

21. (a) We are *sorry about* that man.	We are *sorry for* that man.
(b) We are *sorry for* your misfortune.	We are *sorry about* your misfortune.

Note : We are sorry *for* a person, but *about* something that has happened. किंतु sorry के बाद infinitive *to* रहे तो preposition नहीं लगता। जैसे :

We are *sorry to hear* that you have not been well.
I am *sorry to say* that he did not keep his word.

22. (a) This will be very *useful for* me.	This will be very *useful to* me.
(b) A map is *useful to* find one's way about.	A map is *useful for* finding one's way about.
(c) This tool is quite *useless for* me.	This tool is quite *useless to* me.
(d) This tool is quite *useful to* my purpose.	This tool is quite *useful for* my purpose.
(e) A small saw is *useless to* cut down trees.	A small saw is *useless for* cutting down trees.

Note : Useful *to* a person, but *for* a purpose. उसी तरह useless *to* a person, but *for* a purpose.

23. (a) He wrote *with ink.*	He wrote *in ink.*
(b) She writes *with pencil.*	She writes *in pencil.*
(c) Write the exercise *with ink.*	Write the exercise *in ink.*

Note : किंतु—The note was written *with* a pencil/*with* a pen.
She writes *with* her left hand.

Incorrect	Correct
24. (a) I *agree to* you.	I *agree with* you.
(b) We *agree with* your proposal.	We *agree to* your proposal.
(c) Let us *agree with* a date.	Let us *agree on* a date.

Note : Agree *with* a person, agree *on* a matter for decision, *agree to* a suggestion or proposal.

Incorrect	Correct
25. (a) He is *bad in* tennis.	He is *bad at* tennis.
(b) I am *good in* history.	I am *good at* (=skilful) history.
(c) She is *clever in* cooking.	She is *clever at* cooking.

Note : Bad *at, good at,* skilful *at,* clever *at* इत्यादि कहा जाता है। यहाँ clever at का अर्थ होता है : quick in learning and understanding things; skilful (कुशल, निपुण)

Incorrect	Correct
26. (a) I am *disappointed about* him.	I am *disappointed with* him.
(b) We had a *discussion to* the budget.	We had a *discussion on/about* the budget.
(c) *Divide* it *in* three parts.	Divide it *into* three parts.
(d) Please *explain* me the reason.	Please *explain to* me the reason.

Note : Disappointed *with* somebody; *with/at/about* something; discussion *about, on, of;* divide *into;* explain something *to* somebody.

Incorrect	Correct
27. (a) He is *ill from* flu.	He is *ill with* flu.
(b) He has no *influence about* me.	He has no *influence on* me.
(c) His father *insisted in* paying.	His father *insisted on* paying.
(d) I am not *interested on* your case.	I am not *interested in* your case.

Note : Ill *with;* influence *on,* insist *on,* interested *in.*

Incorrect	Correct
28. (a) He was *kind with* me.	He was *kind to* me.
(b) I am very *impressed on* your work.	I am very *impressed with* your work.
(c) Her *marriage with* Ramu did not last long.	Her *marriage to* Ramu did not last long.

Note : Kind *to,* impressed *with* or *by;* marriage *to,* nice *to,* polite *to,* rude *to,* disgusted *with* होता है।

Incorrect	Correct
29. (a) He *prevented* me *to* go there.	He *prevented* me *from* going there.
(b) What is the *reason of* his departure ?	What is the *reason for* his departure ?
(c) She was *shivering from* cold.	She was *shivering with* cold.
(d) Can he *succeed at* business ?	Can he succeed *in* business ?

Note : Prevent *from;* reason *for;* shiver *with,* succeed *in,* tremble *with* fear; shaking *with* anger; successful *in/at* होता है।

	Incorrect	Correct
30. (a)	Who is *responsible of* this ?	Who is *responsible for* this ?
(b)	He *reminded* me *to* this.	He *reminded* me *of* this.
(c)	She *suffers at* fever.	She *suffers from* fever.
(d)	Everybody is *surprised on* our calm.	Everybody is *surprised at* our calm.
(e)	What is *wrong* to Hari ?	What is *wrong with* Hari ?

Note : Responsible *for,* remind *of,* suffer *from,* surprised *at,* speak *to/with;* think *of,* talk *to/with;* wrong *with;* write *to* (a person) का प्रयोग किया जाता है।

	Incorrect	Correct
31. (a)	Stop *throwing* stones *to* the cars.	Stop *throwing* stones *at* the cars.
(b)	*Throw* it straight *at* the wicket-keeper.	*Throw* it straight *to* the wicket-keeper.

Note : Throw+object+at (aggressive); throw+object+to (in a game, etc.)

	Incorrect	Correct
32. (a)	Don't *discuss about* your plan.	Don't *discuss* your plan.
(b)	He *describes about* Nature.	He *describes* Nature.

Note : *Discuss* तथा *describe* के बाद कोई preposition नहीं लगता।

	Incorrect	Correct
33. (a)	I have no *experience to* teach.	I have no experiene *of/in* teaching.
(b)	He *entered in* the house.	He *entered* the house.
(c)	I *told to* him to come.	I *told* him to come.
(d)	The workers are *at strike.*	The workers are *on strike.*
(e)	We come *at* school at 10.	We come *to* school at 10.

Note : किंतु enter के साथ into का प्रयोग enter *into* an agreement, *into* a contract के अर्थ में होता है।

	Incorrect	Correct
34. (a)	I *came in* a village.	I came *to/into* a village.
(b)	He returns *in* his town.	He returns *to* his town.
(c)	They are *joking to* each other.	They are *joking with* each other.
(d)	He asked *from* me a question.	He *asked me* a question.
(e)	I *congratulate* you *for* your success.	I *congratulate* you *on* your success.
35. (a)	The glass is *full with* water.	The glass is *full of* water.
(b)	Are you *satisfied from* her ?	Are you *satisfied with* her ?
(c)	My pen is *superior from* yours.	My pen is *superior to* yours.
(d)	Translate this passage *to* Hindi.	*Translate* this passage *into* Hindi.
(e)	I have two, three books.	I have two *or* three books.
36. (a)	He has lived here *since* two months.	He has lived here *for* two months.
(b)	He has been here *from* Friday.	He has been here *since* Friday.

Note : For का प्रयोग period of time (जैसे : for two days, for five months, etc.) के लिए तथा since का प्रयोग point of time (जैसे: since Monday, since 2 o'clock; etc.) के लिए किया जाता है।

37\. (a) I have no house to *live.* — I have no house to *live in.*

(b) We *should obey to* our teacher. — We should *obey* our teacher.

(c) He got down the train. — He got down *from* the train. / He got *off* the train.

(d) He has oil *in* hair. — He has oil *on* hair.

(e) I am a *teacher in* English. — I am a *teacher of* English.

38\. (a) I am *tired from* this work. — I am *tired of* this work.

(b) He came to school *with* bicycle. — He came to school *by bicycle.* / He came to school *on a bicycle.*

(c) I don't *care of* this. — I don't *care for* this.

(d) I can see two boys *on* the picture. — I can see two boys *in* the picture.

(e) I listened to the music *by the radio.* — I listened to the music *on* the radio.

39\. (a) He fell in love *of* her. — He fell in love *with* her.

(b) The garden was covered *from* flowers. — The garden was covered *with* flowers.

(c) *Compare* this bag *to* a really good one. — Compare this bag *with* a really good one.

(d) The poet *compared* her lips *with* roses. — The poet *compared* her lips *to* roses.

Note : You *compare* one thing *with* (or *to*) another. You compare A *with* B to see in what ways they are alike and in what ways they are different. You compare A *to* B when you say that A is like B in certain ways.

12. CORRECT USAGE OF CONJUNCTIONS

	Incorrect	*Correct*
1. (a)	He had *scarcely* gone *than* or *but* his friend arrived.	He had *scarcely* gone *when* his friend arrived.
(b)	He had *scarcely* or *hardly* heard the news *than* he wept aloud.	He had *scarcely* or *hardly* heard the news *when* or *before* he wept aloud.

Note : Scarcely और hardly के बाद when या before का प्रयोग किया जाता है, than, but या that का नहीं।

2.	*No sooner* had he returned *but* he was off again.	*No sooner* had he returned *than* he was off again.

Note : No sooner के बाद than का प्रयोग किया जाता है, but का नहीं।

3.	(a) *Unless* you do not work hard, you will fail.	*Unless* you work hard, you will fail. *If* you do not work hard, you will fail.
	(b) *Unless* you have no objection, I shall see you tomorrow.	*If* you have no objection, I shall see you tomorrow.

Note : Unless का अर्थ होता है—'if not', अतः इसके बाद पुनः no, not नहीं लगाना चाहिए।

4.	(a) He went to Patna *because* he might see Mr Mitra.	He went to Patna *in order that* he might see Mr Mitra.
	(b) He takes medicine *because* he may get better.	He takes medicine *so that* he may get well.

Note : कारण बताने के लिए because का प्रयोग किया जाता है, किंतु purpose सूचित करने के लिए in order that या so that का प्रयोग करते हैं।

5.	(a) He *called* me *as* a fool.	He *called* me a fool.
	(b) I *regard* him my brother.	I *regard* him *as* my brother. I *consider* him my brother.
	(c) He was *appointed as* a clerk.	He was *appointed* clerk.

Note : Regard, describe, represent, portray, depict, mention, define, treat के बाद as का प्रयोग किया जाता है, किंतु name, dub, call, appoint, elect, make, choose, think, consider के बाद as या be का प्रयोग नहीं किया जाता।

6.	(a) *Because* he is rude, *therefore* he is punished.	*Because* he is rude, he is punished.
	(b) *Because* you are poor, *therefore* I shall help you.	*Because* you are poor, I shall help you.

Note : एक ही वाक्य में because तथा therefore का प्रयोग नहीं किया जाता।

7.	(a) *Supposing if* she fails, what will she do ?	*Suppose* she fails, what will she do ?
	(b) *Supposing if* she comes late, where will she go ?	*Suppose* she comes late, where will she go ?

Note : एक ही वाक्य में suppose के बाद if का प्रयोग नहीं किया जाता।

8.	(a) *Until* you work hard, you will improve.	*So long as* you work hard, you will improve.
	(b) Wait here *as long as* five o'clock.	Wait here *until* five o'clock.
	(c) *Until* it rains, I won't go.	*As long as* it rains, I won't go.

Note : Until से point of time का बोध होता है; as long as/so long as से period of time का।

	Incorrect	Correct
9. (a)	He is *as* good if not *better* than his brother.	He is *as* good *as,* if not *better than,* his brother.
(b)	He is *more* polite, but not *so* intelligent *as* Tom.	He is *more* polite *than,* but not *so* intelligent *as* Tom. He is *more* polite *than* Tom, but not *so* intelligent (*as* he).

Note : एक ही वाक्य में यदि दो adjectives एक positive degree और दूसरा comparative में हो तो उनके लिए दो conjunctions—positive के लिए as....as, so...as तथा comparative के लिए comparative degree of adjective + than का प्रयोग किया जाता है। एक ही conjunction दोनों degrees के लिए प्रयुक्त नहीं हो सकता।

	Incorrect	Correct
10. (a)	*If* you do not labour, *then* you cannot pass.	*If* you do not labour, you cannot pass.
(b)	*As* he entered the room, *then* he met me.	*As* he entered the room, he met me.
(c)	*When* he saw the tiger, *then* he was afraid.	*When* he saw the tiger, he was afraid.
(d)	*As* you are intelligent, *so* you will pass the exam.	*As* you are intelligent, you will pass the exam.

Note : As, when, if के साथ so या then नहीं लगाया जाता।

When the conjunction is *as, since, seeing that,* etc. the subordinate clause usually comes first. There is less emphasis on the cause and more emphasis on the result (stated in the main clause).

—A. S. HORNBY : A GUIDE TO PATTERNS AND USAGE IN ENGLISH

	Incorrect	Correct
11. (a)	He said *that,* "I am reading a book."	He said, "I am reading a book."
(b)	He asked me *that* how much it cost.	He asked me how much it cost.
(c)	He enquired *that* who had done it.	He enquired who had done it.
(d)	Tell me *that* whether you will do it.	Tell me whether you will do it.

Note : (i) Direct narration में *that* conjunction का प्रयोग नहीं किया जाता। साथ ही, indirect narration में भी how, what, which, whom, why, where, whether, who, whose, when के पहले that नहीं लगता।

(ii) That के प्रयोग में यह ध्यान रखें :

(a) *That* का प्रयोग प्रायः होता है : *agree, assert, assume, calculate, conceive, hold, learn, maintain, reckon, state, suggest* के बाद;

(b) *That* का प्रयोग प्रायः नहीं होता : *believe, presume, suppose, think* के बाद;

(c) *That* का प्रयोग हो सकता या नहीं भी : ***be told, confess, consider, declare, hear, know, propose, say, see, understand*** **के बाद।**

12.	(a) I have *neither* written to her *or* spoken to her.	I have *neither* written to her *nor* spoken to her.
	(b) He has *either* a pen *nor* a pencil.	He has *either* a pen *or* a pencil.
	(c) He speaks *neither* English *or* French.	He speaks *neither* English *nor* French.

Note : Neither के साथ nor; either के साथ or का प्रयोग किया जाता है।

13.	(a) *Either* he will obey me *or* take the consequences.	*Either* he will obey me *or he will* take the consequences.
	(b) He *neither* speaks English *nor* French.	He speaks *neither* English *nor* French.
	(c) He *not only* cheated me *but also* my friend.	He cheated *not only* me *but also* my friend.
	(d) *Either* the step taken was right *or* wrong.	The step taken was *either* right *or* wrong.
	(e) He was *both* strong in power *and* will.	He was strong in *both* power *and* will.

Note : Either...or, neither...nor, both...and, not only...but also हमेशा साथ-साथ रहते हैं तथा इनके बाद प्रयुक्त words में balance रखा जाता है।

14.	(a) She did *not* break it *nor* lose it.	She did *not* break it *or* lose it.
	(b) I have *never* spoken to her *nor* written to her.	I have *never* spoken to her *or* written to her.

Note : *Not* तथा *never* के बाद *or* का प्रयोग किया जाता है।

15.	(a) Come here *between* ten *or* twelve.	Come here *between* ten *and* twelve.
	(b) *Both* Ram *as well as* Hari were there.	*Both* Ram *and* Hari were there.

Note : Between तथा both के बाद and का प्रयोग किया जाता है।

16.	(a) Walk slowly, *lest* you *shall not* fall.	Walk slowly, *lest* you *should* fall.
	(b) Work hard *lest* you *may not* fail.	Work hard, *lest* you *should* fail.

Note : Lest से negative purpose सूचित होता है। Lest का अर्थ है : 'in order that....not, for fear that' तथा इसके साथ should का प्रयोग किया जाता है, may, shall अथवा ought का नहीं।

17.	Though he is poor *but* he is happy.	Though he is poor *yet* he is happy. Though he is poor, he is happy.

Note : Though के साथ yet का प्रयोग करें, but का नहीं। लेकिन first statement के बाद comma दे देने से yet को लुप्त किया जा सकता है।

18. (a) I have *no other* friend *but* you. — I have *no other* friend *than* you.
    (b) There is no one *else than* you. — There is no one *else but* you.

Note : No other के बाद than का प्रयोग किया जाता है, from, but, except का नहीं; और else के बाद but आता है, than नहीं।

19. She loves you more *than me.* — She loves you more *than I.* / She loves you more *than she does me.*

Note : ऐसे वाक्यों में लुप्त शब्दों को than के बाद supply कर देखना चाहिए कि pronoun का कौन-सा रूप ठीक लगता है। जैसे :

You like him better than I (do).
You can do it better than I (can).
He is two years older than I (am).
You like him better than (you like) me.
That is a task for you rather than (for) me.

किंतु—His wife was several years younger than him को शुद्ध माना जाता है।

13. MISCELLANEOUS ERRORS

	Incorrect	*Correct*
1.	(a) I *advice* you to go home.	I *advise* you to go home.
	(b) I know him very *good.*	I know him very *well.*
	(c) Its raining.	*It's* raining.
	(d) *His room's window* is open.	*The window of his room* is open.
	(e) I have a brother *which* is at school.	I have a brother *who* is at school.

Note : Its= इसका, उसका; किंतु it's= it is.

	Incorrect	*Correct*
2.	(a) He *did* one mistake in dictation.	He *made* one mistake in dictation.
	(b) A boy's hat is different from a *girl.*	A boy's hat is different from a *girl's.*
	(c) I am going *to cut my hair.*	I am going *to have my hair cut.*
	(d) Why *you were* absent last Friday ?	Why *were you* absent last Friday ?
	(e) Are you *alone* or married ?	Are you married or *single* ?

	Incorrect	Correct
3. (a)	My health is *alright* these days.	My health is *all right* these days.
(b)	He is my *cousin brother.*	He is my *cousin.*
(c)	She did not see me *nor* my friend.	She did not see me *or* my friend.
(d)	*You were* at the cinema yesterday ?	*Were you* at the cinema yesterday ?
(e)	Be careful not *to loose* your money.	Be careful not *to lose* your money.

Note : Cousin का अर्थ होता है: चचेरा, ममेरा, मौसेरा, फुफेरा भाई या बहन। अतः, cousin brother/cousin sister नहीं कहा जाता।

	Incorrect	Correct
4. (a)	*This* mistakes are made by the foreigners.	*These* mistakes are made by the foreigners.
(b)	You are coming with me, isn't *it* ?	You are coming with me, *aren't you* ?
(c)	He asked me what games did I *play* ?	He asked me what games *I played.*
(d)	I think his grandfather is *died.*	I think his grandfather *died.*
(e)	I *past* by your house yesterday.	I *passed* by your house yesterday.
5. (a)	*Walking* through a jungle, a snake bit him.	*As he was* walking through a jungle, a snake bit him.
(b)	He is the *Principle* of our college.	He is the *Principal* of our college.
(c)	*The whole* people were poor at that time.	*All the* people were poor at that time.
(d)	It happened *in the March month.*	It happened *in the month of March.*
(e)	He came *by walking.*	He came *on foot.*
6. (a)	He went there *by horse.*	He went there *on a horse.*
(b)	There was a house *at two mile's distance.*	There was a house *at a distance of two miles.*
(c)	India has a Shakespeare of *his* own.	India has a Shakespeare of *her/its* own.
(d)	I have just met a lady *which* I saw last week.	I have just met a lady *whom* I saw last week.
(e)	I have an account *on* this bank.	I have an account *at/with* this bank.
7. (a)	They were in doubt *in* it.	They were in doubt *about it.*
(b)	My house is changed *in* a hospital.	My house is changed *into* a hospital.

(c) Please excuse me *to be* so late.	Please excuse me *for being* so late.
8. (a) He did nothing *but to* laugh.	He did nothing *but laugh.*
(b) He is better able to walk *than* to run.	He is better able to walk than *run.*
(c) He is taught to read rather than *to write.*	He is taught to read rather *than write.*
(d) He did nothing except *to* give a stfaight answer.	He did nothing *except* give a straight answer.

Note : But, except, than तथा as के बाद बिना to का ही infinitive आता है।

9. (a) You *had better to* go home.	You *had better go* home.
(b) I *had rather* not *to accept* the offer.	I *had rather* not *accept* the offer.

Note : Had better, had rather, had sooner के बाद बिना to का ही infinitive का प्रयोग होता है।

EXERCISE 1

Correct the following sentences :

EXAMPLES : (i) He is a worst scholar.
= He is *a very bad* scholar.
(ii) Did you hear of him being killed ?
= Did you hear of *his* being killed.

1. He is a worst scholar.
2. I am senior than him.
3. I am confident to win.
4. I will inform to your father.
5. It is a nice poetry.
6. The rain has stopped yesterday.
7. Your informations are false.
8. This book is preferable than that.
9. One ought to love his country.
10. A number of boys has come.
11. Ganga is sacred river.
12. He describes about nature.
13. Where you are going ?
14. She does not love his husband.
15. Are you ill ? Yes, I am not ill.
16. He is more taller than his brother.
17. This is the only book whom I like.
18. The sceneries are lovely.
19. He is M.A.
20. He has passed last year.
21. He said that he will go after a week.
22. He says English fluently.

EXERCISE 2

Correct the following sentences :

EXAMPLES : (i) When you wrote him a letter ?
= When *did* you *write* him a letter ?
(ii) The whole facts must be considered.
= *All the facts* must be considered.

1. When you wrote him a letter ?
2. It is the most unique thing.

3. He has no any problems.
4. She resembles with my daughter.
5. Ten rupees are a small sum.
6. She gave me the book I want.
7. We availed of the offer.
8. He has three aircrafts.
9. He as well as I am guilty.
10. I know him for a long time.
11. I know to speak English.
12. I will come yesterday.
13. Do not speak a lie.
14. The man is mortal.
15. I wish it was possible.
16. He is taller than her.
17. He gave a speech.
18. His health is too good.
19. Either you or I are wrong.
20. He has given his examination.
21. He ordered for my dismissal.
22. You have done it quick.

EXERCISE 3

Correct the following sentences :

EXAMPLES : (i) I am short in funds.
= I am short *of* funds.

(ii) Let us avail the opportunity.
= Let us avail *ourselves of* the opportunity.

1. I past my driving test.
2. This mango tastes sweetly.
3. He gave me a most perfect answer.
4. Let me write it by a pen.
5. Did you buy two breads ?
6. Science has and will help man.
7. He drunked two glasses of water.
8. He is comparatively better today.
9. It is time we go home.
10. I am tired with this work.
11. My brother is too smart.
12. I believe upon God.
13. He said me this.
14. Here is a chair to sit.
15. He called me as a fool.
16. Ram said that he will do it.
17. It was bitter cold.
18. It is a five-members committee.
19. I have rang the bell.
20. He is a foolish.
21. He wrote a best book.
22. He does not know to swim.

EXERCISE 4

Correct the following sentences :

EXAMPLES : (i) I prefer to do this than that.
= I prefer *doing* this to that.

(ii) They go to fish every day.
= They go *fishing* every day.

1. He is ill since a week.
2. The prisoner was hung.
3. He had come here yesterday.
4. I am too glad to see you.
5. My shoes are finer than you.
6. Quote the poem from heart.
7. He and I am neighbours.
8. Every man are mortal.
9. He is my cousin brother.
10. The gold is yellow.
11. Tell me what is your name.
12. He prevents me to go there.
13. He only died yesterday.
14. You should act like I do.
15. She came here today morning.
16. English often fought French.
17. Good night, Sir, have a seat.
18. You are junior than him.
19. We should not do noise.
20. We had a picnic tomorrow.
21. He works hard, isn't it ?
22. He is a worst student.

EXERCISE 5

Correct the following sentences :

EXAMPLES : (i) Either of you are responsible for this.
= Either of you *is* responsible for this.

(ii) I have no interest that he should go.
= I have no interest *in his going*.

1. Either he or I are to blame.
2. I fear its going to rain.
3. We believe to God.
4. Neither he laughs nor sings.
5. Camel is a beast of burden.
6. We enjoyed the theatre.
7. He speaks well English.
8. Why you study English ?
9. She is ill for some days.
10. He is good in health.
11. I didn't see nobody there.
12. I have less friends than you have.
13. Don't be fool.
14. Please shut the light.
15. I think to go to home.
16. Cow's milk are good for you.
17. John gave false witness.
18. It is half-passed two.
19. He has not ate nothing.
20. I have not time to play.
21. It is ten in my watch.
22. Never tell lie.
23. She loves with her husband.
24. Leela was her oldest daughter.

EXERCISE 6

Correct the following sentences :

EXAMPLES : (i) I enjoyed very much at the party.
= I enjoyed *myself* very much at the party.

(ii) Too great a variety of objects distract the mind.
= Too great a variety of objects *distracts* the mind.

1. I am born in 1975.
2. Sita did her work good.
3. It costs two, three rupees.
4. Does he speaks Bengali ?
5. The peon is in leave today.
6. She is very clever girl.
7. Gandak is a small river.
8. I listened his speech.
9. Let us run fastly.
10. Ram is a NCC cadet.
11. It's belong to me.
12. I replied his letter once.
13. I and Moti are friends.
14. I like very much music.
15. When the post will come.
16. A woman lost his son.
17. He enjoys bad health.
18. He is wiser than all.
19. She is bent to take revenge.
20. I prefer to read than to write.

EXERCISE 7

Correct the following sentences :

EXAMPLES : (i) I made her to cry.
= I made her cry.

(ii) He is Daniel in wisdom.
= He is *a* Daniel in wisdom.

1. He is very proudy.
2. He was born at 1980.
3. He never listens his mother..
4. The aeroplane makes noise

5. He wrote very good letter.
6. He hasn't many money.
7. I couldn't find him nowhere.
8. The man who came here he is rich.
9. This is the man which did it.
10. I saw dog coming towards me.
11. Many a man run after wealth.
12. He came in 10th July.
13. He was hung for murder.
14. He said me, "I will not come."
15. I saw many sheeps there.
16. You may either go or to stay.
17. I am sitting here for hours.
18. I asked from him a question.
19. They want to become a doctor.
20. Mathematics are easy to learn.
21. The two first pages are lost.
22. Will I go at the post office ?

EXERCISE 8

Correct the following sentences :

EXAMPLES : (i) He said to me a liar.
= He *called* me a liar.

(ii) My hairs stood on end.
= My *hair* stood on end.

1. I only eat when I am hungry.
2. He ordered for my dismissal.
3. I am looking forward to meet him.
4. He gave a speech.
5. Sita is ill since Monday.
6. Mother Teressa helps poors.
7. Please excuse me being late.
8. All the furniture were lost.
9. This novel is too interesting.
10. He will not listen what you say.
11. I bought four dozens mangoes.
12. He took admission in our school.
13. Not only he was injured but ruined.
14. He was angry upon me.
15. He only died this morning.
16. I know him for a long time.
17. She committed suicide twice.
18. He does not obey to my words.
19. Bring me any water to drink.
20. One should take care of his health.

EXERCISE 9

Correct the following sentences :

EXAMPLES : (i) Is there any use to try to phone him ?
= Is there any use *trying* to phone him ?

(ii) Bird in hand is worth two in bush.
= *A bird* in hand is worth two in *the* bush.

1. I am better of all the students.
2. He said that she has done it.
3. She had died ten years ago.
4. I have been ill since a week.
5. Columbus invented America.
6. Which is easiest—Hindi or Telgu ?
7. I neither met Tom nor his brother.
8. She had been married in 1980.
9. Boys fear from snakes at night.
10. He told me that he was alright.
11. He died from cholera.
12. He is a disgrace for all of us.
13. Everest is highest peak in the world.
14. Neither of the five roads is good.
15. My car is much different from yours.
16. I have lost a ten-rupees note.
17. Dr Sen saw the patient's pulse.
18. My English knowledge is sound.
19. Ram has been accused with theft.
20. This book is much interesting.

EXERCISE 10

Correct the following sentences :

EXAMPLES : (i) My husband is a very good cooker.
= My husband is a very good *cook*.

(ii) Being a wet day, we remained indoors.
= *It being* a wet day, we remained indoors.

1. I have not any books to read.
2. His advices were very wise.
3. Patna is smaller from Delhi.
4. The train left half hour ago.
5. Why he comes here every day ?
6. Who discovered the telephone ?
7. What film will be played tomorrow ?
8. This cloth is superior from that.
9. I am not pleased from him.
10. He has been ill from last Monday.
11. Open page 15 of this book. (Open at........)
12. He came to me every six hour.
13. He brought all his luggages.
14. Have they much books ?
15. (At) what time is the lunch ?
16. I speak English better than him.
17. He can speak very well English.
18. His answer is full with mistakes.
19. He goes at market every day.
20. The man jumped in the river.
21. Somebody is knocking the door.
22. He came in the room at 5.
23. I bought this pen in six rupees.

EXERCISE 11

Correct the following sentences :

EXAMPLES : (i) The fruit tastes sourly.
= The fruit tastes *sour*.

(ii) Please excuse me for giving you this trouble.
= Please excuse *my giving* you this trouble.

1. He hasn't come since a long time.
2. She is the best of the two students.
3. Each of the students were given pencils.
4. Chairs are bought for scholars with handles.
5. We decided to at once call for the police.
6. I had passed the Intermediate Exam. in 1960.
7. Not only I am a learner but I am also an earner.
8. He took admission into Darbhanga Medical College.
9. She has been reading French from 1970.
10. The news of his death are too deep for tears.
11. Please excuse me for giving you this trouble.
12. The patient is getting from worse to bad.
13. Candidates will be determined between 2 p.m. to 5 p.m.
14. I am reading this novel for three days.
15. Either of the two boys have done this.
16. The Mount Everest is highest in the world.
17. This is an useful thing for a traveller.
18. He came here with his family members.
19. The climate of Ranchi is better than Patna.
20. The patient died before the doctor came.

EXERCISE 12

Correct the following sentences :

EXAMPLES : (i) He asked me how did I know him ?
= He asked me how I *had known* him.
(ii) I do not know *that how* you are these days.
= I do not know *how* you are these days.

1. He is the best of the two boys.
2. He asks me why have I beaten him.
3. Neither he has a pen or a pencil.
4. He asked me that what was his name.
5. There is not any place in this compartment.
6. Milk and Soda are a refreshing drink.
7. United States of America have a big army.
8. I am living in Bombay for the last ten years.
9. Who has discovered the steam engine ?
10. Each of the boys were rewarded.
11. Bread and butter are ideal for breakfast.
12. Why you didn't answer my letter ?
13. Neither of the two brothers are married.
14. Lay down, you have high temperature.
15. The poors say that the riches are happy.
16. He is in this school for two years.
17. He past his examination last year.
18. Though he is poor, but he is happy.
19. It is I who is going to Madras.
20. He cut the apple by a new knife.

EXERCISE 13

Correct the following sentences :

EXAMPLES : (i) Why you study English ?
= Why *do* you study English ?
(ii) My English knowledge is sound.
= My *knowledge of English* is sound.

1. The English is the mother-tongue of English.
2. Neither you nor he are the owner of the book.
3. I did not see him since he has come.
4. I have collected five hundreds rupees.
5. She finished her work when I met her.
6. The headmaster denied his application for leave.
7. The news I have received are good.
8. John is more stronger than his brother.
9. There aren't some flowers in the garden.
10. The father called her daughter to come.
11. Sunshine is necessary for a good health.
12. The football is more popular than the hockey.
13. The girl whom mother is ill has left school.
14. One should mind his own business.
15. The man to which I spoke is my brother.
16. I thought that she can run much faster.
17. I asked him whether he wants anything.

18. Every morning I go to school from the bicycle.
19. Can you translate this letter to English ?
20. I did not buy either of the three books.

EXERCISE 14

Correct the following sentences :

EXAMPLES : (i) Neither his action was just nor unjust.
= His action was *neither* just *nor* unjust.
(ii) I have some milk, but I don't have some sugar.
= I have some milk, but I don't have *any* sugar.

1. We reached Ranchi on nine o'clock.
2. The children are playing into the field.
3. The property has been disposed off.
4. I cannot agree with your proposal.
5. I insist upon him going at once.
6. Kalidas is greater than any poet.
7. Ram is as good or better than Shyam.
8. Either of the six teams might win the cup.
9. Ram knows the alphabets of English.
10. The youngest of the three children are a girl.
11. Politics give a number of theories about the state.
12. His knowledge of many languages are remarkable.
13. Let us discuss about the poems we have just read.
14. It is one of the best books that has been written.
15. Please tell me that why you have done it.
16. Ram informed his father that he will come soon.
17. Five boys of my class want to become a farmer.
18. All your's books were stolen by thieves.
19. My friend came here with the train.
20. A large number of cattle is grazing in the field.

EXERCISE 15

Correct the following sentences :

EXAMPLE : I have many works to do this morning.
= I have many *pieces of work* to do this morning.
or, I have *lots of work* to do this morning.

1. This pen is much more cheaper than that.
2. The exhibition has been over ten days ago.
3. The most of the people are fond of the cinema.
4. Everything in the room was covered by dust.
5. He did not obey to his advices.
6. Not only he was injured but ruined.
7. You will get here boarding and lodging.
8. You are the man who have been chosen.
9. Your watch is better than that of mine.
10. Between you and I there is no secret.
11. He insisted to pay my school fees.

12. This is a most unique opportunity for you.
13. I could not catch up his words.
14. He was cowed down by the threat.
15. I don't hardly think it will rain.
16. He picked up a quarrel with me.
17. Each of the boys have homeworks to do.
18. Five students have passed and one failed.
19. He was the man whom I thought was very honest.
20. Mr John, with his wife and children, were present at the show.

EXERCISE 16

Correct the following sentences :

EXAMPLE : Unless you *do not work* hard, you will fail.
= Unless you *work* hard, you will fail.

1. I, you and he are students.
2. Nobody cannot do this work.
3. He is running as if he is mad.
4. The thief was sent to the prison.
5. He gave me many good advices.
6. Each of us have separate books to read.
7. He soon will return home.
8. We had gone to the cinema last night.
9. I have applied for lecturership.
10. There is no reason for me going there.
11. A picture has been hanged on the wall.
12. The population of Delhi is greater than Patna.
13. I wish I was as intelligent as my brother.
14. I did not buy any of the two books.
15. I have not had some breakfast.
16. Do not prevent me to work.
17. This school was closed since yesterday.
18. Bring me any coffee to drink.

EXERCISE 17

Correct the following sentences :

EXAMPLE : The lames and the blinds deserve our sympathy.
= The *lame* and the *blind deserve* our sympathy.

1. Knowledge is more preferable than riches.
2. Little money is better than none.
3. I had written a letter to him last week.
4. In a few years he became a richest.
5. Shakespeare is Kalidas of England.
6. Neither of them could finish their work.
7. I have been ill since three weeks.
8. Where you spent the last summer vacation ?
9. The magistrate and collector were present there.
10. He asked me how have you done in the examination.

11. It is one of the best books that has been written.
12. I am waiting here for the last two hours.
13. He said that he has never gone to Bombay.
14. When he will come I will say him everything.
15. Tell me that whether you will attend the meeting.
16. Not only he is my uncle, but also my teacher.
17. He is one of the most brilliant man of the country.
18. I fail to understand why has he not done this work.
19. If you will steal again, I shall beat you.
20. However hard he tried, he cannot answer the question.

EXERCISE 18

Correct the following sentences :

EXAMPLE : Lying under a tree, a snake bit her.
= *As she was* lying under a tree, a snake bit her.

1. Two years passed since I returned from Bombay.
2. He has more than two dozens of books with him.
3. How long did you awaited for me last evening ?
4. He said that he was suffering from fever for three days.
5. The train will arrive at Tuesday on eleven o'clock at the morning.
6. Unless you will not work hard, you will fail.
7. He has married a woman five years' elder than him.
8. There was very disturbance both in Delhi as well as Pune.
9. No sooner had he reached the station when the train had started.
10. Choose only such friends whom you can trust.
11. Lions are both found in Asia and Africa.
12. I have not and will not give up smoking.
13. He asked if the meeting can be put off till Saturday.
14. My camera is superior and more expensive than yours.
15. She has great respect and unlimited faith in her physician.
16. The minister suddenly stoped his speach and sat down.
17. He was appointed and dismissed from the post.
18. The book is no better, and not even as good as yours.
19. I always have and always shall be faithful.
20. He has been offered, and accepted, the Tagore lectureship.
21. *The Times of India* has the largest circulation than any newspaper.
22. As to how far he will succeed in his attempt it is a hard problem.
23. I am one of those who cannot describe what I feel.
24. The teacher explained them that science comprised of many branches of learning.
25. What to talk of wine, he does not even take tea.

EXERCISE 19

Correct whatever is wrong in the following. Re-write the passage.

1. "Subject : For Ex-student Permetion in Vocational College.

"Sir ;

"Due to respectfully I beg to say that last year I was read in (B.A.) Ist year in College of Vocational College, Sheikh-Sarai. Unfortunately I did failed in B.A.

this year 1986. My principal are not allowed for sitting Ex-student. Kindly I request to you to please give me permission in vocational college for Ex-student..I think you understand my problem. So I will hope, you will done my request.

Thanking you. etc...."

The student who wrote this letter happens to be studying in "the English medium." ! It is addressed to the Dean of Students' Welfare, University of Delhi.

—THE TIMES OF INDIA, OCT. 27, '86.

EXERCISE 20 (With Answer)

1. Each of the following sentences contains only one error Re write the sentences in the correct form :

(a) He behaves as if he is the boss. (b) Hari as well as his father are coming. (c) He is a man whom I know is trustworthy. (d) I have heard the news an hour ago. (e) He has gone to the market for buying vegetables. (f) He asked that why he should be punished. (g) The teacher insisted upon him to go. (h) Please tell me where does the director live. (i) He suggested me that I go home early.

2. Correct the errors in the following sentences and rewrite them :

(a) He never has, and never will, take such strong measures. (b) The sceneries here are not good. (c) Each of these boys play games. (d) Raipur is hot than Simla. (e) He said that he saw him last year.

3. Correct the following sentences :

(a) The quality of films today are inferior. (b) One learns to respect himself in the army. (c) Panting for breath, the lifebelt eluded his grasp. (d) The road was lined with poplars just like Kashmir. (e) I cannot open the drawer in which I put the paper in. (f) She dances better than any girl in her class.

4. Correct the errors in the following sentences and rewrite them :

(a) Tell me where have all the cadets gone. (b) Neither he studies nor plays. (c) Hardly he had reached home than his brother left for the station. (d) Himalayas and Ganga inspire the people of India. (e) He is one of the wisest man that has ever lived.

5. Each of the following sentences contains only one error. Rewrite the sentences in the correct forms :

(a) After returning from the post office, I laid down on the couch to rest. (b) He was not used to eat breakfast at seven in the morning. (c) It is I who is going to Madras. (d) He was found guilty and sent to the prison. (e) Twenty miles are not a long distance in these days of rapid travel. (f) It's high time you start earning your living. (g) I look forward to meet you tomorrow. (h) It is a bad form to put up too many questions during a lecture. (i) The teacher emphasized on the importance of speaking the truth. (j) No sooner had we set out when the thunderstorm broke.

6. Correct the following where necessary :

(a) I love to read sad poetries. (b) She sat on the table for a meal. (c) The parents were discussing about their future plans. (d) My brother is going foreign tomorrow.

7. Correct the following sentences :

(a) Give attention to what I am saying. (b) The flood caused many damages. (c) My uncle denied my invitation to visit Agra. (d) We will discuss about your problems later. (e) We have bought some furnitures. (f) Do you know to make bread ? (g) I have been living in Madras since ten years. (h) Don't have too many luggages while travelling. (i) Your sister is too beautiful. (j) She had scarcely recovered from one illness than she had another.

8. Rewrite the following sentences correctly :

(a) Nobody offered to give up their seat to her. (b) People do not save money like they used to. (c) Woodhouse was more amusing than any humorist. (d) He laid unconscious for over an hour.

9. The following sentences have one error each. Write the corrected sentences :

(a) Do you know the English alphabets ? (b) The delegates discussed about the problem at length. (c) Didn't you avail of the opportunity ? (d) Please speak to the concerned clerk. (e) Not only he was a thief but also a murderer. (f) She denied to say where she had bought the ring. (g) I do not understand why did he speak so softly. (h) He cut the apple by a new knife. (i) He hired a porter to carry his luggages. (j) She has great respect and unlimited faith in her physician. (k) The objectives of this school are different from most schools. (l) He takes pride in whatever work he is engaged. (m) Have either of the patients improved since yesterday ? (n) Reading pages after pages he went through the book quickly. (o) He took great pain to clean your room. (p) We will go on a holiday when the examination will be over. (q) He finds faults with everybody. (r) He is hard to be pleased. (s) The tea is very cold to drink. (t) He is owning a big house.

10. Rewrite the following sentences in the correct grammatical form :

(a) Do you know that he is having a lot of money ? (b) All informations given by him are wrong. (c) The economical condition of our country is bad. (d) Do you know who am I ? (e) I am too glad to see a fine man like you. (f) Flying over Switzerland, the Alps were seen by us. (g) Please explain me this point. (h) Come and sit down for a while, Ashok, you are digging since lunch time. (i) Nalini is quite impossible to carry such a heavy suitcase.

11. Rewrite the following sentences correctly :

(a) Each of us have something to say on this. (b) Please write your name with ink. (c) You must secure at least passable marks. (d) You are stronger than me. (e) The chair cost fifty rupees on which he sat. (f) Chaucer was the greater of all the poets of his age. (g) I and Herbert return to school tomorrow. (h) I don't hardly know how to answer you. (i) The more one gets the greater he demands. (j) "Eat us ! eat us !" cried the hungry children at the sight of the officer, carrying food on a tray.

12. Correct the prepositions in the following sentences :

(a) The boys threw stones on the frogs. (b) He is an asset in the institution. (c) I acquainted him about the facts of the case. (d) Let us go out on a walk. (e) He should refrain on harming others.

13. Rewrite each of the following sentences in its corrected form :

(a) After I answered the questions, I rushed home to check my notes. (b) The medical test at our college includes measurement of chest, height and what the blood pressure is. (c) Although Sheela was not invited to the party, she would have liked to have gone. (d) Roses smell sweetly in January. (e) There was only a boy and a girl in the class when the headmaster arrived. (f) As his involvement in the crime

could not be established he was given the benefit of doubt. (g) Rima is as sharp, if not sharper, than Vinit. (h) I wonder if she will play piano tonight. (i) Walking across the garden, there were a number of fruit trees besides a variety of flower plants. (j) The examination has been postponed to April.

14. Correct the following sentences :

(a) We had written this essay on monday. (b) We should help poors. (c) I am going foreign next month. (d) Sanjay Kumar is a great actor. Isn't it ? (e) I, you and Ram will go to the cinema today. (f) Unless you do not work hard, you will not pass. (g) He knew that I am coming. (h) He got passing marks in the examination. (i) Could you lend me your pen to write ? (j) The two first columns of the newspaper are badly printed.

Ans. 1. (a) *he were.* (b) *is.* (c) *who I know.* (d) *remove 'have'.* (e) *gone to market.* (f) *remove 'that'.* (g) *upon his going.* (h) *.....where the director lives.* (i) *suggested to me that I should go....*

2. (a) *He has never taken, and will never take....* (b) *scenery, here is.* (c) *plays.* (d) *hotter than.* (e) *had seen.*

3. (a) *is.* (b) *oneself.* (c) *while he was panting...* (d) *just as the road in Kashmir.* (e) *remove 'in' at the end.* (f) *any other girl.*

4. (a) *Tell me where all the cadets have gone.* (b) *He neither studies nor plays.* (c) *when his brother.* (d) *The Himalayas and the Ganga.* (e) *men that have....*

5. (a) *lay down.* (b) *to eating.* (c) *am going.* (d) *was sent.* (e) *is not.* (f) *started.* (g) *to meeting.* (h) *remove 'up'.* (i) *remove 'on'.* (j) *than the thunderstorm broke.*

6. (a) *poems.* (b) *at the table.* (c) *remove 'about'.* (d) *to a foreign country tomorrow.*

7. (a) *Pay attention...* (b) *lots of damage.* (c) *refused.* (d) *remove 'about'.* (e) *some furniture.* (f) *how to make bread ?* (g) *for ten years.* (h) *too much luggage.* (i) *very beautiful.* (j) *.....when she had another.*

8. (a) *remove 'up'.* (b) *as they....* (c) *any other humorist.* (d) *lay.*

9. (a) *English alphabet.* (b) *remove 'about'.* (c) *avail yourself of....* (d) *to the clerk concerned.* (e) *He was not only a thief but....* (f) *refused to say.* (g) *why he spoke so softly.* (h) *with a new knife.* (i) *luggage.* (f) *respect for and unlimited faith in.* (k) *from the objectives of the most of the schools.* (l) *engaged in.* (m) *Has either...* (n) *page after page.* (o) *great pains.* (p) *is over.* (q) *finds fault with.* (r) *hard to please.* (s) *too cold to drink.* (t) *He owns....*

10. (a) *he has a lot of.* (b) *All information....is....*(c) *The economic condition.* (d) *.....who I am ?* (e) *very glad.* (f) *While we were flying....*(g) *Please explain this point to me.* (h) *....you have been digging....*(i) *It is quite impossible for Nalini to carry such a heavy suitcase.*

11. (a) *has.* (b) *in ink.* (c) *pass marks.* (d) *than I.* (e) *The chair on/in which he sat cost fifty rupees.* (f) *the greatest of all.....*(g) *Herbert and I will return....*(h) *Remove 'don't,* (i) *one demands.* (j) *"Feed us ! feed us !"*

12. (a) *....at the frogs.* (b)*....an asset to...*(c) *....with the fact....*(d)*....for a walk.* (e)*....refrain from harming.*

13. (a) *After I had answered....*(b) *.....the measurement of the chest, height and blood pressure.* (c) *Although Sheela was not invited to the party, she liked to go.* (d) *Roses smell sweet in January.* (e) *There were only.....*(f)*...given the benefit of the doubt.*

(g) ***Rima is as sharp as, if not sharper than, Vinit.*** (h) ***I wonder if she will play the piano tonight.*** (i) ***Walking across the garden, I found a number of fruit trees besides a variety of flower plants.*** (j) ***The examination has been postponed until April.***

14. (a) *We wrote...Monday.* (b)....*the poor.* (c) ....*to a foreign country*....(d) ....*Isn't he ?* (e) *You, Ram and I*....(f) *Unless you work,*....(g) ....*I was*....(h) ....*pass marks*....(i) ....*to write with ?* (j) *The first two columns*....

EXERCISE 21 (With Answer)

1. There is a mistake in one of the parts (A, B) of each of the following sentences (a to h). Find the mistakes and rewrite the corrected parts :

	A	B
(a)	He pulled his belt tightly	and started off.
(b)	All what you say	is certainly true.
(c)	He needs a place	to live in it.
(d)	I wondered	that where she lived.
(e)	You know	that I go often to the theatre.
(f)	It was cruel of him	to have killed the birds by a stone.
(g)	It's best book	I have ever read.
(h)	Did you notice	that he was wearing a national dress ?

2. Spotting errors :

(i) (a) I and my colleague (A) have carefully considered the important issues raised by (B) the report which (C) you sent me and we have decided (D) to take the following action. No error (E)

(b) I do (A) all the cooking and cleaning and beside (B) that I help my husband in (C) his bookwork. (D) No error (E)

(c) I had just posted (A) the letter when (B) I remembered that I haven't (C) enclosed the cheque which I had meant to send. (D) No error (E)

(d) He is thought (A) to have (B) information which will be (C) useful for the (D) police. No error (E)

(ii) (a) I was thinking inside myself (A) that if the clock had been invented (B) by someone south of the Equator, (C) clock hands would go round the (D) other way. No error (E)

(b) I have given you (A) all necessary directions (B) now don't loose (C) the way. (D) No error (E)

(c) He had no objection (A) to forward (B) my application (C) to the higher authorities. (D) No error (E)

(d) Students should take up (A) such courses of study (B) which will fit them (C) for trade and industries. (D) No error (E)

Ans. 1. (a) *He fastened his belt tightly.* (b) *All that you say.* (c) *to live at* (d) *where she lived.* (e) *that I often go to the theatre.* (f) *to have killed the bird with a stone.* (g) *It's the best book.* (h) *that he was putting on national dress.*

2. (i) (a)—A. My colleague and I. Error in the order of pronouns.

(b)—B. 'besides' means 'in addition to';
'beside' means 'by the side of.'

(c)—(C). I hadn't. Error in the use of tenses

(d)—(D). Useful *to* a person. Useful *for* something.

(ii) (a)—A. 'inside myself' is superfluous.

(b)—C. 'lose' not loose

(c)—B. to forwarding. Error in the verb-form

(d)—C. as will fit....... We say—such.......as. Error in conjunction.

EXERCISE-22 (With Answer)

Read the following sentences carefully and mark the part in which you find an error. If there is no error, the answer is (5).

(i) 1. It is common (1) knowledge that each (2) of us (3) loves our (4) home. No error (5).

2. The teacher repeatedly warned the students (1) not to (2) make noise (3) but the students did not (4) obey. No error (5)

3. The Education Council (1) is consisted of (2) ten members (3) all of whom (4) are experienced men. No error (5).

4. My left leg has (1) just been (2) operated (3) by the surgeon in a big (4) hospital. No error (5).

5. Before long (1) there was no one (2) on the (3) lush green (4) lawn. No error (5).

6. The woman who has been perpetually (1) hesitating (2) which of the two books (3) she will read first will probably read none (4) and will suffer. No error (5).

7. Summons (1) were (2) issued yesterday by the Sessions Judge (3) against the suspected (4) thief. No error (5).

8. Teaching in this school (1) would certainly improve (2) if it had less (3) boys in all the high (4) classes. No error (5).

9. This tall and well-built (1)American girl (2) is sixteen complete (3) though she does not look (4) her age. No error (5).

10. When this was (1) searched (2) it was found (3) and the young servant (4) promptly cleaned it. No error (5).

Ans. 1. (4) his (not our or their) home. The pronoun 'his' must correspond to the subject each of us, implying singular.

2. (3) make a noise.Indefinite article missing.

3. (2) consists of, not consisted of. The verb indicates present tense.

4. (3) operated on. Preposition missing. The verb operated in a surgical sense when used in the active voice must be followed by 'on'.

5. (1) Long ago there was...'Before long' means soon; 'ago' means 'counting from now'. Wrong usage.

6. (4) neither. When the choice is between two persons or things, 'neither' is applicable, not 'none' which is used when there are many things.

7. (1) A summons was issued. The word 'summons' is singular and should carry a singular verb.

8. (3) fewer boys, not less which is used for quantity. 'Fewer' is the correct word when the reference is to numbers.

9. (3) over 16. Wrong construction.

10. (2) searched for. Preposition missing.

(ii) 1. Because of the cricket tournament organisational work (1) hardly (2) I have had (3) any rest since (4) one week. No error (5).

2. P. T. Usha is the fastest (1) runner and (2) she came last (3) in the race at (4) the Seoul Olympics. No error (5).

3. In some ways (1) the Diwali festival corresponds with (2) Christmas which is celebrated (3) with enthusiasm by Christians all (4) over the world. No error (5).

4. If I would have (1) done this, I would have (2) done wrong (3) and would have disappointed (4) my parents. No error (5).

5. Much and consistent (1) efforts always (2) bring their (3) sweet reward (4); so do not give up. No error (5).

6. Have you a sharp (1) pencil in your (2) bag ? I have not (3) got (4); please help. No error (5).

7. I happened (1) to see (2) three comely females (3) at the well-decorated (4) railway station. No error (5).

8. The size of (1) the new shoe (2) should be the same (3) as this (4) shoe; do make sure. No error (5).

9. Each and every (1) person (2) present (3) at the fair (4) wore a hat. No error (5).

10. I am happy (1) for tomorrow (2) is holiday (3) in our (4) school. No error (5).

Ans. 1. (3) have I had, *not* I have had. Error of adverb.

2. (2) but, *not* and. Error of conjunction. But is the right conjunction when the second main clause gives unexpected information.

3. (2) Corresponds to, *not* with. Wrong preposition.

4. (1) If I had done this, I should have done wrong. Error of verb.

5. (3) Its reward, *not* their reward. Error of adjective.

6. (4) got one. Mistake of pronoun. 'it' is needed after 'got'.

7. (3) 'women' is the right word, *not* females. Moreover, the word 'lady' means she is a woman of good birth, breeding and taste. Woman is the usual word and is polite enough.

8. (4) the same as that of this shoe. In comparative sentences 'that of' is necessary. Error of pronoun.

9. (1) Each person or everybody wore a hat. The use of both adjectives together is unnecessary.

10. (3) a holiday. Indefinite article missing. Moreover, because is better than 'for' to introduce casual clause.

(iii) 1. When he went (1) to the zoo, he found there were lions (2) on either side (3) of inner enclosure and they were ferocious (4) indeed. No error (5).

2. The houseowners forget that even (1) so simple a matter (2) as cleaning and maintaining (3) a lawn affects ecology (4) and should not be neglected. No error (5)

3. I took a day's leave from (1) my college to attend a dear (2) departed friend's (3) funeral service (4) which was conducted by his family priest. No error (5).

4. Going round (1) the street corner (2) yesterday afternoon (3), an unbearable sight was (4) seen. No error (5).

5. Considering (1) all the viewpoints (2) he was quite right (3) in rejecting (4) the offer. No error (5).

6. The expert mason (1) reported to the contractor (2) that there was no question (3) of the wall's (4) falling down. No error (5).

7. The politician (1) and the town administrator (2) has (3) arrived at (4) the meeting. No error (5)

8. Raman did not (1) attend the function (2) because he (3) went for riding (4) along with his friend. No error (5).

9. Not only (1) she will (2) go to her dear friend's house (3) but also she will (4) remain there for the day. No error (5).

10. Hardly I have (1) had any rest (2) for (3) two weeks (4) so I feel tired. No error (5).

Ans. 1. (3) on each side of the door. 'Either' means one or the other, not both. Wrong usage.

2. (4) enviroment, not ecology, which is the study of the relation between organisms and their enviorment. Wrong noun.

3. (4) funeral, not funeral service. The word service is redundant. A funeral is itself a service.

4. (4) Going round the street corner..... I saw a terrible sight. Wrong use of present participle.

5. (5) No error. The impersonal absolute in this case is correctly used.

6. (4) of the wall falling down. Possessive case is incorrect with the gerund in such cases.

7. (3) have arrived. Plural verb required because the reference is to two persons, not one; the definite article is mentioned twice.

8. (4) he went for a ride (or he went riding). Incorrect use of the preposition "for".

9. (2 & 4) Not only will she go, but she will also.... Error of conjunction and of construction.

10. (1) Hardly have I had... Mistake of adverb and wrong usage.

(iv) 1. One hundred children, possibly more (1), have died (2) from Cholera (3) in a Bihar rural district (4). No error (5).

2. Mahatma Gandhi taught, (1) by both precept and example (2), that untouchability is a major sin (3) before God (4) and man. No error (5).

3. You were too wise (1) in acting on the employer's letter (2) promptly and got (3) the job you wanted (4). No error (5).

4. When the century's worst drought (1) hit the countryside, (2) thousands of Rajasthan farmers migrated (3) to towns with a view to earn (4) their living. No error (5).

5. Arriving late (1) the old classic film had already (2) started in (3) the city's largest cinema hall (4). No error (5).

6. Of course I will (1) know what my (2) duty in (3) the workshop is (4). No error (5).

7. I clothe myself (I) properly and wear a three-piece (2) suit before I go to office (3) where my brother also goes in the morning (4) at 9. No error (5).

8. Ram has a black and white (1) dog and intends (2) to sell both (4) next week. No error (5).

9. She should have (1) realised long ago (2) that the honesty (3) is the best policy (4). No error (5).

10. Radha is very fond of these (1). kind of flowers (2) and bought some (3) from the florist (4). No error (5).

Ans. 1. (3) of cholera, not from. Wrong preposition.

2. (4) against God. Wrong preposition.

3. (1) very wise, not too wise. Too wise is wrong usage here and carries a contrary meaning.

4. (4) with a view to earning. Wrong construction. With a view to...is followed by "ing".

5. (2) he found that the old.... Wrong use of present participle. The correct construction is "Arriving late, he found that the...."

6. (1) would, not will. Would, past form of will, is used to express a wish.

7. (3) go to the office. Definite article missing. The reference is to a particular office.

8. (1) a black and a white dog. Article missing in second case. The sentence shows that he has two dogs, one black and the other white.

9. (3) Article 'the" not required before honesty. The definite article is omitted when an abstract noun is used in a general sense.

10. (1) 'kind' is used as singular. 'this' is the correct word here, not these.

(v) 1. Rakesh Sharma, the Indian space hero, is much sought after (1) by college students and is invited for (2) various functions at which (3) he is asked to (4) describe his experiences. No error (5).

2. My sister bought a bright red (1) *saree;* she preferred (2) it than (3) the blue one which her husband liked (4) very much. No error (5).

3. Every one (1) of the flood victims (2) whom journalists interviewed have related (3) the same (4) sad story. No error (5).

4. The freedom of speech is (1) one of the most precious right (2) of citizens in a democratic (3) country such as (4) India. No error (5).

5. My father would not (1) have written (2) this letter if (3) he would not have (4) listened to the latest TV news-bulletin. No error (5).

6. Yesterday in the night (1) he came to dinner (2) but ate very little (3) because he was emotionally (4) disturbed. No error (5).

7. Since my left foot is paining (1), I cannot run about (2) along with (3) hockey team mates (4) from my school. No error (5).

8. It is a pity (1) that college boys and girls often (2) spend his or her (3) leisure (4) in cinemas. No error (5).

9. Whoever does (1) best he (2) will get a cash prize (3) from the sports body (4) chairman; he happens to be the district's Deputy Commissioner. No error (5).

10. The beautiful lady (1) tested the boy (2) to see if (3) he could speak (4) English fluently. No error (5).

Ans. 1. (2) invited to, *not* for, which is wrong preposition here.

2. (3) to, *not* than. Appropriate preposition.

3. (3) has related. 'Everyone' carries a singular verb.

4. (2) precious rights, *not* right. Plural required.

5. (4) had, *not* 'would not have' That makes a double negative which is grammatically incorrect.

6. (1) Yesterday evening, *not* 'in the night' Wrong expression and faulty adverb.

7. (1) I have a pain in my left foot (or my left foot is hurting.) Wrong form of verb.

8. (3) their leisure. Mistake of pronoun; "boys and girls" require a plural pronoun.

9. (2) 'he' is superfluous. Mistake of pronoun.

10. (5) No error. "Tested the boy to see if he could speak English fluently"

(vi) 1. No sooner did he reach (1) the platform (2) than the train moved (3) out of the station (4). No error (5).

2. As soon as he saw (1) his mother (2) he ran to her (3) and embraced (4). No error (5).

3. She is wealthy (1) and can afford (2) all the pleasures (3) of life without care (4). No error (5).

4. Everyone expected (1) the bold officer (2) will face the situation (3) with courage (4). No error (5).

5. She is going (1) to her aunt (2) for the weekend (3) and after to Bombay (4). No error (5).

6. The king made him (1) his bodyguard (2) considering his (3) honesty and bravery (4). No error (5).

7. Why are you (1) angry on her (2) when she has done (3) nothing wrong (4). No error (5).

8. You could have been (1) selected for the post (2) if you had (3) applied in time limit (4). No error (5).

9. I will give you (1) an award if you (2) do your work (3) satisfactory (4). No error (5).

10. A bundle of 60 blankets (1) were distributed (2) in five shops (3) in the village (4). No error (5).

11. She got hurt (1) when the transistor (2) in the hand (3) explodes with a bang (4). No error (5).

12. This is one of (1) the rare book (2) which will never (3) be disliked by readers (4). No error (5).

13. Our people are (1) unable to speak (2) English fluently (3) as the American's do (4) No error (5).

14. Was it him (1) who got injured (2) in an accident (3) this morning (4) No error (5).

15. Suresh was suffering (1) from cholera (2) and ultimately (3) he died by it (4). No error (5).

Ans. 1. (1) No sooner *had he reached.* Wrong construction. "No sooner" is followed by "had", or in another type of construction, by "than".

2. (4) embraced *her.* Pronoun needed after verb.

3. (4) without *a* care. Indefinite article missing.

4. (3) would face the situation—Correct usage after past tense (expected).

5. (4) afterwards to Bombay. Correct adverb.

6. (3) comma needed before "considering". Punctuation mark missing.

7. (2) angry *with her* (not on). Correct preposition.

8. (4) applied *in time.* "Limit" is superfluous. An alternative construction is "applied within the time limit".

9. (4) *satisfactorily* not "Satisfactory". Adverb is needed, not adjective..

10. (2) *was* distributed. Bundle is used as singular and therefore requires a singular verb.

11. (4) exploded with a bang. Wrong verb."Got hurt" is past tense.

12. (2) *books;* plural required when choice is indicated "One of the..."

13. (4) *Americans,* not American's." Our people" requires a plural, not a possessive case.

14. (1) *he,* not him. Personal pronoun, object form "him" wrongly used.

15. (4) died *of,* not by. Wrong preposition used.

(vii) 1. In her hour of distress (1) she requested Mohan to lend (2) her some money (3) but he refused to do so (4). No error (5).

2. In some Far Eastern (1) countries the members of various racial (2) groups always remain (3) at dagger drawn (4). No error (5).

3. Although all my brothers (1) found themselves in trouble (2), I felt confident that ultimately everything would turn all right (3) because they had not (4) done anything wrong. No error (5).

4. Since the day the lockout was declared (1) by the factory employees (2), over 20 workers have been (3) dismissed and 10 resigned (4). No error (5).

5. The students were officially (1) told that they (2) are not to cross (3) the road against (4) the red light. No error (5).

6. On my way to (1) office, I shall (2) generally come across (3) many children wearing (4) blue uniforms. No error (5).

7. The well-clad servant lays (1) the table (2) while the lady of the house (3) was busy with (4) her guests. No error (5).

8. The tutor cautioned (1) the girl's guardian (2) that she would not (3) be able to get through the examination until she did not (4) work hard. No error (5).

9. Though the first portion (1) of the book was dull (2), the later (3) part was quite (4) interesting. No error (5).

10. Such a deep-rooted (1) prejudice, like (2) her anger, was bound (3) to affect (4) her judgement. No error (5).

Ans. 1. (4) but he refused. The words "to do so" are superfluous.

2. (4) at *daggers* drawn. Plural required since almost everyone referred to in the sentence supposedly has a dagger.

3. (3) turn out all right. Wrong phrase; 'out' required after 'turn'.

4. (4) 10 *have resigned.* Separate, independent verb required.

5. (5) No error. All eternal truths and permanent rulings may remain in the simple present.

6. (2) 'shall' is both wrong and unnecessary.

7. (1) *laid* the table. Past tense required because the reference is to a past occurrence (lady was busy).

8. (4) "until she worked hard." Double negative incorrect.

9. (3) The *latter* part. The word 'later' refers to time.

10. (1) *such .. as,* is the correct idiom.

(viii) 1. The Indian people, (1) especially in the 20th (2) century, waste much time in (3) trifles and so are behind (4) other nations in many respects. No error (5).

2. Ram was able to (1) prevent (2) Mohan from (3) harm throughout (4) the incident. No error (5).

3. At long last (1) he got (2) an employment (3) in South (4) Delhi, which is a posh colony. No error (5).

4. The old teacher (1) tested (2) the boy if (3) he could read (4) English fluently. No error (5).

5. He got (1) a bad companionship (2) and, as a result (3) ruined (4) his career. No error (5).

6. He as well as (1) his parents were (2) fond of (3) reading Ramayana (4) and derived much benefit from it. No error (5).

7. The woman (1) is the ornament (2) of the home (3) and should always (4) be regarded as such. No error (5).

8. He was clever (1) to see (2) through (3) her game and thus (4) escaped damage. No error (5).

9. He is as strong (1) if not stronger than (2) Mr Suri and therefore (3) carries (4) the day. No error (5).

10. He said that (1) "I am not feeling well"; (2) so he was (3) not able to play (4) the match. No error (5).

Ans. 1. (3) on (or over) trifles. Wrong preposition.

2. (2) protect, not prevent. Wrong verb.

3. (3) 'got employment' not 'an employment', Error in article.

4. (3) Wrong pronoun.

5. (2) got into bad company. Error in noun-phrase.

6. (4) *the* Ramayana. The definite article must be used before certain famous books (the Vedas, the Koran).

7. (1) Woman, not the woman. The article is omitted before common nouns used in the widest sense.

8. (1) clever enough. Adverb missing. The adverb 'enough' is always placed after the adjective which it modifies.

9. (1) as strong as, if not stronger than... error in placement of conjunction.

10. (1) 'That' should not be used before a sentence in direct narration. Relative pronoun wrongly placed.

(ix) 1. Even though he has been (1) regularly receiving financial help (2) from his elder brother (3) he is poor (4) than before. No error (5).

2. Expert dramatists rightly claim (1) that the plays of Shakespeare (2) were greater (3) than any plays (4) written in English. No error (5).

3. Ram Lal accompanied with (1) his friends when (2) the latter went (3) to the Simla hills (4) for a holiday. No error (5).

4. His father was surprised to know (1) that his grown-up son Rakesh, (2) who had travelled a lot (3), said "Never I have (4) seen such a sight." No error (5).

5. In my opinion (1) I think (2) this proposal is (3) totally wrong and must (4) be rejected. No error (5).

6. (5) Remember that (1) dust commonly triggers of asthma attacks (2) so try to keep the house (3) free of all dust (4). No error (5).

7. Much to the disappointment (1) of the teacher, none (2) of the boys had (3) learnt their (4) lesson. No error (5).

8. I repeatedly (1) asked for my pencil (2) but my friend did (3) not give (4) me. No error (5).

9. My teacher does not (1) know that (2) I and Krishan (3) are brothers and therefore (4) we live together. No error (5).

10. Last Sunday I (1) with some friends (2) went for a long (3) walk in (4) the hills. No error (5).

Ans. 1. (4) poorer than before. Comparative degree required because of the words "than before".

2. (4) greater than any other plays. Shakespeare's works have to be excluded to conform with the sense sought to be conveyed.

3. (1) accompanied his friends. The proposition 'with' is superfluous.

4. (4) "Never have I seen...." Wrongly placed adverb.

5. (2) The words " I think" are superfluous. " In my opinion" conveys the same sense.

6. (2) triggers *off,* not of. Wrong preposition. When used as transitive verb, *trigger off* is the idiomatic usage.

7. (4) learnt his lesson. 'None' is used as singular and 'their' is therefore incorrect. Wrong adjective.

8. (4) did not give it to me. Transitive verbs like 'give' and 'lend' must have an expressed object.

9. (3) Krishan and I. When there are two subjects the other person's name comes first and 'I' comes later. He and I, not I and he. Putting 'I' first indicates conceit !

10. (2) I went for a long walk with some friends. A pronoun used as a subject should not be separated from the verb if possible.

(x) 1. He made it (1) clear to his friends (2) that he preferred (3) reading than (4) playing cards. No error (5).

2. There are plenty (1) refreshments at (2) the Sunday (3) carnival being held at (4) Calcutta. No error (5)

3. He was angry (1) and looked like (2) he would gladly (3) attack me right (4) in front of my house. No error (5)

4. Aren't you most (1) ready to (2) leave for Delhi (3) to see (4) the match ? No error (5).

5. We stopped (1) at the International Hotel (2) for three days (3) in order to (4) attend a wedding. No error (5).

6. It was clear (1) that the committee's recommendations (2) will neither (3) bring good government nor contentment (4) to the country. No error (5).

7. He was an expert batsman (1) but through an error (2) he lifted the ball highly (3) in the air and gave a simple catch (4) to a fielder. No error (5).

8. Ram must take regular (1) exercise lest (2) his health would (3) break down (4) at the age of 40 or 45. No error (5).

9. When the stranger (1) entered the hotel and ordered (2) lunch he spoke (3) in a decided (4) American accent. No error (5).

10. The economic situation (1) now is no better (3) good as (2) and not even as it was (4) in 1987. No error (5).

Ans. 1. (4) preferred reading to playing cards. Wrong preposition and wrong construction.

2. (1) 'plenty refreshments' is colloquial. The correct construction is "There are plenty of refreshments.."

3. (2) He looked as if he would gladly attack me. 'Like' should not be used in place of 'as' or 'as if'. Wrong usage.

4. (1) *Almost,* not most. Wrong usage. 'Most' should not be used in place of almost.

5. (1) *stayed* not stopped. Wrong, unidiomatic expression.

6. (3) bring neither good government nor... Wrong construction.

7. (3) high in the air, not highly. Misuse of adverb.

8. (3) Should, not would. Lest is followed by should. Wrong usage.

9. (4) *decidedly,* not decided. Adverb needed here.

10. (2) no better than. Conjunction.

(xi) 1. Ram Lal is a better (1) mason than a (2) painter; hence (3) he is eagerly sought (4) by house-builders. No error (5).

2. There was little (1) food in the house (2) and the elderly (3) woman ate it when (4) she felt hungry. No error (5).

3. The school teacher reported (1) after the function that the (2) behaviour of (3) the children were (4) excellent. No error (5)

4. These are the the street (1) dogs who (2) bit the school children (3) on the grassy (4) lawn yesterday evening. No error (5).

5. Ashok is rather (1) rich, but his elder (2) brother is fairly (3) poor and is in fact (4) utterly helpless. No error (5)

6. The angry boatman (1) threw the cracked (2) oar in (3) the river and returned (4) home. No error (5).

7. Because he is (1) intelligent, therefore (2) he gets (3) good marks (4) in exminations. No error (5).

8. She had no other (1) hobby than (2) that of collecting (3) flowers and arranging (4) them nicely. No error (5).

9. The annual examination (1) results indicate (2) that girls are superior than (3) boys in the academic (4) field. No error (5).

10. Left to him (1) he would (2) donate his entire collection (3) of books to the Ashram (4) library. No error (5).

11. If he has taken (1) a taxi (2) he wouldn't have (3) missed the (4) train. No error (5).

Ans. 1. (2) 'a' is incorrect here. When two nouns in a comparison refer to the same person or thing, the article is used before the first noun only.

2. (1) a little. not little. Mistake of indefinite article and adjective. "Little" food means hardly any (or no) food, while "a little" means a small quantity of food which the woman ate.

3. (4) was excellent. Error of proximity. The verb must agree with the noun near it.

4. (2) *which,* not who. For animals and things 'which' is used as a relative pronoun.

5. (3) *quite,* not fairly. Fairly is generally used with favourable adjectives and adverbs.

6. (3) *into,* not in. Error of preposition.

7. (2) because ...., he gets good marks. Error of conjunction. 'Because' and 'therefore' are not used together.

8. (5) No error; but that of .... would have been incorrect.

9. (3) *to,* not than. Error of preposition.

10 (1) *himself,* not him. Emphatic pronoun is needed here.

11. (1) *had,* not has. Past tense required. Mistake of tense. The sentence refers to an event that has already occurred. The corrected sentence would read "If he had taken a taxi he wouldn't have......."

□ □ □

11. DIRECT AND INDIRECT SPEECH

(i) INTRODUCTION

किसी की कही हुई बात दो भिन्न-भिन्न तरीके से कही जा सकती है :

(a) जब speaker के मूल कथन को हम दूसरे से हू-बहू उन्हीं शब्दों में कहते हैं तब इसे *Direct Speech* कहा जाता है।

(b) Speaker के मूल कथन में कुछ हेरं-फेर कर किंतु आशय को अक्षुण्ण रखते हुए हम जो कुछ कहते हैं उसे *Indirect Speech* या *Reported Speech* कहा जाता है।

Indirect Speech के अध्ययन से केवल परीक्षा की तैयारी में ही मदद नहीं मिलती वरन् शुद्ध अंगरेजी जानने के लिए इसका practice आवश्यक है। English के बहुत सारे वाक्य indirect speech में ही होते हैं।

अगर हमसे कोई पूछे 'What did he say ?' तो इसका उत्तर देने के लिए हमें indirect speech के तरीके की जानकारी आवश्यक है।

(a) Difference between direct and indirect speech

Look at these sentences :

Direct	*Indirect*
He said, 'I am hungry'.	He said *that he was* hungry.
She said, 'Hurry up !'	She *told me to* hurry up.
Rekha said, 'Is anyone there ?'	Rekha *asked if* anyone *was* there.

ऊपर दिए गए वाक्यों को देखने से स्पष्ट हो जाता है कि

(i) Direct speech को quotation marks या inverted commas के अंदर रखा जाता है, किंतु indirect speech में quotation marks हटा दिए जाते हैं।

(ii) Direct speech में reporting verb (said) के बाद एक comma रहता है, किन्तु indirect speech में वह comma हट जाता है।

(iii) Indirect speech में reporting verb के बाद आवश्यकतानुसार *that, if, whether, to* इत्यादि का प्रयोग किया जाता है।

(iv) Direct speech का पहला letter capital होता है, किंतु indirect speech को capital letter से तभी शुरू करते हैं जब वह शब्द कोई proper name (Tom, Patna, India इत्यादि) हो।

(v) Indirect speech में आवश्यकतानुसार tense of the verb तथा pronoun में भी change करना पड़ता है।

Note : **(i) Direct speech में quotation marks (' ') के बाहर भी एक clause (He said इत्यादि) रहता है जिसे *reporting clause* कहते हैं और इसके verb (said) को *reporting verb* कहते हैं।**

(ii) Reported speech में double quotation marks (" ") का भी प्रयोग किया जाता है। किंतु Modern English में आजकल single quotation mark ('........') का ही प्रयोग चलता है।

(b) Direct speech के वाक्यों को लिखने के भिन्न-भिन्न तरीके

1. *Look at these sentences :*

He says, 'I shall be there.'
He asked, 'What is the time ?'
She said to her father, 'Please give me some money.'

इन वाक्यों में *He says, He asked* तथा *She said to her father* के बाद direct speech के वाक्य आए हैं अर्थात यहाँ reporting clause + direct speech है।

2. *Look at these sentences :*

'Where has she gone ?' { *he asked me.* / *Rajeev said.* / *he said.* }

'I am your friend', *said Rajeev.*

(i) ऊपर के वाक्यों में direct speech के वाक्य पहले और reporting clause बाद में आए हैं अर्थात इनमें direct speech + reporting clause है।

(ii) याद रखना चाहिए ऐसे वाक्यों में *he said* का अकसर प्रयोग किया जाता है, *said he* का नहीं। Rajeev said या said Rajeev लिखने के ये दोनों ढंग चलते हैं।

(iii) ऐसे वाक्यों को indirect में बदलने के पहले reporting clause (Rajeev said, he said, said Rajeev, he asked me) को वाक्य के शुरू में रख देते हैं। जैसे : *Rajeev said* that he was his friend.

3. *Look at these sentences :*

'Tuesday', *he said,* 'is not a good day'.
'The boy', *said the teacher,* 'is very intelligent'.
'Of course', *said Mr Bose,* 'we're very grateful'.

(i) इन वाक्यों में देखते हैं कि inverted commas को दो टुकड़ों में बाँट दिया गया है तथा reporting clause *(he said, said the teacher, said Mr Bose)* को उन दोनों के बीच रख दिया गया है। *('The medial placing of the reporting clause is very frequent.'*—R. Quirk & others)

(ii) ऐसे वाक्यों में punctuation (जो inverted commas के अंदर full stop, commas etc. हैं) तथा verb के position (he said, said the teacher, said Mr Bose) पर ध्यान दें।

(iii) ऐसे वाक्यों को indirect में बदलने के पहले हम reporting clause को वाक्य के शुरू में रख देते हैं। जैसे : *Mr Bose said* that of course they were very grateful.

4. *Look at these sentences :*

Ruby : Hello. How are you ?
Mira : Pretty well, thanks. And you ?
Ruby : I'm fine, thanks.
Mira : It's good to see you again.

(i) इन वाक्यों में speakers के नाम हैं किंतु reporting verbs नहीं हैं।

(ii) ऐसे वाक्यों को indirect speech में बदलने के पहले हम अपनी ओर से उपयुक्त reporting verb जोड़ देते हैं। जैसे : Ruby *asked* Mira how she was.

(c) Kinds of sentences in direct speech

Look at these sentences :

He said, 'I have lost my umbrella.' (*Statement*)
She said, 'What do you want ?' (*Question*)
He said, 'Shut the door.' (*Command*)
Tom said, 'Nonsense !' (*Exclamation*)

(i) Speaker द्वारा बोले गए वाक्य *statement, question, command* या *exclamation* हो सकते हैं।

(ii) Direct से indirect speech में बदलने के पहले छात्रों को inverted commas में आए वाक्यों को अच्छी तरह पहचान लेना चाहिए कि वे *statement* हैं या *question, command* या *exclamation.*

(iii) जिस प्रकार के वाक्य होंगे indirect speech में reporting verb *(told, asked, prayed* इत्यादि) उसी के अनुसार होंगे।

(ii) CHANGING FROM DIRECT TO INDIRECT

(a) INDIRECT STATEMENTS

किसी statement के direct से indirect में बदलने पर निम्नलिखित changes होते हैं :

A. Punctuation

1. *Look at these sentences :*

Direct	*Indirect*
Hari says, 'Sita is ill.'	Hari says *that* Sita is ill.
Moti says, 'Sudha is tall.'	Moti says *that* Sudha is tall.

(i) Direct speech में inverted commas का प्रयोग किया जाता है, किंतु indirect में नहीं।

(ii) Direct speech में reporting verb जैसे—*say, says, said* इत्यादि के बाद comma रहता है जो indirect speech में हट जाता है।

B. Conjunction : That

2. *Look at these sentences :*

Direct	*Indirect*
He says, 'He has lost his pen.'	He says *that* he has lost his pen.
Tom says to Moti, 'Hari is intelligent.	Tom tells Moti *that* Hari is intelligent.
She says, 'The train will be late.'	She says *that* the train will be late.

Direct speech में reporting verb *(says, say, said.....)* के बाद कोई conjunction *(that)* नहीं रहता; किंतु indirect speech में *say/says/said/told* इत्यादि के बाद *that* लगाया जाता है।

C. Pronouns and Determiners

3. *Look at these sentences :*

Direct	*Indirect*
I say, 'I write a letter.'	*I* say that *I* write a letter.
I say, 'I work hard.'	*I* say that *I* work hard.
I say, 'You are a fool.'	*I* say that *you* are a fool.
I say, 'He is ill.'	*I* say that *he* is ill.

(i) ऊपर के वाक्यों में *I, you* तथा *he* pronouns हैं।

(ii) अगर reporting clause का subject *I* रहे तो indirect में बदलते समय reported speech के subject में कोई परिवर्तन नहीं होता।

4. *Look at these sentences :*

Direct	*Indirect*
You say, 'I cut the finger.'	*You* say that *you* cut the finger.
You say, 'He will play.'	*You* say that *he* will play.

(i) अगर reporting clause का subject *you* रहे और reported speech का subject *I* तो indirect speech में *I* को *you* में बदल दिया जाता है।

(ii) परंतु reported speech का subject *he* नहीं बदलता।

5. *Look at these sentences :*

Direct	*Indirect*
He says, 'She is here.'	*He* says that *she* is here.
Sita says, 'He has a car.'	*Sita* says that *he* has a car.

अगर reported speech का subject third person *(he, she, it, they, Ram etc.)* हो तो उसे indirect speech में ज्यों-का-त्यों छोड़ देते हैं।

6. *Look at these sentences :*

Direct	*Indirect*
He says, 'I am a student.'	He says that *he* is a student.
She says, 'I play ludo.'	*She* says that *she* plays ludo.
Sima says, ' I like sweets.'	*Sima* says that *she* likes sweets.

(i) अगर reporting clause का subject third person *(he, she, Sima etc.)* हो तो indirect speech में reported specch का subject (I) third person में बदल दिया जाता है

(ii) अतः, he, she तथा Sima के अनुसार *I* को *he* तथा *she* में बदल दिया गया है।

7. *Look at these sentences :*

Direct	*Indirect*
Ram says to me, 'You are dull.'	Ram tells *me* that *I* am dull.
Tom says to you, 'You are tall.'	Tom tells *you* that *you* are tall.
Amar says to Rana, 'You are ill.'	Amar tells *Rana* that *he* is ill.
Sita says to Rekha, 'You can sing.'	Sita tells *Rekha* that *she* can sing.

(i) Reported speech का subject *(you)* indirect speech में reporting verb के *object (me, you, Rana, Rekha)* के अनुसार बदलता है।

(ii) *You* को *me* के अनुसार *I* में, *you* के अनुसार *you* में, *Rana* के अनुसार *he* में तथा *Rekha* के अनुसार *she* में बदल दिया गया है।

8. *Look at these sentences :*

Direct	*Indirect*
He said, "*You* like this."	He told *me* that *I* liked it.
He said, "*You* must be silent."	He told *me* that *I* must be silent.

जब reporting verb का object (me, you, him, her etc.) स्पष्ट नहीं हो तो *You* को प्रायः *I* में बदलते हैं तथा स्पष्टता के लिए reporting verb के बाद indirect speech में *told me/ asked me* लिख देते हैं।

9. *Look at these sentences :*

Direct	*Indirect*
Hari says, 'My book is new.'	*Hari* says that *his* book is new.
I say, 'Your pen is old.'	*I* say that *your* pen is old.
She says, 'His car is blue.'	She says that *his* car is blue.

Reporting clause के subject *(Hari, I, She,* etc.) के अनुसार ही indirect speech में determiners *(my, your, his)* को बदलना पड़ता है।

10. *Look at these sentences :*

Direct	*Indirect*
The *Times of India says,* 'We shall discuss the matter in our next issue.'	The *Times of India says* that *it will* discuss the matter in *its* next issue.

(i) Editorial *we* को third person में बदल दिया जाता है।

11. *Look at these sentences :*

Direct	*Indirect*
Tara says to Sita, 'She is young.'	Tara tells Sita that *she (Tara/Sita/*or *third person)* is young.

(i) ऊपर indirect speech में *she* का प्रयोग किसके लिए हुआ है पता नहीं चलता।

(ii) अतः, स्पष्टता के लिए ऐसे वाक्यों में उपयुक्त व्यक्ति का नाम brackets में लिख दिया जाता है।

(iii) Change of Pronouns से सम्बन्धित कुछ और उदाहरण देखे :

	Direct	*Indirect*
(i)	*I* say, '*I* cut *my* finger.'	*I* say *I* cut *my* finger.
(ii)	*You* say, '*I* cut *my* finger.'	*You* say *you* cut *your* finger.
(iii)	*He* says, '*I* cut *my* finger.'	*He* says *he* cuts *his* finger.
(iv)	*She* says, '*I* cut *my* finger.'	*She* says *she* cuts *her* finger.
(v)	Ram says to *me, 'You* should mind *your* own business.'	Ram tells *me* that *I* should mind *my* own business.
(vi)	Ram says to *you, 'You* should mind *your* own business.'	Ram tells *you* that *you* should mind *your* own business.
(vii)	Ram says to *him, 'You* should mind *your* own business.'	Ram tells *him* that *he* should mind *his* own business.
(viii)	Ram says to *her, 'You* should mind *your* own business.'	Ram tells *her* that *she* should mind *her* own business.
(ix)	Ram says to *them, 'You* should mind *your* own business.'	Ram tells *them* that *they* should mind *their* own business.
(x)	Ram says to *us, 'You* should mind own business. '	Ram tells *us* that *we* should mind *our* own business.
(xi)	Ram says to *me, 'He* should mind *his* own business.'	Ram tells *me* that *he* should mind *his* own business.
(xii)	Ram says to *him, 'They* should mind *their* own business.'	Ram tells *him* that *they* should mind *their* own business.

D. Tenses of verbs (sequence of tenses)

वाक्य को direct से indirect speech में बदलने के लिए sequence of tense की जानकारी आवश्यक है। Sequence of tense बतलाता है कि किसी complex

sentence में principal clause के verb के tense के अनुसार subordinate clause के verb का tense होगा। Indirect speech में जितने वाक्य होते हैं वे सदा complex sentences होते हैं। अतः, sequence of tenses के नियम उनमें भी लागू होते हैं।

12. *Look at these sentences :*

Direct	*Indirect*
I say, 'I *am reading.*'	I *say* that I *am reading.*
He will say, 'He *is* ill.'	He *will say* that he *is* ill.
Raju *says,* 'Rana *was* there.'	Raju *says* that Rana *was* there.

(i) इन वाक्यों में reporting verbs *say/says* present tense में हैं तथा *will say* future tense में।

(ii) अगर reporting verb present या future tense में रहे तो reported speech के tense of the verb में कोई परिवर्तन नहीं होता।

13. *Look at these sentences :*

Direct	*Indirect*
He *said,* 'He *is playing* tennis.'	He *said* that he *was playing* tennis.
She *said,* 'Sita is *reading,*'	She *said* that Sita *was reading.*
Reeta *said,* 'Moti *has done* the work.'	Reeta *said* that Moti *had done* the work.
Tom *said,* 'Jack *has been reading* the book since morning.'	Tom *said* that Jack *had been reading* the book since morning.
Meera *said,* 'She *will sing* a song.'	Meera *said* that she *would sing* a song.
Mr Gupta *said,* 'I *shall write* a story.'	Mr Gupta *said* that he *would write* a story.

(i) ऊपर के वाक्यों में आए reporting verbs *(said) past tense* में हैं।

(ii) अगर reporting verb past tense में रहे और reported speech का verb present या future tense में, तो indirect speech में reported speech के verb को past tense में बदल देते हैं।

(iii) अंतिम वाक्य में I को he में बदल दिया गया है; फलतः third person के साथ shall का would हो गया है : *I shall=he would.*

14. *Look at these sentences :*

Direct	*Indirect*
She *said,* 'He *came* at dinner-time.'	She *said* that he *had come* at dinner-time.
He said, 'Ramu *was playing* football.'	He *said* that Ramu *had been playing* football.

(i) ऊपर के Direct speech के वाक्यों में reporting verb *(said)* past tense में है तथा reported speech के verb *(came /was playing)* क्रमशः simple past एवं past continuous में हैं।

(ii) ऐसे वाक्यों में simple past *(came)* past perfect *(had come)* में तथा past continuous *(was playing)* past perfect continuous *(had been playing)* में बदल जाता है।

Note : (i) कभी-कभी ऐसे वाक्यों में tense form नहीं भी बदलता है। जैसे :

Direct	*Indirect*
He *said,* 'India *became* independent in 1947.'	He *said* that India *became* independent in 1947.
She *said,* 'I *was* not at home when the postman *came.*'	She *said* that she *was* not at home when the postman *came.*

अगर *reporting verb* past tense में रहे तो indirect speech के verb में निम्नलिखित ढंग से change होता है :

in direct speech	*in indirect speech*
he *is*	he *was*
he *can*	he *could*
he *may*	he *might*
he is *making*	he was *making*
he *makes*	he *made*
he *made*	he *had made*
he *was playing*	he *had been playing.*
he *has* found	he *had* found
he *will* write	he *would* write
he *will have* finshed	he *would have* finished
he *would help*	he *would have helped*
he *was* injured	he *had been* injured

15. *Look at these sentences :*

Direct	*Indirect*
He *said,* 'Honesty *is* the best policy.'	He *said* that honesty *is* the best policy.
He *said,* 'Two and two *make* four.'	He *said* that two and two *make* four.
We *said,* 'The earth *moves* round the sun.'	We *said* that the earth *moves* round the sun.
I *said,* 'I always *walk* in the morning.'	I *said* that I always *walk* in the morning.

(i) ऊपर direct speech में reporting verb *(said)* past tense में है तथा inverted commas के भीतर ऐसे वाक्य हैं जो universal truth (चिरंतन सत्य) या habitual fact (आदत-संबंधी सत्य) व्यक्त करते हैं।

(ii) Indirect speech में universal truth या habitual fact वाले वाक्यों के verb का tense नहीं बदलता।

E. Time Expression

16. *Look at these sentences :*

Direct	*Indirect*
He *said*, 'I saw her *yesterday*.'	He *said* that he had seen her *the previous day*.
She *said*, 'I will dance *tomorrow*.'	She *said* that she *would* dance the *next day*.

(i) ऊपर direct speech के वाक्यों में reporting verb *(said)* past tense में है तथा reported speech में समयसूचक शब्द (yesterday, tomorrow) हैं।

(ii) अर्थ को स्पष्ट करने के लिए indirect speech में उन्हें निम्नलिखित ढंग से बदल दिया जाता है :

in direct speech	*in indirect speech*
this	that
these	those
now	then
ago	before
today	that day
tomorrow	the next day
yesterday	the previous day; the day before
tonight	that night
next week	the following week

F. Modification of Place

17. *Look at these sentences :*

Direct	*Indirect*
He said, 'I saw a book *here*.'	He said that he had seen a book *there*.

(i) यहाँ *here* को indirect speech में *there* में बदल दिया गया है।

18. *Look at these sentences :*

Direct	*Indirect*
He said, 'Everybody is *here*.'	He said that everybody was *here*.
Ram said, 'I may go to a film *tomorrow*.'	Ram said that he might go to a film *tomorrow*.

(अगर यह वाक्य Sunday के 3 p.m. में कहा जाए।)	(अगर वही वाक्य Sunday के 5 p.m. में कहा जाए अर्थात उसी दिन कहा जाए।)
He said, 'I bought *this* book for my brother.'	He said that he had bought *the* book for his brother.

(i) ऊपर indirect speech में time तथा place expressions को बदला नहीं गया है।

(ii) अगर कोई व्यक्ति किसी बात को उसी समय या स्थान पर report करे तो time तथा place सूचित करनेवाले शब्द नहीं बदलते। ऐसे शब्दों को बदलते समय अपना common sense लगाना होगा।

Tomorrow को प्रायः *next day* में बदल दिया जाता है किंतु जब speech को उसी दिन report किया जाता है तब *tomorrow* ही रह जाएगा।

(iii) *This* को *that* में बदला जाता है किंतु कभी-कभी *this* तथा *that* की जगह indirect speech में अर्थानुसार *the* का प्रयोग करते हैं।

(iv) अतः, ऐसे शब्दों को बदलने में सावधानी बरतने की जरूरत है। कभी उनके बदलने की जरूरत होती है और कभी नहीं भी।

G. Say/Said, Tell/Told

19. *Look at these sentences :*

Direct	*Indirect*
He *said,* 'Man is mortal.'	He *said* that man is mortal.
She *says,* 'I am ill.'	She *says* that she is ill.
You *said to me,* 'He has lost his pen.'	You *told me* that he had lost his pen.
He *says to me,* 'You are dull.'	He *tells me* that I am dull.

(i) अगर say या said के बाद कोई object नहीं रहे तो indirect speech में *say/said* को change नहीं करते।

(ii) अगर say या said+to+object *(say/said to me)* रहे तो *say* को *tell* में और *said* को *told* में बदल दिया जाता है।

Note :

wrong	*right*
say me	say *to* me
said	said *to* him
tell *to* me	tell me
told *to* her	told her

ध्यान दें : (i) किस verb में *to* लगता है और किसमें नहीं;

(ii) Tell का प्रयोग object (you/me/him/ her/us /Hari इत्यादि) के बिना नहीं होता। अतः, He *told* that he was wrong गलत है। यहाँ *told* की जगह *said* का प्रयोग करें।

(iii) किंतु say या said के बाद to+object का प्रयोग किया जाता है (he said *to me)* या say/said के बाद that-clause लगता है (I say/said *that* he...) Say/ said के तुरत बाद object नहीं लगाना चाहिए। जैसे : he said me गलत है; he said *to* me होना चाहिए।

Statements को Direct से Indirect में बदलने के नियमों का सारांश

(i) *Say* या *said* को अगर आवश्यक हो तो *tell* या *told* में बदल दें अन्यथा उसे छोड़ दें।

(ii) Commas और inverted commas को हटा दें तथा reported speech को *that* से शुरू करें।

(iii) आवश्यकतानुसार reported speech के verb के tense को बदल दें।

(iv) अगर आवश्यक हो तो indirect speech में pronoun तथा determiner को भी बदलें।

(v) आवश्यकतानुसार place तथा time सूचक शब्दों को भी बदलें।

Some more examples

Direct	*Indirect*
Mohan said, '*I am* ill *today.*'	Mohan said *he was* ill *that day.*
Ramu said to Hari, '*I will* write *these* letters *now.*	Ramu *told* Hari that *he would* write *those* letters *then.*

(b) INDIRECT QUESTIONS

1. *Look at these sentences :*

A	*B*
What is this ?	*Are* you a player ?
Who is he ?	*Is* he here ?
Where does he live ?	*Was* she at home ?
How have you come ?	*Do* you run ?
When will she go ?	*Can* they sing ?
Why do you cry ?	*Have* you a car ?

(i) ऊपर A तथा B के नीचे दिए गए वाक्य questions हैं। इन्हें *direct questions* कहा जाता है। जब questions को direct speech से indirect speech में बदला जाता है तब वे *indirect questions* कहलाते हैं। जैसेः He asked *who he was.*

(ii) Questions दो तरह से पूछे जाते हैं :

(a) Who, what, where, how, when, why, whom, whose तथा which का प्रयोग कर। इन्हें *wh-questions* कहते हैं।

(b) Is, are, am, was, were, do, did, does, has, have, had, can, may, should, shall, will इत्यादि का प्रयोग कर जो प्रश्न पूछे जाते हैं उन्हें *yes-no questions* कहते हैं क्योंकि ऐसे questions के उत्तर yes या no में दिए जा सकते हैं। जैसे : 'Are you very ill ?' 'Yes' या 'No'.

Direct Questions को Indirect questions में बदलने के नियम

A. Punctuation

2. *Look at these sentences :*

Direct	*Indirect*
'Where has she gone ?' he asked me.	He asked me where she had gone.
He said, 'Where do you live ?'	He asked (me) where I lived.
She said to Reeta, 'Is it raining ?'	She asked Reeta if it was raining.

(i) Indirect question में inverted commas का प्रयोग नहीं किया जाता।

(ii) Indirect question के अंत में full stop दिया जाता है; question mark (?) नहीं।

(iii) Indirect speech में reporting verb *asked* इत्यादि के बाद comma नहीं दिया जाता।

B. Conjunction : If/Whether

3. *Look at these sentences :*

Direct	*Indirect*
He said, 'Where is the book ?'	He asked me *where* the book was.
She said, 'What is your name ?'	She asked me *what* my name was.
'How far is the station ?' he inquired.	He inquired *how* far the station was.
He said to me, 'When will he sleep ?	He asked me *when* he would sleep.

(i) ऊपर direct speech में *where, what, how* तथा *when* से प्रश्न पूछे गए हैं।

(ii) Indirect speech में where, what, how, when, why, which, who, whom तथा whose से शुरू होनेवाले question के पहले कोई conjunction *(if, whether* या *that)* नहीं लगाया जाता।

4. *Look at these sentences :*

Direct	*Indirect*
He said to me, 'Is Mukul your brother ?'	He asked me *if* Mukul was my brother.

The stranger said, 'Is this an inn ?'	The stranger wanted to know *if* that was an inn.
John said, 'Are the boys playing ?'	John asked (me) *whether* the boys were playing.
She said to me, 'Have you a car ?	She asked me *if I* had a car.
They say, 'Was Hari ill ?'	They ask me *whether* Hari was ill.

(i) ऊपर direct speech में is, are, have तथा was से question पूछे गए हैं।

(ii) Is, are, am, was, were, has, have, had, do, does, did, can, could, may, should, will, shall इत्यादि से शुरू होनेवाले reported question के पहले *if* या *whether* का प्रयोग किया जाता है।

C. Dummy 'Do'

5. *Look at these sentences :*

Direct	*Indirect*
He said, '*Do* they play hockey ?'	He asked me *if* they *played* hockey.
She says, '*Does* he like sweets ?'	She asks me *whether* he *likes* sweets.
Tom says to Mary, '*Did* Hari buy a pen ?'	Tom asks Mary *if* Hari *bought* a pen.

(i) ऊपर direct speech के question *do, does* तथा *did* से शुरू होते हैं। Do के इस रूप को *dummy 'do'* कहा जाता है क्योंकि इसका प्रयोग केवल question form करने के लिए किया जाता है और dummy 'do' का वाक्य में कोई अर्थ नहीं होता।

(ii) Indirect speech में इस dummy 'do' *(do/does/did)* को हटा दिया जाता है और if या *whether* का प्रयोग किया जाता है।

D. Word Order

6. *Look at these sentences :*

Direct (Verb+Subject)	*Indirect (Subject+Verb)*
He says, 'What *is* **she** doing ?'	He asks me what **she** is *doing*.
She said, '*Is* **anyone** there ?	She asked me if **anyone** *was* there.
Rani said, 'Who *are* **they** ?'	Rani asked me who **they** *were*.

(i) ऊपर quotation marks के भीतर direct questions हैं; direct questions में verb *(is, are, am etc.)* पहले आता है और subject (she, he, anyone, they etc.) उसके बाद। Direct question में *verb + subject* का word order रहता है।

(ii) **Indirect speech में direct question को indirect बना दिया जाता है अर्थात subject को पहले और verb को बाद में किया जाता है। Indirect question में *subject + verb* का word order रहता है जैसा हम statement में पाते हैं।**

E. Tenses of Verbs

7. *Look at these sentences :*

Direct	*Indirect*
My father said, 'Where is Tom ?'	My father *asked* me where Tom *was*.
Sima said to me, 'Is the iron hot ?'	Sima *asked* me if the iron *was* hot.
Reskha says to Hari, 'Are you thirsty ?'	Rekha *asks* Hari whether he *is* thirsty.

(i) ऊपर के वाक्यों को पढ़ने से पता चलता है कि अगर reporting verb *(said)* past tense में रहे तो reported speech का verb भी past tense में बदल जाता है। Sequence of Tenses के नियम यहाँ भी लागू होते हैं।

(ii) *Ask/Asked* के बाद अकसर कोई object रहता है। जैसे : Ask *him* his name. He asked *me* for help.

(iii) किंतु *ask/asked* के बाद कभी-कभी object न भी रह सकता है। जैसे : He was *asked* to go there. I must *ask* to be excused.

लेकिन narration change में ask/asked के बाद कोई **object** लग सके तो लगा दें।

जैसे : He asked *me*....she asked *you*.... I ask *her*....इत्यादि।

F. Pronouns, Place and Time

8. *Look at these sentences :*

Direct	*Indirect*
He said to Rani, 'Am *I* ill ?'	*He* asked Rani if *he* was ill.
He said, 'Is it *my* watch ?'	*He* asked me whether it was *his* watch.
Tom said to *me*, 'Will *you* stop ?'	Tom wanted to know of *me* if *I* would stop.
Hari said, 'Is Rekha *coming here this* week ?	Hari enquired of me whether Rekha was *going there that* week.

(i) ऊपर के वाक्यों को पढ़ने से पता चलता है कि indirect speech में pronouns, determiners, place तथा time सूचित करनेवाले शब्दों में भी changes होते हैं।

(ii) Reporting verb *said* की जगह *asked, enquired, wanted to know* आदि का प्रयोग किया जाता है।

(c) INDIRECT COMMANDS

1. *Look at these sentences :*

He said, *'Hurry-up !'*	(Order)
She said, *'Please help me.'*	(Request)
Mukul said, *'Don't shout.'*	(Negative command)

(i) ऊपर दिए गए प्रथम वाक्य से order (आज्ञा), दूसरे से request (अनुरोध) तथा तीसरे से negative command (नकारात्मक आज्ञा) का बोध होता है।

(ii) ऐसे सारे वाक्यों को हम *commands* कहते हैं। अब हम ऐसे वाक्यों के narration change के नियमों को एक-एक कर देखें :

A. Orders

2. *Look at these sentences :*

Direct	*Indirect*
The farmer *said to* Jack, 'Go away !'	The farmer *asked/ordered* Jack *to* go away.
He *said,* 'Hurry up !'	He *asked* me *to* hurry up.
The teacher *said to* Mohan, 'Do it at once.'	The teacher *told/asked/ ordered* Mohan *to* do that at once.
The Principal *said to* him, 'Call the boy.'	The Principal *ordered* him *to* call the boy.

(i) ऊपर inverted commas के भीतर के वाक्यों से order का बोध होता है।

(ii) Indirect speech में अर्थ के अनुसार reporting verb *(say/said)* को *ask/ asked, order/ ordered, tell/ told, command/ commanded* में बदल देना चाहिए।

(iii) Command प्रायः verb (Go, Run, Do, Call, etc.) से शुरू होते हैं। Indirect speech में उनके पहले *to* लगता है।

याद रखें : *to* के बाद आनेवाला verb अपने simple रूप में रहता है। जैसे : *to go, to play, to run, to call, to write* इत्यादि।

(iv) Indirect speech के अंत में full stop दें।

B. Requests

3. *Look at these sentences :*

Direct	*Indirect*
He said, *'Please* give me another chance.'	He *requested* them *to* give him another chance.

She said to me '***Kindly*** **help me.'**	**She** ***asked/requested*** **me** ***to*** **help her.**
Rekha said to Reeta, 'Sing a song, *please.'*	Rekha *asked/ requested* Reeta *to* sing a song.

(i) ऊपर Inverted commas के अंदरवाले वाक्य से request का भाव व्यक्त होता है।

(ii) Indirect speech में reporting verb को *request, ask, tell, beg* इत्यादि में बदल देना चाहिए।

(iii) *Please* तथा *kindly* को indirect speech से हटा दिया जाता है।

(iv) Indirect speech में reporting verb के बाद *to* लगाया जाता है।

C. Negative Commands

4. *Look at these sentences :*

Direct	*Indirect*
He said to the boys, *Don't* make a noise.'	He *asked* the boys *not to* make a noise.
She said to Moti, *'Don't* move.'	She *told* Moti *not to* move.
He said, *'Don't* be foolish.'	He *told* me *not to be* foolish.
Hari said, *'Do not* forget to tell her.'	Hari *told/asked/reminded* me *not to* forget to tell her.
The guide said to the students, *'Please don't* touch the wall.'	The guide *requested/asked* the students *not to* touch the wall.

(i) Inverted commas के अंदर के वाक्य *Don't/Do not* से शुरू होते हैं जो negative commands हैं।

(ii) Indirect speech में *do* को हटा दिया जाता है।

(iii) Negative word *not* को *to* के पहले रखा जाता है।

(iv) *Please/kindly* को भी indirect speech से हटा दिया जाता है।

(d) INDIRECT EXCLAMATION AND WISHES

1. *Look at these sentences :*

Direct	*Indirect*
He said, 'What a pity !'	He *exclaimed that* it was a great pity.
They said, 'How silly of him !	They *exclaimed that* it was very silly of him.
'What a terrible storm it is !' he said.	He *exclaimed that* it was a very terrible storm.

He said, 'How dreadful !'	He *exclaimed that* it was very dreadful.

(i) ऊपर inverted commas के अंदर आए वाक्य exclamatory sentences है जो What a .../How...से शुरू हुए हैं।

(ii) Indirect में reporting verb *said* की जगह *exclaimed* का प्रयोग किया जाता है।

(iii) Indirect में exclamation का भाव statement *(subject + verb)* के रूप में व्यक्त किया जाता है।

(iv) Indirect speech को *that* से प्रारंभ किया जाता है तथा वाक्य के अंत में full stop दिया जाता है।

2. ***Look at these sentences :***

Direct	*Indirect*
The boys said, 'Hurrah ! The cup is ours.'	The boys *exclaimed with joy* that the cup was theirs.
Sethji said, 'Alas ! I am undone.'	Sethji *exclaimed with sorrow* that he was undone.
He said, 'O that I were young again !'	He *eargerly wished* that he were young again.
I said, 'Nonsense !'	I *exclaimed* that it was nonsense.
The teacher said, 'Well done ! my boys.'	The teacher *shouted with applause* that the boys had done well.

(i) Exclamations में प्राय: *Hurrah, Alas, Oh, Heavens, Bravo* इत्यादि शब्द रहते हैं।

(ii) Indirect speech में इन शब्दों को हटा दिया जाता है।

(iii) तथा इनके बदले अर्थ के अनुसार reporting verb का प्रयोग किया जाता है। जैसे *said* के बदले—*exclaimed with joy, exclaimed with sorrow, exclaimed with surprise* इत्यादि प्रयुक्त होते हैं।

(iv) कभी-कभी reporting verb *said* को *cried out, shouted, wished, prayed* इत्यादि में भी बदल दिया जाता है।

3. ***Look at these sentences :***

Direct	*Indirect*
He said, 'May God bless you.'	He *prayed that* God might bless *me.*
My friends said, 'May you succeed in your examination.'	My friends *wished/prayed that* I might succeed in my examination.

He said, 'God save the President.'	He *prayed that* God might save the President.
The audience said, 'Long live the king.'	The audience *wished/prayed that* the king *should* live long.

(i) ऊपर inverted commas के अंदरवाले वाक्यों से desires या wishes (कामना, आशीर्वाद आदि) के भाव व्यक्त होते हैं। ऐसे वाक्य प्रायः *may* से प्रारंभ होते हैं।

(ii) इन्हें indirect में बदलने के लिए reporting verb *(say* etc.) को *wish, pray* आदि में बदल देते हैं।

(iii) Indirect speech को *that* से आरंभ करते हैं।

(iv) Reported speech के शब्द-क्रम को जिसमें verb पहले रहता है और subject बाद में, statement के शब्द-क्रम (subject+verb) में बदल देते हैं।

(v) आवश्यकतानुसार *should, might* का प्रयोग करते हैं।

SUMMARY

Indirect Statements, Questions, Commands and Exclamations

संक्षेप में दुहरा लें :

Indirect statement	:	(a) *that*-clause से शुरू होता है।
Indirect question	:	(a) *wh-clause* से शुरू होता है।
		(b) *if/whether* clause से शुरू होता है।
Indirect command	:	(a) *to* से शुरू होता है।
Indirect exclamation	:	(a) *wh*-clause से शुरू होता है।
		(b) वाक्य के भाव से शुरू होता है।

For example :

Direct	*Indirect*	*Type of Sentence*
(i) He said, 'I write homework every week.'	He said *that he wrote* homework every week.	(i) Statement
(ii) 'When will the plane leave ?' I wondered.	I wondered *when* the *plane would* leave.	(ii) Wh-question
(iii) 'Are you ready ?' asked Tom.	Tom asked *(me) whether I was ready.*	(iii) Yes-no question
(iv) 'Be quiet !' I told him.	I told him *to be quiet.*	(iv) Command
(v) 'How brave you are !' Sita told him.	Sita told him *how brave he was.* *Or,* Sita told him *that he was very brave.*	(v) Exclamation

MISCELLANEOUS SENTENCES

1. Sentences Beginning with Terms of Address in Reported Speech

1. *Look at these sentences :*

Direct	*Indirect*
He said, '*Rajeev,* when is the next train ?"	He asked *Rajeev* when the next train was.
Tara told, '*Brother,* I am going.'	Tara told her *brother* that she was going.
He said, 'Get your coat, *Tom.*'	He told *Tom* to get his coat.
The teacher said, '*Moti,* what are you doing ?'	The teacher asked *Moti* what he was doing.

(i) ऊपर Direct speech में Rajeev, Brother, Tom तथा Moti संबोधन के शब्द (terms of address) हैं।

(ii) Indirect speech में terms of address को reporting verb के बाद रख दिया जाता है।

2. *Look at these sentences :*

Direct : Brutus said, '*Friends, Romans and countrymen,* lend me your ears.'

Indirect : *Addressing the citizens as friends, Romans and countrymen,* Brutus appealed to them to lend him their ears.

Or, Brutus *addressed the citizens as friends, Romans and countrymen* and appealed to them to lend him their ears.

Direct : The chairman said, '*Ladies and gentlemen,* I should thank you all.'

Indirect : *Addressing the public as ladies and gentlemen,* the Chairman said that he should thank them all.

Or, The Chairman addressed the public as ladies and gentlemen and said that he should thank them all.

संबोधन के शब्दों को *Addressing as..*या *Addressed as* का प्रयोग कर indirect speech में लिखा जाता है।

2. Sentences with 'Sir' or 'Madam'

3. *Look at these sentences :*

Direct	*Indirect*
The boy said, '*Sir,* may I go home ?'	The boy *respectfully* asked whether he could go home.

Reeta said to the Headmistress, '*Madam,* I have done my homework.'	Reeta told the Headmistress *respectfully* that she had done her homework.

(i) कभी-कभी reported speech में संबोधन के शब्द *Sir, Madam, Your honour* आदि का प्रयोग होता है। साधारणतः, इनका प्रयोग संबोधित व्यक्ति के प्रति आदर व्यक्त करने के लिए होता है।

(ii) Indirect speech में ऐसे शब्दों को हटा दिया जाता है तथा reporting clause में *respectfully* का प्रयोग किया जाता है।

3. Sentences with 'Yes' or 'No'

4. *Look at these sentences :*

Direct	*Indirect*
He said, 'Can you sing ?' And I said, '*No*'.	He asked me if I could sing and I said that I *couldn't.*
She said, 'Will you have time to do it ?' And I said '*Yes*'.	She asked if I would have time to do it and I said that I *would.*

(i) ऊपर inverted commas के भीतर 'yes' तथा 'no' का प्रयोग है।

(ii) 'Yes' या 'No' में एक पूरा वाक्य छिपा है। जैसे :
'Can you sing ?' I said 'No'. *No = I cannot sing or I cannot.*
'Will you play ?' I said 'Yes'. *Yes = I will play* or *I will.*

(iii) अतः, yes/no को indirect में बदलते समय yes/no को short answer (जैसे : I cannot, I will इत्यादि) में बदल दें।

(iv) फिर आवश्यकतानुसार उसमें pronouns, tense, determiners को change करें।

4. Sentences with Emphatic 'Do'

5. *Look at these sentences :*

Direct	*Indirect*
I said to Rana, '*Do* have a cup of tea.'	I *requested* Rana *to have* a cup of tea.
He said to me, '*Do* write to me soon.'	He *asked/requested* me *to write* to him soon.

(i) ऊपर inverted commas के अंदर *do* का प्रयोग अनुरोध को जोरदार बनाने के लिए किया गया है। इसे *emphatic 'do'* कहते हैं।

(ii) इस *do* को भी *kindly/please* की तरह indirect speech से हटा दिया जाता है।

(iii) *Do* के बाद आनेवाले verb के पहले *to* का प्रयोग करते हैं।

5. Sentences with 'Well', 'You see', 'You know', 'Okay', etc.

6. *Look at these sentences :*

Direct	*Indirect*
The Manager said, *'Well,* what can I do for you ?'	The Manager *wanted to know* what he (Manager) could do for him.
He said to Rani, *'You see,* finish the work quickly.'	He *told Rani to finish* the work quickly.
'Okay,' he said, 'I will come again tomorrow.'	He said that *he would* go again the next day.

(i) कभी-कभी inverted commas के अंदर *well, so, you know, you see, okay* आदि का प्रयोग होता है जिनका वास्तव में कोई विशेष अर्थ नहीं होता।

(ii) Indirect speech में इन शब्दों को हटा दिया जाता है।

6. Sentences with 'must', 'mustn't or needn't'

7. *Look at these sentences :*

Direct	*Indirect*
He said, 'Children *must* obey their parents.'	He said that children *must* obey their parents.
He said, 'One *must* always be careful.'	He said that one *must* always be careful.

जब *must* में नैतिकता, natural law या universal truth का भाव व्यक्त हो तब *must* को indirect speech में बदला नहीं जाता।

8. *Look at these sentences :*

Direct	*Indirect*
He said, 'I must go at once.'	He said that he *had to go at once.*
He said, 'I *must* go next week.'	He said that he *would have to* go the following week.
He says, 'I *must* go tomorrow.'	He says that he *has to* (or *will have to)* go tomorrow.

अगर *must* से present या future meaning व्यक्त हो तो *must* को क्रमशः *had to* तथा *would have to, has to/will have to* में बदल दिया जाता है।

9. *Look at these sentences :*

Direct	*Indirect*
He said to her, 'You *mustn't* tell anyone.'	He told her that she *mustn't* tell anyone.
He said, 'You *needn't* wait.'	He told me that I *needn't* wait.

Mustn't तथा *needn't* को indirect speech में प्रायः नहीं बदला जाता।

7. Sentences with 'would', 'should', 'could', 'might', 'ought'

10. *Look at these sentence :*

Direct	*Indirect*
He said, 'I *would* be there.'	He said that he *would* be there.
She said, 'I *might* be there.'	She said that she *might* be there.
She said, 'I *would* help him if I *could*.'	She said that she *would* help him if she *could*.
'*Could* I use your phone ?' he said.	He asked me if he *could* use my phone.

Would, should, could, might, ought, had better तथा used to को indirect speech में साधारणतः नहीं बदला जाता।

8. Sentences with 'Let'

11. *Look at the following sentences :*

Direct	*Indirect*
He said, '*Let* us go home.'	He *proposed/ suggested* to his friends that they *should* go home.
I said to him, '*Let* us go out for a walk.'	I *proposed* to him that we *should* go out for a walk.

(i) *Let* के कई अर्थ होते हैं। इसका एक अर्थ है : to make a proposal (सलाह, सुझाव देना)।

(ii) यदि *let* से सलाह, सुझाव का भाव व्यक्त हो तो

(a) reporting verb को *proposed* या *suggested* में बदल दें, तथा

(b) *let* के स्थान पर *should* का प्रयोग करें।

12. *Look at the following sentences :*

Direct	*Indirect*
They said to the teacher, '*Let* us go home.'	They *requested* the teacher *to allow* them to go home.
The Headmaster said to the peon, '*Let* the boy come in.'	The Headmaster *ordered* the peon *to allow* the boy to come in.

(i) Let का अर्थ *to allow* (अनुमति देना) भी होता है।

(ii) Indirect speech में reporting verb को *requested* या *ordered* में बदल देते हैं, तथा

(iii) Reported speech को *to* से शुरू करते हैं।

Note : कभी-कभी *let* को Indirect speech में *to let* कर दिया जाता है। जैसे :
Direct : He said to Raman, '*Let* the boy go home.
Indirect : He *ordered* Raman *to let* the boy go home.
Or, He *told* Raman *that* the boy *might be allowed* to go home.

9. Sentences with question tags

13. *Look at these sentences :*

Direct	*Indirect*
He said to me., 'You are going to the cinema, *aren't you ?*'	He *asked* me whether *I was going to the cinema.*
She said to me., 'You didn't break this mirror, *did you ?*'	She *asked* me *whether I had broken the mirror.*

(i) ऊपर inverted commas के अंदर question tags है।
(ii) Indirect speech में question tags को प्रायः छोड़ दिया जाता है।

10. Sentences with 'have to,' 'had to'

14. *Look at these sentences :*

Direct	*Indirect*
He said, 'I *have to* play a match.'	He said that he *had to* play a match.
He said, 'After the lecture I *had* to rush home.'	He said that after the lecture he *had had* to rush home.

(i) Have to को तो indirect speech में सामान्य नियम के अनुसार बदलते है,
(ii) लेकिन *had to* indirect में had had to बन जाता है।

11. Mixed Type

15. *Look at these sentences :*

Direct	*Indirect*
He said, 'I am a student. I have studied for there years.'	He said that he was a student. *He added that* he had studied for three years.
Moti said, 'I have to be back this evening. A friend of mine is coming to see me.'	Moti said that he had to be back that evening. A friend of his was coming to see him.

(i) ऊपर inverted commas के भीतर एक से अधिक statements है।
(ii) Indirect speech में आवश्यकतानुसार वाक्यों में संबंध कायम रखने के लिए *added, further added, went on to say* आदि का प्रयोग किया जाता है।
(iii) कभी-कभी added, further added इत्यादि को छोड़ भी दिया जाता है।

16. *Look at these sentences :*

Direct	*Indirect*
He said, 'Do you know who is coming ?'	He asked (me) if I *knew* who *was* coming.
He said, 'Do you know who killed him ?'	He asked (me) if I *knew* who *had killed* him.

ऐसे वाक्यों को indirect speech में बदलते समय यह याद रखना चाहिए कि इन वाक्यों के दोनों parts के verb का tense change किया जाता है। ('The only point to remember is the *change of tense in* both parts.')

17. *Look at these sentences :*

Direct	*Indirect*
'I didn't know the way. Do you ?' he asked.	He *said* that he didn't know the way and *asked* me *if I* did.
He said, 'Someone is coming. Get behind the door.'	He *said* that someone was coming and *told me to* get behind the door.
She said, 'I am going to the pictures. Where are you going ?'	She *said* that she was going to the pictures and *wanted to know* where I was going.
He said, 'Where is your pen ? I have lost mine.'	He asked me where my pen was *and added that* he had lost his.

(i) ऊपर inverted commas के अंदर statement, question तथा command हैं।

(ii) Indirect speech में बदलते समय प्रत्येक प्रकार के वाक्य के लिए उपयुक्त verb का प्रयोग किया जाता है।

(iii) (a) Statement के लिए *say, tell, explain, remark* आदि।

(b) Question के लिए *ask, enquire, want to know* आदि।

(c) Command के लिए *tell, ask, order, request* आदि।

(iv) Indirect speech में question + statement या command को प्रायः *adding that......* से जोड़ा जाता है।

Examples Worked Out

Change the following into indirect speech :

Direct	*Indirect*
1. Mukul says, 'I am going to Delhi.'	Mukul says *that he* is going to Delhi.
2. Rana says, 'Sita will dance.'	Rana says *that* Sita will dance.
3. He said, 'I will try it.'	He said that *he would* try it.'

	Direct	*Indirect*
4.	She said, 'I don't like this.'	She said that *she didn't* like that.
5.	He said, 'My mother cooks our breakfast.'	He said that *his* mother *cooked* *their* breakfast.
6.	She said, 'He is taking his examination.'	She said that he *was* taking his examination.
7.	He said, 'I have finished the work.'	He said that he *had* finished the work.
8.	He said, 'Hari has been giving us very good milk.'	He said that Hari *had been* giving *them* very good milk.
9.	Mr Jha said, 'I saw the Taj Mahal.'	Mr Jha said that he *had seen* the Taj Mahal.
10.	She said, 'I had waited for the bus for an hour.'	She said that she *had* waited for the bus for an hour.
11.	The boys said, 'We were watching the game.'	The boys said that *they had been watching* the game.
12.	He said, 'God is everywhere.'	He said that God *is* everywhere.
13.	Mohan will say, 'I want two persons to help me.'	Mohan will say that *he wants* two persons to help *him*.
14.	He said, 'I can do it myself.'	He said that *he could* do it *himself*.
15.	He said, 'We must wait for the result.'	He said that we *must* (or, *had to*) wait for the result.
16.	I said, 'I am tired.'	I said that I *was* tired.
17.	He said to me, 'You may go.'	He told me that I *might* go.
18.	Tom said to me, 'I shall meet you at the station.'	Tom *told* me that he would meet *me* at the station.
19.	He said, 'Man is mortal.'	He said that man *is* mortal.
20.	He said to me, 'Where is your book ?'	He *asked* me *where* my book *was*.
21.	He said to me, 'What is your name ?	He *asked* me what my name *was*.
22.	He said to me, 'Do you know the way ?'	He *enquired of* me *if I knew* the way.
23.	The teacher said to me, 'What are you doing ?'	The teacher *asked* me *what I was doing*.
24.	He asked, 'What is the time ?'	He asked (me) *what the time was*.
25.	Mohan asked, 'Are the boys here ?'	Mohan asked (me) *whether* the boys were there.
26.	Reeta asked, 'Where were you ?'	Reeta asked (me) where I *had been*.
27.	'Can you see me tomorrow ?' he asked me.	He asked me *if I could see him the next day*.

Direct	Indirect
28. He said, 'Is Raju your brother ?'	He asked (me) *whether* Raju was his brother.
29. He said, 'Good morning.'	He *wished* me a *good morning.*
30. He said to his servant, 'Leave my house at once.'	He *ordered* his servant *to leave* his house at once.
31. He said, 'May God bless you.'	He *prayed that God might bless* me.
32. I said, 'Go home.'	I *asked (ordered/told)* him to go home.
33. He said, 'Has Ramesh spent all the money ?'	He *wanted to know* (or, *enquired*) *if Ramesh had spent all the money.*
34. The teacher said to the boys, 'Take back your books.'	The teacher *asked* the boys *to take* back *their* books.
35. He said, 'Lie down, Mukul.'	He *told Mukul to* lie down.
36. He said, 'Please say anything about it.'	He *asked me* to tell anything about it.
37. He said, 'Don't move, boys.'	He *told the boys* not to move.
38. 'Please grant me leave for a day,' the peon said to the Principal.	The peon requested the Principal *to grant* him leave for a day.
39. 'Don't let anybody in,' said the master to the servant.	The master *ordered (told)* the servant *not to let* anybody in.
40. 'What a beautiful view !' my friend said.	My friend *exclaimed that it was a very beautiful view.*
41. He said, 'What a lovely garden ?'	He *remarked what a lovely garden it was.*
42. 'What a terrible storm it is !' he said.	He *exclaimed that* it *was a very* terrible storm.
43. He said, 'Good-bye, my friend.'	He *bade* good-bye *to* his friend.
44. He said, 'God save the King.'	He *prayed that* God might save the King.
45. They said, 'Hurrah ! We have won the cup.'	They *exclaimed with delight that* they had won the cup.
46. He said, 'Bravo ! You have done well.'	He *applauded (or praised) him saying* that he had done well.
47. Moti said, 'Alas ! I am undone.'	Moti *exclaimed with sorrow* that he was undone.
48. 'Hello ! How are you ?' he said.	He greeted *me* and asked *me* how I was.
49. She said, 'Alas !' How foolish I have been.'	She *confessed with regret that* she had been very foolish.

	Direct	*Indirect*
50.	He said, 'Farewell, my countrymen.'	*He bade farewell to* his countrymen.
51.	He said, 'May God bless her with long life and prosperity.'	He *prayed* that *God* might bless her with long life and prosperity.
52.	'Oh dear ! I have lost my money.' he said.	He *exclaimed that* he had lost his money.
53.	'What a lot of food there is to eat !' she said.	She *exclaimed what a lot of food there was to eat.* Or, *She exclaimed that there was a lot of food to eat.*
54.	He said, I'll come here again tomorrow.'	He said that he would *go there* again *the next day*.
55	The teacher said to the boys, 'Don't write on both sides.'	The teacher asked the boys *not to* write on both sides.
56.	The clerk said to the Manager, 'Please don't refuse leave to me.'	The clerk *requested* the Manager *not to* refuse leave to him.
57.	He said, 'Congratulations.'	He *congratulated* me.
58.	He said, 'You needn't wait.'	He told me that I *needn't* wait.
59.	He said, 'Hello ! Where are you going ?'	He *greeted me* and asked me where *I was going*.
60.	He said, 'Let me have some tea.'	He *wished that* he *might* have some tea.
61.	Ali said to his friends, 'Let me do my work, please.'	Ali *requested* his friends *that he might be allowed* to do his work.
62.	She said to us, 'Let us have some music.'	She *proposed (or suggested)* to us that *we should* have some music.
63.	He said to me, 'Please wait here till I return.'	He *requested* him *to* wait *there* till *he* returned.
64.	He said, 'After the class I had to return home.'	He said that after the class he *had had to* return home.
65.	He said, 'Thank you.'	He *thanked* me.
66.	He said, 'Curse the fog.'	He *cursed* the fog.
67.	He said, 'Happy Christmas.'	He *wished* me a happy Christmas.
68.	He said, 'Liar.'	He *called* me a liar.
69.	He said, 'Do you like it ?' She said, 'Yes.'	He *asked* her if she liked it *and* she said *that she did.*
70.	He said, 'Let's go.'	{He *suggested going.* He *suggested that* they should go.
71.	'Let me go !' the boy said to the policeman.	The boy *asked* the policeman *to let* him go.
72.	He said, 'You must be silent.'	He asked me *to be* silent.

	Direct	*Indirect*
73.	He said, 'What a fool Tom is !'	He *exclaimed* that Tom was a big fool.
74.	The teacher asked the boys, 'Where do you want to go !'	The teacher asked the boys where *they wanted* to go.
75.	'Why does the child cry ?' Mr Shinha asked his servant.	Mr Sinha asked his servant why the *child cried.*
76.	'What a nice man Mr Prasad is !' one of the guests at the party said.	One of the guests at the party *remarked with appreciation* that Mr prasad was a very nice man.
77.	He said, 'Thank you very much for your help.'	He thanked *me (him)* very much for *my (his)* help.
78.	He said, 'Do you know who is coming ?'	He asked (me) if *I knew* who *was* coming.
79.	She said, 'I've lost my key. Can I borrow yours ?'	She said that she had lost her key and *asked* me whether *she could* borrow *mine.*
80.	He said, 'Will you come out with me ?' 'No,' I said.	He *asked me* if I would go out with him *but* I *said* I *wouldn't.*
81.	He asked me, 'Do you like this ?' and I said 'Yes.'	He asked (me) if I liked it *and* I *said (that) I did.*
82.	He asked, 'Are you a student ?' and I said, 'No.'	He asked (me) *if I* was a student and I said *that I wasn't.*
83.	The teacher said, 'Don't sleep late and miss the train.'	The teacher *advised (warned)* us not *to* sleep late and miss the train.
84.	Prospero said, 'Can you remember a time before you came to this cell ? I think you cannot, for you were not then three years of age.'	Prospero *asked* (her) whether she could remember a time before she had come to that cell. He *further added that* he thought she could not, for she was not then three years of age.
85.	She called out angrily, 'So you have been hitting Makhan again ?' Phatik answered indignantly, 'No, I havn't; who told you that ?'	She called out angrily and *asked (him) whether* he *had been hitting* Makhan again. Phatik answered indignantly that he hadn't. He *further asked* (her) who told *her* that.
86.	The robber said to Alexander, 'I am thy captive; I must hear what thou art pleased to say, and	The robber *told* Alexander *that* he was his captive and *that* he must *hear* what he (Alexander) was

	Direct	*Indirect*
	endure what thou art pleased to inflict.'	pleased to say and *that* he (must) endure what he was pleased to inflict.
87.	The teacher became angry and said to the student, 'Why have you disturbed the class again ? I have told you before that you should be silent when I am speaking. Leave the room and do not return again today.'	The teacher became angry and *asked* the student why *he had disturbed the class again. He further said* he had told him before that he should be silent when he (teacher) was speaking. *He ordered him* to leave the room. and not to return again *that day*.

EXERCISE 1

Fill in the blanks with the correct tense of the verb given in brackets :

EXAMPLE : We felt that she ....miss the the train. *(may)*
= We felt that she *might* miss the train.

1. We felt that she.....miss the train. (*may*)
2. I thought that you....me yesterday. (*see*)
3. He said that he ......go to Delhi soon. (*will*)
4. When I saw her, I.....to her. (*speak*)
5. I was told that he ....better now. (*is*)
6. Is there anything that I......do for you ? (*can*)
7. He was surprised when he............... the story. (*hear*)
8. He ordered that the window.........be opened. (*shall*)
9. He told me how dangerous the journey.............. (*is*)
10. I was ready when they..........me. (*call*)
11. It was twelve o'clock last night when I...........to bed. (*go*)
12. I did not know whether he...........it or not. (*like*)
13. They said that the teacher had...........him. (*pardon*)
14. She said that she..........never heard of the place. (*have*)
15. I hope you...........be punctual. (*will*)
16. I wrote to find out whether the car.........arrived. (*have*)
17. He asked me why I..........to go there. (*wish*)
18. He did not say when he............come. (*will*)
19. Did you know what his name.......... (*is*)
20. The teacher said that the earth........round the sun. (*move*)

EXERCISE 2 (Statements)

Change the following statements into indirect speech :

EXAMPLE : She said, 'I want a dictionary.'
= She said *that she wanted* a dictionary.

1. She said, 'I want a dictionary.'
2. You said, 'I shall leave at twelve o'clock.'
3. They said, 'We can speak English.'

4. He says, 'I am too busy to help you.'
5. He has just said to me, 'I have been very busy this week.'
6. I shall say to him, 'I cannot give you the money.'
7. He said, 'I write home every week.'
8. She said to me, 'I am learning English.'
9. Tom said, 'I shall see her in London.'
10. Hari said to me, 'I may be able to run.'
11. She said to Reeta, 'I don't write every week.'
12. He said, 'I wrote a letter to my friend.'
13. The boy said, 'I have been playing cricket.'
14. I said, 'I get up at 6 o'clock every morning.'
15. She said to me, 'I bring my book every day.'
16. The teacher said, 'I will see these boys now.'
17. The saint said, 'God is everywhere.'
18. Rekha said, 'I want to become a doctor.'
19. He said, 'I bought a car in Calcutta.'
20. They said, 'Ramu was swimming in the river.'

EXERCISE 3 (statements)

Change the following statements into indirect speech :

EXAMPLE : The boy said, 'Mother, I am hungry.'
= The boy *told his mother* that he was hungry.

1. The boy said, 'Mother, I am hungry.'
2. He said, 'Rekha, I am going to school.'
3. He said, 'I had a wonderful dream last night.'
4. She said, 'Rani will be in Delhi on Monday.'
5. 'I never eat meat,' he explained.
6. He said, 'Reeta arrived on Sunday.'
7. I said, 'I like my house.'
8. 'You have taken my pen, Rajeev,' he said.
9. He said, 'We will discuss the matter tomorrow.'
10. 'I'll do it today,' he promised.
11. She said, 'My father died a year ago.'
12. At breakfast this morning he said, 'I'll be very busy today.'
13. She said, 'You can sit here, Mohan.'
14. He said, 'I wrote three letters yesterday.'
15. 'I shall not wait for more than five minutes,' she said.
16. He said, 'I will come as soon as I can.'
17. 'You have all done very well in the test,' the teacher said to the boys.
18. 'Those who have written the essay can go home,' the teacher said.
19. 'If it rains we will have to cancel the match,' the captain said.
20. She said, 'We are very busy now but we shall have more time next week.'

EXERCISE 4 (Questions)

Change the following questions into indirect speech :

EXAMPLE : He said to me, 'Where are you going?'
= He *asked* me *where I was* going.

1. He said to me, 'Where are you going?'

2. The teacher said to me, 'What are you doing ?'
3. Ahmad said to me, 'When will you return ?'
4. The old man said to me, 'Where do you live ?'
5. My friend said to Radhika, 'When do you start for school ?'
6. The teacher said to his pupils, 'Why have you made a noise like this ?'
7. Mohan asked, 'Where were you ?'
8. He asked, 'What time is it ?'
9. She asked, 'How old is he ?'
10. 'Where is the bus-stand ?' he inquired.
11. He said, 'What have you got in your bag ?'
12. She said, 'Madan, when is the next train ?'
13. She said to Tom, 'What do you want ?'
14. He said, 'How many brothers have you ?'
15. The teacher said to me, 'Why do they go to Delhi ?'
16. She said, 'Who has broken this cup ?'
17. The teacher said, 'Ruby, what are you doing ?'
18. The peon said to the visitor, 'Whom do you want to see ?'
19. Mr Jha said to me, 'Whose answer are you writing ?'
20. My father said to him, 'When does the postman come every day ?'

EXERCISE 5 (Questions)

Change the following questions into indirect speech :

EXAMPLE : I said to her, 'Did you go away last year ?'
= I *asked* her *whether (if) she had gone* away *the previous year.*

1. I said to her, 'Did you go away last year ?'
2. Sima said, 'Is the Headmaster in the office ?'
3. He said to me, 'Are you going to the cinema ?'
4. She said to Rekha, 'Do you play tennis ?'
5. The teacher said, 'Has Mukul many friends ?'
6. He said to me, 'Can Amar speak English ?'
7. Mr Gupta said to me, 'Will you help me ?'
8. He said, 'Did you see Mukul at the football match ?'
9. The teacher said to me, 'Did you do all the exercises correctly ?'
10. My father said, 'Have you done your homework ?'
11. Tom said, 'Will you come and play badminton with me ?'
12. 'Have you no manners ?' shouted the woman angrily.
13. 'Do you write a good hand ?' asked the teacher.
14. 'Is anyone there ?' he asked.
15. 'Will you post this letter for me ?' he said.
16. 'Shall we meet at the station ?' they said.
17. Rani asked, 'Are the boys here ?'
18. 'Is this seat reserved ?' he asked me.
19. 'May I come in ?' the student asked the teacher.
20. The doctor said to the patient, 'Do you have a headache ?'

EXERCISE 6 (Commands)

Change the following commands into indirect speech :

EXAMPLE : The teacher said to the students, 'Write your answers soon.'
= The teacher *told* the students *to write their* answers soon.

1. The teacher said to the students, 'Write your answers soon.'
2. He said to me, 'Give me your pen.'
3. He said to the boys, 'Do not make a noise.'
4. I said to the teacher, 'Please explain the question to me.'
5. He said to his servant, 'Leave my house at once.'
6. 'Shoot the enemy,' said the Captain.
7. He said to me, 'Do try your luck.'
8. 'Waiter, please bring me a cup of tea,' said the man.
9. He said, 'Don't say a word.'
10. He said, 'Never talk to me again.'
11. The boy said to the teacher, 'Please mark me present.'
12. My father said, 'Work hard, if you want to get a first division.'
13. I said, 'Go home.'
14. He said, 'Get your book, Mahesh.'
15. He said, 'Go away.'
16. She said, 'Please say nothing about it.'
17. He said, 'Don't move, boys.'
18. 'Don't go near the fire, children,' she said.
19. 'Stop taking medicines,' I said.
20. I said, 'Don't leave the place without my permission.'

EXERCISE 7 (Commands)

Change the following commands into indirect speech :

EXAMPLE : He said to me, 'Do write to me soon.'
= He *asked (requested)* me *to write* to him soon.

1. He said to me, 'Do write to me soon.'
2. She said to Rekha, 'Switch the radio on, please.'
3. They said, 'Don't shut the door.'
4. 'Keep quiet,' said the mother to the child.
5. 'Please take me to the Principal,' said the visitor.
6. He said, 'Please let me go.'
7. She said, 'Let us have a picnic on Sunday.'
8. 'Tell the truth,' the teacher said to the boy.
9. 'Do forgive me,' said Rana to Sita.
10. He said, 'Mohan, sit still.'
11. I said to her, 'Please shut the door.
12. He said to the servant, 'Please bring me some hot water.'
13. The officer gave the order, 'Fire !'
14. He said to me, 'Please, wait until I come back.'
15. He said, 'Don't open the door.'
16. He said, 'Please, please give me another chance.'
17. He said, 'Be quiet and listen to my words.'
18. They shouted, 'Let them go.'

19. He said to me, 'Take a look at yourself in the mirror.'
20. The teacher said, 'Write your name clearly on the blackboard.'

EXERCISE 8 (Exclamations)

Change the following exclamations and wishes into indirect speech :

EXAMPLES : (i) He said, 'Alas ! I am ruined.'

= He *exclaimed with sorrow* that he was ruined.

(ii) She said, 'What a fine picture it is !'

= She *exclaimed with joy* that it was a very fine picture.

1. He said, 'Alas ! I am ruined.'
2. She said, 'What a fine picture it is !'
3. He said, 'Ah ! He is dead.'
4. Sita said, 'How clever I am !'
5. He said, 'Bravo ! You have done well.'
6. She said, 'Good-bye, my brother.'
7. He said, 'Alas ! How foolish I have been !'
8. He said to her, 'May you succeed.'
9. She cried, 'O that I were dead !'
10. They said, 'Hurrah ! We have won the match.'
11. He said to me, 'May God bless you.'
12. The audience said, 'Long live the President.'
13. We said, 'What a pity !'
14. They said, 'How foolish of him !'
15. The boy said, 'Wish you a happy journey !'
16. He said, 'What a fool Sima is !'
17. The teacher said to the boys, 'Well done !'
18. I said, 'Enough !'
19. He said, 'Thank you !'
20. He said, 'Happy New year !'

EXERCISE 9 (Revision)

Change the following (miscellaneous) sentences into indirect speech :

EXAMPLE : He said, 'We must all die.'

= He said *that we must* all die.

1. He said, 'We must all die.'
2. He said, 'Where is the station ?'
3. He said, 'The horse died in the night.'
4. John said to me, 'Go there.'
5. He said, 'Man is mortal.'
6. Ram said to me, 'You are a coward.'
7. He said to me, 'Why did you not come ?'
8. He said to me, 'Work steadily.'
9. He said to them all, 'Good-bye, my friends.'
10. The teacher said, 'The earth is round.'
11. I said to him, 'Will you follow me ?'
12. He said to the students, 'Do not sit there.'
13. He has told them, 'I did not make this mistake.'

14. **The old man said to me, 'May you live long !'**
15. **He said, 'The dog died yesterday.'**
16. **He said to me, 'Have you done this work ?'**
17. **The poet said, 'How beautiful the sunrise is !'**
18. **She said to him. 'Please give me a book.'**
19. **Akbar said to us, 'Let us play.'**
20. **He said to Abhoy, 'Why do you weep ?'**

EXERCISE 10 (Revision)

Change the following into indirect speech :

EXAMPLES : (i) "Please, please, do as I say," I said.
= I *begged* him to do as I said.
(ii) "Welcome home, my dear," said his wife.
= His wife *welcomed* him warmly.

1. "What a fool I am !" said she.
2. "Don't go out in the sun," cried the mother.
3. The woman said, "May you die of cholera."
4. Sita said, "I didn't know it was your table."
5. He said to him, " Isn't your name Jones ?"
6. "What makes you cry ?" asked her sister.
7. "Go there at once," said the Lieutenant.
8. I said to him, "It was raining last night when you left."
9. "Stop ! Wait for me !" he said to me.
10. The young sparrow said, "Mother, what is that queer object ?"
11. The prince said, "It gives me great pleasure to be here this evening."
12. He said, "I shall go as soon as it is possible."
13. He said, "I do not wish to see any of you, go away."
14. He said, "The rainy season lasts for four months."
15. "What is the matter ?" my aunt asked.
16. "Bring them here quickly, Anil," said Rajendra.
17. He said, "Where shall I be in 1990 ?"
18. "Take your things and be gone !" he ordered.
19. He said, "Alas ! What a fool I was !"
20. "Who are you, Sir, and why have you come here ?" they said to the stranger.

EXERCISE 11 (Revision)

Change the following into indirect speech :

EXAMPLE : He said, "Good-bye, my friend."
= He *bade* good-bye to his friend.

1. He said to me, "You alone can save her."
2. Tom said, "Mother, I am in a hurry."
3. "Hurrah ! We have overtaken them," said the boys.
4. He said, "Please let me go."
5. She said, "Let us have a picnic on Saturday."
6. He said, "Sudhir was swimming in the pool."
7. "Have you done your homework ?" the teacher asked.
8. He said, "Where can I get an application form ?"

9. He said, 'How many brothers have you ?'
10. 'Keep quiet,' said the mother to the child.
11. 'Where do you live and where are you going ?' asked the fellow passenger.
12. The old man said, 'O, that I could see my dear son !'
13. 'You have done it very badly,' remarked the teacher.
14. He said, 'Will you listen to such a man ?'
15. The teacher said to us, 'The prizes will be presented tomorrow.'
16. He said, 'May God pardon this sinner.'
17. He said to his teacher, 'Sir, I am a poor boy.'
18. The Holy Bible says. 'Do not steal.'
19. The man said, 'Ah ! the poor man is undone.'
20. He said, 'Who has stolen my book ?'

EXERCISE 12

Change the following sentences into indirect speech :

EXAMPLE : He said, 'Good heavens ! What you have done !'
= He *exclaimed* what he had done.
Or, He *exclaimed with sorrow that* he had done it badly.

1. He said, 'Good heavens ! What you have done !'
2. My friend said to me, 'Please lend me a rupee.'
3. He said to us, 'Are you going away today ?'
4. Ram said to me, 'I met your friend yesterday.'
5. The teacher said to the boys, 'The earth moves round the sun.'
6. The captain said to the sailor, 'Leave the cabin at once.'
7. Mannu said to him, 'You are a liar.'
8. Madhu said to his friend, 'Please lend me your book.'
9. Suman said to me, 'You are a coward.'
10. 'Keep quiet,' said the mother to the child.
11. 'Let the gate be left open,' said the Commander.
12. The father said, 'Light runs faster than sound.'
13. You said to me, 'I went to Patna last week.'
14. The man said, 'Alas ! What a fool I have been.'
15. 'May I have a little more sugar ?' said the girl.
16. She said to her husband, 'What is it that makes you so sad and gloomy ?'
17. 'Good-bye, father,' said Tom, as he got into the train.
18. The teacher said to the students, 'Why have you disturbed other classes ?'

EXERCISE 13

Change the following dialogues into indirect speech :

EXAMPLE : (a) Ruby said to Reeta, 'Are you coming with me ?'
(b) Reeta said, 'Yes.'
= Ruby *asked* Reeta *whether* she *was going* with her.
Reeta *replied* that she was.

1. (a) Ruby said to Reeta, 'Are you coming with me ?'
   (b) Reeta said, 'Yes.'
2. (a) The teacher asked the student, 'Who is the President of America ?'
   (b) The student said, 'I don't know, Sir.'

3. (a) **My father asked me, 'Why are you so worried ?'**
   (b) **I said, 'I have an examination tomorrow.'**
4. (a) **The teacher asked me, 'How well can you speak English ?'**
   (b) **I said, 'Not like an Englishman.'**
5. (a) **Shylock said to Portia, 'Is that the law ?'**
   (b) **Portia said, 'Yes.'**
6. (a) **The Judge said, 'What is your situation in life ?'**
   (b) **The witness said, 'A labourer, my lord nothing but a day labourer.'**
7. (a) **My father said to me, 'Where has Amrit gone ?'**
   (b) **I said, 'To school.'**
8. (a) **Rajeev said to Mukul, 'Will the radio work ?'**
   (b) **Mukul said, 'No.'**
9. (a) **Mohan said, 'May I borrow your bicycle, Lalan ?'**
   (b) **Lalan said, 'Yes, but it is not in good order.'**
10. (a) **The stranger said to Ramu, 'Can you tell me which is the road to the station ?'**
    (b) **Ramu said, 'Well, I am myself a new man here.'**
11. (a) **He said to me, 'Will you help me ?'**
    (b) **I said, 'Yes, gladly.'**
12. **(Mrs Sen, newly married, has just employed Anita, a young village girl, as a servant :)**
    (a) **Anita : How do you make a cup of tea ?**
    (b) **Mrs Sen : First of all put some cold water in the kettle.**
    (c) **Anita : Which kettle should I use ?**
    (d) **Mrs Sen : Use the small one.**
    (e) **Anita : What should I do now ?**
    (f) **Mrs Sen : Put in two spoons of tea.**
    (g) **Anita : And then ?**
    (h) **Mrs Sen : When the water boils, pour the boiling water into the tea-pot.**

EXERCISE 14

Change the following into indirect speech :

EXAMPLE : *Direct :* They said to me, 'We have just arrived in the town. Can you tell me the name of a good hotel ?'

Indirect : They *told* me that they had just arrived in the town *and asked* me whether I could give them the name of a good hotel.

[Note : (i) कभी-कभी direct speech में एक से अधिक sentences रहते हैं।

(ii) अगर direct speech में statements, questions, commands तथा exclamations हों तो हमें प्रत्येक part के लिए अलग-अलग reporting verb (tell, say, ask, order, exclaim etc.) का प्रयोग करना चाहिए।

(iii) Indirect speech में, अगर संभव हो, तो उन वाक्यों को and, add, go on इत्यादि का प्रयोग कर जोड़ दिया जा सकता है।]

1. They said to me, 'We have just arrived in the town. Can you tell me the name of a good hotel ?'
2. He said, 'What is the time ? I don't want to be late.'
3. My friend said to me, 'Are you doing anything this evening ? Let us go and have a talk somewhere.'

4. **He said to me, 'Please ask Ranjan to take a seat. I shall be coming in a moment.'**
5. **The teacher said, 'Do keep quiet for a moment, children. I am going to answer the telephone.'**
6. **He said, 'What kind of man is your brother ? I hope he is as kind as you are.'**
7. **The teacher said to Moti, 'Get out of the class. You ought to be ashamed of yourself.'**
8. **He said, 'Why does she wear that coat ? I can't stand that colour.'**
9. **He said to Hari, 'Good boy, labour hard to become first in the next chance, you needn't lose heart.'**
10. **Antonio said to Bassanio, 'My dear friend, I can spare my wife, my life and everthing for you. Be bold and face life.'**
11. **An old lion said to a fox, 'Please come near me in my cave. Come, let us talk of your health.'**
12. **The astrologer said to Mintu, 'Take your child dressed in red to the river and bathe him. After that throw away the red clothes into the river.'**
13. **He asked, 'What time is it ? My watch has stopped.'**
14. **He asked, 'How old is he ? Can he read yet ?'**
15. **Dasharath said to Vishwamitra, 'Please do not insist on taking Ram and Lakshman with you. I am prepared to send my whole army with you.'**
16. **The father said to the child, 'Don't waste your time. Work hard to get success at the examination.'**
17. **The father said to his son, 'Didn't I tell you to attend your school regularly ? Why do you keep away from school two days in a week ? You think that it is no use going to school.'**
18. **The teacher said to me very angrily, "Why have you come ? Have I not told you never to see my face again ? Either leave the room at once or stand up on the bench.'**

EXERCISE 15

Use the sentences given below the paragraph and fill in the gaps numbered 1 to 4. (Use the appropriate reported speech.) :

EXAMPLE : The Headmaster asked Mohan......[1] ...and the boy said.....[2]..... Then the Headmaster enquired whether....[3].......Mohan answered that.....[4]..

1. 'How old are you ?'
2. 'Fifteen and a half.'
3. 'Do you know what you want to do if you leave school ?'
4. 'I want to join the Army.'

Ans. The Headmaster asked Mohan *how old he was* and the boy said *that he was fifteen and a half.* Then the Headmaster enquired *whether he knew what he wanted to do if he left school.* Mohan answered that *he wanted to join the Army.*

1. When the Headmaster discovered that one of the boys in his class, Mohan, had been playing truant, he called him to his office. He looked at the boy sternly and asked him......[1]....Mohan replied that......[2] ....The Headmaster looked astonished and asked him........[3].......Mohan explained......[4]........

   1. 'What did you run away for ?'
   2. 'I don't know.'
   3. 'What do you mean ?'
   4. 'I haven't any particular reason.'

2. The Headmaster thought for a moment and asked Mohan whether.....[1]..... Mohan said that......[2]........because he had to join the army. The Headmaster remarked that.....[3]........He went on to say, however, that.....[4]......

1. 'Do you like school ?'
2. 'I don't like school and want to leave.'
3. 'Perhaps that is the best thing you can do.'
4. 'I am still going to punish you for taking the law into your own hands.'

3. One day an old man called me and asked me.......1.........I told him that........2 ....Then he asked me whether.....3.....I replied to him that.......4..........

1. 'Who are you ?'
2. 'I am a student.'
3. 'Do you know English ?'
4. 'Yes.'

4. Sometime ago Ramesh applied for the post of clerk in a bank. Last Monday he was called for an interview. When he went into the Manager's office, the Manager told him.....1...........and asked him.....2........ Ramesh told him.........3............ Then the Manager asked him......4.......

1. Please sit down.'
2. 'What is your name ?'
3. 'My name is Ramesh.'
4. 'Do you take tea '?

5. The Manager of the bank asked Ramesh.....1...Ramesh replied to him.....2... Then the Manager wanted to know....3...and Ramesh repied....4....

1. 'Do you know typewriting ?'
2. 'I am good at typewriting.'
3. 'Where have you worked before ?'
4. 'I worked for six months in a private firm.'

6. The Manager asked Ramesh........1 ....and Ramesh replied........2........The Manager gave him a test and said........3........Ramesh said......4.....

1. 'Can you type a letter ?'
2. 'Yes, I can.'
3. 'You have done very well, Ramesh.'
4. 'Thank you, Sir.'

7. The Manager was pleased with Ramesh. Ramesh asked......1.......The Manager replied that he could start.......2.......and Ramesh promised......3.......Then the Manager said......4.......

1. 'When shall I start work ?'
2. 'As soon as you wish.'
3. 'I will be here on Friday.'
4. 'I have no objection to it.'

8. A man went into a restaurant and ordered a cup of tea. He got the tea. He had a sip and then he shouted.......1......... The waiter asked him politely......2........ The man replied.......3....... The waiter said......4........

1. 'Is this tea or coffee ?'
2. 'What does it taste like ?'
3. 'Kerosene.'
4. 'Then it must be coffee.'

9. One morning Akbar, Prince Salim and Birbal went to the bank of a river. A few minutes later Akbar said........1..........Birbal put his hand into the water and said......2........ Akbar and Salim gave their clothes to Birbal. Akbar said to Prince Salim.......3.......Birbal bowed his head and respectfully said......4.........

1. 'Shall we go and bathe in the river ?'
2. 'I don't like to bathe.'
3. 'Birbal looks like a washerman's donkey.'
4. 'No, Sir, I am carrying the loads of two donkeys.'

EXERCISE 16 (with Answer)

1. Rewrite the following sentences in Indirect speech :

(a) He said to me, "I have often told you not to play with fire." (b) "My children, this is the last lesson I shall give you," said the teacher. (c) "Go to your place quickly," his brother said. (d) The minister said, "It gives me great pleasure to be here this evening." (e) "Alas ! my dear son, why do you ask for the thing I cannot grant you ?"

2. Rewrite the following sentences in indirect speech :

(a) "What a rare article milk is in London !" said Mohan with a sigh. (b) He said, "Daughter, sit down at the desk and stay there until your work is finished." (c) He demanded of me, "When will you mend your ways ?" (d) The teacher said to the student, "Did you solve that question yesterday ?" (e) The judge said, "You must have stolen the money."

3. Complete the following sentences using the Indirect form of narration for the words given in brackets :

(a) He remarked...................... ("What a great discovery !") (b) The teacher asked the girl...............("Why didn't you complete your work in time ?") (c) My friend asked me..............("Can you remember when you last heard that tune ?") (d) I was told..............("When you get there, enter the second room.") (e) The headmaster told her..............("You must have stolen the money before you left the hostel.")

4. Turn the following into Indirect speech :

He wrote and said, "I am unable to come just now because I am ill, but I will certainly start as soon as I am well enough to do so. I am greatly looking forward to meeting you both soon."

5. Turn the following into Indirect speech :

"What shall I bring you when I return ?" said the Merchant to his daughters.

"Papa, I want a new dress," cried each of the elder sisters.

"And you Beauty, what would you have ?" Beauty said very quietly, "A rose, father, just a beautiful rose, if you can find one."

Ans. 1. (a) He reminded me that he had often told me not to play with fire. (b) The teacher told the children that it was the last lesson he would give them. (c) His brother ordered him to go to his place quickly. (d) The minister said that it gave him great pleasure to be there that evening. (e) The father told his son with sorrow that he asked for the thing that he (father) could not grant him.

2. (a) Mohan exclaimed with a sigh that milk was a very rare article in London. (b) He told his daughter to sit down at the desk and stay there until her work was finished, (c) He demanded of me when I would mend my ways. (d) The teacher asked the student whether he had solved that question the previous day. (e) The judge told him that he must have stolen the money.

3. (a) He remarked with surprise that it was a great discovery. (b) The teacher asked the girl why she had not completed her work in time. (c) My friend asked me if I could remember when I had last heard that tune. (d) I was told when I got there, I should enter the second room. (e) The headmaster told her that she must have stolen the money before she had left the hostel.

4. He wrote and said that he was unable to come just then because he was ill, but he would certainly start as soon as he was well enough to do so. He added that he was greatly looking forward to meeting them soon.

5. The Merchant asked his daughters what he would bring them when he returned. Each of the elder sisters told her Papa that she wanted a new dress. Then the Merchant asked Beauty what she would have. Beauty replied to her father very quietly that she wanted a rose, just a beautiful rose, if he could find one.

□ □ □

12. SENTENCE PATTERNS

(a) Simple (b) Compound (c) Complex and (d) Compound-Complex

(a) Meaning और word order के आधार पर sentence चार प्रकार के होते हैं :

(i) Statement (ii) Question
(iii) Command (iv) Exclamation

(b) Sentence pattern का अर्थ होता है : sentence का structure. Structure के आधार पर sentence के चार भेद होते हैं :

(i) Simple (ii) Compound
(iii) Complex (iv) Compound-complex

(A) Simple Sentence

1. *Look at these sentences:*

Dogs bark. Boys laughed.
He will go. The children were playing.

ऊपर के प्रत्येक वाक्य में एक subject और एक verb है।

Subject	*Verb*	*Subject*	*Verb*
Dogs	bark.	Boys	laughed.
He	will go.	The children	were playing.

(i) Subject कभी एक शब्द का होता है या कभी एक से अधिक शब्दों का।

(ii) Verb कभी एक शब्द का होता है या कभी एक से अधिक शब्दों का।

(a) Subjects

2. *Look at these sentences:*

Shekespeare was a great dramatist. (*noun*)
He was a rich man. (*pronoun*)
The rich helped the poor. (*adjective*)
Walking is a good exercise. (*gerund*)
Well begun is half-done. (*phrase*)
To read is useful. (*infinitive*)
Slow and steady wins the race. (*phrase*)
What he does is difficult to know. (*clause*)

वाक्य का subject कोई *noun, pronoun, adjective, gerund, infinitive, phrase* या *clause* हो सकता है।

(b) Finite Verbs

3. *Look at these sentences:*

We *read* a lesson, (*plural subject+plural verb*)

Gopal *reads* a lesson, (*singular subject + singular verb*)

(i) *We* plural subject है इसके साथ plural verb *read* का प्रयोग हुआ है और *Gopal* sigular subject है इसके साथ singular verb *reads* का प्रयोग हुआ है।

(ii) इन वाक्यों में *read* और *reads* Finite verbs हैं।

(iii) Finite का अर्थ होता है—'limited'. Finite verb वह verb है जिसका *number* और *person* उसके subject के *number* और *person* के अनुसार होता है।

Note: (i) जो verb अपने subject के number और person से अनुशासित नहीं होता है, उसे non-Finite verb कहते हैं। जैसे :

He likes *to walk* (*non-finite verb*) He is fond of *walking*. (*non-finitive verb*)

(ii) कभी-कभी वाक्य में *S*ubject छिपा रहता है, केवल verb रहता है, वैसे वाक्य को verb sentence कहते हैं। जैसे :

Open the door. *Go* there. *Read* this book carefully.

जब वाक्य में एक subject और एक verb रहे तब उसे Simple Sentence कहते हैं। कभी-कभी Simple Sentence में subject छिपा रहता है और केवल Finite verb ही रहता है।

Some examples of simple sentence

I am sure of my success.
Honesty is the best policy.
How to do this is doubtful.
Father gave me some money.
I don't know the year of my birth.
He acted according to your instructions.
Good students do their homework regularly.

Compound और Complex sentence के संबंध में पढ़ने से पहले यह जान लेना आवश्यक है कि Clause किसे कहते हैं तथा Clause के कितने भेद होते हैं।

(a) Clause

1. *Look at these sentences:*

I shouted and he ran up. I called her but she gave no answer.

(i) प्रथम वाक्य में *I shouted* और *he run up* में एक-एक subject और एक-एक finite verb हैं।

(ii) उसी प्रकार दूसरे वाक्य में *I called her* तथा *she gave no answer* में भी एक-एक subject और एक-एक finite verb है।

(iii) इस प्रकार प्रत्येक subject + verb वाले अंश को clause कहते हैं।

(iv) ऊपर के वाक्यों में *and* तथा *but* से दोनों clauses को जोड़ा गया है।

Clause शब्दों के उस समूह को कहते हैं जो किसी वाक्य का अंश (part) हो और जिसमें एक Subject और एक Finite verb हो।

(b) Kinds of Clauses

Clause मूलतः तीन प्रकार के होते हैं :

(i) Main clause या Principal clause

(ii) Subordinate clause या Dependent clause

(iii) Co-ordinate clause

(c) Main Clauses

2. *Look at these sentences:*

This is the pen which I like.

Sunday is the day when I am least busy.

(i) इन वाक्यों में *This is the pen/Sunday is the day*—Main clauses हैं। Main clause को Principal clause या Independent clause भी कहा जाता है।

जो Clause स्वतः पूर्ण अर्थ रखता है, और किसी अन्य Clause पर आश्रित नहीं रहता, उसे Main (या Principal) Clause कहते हैं।

(d) Subordinate Clauses

3. *Look at these sentences:*

I do it *because I like it.* I hoped *that was true.*

Don't talk *while she is singing.* He must stay *where he is.*

(i) ऊपर के वाक्यों में टेढ़े अक्षरों में लिखे हुए clauses Subordinate clauses हैं।

जो Clause अपने अर्थ की पूर्णता के लिए Main Clause या अन्य Clause पर आश्रित रहता है उसे Subordinate (या Dependent) Clause कहते हैं।

(ii) निम्नलिखित Conjunctions से शुरू होनेवाले clauses Subordinate clauses होते हैं: *as, because, since, before, till, after, while, when, if, unless, though, although, lest, in order that, as soon as, provided, provided that, as if, that, whether, which, where, why, how, as much as, according as, than* इत्यादि।

(e) Co-ordinate Clauses

4. *Look at these sentences:*

Govern your passion or they will govern you. (*2 clauses joined by* ***or***)

I came, I saw, I conquered. (*3 clauses separated by commas*)

To err is human; to forgive; divine. (*2 clauses separated by a semicolon*)

(i) जो clauses एक ही rank या order (समान महत्त्व) के होते हैं, वे Co-ordinate clauses कहलाते हैं।

(ii) ये साधारणतः Co-ordinate conjunctions *and, or, but* इत्यादि द्वारा जुड़े रहते हैं या कभी-कभी conjuctions के बदले comma या semi-colon का प्रयोग किया जाता है।

(iii) मुख्य Co-ordinating conjunctions निम्नलिखित हैं: *and, but, or, still, yet, as well as, both..... and, either .....or, however, neither .... nor, neither, nor, otherwise, else, for, so, not only...., but also, nevertheless* इत्यादि।

(B) Compound Sentence

1. *Look at these sentences:*

God made the country. —Simple sentence

Man made the town. —Simple sentence

(i) यदि इन दो Simple sentences को किसी conjunction से जोड़ दें तो इनमें प्रत्येक को clause कह सकते हैं। जैसे :

God made the country and man made the town. इस वाक्य में दो clauses हैं और यह Compound sentence है :

(i) God made the country. (ii) (and) man made the town.

Some examples of compound sentence

Main clause	Co-ordinate clause
The fact is true	*and* I can prove it.
He is rich	*but* he is miserly.
Be off	*or* I will thrash you.
It was raining,	*however,* we went for a walk.
Speak	*otherwise* I fire.
He is ignorant	*still* he claims to be wise.
I can't give you any money,	*for* I have none.

जो वाक्य दो या दो से अधिक Main clauses से बना हो वह Compound Sentence कहलाता है।

(a) Shortened Forms of the Compound Sentence

Compound sentence में कभी subject तो कभी verb छिपा रहता है।

(i) Omission of the subject

2. *Look at these sentences:*

He called at my house, *but* left soon after.

(= (a) He called at my house. (b) (but) *he* left soon after.)

He wrote the letter *and* sent it through his brother.

(= (a) He wrote the letter. (b) (and) *he* sent it through his brother.)

कभी-कभी एक ही subject के साथ दो या दो से अधिक verbs रहते हैं।

(ii) Omission of the verb (Predicate)

3. *Look at these sentences:*

Write *as fast as* you can.

(= (a) You write. (b) (As fast as) you can *write.*)

Some played cricket *and* others hockey.

(= (a) Some played cricket. (b) others *played* hockey.)

(i) कभी-कभी दो subjects के साथ एक ही verb का प्रयोग होता है।

(ii) ऐसे वाक्य प्राय: *but, and . therefore, or, nor, as well as, not only.... but also* आदि द्वारा जुड़े रहते हैं।

Some more examples of compound sentence

He *as well as* Hari is guilty.

(= He *is guilty* as well as Hari *is guilty*)

Some like coffee and others tea.

(= Some like coffee and others *like* tea.

A train goes fast, but an aeroplane faster.

(= A train goes fast, but an aeroplane *goes* faster.)

He took out his bicycle, locked the room and went out.

(= He took out his bicycle, *he* locked the room, and *he* went out.)

Note: कभी-कभी जब एक से अधिक subjects को and के द्वारा जोड़ा जाता है, तब उन सभी subjects को एक ही माना जाता है और इसलिए उन्हें अलग-अलग clauses में नहीं बाँटना चाहिए। जैसे :

Mukul, Rajeev and Raja are friends.

इस वाक्य में एक ही clause है, तीन नहीं।

(a) Mukul is a friend. (b) Rajeev is a friend. (c) Raja is a friend. कहना तो अनुचित होगा।

(b) Use of Co-ordinating Conjunctions

आगे कुछ Co-ordinating conjunctions का list और उनसे शुरू होनेवाले compound sentences के उदाहरण दिए जा रहे हैं :

and: Man discovered fire *and* learnt to cook.

but: We knocked at the door, *but* no one answered.

or: Hurry up *or* you will be late.

Yet: He is poor, *yet* he is happy.

still: The best doctors are attending on him, *still* he is not out of danger.

for: The old lady does not go out in the winter, *for* she feels the cold a great deal.

so: The man had a stomach pain, *so* we took him to a doctor.

otherwise: You should better go now, *otherwise* you will miss your train.

either.... or: You may *either* stay in the hostel *or* stay at home.

not only... but also: The enemy *not only* captured the city, *but also* killed several soldiers.

as well as: He was punished *as well as* fined.

therefore: He is laborious, *therefore* he will succeed.

neither.... nor: The old man could *neither* read *nor* write.

nor: He cannot speak, *nor* can he write.

else: Walk quickly, *else* he will overtake you.

nevertheless: I did my best, nevertheless I failed.

(c) Complex Sentence

1. *Look at these sentences:*

I know the reason *why he was so angry.*

That is the house *that I would like to buy.*

(i) ऊपर के वाक्यों में *I know the reason* तथा *That is the house* Main clauses हैं।

(ii) इन्हीं वाक्यों में *why he was so angry* तथा *that I would like to buy* subordinate clauses हैं।

(iii) Subordinate clauses *why* तथा *that* से शुरू हुए हैं। *Why* तथा *that* Subordinate conjunctions हैं।

ऊपर के दोनों वाक्य Complex sentences हैं।

जिस वाक्य में एक Main clause (या Principal clause) और एक या एक से अधिक Subordinate clauses रहें उसे Complex Sentence कहते हैं।

Some more examples of complex sentences

Main clause	Subordinate clause
Some people eat	*so that* they may live.
I will do it	*when* I am fit.
He is the man	*whom* we all respect.
I gave him the money	*because* he needed it.
She said	*that* she would come early.
He said	*that* he would pass.
He was glad	*when* he heard the news.

(a) Omission of the Subject or Predicate in Complex Sentences

Complex sentence में भी कभी subject तो कभी verb (या Predicate) छिपा रहता है।

2. *Look at these sentences:*

He is better *than* his brother.

(= (a) He is better. (b) than his brother *is*.)

I like you no less *than* him.

(= (a) I like you. (b) no less than (*I like*) him.)

Play *as fast as* you can.

(= (a) *You* play. (b) (as fast as) you can *play*.)

कभी-कभी *than* और *as* के बाद subject या verb छिपा रहता है।

3. *Look at these sentences:*

Though happy, he does not spend much.

(= (a) Though *he is* happy, (b) he does not spend much.)

He fell to the ground while running in the dark.

(= (a) He fell to the ground, (b) while *he was* running in the dark.)

If, though, when, till, while आदि के बाद कभी-कभी subject या verb छिपा रहता है।

(b) Kinds of Subordinate Clauses

Subordinate clause के तीन भेद होते हैं?

(i) **Noun clause**. जो clause *noun* का काम करे उसे *Noun clause* कहा जाता है। जैसे :

He said *that he would buy a house.*

(ii) **Adjective** या **Adjectival clause**. जो clause *adjective* का काम करे उसे *Adjective* या *Adjectival clause* कहा जाता है। जैसे :

This is the man *who helped me yesterday.*

(iii) **Adverb** या **Adverbial clause.** जो clause *adverb* का काम करे उसे *Adverb* या *Adverbial clause* कहा जाता है। जैसे :

He cannot go to college *because he is ill.*

(i) Noun Clause

Noun clause को आरंभ करने के लिए निम्नलिखित connective words का प्रयोग किया जाता है :

(a) That-clauses

1. *Look at these sentences:*

I hoped *that it was true.* You said *that he was busy.*
He says *that he won't go.* I feel *that it is wrong.*
We were certain *that he will pass.* My belief is *that he will come.*

अगर कोई clause *that* से शुरू हो और उस *that* का अर्थ 'कि' हो तो वह प्रायः Noun clause होता है।

2. *Look at these sentences:*

It seems *he is rich.* He says *it is meaningless.*
I believe *he was wrong.* I think *she was right.*

(i) कभी-कभी कुछ verbs के बाद *that* का प्रयोग नहीं होता है। फिर भी, ऐसे verb के बाद आनेवाला clause होता है—Noun clause.

(ii) इस छिपे हुए *that* के लिए भी हिंदी अनुवाद में **कि** का प्रयोग अवश्य होता है : "It seems he is rich."—

इसका अर्थ है—"लगता है **कि** वह धनी है।"

(b) Wh-clauses as Noun Clauses

3. *Look at these sentences:*

No one knows *who he is.* (कौन) I know *how he got it.* (कैसे)
Tell me *where he lives.* (कहाँ) Tell me *why you do this.* (क्यों)
I know *which pen you want.* (कौन) Inform him *when he will come.* (कब)
I don't follow *what you say.* (क्या) I know *how it came about*. (कैसे)

---

1. *Connective: A word whose function is to connect other words or groups of words. Two of the parts of speech, Conjunctions and Prepositions, regularly function as connectives.*

(i) Wh-से शुरू होनेवाले शब्द को Wh-words कहते हैं। इनमें *who, what, why, where, how, when, which* आदि शब्द होते हैं।

(ii) *Who, where, which, how, why, when* आदि से शुरू होनेवाले clauses Noun clauses होते हैं, जब उनका हिंदी में अर्थ 'क' अर्थात कहाँ, कैसे, क्यों, कब होता है।

4. *Look at these sentences:*

What you say is true.
When he will come is uncertain.
Where he lives is a mystery.
How he comes here is not known.
That you should say so surprises me.
Why he left is not known to anybody.

What, where, when, that, how, why आदि से शुरू होनेवाले clauses जब किसी sentence के आरंभ में रहते हैं और जब उनके पहले कोई noun नहीं आता है तब वे Noun clauses होते हैं।

(c) If/Whether Clauses as Noun Clauses

5. *Look at these sentences:*

Do you know *if the banks are open*? (कि)
Can you say *whether Hari is in the garden*? (कि)

Yes or *No* question में *if* या *whether* से Noun clause शुरू होता है।

6. *Look at these sentences:*

I don't know *whether it will rain or be sunny.* (कि)
I don't care *if your car breaks down or not.* (कि)

कुछ अन्य तरह के वाक्यों में *whether* और *if* से शुरू होनेवाले *clauses* Noun clauses होते हैं जब उनका हिंदी में अर्थ कोई ऐसा शब्द होता है जो 'कि' से शुरू होता है।

(d) Sentences in Direct Speech as Noun Clauses

7. *Look at these sentences:*

He said, "*What do you want?*"
He said to me, "*I shall come.*"

जो वाक्य Direct Speech में quotation marks के अंदर रहता है वह Noun clause होता है।

(ii) Adjective Clause

Adjective clause, एक Adjective के समान, अपने से पूर्व आनेवाले noun/pronoun की विशेषता बताता है। Adjective clause निम्नलिखित Connective words से शुरू होते हैं :

(a) who, which, that, whom, whose

1. *Look at these sentences:*

This is the man *who gave me money.* (जो)
She gave me the pen *which I wanted.* (जो)
This is the house *that Jack built.* (जो)
The man *whom you saw* is a professor. (जिसे)
The boy *whose bicycle was lost* came to see me. (जिसका)

(i) *Who, which, that, whom, whose,* इत्यादि से शुरू होनेवाले *clauses* Adjective clauses होते हैं जब इनके पहले कोई noun रहता है।

(ii) इनका अर्थ हिंदी में कोई ऐसा शब्द होता है जो **'ज'** अर्थात *जो*, *जिसने*, *जिनको*, *जहाँ*, *जब* इत्यादि से आरंभ होता है।

(iii) ऐसे Noun और Adjective clause के बीच कोई comma नहीं रहता।

2. *Look at these sentences:*

The man ^ (*whom*) *you saw* is my teacher.

The book ^ (*that/which*) *you gave me* is very interesting.

The reason ^ (*why*) *I have* come is to ask for money.

That was the time ^ (*when*) *you should have done it.*

(i) You saw, you gave me, I have come तथा you should have done it—Adjective clauses हैं। Adjective clause किसी Noun के बाद आता है और उसकी विशेषता बताता है।

(ii) ऐसा Adjective clause किसी Conjunction से आरंभ नहीं होता क्योंकि वह Conjunction छिपा रहता है।

(iii) *Who/whom/which/that* आदि के छिपे रहने पर भी अनुवाद करने पर इसका अर्थ हिंदी में ऐसा शब्द होता है जो **'ज'** से आरंभ होता है।

(iv) *Who* का प्रयोग किसी व्यक्ति के लिए, *which* का प्रयोग किसी वस्तु या पशु के लिए तथा *that* का प्रयोग व्यक्ति या *निर्जीव* वस्तु के लिए किया जाता है।

(b) where, when, why

3. *Look at these sentences:*

This is the house *where I was born.* (जहाँ)

He arrived on the day *when the bank was closed.* (जब)

You can't tell me the reason *why he left so suddenly.* (जिस)

(i) *Where, when, why* आदि से शुरू होनेवाले clauses भी Adjective clauses होते हैं अगर इनके पहले कोई noun रहता है।

(ii) इस *where, when, why* आदि का अर्थ हिंदी में कोई ऐसा शब्द होता है जो **'ज'** से शुरू होता है।

(c) as

4. *Look at these sentences:*

This is the same book *as I wanted.* (जो)

He is not such a fine man *as I thought.* (जैसाकि)

You are making the same kind of mistakes *as the last speaker made.* (जिस तरह से)

(i) As से आरंभ होनेवाला *clause* Adjective clause तब होता है जब यह Principal clause में प्रयुक्त Noun के बाद आता है और उस Noun की विशेषता बताता है।

(ii) *As* का प्रयोग *such* या *the same* के बाद होता है।

(iii) *As* का अर्थ हिंदी में **ज अर्थात जो, जैसाकि, जिस तरह से** आदि से प्रारंभ होता है जैसाकि *who/which/that* का अर्थ होता है।

(iii) Adverbial Clause

Adverbial clause वाक्य में Adverb का काम करता है और Principal clause में व्यवहार किए गए किसी adjective, adverb या verb की विशेषता बताता है। कभी-कभी यह पूरे clause की भी विशेषता बताता है।

Kinds of Adverbial Clauses

Adverb clauses कई प्रकार के होते हैं :

(a) Aderbial Clause of Time

1. *Look at these sentences:*

They stood up *when you left the room.*

I learned a lot of things *while I was at school.*

He went home *after he had finished his work.*

There was silence *as the leader spoke.*

One of them began to cry *before I opened the door.*

He has not written to me *since he went to Delhi.*

(i) Adverbial clause of Time से Principal clause में क्रिया के होने के समय (time) का बोध होता है।

(ii) Adevrbial clause of Time इन Subordinating Conjucntions से आरंभ होता है : *when, while, after, as* (ज्योंही), *before, since* (तबसे), *till, until, whenever, as long as, than, as soon as.*

(b) Adverbial Clause of Place

2. *Look at these sentences:*

Please go *where you are.*

You should stay *where he is.*

Wherever the piper went, the children followed.

(i) Adverbial clause of Place से क्रिया के होने का स्थान (place) का बोध होता है।

(ii) यह clause इन Subordinating Conjunctions से आरंभ होता है :

where, wherever, whither, wherein, wherefrom, whence

(c) Adverbial Clause of Cause or Reason

3. *Look at these sentences:*

He will succeed *because he works hard.*

Since she says so, I must believe it.

As he was not there, I spoke to his brother.

Now that he is dead, we should not criticize him.

(i) Adverial clause of Cause or Reason से किसी काम के होने के कारण (cause) का बोध होता है।

(ii) ऐसे clause को प्रधानतः *because, as* (क्योंकि), since (चूँकि), in that (क्योंकि), *now that, considering that* आदि से आरंभ किया जाता है।

(d) Adverbial Clause of Condition

4. *Look at these sentences:*

I shall go *if he asks me.* (यदि)

If the weather is fine, we will go for a picnic.

Unless (जब तक नहीं) *you work harder,* you will fail.

Supposing that he asks you, will you go?

I will do it, *whether* (चाहे) *you like it or not.*

Take an umbrella with you, *in case it rains.*

(i) Adverbial clause of Condition से शर्त्त (condition) का बोध होता है।

(ii) ऐसे Adverbial clause इन Subordinating Conjunctions से आरंभ होते हैं :

if, unless, supposing, provided, provided that, in case, whether....or, on condition that

(e) Adverbial Clause of Comparison

5. *Look at these sentences:*

She is as wise *as she is beautiful.*

She is not taller *than her husband.*

He speaks better *than he writes.*

He is not so clever *as you think.*

(i) Adverbial clause of Comparison से तुलना (comparison) का बोध होता है।

(ii) ऐसे Adverial clause इन Subordinating Conjuctions से आरंभ होते हैं : *As, than*

(f) Adverbial Clause of Purpose

6. *Look at these sentences:*

We eat *that we may live.*

Some people eat *so that they may live.*

Others seem to live *in order that they may eat.*

He worked hard *so that he might win the prize.*

Make a note of it *lest you should forget it.* (ऐसा नहीं हो कि)

(i) Adverbial clause of Purpose से उद्देश्य (purpose) का बोध होता है।

(ii) यह clause इन Subordinating Conjunctions से आरंभ होते हैं :

that, so that, in order that, lest

(g) Adverbial Clause of Result/Consequence

7. *Look at these sentences:*

Strict laws were passed *so that this cruel custom was no more.*

He speaks *so* fast *that I cannot follow him.*

She spoke in *such* a low voice *that few could hear her.*

He is *so* brave *that he is not afraid of any danger.*

(i) Adverbial clause of Result/Consequence से कार्य होने के परिणाम/फल (result/consequence) का बोध होता है और Main clause से कारण (cause) का भाव व्यक्त होता है।

(ii) यह clause इन Conjunctions से आरंभ होते हैं :

so that, so.... that., such....that

(h) Adverbial Clause of Manner

8. *Look at these sentences:*

You do *as I tell you.*

He looks *as if he were frightened.* (मानो)

It looks *as though it might rain.* (मानो)

(i) Adverbial clause of Manner से कार्य करने का ढंग/रीति (manner) का बोध होता है।

(ii) यह clause साधारणत: इन Conjuctions से आरंभ होते हैं :

as, as if, as though

(i) Adverbial Clause of Concession

9. *Look at these sentences:*

Though he is poor, he is honest.

Although he tried hard, he was not successful.

However hard he tries, he cannot get success.

Whether he works or not, he will be promoted.

Whatever you may say, I still think I did the right.

Poor as he was (Though he was poor), he was sincere.

(i) Adverbial clause of Concession से यद्यपि-तथापि (concession) का बोध होता है।

(ii) इस clause को Adverbial clause of Contrast (विपरीत) भी कहा जाता है क्योंकि Adverbial clause में जो कुछ कहा जाता है उसके विपरीत Principal clause में कहा जाता है।

(iii) यह clause साधारणत: इन Conjunctions से आरंभ होता है :

though, although, however, whether....or not, no matter, even if, notwithstanding

(D) Compound-Complex Sentences

Look at these sentences:

I came/*but* I did not see the boy/*who* stood first in the exam.

(*Main clause+Main clause+Adjective clause*)

When I went to him/ he saw me,/*but* he did not get up from his seat.

(*Adverb clause+Main clause+Main clause*)

(i) ऊपर के वाक्यों में दो Main clauses और एक subordinate clause है, इसे compound-Complex sentence कहते हैं।

जिस sentence में कम-से-कम दो main clauses और एक subordinate clause रहे उस sentence को Complex-Compound या Mixed Sentence कहते हैं।

Examples Worked Out

(A) *State, which of the following sentences are 'Compound' and which are 'Complex':*

1. She must weep or she will die. —*Compound sentence*
2. I know Rani who is a clever girl. —*Complex sentence*
3. The city in which I live is very large. —*Complex sentence*
4. He returned home because he was tired. —*Complex sentence*
5. I will treat him as he has treated me. —*Complex sentence*
6. God made a river and man made a machine. —*Compound sentence*
7. A guest is unwelcome when he stays too long. —*Complex sentence*
8. She is not only pretty but also clever. —*Compound sentence*
9. He liked what I suggested. —*Complex sentence*
10. He was ill, but still he attended classes. —*Compound sentence*
11. As he was sick, he could not work. —*Complex sentence*
12. He is very learned, yet humble. —*Compound sentence*
13. I have no money that I can lend you. —*Complex sentence*
14. Whoever is learned is respected. —*Complex sentence*
15. He was tired and fell asleep. —*Compound sentence*
16. I wish that he should succeed. —*Complex sentence*
17. He is so weak that he cannot walk. —*Complex sentence*
18. He was ill, therefore, he could not continue his studies. —*Compound sentence*
19. They criticized what we did. —*Complex sentence*
20. Though it was very hot, we started on foot. —*Complex sentence*
21. When they were challenged they ran away. —*Complex sentence*
22. I have no advice that I can offer you. —*Complex sentence*
23. Waste not, want not. *Compound sentence*
24. If you do your best, you will never regret it. —*Complex sentence*

25. There is no student but (=जो नहीं) loves good teachers. —*Complex sentence*
26. He is rich but he is miserly. —*Compound sentence*
27. He is more a fool than a cheat. —*Complex sentence*
28. I can prove that this is a fact. —*Complex sentence*
29. Were I rich, I would help you. —*Complex sentence*
30. I will help you with money you need. —*Complex sentence*
31. The higher we go, the cooler it is. —*Complex sentence*

(B) *Fill in the blanks with right words from brackets:*

1. Work hard...... you will fail. (*unless, or, and*)	Work hard *or* you will fail.
2. It is he..... said so. (*which, whom, who*)	It is he *who* said so.
3. He neither drinks...... smokes. (*or, nor, and*)	He *neither* drinks *nor* smokes.
4. Tell me...... I should sign. (*where, after, while*)	Tell me *where* I should sign.
5. Can you explain........a computer works? (*how, as, so*)	Can you explain *how* a computer works?
6. Northing happened..... we have feared. (*since, as, though*)	Nothing happened *as* we have feared.
7. He is the man ..... we all respect. (*which, whom, how*)	He is the man *whom* we all respect.
8. Do it ...... you forget it. (*before, after, that*)	Do it *before* you forget it.
9. We love them...... love us. (*where, whom, who*)	We love them *who* love us
10. They can stay..... they are. (*whether, where, if*)	They can stay *where* they are.
11. I am glad .... you like it. (*than, although, that*)	I am glad *that* you like it.
12. He is rich ...... dishonest. (*as well as, but, or*)	He is rich *but* dishonest.
13. He is older........ he looks. (*as, than, as if*)	He is older *than* he looks.
14. He is as stupid.... he is lazy, (*as, so, and*)	He is as stupid *as* he is lazy.
15. ..... it rains, I shall come. (*Even if, After, Since*)	*Even if* it rains, I shall come.

16. I know...... he lives. (*whom, why, where*)	I know *where* he lives.
17. He is absent...... he is not here. (*provided, because, where*)	He is absent *because* he is not here.
18. Let me know..... has come. (*who, where, whose*)	Let me know *who* has come.
19. He said...... he was well. (*that, since, because*)	He said *that* he was well.
20. I gave him...... help... I could. (*so.... as, so.... that, such...that*)	I gave him *such* help *that* I could.
21. ....he says is correct. (*Where, What, That*)	*What* he says is correct.
22. This is the place...he lives. (*that, where, which*)	This is the place *where* he lives.
23. Make hay..... the sun shines. (*while, when, unless*)	Make hay *while* the sun shines.
24. Run, ... you will be caught. (*or, still, but*)	Run, *or* you will be caught.
25. He is poor, ...he is honest. (*while, yet, as well as*)	He is poor, *yet* he is honest.
26. He works.... hard ...he fell ill. (*as...if, so... that, as .... that*)	He works so hard *that* he fell ill.
27. Many of us can read English... can't speak English. (*and, or, but*)	Many of us can read English *but* can't speak English.
28. I read the book.... I was in hospital. (*because, if, while*)	I read the book *while* I was in hospital.
29. I did it ..... I had to do it. (*though, unless, because*)	I did it *because* I had to do it.
30. You may come .... you like. (*as if, if, until*)	You may come *if* you like.

(C) *Join the following separate sentences into compound sentences using the words in brackets:*

Separate Sentences	**Compound Sentences**
1. She must weep. She will die. (*or*)	She must weep *or* she will die.
2. He is slow. He is sure. (*but*)	He is slow, *but* he is sure.
3. Rajeev worked hard. He won a scholarship. (*and*)	Rajeev worked hard *and* won a scholarship.
4. I went to his house. I did not meet him. (*but*)	I went to his house *but* I did not meet him.

Separate Sentences	Compound Sentences
5. He is very rich. He is unhappy. (*yet*)	He is very rich, *yet* he is unhappy.
6. You should learn how to read English. You should learn how to speak English. (*not only.... but also*)	You should learn *not only* how to read English *but also* how to speak it.
7. He was punished. He was fined also. (*as well as*)	He was punished *as well as* fined.
8. Priya can come early. Rahul can't come early. (*but*)	Priya can come early *but* Rahul can't.
9. Do not do this. Do not do that. (*neither, nor*)	*Neither* do this *nor* (do) that.
10. He cried. He wept. (*both ... and*)	He *both* cried *and* wept.
11. I cannot see. It is very dark. (*for*)	I cannot see, *for* it is very dark.
12. You may study here. You may play in the field. (*either ... or*)	You may *either* study here *or* play in the field.
13. He gave me food. He comforted me. (*not only ..... but also*)	He *not only* gave me food *but also* comforted me.
14. God made the country. Man made the town. (*and*)	God made the country *and* man made the town.
15. Do not be a borrower. Do not be a lender. (*Neither. nor*)	*Neither* a borrower *nor* a lender be.
16. He failed twice. He would not stop. (*yet*)	He failed twice, *yet* he would not stop.
17. Correct your habits. You will suffer. (*else/otherwise*)	Correct your habits *else/otherwise* you will suffer.
18. He is a dacoit. He is jailed. (*so/therefore/hence*)	He is a dacoit *so/therefore/hence* he is jailed.

(D) *Join these separate sentences into complex sentences using the words in brackets:*

Separate Sentences	Complex Sentences
1. Don't eat too much. You will be ill. (*If*)	*If* you eat too much, you will be ill.
2. You are strong. I am equally strong. (*as...as*)	I am *as* strong *as* you are.
3. He began late. He finished first. (*though*)	He finished first *though* he began late.
4. He is very dishonest. Nobody likes him. (*because*)	Nobody likes him *because* he is very dishonest.

Separate Sentences	Complex Sentences
5. He heard the news. He was glad. *(When)*	*When* he heard the news, he was glad.
6. Lalan is brave. Mukul is braver. *(than)*	Mukul is braver *than* Lalan.
7. This is the letter. Sohan wrote it. *(which)*	This is the letter *which* Sohan wrote.
8. This is the house. Jack built it. *(that)*	This is the house *that* Jack built.
9. He is ill. He can't attend office. *(As)*	*As* he is ill, he can't attend office.
10. He may fail. This is his great fear. *(that)*	His great fear is *that* he may fail.
11. This is the village. I was born here. *(where)*	This is the village *where* I was born.
12. You finish writing the letter. I shall wait here. *(until)*	I shall wait here *until* you finish writing the letter.
13. You must work hard. Otherwise you won't pass. *(unless)*	You won't pass *unless* you work hard.
14. This is the boy. His parents are teachers. *(whose)*	This is the boy *whose* parents are teachers.
15. I must know all the facts. I cannot help you otherwise. *(Before)*	*Before* I can help you, I must know all the facts.
16. He was very clever. His brother was very dull. *(as.....as)*	He was *as* clever *as* his brother was dull.
17. I met my old friend. He is now an officer. *(who)*	I met my old friend *who* is now an officer.
18. It is true. She will succeed. *(that)*	It is true *that* she will succeed.
19. He may be at home. I do not know. *(if/whether)*	I do not know *if/whether* he is at home.
20. He is poor. He is honest in spite of it. *(Though)*	*Though* he is poor, he is honest.
21. I will get ready. Wait till then. *(till)*	Wait *till* I get ready.
22. The bell rang. They all came up at once. *(As soon as)*	*As soon as* bell rang, they all came up.

EXERCISE 1

State, which of the following sentences are 'Compound' and which are 'Complex':

EXAMPLE: I have been busy ever since I arrived here. *Ans.—Complex sentence.*

1. He is ill but he is cheerful.
2. This is where I live.
3. Please see me before you go.
4. He works hard though he is weak.
5. He has not come, neither has he sent any letter.
6. He is not so bad as you think.
7. It looks as if it might rain.
8. The time was short but he completed the work.
9. She can neither read nor write.
10. I know who is there.
11. I make friend wherever I go.
12. He is more foolish than he looks.
13. Don't talk while she is reading.
14. He lifted a gun and fired.
15. He neither drinks nor smokes.
16. Wait here as long as you can.

EXERCISE 2

State, which of the following sentences are 'Compound' and which are 'Complex':

EXAMPLE: How can one eat the cake as well as have it, too? *Ans.—Compound sentence.*

1. This is the place where I live.
2. Tell me where I should sign.
3. You can go wherever you like.
4. It looks as if it will rain.
5. It is as large as you thought.
6. They neither sleep nor read.
7. The boy got up and walked away.
8. Ram as well as Mohan qualified for the finals.
9. He is very wealthy yet he is very unhappy.
10. I do not care if he comes or not.
11. Tell me how you managed it.
12. He will help me when I am in trouble.
13. He can't attend school because he is ill.
14. It is a year since we left Bombay.
15. Neither you nor I am wrong.
16. This is the person who helped me.

EXERCISE 3

State, which of the following sentences are 'Compound' and which are 'Complex':

EXAMPLE: I am very tired for I have been working all day. *Ans.—Compound sentence.*

1. He is lazy, therefore, he will fail.
9. It is not as large as I thought.

2. As you sow, so shall you reap.
3. I know the man who is there.
4. If it rains, we shall stay at home.
5. The boy who ran away was a thief.
6. He is as wicked as he is lazy.
7. Ask them where they are going.
8. He learnt to speak and to write Tamil.
9. Can you tell me what she wants?
10. This is the book which I bought.
11. He will do it as soon as he comes home.
12. I finished my breakfast and went out for a walk.
13. Since you were very busy, I didn't call you.
14. He took off his clothes and jumped into the well.
15. I know what he said to be false.

EXERCISE 4

State, which of the following sentences are 'Compound' and which are 'Complex':

EXAMPLE: Take whatever you want. *Ans.—Complex sentence.*

1. He paid no attention to what I said.
2. This is the school that they built.
3. He is a man everybody likes.
4. I found it as I was walking to school.
5. Men like dogs, for dogs are faithful animals.
6. Walk fast or else you will miss the train.
7. I left home before she came.
8. Unless you work harder, you will not pass.
9. Take all you want.
10. He worked hard and passed in the first division.
11. When the sun set, we returned home.
12. I do not know whether he is at home.
13. He worked so hard that his health broke down.
14. Come in time otherwise you shall be marked absent.
15. He made a mistake, however, he was pardoned.
16. It looked as though it might rain.

EXERCISE 5

State, which of the following sentences are 'Compound' and which are 'Complex':

EXAMPLE: I am sure that he has gone mad. *Ans.—Complex sentence.*

1. It is certain that we are late.
2. Don't talk while you are eating.
3. Wait here till I come back.
4. Strike the iron while it is hot.
9. Wherever you go, I shall follow you.
10. He looks as if he is frightened.
11. We eat that we may live.
12. I laugh, I run, I leap, I sing for joy.

5. I paint because I like painting.
6. He is a fool and you are a bigger fool.
7. He cannot speak nor can he hear.
8. You should neither borrow nor lend.
13. You must either stay here or go to your father's house.
14. Go back wherefrom you have come.
15. Stop where you are.
16. I must come even if it is raining.

EXERCISE 6

Fill in the blanks with right words from brackets:

EXAMPLE: Wise men welcome advice, ...fools hate it. *(and, whereas, or)*
= Wise men welcome advice, *whereas* fools hate it.

1. I tried my best, ... I couldn't pass the test. *(since, and, still)*
2. Ramesh is a scientist, ... Shyam is a politician. *(still, and, as)*
3. He is ill ...... he is cheerful. *(and, but, yet)*
4. He has influence, ... he may be able to do it. *(as, so, that)*
5. Students stood up ..... the teacher came. *(and, as, but)*
6. He may see your point ... he is a reasonable man. *(for, as, so)*
7. Some played cricket ...... others played hockey. *(or, and, so)*
8. He worked hard, ... he failed. *(until, unless, nevertheless)*
9. Don't get off .... the bus stops. *(when, before, after)*
10. Sita is reading ..... Lata is dancing. *(and, but, therefore)*
11. He is rich and ...... he is prosperous. *(therefore, as, so)*
12. He came here..... gave me a postcard. *(or, still, and)*
13. Start early ...... you should miss the train. *(so that, lest, as)*
14. Many are called, ...a few are chosen. *(since, after, but)*
15. Work hard ...... you will fail. *(and, else, as well as)*
16. He behaved .... he had seen a ghost. *(as though, while, how)*

EXERCISE 7

Fill in the blanks with right words from brackets:

EXAMPLE: He does ...... he is told to do. *(so, when, whatever)*
= He does *whatever* he is told to do.

1. I expect ..... he will come. *(that, though, whose)*
2. ...... he said was true. *(Where, Because, What)*
3. I shall do .... I like. *(as, who, than)*
9. You can come, ... you like. *(that, if, after)*
10. She is .... pretty .... a doll. *(such ... that, as ... as, so... that)*
11. Nobody knows better ..... you. *(that, than, which)*

4. Take .... you want. *(before, though,whatever)*
5. This is a matter of .... I am proud. *(where, that, which)*
6. .... he was tired, he offered to carry her. *(Though, Unless, If)*
7. He is the man ..... saved my life. *(since, whose, who)*
8. She failed ..... she did not work. *(though, as if, because)*
12. Put the book. .... you found it. *(how, where, since)*
13. They arrived.... he was reading. *(as if, that, while)*
14. ..... I took every care, I was completely deceived. *(But, Although, And)*
15. He worked ...... hard ... he fell ill. *(Such...as, so...that, even if)*
16. ..... hard he may try, he will not succeed. *(Yet, However, Still)*

EXERCISE 8

Fill in the blanks with right words from brackets:

EXAMPLE: It began to rain, ... we went indoors. *(whereas, therefore, and)*
= It began to rain, *therefore* we went indoors.

1. He writes the same way .... I do. *(that, as, when)*
2. His words were respected ... he was honest. *(that, if, because)*
3. I am sorry ...... I missed the chance. *(than, that, so)*
4. You may go to college ....stay at home. *(although, or, whether)*
5. He reached late ...... it was raining. *(when, since, that)*
6. The police did not tell him ... he was arrested. *(why, because, as)*
7. We sat in the canteen ..... the meeting was over. *(after, so that, since)*
8. We shall go ..... you desire it. *(since, than, that)*
9. We came here .... they had left. *(if, after, where)*
10. Look ... you leap. *(after, before, since)*
11. He tried, ... did not succeed. *(and, or, but)*
12. ...... he is there, I shall meet him. *(Unless, If, Where)*
13. ...... we were eating, the telephone rang. *(Though, While, That)*
14. I will wait .... the next train comes. *(until, unless, if)*
15. I know the place .... roses grow. *(that, where, lest)*
16. Sohan met me .... talked about you. *(but, and, while)*

EXERCISE 9

Join the following separate sentences into compound sentences using the words in brackets:

EXAMPLE: He was punished. He was fined also. *(as well as)*
= He was punished *as well as* fined.

1. Walk fast. You will miss the train. *(or)*
2. I can read English. I can write English. *(and)*
9. I know Ruby. I don't know Rupa. *(but)*
10. Correct your habits. You will suffer. *(otherwise)*

3. She smiled. She refused. (*but*)
4. We do our work during the day. We take rest at night. (*and*)
5. He attacked us. He robbed us. (*not only ..... but also*)
6. I knocked. No one came to open the door. (*but*)
7. He is mad. He pretends to be mad. (*Either ...... or*)
8. He took bribe. He was dismissed. (*therefore*)
11. He may cheat me. I will love him. (*yet*)
12. You must apologize. You will be punished. (*else*)
13. He is unwell. He can't attend college. (*so*)
14. It is dark. We can't see. (*therefore*)
15. We will die one day. All men are mortal. (*for*)
16. We lost our way. We asked the policeman to help us. (*but*)

EXERCISE 10

Join the following separate sentences into complex sentences using the words in brackets:

EXAMPLE: He writes well. He speaks better. (*than*)
= He speaks better *than* he writes.

1. I will help you. You must be polite. (*if*)
2. I trust him. He is honest. (*because*)
3. This is the garden. The finest roses grow here. (*where*)
4. The sun set. We returned home. (*when*)
5. He is hard-working. Everybody knows it. (*that*)
6. He may be at home. I do not know. (*whether*)
7. This is the new car. I like it most. (*which*)
8. This is the boy. He stood first in the examination. (*who*)
9. This is the book. I bought it yesterday. (*that*)
10. He is ill. He can't go to school today. (*As*)
11. We entered the room. The boy was weeping. (*When*)
12. This is the hole. A snake lives here. (*where*)
13. The sun comes out. Then the stars disappear. (*When*)
14. He was very tired. He could not walk any further. (*so ... that*)
15. He used very bad words. I don't want to repeat them. (*such ... that*)
16. Take exercise every day. Then you can keep fit and healthy. (*If*)

EXERCISE 11 (With Answer)

Join the following separate sentences into either Compound or Complex sentences whichever you find suitable:

1. I called on you. You were out.
2. Make haste. You will be late.
9. He switched off the lights. He went to bed.
10. The days are warm. The nights are cool.

3. We eat. We may live.
4. He was tired. He went on working.
5. It is twelve. I must go to bed.
6. I met my friend. He recongnized me at once.
7. He came very late. I did not lose my temper.
8. The whistle blew. The train left the station.
11. She had a pleasant manner. So we all liked her.
12. He is hard-working. He is equally intelligent.
13. Mend your ways. You may suffer.
14. I was waiting for a man. He did not turn up.
15. He does not tell a lie. He does not tolerate it.
16. This is the town. My brother lives in it.

EXERCISE 12 (With Answer)

State which of the following sentences are 'Compound' and which are 'Complex'.

1. I do not know whether he is guilty.
2. This is the nice place where he met me.
3. Either do it yourself or let me do it.
4. He travelled without a ticket, so he was fined.
5. After the school is over, we all go home.
6. Don't open the door unless I tell you.
7. Don't talk while I am speaking.
8. They began as well as ended badly.
9. The paper was lengthy; however, we did all the questions.
10. He was tired; nevertheless he went on working.
11. Do you know who has taken away my pen?
12. The chair on which I was sitting broke.
13. When the guard gave the signal, the train moved.
14. If you tease the dog, it will bite you.
15. He is so dull that he can't understand the poem.
16. I will give you whatever you wish to have.

EXERCISE 13 (With Answer)

Fill in the blank in each of the following sentences with the best of the alternatives given:

1. She must be over forty, ... she looks charming.
   A. *although* **B.** *still* **C.** *while* **D.** *that*
2. I am giving him some money ..... that he may buy a dictionary.
   A. *when* **B.** *as* **C.** *so* **D.** *such*
3. I couldn't take a bath .... there was no water.
   A. *while* **B.** *if* **C.** *when* **D.** *because*

4. He spends money .... it grew in his garden.
   A. *as far as* **B.** *as if* **C.** *in case* **D.** *in spite of*
5. He refuses to attend the party ..... he is properly invited.
   A. *though* **B.** *in case* **C.** *unless* **D.** *if*
6. He ran away .... he should be sent to prison.
   A. *than* **B.** *lest* **C.** *till* **D.** *if*
7. ..... you see him, tell him to come to my room.
   A. *If* **B.** *That* **C.** *As if* **D.** *Before*
8. He will never succeed, ... hard he works.
   A. *after* **B.** *as* **C.** *so* **D.** *however*
9. You can borrow it ...... you don't get it dirty.
   A. *as much as* **B.** *as long as* **C.** *whether* **D.** *even if*
10. .... what you say is true, I still admire the man.
   A. *That* **B.** *Until* **C.** *Lest* **D.** *Even if*
11. He went out .... the fact that he had a bad cold.
   A. *in spite of* **B.** *as far as* **C.** *as much as* **D.** *provided that*
12. He speaks English perfectly, ... has never been to England.
   A. *when* **B.** *that* **C.** *if* **D.** *although*

ANSWERS

EX. 11. 1. *When* I called on you, you were out. 2. Make haste *or* you will be late. 3. We eat *that* we may live. 4. He was tired, *still* he went on working. 5. It is twelve, *so* I must go to bed. 6. I met my friend *who* recognized me at once. 7. He came very late, *yet* I did not lose my temper. 8. *As soon as* the whistle blew the train left the station. 9. He switched off the lights *and* went to bed. 10. The days are warm, *but* the nights are cool. 11. She had *such* a pleasant manner *that* we all liked her. 12. He is *as* intelligent *as* he is hard-working. 13. Mend your ways, *otherwise* (or *else*) you may suffer. 14. The man *whom* I was waiting for did not turn up. (or, I was waiting for a man *who* did not turn up.) 15. He *neither* tells a lie *nor* tolerates it. 16. This is the town *where* my brother lives.

EX. 12. 1. Complex sentence 2. Complex sentence 3. Compound sentence 4. Complex sentence 5. Complex sentence 6. Complex sentence 7. Complex sentence 8. Compoud sentence 9. Compound sentence 10. Compound sentence 11. Complex sentence 12. Complex sentence 13. Complex sentence 14. Complex sentence 15. Complex sentence 16. Complex sentence

EX. 13. 1. still 2. so 3. because 4. as if 5. unless 6. lest 7. If 8. however 9. as long as 10. Even if 11. in spite of 12. although

□□□

13. SYNTHESIS

Synthesis (संयोजन) का अर्थ है : 'the joining together of parts so as to form a whole.' Synthesis को combination भी कहा जाता है।

1. *Look at these sentences :*

	Separate	*Combined*
(i)	(a) I went to the market. (b) I bought several things.	I went to the market *and* bought several things.
(ii)	(a) He did it. (b) He had to do it.	He did it *because* he had to do it.
(iii)	(a) Mr Prasad is our Principal (b) He is a great scholar.	Mr Prasad, *our Principal*, is a great scholar.

ऊपर के वाक्यों को पढ़ने के बाद आप समझ गए होंगे कि synthesis वह प्रक्रिया है जिसके द्वारा हम कई छोटे-छोटे वाक्यों को मिलाकर एक लंबा वाक्य बनाते हैं।

छात्रों को synthesis की अच्छी जानकारी आवश्यक है क्योंकि

(i) इससे अनेक छोटे-छोटे sentences लिखना नहीं पड़ता;

(ii) छोटे-छोटे sentences को जोड़कर लिखने का अभ्यास होता है;

(iii) इससे joining words *(and, but, so* etc.) के प्रयोग की विधि सीखते हैं।

किंतु, इसका अर्थ आप यह नहीं समझ लें कि long sentences ही लिखना अच्छा माना जाता है। वास्तव में, अनावश्यक लंबा वाक्य नहीं लिखना चाहिए। दस से पंद्रह शब्दों का वाक्य अच्छा समझा जाता है।

Simple, Compound and Complex Sentences

Synthesis करके जब हम कई वाक्यों को मिलाकर एक वाक्य बनाते हैं तो वह वाक्य simple हो सकता है या compound या complex.

2. *Look at these sentences :*

	Separate *(Simple Sentences)*	*Combined* *(Simple Sentences)*
(i)	(a) He heard a noise. (b) He got up.	*Hearing* a noise, he got up.
(ii)	(a) He has three sons. (b) He has to educate them.	He has three sons *to educate*.

(iii) (a) You will win the election.	You will *certainly* win the
(b) That is certain.	*election.*

(i) ऊपर दो simple sentences को मिलाकर एक simple sentence बनाया गया है।

(ii) Simple sentence में एक subject और एक finite verb[1] होता है।

3. *Look at these sentences :*

Separate *(Simple sentences)*	*Combined* *(Compound sentences)*
(i) (a) I went to the fair.	I went to the fair *but* did not buy
(b) I did not buy anything.	anything.
(ii) (a) Tom got up.	Tom got up *and* went to the post
(b) He went to the post office.	office.
(iii) (a) You can have tea.	You can have tea *or* coffee.
(b) You can have coffee.	

(i) ऊपर प्रत्येक दो simple sentences को जोड़कर एक compound sentence बनाया गया है।

(ii) Compound sentence में दो या दो से अधिक main clauses या statements होते हैं; प्रत्येक में subject + verb रहता है।

(iii) Compound sentece के parts मुख्यतः निम्नलिखित connectors द्वारा जुटे रहते है :

and	still	however	both........and
or	yet	neverthless	neither...........nor
but	nor	therefore	not only...........but also

4. *Look at these sentences :*

Separate *(Simple sentences)*	*Combined* *(Complex sentences)*
(i) (a) I went there.	*When* I went there, the door was
(b) The door was locked.	locked.
(ii) (a) This is the letter.	This is the letter *which* Mukul
(b) Mukul wrote it.	wrote.
(iii) (a) I was right.	The teacher told me *that* I was
(b) The teacher told me this.	right.

1. जो verb अपने subject के number और person द्वारा अनुशासित होता है, उसे finite verb कहते हैं। जैसे :

Hari *plays* football.

Boys *play* football.

(i) **ऊपर प्रत्येक दो simple sentences को जोड़कर एक complex sentence बनाया गया है।**

(ii) Complex sentence में कितने भी main clauses हो सकते हैं, किंतु उसमें कम-से-कम एक subordinate clause (adjective clause, adverb clause, noun clause) अवश्य रहता है।

(iii) Subordinate clause प्राय: निम्नलिखित शब्दों से शुरू होते हैं :

Adjective Clause	*Adverb Clause*	*Noun Clause*
who, which, whom that, whose, why, etc.	if, when, while, though although, so, as, before, after, because, until, since etc.	that, whether, what, if etc.

अगर परीक्षा में कोई स्पष्ट आदेश नहीं रहे तो आप वाक्यों को simple, compound या complex किसी में जोड़ सकते हैं। किंतु यथासंभव कम-से-कम finite verb का प्रयोग करें। अर्थात, पहले आप उन्हें मिलाकर simple sentence बनाने की चेष्टा करें। अगर यह संभव नहीं हो सके तो compound sentence बनाने की चेष्टा करें और अगर यह भी संभव नहीं हो तो अंत में complex sentence बनाएँ।

नीचे अब हम भिन्न-भिन्न तरीके से simple sentences को जोड़ना सीखेंगे।

1. And; as well as; both...........and; not only..........but also

5. *Look at these sentences :*

Separate	*Combined*
(i) (a) I finished my breakfast. (b) I went for a walk.	I finished my breakfast *and* went for a walk.
(ii) (a) Moti was punished. (b) Hari was punished.	Moti *as well as* Hari *was* punished.
(iii) (a) He speaks Hindi. (b) He speaks English.	He speaks *both* Hindi *and* English.
(iv) (a) Tom was fined. (b) Tom was expelled.	Tom was *not only* fined *but also* expelled.

अगर दिए हुए simple sentences से यह भाव झलके कि एक statement के बाद दूसरा statement आया है तो उन्हें जोड़ने के लिए हम *and, as well as, both.........and* तथा *not only............but also* का प्रयोग करते हैं।

(i) *And* का प्रयोग words, pharases, clauses तथा sentences को जोड़ने के लिए किया जाता है।

(ii) *As well as* का अर्थ होता है 'अतिरिक्त, अलावा' *(in addition to)*. इसका भी प्रयोग दो words या phrases को जोड़ने के लिए किया जाता है। यादं रखें : दो singular subjects *as well as* से जुटे हों तो verb singular होता है।

(iii) *Both............and* से जुटनेवाले subjects के बाद verb plural होता है।

(iv) *Not only* के बाद *but also* का प्रयोग अवश्य किया जाता है।

2. Or; nor; neither; else; otherwise; either....or; neither......nor.

6. *Look at these sentences :*

		Separate	*Combined*
(i)	(a)	Will you have tea ?	Will you have tea *or* coffee ?
	(b)	Will you have coffee ?	
(ii)	(a)	He does not play football.	He does not play football *nor* does he play cricket.
	(b)	He does not play cricket.	
(iii)	(a)	Tom does not smoke.	Tom does not smoke, *neither* does he drink.
	(b)	He does not drink.	
(iv)	(a)	Run fast.	Run fast, *else* you will be late.
	(b)	You will be late.	
(v)	(a)	Mend your ways.	Mend your ways *otherwise* you will suffer.
	(b)	You will suffer.	
(vi)	(a)	Rekha can do it.	*Either* Rekha *or* Ruby can do it.
	(b)	Ruby can do it.	
	(a)	The banks are not open today.	*Neither* the banks *nor* the post offices are open today.
	(b)	The post offices are not open today.	

यदि दिए गए simple sentences में choice का या विकल्प का भाव झलके तो उन्हें जोड़ने के लिए *or, nor, neither, else, otherwise, either...............or* या *neither..........nor* का प्रयोग करते हैं।

(i) Or का प्रयोग choice (विकल्प) सूचित करने के लिए होता है।

(ii) Nor (और न) का प्रयोग (बिना *neither* का) तब होता है जब उसके पहलेवाला clause negative हो या उसमें negative word हो। याद रखें *nor* के बाद verb+subject का शब्द-क्रम रहता है।

(iii) Neither (और न) का प्रयोग भी nor की तरह अकेले (बिना nor के) भी हो सकता है। Neither के पहलेवाला clause भी negative होता है तथा neither के बाद भी, verb+subject का शब्द-क्रम रहता है। वाक्य में जहाँ *nor* का प्रयोग हो सकता है वहाँ हम *neither* का भी प्रयोग कर सकते हैं।

(iv) Else (अगर नहीं तो)।

(v) Otherwise (अगर नहीं तो) एवं else के समान अर्थ होते हैं तथा एक की जगह दूसरे का प्रयोग किया जा सकता है।

जैसे : Do what you've been told, *else/or/otherwise* you will be punished.

(vi) Either...........or (या.............या) दो choices (विकल्प) के बीच चुनाव का भाव व्यक्त करने के लिए प्रयुक्त होता है।

Either...............or की जगह कभी-कभी whether.............or का भी प्रयोग किया जाता है।

जैसे : *Either* out of anger *or* jealousy, he wanted to harm me. *Whether* out of anger *or* jealousy, he wanted to harm me.

(vii) Neither..........nor=दोनों में से कोई नहीं।

3. But; still; yet; nevertheless; however

7. *Look at these sentences :*

		Separate	*Combined*
(i)	(a)	Many of you can read English .	Many of you can read English
	(b)	You cannot speak English.	*but* you cannot speak English.
(ii)	(a)	He is rich.	He is rich *still* he is unhappy.
	(b)	He is unhappy.	
(iii)	(a)	Ramu worked hard.	Ramu worked hard, *yet* he
	(b)	He failed.	failed.
(iv)	(a)	He has a lot of faults.	He has a lot of faults;
	(b)	I admire him very much.	*nevertheless* I admire him very much.
(v)	(a)	He was ill.	He was ill, *however*, he
	(b)	He decided to go.	decided to go.

जब दिए गए simple sentences से विरोधाभास (contrast) का भाव व्यक्त हो तो *but, still, yet, nevertheless* या *however* का प्रयोग कर simple sentences को जोड़ा जाता है।

(i) *But* से contrast (विरोध) का भाव व्यक्त होता है। किंतु कभी-कभी हल्का विरोध भाव व्यक्त करने के लिए *but* की जगह *and* का भी प्रयोग किया जाता है। जैसे :

My pen is here *but* yours is on the table.

My pen is here *and* yours is on the table.

(ii) Still = तो भी।

(iii) Yet (फिर भी) का प्रयोग प्राय: negative या conditional sentences में होता है। 'Yet, is stronger than 'but' in expressing contrast.

(iv) Nevertheless=किन्तु, तथापि, तो भी।

(v) However=तो भी, तथापि।

4. Therefore; so; for; consequently; hence

8. *Look at these sentences :*

		Separate	*Combined*
(i)	(a)	He was found guilty.	He was found guilty; *therefore*,
	(b)	He was hanged.	he was hanged.

		Separate	*Combined*
(ii)	(a)	It was getting dark.	It was getting dark, *so* we went home.
	(b)	We went home.	
(iii)	(a)	We will die one day.	We will die one day, *for* all men are mortal.
	(b)	All men are mortal.	
(iv)	(a)	They would not believe me.	They would not believe me; *consequently I* had to give them proofs.
	(b)	I had to give them proofs.	
(v)	(a)	Gandhijee died for us.	Gandhijee died for us, *hence* we honour him.
	(b)	We honour him.	

जब दिए गए simple sentences में 'कारण-परिणाम' ('one thought is inferred or proved from another') का भाव व्यक्त हो तो उन simple sentences को जोड़ने के लिए *therefore, so, for, consequently* तथा *hence* का प्रयोग किया जाता है।

(i) Therefore=इसलिए; (ii) so=इसलिए; (iii) यहाँ for=क्योंकि;

(iv) Consequently=फलतः, अतः (v) hence=अतएव; इसलिए।

5. As.............as; so...............as; than

9. *Look at these sentences :*

		Separate	*Combined*
(i)	(a)	She is pretty.	She is *as* pretty *as* her sister.
	(b)	Her sister is pretty.	
(ii)	(a)	She did not run quickly.	She did not run *so* quickly *as* her sister.
	(b)	Her sister ran quickly.	
(iii)	(a)	This book is easier.	This book is easier *than* that book.
	(b)	That book is easy.	

जब simple sentences में comparison (तुलना) का भाव हो तब उन्हें *as........as, so.......as* या *than* का प्रयोग कर जोड़ते हैं।

(i) जब simple sentences से समानता (equality) का भाव व्यक्त हो तब उन्हें as...........as का प्रयोग कर जोड़ते हैं।

(ii) किन्तु simple sentences से जब नकारात्मक समानता की तुलना (negative comparison of equality) का बोध हो तब *not so..........as* या *not as..........as* का प्रयोग किया जाता है।

(iii) जब simple sentences से अधिक अच्छा या अधिक खराब जैसी तुलना का भाव व्यक्त हो तब comparative degree + *than* का प्रयोग कर उन्हें जोड़ा जाता है।

6. Who; whom; whose; which; that

10. *Look at these sentences :*

		Separate	*Combined*
(i)	(a)	I met my friend.	I met my friend *who* is in London now.
	(b)	He is in London now.	

		Separate	Combined
(ii)	(a)	Here is the boy.	Here is the boy *whom* you
	(b)	You wanted to see.	wanted to see.
(iii)	(a)	This is the girl.	This is the girl *whose* parents
	(b)	Her parents are in Canada.	are in Canada.
(iv)	(a)	I have a car.	I have a car *which* is blue.
	(b)	It is blue.	
(v)	(a)	This is the house.	This is the house *that* Jack
	(b)	Jack built it.	built.

कभी-कभी simple sentences को *who, whom, whose, which* तथा *that* का प्रयोग कर जोड़ा जाता है। इन शब्दों से शुरू होनेवाले clauses, adjective clauses होते हैं तथा उस वाक्य को complex sentence कहा जाता है।

(i) Who (जो, जिसने) का प्रयोग केवल व्यक्ति (person) के लिए होता है।

(ii) Whom (जिसे, जिसको) who का ही एक रूप है जिसका प्रयोग व्यक्ति (person) के लिए होता है।

(iii) Whose (जिसका) भी who का ही एक रूप है जिसका प्रयोग व्यक्ति के लिए होता है। कभी-कभी whose का प्रयोग निर्जीव वस्तुओं के लिए भी होता है किंतु ऐसे वाक्य में हमें whose की जगह which का प्रयोग करना चाहिए। जैसे :

This is the house *whose* windows are broken.

इसके बदले हम कहें :

This is the house *which* has the broken windows.

(iv) Which (जो, जिसको) का प्रयोग प्रायः वस्तुओं तथा छोटे-छोटे जीवों के लिए होता है; किंतु कभी-कभी चुनाव (selection) के अर्थ में व्यक्ति के लिए भी which का प्रयोग होता है। जैसे :

This is the book *which* I like.
This is the dog *which* bit me.
Which of you did it ?

(v) That (जो, जिसे, जिसने, जिन्होंने) का प्रयोग वस्तु, छोटे जानवर तथा व्यक्ति के लिए भी किया जाता है।

The letter *that* came this morning is from my father. (वस्तु)
Those dogs *that* attacked you ought to be shot. (जानवर)
The man *that* (किंतु यहाँ *who* का प्रयोग अच्छा होता) sold you the camera is a thief. (व्यक्ति)

7. When; whenever; while; before; after; as; since; as soon as

11. *Look at these sentences :*

		Separate	*Combined*
(i)	(a)	The sun set.	*When* the sun set, we returned
	(b)	We returned home.	home.
(ii)	(a)	I want to go.	*Whenever* I want to go, the
	(b)	The child begins to cry.	child begins to cry.

	Separate	Combined
(iii)	(a) I wrote the letter. (b) I was in hospital.	I wrote the letter *while* I was in hospital.
(iv)	(a) I had left home. (b) He came later.	I had left home *before* he came.
(v)	(a) I arrived. (b) He had left.	*I* arrived *afer* he had left.
(vi)	(a) I found it. (b) I was going to college.	I found it *as* I was going to college.
(vii)	(a) Mr Sinha is ill. (b) He cannot attend the meeting.	*Since* Mr Sinha is ill, he cannot attend the meeting.
(viii)	(a) He will do it. (b) He comes home.	He will do it *as soon as* he comes home.

अगर simple sentences से कब (when) अर्थात time का भाव व्यक्त हो तो उन्हें *when, whenever, while, before, after, as, since* तथा *as soon as* का प्रयोग कर जोड़ते हैं।

(i) When=कब, जब; (ii) whenever=जब कभी; (iii) while=जिस समय में, जिस बीच में; (iv) before=के पहले; (v) after=के बाद; (vi) as=ज्योंही, जब, जिस समय, जबकि; (vii) since=से, क्योंकि, इसलिए कि; (viii) as soon as= ज्योंही।

8. Till; until; as long as

12. *Look at these sentences :*

	Separate	Combined
(i)	(a) Let us wait. (b) The rain stops.	Let us wait *till* the rain stops.
(ii)	(a) I told him to stay. (b) I returned.	I told him to stay *until* I returned.
(iii)	(a) You can keep the book. (b) You like.	You can keep the book *as long as* you like.

अगर simple sentences से समय की अवधि अर्थात how long (कब तक) का बोध हो तो उन्हें *till, until* या *as long as* से जोड़ा जाता है।

(i) Till=जब तक कि, जबकि, यहाँ तक कि।

(ii) Until का भी वही अर्थ होता है जो till का। Till का प्रयोग sentence के बीच में किया जाता है किंतु until का प्रयोग sentence के शुरू तथा बीच दोनों position में होता है। जैसे :

She won't go away *till* you promise to help her.
Until you told me, I had heard nothing of what happened.
Go straight on *until* you come to the post office.

(iii) As long as=जब तक कि।

9. Because; if; unless; though; although

13. *Look at these sentences :*

	Separate	*Combined*
(i)	(a) I did it. (b) I had to do it.	I did it *because* I had to do it.
(ii)	(a) Don't eat too much. (b) You will be ill.	*If* you eat too much, you will be ill.
(iii)	(a) You must work hard. (b) Otherwise you won't pass.	You won't pass *unless* you work hard.
(iv)	(a) He is contented. (b) He is poor.	He is contented *though* he is poor.
(v)	(a) He did not have much wealth. (b) He was not unhappy.	*Although* he did not have much wealth, he was not unhappy.

(i) Because (क्योंकि) से कारण का भाव व्यक्त होता है।

(ii) If (अगर) से शर्त सूचित होती है।

(iii) Unless (जब तक, if not) से भी शर्त (condition) का भाव व्यक्त होता है।

(iv) Though=यद्यपि।

(v) Although (यद्यपि) तथा though इन दोनों के अर्थ एक-जैसे हैं।

Though तथा *although* अगर वाक्य के शुरू में रहें तो *though/although* clause के बाद comma (,) दिया जाता है तथा *yet* का प्रयोग नहीं किया जाता।

Note : अगर कोई वाक्य because, if, unless, though, although से शुरू हो तो उस clause के बाद comma दिया जाता है; किंतु अगर principal clause पहले आए और बादवाला clause इन शब्दों से शुरू हो तो इन दोनों clauses के बीच comma नहीं आता। जैसे :

If you labour hard, you will succeed. (comma)
You will succeed *if* you labour hard. (no comma)

10. As if; where; why

14. *Look at these sentences :*

	Separate	*Combined*
(i)	(a) It looks. (b) It will rain.	It looks *as if* it will rain.
(ii)	(a) There is heavy rainfall there. (b) Maize will not grow at such a place.	Maize will not grow *where* there is heavy rainfall.
(iii)	(a) She refused to sing. (b) Can she tell me the reason ?	Can she tell me the reason *why* she refused to sing ?

(i) As if (मानो) के बाद *verb* present, future या past tense में हो सकता है।

He speaks *as if* he *was* (or *were*) my boss.
He speaks as if he *is* my boss.

(ii) Where= जहाँ; (iii) why= क्यों।

11. That; whether; how; what

15. *Look at these sentences :*

		Separate	*Combined*
(i)	(a)	He is hard working.	Everybody knows *that* he is hard working.
	(b)	Everybody knows it.	
(ii)	(a)	She may be in the office.	I do not know *whether* she is in the office.
	(b)	I do not know.	
(iii)	(a)	How should I do this sum ?	I don't know *how* I should do do this sum.
	(b)	I don't know this.	
(iv)	(a)	What did she say ?	This was *what* she said.
	(b)	This was it.	

कभी-कभी simple sentences को *that* (कि), *whether* (कि), *how* (कैसे) तथा *what* (जो कुछ) से जोड़ा जाता है।

12. To; too..............to

16. *Look at the following sentences :*

		Separate	*Combined*
(i)	(a)	He is going to Bombay.	He is going to Bombay *to* start business.
	(b)	He will start business..	
(ii)	(a)	You must help your friend.	It is your duty *to* help your friend.
	(b)	It is your duty.	
(iii)	(a)	It is very heavy.	It is *too* heavy *for* me *to* lift.
	(b)	I can't lift it.	
(iv)	(a)	She is too weak.	She is *too* weak *to* attend school.
	(b)	She cannot attend school.	

कभी-कभी simple sentences को *to* या *too.........to* का प्रयोग कर जोड़ते हैं।

13. Verb+ing; having+v^3., being+v^3

17. *Look at the following sentences :*

		Separate	*Combined*
(i)	(a)	I saw a tiger.	*Seeing* a tiger, I cried out.
	(b)	I cried out.	
(ii)	(a)	She took a pencil.	*Taking* a pencil, she began to write.
	(b)	She began to write.	
(iii)	(a)	I read the book.	*Having read* the book, I returned it to Mohan.
	(b)	I returned it to Mohan.	
(iv)	(a)	He lost his fortune.	*Having lost* his fortune, he is now a beggar.
	(b)	He is now a beggar.	
(v)	(a)	He is tired of play.	*Being tired* of play, he wants rest.
	(b)	He wants rest.	

(i) अगर simple sentences के verbs present tense में हों तो उनमें से किसी उपयुक्त verb में *ing* लगाकर simple sentences को जोड़ते हैं।

(ii) Simple sentences को *having* तथा *being* का प्रयोग कर भी जोड़ते हैं। *Having/Being* के बाद verb का तीसरा रूप यानी v^3 का प्रयोग किया जाता है।

14. By using a noun or phrase in apposition

18. *Look at these sentences :*

		Separate	*Combined*
(i)	(a)	Ramesh is my friend.	Ramesh, *my friend*, plays
	(b)	He plays badminton with me.	badminton with me.
(ii)	(a)	Patna is the capital of Bihar.	Patna, *the capital of Bihar*, is
	(b)	It is situated on the bank of the Ganga.	situated on the bank of the Ganga.

Apposition का अर्थ होता है : अगल-बगल। कभी-कभी simple sentences में एक ही noun के विषय में कुछ और बातें बताई जाती हैं। तब noun या phrase को उस noun या phrase के बगल में रखा जाता है जिसके विषय में कुछ कहा गया हो।

SUMMARY

जिन शब्दों से simple sentences को जोड़कर एक किया जाता है उन्हें linking words कहते हैं। Linking words—*words* को *words* से, *phrases* को *phrases* से तथा *clauses* को *clauses* से जोड़ते हैं। English के कुछ मुख्य linking words इस प्रकार हैं :

Linking Words

and	but	or	so
for	yet	till	until
who	when	as	if
that	which	since	how
what	while	hence	else
nor	after	before	than
when	whose	why	where
though	although	unless	because
whether	therefore	still	neither
otherwise	whenever	nevertheless	consequently
however	as if	as well as	as long as
as soon as	both......and	as......as	so......as
even if	neither......nor	either.......or	not only......but also

हम इन शब्दों का प्रयोग कर छोटे-छोटे वाक्यों को जोड़कर बड़ा वाक्य बनाते हैं।

Examples Worked Out

Combine each of the following sentences :

I

	Separate	Combined
1.	(a) It is clear. (b) He did not want to go.	It is clear *that* he did not want to go.
2.	(a) He can understand English. (b) He can speak English.	He can understand *and* speak English.
3.	(a) He was poor. (b) He was happy.	He was poor *but* happy.
4.	(a) She heard the news. (b) She was glad.	*When* she heard the news, she was glad.
5.	(a) I trust him. (b) He is honest.	I trust him *because* he is honest.
6.	(a) Rajeev is brave. (b) Mukul is equally brave.	Rajeev is *as* brave *as* Mukul.
7.	(a) He was poor. (b) Yet he was proud.	*Although* he was poor, he was proud.
8.	(a) Are you an artist ? (b) Are you a photographer ?	Are you an artist *or* a photographer ?
9.	(a) He did not come. (b) He did not inform me.	He did not come, *nor* did he inform me.
10.	(a) I have some work. (b) I must do it today.	I have some work *to* do today.
11.	(a) Ravi passed the test. (b) Reeta also passed the test.	Ravi *as well as* Reeta passed the test.
12.	(a) He is rich. (b) He is miserable.	He is rich *yet* miserable.
13.	(a) You want me to go with you. (b) I will do so.	*Since* you want me to go with you, I will do so.
14.	(a) It may rain. (b) Then the match may be cancelled.	*If* it rains, the match will be cancelled.
15.	(a) He is very weak. (b) He cannot walk.	He is *too* weak *to* walk.
16.	(a) He will pass. (b) It is certain.	It is certain *that* he will pass.
17.	(a) She writes well. (b) She speaks better.	She speaks better *than* she writes.
18.	(a) He was a dacoit. (b) He was jailed.	He was a dacoit, *so* he was jailed.

	Separate	Combined
19.	(a) Gandhijee died for us. (b) We honour him even today.	*As* Gandhijee died for us, we honour him even today.
20.	(a) Life is short. (b) It is sweet.	Life is short *but* sweet.
21.	(a) I am very tired. (b) I have been working all day.	I am very tired, *for* I have been working all day.
22.	(a) Ruby bought a watch. (b) It shows the date.	Ruby bought a watch *which* shows the date.
23.	(a) I gave him the money. (b) He needed it.	I gave him the money *because* he needed it.
24.	(a) Mr Sen was very tired. (b) He could not walk any further.	Mr Sen was *so* tired *that* he could not walk any further.
25.	(a) Get one hundred marks. (b) Then you will get a prize.	*If* you get one hundred marks, you will get a prize.
26.	(a) You said something. (b) It is true.	*What* you said is true.
27.	(a) The bus was full. (b) I managed to get into it.	*Although* the bus was full, I managed to get into it.
28.	(a) A thief entered the room. (b) He found it empty.	*Entering* the room, the thief found it empty.
29.	(a) He did not help me. (b) He was angry with me.	*Being* angry with me, he did not help me.
30.	(a) He finished his work. (b) He left for home.	*Having* finished his work, he left for home.
31.	(a) You were not present there. (b) This was unfortunate.	*Unfortunately*, you were not present there.
32.	(a) You must succeed in life. (b) I expect this of you.	I expect you *to* succeed in life.
33.	(a) My father was ill. (b) I had to do everything myself.	My father *being* ill, I had to do everything myself.
34.	(a) Dashrath was the king of Ayodhya. (b) He had four sons.	Dasharath, *the king of Ayodhya.* had four sons.
35.	(a) I have rented this house. (b) It belongs to my friend.	I have rented *the house of* my friend.
36.	(a) He is a rich man. (b) It is known to all.	*That he is a rich man* is known to all.
37.	(a) A boy said this. (b) I know him.	I know the boy *who* said this.
38.	(a) This is the school. (b) I taught here.	This is the school *where* I taught.

	Separate	Combined
39.	(a) He taught me a lesson. (b) I cannot forget it.	He taught me a lesson *which* I cannot forget.
40.	(a) He may come. (b) Please request him to wait for me.	Please request him to wait for me *when* he comes.
41.	(a) You can stay. (b) You can come with us.	You can *either* stay *or* come with us.
42.	(a) He was surprised. (b) He was pleased.	He was *both* surprised *and* pleased.
43.	(a) The camera was not cheap. (b) It was not very useful.	The camera was *neither* cheap *nor* very useful.
44.	(a) I went to the market. (b) I did not buy anything.	I went to the market *but* did not buy anything.
45.	(a) The boy sits near me. (b) His father is a doctor.	The boy *whose* father is a doctor sits near me.
46.	(a) You did not come to my house yesterday. (b) Can you tell me the reason ?	Can you tell me the reason *why* you did not come to my house yesterday ?
47.	(a) You are there. (b) You can stay there.	You can stay *where* you are.
48.	(a) He is ill. (b) He cannot attend classes.	*As* he is ill, he cannot attend classes.
49.	(a) I will return. (b) Do not go till then.	Do not go *until* I return.
50.	(a) I had left home. (b) he came later.	I had left home *before* he came.
51.	(a) The sun set. (b) Darkness came.	The sun *having* set, darkness came.
52.	(a) You may be wrong. (b) I cannot say.	I cannot say *whether* you are wrong.
53.	(a) He was guilty. (b) He was punished.	He was guilty *therefore* he was punished.
54.	(a) He is very fat. (b) He cannot run.	He is *too* fat *to* run.
55.	(a) Tell the truth. (b) Be silent.	Tell the truth *or* be silent.
56.	(a) The thief ran away somehow. (b) I do not know how.	I do not know *how* the thief ran away.
57.	(a) He is lazy. (b) He is equally foolish.	He is *as* foolish *as* lazy.

	Separate	*Combined*
58.	(a) Mr Sinha is my neighbour. (b) He is on the telephone.	Mr. Sinha, *my neighbour*, is on the telephone.
59.	(a) Rekha is a 20 year-old singer on television shows. (b) She is being invited to the party.	Rekha, *who is a 20 year-old singer on television shows*, is being invited to the party.
60.	(a) He is poor. (b) He is honest in spite of it.	*Though* he is poor, he is honest.
61.	(a) You must do your homework. (b) You will be punished.	You must do your homework *otherwise* you will be punished.
62.	(a) How old am I ? (b) That's none of your business.	*How old I am* is none of your business.
63.	(a) How many times did you knock ? (b) Tell me this.	Tell me *how many times you knocked.*
64.	(a) He lost his watch. (b) He lost his money.	He lost *not only* his watch *but also* his money.
65.	(a) She was sleeping. (b) They arrived.	*While* she was sleeping, they arrived.
66.	(a) You must write correctly. (b) You will not pass.	*Unless* you write correctly, you will not pass.
67.	(a) Mr Reddy was the President of India. (b) He addressed the nation last year. (c) There were violent demo-nstrations in the streets of Delhi.	*While the President of India,* Mr Reddy, addressed the nation last year, there were violent demonstrations in the streets of Delhi.
68.	(a) Reeta washed the shirts. (b) Rekha ironed the shirts. (c) Ruby folded the shirts.	Reeta washed, Rekha ironed *and* Ruby folded the shirts.
69.	(a) He was absent. (b) He was ill. (c) His illness was serious.	He was absent *as he was seriously ill.*
70.	(a) Take exercise regularly. (b) Then you can keep fit. (c) Then you can do a lot of work.	*If* you take exercise regularly, you can keep fit *and* do a lot of work.

II

71.	He struck his foot against a stone. He fell to the ground.	*By striking* his foot against a stone *and* falling to the

	Separate	*Combined*
	He made his clothes very dirty.	ground, he made his clothes very dirty.
72.	He was helping his friend. His friend was learning how to ride a scooter. The scooter was new.	He was helping his friend *(to) learn* how to ride a new scooter.
73.	Portia was the wife of Bussanio. She saved the life of Antonio. Antonio was a merchant of Venice.	Bassanio's wife, *Portia,* saved the life of Antonio, a *marchant of Venice.*
74.	The wind was strong. It drove the ship ashore. The ship ran on to the sand. It remained there for several days.	The wind *being* strong drove the ship ashore, *which* ran on to the sand *and* remained there for several days.
75.	Mohan came here on Tuesday. He is an officer in the revenue department. He came here to meet his father. His father is ailing.	Mohan, *an officer in the revenue department*, came here on Tuesday *to* meet his ailing father.
76.	King Lear was found by some men. He was wandering about the fields near Dove. His condition was pitiable.	King Lear, *who* was wandering about the fields near Dove, was found by some men in pitiable condition.
77.	A man had lost a purse. He was passing through a jungle He entered the jungle again. He found it.	*While* passing through a jungle, a man had lost a purse *which* he found on entering the jungle again.
78.	A lion was once king of the beasts of the forest. At last, he became weak from old age. He was unable to obtain food. He died of hunger.	A lion, *once* king of the beasts of the forest and at last weak from old age, was unable to obtain food and died of hunger.
79.	There was an old man. He was dying. He had four sons. He advised them to live in peace together after his death.	There was a *dying old man who* advised his four sons to live in peace together after his death.
80.	I am young. You are old and experienced. I was afraid of your age and dignity.	I, *being* young and you, old and experienced, was afraid of your age and dignity.

	Separate	*Combined*
81.	Robert Bruce was lying in bed. His bed was a very poor one. He looked up at the ceiling and saw a spider.	*Lying* in a poor bed, Robert Bruce looked up at the ceiling and saw a spider.

EXERCISE 1

Underline the linking words in the following sentences :

EXAMPLE : Do you know *if* Mr Kujur is at home ?

1. Do you know if Mr Kujur is at home ?
2. As a child he lived in India.
3. Is it green or blue ?
4. It was raining when we arrived.
5. The river which flows through London is called the Thames.
6. While in Delhi, she studied music.
7. There was a man who came to see you yesterday.
8. My brother whom you met has written a book.
9. This is the reason why I left early.
10. Unless compelled to stay in, I go for a walk every day.
11. I did not go there because I was ill.
12. It will be five years before we meet again.
13. I shall arrive after you leave.
14. It is just a week since we arrived here.
15. Although it was very cold, he went out without a coat.

EXERCISE 2

Copy the following sentences. Fill in the blanks with suitable linking words given in the brackets :

EXAMPLE : Try.........come early. *(for/so/and)*
Try *and* come early.

1. Try......come early. *(for/so/and)*
2. Tom was not there......his brother was. *(or/but/that)*
3. Go......buy one. *(as/and/nor)*
4. We tried to do it......couldn't. *(but/as/if)*
5. She asked me to go......I went. *(or/for/so)*
6. ......you ask him, he will help you. *(And/But/If)*
7. He is a hardworking......not very intelligent boy. *(or/but/so)*
8. ......it is necessary, I can come at six. *(That/If/So)*
9. They cost a lot of money,.......use them carefully. *(or/so/that)*
10. Sunday is the day.......I am least busy. *(what/why/when)*
11. ......he grew older, he became less active. *(So/How/As)*
12. Are you coming......not ? *(and/or/but)*
13. He said......he would come. *(that/what/and)*
14. Do it now......you forget. *(before/how/where)*
15. He worked hard......he failed. *(so/as/yet)*

EXERCISE 3

Copy the following sentences. Fill in the blanks with suitable linking words given in the brackets :

EXAMPLE : This is the man....... wanted to see you. *(which/who/whom)*
This is the man *who* wanted to see you.

1. This is the man......wanted to see you. *(which/who/whom)*
2. It is not so difficult......I expected. *(so/or/as)*
3. Hurry up......you will be late. *(or/if/as)*
4. This is the boy......father is a lawyer. *(who/whose/which)*
5. You can either stay......come with me. *(or/as/for)*
6. That's the place......the accident took place. *(which/why/where)*
7. The reason......he did it is unknown. *(who/why/when)*
8. ......we have no money, we can't buy it. *(Yet/Nor/Since)*
9. He must be either mad......drunk. *(nor/or/as)*
10. Please come in......go out. *(or/so/too)*
11. Take the book......is lying on that table. *(who/when/which)*
12. Meena was dressed in blue......Veena was dressed in red. *(both/while/otherwise)*
13. I know the man......you mean. *(what/whose/whom)*
14. I saw him......he was getting off the bus. *(as/so/but)*
15. I don't care......he stays or goes. *(what/whether/which)*

EXERCISE 4

Combine each of the following pairs of sentences. Use the linking word given in the brackets :

EXAMPLE : Sima can come early. Rekha can't come early. *(but)*
Sima can come early *but* Rekha can't.

(Rekha can't come early की जगह Rekha can't से ही काम चल जाएगा क्योंकि come early पहले part में आ चुका है। अतः, शब्दों को repeat नहीं करना ही अच्छा माना जाता है।)

1. Sima can come early. Rekha can't come early. *(but)*
2. She wants tea. I will have coffee. *(but)*
3. I can read English. I can write English. *(and)*
4. You can go. You can stay. *(or)*
5. He is hardworking. He is intelligent. *(and)*
6. You may speak English. You may speak Bengali. *(or)*
7. Today is cloudy. Yesterday wasn't cloudy. *(but)*
8. He is greedy. He is dishonest. *(as well as)*
9. Everybody stood up then. Mr Sinha entered the room. *(when)*
10. I will wait here. You come back. *(till)*
11. The thief saw the police. He ran away at once. *(when)*
12. She is walking slowly. She is old. *(as)*
13. I will get ready. Wait till then. *(till)*
14. He has not done any work. He will fail in the examination. *(As)*
15. I didn't speak to him. He was in a hurry. *(as)*

EXERCISE 5

Combine each of the following pairs of sentences. Use the linking word given in the brackets :

EXAMPLE : I fell asleep. I was reading. *(while)*
While I was reading, I fell asleep.
Or, I fell asleep *while* I was reading.
(इन दोनों वाक्यों में comma के प्रयोग पर ध्यान दें।)

1. I fell asleep. I was reading. *(while)*
2. We decided not to buy it. The price was high. *(because)*
3. You want me to go with him. I will do so. *(Since)*
4. It is raining. I shall not go out today. *(Since)*
5. Take exercise every day. Then you can keep fit. *(If)*
6. It was late. We decided not to play any more. *(so)*
7. This is the boy. He stood first in the examination. *(who)*
8. That is the letter. Rajeev wrote it. *(which)*
9. Read a large number of books. Then you can improve your English. *(If)*
10. We went to bed at once. We were very tired. *(since)*
11. I gave him the book. He needed it. *(because)*
12. Once there lived a farmer. He had a big elephant. *(who)*
13. He cut himself. He was shaving. *(while)*
14. This is the new book. I like it most. *(which)*
15. He is not going to college. There is a strike. *(because)*

EXERCISE 6

Combine each of the following pairs of sentences. Use the linking word given in the brackets :

EXAMPLE : He is hardworking. Everybody knows it. *(that)*
Everybody knows *that* he is hardworking.

1. He is hardworking. Everybody knows it. *(that)*
2. He is poor. He is contented. *(but)*
3. Come in. Go out. *(or)*
4. He can't go. He has no suitable clothes. *(Since)*
5. He is past ninety. His senses are still keen. *(Although)*
6. I want to tell you something. I may forget it. *(before)*
7. It is true. She will succeed. *(that)*
8. We go to the post office. We buy stamps there. *(to)*
9. He helped me. I was about to fall down. *(when)*
10. He is very helpful. He is very rich. *(although)*
11. He was fined. He was jailed. *(as well as)*
12. He was very busy last week. I called on him. *(when)*
13. Don't get down. The bus must stop. *(till)*
14. He stopped talking. He had nothing more to say. *(as)*
15. He injured himself. He was climbing a tree. *(while)*

EXERCISE 7

Combine each of the following pairs of sentences. Use the linking word(s) given in the brackets :

EXAMPLE : He may come by train. He may come by taxi. *(either.......or)*

He may come *either* by train *or* by taxi.

1. He may come by train. He may come by taxi. *(either.....or)*
2. She wasn't hungry. She wasn't thirsty. *(neither......nor)*
3. The dog isn't white. The dog isn't black. *(neither.....nor)*
4. He lost his pen. He lost his pencil. *(not only...but also)*
5. She is tall. She is beautiful. *(not only...but also)*
6. God is with you. You may go to any place. *(wherever)*
7. I went to her room. She was sitting on a chair. *(when)*
8. This is the garden. The finest roses grow here. *(where)*
9. I will follow you. You may go to any place. *(wherever)*
10. My mother gave me a camera. I was twelve at that time. *(when)*
11. It is Sunday tomorrow. We needn't go to college. *(as)*
12. He used very bad words. I don't want to repeat them. *(such......that)*
13. He walked very fast. I couldn't keep up with him. *(so......that)*
14. It was a very cold night. We did not go out. *(such......that)*
15. I asked him to make a fire. It was very cold. *(since)*

EXERCISE 8

Combine each of the following pairs of sentences. Use the linking word(s) given in the brackets :

EXAMPLE : The poem is very difficult. I can't understand it. *(too......to)*

The poem is *too* difficult *for me to* understand.

1. The poem is very difficult. I can't understand it. *(too......to)*
2. He is very lazy. He will not revise his work. *(too......to)*
3. We go to a shop. We buy things there. *(to)*
4. She is tall. She is beautiful. *(both......and)*
5. The table is heavy. I cannot lift it. *(too.....to)*
6. You must write correctly. You will not pass. *(unless)*
7. I reached the station. The train had left. *(after)*
8. I don't know. He gets good marks. *(how)*
9. I went home. I took Tom with me. *(with)*
10. He lost his time. He did not read. *(without)*
11. He has bought a book. He has lost the money. *(either......or)*
12. London isn't the capital of India. It isn't the capital of America. *(neither......nor)*
13. I am tired. I am unhappy. *(not only...but also)*
14. I found the bag in a certain place. I left it there. *(where)*
15. You may like a certain place. Sit there. *(wherever)*

EXERCISE 9

Combine each of the following pairs of sentences. Use the linking word(s) given in the brackets :

EXAMPLE : You are walking slowly. You are an old man. *(as)*
You are walking slowly *as* you are an old man.

1. You are walking slowly. You are an old man. *(as)*
2. She was able to go home. Her dress was dry. *(only when)*
3. I ran to look for a rickshaw. It was raining heavily. *(even though)*
4. He forgot to bring the book. That was unfortunate. *(unforunately)*
5. He is lazy. He is stupid. *(both......and)*
6. It goes on raining. It is never going to stop. *(as if)*
7. You may go to any place. I shall go with you. *(wherever)*
8. Rani is studying very hard. She wants to pass. *(in order to)*
9. You may need money. Take this cheque with you. *(in case)*
10. Tom is brave. Jack is braver. *(than)*
11. Amar is tall. Abdul is equally tall. *(as......as)*
12. He failed. I asked him the rason. *(why)*
13. He is very bright. There is no doubt about it. *(that)*
14. There are two more shirts. They must be repaired. *(to)*
15. It is very late. We can't go there now. *(too....for....to)*

EXERCISE 10

Combine each of the following pairs of sentences :

EXAMPLE : He has come. We know it.
We know *that* he has come.

1. He has come. We know it.
2. I have lost the book. You gave it to me.
3. I may grant you your prayer. You shall have to ask for it.
4. He is ill. It is known to all.
5. He saw me come. He ran away.
6. He was tired. He rested for a while.
7. He has many sons. He has to educate them.
8. He is very weak. He can't walk.
9. She failed. It was unfortunate.
10. He returned home. It was evening at that time.
11. The dinner was over. We left the place.
12. The sun set. We began our march.
13. Akbar was the Emperor of India. He was one of the greatest kings of his time.
14. Delhi is the capital of India. It is one of the best cities in the world.
15. He came. You had left before that.

EXERÇISE 11

Combine the following pairs of sentences :

EXAMPLE : It is dark. We cannot see.
As it is dark, we cannot see.
Or, It is dark, *so/hence/therefore* we cannot see.

1. It is dark. We cannot see.

2. **He is unwell. He cannot attend college.**
3. **He is slow. He is sure.**
4. He is a thief. He is jailed.
5. He is not a fool.He is not an idiot.
6. She is rich. She is unhappy.
7. They may cheat me. I will love them.
8. Wise men love truth. Fools hate it.
9. It is true. She will succeed.
10. He will go there. It is certain.
11. She may be at home. I do not know.
12. He is ill. He cannot go to college today.
13. The teacher entered the classroom. The students stood up.
14. This is the village. I was born here.
15. This is the new book. I bought it yesterday.

EXERCISE 12

Combine the following sentences. (Use as few finite verbs as possible.) :

EXAMPLE : He would win the first prize. That was his hope. His hope was not fulfilled.
His hope *that he would win the first prize* was not fulfilled.

1. He would win the first prize. That was his hope. His hope was not fulfilled.
2. His mother died. He heard the news. He left at once.
3. She lost her time. She did not read. She did not write.
4. He defended himself against the charge. His defence was clever. His defence was strong.
5. Rajeev works day and night. He wishes to win a scholarship. We all know it.
6. We saw the boy on the road. We stopped to speak to him. We gave him a toy.
7. Valmiki compiled the *Ramayana*. It is one of the most ancient epics. Valmiki had once been a dacoit.
8. I have engaged a servant. He will clean the house. He will cook my food.
9. He was honest. He was sincere. He was punctual.
10. I gave him books. I gave him pencils. I gave him some money.
11. Renu died at the age of six. She was the only child of her parents. Cancer was the cause of her death.
12. There was an old man. He had four sons. He advised them to live in peace together after his death.
13. This is the boy. He is poor. His parents are dead.
14. He was absent. He was ill. His illness was serious.
15. Mr Singh was hurt by a car. He was returning from the market. A man told me this.
16. This is the house. He lives in it. He lives with his family.
17. It may rain. It may not rain. You must reach your school in time.
18. It was now seven o'clock in the evening. It was too late to start on our journey. We postponed starting till the following morning.
19. The criminals were approaching. The policemen saw them. The policemen resorted to blank fire.
20. You have finished the job before time. You have done it in a good style. This is more than I expected from you.

EXERCISE 13

Combine the following sentences. Use as few finite verbs as possible :

EXAMPLE : I was ill. He heard of it. He at once went to the doctor.
Hearing of my illness, he at once went to the doctor.

1. I was ill. He heard of it. He at once went to the doctor.
2. He is rich. I was in difficulty. He did not help me.
3. You may agree. You may disagree. I shall certainly try to win the match.
4. I went to your father. He received me kindly. He promised to help me.
5. The man is very brave. You saw him. He once killed a tiger with an axe.
6. She had failed. She heard the news. She fainted.
7. You will be sent up to the university examination. Your doing well in the college examination is a condition. The Principal has issued these orders.
8. In private life he was kind. In private life he was even generous. But in public life he was very strict.
9. The sun rose. The fog dispersed. The General gave the order to advance.
10. The peasants were rich. They lived in a village. The village was in Bengal.
11. He is wicked. We must keep him at a distance. We must avoid him.
12. The monsoon failed. The tanks became empty. The fields could not be irrigated.
13. The people of that place are dirty. They are dishonest. They are hardworking.
14. He may accept our invitation. He may not accept our invitation. We shall invite him.
15. His parents may agree. They may not agree. He is determined to marry this girl.
16. He received all the pay promised him. He was dissatisfied. He filed a petition in court.
17. Two cats had stolen some cheese. They could not decide how to divide it equally between them. They decided on asking a monkey to settle the dispute for them.
18. I offered him help on all occasions. He went on refusing help. I left him to his fate.
19. The man with his son lived in a large house. His son was named John. The house was by the side of the hill.
20. English is a foreign language. It is not difficult to learn English. It has been made an optional subject now.

EXERCISE 14

Combine the following sentences into one :

EXAMPLE : He turned over the cradle. He found his child unhurt. He found a big snake lying dead on the floor.
= *Turning over* the cradle, he found his child unhurt *and* a big snake lying dead on the floor.

1. He has found out his mistake. He was very sorry. It was then too late.
2. The whole house was happy. Someone had brought good news. This was the cause of the happiness.
3. Some things are known. Others are unknown. The former help us to understand the latter.

4. The weather was hot. Elizabeth bought an ice-cream for fifty paise. She quenched her thirst with it.
5. The prince was ill. The people heard of it. They crowded to the palace.
6. You have succeeded very well. This was news to us. It gave us much pleasure.
7. I worked hard to earn money. I built this house. The house is close to the river.
8. I spoke to the teacher. I sat at the table. I held the book in my hand.
9. The man talks most. That man does least. This often happens.
10. Cowper's pet dog plunged into the river. It swam out to get a lily. This lily was the one especially admired by the poet.
11. The boy was drowning. He shouted for help. A workman plunged into the river to save him.
12. I was sitting at the window. I caught sight of a bear. He was wounded.
13. He attends classes regularly. He reads hard at home. He is sure to do well at the examination.
14. Duncan was the king of Scotland. He was put to death by Macbeth. Macbeth was his kinsman.
15. The rain stopped. We continued the match. We played till the sun set.
16. The strike was called off. The workers went back to work. The management increased their wages.
17. Milton was the Homer of England. He wrote *Paradise Lost*. It is the greatest epic poem in English.
18. Gandhiji was the Father of the Nation. He realized the danger of violent communal conflicts. He sacrificed his life to bring about unity.
19. One tongue is enough for a woman. Milton thought so. Therefore he taught his daughters only English.
20. She spoke very clearly. There were people standing at a distance. Even they could hear her well.
21. They were very poor. They had insufficient food for themselves. They invited the stranger to dinner.

EXERCISE 15

Combine into one sentence, using as few finite verbs as possible :

EXAMPLE : You will be sent up to the university examintion. Your doing well in the college examination is a condition. These are the orders. The Principal has issued these orders.

= The orders *which* the principal has issued are *that* you will be sent up to the university examination *provided that* you do well in the college examination.

1. I saw two beautiful birds. Both of them were of deep red colour. They were sitting on the topmost branch of a tree. They were indulging in a singing competition. I was charmed by the sight.
2. Two cats had stolen some cheese. They could not decide how to divide it equally between them. They decided on asking a monkey to settle the dispute for them. They went to the monkey at once for that purpose.
3. I left the place. I took the boy with me. The reason of my going was the unhealthiness of the neighbourhood. I was glad to go. We left in the afternoon.
4. Every boy should learn how to swim. Swimming is a fine, healthy exercise. Swimming is often the means of saving one's own life. Swimming is often the means of saving the lives of others.

5. **A certain rumour was current. He was said to have been taken seriously ill. He was quite well. He wrote to me that every day. He informed me by letter of his intention to extend his business.**
6. **Socrates was given a cup of hemlock. He drank it. His friends were standing near him then. So History says.**
7. **A fox saw a crow sitting on a tree. It had a piece of cheese in its mouth. The fox praised the crow's singing. The crow began to sing. It dropped the cheese.**
8. **A fox wanted to quench his thirst. He tried to get at the grapes. He failed in his attempts. The grapes were beyond his reach. He went away disappointed. He said that the grapes were sour.**
9. **The monkey agreed to hear and dicide the case. He called the two cats before him. He held out a pair of scales. He put one piece of cheese in one scale and one in another.**
10. **Shakespeare wrote comedies and tragedies. His comedies are the better of the two. So Dr Johnson said. We cannot agree.**

□ □ □

14. TRANSFORMATION

Look at these sentences :

A	B
Did I not help you ?	I did help you.
He is no fool.	He is wise.
Never tell a lie.	Always speak the truth.
He is as dull as an ass.	An ass is not duller than he is.

(i) स्तंभ A के नीचे दिए गए वाक्यों तथा ठीक उनके सामने स्तंभ B में दिए गए वाक्यों को देखें, अर्थ की दृष्टि से दोनों समान हैं।

(ii) किंतु एक ही बात को हम दो तरह से कह सकते हैं और तब वाक्यों के words तथा word-order भी अलग-अलग हो सकते हैं।

अतः, हम कह सकते हैं कि किसी वाक्य के meaning को अक्षुण्ण रखते हुए उसके form (रूप) को बदला जा सकता है। अँगरेजी व्याकरण में इसे Transformation कहते हैं। Transformation का अर्थ होता है—रूप-परिवर्तन यानी To transform a sentence is to re-write it to change its form without any change of meaning.

अँगरेजी में वाक्यों के मुख्यतः निम्नलिखित forms हो सकते हैं :

(a) (i) Statement या Assertive (affirmative or negative), (ii) Question या Interrogative, (iii) Desires या Imperative and Optative तथा (iv) Exclamations.

(b) Voice : Active and Passive

(c) (i) Simple, (ii) Complex, (iii) Double and Multiple (Compound).

(d) Direct and Indirect (Narration).

Voice तथा Narration के विषय में आप पढ़ चुके हैं। यहाँ हम Transformation की अन्य विधियों पर एक-एक कर विचार करेंगे।

(a) Transforming interrogative into assertive

Look at these sentences :

Interrogative	*Assertive*
Am I a fool ?	*I am not* a fool.
Did I *not write* to you ?	I *wrote* to you.
Can a man live for ever ?	A man *cannot* live for ever.

Interrogative	*Assertive*
Shall I *ever forget* those happy days ?	I ***shall never forget*** those happy days.
Who would not love his country ?	*Everyone would* love his country.
Can the leopard change its spots ?	A leopard *cannot* change its spots.
Who does not know Mahatma Gandhi ?	*Everyone* knows Mahatma Gandhi.

Interrogative sentence में पहले verb तब subject रहता है, किंतु assertive sentence में subject + verb का word-order रहता है। Interrogative sentence को assertive में बदलने के लिए :

(i) Verb + subject के word-order के बदले वाक्य में subject + verb का word-order लगाते हैं;

(ii) Interrogative mark की जगह full stop देते हैं;

(iii) यदि interrogative sentence में not नहीं रहे तो assertive में not लगाते हैं, पर यदि interrogative में not हो तो assertive में not का प्रयोग नहीं करते हैं।

(iv) कुछ ऐसे interrogative sentences होते हैं जो अर्थ के अनुसार assertive होते हैं, उन्हें rhetorical questions कहते हैं। ऐसे वाक्यों को अर्थ के अनुसार assertive में बदलते हैं। जैसे :

Isn't India a big country ?	India is a big country.

(b) Transforming assertive sentences into interrogative

Look at these sentences :

Assertive	*Interrogative*
It is very strange.	*Isn't* it very strange ?
Everyone knows you.	*Who* doesn't know you ?
I am a fly like thee.	*Am* I *not* a fly like thee ?
Nobody else could have done it.	*Who else* could have done it ?
There is nothing wrong with me.	*Is there anything* wrong with me ?
That is not the way to do it.	*Is* that the way to do it ?

Assertive sentence को interrogative बनाने के लिए :

(i) सबसे पहले assertive sentence के subject + verb के शब्द-क्रम को verb + subject के शब्द-क्रम में बदलें;

(ii) फिर full stop की जगह question mark लगाएँ; तथा

(iii) अगर assertive sentence में not नहीं हो तो interrogative में not लगाएँ, अगर assertive में not हो तो interrogative में इसका प्रयोग नहीं करें।

(c) Transforming exclamatory sentences into assertive

Look at these sentences :

Exclamatory	*Assertive*
What a lovely rose !	*It is* a very lovely rose.
O that I were young again !	*I wish* I were young again.
What a piece of work is man !	*Man is a strange* (or *wonderful*) piece of work.
O that I were at home again.	*I wish* I were at home again.
If only I could win the first prize !	*My greatest ambition* is to win the first prize.
To think of my seeing you here ?	*I never* thought I would see you here.
Alas ! Mr Oraon is dead.	*It is sad* that Oraon is dead.

Exclamatory sentence को assertive में बदलने के लिए :

(i) सबसे पहले subject + verb का शब्द-क्रम करें;

(ii) लुप्त शब्दों को जोड़ दें; जैसे : What a lovely rose ! = What a lovely rose it is !

(iii) अगर exclamation *how, what, such* आदि से प्रारंभ हो तो very या great + adjective या उपयुक्त adjective + noun का प्रयोग करें;

(iv) अगर exclamation *o that, would that, if I were, if only, alas that* से प्रारंभ हो तो assertive वाक्य में I wish, I earnestly desire, I am sad आदि का प्रयोग करें;

(v) Exclamation के चिह्न के स्थान पर full stop का प्रयोग करना चाहिए।

(d) Transforming affirmative sentences into negative

1. Look at these sentences :

Affirmative	*Negative*
Look before you leap.	*Do not* leap before you look.
Everyone will like it.	*No one* will dislike it.
Man is mortal.	*No man* is immortal.
He is sometimes wise.	He is *not always* foolish.
I always write to him.	I *never forget* to write to him.
All these boys are intelligent.	*None of* these boys is dull.
Every rose has a thorn.	There is *no* rose *without* a thorn.

Affirmative से negative बनाने के लिए कभी-कभी no/not तथा अन्य नकारात्मक भाव व्यक्त करनेवाले शब्दों का प्रयोग किया जाता है। जैसे : doubtful = not sure; always = never; as soon as = no sooner than; all = none; cruel = not kind आदि। कभी-कभी affirmative ध्वनिवाले शब्दों की जगह negative ध्वनिवाले विपरीतार्थक शब्दों के प्रयोग से भी काम चल जाता है।

2. ***Look at these sentences :***

Affirmative	*Nagative*
He is wise.	He is *not without* wisdom.
He was sure about his success.	He was *not doubtful* about his success.
Every man has his failings.	There is *no man* who has *no* failings.

कभी-कभी affirmative से negative बनाने के लिए double negative (negative + negative) की आवश्यकता पड़ती है। आप जानते हैं कि double negative = affirmative.

(e) Transforming negative sentences into affirmative

Look at the sentences :

Negative	*Affirmative*
Never tell a lie.	*Always* speak the truth.
He is *no mean* man.	He is a *good* man.
I am *not so rich* as he.	He is *richer* than I.
There is *no smoke* without fire.	Fire always causes *smoke*. *Or,* Wherever there is *smoke*, there is fire.
That is *not* a *new* book.	That is an *old* book.
None but a Hercules could do this.	*Only* a Hercules could do this.
I am *not a little* tired.	I am *very* tired.
No sooner did he see the tiger than he fled.	*As soon as* he saw the tiger, he fled.

Negative से affirmative बनाने की प्रक्रिया affirmative से negative बनाने की प्रक्रिया के ठीक विपरीत है। जैसे : not always = sometimes; no one = everyone; not good = bad; not kind = cruel; not getting help = helpless; no sooner than = as soon as आदि।

(f) Use of one part of speech for another

Look at these sentences :

(i) The *cost* of this pen is ten rupees. (Use verb for 'cost')
This pen *costs* ten rupees.

(ii) Tea and milk *differ* in colour. (Change verb into adjective)
Tea and milk are *different* in colour.

(iii) He will *certainly* succeed. (Use adjective for 'certainly')
His success is *certain*.

(iv) **His attitude *surprised* us. (Use noun for 'surprised')**
His attitude caused *surprise* in us.

(v) He is a man of *scholarship*. (Use adjective for 'scholarship')
He is a *scholarly* man.

(vi) We were present when he *arrived*. (Use noun for 'arrived')
We were present at the time of his *arrival*.

कभी-कभी एक ही शब्द को विभिन्न parts of speech में प्रयोग किया जाता है, तो ऐसी अवस्था में word का मूल अर्थ तो समान रहता है किंतु उसका रूप बदल जाता है।

(g) Transforming simple sentences into double or compound sentences

Look at these sentences :

Simple	*Double (Compound)*
Seeing a tiger coming, he ran away	He saw a tiger coming *and* he ran away.
In spite of his wealth, he is unhappy.	He is wealthy *but* he is unhappy.
I shall succeed with your help.	Help me, *and* I shall succeed.
Work hard to pass the examination	Work hard *and* you will pass the examination.
Besides being laborious, he is clever.	He is not only laborious but he is also clever.
Leaning on my arm, he stood up.	He leaned on my arm *and* stood up.
Match over, we left for home.	The match was over *and* we left for home.

(i) Simple sentence में एक ही principal clause रहता है, किंतु double sentence में दो;

(ii) And, but, still, yet, or, both...........and, not only..................but also, otherwise, either....................or आदि द्वारा जोड़कर simple से double sentence बनाया जाता है।

(h) Transforming double or compound sentences into simple sentences

Look at these sentences :

Double (Compound)	*Simple*
He came and took away my pen.	*Coming* here he took away my pen.
He worked hard, for he wanted to succeed.	He worked hard *for success*.

Double (compound)	*simple*
He bought a book and read it.	*After buying* a book he read it.
He was poor and so he was handicapped.	*Owing* to poverty he was handicapped.
You may take this pen or you may take that pen.	You may take *either of* the pens.
John did his best but could not succeed.	*In spite of* doing his best, John could not succeed.

Double sentence को simple में बदलने के लिए :

(i) Double sentence के finite verb को participle (verb + ing) में बदल दिया जाता है; या

(ii) आवश्यकतानुसार उस जगह to, for, after, by, unless, owing to, in spite of आदि का प्रयोग किया जाता है।

(i) Transforming simple sentences into complex sentences

Look at these sentences :

Simple	*Complex*
I wish him *success*.	I wish *that he should succeed.*
India's *victory* is certain.	It is certain *that India will have victory.*
He is a man *of power*.	He is a man *who has power*.
Work hard *for success*.	Work hard *so that you may have success.*
You may go *anywhere*.	You may go *wherever you like*.
His *failure* is almost certain.	*That he will fail* is almost certain.

(i) Simple sentence में एक *principal clause* रहता है, किंतु complex sentence में एक principal clause तथा कम-से-कम एक subordinate clause (noun, adjective या adverb clause) अवश्य रहता है।

(ii) अत:, simple sentence से complex sentence में बदलने के लिए simple sentence के किसी एक word या phrase (शब्द-समूह) को लेकर noun, adjective या adverb clause में who, whom, whose, that, which, when, why, where, unless, till, so.........that इत्यादि की सहायता से बदल दें।

(j) Transforming complex sentences into simple sentences

Look at these sentences :

Complex	*Simple*
I am not a man *who will deceive you*.	I am not a man *to deceive you.*
They criticised *what we did*.	They criticised *our actions*.

complex	*simple*
Though it was very hot, we started on foot.	*Despite the heat*, we started on foot.
The report *that the king was dead* is false.	The report *of the king's death* is false.
Father desired *that I should go*.	Father desired *me to go*.
That he should resign was beyond doubt.	*His resignation* was beyond doubt.

Complex sentence को simple sentence बनाने की कला simple से complex बनाने की कला के ठीक विपरीत है, अर्थात simple sentence में noun, adverb या adjective clause के भाव को एक शब्द या शब्दसमूह (phrase) में व्यक्त करना चाहिए।

(k) Transforming double sentences into complex sentences

Look at these sentences :

Double	*Complex*
Spare the rod and spoil the child.	*If you spare the rod*, you spoil the child.
He was lazy, *therefore, he failed*.	*As he was lazy*, he failed.
Listen and I will tell you all.	*If you listen*, I will tell you all.
She must weep *or she will die*.	*Unless she weeps*, she will die.
Do this *and I shall be satisfied*.	*If you do this*, I shall be satisfied.
He was very tired *and so he fell asleep*.	He fell asleep *because he was very tired*.

Co-ordinate main clause के स्थान पर किसी subordinate clause का प्रयोग कर double sentence को complex में बदला जा सकता है।

(l) Transforming complex sentences into double sentences

Look at these sentences :

Complex	*Double*
Because he was clever, he succeeded.	He was clever, *and so he succeeded*.
Although he did his best, he failed.	He did his best *and yet he failed*.
As he was very tired, he fell asleep.	He was very tired *and so he fell asleep*.
When he saw the tiger, he fled away.	He saw the tiger *and fled away*.
If you speak, you will die.	Speak *and you will die*.

Subordinate clause के स्थान पर co-ordinate clause (and, but इत्यादि) का प्रयोग कर हम complex sentence को double sentence बना सकते हैं।

(m) Interchange of main (principal) and subordinate clauses

Look at these sentences :

A	*B*
Look before you leap.	Do not leap *before you look*.
She is taller than her brother.	Her brother is not as tall *as she*.
It never rains but pours.	It always pours *when it rains*.
He ran away as soon as he saw me.	No sooner did he see me *than he ran away*.
He never began a job which he did not complete.	He always completed the job *which he began*.

कभी-कभी निर्देश रहता है कि main clause (ऊपर A के अंतर्गत वाक्यों में तिरछे अक्षरवाले भाग) को subordinate clause (B के अंतर्गत तिरछे अक्षरवाले भाग) में बदलें और subordinate को main में। ऐसा रूपांतर करने के लिए कोई नियम-विशेष नहीं है। आप, फिर भी, ऊपर दिए गए उदाहरणों को देखें और समझें।

(n) Different ways of expressing condition

Look at these sentences :

(i) *If* you are sincere, you can succeed.
Or, *Unless* you are sincere, you *cannot* succeed.
Or, *Provided* you are sincere, you can succeed.
Or, Be sincere, *and* you can succeed.
Or, *Should* you *be* sincere, you can succeed.
Or, *Supposing that* you are sincere, you can succeed.
Or, *In case* you are sincere, you can succeed.

(ii) *Move or* you will be a dead man.
Or, *Unless you move*, you will be a dead man.
Or, *If you do not move*, you will be a dead man.

(iii) *Speak or* you will die.
Or, *If you do not speak*, you will die.
Or, *Unless you speak*, you will die.

ऊपर के उदाहरणों से पता चलता है कि एक ही conditional (शर्तवाला) वाक्य को कई तरह से व्यक्त किया जा सकता है। Conditional वाक्य प्रायः इन शब्दों से प्रारंभ होते हैं : if, unless, in case, provided, provided that, should, had, supposing, but, for, were, and, or, one more + and, but for इत्यादि।

(o) Ways of expressing concession or contrast

Look at these sentences :

Though he is rich, he is kind.
Or, *Although* he is rich, he is kind.
Or, Rich *as* he is, he is kind.
Or, He is rich *indeed, but* he is kind.
Or, *In spite of* being rich, he is kind.
Or, *Despite* his richness, he is kind.
Or, He is rich *nevertheless* he is kind.
Or, *Admitting* that he is rich, he is kind.
Or, He is rich *yet/still/but* he is kind.

कुछ ऐसे वाक्य हैं जिनमें दो भाग होते हैं—एक भाग में जो कुछ कहा जाता है दूसरे भाग में उसके विपरीत कहा जाता है। ऐसे वाक्य प्रायः इन शब्दों से शुरू होते हैं : though, although, as, indeed, ...but, nevertheless, in spite of, despite, however, all the same इत्यादि।

(p) Interchange of degrees of comparison

वाक्य में जितने adjectives के प्रयोग होते हैं, वे किसी-न-किसी degree में अवश्य ही रहते हैं—positive, comparative या superlative. एक ही गुण या adjective को हम तीन तरह से व्यक्त कर सकते हैं :

(a) बिना तुलना किए हुए—positive degree में;
(b) या दो से तुलना कर—comparative degree में;
(c) सबों से तुलना कर—superlative degree में।

एक प्रकार की degree को दूसरे में बदल सकते हैं और उसके अर्थ में भी कोई अंतर नहीं आता। अब देखें ऐसा परिवर्तन किस प्रकार होता है।

(i) From positive to comparative

Look at these sentences :

Positive	*Comparative*
He is not *so good as* Tom.	Tom is *better* than he.
Ramesh is *as dull as* Moti.	Moti is not *duller* than Ramesh.
This book is not *so good as* that.	That book is *better* than this.
You are *as tall as* I.	I am not *taller* than you.
You are *as intelligent as* Sita.	Sita is not *more intelligent* than you.
Jack is not *so fat as* Tom.	Tom is *fatter* than Jack.

बहुत-से positive degree के adjectives (as......as) या (so......as) के बीच रखे जाते हैं; जैसे : as *dull* as, so *good* as.

ऐसे वाक्यों को comparative में बदलने के लिए :

(i) दोनों as......as या so............as को हटा दें;

(ii) Adjective (जो दो as के बीच में रहता है) comparative में बदल दें;

(iii) यदि वाक्य affirmative हो, तो उसे negative बना दें और यदि negative हो, तो affirmative बना दें; तथा

(iv) वाक्य के दूसरे भाग को नए वाक्य में पहले लिखें और पहले भाग को अंत में।

(ii) From comparative to positive

Look at these sentences :

Comparative	*Positive*
She is not *more beautiful* than I.	I am *as beautiful as* she.
Tom is *taller* than Jack.	Jack is not *as tall as* Tom.
That book is *better* than this.	This book is not *so good as* that.
The aeroplane flies *faster* than birds.	Birds do not fly *so fast as* the aeroplane.

Comparative degree को positive degree में बदलने के लिए :

(i) Comparative degree के adjective को positive में बदल दें;

(ii) Adjective को दो as (as......as) या so.............as के बीच में रखें;

(iii) यदि वाक्य affirmative हो तो उसे negative बना दें और यदि negative हो तो affirmative.

(iv) वाक्य के दूसरे भाग को नए वाक्य में पहलें रखें और पहले को अंत में।

(iii) From positive to superlative

1. *Look at these sentences :*

Positive	*Superlative*
No other boy is *as good as* Hari.	Hari is *the best* boy.
No other man is *as tall as* Moti.	Moti is *the tallest* man.
No other English poet is *as great as* Shakespeare.	Shakespeare is *the greatest* English poet.

as........as जब वाक्य में positive degree को के बीच रखा जाता है और उसके पहले no other का प्रयोग होता है, तब उसकी superlative degree इस प्रकार बनाई जाती है :

(i) No other तथा as..........as को हटा दें; तथा

(ii) Adjective को superlative degree में बदल दें।

(iii) वाक्य के अंतवाले noun को पहले रखें और पहले noun को बाद में।

2. *Look at these sentences :*

Positive	*Superlative*
Very few flowers are *as sweet as* the rose.	The rose is *one of the sweetest* flowers.
Very few Indian rulers were *so great as* Asoka.	Asoka was *one of the greatest* of Indian rulers.
Very few Hindi poets were *as great as* Dinkar.	Dinkar was *one of the greatest* Hindi poets.

यदि वाक्य में positive degree को as.........as या so.........as के बीच रखा जाए और वाक्य के शुरू में very few का प्रयोग हो, तो positive degree को superlative में इस प्रकार बदलना चाहिए :

(i) As............as तथा very few के बदले one of the का प्रयोग करें; तथा

(ii) Adjective को superlative degree में बदल दें;

(iii) वाक्य के पहले noun को अंत में और अंत के noun को पहले के स्थान में रखें।

(iv) From comparative to superlative

1. *Look at these sentences :*

Comparative	*Superlative*
The Pacific is *deeper than any other* ocean.	The Pacific is *the deepest* ocean.
This pen is *better than any other* pen here.	This is *the best* pen here.
This book is *more useful than any other* in the market.	This is *the most useful* book in the market.

यदि comparative degree में any other या all other का प्रयोग हो, तो उसे superlative degree में बदलने के लिए :

(i) Any other या all other को हटा दें; तथा

(ii) Comparative degree के adjective को superlative में बदल दें।

Note : इसी प्रकार superlative degree को भी comparative में बदलना चाहिए।

2. *Look at these sentences :*

Comparative	*Superlative*
He is *more wicked* than *most other* boys.	He is *one of the most wicked* boys.
Iron is *more useful* than *most other* metals.	Iron is *one of the most useful* metals.

यदि comparative degree के साथ most other लगा रहे, तो इसको superlative degree में बदलने के लिए :

(i) Most other के बदले one of the का प्रयोग करें; तथा

(ii) Comparative degree के adjective को superlative में बदल दें।

Note : इसी प्रकार superlative degree को भी comparative में बदलना चाहिए।

(v) Interchange of positive, comparative and superlative

Look at these sentences :

(i) Bombay is the *best* city in India. *Superlative*
Bombay is *better than any other* city in India. *Comparative*
No other city in India is *so good as* Bombay. *Positive*

(ii) Love is the *greatest* thing in the world. *Superlative*
Love is *greater than any other* thing in the world. *Comparative*
No other thing in the world is *as great as* love. *Positive*

(iii) Mahatma Gandhi was *one of the greatest* leaders of India. *Superlative*
Mahatma Gandhi was *greater* than *most other* leaders of India. *Comparative*
Very few leaders of India were *so great as* Mahatma Gandhi. *Positive*

कुछ ऐसे वाक्य होते हैं जिन्हें हम positive, comparative या superlative degrees में व्यक्त कर सकते हैं।

(i) Positive degree में as........as; so..........as का प्रयोग किया जाता है;

(ii) Comparative degree में better/more.......than और कभी-कभी other का भी प्रयोग किया जाता है;

(iii) Superlative degree में adjective, superlative degree में रहता है।

Note : कभी-कभी ऐसे भी वाक्य होते हैं जिनका degree of comparison किसी निश्चित फॉर्मूले पर निर्भर न होकर, आपके तर्क (logic) पर निर्भर करता है। अतः, वाक्य का अर्थ समझकर निर्देशानुसार वाक्य का रूपांतर करें। जैसे :

Very few countries are *as great as* India. *Positive*
= *Some* countries are *as great as* India. *Positive*
= *Some* countries are *greater than* India. *Comparative*
= India is *greater than most* countries. *Comparative*
= India is *one of the greatest* countries. *Superlative*

(q) Removal of 'too'

जिन वाक्यों में too का प्रयोग होता है वे साधारणतः चार प्रकार के होते हैं :

1. *Look at these sentences :*

A	*B*
I, *too*, have been to Delhi.	I *also* have been to Delhi.

Cotton is grown in India, *too*.	Cotton is grown in India *also*.

जिन वाक्यों में too का प्रयोग noun/pronoun के बाद 'भी' के अर्थ में होता है उनमें आप too के स्थान पर also का प्रयोग कर सकते हैं। लेकिन ध्यान रहे कि अगर too दो comma के बीच रहे तो also का प्रयोग करने पर वे comma लुप्त हो जाएँगे।

2. *Look at these sentences :*

A	*B*
You are being *too* kind.	You are being *extremely* kind.
Tea is *too* sweet.	Tea is *sweeter than it should be*.
He is *too* intelligent.	He is *more intelligent than it is proper* या *than he should be*.

(i) इन वाक्यों में too+adjective (जैसे : too kind, too sweet) का प्रयोग हुआ है। ऐसे प्रयोग में too का अर्थ है 'अत्यंत अधिक'।

(ii) अतः, इस too के स्थान पर हम very या extremely का तथा कभी-कभी अर्थ के अनुसार more......than it is proper, more.........than it should be का प्रयोग करते हैं।

3. *Look at these sentences :*

A	*B*
He is *too* strong for me.	He is *so strong* that I am *no match for him*.
This house is *too* small for me.	This house is *so small that it cannot serve my purpose*.
He is *too* dull for a sportsman.	He is *so dull that he cannot be a sportsman*.

(i) जब किसी वाक्य में too+adjective+for का प्रयोग हो, तब too का अर्थ होता है—'आवश्यकता से अधिक' और इससे नकारात्मक भाव व्यक्त होता है।

(ii) ऐसे वाक्यों से too को हटाने के लिए so+adjective+that clause का प्रयोग किया जाता है; तथा

(iii) That clause में no/not का भी प्रयोग किया जाता है।

4. *Look at these sentences :*

A	*B*
The news is *too* good to be true.	The news is *so* good *that it cannot* be true.
He is *too* proud to learn.	He is *so* proud *that he cannot learn*.
I am *too* busy to go out.	I am *so* busy *that I cannot go out*.
It is never *too* late to mend.	It is never *so late that one cannot mend oneself (or, mend it)*.

The fact is *too* evident to require proof.	The fact is *so evident that it does not require any proof.*

इन वाक्यों में too का अर्थ है—'इतना अधिक जितना नहीं होना चाहिए'। जब वाक्य में too+adjective+to....... रहे तब इससे नकारात्मक भाव व्यक्त होता है। ऐसे वाक्यों से too हटाने के लिए :

(i) Too की जगह so लगाएँ;

(ii) ....too + adjective + to........को so + adjective + that clause में बदलें; और

(iii) फिर that clause में verb के पहले अर्थानुसार cannot, should not, will not, could not आदि का प्रयोग करें।

Examples Worked Out

Transform the following sentences as directed :

(i) Interrogative into Assertive

Interrogative	*Assertive*
1. *Is* it a foolish idea ?	It is *not* a foolish idea.
2. *When* can their glory fade ?	Their glory can *never* fade.
3. *Did I not* tell him not to go there ?	*I told* him *not* to go there.
4. Shall I *ever* forget his kindness ?	I shall *never* forget his kindness.
5. *Who will* not help a man in distress ?	*Everybody will* help a man in distress.
6. *Is* that the way a gentleman should behave ?	That is *not* the way a gentleman should behave.
7. *Can* the Ethiopian change his skin ?	The Ethiopian *cannot* change his skin.
8. Does *anyone* like paying taxes ?	*No one* likes paying taxes.
9. *What does* it matter if we lose ?	It does *not* matter if we lose.
10. *Why* go to him ?	It is *useless* to go to him.
11. *Can* anyone put up with such an insult ?	*No one* can put up with such an insult.
12. *Why* waste time in reading trash ?	*It is extremely foolish* to waste time in reading trash.

(ii) Assertive into Interrogative

Assertive	*Interrogative*
13. That is nothing to you.	*What* is that to you ?
14. It is useless to blame him.	*Why* blame him ?

Assertive	Interrogative
15. Everyone knows you.	*Who* does not know you ?
16. Everybody wishes to be happy.	*Who* does not wish to be happy ?
17. His condition is hopeless.	*Isn't* his condition hopeless ?
18. The deaf cannot hear.	Can the deaf hear ?
19. Human nature cannot change.	*Can* human nature change ?
20. If you prick us, we bleed.	If you prick us, *don't we bleed* ?
21. This is not the kind of dress to wear in school.	*Is* this the kind of dress to wear in school ?
22. I have warned you of this danger over and again.	*Haven't* I warned you of this danger over and again ?

(iii) Exclamatory into Assertive

Exclamatory	Assertive
23. How odd !	*It is very* odd.
24. If I could only gain the first prize !	*I earnestly desire* to gain the first prize.
25. How sweet were your kisses, mother !	Mother, your kisses were *very* sweet.
26. Alas, that ever a friend should be false !	*It is extremely sad* that a friend should ever be false.
27. Oh for a little cottage in some village !	I *ardently wish* for a little cottage in some village.
28. What an unhappy life he leads !	He leads *a most/very unhappy* life.
29. Was any man ever immortal !	*No man* was ever immortal.
30. If only I could raise the cover and look inside !	*I wish* I could raise the cover and look inside.
31. To think of our meeting here !	*It is strange* that we should meet here.

(iv) Affirmative into Negative

Affirmative	Negative
32. This sum is *easy*.	This sum is *not difficult*.
33. Please *remember* it.	Please *do not forget it*.
34. Everybody *admits* it.	*Nobody denies* it.
35. It *always* pours when it rains.	It *never* rains *but* pours.
36. You are *tallller* than I.	I am *not* so *tall* as you.
37. He is *wise*.	He is *not without* wisdom.
38. He is *sometimes* foolish.	He is *not always* wise.
39. *Every man* has his failings.	There is *no man* who has *no* failings.

	Affirmative	*Negative*
40.	He is *greater* than I.	I am *not* so great as he.
41.	*As soon as* he came he made objections.	*No sooner* did he come *than* he made objections.
42.	He was more worthy of praise than *anyone else*.	*None* was more worthy of praise than he.
43.	Calcutta is the *biggest* city.	There is *no bigger* city in India than Calcutta.

(v) Negative into Affirmative

	Negative	*Affirmative*
44.	A good boy *never neglects* his lessons.	A good boy *always minds* his lessons.
45.	We did *not* find the road very *bad*.	We found the road fairly *good*.
46.	*No one* can *deny* that he was a great man.	*Everybody* must *admit* that he was a great man.
47.	I was *not sure* about the result.	I was *doubtful* about the result.
48.	*None but* the brave deserves the fair.	*Only* the brave deserve the fair.
49.	*No sooner* had he seen the tiger *than* he fled.	*As soon as* he saw the tiger he fled.
50.	This is *not impossible*.	This is *possible*.
51.	We *did not find many* boys in the class.	We *found a few* boys in the class.
52.	It is *not always* easy in company to speak frankly.	It is *often difficult* in company to speak frankly.

(vi) Simple into Double

	Simple	*Double*
53.	Don't desire *without deserving*.	First deserve, *then desire*.
54.	*Besides making* a promise, he kept it.	He *not only made* a promise, *but* he *also* kept it.
55.	*Owing* to ill-health, he could not work.	He *was* in ill-health, *and so* he could not work.
56.	*Notwithstanding his sorrow*, he is hopeful.	He is *sorrowful, but yet* hopeful.
57.	*For all his troubles*, he is cheerful.	*He is in great troubles*, still he is cheerful.
58.	You must work hard *to pass* the examination.	You must work hard *or you will not pass* the examination.

	Simple	*Double*
59.	The teacher punished the boy *for disobedience*.	The boy *was disobedient*, and so the teacher punished him.

(vii) Double into Simple

	Double	*Simple*
60.	*The sun rose and* the fog dispersed.	*The sun having risen*, the fog dispersed.
61.	You must work hard, *or you will not get promotion*.	Hard work is necessary *for you to get promotion*.
62.	*He finished his exercise* and put away his books.	*Having finished his exercise*, he put away his books.
63.	*He must not be late* or he will be punished.	*In the event of his being late*, he will be punished.
64.	*His father died and this* multiplied his problems.	*His father's death* multiplied his problems.
65.	*I gave him not only money* but also good advice.	*Besides* giving him money, I gave him good advice.

(viii) Simple into Complex

	Simple	*Complex*
66.	The captain wished *to win the* match.	The captain wished *that he should win the match*.
67.	I paid off *my father's debts*.	I paid off the debts *which my father had contracted*.
68.	*For all his experience* he is still incompetent.	*Although he is experienced*, he is still incompetent.
69.	I am certain *of giving* you satisfaction.	I am certain *that I shall give* you satisfaction.
70.	His offence was *unpardonable*.	His offence was such *as could not be pardoned*.
71.	He started by night to *escape being seen by any one*.	He started by night *lest he should be seen by anyone*.
72.	*On reaching manhood* you will have to work for your living.	*As soon as you have reached manhood*, you will have to work for your living.
73.	He confessed *his crime*.	He confessed *that he was guilty*.
74.	*His silence* proves his guilt.	*The fact that he is silent* proves his guilt.
75.	He owed *his success* to his father.	It was owing to his father *that he succeeded*.

(ix) Complex into Simple

Complex	*Simple*
76. He said *that he was innocent*.	He declared *his innocence*
77. Tell me *where you live*.	Tell me *your address*.
78. *How long I shall stay* is doubtful.	*The duration of my stay* is doubtful.
79. It is sad *that he died so young*.	*His death at so early an age* is sad.
80. Tell me *when and where you were born*.	Tell me *the date and place of your birth*.
81. We need not disbelieve *what he said*.	We need not disbelieve *his word*.
82. Pupils *who work hard* may win a prize.	*Hard-working* pupils may win a prize.
83. I have no money *that I can spare*.	I have no money *to spare*.
84. The boy was pleased *that he had won a prize*.	The boy was pleased at *having won a prize*.
85. They were surprised *when they heard him sing*.	They were surprised *to hear him sing*.
86. This rule, from *which all our troubles have come*, is much disliked.	This rule, *the source of all our troubles*, is much disliked.

(x) Double into Complex

Double	*Complex*
87. Speak the truth *and* you will never regret it.	*If you speak the truth*, you will never regret it.
88. Hold your tongue *or* you will repent it.	*If you do not hold your tongue*, you will repent it.
89. He was a poor man, *but* he was always honest.	He was always honest, *although he was poor*.
90. Either you *or* I must write the report.	*If you do not write* the report, I must do so.
91. He is still in his teens, *but* he has the sense of a man.	He has the sense of a man, *although he is still in his teens*.
92. Drink this medicine, *or* I will make you do so.	*Unless you drink this medicine*, I will make you do so.
93. Waste not, want not.	*If you do not waste*, you will not want.
94. Do it *or* you will be punished.	*Unless you do it*, you will be punished.

	Double	*Complex*
95.	He was very tired *and* so he fell asleep.	*As he was very tired*, he fell asleep.

(xi) Complex into Double

	Complex	*Double*
96.	I am certain *you have made a mistake*.	You have made a mistake, *and* of this I am certain.
97.	*If he is at home*, I shall see him.	He may be at home, *and* in that case I shall see him.
98.	He lost more *than he could afford*.	He could afford to lose something, *but* he lost somewhat more.
99.	I am sure *that you are doing your best*.	You are doing your best, *and* I am sure of it.
100.	I loved her *because she pitied me*.	She pitied me, *and* so I loved her.
101.	I have found the money *that I had lost*.	I had lost the money *but* I have found it again.
102.	*If he acts foolishly*, he will certainly be ruined.	He must not act so foolishly, *or* he will certainly be ruined.
103.	He works hard *in order that he may become rich*.	He wants to become rich, *and* therefore he works hard.
104.	*If he were here*, I would explain everything to him.	He is not here, *or* I would explain everything to him.
105.	I have lost the pen *which my father gave me*.	My father gave me a pen *and* I have lost it.

(xii) Positive into Comparative

	Positive	*Comparative*
106.	I am not *as* tall *as* he.	He is *taller than* I.
107.	Platinum is *as* heavy *as* gold.	Gold is not *heavier than* platinum.
108.	This radio is not *so* good *as* that.	That radio is *better than* this.
109.	Tom is not *so* clever *as* Hari.	Hari is *cleverer than* Tom.
110.	Very few metals are *as* heavy *as* gold.	Gold is *heavier than* most other metals.
111.	Ram is *as* dull *as* Shyam.	Shyam is *not duller than* Ram.
112.	You are *as* good *as* I.	I am *not better than* you.
113.	Sita is not *so* fat *as* Moti.	Moti is *fatter than* Sita.

(xiii) Comparative into Positive

	Comparative	*Positive*
114.	Rana is *taller* than Mohan.	Mohan is *not so* tall *as* Rana.
115.	Sima is *more* beautiful *than* you.	You are *not as* beautiful *as* Sima.
116.	My house is *better than* your house.	Your house is *not so* good *as* my house.
117.	He is *fatter than* you.	You are *not so* fat *as* he.
118.	That man has *more* money *than* brain.	That man has *not as* much brain *as* he has money.
119.	I would *rather* die *than* beg.	I would *as* soon die *as* beg.
120.	A live ass is *stronger than* a dead lion.	A dead lion is *not so* strong *as* a live ass.
121.	She is *taller than her sister.*	*Her sister is not so* tall *as* she.

(xiv) Comparative into Superlative

	Comparative	*Superlative*
122.	Akbar was *greater* than many other kings.	Akbar was *one of the greatest* kings.
123.	Amar is *more* intelligent than many other boys.	Amar is *one of the most* intellligent boys.
124.	This newspaper has a *bigger* circulation than any other morning paper.	This newspaper has *the biggest* circulation among morning papers.
125.	Tom is *better* than most other boys in the class	Tom is *one of the best* boys in the class.
126.	The rose is *sweeter than* other flowers.	The rose is *the sweetest* of all flowers.

(xv) Positive into Comparative and Superlative

127. *Positive—Very few* countries are *as* hot *as* India.
Comparative—India is *hotter than many other* countries.
Superlative—India is *one of the hottest* countries.

128. *Positive—Very few* countries are *as* rich *as* Japan.
Comparative—Japan is *richer than most other* countries.
Superlative—Japan is *one of the richest* countries.

129. *Positive—No other* boy is *so* intelligent *as* Ramu.
Comparative—Ramu is *more intelligent than any other* boy.
Superlative—Ramu is *the most intelligent* boy.

130. *Positive—Very few* poets of England were *so* great *as* Milton.

Comparative—Milton was *greater than most other* poets of England.
Superlative—Milton was *one of the greatest* poets of England.

131. *Positive—No other* flower is *as* sweet *as* the rose.
Comparative—The rose is *sweeter than any other* flower.
Superlative—The rose is *the sweetest of all* flowers.

132. *Positive—Very few* metals are *as* heavy *as* gold.
Comparative—Gold is *heavier than most other* metals.
Superlative—Gold is *one of the heaviest* metals.

133. *Positive—No other* city in the world is *so* big *as* London.
Comparative—London is *bigger than any other* city in the world.
Superlative—London is *the biggest city* in the world.

134. *Positive*—Bangalore is *as beautiful as* any capital city in India.
Comparative—No capital city in India is *more beautiful than* Bangalore.
Superlative—Bangalore is one of *the most beautiful* capital cities in India.

(xvi) Removal of 'Too'

	Sentences with 'too'	*Sentences without 'too'*
135.	The news is *too* good to be true.	The news is *so* good that it *cannot* be true.
136.	You are *too* lazy to walk.	You are *so* lazy that you *cannot* walk.
137.	She is *too* shy to ask for help.	She is *so* shy that she *cannot* ask for help.
138.	He was *too* honest to accept a bribe.	He was *so* honest that he *could not* accept a bribe.
139.	The results were *too* bad to be published.	The results were *so* bad that they *were not* fit to be published.
140.	The tree is *too* high for me to climb.	The tree is *so* high that I *cannot* climb.
141.	This cup of milk is *too* hot for me.	This cup of milk is *so* hot that I *cannot* drink it.
142.	Don't make yourself *too* cheap.	Don't make yourself *more cheap than it is proper.*
143.	The sight was *too* dreadful to be seen.	The sight was *so* dreadful that it *could not* be seen.

EXERCISE 1

Transform the following questions into assertive sentences (statements) :

EXAMPLE : What is the use of going to him ? *(interrogative)*
= There is *no use* going to him. *(assertive)*

1. What is the use of sitting here ?
2. Does anyone like paying taxes ?
3. Shall we ever forget her beauty ?
4. Can a tiger change its nature ?
5. Isn't blood thicker than water ?
6. Why waste time in reading novels ?
7. What does it matter if we lose ?
8. Can anyone bear such an insult ?
9. If you prick us, do we not bleed ?
10. Can a Negro cnange his skin ?
11. Are we born simply to eat ?
12. Who does not love his country ?
13. Does man live by bread alone ?
14. If you poison us, do we not die ?
15. Can you fly like a bird ?
16. Are we going to lose the battle ?
17. Does he look like a gentleman ?
18. Did I not warn you yesterday ?
19. Is there anything greater than love ?
20. Was I not sure about my result ?

EXERCISE 2

Transform the following statements into interrogative sentences (questions) :

EXAMPLE : Everybody wishes to live long. *(assertive)*
= *Who does not* wish to live long ? *(interrogative)*

1. I like you.
2. It cannot be useful.
3. It is really very sweet.
4. A lie has no legs.
5. Tagore was a great poet.
6. You do not read everyday.
7. This is not the way to speak.
8. I am the first speaker today.
9. America is richer than India.
10. He was not very poor.
11. His condition is hopeless.
12. He always plays in the evening.
13. There is nothing else to do.
14. It is indeed very sweet.
15. It cannot be true.
16. Everybody has his likes and dislikes.
17. It is useless to go to him.
18. That is not the way to teach a child.
19. I have always helped you.
20. His health grew worse with age.

EXERCISE 3

Transform the following exclamatory sentences into assertive forms :

EXAMPLES : (i) O to be at home ! *(exclamatory)*
I wish I were at home. *(assertive)*
(ii) Alas, that ever a friend should be false ! *(exclamatory)*
= *It is extremely sad* that a friend should ever be false. *(assertive)*

1. What a lovely rose !
2. How sad she looks !
3. How hot it is !
4. How sweet she sings !
5. What a lame excuse !
6. What a beautiful night it is !
7. How lovely these flowers are !
8. If I could only see him again !
9. What a happy ending !
10. O that I had the wings of a dove !
11. O that I were young again !
12. What a piece of work is man !

13. If I could see him again !
14. How dreadful was the dream !
15. What a fool you are !
16. O that he had a son !
17. What a foolish question to ask !
18. Alas, my friend is no more !
19. What a miserable life he leads !
20. If only I had known him !

EXERCISE 4

Transform the following affirmative sentences into negative :

EXAMPLE : Only a fool would do such a thing. *(affirmative)*
= *None but* a fool would do such a thing. *(negative)*

1. Please remember it.
2. This is possible.
3. He is a bad man.
4. He is sometimes foolish.
5. Only a fool would say so.
6. Few students are present today.
7. I am doubtful whether it was true.
8. Everybody admits it.
9. You are a fool.
10. A wise man keeps silent.
11. Every rose has a thorn.
12. Brutus loved Caesar.
13. I am not sure about his result
14. Old men are always wise.
15. He tried every plan.
16. He believed me.
17. The book on geography is easy.
18. You are taller than I.
19. Man is mortal.
20. Look before you leap.

EXERCISE 5

Transform the following negative sentences into affirmative :

EXAMPLE : I am not ungrateful. *(negative)*
= I am *grateful.* *(affirmative)*

1. He is not a good man.
2. He left no work undone.
3. I do not like his behaviour.
4. The station is not far off.
5. He did not live many years in India.
6. You are not taller than he is.
7. None but the brave deserves the fair.
8. No one will deny it.
9. He is seldom punctual.
10. This was not unexpected.
11. Man is not immortal.
12. I shall never forget your kindness.
13. He does not remember you now.
14. Our car is not small.
15. The radio is not costly.
16. Brutus was not without love for Caesar.
17. There is no smoke without fire.
18. He was asked not to smoke.
19. I never disoblige a friend.
20. The rumour has no basis.

EXERCISE 6

Transform the following simple sentences into compound/double ones :

EXAMPLE : To avoid punishment, you must beg pardon. *(simple)*
= *Either* you must beg pardon or you will be punished. *(compound)*

1. Labour hard to stand first.
2. Besides being laborious, he is clever.
3. Because of poverty, he is sorry.
4. Seeing a tiger coming, he ran away.
5. In spite of wealth he is unhappy.
6. He worked hard to pass the exam.
7. To avoid punishment he left home.
8. To everyone's surprise, he failed.

9. **Drawing his sword he rushed at John.**
10. **He fell ill after taking his exam.**
11. I shall succeed with your help.
12. He received praise and reward.
13. Despite his sorrow, he is hopeful.
14. Being dissatisfied he resigned his post.
15. In spite of several efforts, he failed.
16. Besides giving me advice, he helped me.
17. He has not finished his work by sunset.
18. Seeing his friend, he was very happy.
19. Besides making a promise he kept it.
20. I went home to see my father.

EXERCISE 7

Transform the following compound/double sentences into simple ones :

EXAMPLE : Turn to the left and you will find his house. *(compound)*
= *Turning* to the left, you will find his house. *(simple)*

1. He made a promise and kept it.
2. He must work hard or he will fail.
3. Be good and you will be happy.
4. He came and took away the pen.
5. She took her books and went to school.
6. He worked hard, for he wanted to succeed.
7. He finished his work and went home.
8. They go to the library and they borrow books.
9. I bought a book and read it.
10. He is rich yet he is not happy.
11. He took every care yet he died.
12. He saw a tiger and he ran away.
13. I disliked him still he was here.
14. He beat not only the boy but also the girl.
15. Tom took his bath and had tea.
16. The sun set and they came here.
17. He paid for the car and gave it to me.
18. He has suffered loss, but yet he is cheerful.
19. You must act well or you will be laughed at.
20. The sun rose and the fog dispersed.

EXERCISE 8

Transform the following simple sentences into complex ones :

EXAMPLE : For all his experience he is still incompetent. *(simple)*
= *Although* he is experienced, he is still incompetent. *(complex)*

1. I heard of his arrival.
2. He is believed to be rich.
3. She taught me to play chess.
4. A woman will not tell us her age.
5. Let me know your opinion about this.
6. I will not rise without your pardon.
7. He was not a man to tell a lie.
8. That was the act of a coward.
9. That was the fault not to be forgiven.
10. I am not a man to cheat you.
11. I cannot do it without risk.
12. It resulted according to my hope.
13. It never thunders without lightning.
14. We know the time of his arrival.
15. He hoped to win the prize.
16. She has hopes of success.

17. They soon forgot their past troubles.
18. We must hope for better times.
19. A man of wisdom in loved by all.
20. He is a man of great power.

EXERCISE 9

Transform the following complex sentences into simple ones :

EXAMPLE : This proved that he was innocent. *(complex)*
= This proved his *innocence.* *(simple)*

1. We eat that we may live.
2. No one knows when he died.
3. He shows that he is intelligent.
4. There is no boy who is rich.
5. That he will come is certain.
6. We all know that you are poor.
7. A boy who is good labours hard.
8. Whatever you do I will support.
9. I believe that he is innocent.
10. They guessed what he meant.
11. I have come that I help you.
12. Everyone who knows you likes you.
13. Tell me where Tom lives.
14. The man who wrote it was a poet.
15. He never does a thing that is foolish.
16. The boy who stood first got a prize.
17. When the sun rose, he started for home.
18. We believe that God is kind.
19. Time which is lost is lost for ever.
20. I have no money that I can spare.

EXERCISE 10

Transform the following complex sentences into compound ones :

EXAMPLE : If you speak the truth, you will never regret it. *(complex)*
= Speak the truth, *and* you will never regret it. *(compound)*

1. If you spare the rod, you will spoil the child.
2. Unless you leave the room, I will compel you to do so.
3. If you do not hold your tongue, you will repent it.
4. He was always honest, although he was poor.
5. He fell sound asleep, so he felt much better next day.
6. If he acts foolishly, he will certainly be ruined.
7. I am sure that you are doing your best.
8. Though I saw him, I did not speak to him.
9. When you have finished your work you can go out to play.
10. I know the car which you are buying.

EXERCISE 11

Transform the following compound sentences into complex ones :

EXAMPLE : He wanted to save money; therefore he walked all the way. *(compound)*
= He walked all the way *as* he wanted to save money. *(complex)*

1. Pay attention to your work, or I will punish you.
2. He has many acquaintances, but few friends.
3. I will keep my promise or die.
4 She loved you most and me least.

5 I dropped a coin on the floor and it is still there.
6 Pay the fine or go to prison.
7. He wants to become rich, and therefore he works hard.
8. He must speak the truth, or he will not be freed.
9. He is eighty years old, and yet he still has good sight.
10. Mr Sen was a poor man, but he was always honest.

EXERCISE 12

Rewrite the following sentences making the principal and subordinate clauses change places :

EXAMPLES : (i) He never began a job which he did not complete.
= He always completed the job which he began.

(ii) Another such shock, and the house will collapse.
= If there is another such shock, the house will collapse.

1. Look before you leap.
2. He never began a job which he did not complete.
3. Another such shock, and the house will collapse.
4. This is the most beautiful sight that I have ever seen.
5. He was not such a good teacher as he was reputed to be.
6. He is more eager to accumulate wealth than to earn fame.
7. As soon as the teacher came, the boys stood up.
8. The audience cheered as soon as the President arrived.
9. He cannot walk fast because he is rather lame.
10. Nath read nothing that he did not remember.

EXERCISE 13

Transform each of the following sentences in as many ways as you can :

EXAMPLES : (i) Move or you will lose.
= Unless you move, you will lose.
= If you do not move, you will lose.

(ii) Though he is poor, he is honest.
= Although he is poor, he is honest.
= Despite his poverty, he is honest.
= Even if he is poor, he is honest.
= He is poor, yet he is honest.

1. If you are sincere you will succeed.
2. If he had written to me I could have helped him.
3. But for his help I would have been ruined.
4. One more word, and you will be turned out.
5. Move and you will be a dead man.
6. Supposing that he fails to turn up, what will you do ?
7. Though his father is rich, he is a very miserly boy.
8. However much I try, I cannot defeat you.
9. One more mistake, and I will dismiss you.
10. But for your advice, I should have been a beggar.

EXERCISE 14

Change the degree of comparison of the following in as many ways as possible :

EXAMPLE : Calcutta is the *busiest* port in India. *(superlative)*
= Calcutta is *busier than* any other port in India. *(comparative)*
= No other port in India is *so busy as* Calcutta. *(positive)*

1. Ashoka was the greatest king of India.
2. Tagore was the best poet of modern India.
3. Platinum is as heavy as gold.
4. That horse is better than this.
5. He runs as fast as the deer.
6. Nirala is the greatest Hindi poet.
7. Very few countries are as hot as India.
8. Hari is not wiser than his brother.
9. Bombay is the best seaport in India.
10. He is not so learned as his sister.
11. Jack is the strongest boy in the class.
12. No other metal is as heavy as lead.
13. Very few Indian towns are as big as Calcutta.
14. The princess is not so tall as the prince.
15. A live ass is stronger than a dead lion.
16. Hari is not wiser than his brother.
17. This is the best book that I have read.
18. This is the most beautiful picture.
19. Our goods are the cheapest in the market.
20. It is easier than most poems.

EXERCISE 15

Transform the following sentences as directed :

EXAMPLES : (i) I have not seen him for six months. (Replace *for* by *since*)
= Six months have passed *since* I saw him.
(ii) The news gave him much pleasure.
(Use the verb form of *pleasure*)
= The news *pleased* him much.

1. (a) It is too late to begin the work. (Remove *'too'*)
   (b) He sent no reply to my letter. (Use verb form of *'reply'*)
   (c) Health is far better than wealth. (Use *'preferable'*)
   (d) Men eat to preserve life. (Change into *Complex*)
   (e) Take care of your purse. (Change the *Voice*)
2. (a) She is sometimes sad. (Use *Negative*)
   (b) He is too old for the job. (Remove *'too'*)
   (c) Only Madan came to see me. (Use *'but'*)
   (d) It was a very narrow escape. (Change into *Exclamatory*)
   (e) Kalidas was as great as Shakespeare. (Change *Degree*)
3. (a) It is no joke. (Change into *Affirmative*)
   (b) Do not go away until I return. (Use *'as long as'*)
   (c) He was so strong that he lifted the box easily. (Use *'enough'*)
   (d) It is likely that he will get success. (Change into *Simple*)
   (e) The house has none to look after it. (Use *'there'*)

4. (a) Who is looking after the child ? (change *Voice*)
 (b) They rejected our suggestions. (Change into *Negative*)
 (c) He is not the best boy in the class. (Change *Degree*)
 (d) He is intelligent; moreover, he is sincere. (Change into *Simple*)
 (e) We have not heard from him for a long time. (Change into *Affirmative*)

5. (a) He is too old for the job. (Remove *'too'*)
 (b) Tell me why you have come here. (Change into *Simple*)
 (c) The boy is strong and intelligent. (Use *nouns* for *adjectives*)
 (d) He was more to blame than anyone else. (Use *Negative*)
 (e) After a storm the weather is generally calm. (Change into *Complex*)

6. (a) You can do it easily. (Use the noun form of *'easily'*)
 (b) Students who work hard are sure to succeed. (Change into *Simple*)
 (c) I will do this, if you allow me. (Remove *'if'*)
 (d) Poor as he is, he is honest. (Use *'though'* for *'as'*)
 (e) English is spoken by people all over the world. (Change *Voice*)

7. (a) All human beings are mortal. (Change into *Interrogative*)
 (b) Only a little child could talk like that. (Change into *Negative*)
 (c) Each part has a day that lasts two weeks. (Change into *Simple*)
 (d) Can a crow change its colour ? (Change into *Assertive*)
 (e) The audience applauded as the Prime Minister arrived. (Use noun form for *'arrive'*)

8. (a) O that you had more sense ! (Change into *Assertive*)
 (b) Hercules was stronger than any wild beast. (Change into *Positive Degree*)
 (c) John was captured by his enemies. (Change into *Active voice*)
 (d) Madan is fatter than any other boy in the class. (Change into *Superlative Degree*)
 (e) As soon as he came, everybody became silent. (Replace *'as soon as'* by *'no sooner.....than'*)

EXERCISE 16 (With Answer)

Rewrite the following sentences as directed :

1. (a) The key was discovered in the cupboard. (Rewrite it in the *Active Form*)
 (b) "Is the earth flat ?" The chairman asked the candidate. (Rewrite it in the *Reported speech*)
 (c) "You can't eat all that." (Frame a sentence in reply to express your disagreement with the given statement)
 (d) We carried the umbrella thinking it might rain. (Rewrite it using *'lest'*)
 (e) She is the best teacher of this college. (Rewrite it changing the Superlative Degree into the *Comparative*)
 (f) It is easy to please Govind. (Rewrite it beginning with Govind)
 (g) Patel was in his sixtieth year when he died. (Use *'sixty'*)
 (h) I cannot help complying with his wishes. (Use *'but'* for *'help'*)

Ans. 1. (a) Someone discovered the key in the cupboard. (b) The chairman asked the candidate whether the earth was flat. (c) Of course, I can. (d) We carried the umbrella lest it should rain. (e) She is better than any other teacher of this college. (f) Govind is easy to be pleased. (g) Patel was sixty when he died. (h) I cannot but comply with his wishes.

□□□

15. PUNCTUATION AND THE USE OF CAPITALS

जब हम बोलते हैं, अपने भावों को स्पष्ट करने के लिए कहीं-कहीं रुकते हैं। किंतु जब हम लिखते हैं, तब अपनी लिखावट में punctuation marks का प्रयोग करते हैं ताकि पाठक वहीं रुकें जहाँ हमारी भाषा के अर्थ को समझने के लिए उन्हें रुकने की आवश्यकता हो।

Punctuation के संबंध में आधुनिक धारणा यह है कि punctuation marks का प्रयोग वहीं करें जहाँ अभिव्यक्ति की समझ तथा स्पष्टता के लिए आवश्यक हो।

अँगरेजी में मुख्य punctuation marks इस प्रकार हैं :

Full stop [.]	Colon [:]
Question mark [?]	Semi-colon [;]
Exclamation mark [!]	Dash [—]
Comma [,]	Hyphen [-]
Apostrophe [']	Brackets [ ]; ( )
Quotation marks [' ']	Capitals [A, B, C....]

1. Capital Letters के प्रयोग

1. *Look at these words :*

Ram	Sita	Tom	Mary	Abdul
Hari	Meera	Jack	Lucy	Zaheer

किसी व्यक्ति के नाम का पहला अक्षर capital होता है।

2. *Look at these words :*

Bose	Gupta	Sinha	Tiwary	Thakur
Sen	Prasad	Rai	Abbas	Gupta

किसी व्यक्ति के उपनाम (surname) का पहला अक्षर capital होता है।

3. *Look at these words :*

India	Asia	Delhi	Bihar	Sarai
China	Africa	Patna	Punjab	Goraul

किसी देश, महादेश, शहर, राज्य तथा गाँव के नाम का पहला अक्षर capital होता है।

4. *Look at these words :*

Sunday	Tuesday	March	May	July
Monday	Wednesday	April	June	August

किसी दिन तथा महीने के नाम का पहला अक्षर capital होता है।

5. *Look at these words :*

Hindi	Urdu	Tamil	Maithili	French
English	Bengali	Telgu	Bhojpuri	Sanskrit

किसी भाषा के नाम का पहला अक्षर capital होता है।

6. *Look at these words :*

Mr	Miss	Dear Sir	Prof.	Col.
Mrs	Dr	Master	Lt.	Sri

किसी व्यक्ति के नाम के पहले आनेवाले title का पहला अक्षर capital होता है।

7. *Look at these words :*

Hindu	Sikh	Buddhist	Hinduism
Muslim	Christian	Buddhism	Islam

किसी समुदाय या धर्म के नाम का पहला अक्षर capital होता है।

8. *Look at these words :*

Geeta	Vedas	Mahabharata
Ramayana	Bible	Koran

धार्मिक ग्रंथों के नाम का पहला अक्षर capital होता है।

9. *Look at these words :*

Indian	British	Bihari	Kashmiri	Nepalese
American	Russian	Punjabi	Bengali	Japanese

Proper noun से बने हुए शब्द का पहला अक्षर capital होता है।

10. *Look at these words :*

Holi	Bakrid	Id	New Year
Diwali	Dasera	Christmas	Easter

त्योहारों के नाम का पहला अक्षर capital होता है।

11. *Look at these words :*

M.A.	I.Sc.	M.L.A.	UNO	NATO
B.A.	B.Sc.	M.P.	M.B.B.S.	UNESCO

Abbreviation (शब्द का लघु रूप) में प्रयुक्त प्रत्येक letter को capital से लिखा जाता है।

(i) किंतु abbreviation में जब एक से अधिक शब्द रहें तो केवल पहला अक्षर capital होता है। जैसे :

Ph.D. (Ph = philosophy) M.Sc. (Sc. = science)

(ii) कुछ abbreviations small letters से भी लिखे जाते हैं। जैसे : i.e., e.g., etc., m.p.h.

(iii) जब किसी संस्था के नाम का abbreviation होता है तब उसके प्रत्येक letter के बाद full stop नहीं दिया जाता। जैसे : UNESCO.

12. *Look at these words :*

Mahatma Gandhi Road	Town High School	Rajendra Hospital
Nehru Street	Patna College	B.C. Roy Hospital

अगर किसी road, street, school, college, hospital, university इत्यादि के नाम किसी व्यक्ति या स्थान से जुड़े हों तो वैसे नाम में आए प्रत्येक शब्द का पहला अक्षर capital होता है।

13. *Look at these words/phrases :*

the Himalayas	the Ganga	the Taj Express	the Yamuna
the Alps	the Damodar	The Maurya Express	the Sagar Samrat

पहाड़, नदी, train, aeroplane तथा ship के नाम का पहला अक्षर capital होता है।

14. *Look at these words/phrases :*

Independence Day	Republic Day	World War II
the Middle Ages	French Revolution	Cultural Revolution

ऐतिहासिक घटनाओं के नाम में आए प्रत्येक शब्द का पहला अक्षर capital होता है।

15. *Look at these words/phrases :*

the Congress Party	the Socialist Party	the Janata Party
the Communist Party	the Muslim League	the B.J.P.

Political parties के नाम का पहला अक्षर capital होता है।

16. *Look at these sentences :*

I wanted to speak to *Prof./Dr/Col.* Sinha.

I saw a *professor/doctor/colonel* sitting in the office.

(i) अगर किसी व्यक्ति के नाम के पहले उसका title हो तो उस title का पहला अक्षर capital होता है।

(ii) अगर title के बाद किसी व्यक्ति का नाम नहीं रहे तो title को small letter से लिखा जाता है। जैसे :

He is a *doctor.* He is *Dr* Ghosh.

(iii) किंतु अगर title का प्रयोग किसी खास व्यक्ति के लिए किया जाए तो उसका पहला अक्षर capital से शुरू होता है। जैसे :

Our *President* met the *President* of the United States.

17. *Look at these sentences :*

He said, '*My* book is new.'

Hari said, '*His* brother is ill.'

Inverted commas के अंदर शुरू होनेवाले प्रत्येक वाक्य का पहला शब्द capital से शुरू होता है।

Note : अगर quotation दो या दो से अधिक भागों में बँटा हो तो केवल पहले भाग का पहला अक्षर capital letter होगा। जैसे :

'*You* ask me,' he said, 'to work all the time.'

18. *Look at these sentences :*

God is kind to *His* children.
Man is created by *God*.

(i) God का पहला अक्षर हमेशा capital होता है।

(ii) साथ ही, God के लिए प्रयुक्त होनेवाले pronoun (*He*/*Him*/*His*) का पहला अक्षर भी capital होता है।

Note : किंतु अगर God का प्रयोग ईश्वर नहीं देवता के लिए हो तो वह capital letter से नहीं प्रारंभ होता है। जैसे :

The Hindus worship numerous *gods*.

19. *Look at these sentences :*

Some books are very useful.
Those boys are playing cricket.

किसी वाक्य के शुरू के पहले शब्द का पहला अक्षर capital होता है।

20. *Look at these sentences :*

I spoke to *Father* about this.
Father agreed but *Mother* didn't.
I have to consult *Uncle* and *Aunt*.

(i) Father, Mother, Uncle तथा Aunt का प्रयोग जब title की तरह हो तब उसका पहला अक्षर capital होता है।

(ii) अगर इन शब्दों का प्रयोग titles की तरह हो तो इनके पहले कोई determiner (*my, your, his, her* etc.) नहीं आता है। अगर कोई determiner उनके पहले रहे तो उन्हें small letter से लिखा जाता है।

21. *Look at these words :*

Dear Sir	*My* dear Sir
Yours faithfully	*Yours* sincerely

पत्रों में salutation (संबोधन) का पहला अक्षर और complimentary close (अंत पद) का पहला अक्षर capital letter होता है।

22. *Look at these words :*

I	O Death	O Time
O	O Life	

(i) Pronoun *I* हमेशा capital से लिखा जाता है।

(ii) Interjection *O* भी capital होता है।

(iii) Personified words (मानवीकरण जैसे शब्द) भी capital letter से शुरू होते हैं।

23. *Look at these words :*

Chief Justice — District Magistrate
Headmaster — Padma Bibhushan

Title (पदवी) और designation (ओहदा) का पहला अक्षर capital letter होता है।

24. *Look at these words :*

Jupiter — Venus — Mars

ग्रहों (planets) के नाम का पहला अक्षर capital letter होता है, किंतु the earth, the sun, the moon को small letter से लिखा जाता है।

25. *Look at the following :*

The Use of Prepositions — *Water Babies* (Book)
Business in Benares — 'Lucy Gray' (Poem)
The Chamber of Commerce — The Macmillan Company of India

कभी-कभी हमलोगों को title of book, report, article, magazine, poem, play, club, organisation या business firm के नाम लिखने में small तथा capital letters के प्रयोग में दुविधा हो जाती है। इसके लिए सामान्यतः

(i) प्रत्येक main words (*nouns, adjectives, verbs, adverbs*) के प्रथम अक्षर capital होते हैं।

(ii) Articles, conjunctions, prepositions (जो पाँच या पाँच letters से कम के होते हैं) small letter से लिखे जाते हैं।

(iii) पुस्तक, पत्रिका या नाटक के title को underline कर दिया जाता है।

(iv) किंतु story, poem, report, article या chapter of a book के title को quotation marks के अंदर लिखा जाता है।

Note : (i) Season के नाम का पहला अक्षर small होता है। जैसे—in summer; in winter; in autumn; in spring.

(ii) कुछ शब्द जैसे *east, west, north* तथा *south* से जब देश या महादेश के किसी भाग का बोध हो तो उनका पहला अक्षर capital होता है; किंतु जब इनसे दिशा (direction) का बोध हो तब इन्हें small letter से लिखा जाता है।

26. *Look at the following :*

(i) 'No Exit'

Notice इत्यादि के शब्दों का पहला अक्षर capital होता है।

(ii) C/o (in postal address read as 'care of') को capital से लिखा जाता है।

(iii) Mr S. Bose
Govind Mitra Road
Patna

(i) Postal address में हर नई मुख्य बात को नई पंक्ति में capital letter से लिखा जाता है।

(ii) Postal address में comma तथा full stop के प्रयोग के संबंध में America तथा Britain में दो अलग-अलग विचारधाराएँ हैं। जैसे :

(*American use*)	(*British use*)
Mr A. V. Rao 12 Asaf Ali Road New Delhi-110 002	Mr A.V. Rao, 12, Asaf Ali Road, New Delhi—110 002.

27. *Look at the following :*

un-English	*non*-Catholic	*anti*-American
non-Christian	*anti*-British feeling	*pro*-Russian elements

(i) इन शब्दों में un-, non-, anti-, pro-*prefixes* हैं तथा English, Christian *proper nouns* एवं American, Russian *proper noun* से बने adjectives हैं।

(ii) अगर किसी proper noun या adjective के पहले prefix आए तो prefix *small letter* से शुरू होता है किंतु prefix और hyphen के बाद आनेवाला proper noun या adjective का पहला letter सदा capital होता है।

Note : In the titles of literary works, names of organisations, etc. both the prefix and the word to which it is attached must have a capital letter : *Anti-Apartheid Organisation, Anti-Vivisection League*

28. *Look at these sentences :*

She is very interested in *history*.
A good knowledge of *mathematics* is essential to you.
Do you want to study *biology ?*
He is trying to secure good marks in *physics* and *chemistry*.

(i) History, mathematics, biology आदि शैक्षिक विषय के नाम हैं, इन्हें प्रायः small letter से लिखा जाता है, किंतु भाषा के नाम (जैसे—Hindi, English, Urdu, Tamil, etc.) सदा capital letter से शुरू किए जाते हैं।

(ii) लेकिन history, mathematics आदि को capital letter से भी लिखा जा सकता है जब इनसे name of a course in a curriculum या subject in an examination का बोध हो। जैसे :

She passed in *History* but failed in *Mathematics*.

इस संबंध में यह विचार देखें :

The names of academic subjects other than languages (which must, of course, have capitals), are normally written with a small letter, but a capital may be used when the word is thought of as the name of a course in a curriculum or a subject in an examination. F. T. Wood : CURRENT ENGLISH USAGE

2. Full Stop [.] के प्रयोग

1. *Look at these sentences :*

He is a good boy.	(*Statement*)
Don't make a noise.	(*Command*)
He asked me what my name was.	(*Indirect Question*)

Statements, commands तथा indirect questions के अंत में full stop दिया जाता है।

2. *Look at the following :*

B.A.	M.P.	M.L.A.	U.K.	U.S.A.
Ph.D.	Co.	Nov.	Dec.	U.S.S.R.

कुछ शब्दों के abbreviations के बाद full stop दिया जाता है। Initials (नामाक्षर) के बाद भी full stop दिया जाता है। जैसे :

B. C. Roy	B. K. Singh	S. Bose
D.P. Rai	B. N. Tiwari	J. B. Prasad

Note : A full stop *may* follow a person's initials :
F. T. Wood or *F. T. Wood, Messrs T J Jones & Co* or *Messrs T. J. Jones & Co.*
—F. T. Wood : CURRENT ENGLISH USAGE

3. *Look at the following :*

Dr	Mrs	MCC	NATO	PTO	SALT
Mr	Ltd	WHO	UNESCO	UN	OPEC

आजकल बहुत-से abbreviations के बाद full stop नहीं भी दिए जाते हैं।

Note : If the abbreviation ends with the last letter of the word, it is now common practice to omit the stop: *Mr, Mrs, Dr, Maths.* The student must decide for himself whether to write *eg, Prof, ref, Jan* or e.g., Prof., ref., Jan. —F. T. Wood : CURRENT ENGLISH USAGE

4. *Look at the following :*

He is an officer in the P.W.D.
The meeting will be held at 4 p.m.

अगर कोई वाक्य abbreviation से अंत करे तो वाक्य के अंत में एक ही full stop दिया जाता है, दो नहीं।

5. *Look at the following :*

Rs. 10.55	$ 3.40	£ 1.20
6.30 a.m.	5.15 p.m.	7.30 a.m.

(i) रुपए-पैसे, डॉलर-सेण्ट या पौंड-शिलिंग के बीच full stop दिया जाता है।

(ii) घंटा और मिनट के बीच भी full stop दिया जाता है।

(iii) Rs. 10.55 को ten rupees and fifty-five paise पढ़ा जाता है।

$ 3.40 को three dollars and forty cents पढ़ा जाता है।
£ 1.20 को one pound and twenty pence ,, ,, ,,
6.30 को six-thirty या half past six ,, ,, ,,

6. *Look at the following :*

7.8.89 7th August 1989
7/8/89 August 7, 1989

(i) Date लिखने में day तथा month के बीच full stop दिया जाता है। कुछ लोग 7.8.89 की जगह 7/8/89 भी लिखते हैं।

(ii) 7th August 1989 के बीच comma नहीं होगा, किंतु August 7, 1989 में comma लगेगा।

7. *Look at the following :*

I will see you at...in the evening.
You must come to... at that time.

अगर वाक्य से कुछ शब्द या शब्दों को लोप कर दिया जाए तो उसकी जगह तीन full stops दिए जाते हैं। किंतु जब वाक्य के अंत से कोई शब्द लोप किया जाए तो तीन full stops उसके लिए और एक full stop वाक्य के अंत के लिए दिया जाता है। कुल मिलाकर चार full stops दिए जाएँगे। जैसे :

Ramu went to see Rekha at....

8. *Look at the following :*

Yours sincerely, (*comma*)
Ramesh Kumar (*no full stop*)

Mr Rajeev Kumar
S.N. 1120
Sainik School
Tilaiya Dam

(i) पत्र के अंत में अपने हस्ताक्षर के बाद full stop नहीं देना चाहिए।

(ii) Postcard, inland या लिफाफे के ऊपर address के अंत में full stop दिया भी जा सकता है या छोड़ दिया जा सकता है।

3. Question Mark [?] के प्रयोग

1. *Look at these sentences :*

When will he go today ?
Is he leaving for Delhi now ?
'Are we near Bombay ?' he asked.
Is Mr Sharma an M.A. ?

Interrogative sentence के अंत में question mark दिया जाता है। किंतु indirect question के अंत में full stop दिया जाता है। जैसे :

He said to me, 'What is your name ?' (*Direct question*)
He asked me what my name was. (*Indirect question*)

2. *Look at the these sentences :*

Post this letter, *will you* ?
He is a fool, *isn't he* ?
Question tag के अंत में question mark दिया जाता है।

3. *Look at these sentences :*

Mahatma Gandhi was born in 1868 (?)
This is a good (?) tape-recorder.
वैसे वाक्यों में जहाँ किसी प्रकार का प्रश्न, शंका या अनिश्चितता व्यक्त करनी हो वहाँ question mark का प्रयोग किया जाता है।

4. *Look at these sentences :*

Who will be there ? *You ? Your brother ? Your friend ?*
Also : *Will you be there*—or *your brother* or *your friend ?*
अगर एक ही वाक्य में कई questions हों तो उस वाक्य के अंत में (जैसा दूसरे वाक्य में बताया गया है) question mark दिया जाता है। Question marks अलग-अलग भी दिए जा सकते हैं, जैसा ऊपर प्रथम वाक्य में बताया गया है।

4. Exclamation mark [!] के प्रयोग

1. *Look at these sentences :*

What a piece of work is man !
What a wonderful day that was !
How lovely you look !
Exclamatory sentence (जो प्रायः What a...या How से शुरू होते हैं) के अंत में exclamation mark [!] दिया जाता है।

2. *Look at the following :*

'*Oh !*' he exclaimed	What fun !	Nonsense !
How ridiculous !	Good Heavens !	What ! Hello !

अत्यधिक सुख, दुःख, या आश्चर्य व्यक्त करनेवाले शब्दों के बाद exclamation marks दिए जाते हैं।

3. *Look at these sentences :*

Get out ! I don't want to see you again.
Shut up ! I don't want to hear a word.
कभी-कभी short order के बाद exclamation mark दिया जाता है।

4. *Look at these sentences :*

Long live the President !	(कामना)	Stop !	(प्रबल इच्छा)
May you live long !	(कामना)	Get out !	(प्रबल इच्छा)

Imperative sentence के अंत में कामना या प्रबल इच्छा व्यक्त करने के लिए exclamation mark का प्रयोग किया जाता है।

5. Comma [,] के प्रयोग

1. *Look at these sentences :*

If the taxi is here, we must go.
When electricity fails, we can't do anything.

अगर कोई adverb clause किसी principal clause के पहले आए तो उस adverb clause के पहले comma दिया जाता है।

Note : किंतु अगर principal clause पहले हो और adverb clause बाद में तो इन दोनों के बीच comma नहीं दिया जाता। जैसे :

If you ask him, he will help you. (comma)
He will help you *if you ask him.* (no comma)

2. *Look at these sentences :*

He said, 'Sita is a good girl.'
'Sita is a good girl,' *he said.*
'I will do,' *she said,* 'if you like it.'

(i) Direct speech में He said इत्यादि के बाद comma दिया जाता है।

(ii) अगर he said अंत में आए तो direct speech के बाद comma दिया जाता है। किंतु, direct speech में अगर question रहे, तो वाक्य के अंत में question mark दिया जाता है। जैसे :

'Is he very tall ?' said Moti.
'He is very tall,' said Moti.

(iii) अगर he said, said Mukul इत्यादि किसी quotation के बीच में आए तो उसके दोनों ओर comma दिया जाता है।

3. *Look at the following :*

Muzaffarpur,
10th September 1989.

Dear Ramesh,

....
....

Yours sincerely,
....

(i) चिट्ठियों में अभिवादन (salutation) तथा विदाई (words of leave-taking) के बाद comma दिया जाता है।

(ii) पत्र लिखने में स्थान के नाम के बाद comma दिया जाता है।

(iii) Date हम कई तरह से लिखते हैं :

March 19, 1990 (comma)
19th March 1990 (no comma)

4. *Look at the following :*

Sri M.K. Prasad	Sri M.K. Prasad,
118 Vivekanand Marg	118, Vivekanand Marg.
Allahabad	Allahabad.

Address लिखने के ऊपर बताए गए दोनों तरीके के punctuation पर ध्यान दें। ये दोनों तरीके सही माने जाते हैं।

5. *Look at these sentences :*

His shop is in *Patna,* Bihar.
The meeting was held on Monday, *April* 10, 1990.
Please contact Sri D. P. Rai, *Bharati Bhawan, Motijheel,* Muzaffarpur.

Geographical names, dates तथा address की अन्य बातों को अलग करने के लिए comma का प्रयोग किया जाता है।

6. *Look at these sentences :*

Prof. Sinha, *M.A., Ph.D.,* has joined his post.
Sri Kumar, *B.A., B.Ed.,* is our new teacher.

नाम, उपाधियों तथा पदवियों के बीच में comma का प्रयोग किया जाता है।

7. *Look at these sentences :*

They will close the window, *won t they ?*
He has written a letter, *hasn't he ?*

Question tag को main clause से अलग करने के लिए comma का प्रयोग किया जाता है।

8. *Look at these sentences :*

I want *a pen, a book* and *a bag.* (nouns)
She *bathed, dressed* and *went* away. (verbs)
He is *tall, gentle* and *hard-working.* (adjectives)

(i) अगर वाक्य में एक ही part of speech (*noun, verb, adjective, adverb*) के तीन या तीन से अधिक शब्द आएँ तो उनके बीच comma दिया जाता है।

(ii) किंतु अंतिम शब्द में जब *or* या *and* का प्रयोग किया जाए तो *or/and* के पहले comma प्रायः नहीं दिया जाता।

9. *Look at these sentences :*

Ruby, get me a glass of water.
I don't know what to say, *boys.*

Will you please switch off the radio, *Rajeev* ?
I think, *Ramesh,* that you would be wiser not to go.

(i) संबोधन (words of address) को वाक्य से अलग करने के लिए comma का प्रयोग किया जाता है।

(ii) संबोधन का शब्द अगर वाक्य के शुरू में हो तो उसके बाद और अगर अंत में हो तो उसके पहले और बीच में हो तो उसके दोनों ओर comma दिया जाता है।

Note : सम्बोधन यदि जोर देने के लिए रहे तो उसके बाद comma नहीं देकर exclamation mark का प्रयोग किया जाता है। जैसे :
Mohan ! What are you doing ?

10. *Look at these sentences :*

In fact, he is a good teacher.
No, I don't know him.
Slowly, she went to him.
After the war, he lived in India.

अगर वाक्य के शुरू में *No, In fact, Slowly, However, For example, For instance, That is, After the war* जैसे adverbials आएँ तो उनके बाद comma दिया जाता है।

11. *Look at these sentences :*

We know, *of course,* that the prices are rising.
You must, *however,* remember your promise.

अगर *of course, however, moreover, I think, you know, that is* वाक्य के बीच में आएँ तो उनके दोनों ओर comma दिया जाता है।

12. *Look at these sentences :*

Hari, *the son of Govind,* went to England.
Shyam, *not Hari,* has broken the window.
Noun in apposition के दोनों ओर comma दिया जाता है।

13. *Look at these sentences :*

He is not only wise, *but* also clever.
He is not only old, *but* also sickly.
She doesn't smoke, *nor* does she drink.

(i) दो principal clauses जब *or, but, and, nor* इत्यादि से जुटे हों तो इन शब्दों के पहले comma दिया जाता है।

(ii) याद रखें : Comma का प्रयोग तब किया जाता है जब दूसरा principal clause कोई नया या विरोधी विचार व्यक्त करे या उसकी बनावट नए ढंग की हो।

(iii) जब दो छोटे-छोटे independent clauses *and, or, but* इत्यादि से जुटे हों तब उनके बीच comma का प्रयोग नहीं किया जाता। जैसे :
You go ahead *and* I will follow.
Produce *or* perish.

14. *Look at this sentence :*

By night or day, at home or abroad, asleep or awake, Pradeep has no peace of mind.

एक ही part of speech के pairs of words के बीच comma का प्रयोग किया जाता है।

15. *Look at these sentences :*

He lives in *a tall, beautiful* and *newly-built* house.

I bought a *new, red,* and *beautiful* chair.

जब दो या दो से अधिक adjectives किसी noun के पहले आए तब उन्हें अलग करने के लिए comma का प्रयोग किया जाता है।

16. *Look at these sentences :*

The other boy, *Raman,* refused to do it.

He should, *or rather must,* go there.

The job having been completed, everyone relaxed.

Shyam, *to tell you the truth,* is not a good boy.

His method of work is *as good as, or better than,* mine.

He is, *at least in my opinion,* a dishonest man.

The decision, *as you know,* may be taken tomorrow.

(i) वाक्य के बीच में आनेवाले words, phrases या clauses के दोनों ओर comma दिया जाता है।

(ii) Absolute construction (तीसरा वाक्य) के बाद भी comma का प्रयोग किया जाता है।

17. *Look at these sentencese :*

Try, try again.

Come, come; you need not be shy.

जब किसी शब्द को दुहराया जाए तब उसके बीच comma का प्रयोग किया जाता है।

18. *Look at the following :*

5,789; 1,11,425,

हजार, लाख या करोड़वाली संख्याओं की दाहिनी ओर से तीन संख्याओं के बाद comma दिया जाता है ताकि वे गणना की इकाइयों के अनुसार सुगमता से पढ़ी जा सकें।

Note : किंतु वैसी संख्याएँ जिनसे साल या telephone number या house number सूचित हों, उनपर यह नियम लागू नहीं होता। जैसे :

In *1980,* I went to Hyderabad.

If you ring up *3575,* you may talk to me.

19. *Look at these sentences :*

Rajeev is fifteen; *Mukul, eleven.* (is लुप्त है)

Ruby is fourteen; *Soni, ten*. (is लुप्त है)

वैसे वाक्य जिनमें कुछ शब्द लुप्त हों, उन शब्दों को सूचित करने के लिए comma का प्रयोग किया जाता है।

6. Apostrophe ['] के प्रयोग

1. *Look at these sentences :*

Mohan's car is red.
These are *children's* toys.
This is the *buyers'* wish.

(i) जिस singular noun के अंत में *s* नहीं रहता उसमें *'s* लगाकर possessive बनाया जाता है। याद रखें, *'s* का प्रयोग प्रायः सजीव के साथ होता है। जैसे :

the *boy's coat,*	न कि the *table's leg,*
the *girl's bag*	,, ,, the *pen's nib*

(ii) जिस plural noun के अंत में *s* नहीं रहता उसमें *'s* लगाकर possessive बनाया जाता है।

(iii) जिस plural noun के अंत में *s* हो उसमें केवल apostrophe (') लगाकर possessive बनाया जाता है।

Incorrect	*Correct*
This is *your's.*	This is *yours.*
It's importance.......	*Its* importance......
I have a pair of *jean's.*	I have a pair of *jeans.*

2. *Look at the following :*

'81	for	1981
It's	for	it is
o'clock	for	of the clock.

Contractions में (संक्षिप्त शब्दों में) लुप्त अक्षर या अक्षरों के स्थान पर apostrophe का प्रयोग किया जाता है।

3. *Look at the following :*

Your 3's and 8's look alike.
Cross your *t's,* they look like *l's.*

संख्या तथा अक्षरों को plural बनाने के लिए *'s* का प्रयोग किया जाता है।

Note : संख्या यदि शब्दों में लिखी जाए तो उसका plural *s* या *es* लगाकर बनता है; *'s* लगाकर नहीं जैसे :

Kapil hit three *fours* and two *sixes.*

4 *Look at the following :*

B.A.'s	**M.A.'s**	**Ph.D.'s**
M.P.'s	**M.L.A.'s**	**M.L.C.'s**

कुछ abbreviations को plural बनाने के लिए 's का प्रयोग किया जाता है। किंतु जहाँ अस्पष्टता की गुंजाइश नहीं रहती, वहाँ बहुत-से लेखक अंकों तथा अक्षरों के abbreviations के बाद केवल *s* लगाते हैं और apostrophe छोड़ देते हैं। जैसे :

Two *Ph. D. s*	many *F.-16s*
Twenty *M.P.s*	first half of the *1981s*

इस संबंध में आप यह विचार देखें :

An apostrophe may also be used for the plurals of numbers when they are written as figures : *He makes his 8's like 3's; the 1970's,* but the modern tendency is to omit the apostrophe here : *8s like 3s; the 1970s.*

—*F.T.* Wood : *CURRENT ENGLISH USAGE*

7. Quotation Marks [' '] के प्रयोग

1. *Look at these sentences :*

Sita said, 'They think so.'
He said, 'I won't allow it.'
Pope says, 'The proper study of mankind is man.'

(i) Quotation marks को inverted commas भी कहा जाता है। इसका प्रयोग speaker के actual words को घेरने के लिए या quotation को घेरने के लिए किया जाता है।

(ii) Quotation marks single ('....') हो सकता है या double ("...."). आप दोनों में से किसी का प्रयोग कर सकते हैं।

(iii) 'But whichever form is not used for ordinary quotation is then used for quotation within quotation,' e.g.,

'I heard *"keep out"* being shouted,' he said.
"I heard *'keep out'* being shouted," he said.

2. *Look at these sentences :*

'I will return by 8 p.m.,' *Mukul said.*
'I know you can't,' *Rajeev said.*

यदि speaker बदल जाए तो उसका कथन नए para या separate line(s) में देना चाहिए।

Note : (i) यदि quotation कई paragraphs का हो तो प्रत्येक paragraph को quotation mark से प्रारंभ करना चाहिए। लेकिन केवल अंतिम paragraph के बाद quotation की समाप्ति करनी चाहिए।

(ii) कहानी, कविता, लेख, निबंध, अखबार आदि के नाम quotations के भीतर रखे जाते हैं। जैसे :

Have you read 'The Post Master' by Tagore ?

(iii) पुस्तक तथा पत्रिकाओं के नाम के नीचे लकीर खींच दी जाती है या उन्हें वक्राक्षरों (italics) में लिखा जाता है।

3. *Look at these sentences :*

Your meaning of "socialism" is different from mine.

In Linguistics "competence" has a new meaning.

किसी वाक्य में किसी word, phrase या technical expression को सूचित करने के लिए उसे quotation marks के अंदर रखा जाता है।

Note : *Punctuation of Direct Speech*

(i) Direct speech में full stop, exclamation mark, question mark या comma को quotation marks के अंदर रखा जाता है। जैसे :

'I am happy now.'	(full stop)
'Is he very tall ?'	(question mark)
'This boy,' he said, *'is very tall.'*	(comma)
He said, *'Nonsense !'*	(exclamation mark)

(ii) *'Hands up !'* said the General.

'Hands up !' के बाद comma का प्रयोग नहीं किया गया है क्योंकि इसके बाद exclamation mark लगा हुआ है।

(iii) 'Have you seen the boy ?' asked the teacher.

.......boy के बाद comma का प्रयोग नहीं किया गया है क्योंकि वहाँ question mark लगा हुआ है।

(iv) 'I want a cup of tea,' *said Sheela.*

'I want,' *said the boy,* 'a watch as a present.

Comma का प्रयोग said Sheela के पहले तथा said the boy के पहले और बाद में किया गया है क्योंकि वहाँ और कोई punctuation mark का प्रयोग नहीं किया गया है।

(v) *Look at these sentences :*

Did you see 'Are you happy' ?

These words ('Are you happy ?') were on the wall.

I saw the words { 'Are you happy ?' / 'You fools !' }

Did you see the words { 'Are you happy ?' / 'You fools !' } on the wall ?

Did you see the words { 'Are you happy ?' / 'You fools !' }

ऊपर के वाक्यों में punctuation marks पर ध्यान दें। Question तथा exclamation marks के बाद comma या full stop का प्रयोग नहीं किया जाता। जैसे :

Did you see the words *'Are you happy ?'* ?(दो question marks नहीं देना चाहिए।)

These words, *'Are you happy ?'* were on the wall. (Question mark के बाद comma नहीं दिया जाता है।)

4. *Look at these sentences :*

Mr Sen : Do you understand the sentence ?
Sudha : I don't understand it completely.
Mr Sen : All right, then. I'll repeat it.
Sudha : Thank you very much.

(i) किसी की कही हुई बातों को हमेशा quotation marks के अंदर नहीं रखा जाता।

(ii) Dialogue (वार्तालाप), newspaper reports, speeches या court के कामकाज में quotation marks का प्रयोग नहीं किया जाता।

(iii) इनमें speaker का नाम रहता है, उसके बाद colon (:) और फिर quotation.

(iv) Serious writing में दूसरे लेखकों के छोटे-छोटे quotations को quotation marks के भीतर रखा जाता है।

> Only short quotations from other writers will be put in quotation marks in serious writings; longer quotations will be indented and given without quotation marks. —RANDOLPH QUIRK & OTHERS : A GRAMMAR OF CONTEMPORARY ENGLISH

8. Colon [:] के प्रयोग

1. *Look at these sentences :*

I want the following : *books, pens and newspapers.*
I like the following : *poems, stories and novels.*

Colon का प्रयोग किसी सूची (list) को आरंभ करने के लिए किया जाता है।

2. *Look at these sentences :*

Shakespeare said : *'Neither a borrower nor a lender be.*
Justice Sinha observes : *'People in technical fields need to express their ideas clearly....'*

Quotation तथा direct speech के लंबे quotation के पहले colon का प्रयोग किया जाता है। जैसे : The President went on to say : (यहाँ long quotation रहता है।)

3. *Look at these sentences :*

The excuse he gave was this : *he had not properly understood the rules and regulations.*

वाक्य में पहले कही गई बात के बाद अगर उस संबंध में कोई explanation या statement देना हो तो इन दोनों के बीच colon का प्रयोग किया जाता है। यहाँ colon का अर्थ होगा : *that is to say.*

4. *Look at these sentences :*

What really happened was this : the car came and the boy was run over and the car sped away.

(a) Colon का प्रयोग प्रायः *what I suggest is this, what really happened was this, as follows, the following, for example, namely,* इत्यादि के बाद किया जाता है। जैसे :

Please send the items, namely :

(i) birth certificate
(ii) passport
(iii) family report

(b) कभी-कभी list of things के पहले *colon + short dash* (:–) भी दिया जाता है। किंतु इसे heavy punctuation माना जाता है। अतः, आप या तो colon (:) का प्रयोग करें या dash (—) का।

5. *Look at the following :*

Colon के कुछ और प्रयोग देखें :

(i) 5 : 3 : 2 [अनुपात (proportion) बताने के लिए]

(ii) *Journal of Language Teaching : 210-215.* (किसी journal को refer करने के लिए)

(iii) *New Delhi : Nationat Publishers, 1989.*
(Bibliographical details देने के लिए)

9. Semi-colon [;] के प्रयोग

1. *Look at these sentences :*

Please go there; *it is getting late.*
John is writing; *Jack is playing.*
Mukul is a boy; *Ruby is a girl.*

(i) अगर दो independent clauses के बीच कोई linking word (*but, and, so* इत्यादि) नहीं रहे तो उन दोनों clauses को अलग करने के लिए semi-colon का प्रयोग किया जाता है।

(ii) ऐसे वाक्यों में semi-colon का अर्थ *and* होता है।

(iii) Semi-colon, comma तथा full stop के बीच का pause (विराम) है।

10. Dash [—] के प्रयोग

1. *Look at these sentences :*

He looked at a face—*a face which he would never forget.*
A similar exercise—*you would recall—was done last year.*

वाक्य के विचार में रुकावट सूचित करने के लिए dash का प्रयोग किया जाता है।

2. *Look at these sentences :*

The other boy—*Ramesh Tandon*—refused to go there.

The other boy (*Ramesh Tandon*) refused to go there.

कभी-कभी कही हुई बात को स्पष्ट करने के लिए dash का प्रयोग करते हैं। किंतु ऐसी परिस्थिति में dash की जगह brackets भी चल सकता है।

3. *Look at these sentences :*

The policeman stated that *Sri*—was not there.

'I don't know *Mr*—who lived *at*—,' he said.

वाक्य में कुछ शब्द को छिपाने या लुप्त करने के लिए या यह दिखाने के लिए कि वाक्य अधूरा है, dash (—) का प्रयोग किया जाता है।

4. *Look at this sentence :*

'Well,' he said, '*I*—*I*—can't tell you anything more.'

वाक्य में हिचकिचाहट का बोध कराने के लिए dash का प्रयोग किया जाता है।

5. *Look at this sentence :*

There is no date to that letter—*a most significant omission.*

किसी बात पर जोर देने के लिए तथा long pause का बोध कराने के लिए dash दिया जाता है।

6. *Look at these sentences :*

He left them all—*his family, his relatives, his friends and the traditions of a long time.*

We have ordered the following—

(a) *10 steel chairs*

(b) *40 tables*

कभी-कभी जहाँ colon का प्रयोग किया जा सकता है वहाँ dash का भी प्रयोग किया जाता है। List of things या वाक्य में पहले कही हुई बातों को explain करने के लिए dash दिया जाता है।

7. *Look at the following :*

1975—1981

Chapters I—X

Pp 14—23

Dash का प्रयोग दी हुई प्रथम तथा अंतिम संख्या के बीच की लुप्त संख्या या संख्याओं को सूचित करने के लिए किया जाता है। जैसे : 1975—1981, I—X, 14—23 के बीच की संख्याएँ लुप्त हैं।

11. Hyphen [-] के प्रयोग

1. *Look at these sentences :*

If you want to study *gra-mmar,* study it well.

When he was going to *col-lege,* he met me.

(i) अगर sentence का अंतिम शब्द अपूर्ण हो जिसे दूसरी पंक्ति में पूरा किया जाता हो, तो अपूर्ण शब्द के बाद hyphen दिया जाता है।

Note : (i) एक syllable वाले word को divide नहीं किया जाता। जैसेः box; bag; ox इत्यादि।

(ii) जब word का syllable पूरा हो जाए, उसके बाद hyphen दें। जैसे :

phy-si-cs
bo-ta-ny

Physics शब्द में *phy* के बाद hyphen दें या *physi* के बाद और फिर बाकी अक्षरों को दूसरी पंक्ति में लिखें।

(iii) पंक्ति के अंत में किसी शब्द का एक अक्षर लिखकर या केवल एक अक्षर छोड़कर hyphen कभी नहीं देना चाहिए। जैसे :

among को *a-mong* या *amon-g* नहीं लिखें।
again को *a-gain* या *agai-n* ,, ,,।

2. *Look at these words :*

twenty-one	forty-two	sixty-six
thirty-one	fifty-five	eighty-nine

21 से लेकर 99 तक के अंकों को शब्दों में लिखने पर compound numbers को जोड़ने के लिए इनके बीच hyphen दिया जाता है।

3. *Look at the following :*

H-bomb	self-control	half-truth	ex-president
anti-goonda	self-respect	Vice-President	ex-husband
anti-inflation	self-love	non-violence	ex-chairman
bell-like	soft-spoken	absent-minded	un-English
a 4-hour week	a 10-day trip	a 6-foot snake	600-word essays
sister-in-law	brother-in-law	pre-planned	
one-storey house	a first-class hotel	a ten-rupee note	a heart-broken lover

(i) अँगरेजी में बहुत सारे compound तथा complex words हैं; उनके भागों (constituents) को अलग करने के लिए hyphen का प्रयोग किया जाता है। वैसे कुछ और शब्दों को देखें :

go-as-you-please ticket	house-to-house survey
middle-of-the-road policy	single-phase motor
well-planned campaign	out-of-the-way place

4. *Look at this sentence :*

'P-p-p-please t-t-try,' his teeth chattered through fear and cold.

तुतलाहट में अक्षरों की पुनरावृत्ति को बताने के लिए hyphen का प्रयोग किया जाता है।

Note : यदि किसी prefix के लगाने से लगातार दो vowels या तीन consonants हो जाएँ तो इसके निवारण हेतु hyphen का प्रयोग किया जाता है। जैसे :
co-operation; co-ordination; bell-like;
co-operate; co-operative; co-ordinate etc.

12. Brackets [ ], ( ) के प्रयोग

1. *Look at these sentences :*

We have already discussed (*chapter 6*) how to do it.
We shall see (*p.54*) that Mary's first lover was William Bevan. (*1912-81*)

(i) Reference या life-span को बताने के लिए brackets का प्रयोग किया जाता है।

2. *Look at these sentences :*

I spoke to my neighbour (*Mr Sinha*) about it.
You may sell even your immovable property (*land and buildings*) for your children's education.
I saw Ramesh (*my classmate*) when I was in Delhi.

(i) जब हम किसी बात को main sentence से अलग व्याख्या के रूप में जोड़ते हैं तब उस व्याख्या को brackets के अंदर रखते हैं।

(ii) कभी-कभी addition या explanation बड़ा भी हो सकता है। जैसे :

He married Rashmi in 1980. (*His father had forbidden him to do so earlier.*) She was then eighteen.

3. *Look at these sentences :*

(a) These words ('*Are you happy ?*') were on the walls.
(b) The other boy (*Mukul* [*alias Munna*]) was there.
(c) He said that *Monday* was his visiting day [italics—by the editor].
(d) You saw the words $\left\{\begin{array}{l}\text{'Are you happy ?'}\\ \text{'You fools !'}\end{array}\right\}$

(i) Brackets तीन प्रकार के होते हैं : round brackets ( ), square brackets [ ], braces { }.

(ii) अगर round brackets के बीच में कुछ जोड़ना होता है (when inclusions have to be made within inclusions) तो हम square brackets का प्रयोग करते हैं। जैसे : वाक्य (b) को देखें।

(iii) अगर कोई writer या editor वाक्य में कुछ अपनी ओर से जोड़ता है या कुछ बदलता है तो वह square brackets [ ] का प्रयोग करता है, अर्थात square brackets का प्रयोग serious writing में होता है। जैसेः वाक्य (c) को देखें।

(iv) Braces { } का प्रयोग प्रायः mathematics या किसी दूसरे technical writing में या कुछ विशेष स्थानों में होता है; उदाहरणार्थ वाक्य (d) देखें।

Examples Worked Out

Punctuate the following sentences, using capitals where necessary :

1.	he said i wont go	*He* said, *'I won't go.'*
2.	yes please i said	*'Yes, please,' I* said.
3.	he asked me whats your name	He asked me, *'What's your name?'*
4.	i tell you sir i cant give it	*I* tell you, *Sir, I can't* give it.
5.	she is after all a poor girl	*She* is, *after all,* a poor girl.
6.	where are you going	*Where* are you going ?
7.	have you written to your father	*Have* you written to your father ?
8.	he asked me where i was going	*He* asked me where *I* was going.
9.	did you go there he asked	*'Did you go there* ?' he asked.
10.	if you cant understand it tell me	*If* you *can't* understand it, tell me.
11.	no i dont know him	*No, I don't* know him.
12.	in fact mr sinha is a good teacher	*In fact, Mr Sinha* is a good teacher.
13.	he was a student of the town high school in patna	*He* was a student of the *Town High School* in *Patna.*
14.	the children on the whole did well	*The* children, *on the whole,* did well.
15.	try try again for success	*Try,* try again for success.
16.	the answer he said is not easy	*'The answer,'* he said, *'is not easy.'*
17.	shyam not moti did it	*Shyam,* not Moti, did it.
18.	do what you are told	*Do* what you are told.
19.	post this letter will you	*Post* this letter, *will you ?*
20.	this is haris book	*This* is *Hari's* book.
21.	he is an indian she is an african	*He* is an *Indian;* she is an *African.*
22.	whats wrong amar i asked	*'What's* wrong *Amar* ?' I asked.
23.	dont do as i do do as i say	*'Don't* do as *I* do; do as *I say.'*
24.	oh he exclaimed	*'Oh !'* he exclaimed.
25.	i want a pen a watch a notebook and a bag	I want a pen, *a watch, a notebook* and a bag.
26.	usha my brothers daughter is getting married tomorrow	*Usha,* my *brother's* daughter, is getting married tomorrow.
27.	i am good at physics and mathematics but bad at hindi and english	*I* am good at physics and mathematics, but bad at *Hindi* and *English.*
28.	gandhijee the father of the nation lived a simple life	*Gandhijee,* the *Father of the Nation,* lived a simple life.
29.	o lord have mercy upon us	*O Lord,* have mercy upon us.
30.	when the bell rings we shall go to the class	*When* the bell *rings,* we shall go to the class.

31. the poets i like best are milton wordsworth keats and shelley	*The* poets *I* like best are *Milton, Wordsworth, Keats* and *Shelley.*
32. no she said i did nothing	*'No'*, she said, *'I did nothing.'*
33 yes she said i heard the sound	*'Yes'*, she said, *'I heard the sound.'*
34. hands up said the leader of the gang	*'Hands up !'* said the leader of the gang.
35. please tell me what time it is	*Please* tell me what time it is.
36. oh dear what am i going to do	*'Oh dear !' What* am I going to do ?'
37. mr s redddy the president of india went to england	*Mr S. Reddy,* the *President of of India,* went to *England.*
38. follow me cried their leader	*'Follow me !'* cried their leader.
39. having done his work he went home	*Having done his work,* he went home.
40. rich and poor high and low young and old all must die	*Rich and poor, high and low,* young and old—*all must die.*
41. she did not however succeed in the examination	*She* did not, *however,* succeed in in the examination.
42. Heera is a bihari surjeet singh a punjabi	*Heera* is a *Bihari; Surjeet Singh, a Punjabi.*
43. when you are ready we shall start	*When you are ready,* we shall start.
44. we shall start when you are ready	*We* shall start when you are ready.
45. he is handsome intelligent sincere and faithful	*He* is *handsome, intelligent, sincere* and faithful.
46. you expect me he said to work all the time	*'You expect me,'* he said, *'to work all the time.'*
47. the days of the week are sunday monday tuesday wednesday thursday friday and saturday	*The* days of the week are : *Sunday Monday, Tuesday, Wednesday, Thursday, Friday* and *Saturday.*
48. the months of the year are january february march april may june july august september october november and december	The months of the year are : *January, February, March, April, May, June, July, August, September, October, November* and *December.*
49. he cried help help	He cried, *'Help ! Help !'*
50. tell me i said how you know all that	*'Tell me,' I said, 'how you know all that.'*
51. you know of course the way to delhi	*You* know, *of course,* the way to *Delhi.*

52. i saw mr prasad your teacher this morning	*I* saw *Mr Prasad, your teacher,* this morning.
53. what a wonderful day that was	*What* a wonderful day that was !
54. mr bose please listen to him	*Mr Bose,* please listen to him.
55. the meeting will be held on april 17 1982	*The* meeting will be held on *April* 17, 1982.
56. i have some news for you rekha has arrived	*I* have some news for you *Rekha has arrived.*
57. i must i can i will do it	*I* must, *I* can, *I* will do it.
58. you'll succeed if you try	*You'll* succeed if you try.
59. if you try you'll succeed	*If you try,* you'll succeed.
60. he lived in india after the war	*He* lived in *India* after the war.
61. after the war he lived in india	*After the war,* he lived in *India.*
62. what his name is is of no interest to me	*What his name is,* is of no interest to me.
63. whatever he does does not concern me	*Whatever he does,* does not concern me.
64. he slowly carefully moved the the chair	*He slowly,* carefully moved the chair.
65. he can may should and will do it it	*He can, may,* should and will do it.
66. government of by and for the people	*Government of, by* and for the people.
67. she bought eggs butter bread rice and coffee	*She* bought eggs, *butter, bread,* rice and coffee.
68. he wrote down 73 12 14 8 6 and 14 and then added them up	*He* wrote down 73, 12, 14, 8, 6 and 14, and then added them up.
69. i like reading you like playing	*I* like *reading;* you like playing.
70. in one respect government policy has been firmly decided	*In* one respect, government policy has been firmly decided.
71. how silly she is he thought	*'How silly she is !'* he thought.
72. i am delighted to see you he said	*'I am* delighted to see you,' *he* said.
73. he said i am delighted to see you	*He said, 'I* am delighted to see you.'
74. hearing the words keep out he stopped	*Hearing* the words *'keep out,'* he stopped.
75. i saw the words are you happy	*I* saw the words *'Are you happy ?'*
76. k.n. ganesan is a doctor	*K. N. Ganesan* is a doctor.
77. he is doctor k. n. ganesan	*He* is *Dr K. N. Ganesan.*
78. o yes said the father i can at least do that much	*'O, yes,' said the father, 'I can at least do that much.'*

79. listen said he can't you hear a low moaning from that hut there	*"Listen !" said he,* 'can't you hear a low moaning from that hut there ?'
80. yes she whispered i do hear it now let us go and find out what it means	*'Yes,' she whispered,* 'I do hear it now. Let us go and find out what it means.'
81. reading maketh a full man conference a ready man writing an exact man	Reading maketh a full man; conference a ready man; writing an exact man.
82. as caesar loved me i weep for him as he was fortunate i rejoice at it as he was valiant i honour him	As Caesar loved me, *I* weep for him; as he was fortunate, *I* rejoice at it; as he was valiant, *I* honour him.

EXERCISE I

In each row, underline two words which would start with a capital letter when used in a sentence in an essay :

EXAMPLE : road, book, **july,** house, watch, **tom,** table.

1. road, book, july, house, watch, tom, table.
2. chair, bottle, pencil, madan, knife, sun, thakur,
3. word, ink, sohan, earth, moon, india, minister.
4. tagore, poem, essay, story, english, pin, country.
5. stone, bihar, radio, lamp, carbon, mr, clock.
6. shirt, japanese, door, window, america, peon, teacher.
7. star, holi, diwali, letter, friend, brother, class.
8. copybook, ramayana, u.s.a., paper, servant, bed, fan.
9. bible, picture, bag, roof, flower, inkpot, friday.
10. month, september, field, ball, bat, sanskrit, air.
11. history, england, music, bicycle, mrs, coal, boy.
12. tin, prasad, gold, rent, saturday, food, car.
13. bus, u.n.o., state, bench, blackboard, urdu, prose.
14. kitchen, russian, man, woman, girl, delhi, egg.
15. blackboard, peon, shakespeare, garage, sky, sinha, milk.

EXERCISE 2

Select the right answer from A, B, C and D below and then complete each sentence :

[ध्यान दें : अगर आप full stop चुनते हैं तो अगला शब्द capital letter से शुरू होगा ।]

EXAMPLE : She wants to know where you live ( )
A (?) B(!) C (;) D (.)
She wants to know where you live.

1. She wants to know where you live ( )
A (?) B (!) C (;) D (.)

2. He said ( ) 'Moti is a good boy.'
A (.) B (;) C (,) D (—)
3. She is very beautiful, isn't she ( )
A (.) B (?) C (!) D (,)
4. 'Dinner is ready ( )' said Veena.
A (;) B (:) C (,) D (?)
5. He visited Patna ( ) Delhi and Bombay.
A (:) B (,) C (;) D (—)
6. How old he is ( )
A (?) B (.) C (!) D (:)
7. Morarji Desai is our ex ( ) Prime Minister.
A (,) B (;) C (:) D (-)
8. Write carefully and avoid mistakes ( )
A (!) B (?) C (.) D (;)
9. 'Are you writing a letter ?' 'Yes ( )'
A (,) B (.) C (!) D (;)
10. Tell me what he said ( )
A (?) B (.) C (!) D (,)
11. He said to me, 'What's your name ( )'
A (!) B (.) C (?) D (:)
12. Pass the sugar ( ) please.
A (?) B (.) C (;) D (,)
13. 'Be quiet ( ) The baby is asleep.'
A (?) B (.) C (!) D (,)
14. When are we meeting again ( )
A (!) B (,) C (?) D (.)
15. Rani ( ) get me a glass of water.
A (;) B (:) C (,) D (?)

EXERCISE 3

Select the right answer from A, B, C and D below and then complete each sentence :

EXAMPLE : Alas ( ) They know not what they do.
A (.) B (?) C (!) D (—)
Alas ! They know not what they do.

1. Alas ( ) They know not what they do.
A (.) B (?) C (!) D (—)
2. How late you are ( )
A (:) B (.) C (?) D (!)
3. George said ( ) 'I heard it on the radio.'
A (;) B (:) C (,) D (.)
4. 'I have spoken to him,' I said ( ) 'on only one occasion.'
A (,) B (:) C (!) D (?)
5. 'Please tell me what time it is ( ).
A (?) B (!) C (.) D (,)
6. Shut up ( ) I can't hear what they are saying.
A (.) B (,) C (:) D (!)
7. When he comes ( ) give him my love.
A (;) B (,) C (.) D (:)

8. **We, however ( ) have made that mistake.**
   A (:) B (,) C (;) D (—)
9. **The problem is this ( ) which comes first, the hen or the egg ?**
   A (,) B (?) C (:) D (;)
10. **'Where did they go ? ( ) he asked.**
    A (,) B (:) C (;) D (')
11. **What a hot day ( ) Let us stay at home.**
    A (?) B (!) C (,) D (:)
12. **Ramesh, my next door neighbour ( ) went to Kashmir.**
    A (:) B (;) C (,) D (!)
13. **The watch is mine ( ) the radio is yours.**
    A (:) B (.) C (;) D (!)
14. **You, too ( ) can have a new car.**
    A (;) B (,) C (!) D (.)
15. **Send me all you have ( ) the grammars, the dictionaries, the readers.**
    A (,) B (;) C (;) D (:)

EXERCISE 4

Give the full form of each of these contractions:

EXAMPLES : he'll = he *will*   **I'd = I *had* or I *would***

1. he'll	**6. I won't**	**11. didn't**	**16. you're**
2. it's	**7. they've**	**12. can't**	**17. you'll**
3. he'd	**8. they're**	**13. I'll**	**18. that's**
4. I'd	**9. there'll**	**14. aren't**	**19. she's**
5. I shan't	**10.there's**	**15. isn't**	**20. where's**

EXERCISE 5

Punctuate the following, using capital letters wherever necessary :

EXAMPLE : he asked whether it was going to rain
He asked whether it was going to rain.

1. **he asked whether it was going to rain**
2. **those aren't flowers are they**
3. **may we go now**
4. **i wont listen to you she exclaimed**
5. **he told me however that he was going away soon**
6. **as soon as you hear the whistle run up to me**
7. **mr mitra my next door neighbour is in calcutta**
8. **hindi english and tamil are taught in this school**
9. **congratulations when are you getting married**
10. **they wanted to know who he was**
11. **when he comes give him my love**
12. **Where were you when the lights went out**
13. **if i were you i shouldnt do it**
14. **slowly carefully and with definite caution he raised the cover**
15. **i however have never seen him**

EXERCISE 6

Punctuate the following, using capital letters wherever necessary :

EXAMPLE : your son is certainly a boy of ability said the headmaster but it all depends upon you whether he is to do well at school
="Your son is certainly a boy of ability," said the Headmaster, "but it all depends upon you whether he is to do well at school."

1. what an extraordinary statement said the father how can his progress depend upon me
2. you can see replied the headmaster that he does his homework carefully
3. we should live soberly prudently and industriously at all times
4. thank you so much for inviting me and my friend ashok to tea on wednesday at five o clock
5. i have not seen new york but i know it exists then why must i see god before believing that he is there
6. a young rajah once said to his vizier how is it that i am so often ill
7. the shepherd finding his flock destroyed exclaimed i have been rightly served why did i trust my sheep to a wolf
8. i am going to england my mother will accompany me will you like to go with us
9. it was a question of please the complainant entering the lift said top the liftman demanded top please
10. you are tired said the king let me take the spade and work in your place thank you said the hermit giving the king his spade
11. that would be grand certainly said alice but then i shouldnt be hungry for it you know
12. as caesar loved me i weep for him as he was fortunate i rejoice at it as he was valiant i honour him but as he was ambitious i slew him
13. for gods sake said francis tell me who you are and what this means
14. do it yourself said the giant the tailor gave a prod of the knife and he let the broth out of the skin now you do that said he
15. is it me i asked yes he said quietly it is you and he went on looking at it the eyes i said hesitatingly don't look very much like mine
16. some are born great some achieve greatness some have greatness thrust upon them
17. One day walking together up a hill i said to faraday don't you wish yourself in your own country again yes he said what would you do there said i would you turn wild and eat mans flesh again he looked full of concern and shaking his head said no no
18. from all its chapters from all its pages from all its sentences the well written novel echoes and reechoes its own creative and controlling thought to this
19. reading maketh a full man conference a ready man writing an exact man
20. little johnny was not happy it was raining and john did not like rain he kept saying rain rain go away come again another day

EXERCISE 7

Punctuate the following, using capital letters wherever necessary. Arrange the conversation in separate lines :

Note : यदि speaker बदल जाए तो उसका कथन नए para में या नई पंक्ति में शुरू करें।

EXAMPLE : the teacher asked ramesh what time do you get up i get up at five thirty replied ramesh
=The teacher asked Ramesh, 'What time do you get up ?'
'I get up at five-thirty,' replied Ramesh.

1. the teacher asked ramesh what time do you get up i get up at five thirty replied ramesh
2. sita said to rita hello how are you i'm fine thanks said rita
3. mr bose said i cant find my shoes mrs bose said theyre under that chair
4. the salesman said to mr kumar good morning sir good morning i want a secondhand scooter please said mr kumar
5. look mother see what ive caught said vinod whats that asked his mother
6. mukul said why are you going to airport rajeev i m going to meet my friend who is coming from england said rajeev
7. abdul asked mohan is it really you abdul what are you doing in bangalore said mohan
8. radha said what a pretty raincoat where did you get it from rekha at the patna market said rekha
9. mrs prasad said raju raju wake up can you hear a noise what noise asked raju
10. the journalist asked mr prime minister what made you enter politics the prime minister said well i got involved in politics when i was a young man at the university
11. Neelu said have you got a rubber her mother replied i think there is one in the left hand drawer of your table
12. amar said have you got the key of the almirah its in the lock said ruby
13. asha said wheres the sugar father sugar what are you talking about said father
14. mrs jha what do you think of your new neighbour mrs bose i dont think much of her she comes over at least half a dozen times a day and borrows something or other
15. woman inspector i ve lost my handbag inspector can you describe it
16. customer i want some mangoes some good ones shopkeeper i havent got any bad ones madam i only sell the best
17. mr sen congratulations mr srinivasan your son was placed second in the selection list for sri krishna medical college mr srinivasan thank you mr sen
18. wife have you locked the gate dear husband yes i have and i ve checked all the doors and windows
19. justice sinha where were you at midnight on friday last gopal i was at home justice sinha were you in bed gopal no
20. mrs thakur whats your name servant umesh mrs thakur can you cook servant yes madam i can i can cook both vegetarian and non vegetarian food

EXERCISE 8

Write each of the following letters, using capital letters and punctuation marks correctly :

1.

51 ring road
bombay
10th november 1989

dear sujata

will you come to tea with me on wednesday at five o clock in the evening bring your sister anita also with you after tea we shall have some songs from geeta

miss sujata
61 ashoka road
bombay 5

Your loving friend
manju

2.

the headmaster
government high school
tower chowk, darbhanga

sir

as i am down with flu i cannot come to school for three days i request you to be kind enough to grant me leave of absence from school for three days (i.e., 12 13 and 14 august)

12 august 1989

yours faithfully
raghavendrum
class x sec. a

□ □ □

16. IDIOMS PHRASES AND PHRASAL VERBS

दिन-प्रतिदिन व्यवहार किए जानेवाले कुछ idioms, phrases और phrasal verbs को यहाँ निम्नलिखित दो खंडों (Parts I & II) में बाँटा गया है।

PART I: IDIOMS AND PHRASES

(i) "An idiom is a fixed group of words with a special meaning which is different from the meaning of the individual words."

—LONGMAN DICTIONARY OF CONTEMPORARY ENGLISH

Raining cats and dogs (जोर से वर्षा होना) एक idiom है। इस शब्द-समूह का word order fixed है अर्थात raining dogs and cats नहीं होता। साथ ही, इस शब्द-समूह के एक-एक शब्द के अनुसार इसका अर्थ "बिल्ली, कुत्ता बरसना या बरसाना" नहीं होगा।

(ii) A phrase is a group of words, containing neither subject nor predicate, which acts as a single part of speech.

ABC (प्रारंभिक ज्ञान)—I do not know even the *ABC* of Physics.

above board (निष्कपट एवं प्रकट)—My friend's dealings are always frank and *above board*.

above all (सबसे अधिक)—*Above all*, beware of false friends.

after all (याद रहे)—He is a man of wealth *after all*.

all in all (सब मिलाकर)—*All in all* it was a miracle.

all the same (एक ही बात)—It is *all the same* whether he comes or not.

all over (सभी जगह)—Mr Menon has travelled *all over* the world.

along with (साथ-साथ)—Tom came here *along with* Jack.

all along (शुरू से अंत तक; पूरी दूरी तक)—He went on shouting *all along*. There are trees *all along* the road.

all day long (दिनभर)—Ramesh has been reading a novel *all day long*.

at once (तुरत)—You must go and see the Principal *at once*.

at home in (निपुण)—She is quite *at home in* English.

again and again (बार-बार)—Try *again and again* and you will succeed at last.

at random (बिना लक्ष्य के)—He kicked the ball *at random*.

as usual (सदा की भाँति)—*As usual* he went out for a walk.

at the latest (देरी होने पर भी या देर से देर तक)—You must come tomorrow *at the latest.*

at heart (ह्रदय से)—He looks rough, but he is kind *at heart.*

at the top of (one's) voice (उच्चतम स्वर में)—The girl cried *at the top of her voice.*

at all hazards (हर तरह के जोखिम के बावजूद)—He did the work *at all hazards.*

at length (अंत में)—*At length,* he succeeded.

at enmity with (शत्रुता)—Mr Gupta is *at enmity with* his partner.

at a stretch (लगातार)—I can study three hours *at a stretch.*

the apple of (one's) eye (दुलारा, प्यारा)—Mrs Sinha's son is *the apple of her eye.*

an/the apple of discord (झगड़े की वस्तु)—Afghanistan is *an/the apple of discord* between Russia and America.

at the eleventh hour (अंतिम क्षण में)—The patient went to the doctor *at the eleventh hour.*

at bottom (भीतर से)—He is a very helping man *at bottom.*

at daggers drawn (कट्टर दुश्मन)—Once they were friends but now they are *at daggers drawn.*

at a loss (किंकर्तव्यविमूढ़)—I was *at a loss* to see a wolf before me/what to do next.

at sixes and sevens (अस्त-व्यस्त)—My books were *at sixes and sevens* in the room.

add fuel to the fire (flames) (आग मे घी डालना)—The boy failed and his father's chiding had *added fuel to the fire.*

as if (मानो)—He talks *as if* he were my boss.

at hand (नजदीक, आसन्न)—My examination is *at hand.*

as a matter of fact (सचमुच)—*As a matter of fact,* he did not help me.

at the point of (करीब)—The patient was *at the point of* death.

at all costs (किसी भी कीमत पर)—He has to finish this work today *at all costs.*

at stake (खतरे में)—Our life today is always *at stake.*

at variance with (विपरीत)—His acts are *at variance with* his words.

at all (तनिक भी)—He is not guilty *at all.*

at all events (चाहे जो कुछ हो)—You must come here *at all events.*

as a rule (सदा)—*As a rule,* he gets up before sunrise.

apple-pie order (बिलकुल ठीक हालत में)—Everything in this office is in *apple-pie order.*

at a time (एक बार में)—Hand them to me two *at a time.*

at times (कभी-कभी)—*At times* he behaves like a mad man.

as long as (जब तक)—*As long as* you are honest, you have no cause to fear.

as soon as (ज्योंही)—*As soon as* he got the news of his father's illness, he left for home.

at large (स्वतंत्र)—The murderer is still at large.

at the same time (उसी समय)—Both reached the office *at the same time.*

as a result of (के फलस्वरूप)—Two persons died *as a result of* police-firing.

at the instance of (के उकसाने या कहने पर)—He committed the crime *at the instance of* his friend.

at last (अंततः)—*At last*, we reached London.

at any cost (किसी भी कीमत पर)—He was determined to have a house *at any cost.*

as regards (के संबंध में)—*As regards* his qualifications, I have nothing to say now.

a lot of (बहुत)—He earns *a lot of* money by writing books.

at first (शुरू में)—*At first* he did not confess his guilt.

as a whole (पूरे रूप में)—You have to consider the proposal *as a whole,* not piecemeal.

all at once (एकाएक)—*All at once* there was a loud noise and people started running away.

at no time (कभी नहीं)—He was *at no time* a member of the party.

at least (कम-से-कम)—He may be a fool but *at least* he is not a thief.

at fault (गलती में)—My memory was *at fault*. It is difficult to say who is *at fault.*

after a fashion (किसी भाँति, संतोषप्रद ढंग से नहीं)—He can speak and write English *after a fashion.*

all told (सब मिलाकर)—We were twenty *all told.*

all of a sudden (अचानक)—*All of a sudden* a dog came on the road and was run over by a truck.

all the rage (लोकप्रिय)—These white handbags from Japan are *all the rage* this summer.

as well as (के अलावा, साथ-साथ)—He gave me money *as well as* advice. We shall travel by night *as well as* by day.

at any rate (हर हालत में, चाहे जो हो)—I have to see Mr Prasad today *at any rate.*

attend to (ध्यान देना)—I have a lot of work to *attend to.*

all the while (पूरे समय)—I stayed with Hari for an hour; he talked about himself *all the while.*

as far back as (पीछे तक)—If you want to know the history of this college, you will have to go *as far back* as 1950.

duty bound (अपने कार्य या कर्तव्य के लिए जरूरी होना)—I am *duty bound* to visit my old father.

at arm's length (घनिष्ठता से दूर रखना)—He is a straightforward man and keeps flatterers *at arm's length.*

according to (के अनुसार)—*According to* my watch it is 4 o'clock.

at best (हद से हद)—He is *at best* a competent rather than a brilliant officer.

at large (स्वतंत्र, बिना किसी रोक के)—He is a gentleman *at large.* The murderers are still *at large.*

at one's wits' end (कुछ समझ में नहीं आना क्या किया जाए क्या नहीं)—He was *at his wits' end* when I asked questions about his love affairs.

bed of roses (फूलों की सेज)—Life is not a *bed of roses.*

bag and baggage (बोरिया-बधना समेत)—He left the village *bag and baggage.*

by far (बहुत ही अधिक)—Mukul is *by far* the best boy in the class.

at (someone's) beck and call (तुरत (किसी की) आज्ञा या इच्छा पालन हेतु तत्पर)—This man is always *at your beck and call.*

by dint of (के कारण)—He stood first *by dint of* hard labour.

by means of (के द्वारा)—Thoughts are expressed *by means of* words.

by virtue of (के जरिए)—He is appointed to the post *by virtue of* his merit.

black and blue (क्षत-विक्षत, अधमरा)—The thief was beaten *black and blue.*

below the mark (उचित स्तर से नीचे)—His answer is *below the mark.*

by hook or by crook (चाहे जैसे भी हो)—You have to do this work *by hook or by crook.*

by (or in) fits and starts (रुक-रुककर)—Work done *by fits and starts* seldom succeeds.

big gun (बड़ा/प्रभावशाली व्यक्ति)—Nowadays Sitaram Kesri is a *big gun* in the Congress Party.

bosom friend (जिगरी दोस्त)—Have you got any *bosom friend?*

burning question (ज्वलंत प्रश्न)—The Afghan issue is a *burning question* of the day.

by all means (हर तरह से)—If you want to do it, do it *by all means.*

by no means (किसी प्रकार नहीं)—The Principal's job is *by no means* an easy one.

by and by (कुछ समय के बाद)—She will recover *by and by.*

by the by (e) (बात ही बातों में)—*By the by (e)* he told this.

before long (शीघ्र)—They will come home *before long.*

body and soul (पूर्णतया)—She gave herself to study *body and soul.*

by leaps and bounds (दिन दूनी और रात चौगुनी)—India is progressing *by leaps and bounds.*

by chance (संयोगवश)—*By chance,* I met my friend at the station.

by fair means or foul (उचित या अनुचित ढंग से)—Some of the students try to pass the examinations *by fair means or foul.*

by return of post (लौटती डाक से)—Please send a reply to my letter *by return of post.*

by and large (मोटा-मोटी तौर से)—*By and large* this school is better than that.

because of (कारण से)—He did not go to college *because of* illness.

beside the point (असंगत)—Much of what you say is *beside the point.*

bid fair (आशा दिलाना)—The new tax *bids fair* to work well.

bird's eye view (सरसरी निगाह)—From the top of the Golghar we can get a *bird's eye view* of the whole of Patna.

be intimately concerned with (नजदीक से संबंधित होना)—I am *intimately concerned with* your life.

bring to book (दंड देना)—He will be *brought to book* for his misdeeds.

break the ice (चुप्पी तोड़ना)—I *broke the ice* by asking him about his business.

by the way (बातचीत के क्रम में)—I told him *by the way* that I was planning to go to Canada.

by nature (स्वभावत:)—He is very helpful *by nature.*

by fair means (उचित तरीके से)—It is *by fair means* that you should try to get what you want.

break the record (नया कीर्तिमान स्थापित करना)—Sri Ram Singh *broke the record* in 100 metres race.

bad blood (शत्रुता)—There is *bad blood* between these two families.

black sheep (गलत या निकम्मा आदमी, कुलकलंक)—There is *black sheep* in every society.

bone of contention (झगड़े का विषय)—The piece of land is a *bone of contention* between the two brothers.

beat about the bush (घुमा-फिराकर बातें करना)—Please tell me the truth; don't *beat about the bush.*

before long (शीघ्र ही)—He is a talented man and *before long* he will make a mark in his profession.

break the news (उत्तेजक या अशुभ संवाद सुनाना)—Ram's mother is dead, you have to *break the news* to him.

by way of (इरादा से)—I was not serious; I said that *by way of* joke.

bits and pieces (विभिन्न तरह की छोटी-छोटी चीजें)—Let me get my *bits and pieces* together.

be in hot water/get into hot water (झंझट में पड़ना)—If you are not careful, you may *be in hot water shortly.* Try to give up bad company, else you are sure to get *into hot water.*

cat-and-dog life (कलहपूर्ण जीवन)—They always live a *cat-and-dog life.*

come to light (विदित होना)—His evil scheme has *come to light.*

castles in the air (हवाई किला)—He is always building *castles in the air.*

cut a sorry figure (दयनीय स्थिति में होना या व्यंग्य-भाजन होना, अच्छा नहीं करना)—He *cut a sorry figure* in the last examination.

come true (सच्चा सिद्ध होना)—The saint's word *came true* in the long run.

crying in the wilderness (अरण्यरोदन)—The Government's anxiety over the rising prices seems to be *crying in the wilderness.*

crocodile tears (दिखावटी आँसू)—Some leaders shed *crocodile tears* over the defeat of their opponents.

cut and dried (सुस्पष्ट, संदेहातीत, प्रश्नातीत)—There are no *cut and dried* rules for precis-writing.

child's play (आसान काम)—This sum is difficult for you, but it is a *child's play* for me.

come to blows (हाथापाई करना)—From words they soon *came to blows.*

come into force (लागू होना)—The new timetable will *come into force* from next month.

capital punishment (मृत्युदंड)—*Capital punishment* is abolished in some countries.

chicken-hearted (कायर)—A soldier must not be *chicken-hearted.*

cold war (शीत युद्ध)—There is always a *cold war* between America and Russia.

cold-blooded (निर्दय, निर्दयतापूर्ण)—There was a *cold-blooded* murder of a passer-by last night. He is a *cold-blooded* murderer.

close shave (बाल-बाल बचना)—The car ran into the river but the driver jumped out; it was really a *close shave.*

dead against (एकदम विरुद्ध)—I am *dead against* this proposal.

deadline (निर्दिष्ट सीमा)—There is no *deadline* for the submission of applications by freedom fighters.

day in, day out (दिन-रात)—He labours *day in, day out* to pass his examination.

die in harness (कार्य करने की क्षमता रहते हुए मरना)—He was just 40; he *died in harness.*

dead letter (जो कभी लागू था लेकिन अब लागू नहीं है)—This rule is a *dead letter now.*

dark horse (छिपा रुस्तम व्यक्ति)—In the last examination Rajeev proved a *dark horse* as he secured the highest marks.

day-to-day (दिन प्रतिदिन)—We have to solve life's *day-to-day* difficulties.

drop in the ocean (सागर में बूँद के समान)—I needed a hundred rupees and he gave me only two; that was a mere *drop in the ocean.*

dry facts (नीरस तथ्य)—History, some people say, is a mere record of *dry facts.*

do away with (छुटकारा पाना)—Our dog is getting so old that we shall *do away with* him.

do one's utmost (जितना हो सके करना)—You must *do your utmost* for success in the examination.

dog-in-the-manger policy (जिस सिद्धांत से न अपना लाभ हो और न दूसरे का)—I am unhappy with my neighbour's *dog-in-the-manger policy.*

due to (कारण से)—The accident was *due to* careless driving.

even if (चाहे)—I'll get there *even if* I have to sell my watch to get the railway fare.

every now and then (अकसर)—He visits this place *every now and then.*

earning a living (जीविका अर्जन करना)—We have to work very hard for *earning a living* these days.

for want of (कमी से)—The boy could not study further *for want of* money.

far and wide (बहुत दूर तक)—He travelled *far and wide.*

far and near (चारों ओर)—They searched him *far and near.*

for good (हमेशा के लिए)—Those people left the village *for good.*

for fear of (भय से)—He ran away *for fear of* getting killed.

fair and square (निष्पक्ष)—He was *fair and square* in all his dealings.

fair play (ईमानदारी)—We want *fair play* and no favour.

for the sake of (के लिए)—I helped him *for the sake of* friendship.

from head to foot (ऊपर से नीचे तक)—She was dressed in red *from head to foot.*

from time to time (कभी-कभी)—Mr Majumdar helped me *from time to time.*

follow suit (अनुकरण करना)—The teacher laughed and the students *followed suit.*

for the time being (तब तक के लिए, फिलहाल)—She will stay here *for the time being.*

fast living (विलासपूर्ण जीवन)—*Fast living* is responsible for his early death.

fish out of water (कष्टप्रद अवस्था में)—Away from books, he was like a *fish out of water.*

first and foremost (सर्वोपरि)—*First and foremost* a student should maintain discipline.

fancy price (अतिरंजित मूल्य)—He demanded a *fancy price* for his car, and he got it, too.

fool's paradise (कल्पलोक, मूर्ख का स्वर्ग)—If you think that the politician may always help you, you are in a *fool's paradise.*

for nothing (व्यर्थ में)—He wasted all his time *for nothing.*

for instance (उदाहरण के लिए)—I gave you, *for instance*, a new pen last week.

far and away (बहुत अधिक)—This is *far and away* the best.

few and far between (बहुत कम)—His letters to me are *few and far between.*

from bad to worse (बदतर)—In spite of all the medical treatment, his condition turned *from bad to worse.*

from door to door (द्वार-द्वार जाकर)—Candidates are moving *from door to door* for votes.

fair hand (साफ लिखावट)—An examinee gets credit for a *fair hand.*

free-lance (स्वतंत्र)—He is a *free-lance* journalist.

French leave (बिना सूचना के अनुपस्थित होना)—The clerk was punished for taking *French leave.*

face to face (आमने-सामने)—The boy was nervous when he met the Principal *face to face.*

fish in the troubled waters (खलबली से लाभ उठाना)—The two brothers are quarre-lling; their neighbour wants to *fish in the troubled waters.*

from the bottom of one's heart (तहे दिल से)—I thanked him *from the bottom of my heart.*

fair sex (नारी जाति)—We should be courteous to the *fair sex.*

fair weather friends (सुख-समृद्धि का मित्र जो दुर्दिन में छोड़ दे)—*Fair weather friends* are the persons who cease to be friends when we are in trouble.

fall upon (अचानक हमला करना)—They suddenly jumped out of the bush and *fell upon* the travellers.

food and drink (पीने के लिए तरल पदार्थ)—We will die if we do not get *food and drink.*

get rid of (छुटकारा पाना)—We must *get rid of* that selfish fellow.

gala day (आनंदोत्सव का दिन)—15th August is a *gala day* for us.

good-for-nothing (निकम्मा)—adj [attrib] Where is that *good-for-nothing* son of yours?

gift of the gab (प्रभावशोली ढंग से बोलने की शक्ति)—Mere *gift of the gab* is not enough for success in life.

golden mean (मध्यम मार्ग)—You may be happy if you follow the *golden mean* in life.

good Samaritan (दयालु व्यक्ति)—He proved a *good Samaritan* to me in my need.

get the better of (किसी को हराना)—Vijoy Amritraj *got the better of* Shashi Menon in lawn tennis.

get by heart (जबानी याद करना)—He has got the poem *by heart.*

go a long way (बहुत हद तक)—The new Act will *go a long way* towards checking rising prices.

golden opportunity (सुनहला अवसर)—This is a *golden opportunity* for you; don't miss it.

get hold of (समझना, पकड़ना)—I can't *get hold of* the meaning of this telegram. With great difficulty the drowning man *got hold of* the rope.

get no further (आगे नहीं जाना/बढ़ना)—The police will *get no further* into the case without the help of the public.

hard and fast (कठोर, निश्चित)—There are some *hard and fast* rules for promotion to higher posts.

hue and cry (हल्ला-गुल्ला)—The villagers raised a *hue and cry* to see the dacoits.

hand in hand (हाथ में हाथ दिए हुए)—They walked away *hand in hand.*

heart and soul (मन से)—Rekha threw herself into the task *heart and soul.*

hold water (दुरुस्त होना, तर्कसंगत होना)—I am sorry, but your story just does not *hold water.*

here and there (जहाँ-तहाँ)—The garden was neglected; only a few rose plants grew *here and there.*

hand to hand (हाथो-हाथ, हाथ से)—The soldiers of the two armies fought *hand to hand.*

hard cash (नकद)—Mr Singh is a moneyed man and has plenty of *hard cash.*

how and why (क्यों और कैसे)—The children want to know the *how and why* of everything.

hair's-breadth escape (बाल-बाल बचाव)—As the car fell into the river, the driver jumped out and had a *hair's-breadth escape.*

live (from) hand to mouth (मुश्किल से जीवन निर्वाह करना)—During these days of rising prices, salaried people *live hand to mouth.*

hard up (तंगी में)—I have spent a lot over my daughter's marriage, so I am *hard up* these days.

heart to heart (खुले दिल से, अंतरंगता के साथ)—He had a *heart to heart* talk with his son.

high time (उत्तम या सही समय)—It is *high time* we went home.

hard nut to crack (टेढ़ी खीर)—The UNO has found the Afghanistan problem a *hard nut to crack.*

hold good (लागू होना)—The old rules have not yet been amended; they still continue to *hold good.*

iron hand (कड़ाई)—The riots will be suppressed with *an iron hand.*

in the long run (अंततोगत्वा)—He got success *in the long run.*

in favour of (के पक्ष में)—They spoke *in favour of* the proposal.

in front of (के सामने)—My house was *in front of* the river.

in lieu of (के बदले में)—He gave me this pen *in lieu of* that pencil.

in order to (के लिए)—He came here *in order to* help me.

in quest of (खोज में)—He went to Bombay *in quest of* a job.

in short (कुछ शब्दों में, संक्षेप में)—Please tell me everything *in short.*

in vain (बेकार)—Labour never goes *in vain.*

in no way (किसी तरह भी नहीं)—The English cricket team is in *no way* superior to the Indian cricket team.

in the hope of (आशा में)—I went to him two times *in the hope of* getting back my money.

in case (अगर)—Take my umbrella *in case* it rains.

in course of (के क्रम में)—He said all this *in course of* his speech.

in detail (विस्तार में)—Please write to me about your hostel life *in detail.*

in no time (शीघ्र)—He has gone to his next door neighbour; he will come here *in no time.*

in spite of (के बावजूद)—He came to the office *in spite of* illness.

in the teeth of (प्रत्यक्ष विरोध या मुकाबले में)—The Bill was passed *in the teeth of* opposition.

in time (समय रहते, बिलंब से नहीं)—We were *in time* for the train.

in connection with (के संबंध में)—Tell me all you know *in connection with* this case.

in defence of (की प्रतिरक्षा में, बचाव में)—He said all he should *in defence of* his friend.

in consideration of (दृष्टिगत करते हुए, के विचार से)—*In consideration of* his honesty, he must be rewarded.

ins and outs (विस्तृत विवरण)—He knows the *ins and outs* of political life.

in view of (ध्यान रखते हुए)—You must go there *in view of* the urgency of the case.

in proportion to (अनुपात में)—We must pay taxes *in proportion to* our income.

in respect of (के विषय में)—*In respect of* service, he is senior to me.

in the face of (के सामने)—You must be bold *in the face of* dangers.

in point of (की दृष्टि से)—He is junior to me *in point of* age.

in a fix (द्वंद्व, अनिश्चयता या संकट में)—Being *in a fix,* I needed his advice.

in a nutshell (संक्षेप में)—Tell me the whole story *in a nutshell.*

in full swing (पूरे जोर में)—Our classes will run *in full swing* next month.

in regard to (के संबंध में)—He said nothing *in regard to* the case.

in the dark (अंधेरे में या अनवगत)—I am *in the dark* about his next move.

in the nick of time (ठीक समय पर)—He reached the station *in the nick of time.*

instead of (के बदले में)—She went to the market *instead of* going to school.

ill at ease (परेशान)—I am *ill at ease* in the company of politicians.

in vogue (प्रचलित)—A tight dress is much *in vogue* in colleges.

in accordance with (के अनुसार)—The actions of the leaders are seldom *in accordance with* their ideals.

irony of fate (विधि की विडंबना)—It is the *irony of fate* that a millionaire became a beggar.

in all respects (सभी प्रकार से)—Our English teacher is superior to you *in all respects.*

in full (पूरा)—Don't write here the short form; write the word *in full.*

in fact (वस्तुत:)—*In fact,* I came here to ask you for some money.

in the mean time (इस बीच में)—I went out for tea, *in the mean time* my boss called me.

in any case (किसी भी हालत में)—You should not adopt unfair means in the examination *in any case.*

in force (लागू)—This rule has been *in force* for more than a month.

in good faith (सही नीयत से)—He said all that *in good faith* and you should not misunderstand him.

in hot haste (बड़ी जल्दीबाजी में)—Don't write your answer *in hot haste.*

in a hurry (जल्दी में)—I was *in a hurry* to go back home.

in an instant (पलभर में)—The house caught fire and *in an instant* the whole village was burnt down.

in cold blood (जानबूझकर एवं निर्दयतापूर्वक)—When Ramesh said that he had recognized the dacoit, the dacoit turned back and killed him *in cold blood.*

in the wake of (ठीक पीछे, परिणाम स्वरूप)—Epidemics came *in the wake of* the floods.

in name only (नाममात्र का)—He is an officer *in name only;* his PA does everything.

in office (सत्तारूढ़)—The Congress Party has been *in office* once again.

in season and out of season (वक्त-कुवक्त, हर समय)—My relations come to help me *in season and out of season.*

in case of (की स्थिति में)—*In case of* fire, ring up 333.

in defiance of (की अवज्ञा करके)—They took out a procession *in defiance of* Sec. 144.

in honour of (के सम्मान में)—The college was closed *in honour of* the Education Minister's visit.

in keeping with (से मेल खाते हुए)—His conduct is not *in keeping with* the high post he holds.

in the eye of (की नजर में)—All citizens are equal i*n the eye of* law.

in place of (के बदले)—Do you want to study Maithili *in place of* Bhojpuri?

in one's good book (किसी का कृपापात्र होना)—These days he is *in his boss's good book.*

in the twinkling of an eye (पलक झपकते)—The magician brought a packet of sweets *in the twinkling of an eye.*

in the interests of (के हित में)—He should resign *in the interests* of the party.

in the name of (के नाम पर)—Some people commit crimes *in the name of* religion.

in order that (ताकि)—He works hard *in order that* he may please his boss.

in the end (अंत में)—Truth will come out *in the end.*

in one's mind's eye (अन्तश्चक्षु में)—I see the whole scene *in my mind's eye.*

in fault (दोषी)—If you are *in fault,* you must confess it.

in hand (हाथ में)—I have kept fifty rupees *in hand.*

in the hands of (के हाथ में)—Man is playing *in the hands of* fate.

in black and white (लिखित)—The teacher asked him to make a complaint *in black and white.*

in due course (कालक्रम में)—He began life as a clerk and *in due course* he became the headmaster of the school.

in search of (खोज में)—He is *in search of* a new job.

in broad daylight (दिन-दहाड़े)—The murder was committed *in broad daylight* on the main road.

Jack of all trades (सभी कामों में हाथ डालनेवाला, दर्जी की सूई)—He is a *Jack of all trades* but master of none.

jaundiced eye (पक्षपातपूर्ण दृष्टिकोण)—A judge should never have a *jaundiced eye.*

keep an eye on (निगरानी रखना)—We must *keep an eye on* that wicked boy.

keep abreast of (पीछे नहीं पड़ना, साथ-साथ चलना)—We must *keep abreast of* time.

kith and kin (बंधु-बांधव)—Even our *kith and kin* may not help us in bad days.

keep in view (नजर में रखना)—The DM must *keep in view* the difficulties of the public in getting sugar during the marriage season.

keep company (संगति करना या रखना)—If you *keep company* with bad people, you will always suffer.

lose sight of (उपेक्षा करना)—You should not *lose sight of* this point.

lame excuse (फालतू बहाना)—She gave only a *lame excuse* for her absence.

leave in the lurch (विपत्ति या कठिनाई में छोड़ देना)—Don't *leave* your friend *in the lurch.*

look blank (भौंचक्का रह जाना)—When the teacher asked him a simple question, he *looked blank.*

lie in wait (घात में रहना)—They *lay in wait* for the enemy.

life and soul (जान, प्राण)—Mrs Indira Gandhi was the *life and soul* of Congress (I).

long and short (सारांश)—The *long and short* of it is that we have succeeded in our effort.

loaves and fishes (व्यक्तिगत लाभ)—We should not care for the *loaves and fishes* of office.

learn by rote (बिना अर्थ समझे हुए रटकर याद करना)—Do not *learn* it *by rote.*

lion's share (सबसे बड़ा हिस्सा)—The *lion's share* of the illegal money goes into the pockets of some high ups.

long face (मुँह लटकाए हुए)—I found him sitting alone with a *long face.*

left-handed compliment (प्रशंसा के रूप में शिकायत)—To call Gandhi a great leader of the Hindus is to pay him a *left-handed compliment.*

loose tongue (गैरजवाबदेह बातें)—People with a *loose tongue* may make enemies easily.

lump sum (एकमुश्त)—I want payment in a *lump sum*, not in instalments.

lose heart (निराश होना)—Don't *lose heart* even though you fail in the examination.

make a name (नाम कमाना)—He has *made a name* for himself.

maiden speech (जीवन का प्रथम सार्वजनिक भाषण)—It was his *maiden speech* in the Parliament.

make good (क्षति पूरा करना)—You will have to *make good* the loss to me.

make up one's mind (निश्चय करना)—You must *make up your mind* about your next move.

man of letters (विद्वान आदमी)—Vinoba was a *man of letters.*

miss the bus (सुअवसर खो देना)—If you do not try hard for this job, you will *miss the bus.*

man of parts (गुणवान व्यक्ति)—He is a *man of parts* and can never be unhappy.

man in the street (साधारण आदमी)—In the days of elections even a *man in the street* listens to the radio.

man of action (कर्मठ व्यक्ति)—You will not succeed if you are not a *man of action.*

make sure (आश्वस्त होना)—I *made sure* he would be here.

mark the opening (शुरुआत करना)—No War Treaty between India and Pakistan will *mark the opening* of a new chapter of peace and co-operation on the subcontinent.

make the most of (अधिकतम लाभ उठाना)—When I was confined to bed, I decided to *make the most of* it and did a lot of reading.

move one's heart (दया उत्पन्न करना)—His extreme poverty *moved my heart.*

make an ass of oneself (बेवकूफ बनना; गदहपनी करना)—He failed to understand his tricks and *made an ass of himself.*

make the best of both the worlds (दोनों हाथ लड्डू)—It is not easy to *make the best of both the worlds,* for taking bribes results in spiritual poverty.

make a fortune (धन कमाना)—Many dealers *make a fortune* by selling their goods in the black market.

make friends (दोस्ती करना)—You must know how to win people and *make friends.*

make or mar (बनाना या बिगाड़ना)—He is a powerful man; he can *make or mar* your career.

man of the world (दुनियादारी समझनेवाला व्यक्ति)—He is a *man of the world*; he knows what is what.

mind one's own business (दूसरे के काम में दखल नहीं देना)—You needn't advise me; *mind your own business.*

more or less (कम या अधिक, करीब-करीब)—The deal has been *more or less* finalized.

move heaven and earth (आकाश-पाताल एक करना)—He *moved heaven and earth* for admission to a medical college.

make a fool of oneself (बेवकूफ बनना)—By his unwanted suggestions, he has only *made a fool of himself.*

make peace with (समझौता करना)—The king m*ade peace with* the bearded man.

make both ends meet (जीवन की आवश्यकताओं को पूरा करना)—A teacher works hard to *make both ends meet.*

make a mess of (गोलमाल करना)—He had a fine opportunity, but he *made a mess of* the whole thing.

null and void (कानूनन रद्द एवं निष्प्रभावी)—The Act has now become *null and void.*

now and again (कभी-कभी)—I read the Ramayana *now and again.*

nip in the bud (आरंभ में ही नष्ट कर देना)—The plot was *nipped in the bud.*

no end (अनंत)—There is *no end* to man's desire on the earth.

narrow escape (बाल-बाल बचना)—As the roof came down, he rushed out and had a *narrow escape.*

neck and neck (बराबरी में)—These two boys ran *neck and neck* for the first hundred metres.

night and day/day and night (दिन-रात)—They have been working *night and day* to complete the work in time.

nine days' wonder (अल्पकालिक आश्चर्य)—Basic education in India proved to be a *nine days' wonder.*

(every) now and then (again) (कभी-कभी, जब तब)—I go to my uncle *now and then.*

now or never (अभी या कभी नहीं)—I can't miss this chance; it is a question of *now or never* for me.

no love lost (असद्भाव, सुसंपर्क का अभाव)—There is *no love lost* between these two boys.

off and on (कभी-कभी)—He comes to my house *off and on.*

of no avail (व्यर्थ)—His efforts for saving his life were *of no avail.*

on account of (कारण से)—She did not come to college *on account of* illness.

owing to (कारण से)—He met with an accident *owing to* his careless driving.

on the contrary (वरन्)—He never hated me, *on the contrary* he loved me very much.

of late (हाल ही में)—The clerk has been suspended *of late.*

out of question (असंभव)—That Mr Jyoti Bose will become the Prime Minister seems to be *out of question.*

out-and-out (पूर्णत:)—He is *out-and-out* the best boy in the class.

over head and ears (बहुत ज्यादा)—He was *over head and ears* in debt.

on the alert (सतर्क)—Russia ordered its army on the Afghan boarder to be *on the alert.*

on the brink of (किनारे या कगार पर)—The school building was *on the brink of* collapse.

on hand (किसी के आधिपत्य में, उपलभ्य)—We have some new woollen goods *on hand* (in the shop.)

open and above board (स्पष्ट, निश्छल)—Let everything in our deal be *open and above board.*

once again (फिर एक बार)—He read your letter *once again.*

once for all (अंतिम बार)—I tell you *once for all* that the noise must stop.

on the eve of (just before)—He came *on the eve of* our examination.

of course (अवश्य)—'Do you study hard?' '*Of course*, I do'.

out of pocket (बिना पैसे के कपर्दप-शून्य)—I have spent all my money, now I am *out of pocket.*

over and above (के अलावा)—I gave him fifty rupees *over and above* what I had to pay.

of the opinion (मत का)—I am *of the opinion* that women should not join the Army.

on credit on account (उधार)—As I had no ready cash, I bought a coat *on credit on account.*

on an average (औसतन)—*On an average*, he earns Rs 1,000/- a month.

on good terms (मैत्रीभावापन्न, सद्भावयुक्त)—He was not *on good terms* with his neighbour.

on the other hand (दूसरी ओर)—America helps Lebanon on the one hand and Israel *on the other* (*hand*).

odds and ends (टूटी-फूटी फुटकर चीजें)—Most of the articles have already been sent to the new house; now only the *odds and ends* remain.

on the alert (सावधान)—We should be *on the alert* against fresh Chinese attacks.

over and above (के अलावा)—I paid him fifty rupees *over and above* what I had to pay.

on time (निर्धारित समय पर)—The train arrived *on time.*

on and on (निरंतर)—He tried *on and on* until he succeeded.

once upon a time (किसी समय)—*Once upon a time* there was a king in Ayodhya.

on the verge of (कगार पर)—My boss is *on the verge of* retirement.

on the whole (सब कुछ ध्यान में रखते हुए)—*On the whole*, he is one of the best boys in the class.

on no account (किसी हालत में नहीं)—*On no account* can India agree to make a gift of the New Moore Island to Bangladesh.

out of form/off form (अच्छे form में नहीं होना)—Sometimes a player is *out of form/ off form* and then he plays badly.

open secret (वह रहस्य जो सबको मालूम हो)—It is an *open secret* that America never likes the progress of India.

over and over again (बार-बार)—I have helped you *over and over again* but you are ungrateful.

out of the way (गलत ढंग से)—He went *out of the way* to help him find a job.

part and parcel (अभिन्न अंग)—Every man is *part and parcel* of society.

pros and cons (आगा-पीछा, अग्र पश्चात)—You must think of the *pros and cons* of the matter.

put an end to (समाप्त करना)—Death *put an end to* his wicked career.

Pandora's box (दु:ख का भंडार)—The Kosi has been a *Pandora's box* to the people of Saharsa and Darbhanga.

put on flesh (मोटा होना)—You are too slim; you must *put on* some *flesh.*

play the fool (बेवकूफ की तरह हरकत करना)—Don't *play the fool*; be serious in your job.

put someone to death (जान से मार देना)—The dacoit *put the landlord to death.*

play a double game (दुरंगी चाल चलना)—By helping both Israel and Syria, America is *playing a double game.*

play hide and seek (लुका-छिपी खेलना)—Throughout the day the sun has been *playing hide and seek* with the clouds.

pick and choose (छाँटकर चुनना)—He was asked not to *pick and choose* but to allow everybody to come in.

point blank [(i) अत्यंत निकट से : (ii) स्पष्ट रूप से]—He was shot at from the *point blank* range. He refused *point blank* to help me.

poison someone's ears (किसी के विरुद्ध कान भरना)—He has *poisoned my boss's ears* against me.

play false (धोखा देना)—Don't *play* your friend *false.*

plain sailing (आसानी से बढ़ना)—Climbing a mountain is not all *plain sailing.*

put into action (कार्यान्वित करना)—The new scheme has been *put into action.*

point of honour (प्रतिष्ठा की बात)—I shall not withdraw my resignation; it is a *point of honour* for me.

pride oneself on (पर आत्मगौरव करना)—She *prided herself on* her ability to speak eight languages. She *prided herself on* knowing eight languages.

put one's foot down (दृढ़ मोरचा लेना, दृढ़ निश्चय करना)—The Chief Minister has *put his foot down* to have a few new universities.

put up with (बरदाश्त करना, सहना)—I can't *put up with* your rude behaviour any more; leave the room.

rap a tatoo on (लगातार ढोल जैसा पीटना)—Tom was *rapping a tatoo on* the table.

red-letter day (चिरस्मरणीय शुभदिन)—15th August is a *red-letter day* in the history of India.

without rhyme or reason (बिना किसी युक्तिसंगत कारण के)—He left this job *without rhyme or reason.*

for a rainy day (भावी दुर्दिन के लिए)—A wise man saves something *for a rainy day.*

run short (घट जाना, कम होना)—His money *ran short* in the middle of his journey.

red tape (लाल फीता)—Because of *red tape* (rigid formality of intricate official routine), files in Government departments do not move easily.

run amuck (सनक जाना)—The Nepali Durwan *ran amuck* and killed one person.

reap the fruit (का फल भुगतना)—Every man has to *reap the fruit* of his actions.

like a red rag to a bull (डराने-भड़कानेवाली वस्तु)—To many of the landlords, the name of Kanu Sanyal was *like a red rag to a bull.*

royal road (सुगम रास्ता)—There is no *royal road* to success in life.

right-hand man (सर्वाधिक विश्वासयोग्य आदमी)—Mr Prasad is the *right-hand man* of his boss.

run the risk of (खतरा मोल लेना)—When a minister speaks against the Chief Minister, he *runs the risk of* losing his post.

small fry (साधारण आदमी)—He is not a *small fry* at this place.

sine die (अनिश्चित काल के लिए)—The meeting was postponed *sine die.*

sooner or later (कभी-न-कभी, देर-सबेर)—Everybody has to retire *sooner or later*.

set free (आजाद कर देना)—Every prisoner was *set free.*

sleeping partner (निष्क्रिय हिस्सेदार)—He is a *sleeping partner* of our firm.

stuff and nonsense (निरर्थक बकवाद)—What he says is all *stuff and nonsense.*

so far (अब तक)—He has not returned my book *so far.*

spell bankruptcy (दिवालियापन लाना)—Heavy losses in export may *spell bankruptcy* in the business world this year.

set forth (बताना, प्रस्थान करना)—Please *set forth* your political views. They *set forth* in the morning.

sum and substance (सारांश)—This is the *sum and substance* of the whole story.

stand somebody in good stead (किसी के काम आना, उपयोगी होना)—His knowledge has *stood him in good stead.*

snake in the grass (छिपा हुआ दुश्मन)—We can't trust his supporter; he may be a *snake in the grass.*

safe and sound (सुरक्षित)—He reached home *safe and sound.*

slip of the tongue (जबान की फिसलन)—I said 'same' when I actually meant to say 'shame'; it was a *slip of the tongue.*

slip of the pen (कलम की चूक)—Your essay is full of *slips of the pen.*

so long as (जब तक)—*So long as* I am here, you need not fear anyone.

short cut (छोटा रास्ता)—There is no *short cut* to success.

see eye-to-eye (एक ही विचार का होना)—The Vice-chancellor and the Registrar do not *see eye-to-eye* on every issue.

send word (संवाद भेजना)—I was expecting him but he *sent word* that he would not come.

show of hand (हाथ उठाकर)—The motion was passed by a *show of hand.*

tooth and nail (पूरी ताकत से)—We shall fight *tooth and nail* for our rights.

talk big (डींग मारना)—He *talks big* about himself.

time and again (बार-बार)—I came to you *time and again* but you did not listen to me.

to and fro (आगे-पीछे)—He was walking *to and fro* in his drawing-room.

take to one's heels (भाग जाना)—On seeing the police, the thief *took to his heels.*

tall talk (घमंडभरी लंबी-चौड़ी बात)—She often indulges in *tall talk.*

to the letter (अक्षरशः)—I shall carry out your orders *to the letter.*

turn over a new leaf (अच्छी दिशा में जीवनशैली या आचरण बदलना)—It is a matter of satisfaction that he has *turned over a new leaf.*

turn the tables (on someone) (पहले की हार या कमजोरी की स्थिति से मजबूत स्थिति में पहुँचना)—Australia were about to win the first one-day international cricket match in Delhi; but a century by Lamba *turned the tables.*

take a/one's chance (on something) (प्रयास करके देखना)—I don't think I will get the job but I am willing to *take a/my chance* and ask for it.

through thick and thin (सुख-दुःख में)—My friend stood by me *through thick and thin.*

take care of (यत्न करना)—You must *take care of* your health if you want to keep fit.

take (something) for granted (निश्चित या पक्का समझना)—We cannot *take* our success *for granted.*

throw cold water on something (किसी विषय में निरुत्साह करना)—His partner *threw cold water on his scheme.*

through and through (पूर्णत:)—He is a reliable man *through and through*. You are wet *through and through.*

to the last farthing (पैसा-पैसा कर)—He has paid the debts *to the last farthing*.

to his face (मुँह पर ही)—I will call him a liar *to his face.*

to the utmost (यथासाध्य)—I helped him *to the utmost.*

to the point (उपयुक्त)—Your answer is not *to the point.*

take advantage of (लाभ उठाना)—Our boss is absent today; don't *take advantage of* the situation and leave the office early.

take effect (उद्दिष्ट प्रभाव दिखाना)—This medicine will *take effect* and you will be cured of your headache soon.

take something in one's own hand (अपने हाथ में ले लेना)—I have *taken the work in my own hand.*

take heart (हिम्मत करना)—Do not be discouraged by failures, *take heart* and try again.

testing time (परीक्षा की घड़ी)—When the nation is attacked, it is a *testing time* for the army.

this and that (इधर-उधर, यह-वह)—I spent the whole morning doing *this and that.*

think twice (सावधानीपूर्वक सोच समझ लेना)—You should *think twice* before starting a factory.

turn a deaf ear (अनसुनी कर देना)—The minister *turned a deaf ear* to our request for the revision of our pay.

take to heart (अत्यधिक प्रभावित या अभिभूत होना)—He has *taken* his friend's death *to heart.*

teach a lesson (सबक सिखाना, पाठ पढ़ाना)—That accident *taught me a lesson*; I shall not drive too fast again.

take stock of (परिस्थिति पर सावधानीपूर्वक विचार करना)—You must *take stock of* the situation before starting something new.

take part in (भाग लेना)—If you want to keep fit, you must *take part in* games every day.

take some one into confidence (किसी को विश्वास में लेना या किसी का विश्वास प्राप्त करना)—You must *take him into confidence* and seek his advice.

three R's (पढ़ना, लिखना और गणित)—Most of the farmers do not know the *three R's.*

take notice (ध्यान देना)—You must *take notice* of things happening around you.

take the chair (सभापति होना)—The VC was requested to *take the chair* and guide the discussions in the meeting.

up to the mark (संतोषप्रद)—Your answer is *up to the mark.*

ups and downs (उतार-चढ़ाव)—Life is full of *ups and downs.*

up and down (आगे-पीछे)—He was walking *up and down* the station platform.

under one's very nose (के सामने, की उपस्थिति में)—We wonder how such crimes are committed *under the very nose* of the police.

uphill task (बहुत कठिन कार्य)—To learn Chinese is an *uphill task.*

up and doing (सक्रिय)—We must be *up and doing* for success in life.

under consideration (विचाराधीन)—The proposal for a five-day week is *under consideration.*

under lock and key (ताला-चाभी से बंद करके)—This is a valuable document; keep it *under lock and key.*

unless and until (जब तक नहीं········तब तक नहीं)—*Unless and until* he comes to me, I will not help him.

under the nose of (आँखों के सामने)—Crimes are committed every day *under the nose of* the police.

with regard to (के संबंध में)—They said nothing *with regard to* this case.

with a view to (उद्देश्य से)—She labours hard *with a view to* passing her examination.

without fail (नि:संदेह)—I shall come here this evening *without fail.*

with reference to (के संबंध में)—He said nothing *with reference to* that letter.

with an eye to (ध्यान रखते हुए)—He has been working hard *with an eye to* his IAS examination.

ways and means (साधन, उपाय)—The DM discussed the *ways and means* for checking crimes in the town.

the whys and (the) wherefores (हेतु, कारण)—We do not know *the whys and the wherefores* of his dismissal.

worship the rising sun (उगते हुए सूर्य की पूजा करना अर्थात नए प्रभावशाली व्यक्ति का सम्मान करना)—A clever man always *worships the rising sun.*

with respect to (के संबंध में)—I have nothing to say *with respect to* that matter.

with might and main (सारी शक्ति के साथ)—You will succeed only when you work *with might and main.*

with a vengeance (अप्रत्याशित सीमा तक, अत्यधिक)—After remaining an honest officer for years, he has now started taking bribes *with a vengeance.*

wide of the mark (निशाने से दूर)—Most of the bombs fell *wide of the mark.*

white elephant (जिस संपत्ति से लाभ के बदले हानि हो)—A second-hand car is a *white elephant.*

well and good (ठीक है)—If you return the money *well and good,* if not, I will report the matter to the Principal.

with the help of (की मदद से)—He broke the lock *with the help of* a hammer.

wild goose chase (व्यर्थ या निष्फल प्रयास)—To look for happiness in worldly possessions is a *wild goose chase.*

PART II: PHRASAL VERBS

(i) बहुत-सारे verbs के बाद preposition या adverbial particle का प्रयोग होता है। Verb + preposition/verb + adverbial particle के combination (संयोग) को phrasal verbs या two-part verb कहते हैं। जैसे:

put up	put off	put down
put out	put in	put forward

(ii) मुख्य adverb particles हैं : about, away, back, by, down, forward, of, out, over, up इत्यादि।

(iii) Phrasal verb में verb + preposition/adverbial particle के अलग-अलग शब्दों का अर्थ नहीं होता वरन सभी शब्दों को एक unit मानकर उस शब्द-समूह का प्रायः नया अर्थ होता है। जैसे :

call up = दूरभाष पर बातें करना	give up = छोड़ देना
call on = भेंट करना	turn out = निकाल बाहर करना, उत्पादन करना, उड़ेल देना, इत्यादि

Position of the Object

(i) अगर noun या noun phrase वाक्य का direct object हो तो इस direct object को phrasal verb के बाद या main verb और particle के बीच में रखा जाता है।

He *gave away* the books.	He *took off* his coat.
He *gave the* books *away.*	He *took* his coat *off.*

(ii) कुछ phrasal verbs का प्रयोग इस प्रकार तोड़ (split) कर नहीं होता। जैसे :

look for, call on, look after, ask for

(iii) अगर pronoun वाक्य में direct object रहे तो इस pronoun को adverbial particle के पहले रखा जाता है। जैसे :

He *gave up* it.	(Incorrect)
He *gave* it *up.*	(Correct)
She *brought* them *up.*	(,,)
We *called* it *off.*	(,,)

account for (i) (जमाखर्च देना, हिसाब देना)—You must *account for* the money you spend.

account for (ii) (स्पष्टीकरण देना)—Can you *account for* his rude behaviour?

act on (असर करना)—Heat *acts on* metals.

answer back (मुँहलगे जवाब देना)—It is bad for a student to *answer back*

ask for (माँगना)—The man *asked for* more pay and shorter hours.

back out (पीछे हटना)—He *backed out* of the deal at the last moment.

back up (समर्थन देना)—The headmaster did not *back up* his staff

bank on (भरोसा करना)—We can *bank on* the support of our friends.

be off (जाना)—We must *be off* now.

bear out (समर्थन देना; साथ देना)—This report *bears out* my theory.

beat up (खूब पीटना)—The thief who stole my watch was *beaten up.*

blow out (फूँककर बुझाना)—The wind *blew out* the candle.

blow up (विस्फोट होना, बरबाद करना)—They *blew up* the bridge so that the enemy could not follow them.

break down [(i) मशीन इत्यादि खराब हो जाना]—My car *broke down* on the way to Patna.

break down [(ii) स्वास्थ्य खराब हो जाना]—After years of overwork his health *broke down.*

break down [(iii) बेसँभाल हो जाना, temporary emotional collapse]—When he heard the news of his mother's death, he *broke down* completely.

break in (किसी मकान में जबर्दस्ती घुसना)—Thieves had *broken in* while we were away.

break into (जबर्दस्ती घुसना, एकाएक शुरू करना)—Thieves *broke into* his house. His house was *broken into* last night. Hearing the speech the andience *broke into* laughter.

break out (एकाएक फैलना; चाहे वह लड़ाई हो या महामारी)—Flue has *broken out* in Bihar.

break with (दोस्ती समाप्त करना; आदत छोड़ना)—He *broke with* an old friend. You must *break with* old habits.

break open (तोड़कर खोलना या स्वयं झटके से खुल जाना)—The dacoits *broke open* the almirah and decamped with the money. The box *broke open* when it fell.

break up (टूट जाना)—The ship was *breaking up* on the rocks. He *broke up* under the strain.

break away (पकड़ से छूटकर भाग जाना)—The criminal *broke away* from the two policemen who were holding him.

bring in (उत्पन्न करना, लाभ पहुँचाना)—He does odd jobs that *bring* him *in* fifty rupees a month.

bring about (घटित होना, करवाना, लाना)—What *brought* the quarrel *about?* The Indo-Pakistan war was *brought about* by the evil designs of the USA.

bring out (प्रकाशित करना, स्पष्ट रूप से दिखा देना)—When will the publisher *bring out* your new book? *Bring out* the meaning of the passage.

bring round (समझा-बुझाकर सहमत करना)—After a lot of argument I *brought* him *round* to my point of view.

bring up (पालना-पोसना, उठाना)—She has *brought* up five children. These facts can always be *brought up* against you.

brush aside (हटा देना, उपेक्षा करना)—The President *brushed aside* all objections.

brush up (ताजा करना, चमकाना)—If you are going to England, you should brush up your English. Go and have a *brush up*.

build up (बनाना)—He has *built up* a good business.

call at (किसी के घर पर जाना)—I *called at* Sri DP Rai's house.

call on (किसी व्यक्ति के यहाँ जाना)—I *called on* Sri BK Singh.

call out (पुकारना)—The teacher *called out* the names of the students.

call off (समाप्त करना, वापस लेना)—The strike was *called off.*

call up (टेलिफोन करना)—I will *call* you *up* this evening.

call upon (आग्रह करना, अपील करना)—I *call upon* you to keep your promise.

call for (माँगना)—The VC's resignation was *called for* by a large number of citizens.

complain of (शिकायत करना)—Don't always *complain of* lack of resources.

conjure up (दिमाग में चित्र लाना)—We may *conjure up* visions of the past.

care about (चिंतित होना)—Those in power do not *care about* public opinion.

care for (देखभाल करना; परवाह करना)—Who will *care for* the children if their mother dies? He does not *care* much *for* television.

carry on (चालू रखना)—I will *carry on* the business even without your help.

carry out (आज्ञापालन करना)—He *carried out* my orders.

clear off (समाप्त करना, छुटकारा पाना)—You must *clear off* the debt as soon as possible.

close down (दूकान या व्यापार सदा के लिए बंद होना)—The factory was *closed down* because of a lack of orders.

close in (नजदीक आते जाना)—The days are *closing in.*

come to (के लगभग होना)—His monthly expenditure *comes to* nearly a thousand rupees.

come upon (अचानक पाना या भेंट होना)—The farmer in digging a well *came upon* a vessel containing old coins.

catch sight of (कुछ क्षण के लिए देखना)—When we were passing through the forest, we *caught sight of* a tiger.

come back (लौटना)—My friend will *come back* from Japan next month.

come down (मूल्य कम होना)—The prices have come down.

come along/on (जल्दी करो, आना)—*Come along/on* with me. *Come along* and see my sitting-room.

come for (ले जाने के लिए आना)—Has anyone *come for* that book yet?

come in (अंदर आना)—May I *come in*, Sir?

come of (पैदा लेना)—Our Principal *comes of* a repectable Hindu family.

come on (आओ, आना)—You go first: I will *come on* later. *Come on* or we will be late.

come off (घटित होना)—The marriage did not *come off.*

come out (बाहर निकलना, प्रकाशित होना)—He has not *come out* of his house today. His new book will *come out* soon.

come over (दूर से आना)—He *came over* to this place for a picnic.

come across (संयोग से मुलाकात होना या मिलना)—I *came across* my friend in the train.

come round (अनुकूल या सहमत हो जाना)—He will never *come round* to our way of thinking.

come up (सतह से ऊपर उठना; उठाया जाना)—Weeds are *coming up* everywhere. The question has not *come up* yet.

come up to (तक पहुँचना)—The water *came up* to my waist.

compare to[1] (दो चीजों में समानता बताना)—Herrick *compared* the life of the human beings *to* the life of the daffodils.

compare with (दो चीजों में समानता एवं अंतर बताना)—*Compare this* book *with* any other book and you will find out for yourself which is better.

count on (भरोसा करना)—I *count on* your help in the matter.

cut down (काटकर गिराना; छोटा करना)—If you *cut down* all the trees, you will ruin the land. Please *cut down* this article to 1,000 words; it is very long.

cut off (काटकर अलग करना)—*Cut* the chicken's head *off*. The company has *cut off* the electricity supply because we haven't paid our bill.

deal with [(i) निबटना; (ii) विवेचन करना]—We have to *deal with* this firm now. This book *deals with* the problem of unemployment.

deal in (व्यापार करना)—Our firm *deals in* Godrej products.

die out (धीरे-धीरे मिट जाना)—Many old customs are gradually *dying out.*

die away (क्षीण शक्ति, शांत हो जाना)—The noise *died away.*

draw out [(दिन) बड़ा होना])—Christmas passed and the days began to *draw out.*

do with (संबंध रखना, सरोकार रखना)—What did you *do with* my umbrella? (कहाँ रखा या कहाँ छोड़ दिया) What are we *to do with* this naughty boy? (कैसा व्यवहार किया जाए?)

do without (के बिना काम चलाना)—We had to *do without* petrol during the war.

do away with (समाप्त कर देना)—The department was *done away with* a year ago.

draw up (तैयार करना)—We *draw up* a list of things for the party.

drop in (किसी के यहाँ अकस्मात पहुँच जाना)—Some friends *dropped in* on me yesterday.

fade away (गायब हो जाना, धीरे-धीरे हल्का हो जाना या मुरझा जाना)—Daylight *faded away.* She is *fading away.* (शक्तिहीन होते हुए मृत्यु की ओर बढ़ना)

fall back on (आश्रय लेना)—It is always useful to have something to *fall back on* (turn to for support).

---

1. Compare can be followed by *to* or *with* : He *compared London to/with Paris. London is large compared to/with Paris......in/by comparison* is followed by *with, not to : Paris is small in comparison with London.*—LONGMAN DICTIONARY OF CONTEMPORARY ENGLISH

fall upon (अचानक हमला करना)—They suddenly jumped out of the bush and *fell upon* the travellers.

fall behind (पिछड़ जाना)—He always *falls behind* when we are running.

fall out (झगड़ा करना)—He has *fallen out* with the girl he was going to marry.

fall down (गिरना)—He *fell down* and broke his leg.

fed up (with) (तंग आ जाना)—I'm *fed up with* waiting; I'm going home.

fill in (अधूरी लिखावट आदि को पूरा करना)—I had to *fill in* three forms to get my new ration card.

find out (खोजकर पता लगाना)—In the end I *found out* what was wrong with my radio set.

fix up (तय करना, व्यवस्था करना)—The meeting has been *fixed up* for Monday next.

get at (तक पहुँचना)—It was placed on the topmost shelf so that children could not *get at* it.

get back (लौट आना)—When did you *get back* from Delhi?

get up (उठना)—What time do you *get up*?

get down (उतरना)—He *got down* from his horse.

get into (प्रवेश करना)—She *got into* the bus for Darbhanga.

get off (ट्रेन आदि से उतरना)—I am *getting off* the train at the next station. *Get off* (do not stand or walk on) the grass.

get on (चढ़ना)—He *got on* his bicycle or the horse.

get out (बाहर निकलना)—*Get out*! The secret *got out*. The lion *got out* of its cage. Please *get out* of bad habits.

get over (पार करना; कठिनाइयों को जीत लेना; बीमारी आदि से अच्छा होना)—We will *get over* that difficulty somehow. He is just *getting over* a bad heart attack. She can't *get over* her shyness.

get down (उतरना)—Please *get down* from your horse.

get through (पहुँचना)—I started as soon as your letter *got through* to me.

give (something) away (किसी को दे देना; बाँटना)—I will *give* this coat *away*. The Mayor *gave away* the prizes at the sports meeting.

give up (छोड़ देना)—The doctor *gave up* all hope. He *gave up* smoking cigarettes.

give back (लौटा देना)—Please *give* this pen *back* to its rightful owner.

give in (हार मानना; झुकना)—The rebels were forced to *give in*. Anita usually has to *give in* to her big brother.

give out (आउट कर देना; देना)—The batsman was *given out*. The burning of the vegetables *gives out* bad smell.

give way (रास्ता देना)—*Give way* to the traffic coming in from the right.

go away (चला जाना)—Please *go away;* I can't work unless I am alone.

go back (लौटना)—He handed over the letter to me and *went back* immediately.

go on (कोई कार्य जारी रखना)—Please *go on* playing; I like it.

go into (enter)—I will not *go into* the details of the case.

go down (कम हो जाना)—The price of eggs has *gone down.*

go off [(i) विस्फोट होना; (ii) बिना किसी से कहे चला जाना]—As he was cleaning his gun, it *went off* and killed him. He has *gone off* to Madras wih his neighbour's wife.

go out [(i) बाहर जाना; (ii) बुझ जाना; (iii) फैशन में नहीं होना]—She was dressed to *go out*. The fire has *gone out*. All the lights *went out*. The fashion for short skirts is *going out.*

go up (बढ़ना)—The prices are *going up* fast.

go through [(i) सावधानी से जाँच करना; (ii) झेलना; (iii) पुस्तक आदि का प्रकाशित होना]—Let us *go through* the arguments again. If you only knew what she has had to *go through* with that husband of hers! The book *went through* ten editions.

go without (कमी को सहना, से वंचित रहना)—The poor boy often had to *go without* supper.

go in (प्रवेश करना)—The key won't *go in* the lock.

go in for (लग जाना, ग्रहण करना)—He is *going in for* his next examination (परीक्षा देना). She is *going in for* stamp-collecting.

go over [(i) फिर से सावधानीपूर्वक पढ़ना; (ii) जाँचना]—Let us *go over* this chapter again. We must *go over* the accounts before we settle them.

go together (मेल खाना)—Which of these colours would *go* well *together*?

go round [(i) दूर की सड़क से जाना; (ii) किसी से भेंट करने जाना]—The main road to the station was flooded and we had to *go (a long way) round*. I *went round* to see him yesterday evening.

grow up (सयाना होना)—What are you going to do when you *grow up*?

hand over (शासन या जवाबदेही किसी और को हस्तांतरित करना)—The outgoing minister *handed over* the department to his successor.

hold on [(i) प्रतीक्षा करना खासकर टेलिफोन पर; (ii) अपनी पकड़ छोड़ना नहीं]—*Hold on* a minute! You should *hold on* to your shares.

hold out (डटा रहना)—How long can we *hold out* against these determined attacks?

hold up (जबरदस्ती रोकना)—The dacoits *held up* the bus and looted its passengers.

hush up (मामला दबा देना या बात छिपाना)—She tried unsuccessfully to *hush up* the fact that her husband was a criminal.

in sight (देखा जा सके, दृष्टि में)—The train is still *in sight.*

insist on (जोर देना)—Don't *insist on* your going to Kashmir this time.

keep on (जारी रखना)—*Keep on* trying; one day you must succeed.

keep up (बनाए रखना)—He began to walk at six kilometres an hour but he couldn't *keep up* that speed.

keep off (अलग रहना)—*Keep off* the grass.

keep away (निकट नहीं जाना या रखना)—*Keep away* from the fire. *Keep* the child *away* from the water.

keep to (वादा निभाना)—He always *keeps to* his promise.

keep out (बाहर रहना)—Danger! *Keep out*! *Keep out* of their quarrels.

knock out (पछाड़ देना)—In the finals of the boxing championship he *knocked out* his opponent.

knock down (ठोकर मारकर गिरा देना)—The old man was *knocked down* by a jeep.

leak out (ज्ञात हो जाना, रहस्य आदि प्रकाश में आ जाना)—It is said that the questions of BA examinations have *leaked out.*

let off (दंड आदि से रिहा करना)—The wicked students were *let off* with a warning.

let out (भाड़े पर लगाना)—He *let out* his house for a year.

let (someone) down (निराश करना; मदद करने में असफल होना)—Mr Sen will never *let you down*. I have been badly *let down*. (दूसरे की मदद के अभाव में कठिनाई में पड़ना)

lock up (घर या दरवाजे को ताले से बंद करना)—People usually *lock up* before they go to bed at night.

long for (तीव्र इच्छा रखना)—The children are *longing for* the holidays.

look after (देखभाल करना)—He needs a wife to *look after* him.

look at [(i) देखना; (ii) जाँचना]—He *looked at* the ceiling. What are you *looking at*? We must *look* at the question from all sides.

look back (अपने विचार को पीछे ले जाना)—You should not *look back* upon the past.

look down on (घृणा करना)—When she married a rich man, she *looked down on* the office girls she worked with.

look for (खोजना)—Are you *looking for* a job?

look forward to (आनंद के साथ उम्मीद करना)—We are *looking forward to* seeing you again.

look into (जाँचना)—There is a mystery about his death and the police are *looking into* it.

look on [(i) दर्शक की तरह देखना; (ii) समझना)]—Why don't you play cricket instead of just *looking on*? These children *look on* their teachers as their enemies.

look out (बाहर देखना, ताक में रहना)—She stood at the window and *looked out.* The eagle was *looking out* for a prey (शिकार).

look over (जाँचना, दुहराना)—*Look over* what you have written before handing it to the examiner.

look ahead (भविष्य का ध्यान रखना)—Everyone should *look ahead* and save a little money each year for his old age.

look through (पाठ आदि को दुहराना, पढ़ना)—*Look through* your notes before the examination.

look to (भरोसा करना)—They all *look to* you for help.

look up [(i) शब्दकोष आदि में खोजना; (ii) मुँह उठाकर देखना)]—Please *look up* this word in a dictionary. As I entered the room, he *looked up* from his work.

make up [(i) श्रृंगार करना; (ii) पूरा करना; रचित होना]—Most women m*ake up* (their faces) several times a day. We still need Rs 5/- to *make up* the sum we ask for. Are all animal bodies *made up* of cells?

make up for (क्षतिपूर्ति करना)—You'll have to work hard today to *make up for* the time you wasted yesterday. How can we *make up* to you *for* what you have suffered?

make out [अर्थ आदि समझना; केस (case) आदि स्थापित करना]—Can you *make out* the sense of this passage? The lawyer *made out* the case skilfully (to establish by argument).

mix up [(i) मिला देना; (ii) उलझा हुआ; (iii) संबंध रखना]—He *mixed up* the addresses so that no one got the right letters. Don't get *mixed up* in politics. I don't want to be *mixed up* in the affair.

pack up (बोरिया-बिस्तर बाँधकर तैयार होना)—It is time to *pack up* and go away.

pass away (मर जाना)—The old man *passed away* in sleep.

pass into (नाम लिखाना, एक अवस्था से दूसरी अवस्था में बदल जाना)—He *passed into* St Joseph's School. When water boils, it *passes into* steam.

pass off (कोई घटना समाप्त होना)—The meeting of the strikers *passed off* quietly.

pass on (आगे बढ़ाना)—The news was *passed on* from student to student.

pass out (किसी संस्था से पास होकर नौकरी, पेशा आदि के लिए निकलना)—About a hundred medical graduates will be *passing out* this year.

pass over (छोड़ देना)—Let us *pass over* this topic as it is not very important.

pay back (पैसा आदि लौटा देना)—I must *pay back* the money I borrowed from him.

pay (someone) off (पूर्णत: अदा कर देना और उऋण हो जाना)—You must *pay* him *off* as soon as possible.

pay for (खर्च देना, के कारण भुगतना)—You will have to *pay for* music lessons. You have to *pay for* your misdeeds.

pay up (सारे ऋण को चुका देना)—Unless you *pay up*, I shall tell my lawyer to write to you.

pick out (चुनकर अलग करना)—*Pick out* your friend in a crowd. Here are six books; *pick out* the one you like best.

pick up [(i) सीखना; (ii) साथ कर लेना; (iii) अवस्था या स्वास्थ्य सुधरना; (iv) उठना]—Children usually *pick up* foreign languages very quickly. The bus stops here to *pick up* passengers. Book-trade was dull last year; it is now *picking up*. Please *pick up* your hat.

point out (दिखाना, बताना)—As we drove through the city, the guide *painted out* the most important buildings.

play on (वाद्य-यंत्र बजाना)—He is *playing on* the *tabla*.

pull down [(i) गिरा या गिरवा देना; (ii) निस्तेज कर देना]—The new owner *pulled down* the house. You look very much *pulled down.*

pull up (डाँटना-फटकारना)—My peon has of late been very careless; I must *pull* him *up*.

put away (हटाकर अलग रखना)—*Put* your toys *away,* children; it's bedtime.

put (something) back (पूर्ववत कर देना)—When you have finished with the book, *put it back* on the table.

put before (सामने रखना, आगे रखना)—I *put* the facts *before* the Chief Minister.

put down [(i) दबाना; (ii) लिखना; (iii) पक्का निश्चय कर लेना]—Troops were used to *put down* the agitation. Here is my address—*put* it *down* before you forget it. He *put* his foot *down* and got what he wanted.

put forward (प्रतिपादित करना, propose)—He *put forward* a new theory.

put on (पहनना)—She *put on* the glasses and took the letter from my hand.

put out (बुझाना)—*Put out* that light.

put off (स्थगित करना)—The meeting has been *put off* until next week.

put in [(i) पद प्रतिष्ठित करना (ii) आवेदनपत्र देना]—He has *put in* ten years service. He has *put in* an application for the post.

put up [(i) भवन आदि बनाना; (ii) खाना और ठहरना; (iii) किसी को काम पर लगाना; (iv) प्रकाशित करना या ऐसी जगह रखना जिसे सब कोई देख सकें; (v) पेश करना]—He *put up* a shed in the garden to keep his cows. While in Calcutta I *put up* in a hotel. Please *put* the new office-boy *up* to his duties. *Put up* a notice about the classes. He has *put up* the file to the officer.

put up with (बर्दाश्त करना)—We have to *put up with* a lot of noise when the children are at home.

ring up (फोन करना)—I will *ring you* up in the evening. *Ring up* 999 in case of emergency.

round up (धर-पकड़, गिरफ्तारियाँ)—On the day after the riots the police *rounded up* all suspects.

rub out (पेंसिल या स्याही के चिह्न को रबर से मिटाना)—The child wrote down the wrong word and then *rubbed* it *out.*

rule out (असंगत घोषित करना)—That's a possibility that cannot be *ruled out.*

run about (इधर-उधर दौड़ना)—When the guests came, the servants began to *run about* like frightened cattle.

run away (भाग जाना)—Don't *run away*; I have a message for you.

run after (किसी काम में दिन-रात लगे रहना, के पीछे पड़ना)—These days people *run after* wealth.

run down [(i) बीमारी के बाद दुबला हो जाना; (ii) शिकायत करना; (iii) क्षीण हो जाना] He is still *run down* after his illness and unfit for work. He is always *running down* his neighbours. The torch is useless; the battery has *run down.*

run over (कुचल डालना)—The boy was *run over* and had to be taken to hospital.

run into [(i) टकराना; (ii) पहुँचना)]—The bus got out of control and *ran into* a wall. The book *ran into* five editions. He *ran into* debt.

see (somebody) off (विदा करना)—I was *seen off* by many of my friends.

see through (षड्यंत्र या चालाकी का पता पाना)— I *see through* your little game.

see to (ध्यान देकर काम करा लेना)—I will *see to* it that your money is paid to you this week.

sell out (थोड़ा या सब बिक जाना या बेच देना)—All the copies of the book have been *sold out.*

sell off (बचे-खुचे सामान को सस्ते में बेचना)—I am ready to *sell off* the last piece of land.

send for (बुलवाना, बुला भेजना)—The Headmaster *sent for* the boy who had disturbed the class.

set in (आरंभ होना जो कुछ अधिक समय तक चले)—The monsoon has *set in.*

set off (यात्रा पर रवाना होना)—We *set off* just at dawn.

set out (यात्रा शुरू करना)—The two friends *set out* on a long journey.

set up (erect)—They *set up* the stall opposite my house.

shout down (हो-हल्ला करके चुप कर देना)—Some people tried to *shout* the speaker *down.*

show off (ध्यान आकर्षित करने के लिए या लाभ के लिए अपने धन आदि का दिखावा करना)—He always likes to *show off* his wealth. Mothers like to *show off* their daughters.

shut down (कारखाने आदि का काम बंद होना)—They *shut down* their factory.

shut up (चुप रहना)—Tell him to *shut up*. *Shut up*! I don't want to hear anything.

speak for (की सिफारिश करना)—I will *speak* to the Principal *for* you and I hope you will be admitted.

speak out (साफ उच्चारण करके या जोर से पढ़ना)—*Speak out*, boy; I am unable to hear you.

stand for (प्रतिनिधित्व करना)—The letters PO *stand for* post office or postal order.

stand out (श्रेष्ठ या प्रमुख होना, स्पष्ट दिखाई देना)—Does your work *stand out* from that of others?

stand by (साथ देना)—I will *stand by* you whatever happens.

stand up (खड़ा होना)—He looks smart when he *stands up.*

take after (किसी के सदृश होना)—She *takes after* her mother.

take away (ले जाना)—*Take away* that cup; I don't want it.

take back (वापस ले लेना)—The shopkeeper refused to *take back* the already sold goods.

take down [(i) लिखना; (ii) उतारकर लेना]—The reporters *took down* the speech. *Take down* a book from the top shelf.

take off (उतारना)—He *took off* his hat when he entered the house.

take out (निकालना)—The students *took out* a procession.

take up [(i) उठाना; (ii) समय या जगह लेना; (iii) आरंभ करना]—*Take up* your pen and write a letter. The table *takes up* too much room. He has *taken up* the work entrusted to him.

take over (नियंत्रण या स्वामित्व को अपने अधीन लेना)—When Mr Gupta retires, his son will *take over* the business.

tell (up) on (खराब असर डालना, थकाना)—All this hard work is *telling on* him.

think over (किसी निर्णय पर पहुँचने के पहले विषय पर सोचना)—Please *think over* what I have said. Yes, I will *think* it *over.*

think about (विचार करना विशेषकर किसी योजना पर और देखना कि क्या यह उचित या संभव है)—Please *think about* the proposal and let me have your views tomorrow.

think out (सावधानीपूर्वक सोचना और तब कोई योजना बनाना)—It seems to be a well-*thought-out* scheme. Before you take up the work, *think out* the plan of work.

throw away (फेंक देना)—*Throw away* the old shoes; nobody would wear them now.

touch upon (जिक्र करना लेकिन विवेचन नहीं करना)—In course of his address, Mr Gandhi *touched upon* many problems of the world.

try out (जाँचना)—We won't know how the plan works till we have *tried* it *out.*

turn down (अस्वीकार करना)—His application for leave was *turned down.*

turn into [(i) परिणत करना; (ii) बन जाना]—Water *turns into* vapour. When he grew up, he *turned into* a criminal.

turn out (निकाल बाहर करना)—As he was disturbing the class, he was *turned out* of the class.

turn up (पहुँचना)—He promised to come but hasn't *turned up* yet.

turn on (खोल देना, शुरू करना)—*Turn* the lights (radio) *on.*

turn off (बंद कर देना)—*Turn* the water (lights or radio) *off.*

turn over (उलटना, पलटी खाना)—Please *turn over* the pages of the book. The car dashed against the tree and *turned over.*

trace out (रूपरेखा प्रस्तुत करना)—*Trace out* the plan of a house.

turn round (take a new direction)—*Turn round* and let me see your profile.

wind up (चाभी देना, समेटना)—I *wind up* my watch at 8 am every day. They have decided to *wind up* their business without delay.

work out (हिसाब करना)—The details have not yet been *worked out.*

write down (लिखना)—You should *write down* the address before you forget it.

write out (लिख डालना)—*Write out* a copy of an agreement. *Write out* a cheque.

EXERCISE 1

Use the following in sentences of your own:

(i) at home in; in quest of; set out; go round; make up; long and short; open and above board; put up; hold out; taken aback.

(ii) at all; bring up; as soon as; call at; come across; give up; instead of; in order that; put up; with regard to.

EXERCISE 2

Match the verbs on the left with their meanings on the right:

(a) look after (i) leave, stop attending

(b) look for (ii) quarrel
(c) break down (iii) search for
(d) fall out (iv) compensate for
(e) drop out of (v) take care of
(f) make up for (vi) stop because of a mechanical fault

EXERCISE 3 (With Answer)

Each of the following phrasal verbs is followed by alternative meanings of which one is correct. Pick out the best and correct alternative meaning indicating it with a, b, c, d.

1. Break in

(a) disappear (b) destroy (c) enter by force (d) cutting into peices

2. Keep on

(a) admit (b) attend (c) overflow (d) continue

3. Do away with

(a) retain (b) abolish (c) distribute (d) consider

4. Give up

(a) stop (b) rise (c) settle (d) leave

5. Put up with

(a) admire (b) face (c) tolerate (d) contact

Ans. 1.—(c) 2.— (d) 3.— (b) 4.—(d) 5.—(c)

EXERCISE 4 (With Answer)

State which of the following sentences contain phrasal verbs:

1. The sick man has come round.
2. The lady put the lamp out suddenly.
3. We saved the boy from drowning.
4. He is explaining something to the boys.
5. The torch is useless; the battery has run down.
6. She opened the door to let a dog in.
7. The angry mob burnt down the palace.
8. I admired him as my elder brother.
9. He went back on his promise.
10. He used his calculator to work out the cost.

Ans. 1. *come round* 2. *put (something) out* 3. × 4. × 5. *run down* 6. *let (somebody) in* 7. *burnt down* 8. × 9. *went back on* 10. *work out.*

EXERCISE 5. (With Answer)

Complete the verbs in the following sentences with suitable particles:

1. He has given.... smoking. 7. We sold.... the books in two days.

2. Let the dog ....
3. Please ring me...... a bit later.
4. The time is running ......
5. Let me take .... your address.
6. The plane took ..... at 8.30.
8. Please keep .... the grass.
9. Elephants live ..... plants.
10. A truck ran .... the boy.
11. Winter has already set .....
12. White stands ..... purity.

Ans. 1. (*given*) up 2. (*let*) in 3. (*ring*) up 4. (*running*) out 5. (*take*) down 6. (*took*) off 7. (*sold*) out 8. (*keep*) off 9. (*live*) on 10. (*ran*) over 11. (*set*) in 12. (*stands*) for.

□ □ □

17. WORD POWER

VOCABULARY

जिस तरह घर बनाने के लिए ईंट की आवश्यकता होती है उसी तरह अँगरेजी सीखने के लिए अँगरेजी के शब्दों की जानकारी जरूरी है। इस अध्याय में (i) Pairs of words (Synonyms, Homophones, etc); (ii) Antonyms (iii) Single word for a group of words, (iv) The same word used as Different Parts of Speech तथा (v) Word-formation दिए गए हैं।

(i) PAIRS OF WORDS
(Synonyms, Homophones, etc.)

किसी भाषा के वे शब्द जो अर्थ में लगभग समान होते हैं किंतु उनके उच्चारण में विभिन्नता होती है, उन्हें Synonyms (समानार्थक शब्द) कहते हैं। जैसे : ***discover*** (पता लगाना), *invent* (आविष्कार करना).

वैसे शब्द जो उच्चारण में एक-दूसरे से मिलते-जुलते हों या समान मालूम पड़ें, किंतु spelling तथा meaning में विभिन्न हों, Homophones कहलाते हैं। जैसे : *fair* (मेला,सुंदर), *fare* (भाड़ा).

अब नीचे वैसे कुछ मुख्य शब्दों को देखें :

1. **Avenge** (दूसरे के लिए बदला लेना) — Hamlet *avenged* the murder of his father.
   Revenge (प्रतिशोध लेना) — He took *revenge* on him for theft.
2. **Award** (प्रदान करना) — He was *awarded* the first prize.
   Reward (पुरस्कार) — The best boy got the *reward.*
3. **Admit** (स्वीकार करना) — He *admits* that it is true.
   Confess (दोष कबूल करना) — He *confesses* his guilt.
4. **Addicted** (आसक्त, बुरे अर्थ में) — He is *addicted* to smoking.
   Devoted (आसक्त, अच्छे अर्थ में)—He *devotes* his spare time to sport.
5. **Accept** (स्वीकार करना) — I *accept* your advice.
   Except (सिवाय) — Everyone *except* Hari has passed.
6. **Access** (पहुँच) — I have no *access* to the Vice-chancellor.
   Excess (आधिक्य) — *Excess* of anything is bad.
7. **Affect** (प्रभाव डालना) — Overwork may *affect* your health.
   Effect (परिणाम) — Punishment had very little *effect* on him.
8. **Adopt** (ग्रहण करना) — Don't *adopt* unfair means in the examination.
   Adapt (अनुकूल बनाना/बनना) — We must *adapt* ourselves to the new place.
   Adept (निपुण) — She is *adept* in photography.

9. **Artist** (कलाकार) — He is a good *artist.*
Artisan (कारीगर) — A potter is an *artisan.*

10. **Air** (हवा) — The fresh *air* made him feel hungry. We should breathe in fresh *air.*
Heir (उत्तराधिकारी) — The king's eldest son was the *heir* to the throne.

11. **Ascent** (चढ़ाई) — We made a successful *ascent* of the mountain.
Assent (सहमति) — Once we have his *assent* we can start.

12. **Affect** (प्रभावित करना) — Smoking *affects* health.
Affectation (ढोंग) — She is sincere and quiet without *affectation.*

13. **Accept** (स्वीकार करना) — I cannot *accept* your gift.
Agree (सहमत होना) — He *agreed* to my idea.

14. **Advice** (सलाह) — We must act on your *advice.*
Advise (सलाह देना) — I *advise* you to work hard.

15. **Accident** (दुर्घटना) — He was killed in a road *accident.*
Incident (घटना) — This is an important *incident* in his life.

16. **Allusion** (संकेत) — He made an *allusion* to the crime.
Illusion (भ्रम) — I have no *illusions* about his ability.

17. **Altar** (वेदी) — He laid his offerings on the *altar* of goddess Durga.
Alter (बदलना) — I will not *alter* my decision.

18. **Anonymous** (गुमनाम) — It is unpleasant to receive *anonymous* letters.
Unanimous (एकमत) — They were *unanimous* in asking for more holidays.

19. **Avocation** (उपव्यवसाय) — His *avocation* was gardening.
Vocation (पेशा) — Teaching children is his *vocation.*
Vacation (छुट्टी, विशेषत: विद्यालय/विश्वविद्यालय/कचहरी की) — I want to go to Delhi during the Puja *vacation.*

20. **Battle** (लड़ाई) — Many *battles* are fought in the single war.
War (युद्ध) — World *War II* was fought during the forties.

21. **Bill** (विधेयक) — The *bill* is not passed by the Assembly.
Act (अधिनियम) — When the bill is passed, it becomes an *act.*

22. **Beer** (शराब) — Don't take *beer.*
Bear (भालू) — I saw a *bear* last week.

23. **Berth** (गाड़ी में सोने की जगह) — I have reserved *berth* no 9.
Birth (जन्म) — What is your date of *birth?*

24. **Beside** (बगल में) — The boy sat *beside* his mother.
Besides (अलावा) — Please give me a pen, *besides* some paper.

25. **Break** (तोड़ना) — Do not *break* this toy.
Brake (ब्रेक) — He applied the *brake* to stop the car. The Government is determined to put a *brake* on public spending.

26. **Barbarism** (बर्बरता, क्रूरता, गँवारूपन) — *Barbarism* still prevails in some parts of the world.

Barbarity (क्रूरता) — The *barbarities* of the last war must not be repeated.

27. **Brief** (संक्षेप, of short duration) — He gave a *brief* reply.

Short (अल्प, not long in space or time) — He lived a *short* life.

28. **Bloc** (गुट) — Today the world is divided into two major *blocs*.

Block (खंड, कुंदा) — The floor was made of wooden *blocks*.

29. **Bridal** (वधू का, वैवाहिक) — She was in her *bridal* dress.

Bridle (लगाम) — Put the *bridle* on the horse.

30. **Beneficial** (लाभदायक — of non-living things) — His holiday has had a *beneficial* effect.

Beneficent (उपकारी, परोपकारी — of persons) — A *beneficent* man is always respected.

31. **Border** (किनारा) — The *border* of this *sari* is fine.

Boarder (वह जो किसी के साथ उसके घर में रहता और खाता है) — Mrs Sen takes in *boarders* for a living.

32. **Board** (पटरा, फलक, तख्ता) — This is a *cardboard*.

Bored (उबाना) — His long talks *bored* us.

33. **Beach** (समुद्र-तट) — After crossing the sea-scented *beach*, you can come to my farm.

Bitch (कुत्ती) — A female dog is called a *bitch*.

34. **Childlike** (शिशुसुलभ) — She has a *childlike* face.

Childish (बचकाना) — We do not like your *childish* behaviour.

35. **Check** (रोकना) — Please *check* your bad temper.

Cheque (हुंडी) — He gave me a *cheque* for fifty rupees.

36. **Cast** (फेंकना, देना) — Please *cast* your vote in my favour.

Caste (जाति) — We must end the *caste* system.

37. **Council** (सभा) — She is a member of *Council*.

Counsel (राय देना) — Would you *counsel* our giving up the plan?

38. **Cite** (उद्धृत करना) — He *cites* lots of examples from the Bible.

Site (किसी काम के लिए चुनी हुई जगह) — That is the *site* for our new college.

Sight (दृष्टि, दृश्य) — His eye*sight* is very good. This place has a very beautiful *sight*.

39. **Continual** (लगातार, पर रुक-रुककर) — I am tired of this *continual* rain.

Continuous (लगातार) — There has been a *continuous* rain since morning.

40. **Careless** (असावधान) — A *careless* man is never happy.

Carefree (चिंताहीन) — A *carefree* man enjoys life.

41. **Canvas** (मोटा कपड़ा, कैन्वस) — The tent is made of *canvas*.

Canvass (वोट माँगना, पक्ष-प्रचार करना) — He is *canvassing* for votes.

42. **Casual** (आकस्मिक) — He is on *casual* leave today.
Causal (कारण-संबंधी) — There is a *causal* relation between food and health.

43. **Ceremonial** (धर्मानुष्ठान, विधि-विधान) — According to church *ceremonial* the priest kisses the Bible before reading from it.
Ceremonious (आडंबरी) — His manner was rather *ceremonious*.

44. **Cession** (अर्पण, प्रदान, सत्तान्तरण) — The *cession* of the territory was demanded by China.
Cessation (समाप्ति) — We arranged a week-long *cessation* of fighting with the enemy.
Session (सत्र, अधिवेशन) — Parliament is in *session*.

45. **Complement** (पूरक) — A fine wine is a *complement* to a good meal.
Compliment (प्रशंसा, अभिनंदन) — That young man is always ready to pay *compliments* to a young lady.

46. **Comprehensive** (व्यापक) — He gave a *comprehensive* explanation of his plan for development.
Comprehensible (बोधगम्य) — His speech was not *comprehensible* to the public.

47. **Confidant** (विश्वसनीय व्यक्ति) — It is not safe to make everybody your *confidant*.
Confident (विश्वस्त) — I am *confident* of success.

48. **Contemptible** (नीच, घृणित) — He is a *contemptible* fellow who sells official secrets for money.
Contemptuous (तिरस्कारक) — He sent a *contemptuous* reply.

49. **Crops** (फसलें) — *Crops* die for want of rain.
Corps (सेना का एक भाग) — I am in the Army Medical *Corps*.
Corpse (लाश) — The battlefield was full of *corpses*.

50. **Corporal** (शारीरिक) — *Corporal* punishment is prohibited in schools.
Corporeal (मूर्त, शारीरिक) — God is not a *corporeal* Being.

51. **Course** (गति, दिशा, पाठ्यक्रम) — Our *course* is directly south. He is taking a *course* of French lessons.
Coarse (मोटा) — *Coarse* cloth is cheaper than fine cloth.

52. **Credible** (विश्वास करने लायक) — This is a *credible* news report.
Creditable (प्रशंसा करने लायक) — He made a *creditable* effort to establish peace.
Credulous (आशुविश्वासी, भोला, कान का कच्चा) — He was so *credulous* that he readily believed that I had seen a ghost.

53. **Cell** (कोठरी) — When the murderer was arrested, he was put into the *cell*.
Sell (बेचना) — Do you want to *sell* your car?

54. **Crime** (अपराध — कानून की दृष्टि से) — *Crimes* must be checked.

Vice (बुराई, व्यसन, भ्रष्टाचार) — His laziness is so great as to be almost a *vice*.

Sin (पाप — धार्मिक दृष्टि से) — He confessed his *sins* to a priest.

55. Custom (रिवाज) — Social *customs* vary greatly from country to country.

Habit (आदत) — He is in the *habit* of taking bed tea.

56. Cease (रुकना) — The factory has *ceased* making bicycles.

Seize (जप्त करना, पकड़ लेना) — He *seized* Ram's goods for payment of debt.
The policeman *seized* a thief by the collar.

57. Domestic (घरेलू) — His *domestic* life is very happy.

Homely (साधारण) — A *homely* face is one that is plain, not handsome.

58. Differ (मतभेद होना) — I *differ* with you on this point.

Defer (टालना, आस्थगित करना) — You shouldn't *defer* this scheme.

59. Direct (सीधा) — We want *direct* answers.

Directly (अविलंब, सीधे) — Please go there *directly*.

60. Deny (इनकारना) — He *denied* the charges.

Refuse (इनकार करना) — He *refused* to go.

61. Discover (पता लगाना) — Who *discovered* America?

Invent (आविष्कार करना) — Who *invented* the radio?

62. Dairy (दुग्धशाला) — I get milk from the nearby *dairy*.

Diary (डायरी) — He noted my address in his *diary*.

63. Die (मरना) — Every man *dies* in the world.

Dye (रंगना) — I *dye* my sweater in blue.

64. Dying (मरते हुए) — Have you ever seen a *dying* man?

Dyeing (रंगते हुए) — I saw her *dyeing* the dress in red.

65. Deceased (मरा हुआ) — The *deceased* has left no property.

Diseased (रोगग्रस्त) — His *diseased* bone was removed.

66. Decent (उचित, उपयुक्त, भद्र) — I like his *decent* behaviour.

Descent (उतार, नीचे की ओर) — The road makes a sharp *descent* just past the lake.

Dissent (असहमति) — When I asked for agreement, there was no *dissent*.

67. Deficient (अपूर्ण, त्रुटिपूर्ण) — There is a *deficient* supply of water.

Defective (दोषपूर्ण) — This is a *defective* machine.

68. Dependent (निर्भर) — I am *dependent* upon your help.

Dependant (आश्रित) — I am always helpful to my *dependants*.

69. Disinterested (निष्पक्ष, तटस्थ) — His action was not *disinterested* because he hoped to make money out of the affair.

Uninterested (दिलचस्पी या रुचि नहीं रखना) — I am *uninterested* in your activities.

70. Dew (ओस) — The grass was wet with *dew*.

Due (देय) — I don't like him, but, to give him his *due*, he is a good singer.

71. Draft (बैंक ड्राफ्ट) — I sent him a *draft* for Rs 500/-.

Draught (घूँट) — The old man drank a *draught* of medicine.

Drought (सूखा, अनावृष्टि) — The crops died during the *drought.*

72. Drown (डूबना — व्यक्ति का) — He saved a *drowning* boy.

Sink (डूबना — व्यक्ति या वस्तु का) — The ship *sank.* The sick man is *sinking* now.

73. Dual (दोहरा, दुगना) — There is *dual* control over his business.

Duel (द्वंद्व, द्वंद्व-युद्ध) — These boys are fighting a *duel.*

74. Effective (प्रभावशाली) — A crocin is an *effective* medicine for killing pains.

Efficient (कुशल) — Amar is an *efficient* driver.

Efficacious (प्रभावोत्पादक) — Have you found any *efficacious* treatment for your disease?

75. Elemental (तात्त्विक, प्राकृतिक) — Air can be called an *elemental* substance.

Elementary (प्रारंभिक) — He does not have even an *elementary* knowledge of the subject.

76. Elicit (निकालना, प्राप्त करना) — He *elicited* the truth at last, by questioning all the boys in the school.

Illicit (गैरकानूनी, अवैध) — The *illicit* sale of opium must stop.

77. Eligible (योग्य) — You are *eligible* for this post.

Illegible (अपाठ्य, अस्पष्ट) — His handwriting was *illegible.*

78. Emigrant (प्रवासी) — He is an *emigrant* from China.

Immigrant (आप्रवासी, आकर बसनेवाला) — In India all the *immigrants* enjoy the rights of a citizen.

79. Eminent (प्रतिष्ठित, उच्च) — He is an *eminent* scholar of English.

Imminent (सन्निकट) — There is a storm *imminent.*

80. Ensure (सुनिश्चित करना) — This medicine will *ensure* you a good night's sleep.

Insure (वीमा करना) — This house is *insured* against theft and fire.

Assure (विश्वास दिलाना) — I *assure* you that this medicine cannot harm you.

81. Envious (डाही) — She was *envious* of her sister's beauty.

Jealous (ईर्ष्यालु) — Othello was a *jealous* husband. He is *jealous* of their success.

Enviable (ईर्ष्य, स्पृहणीय) — He has everything he wants; he is an *enviable* young man.

82. Eruption (उद्भेदन, विस्फोट) — Several villages were destroyed by a volcanic *eruption.*

Irruption (धावा, चढ़ाई) — There was a violent *irruption* of soldiers into the building.

83. **Fair** (सुंदर, मेला) — Children like the *fair.*
Fare (भाड़ा) — The train *fare* has gone up now.

84. **Further** (और आगे) — I cannot walk *further* in the darkness.
Farther (दूर) — The old man can't go any *farther* without a rest.

85. **Famous** (प्रसिद्ध) — He is *famous* for his fine acting.
Notorious (कुख्यात) — He was a *notorious* thief.

86. **Fetch** (किसी व्यक्ति या वस्तु को लाने जाना) — Run and *fetch* the doctor. Please *fetch* me a clean handkerchief from my bedroom.
Bring (लाना) — *Bring* me the book.

87. **Fight** (संघर्ष) — There was a *fight* between the customer and the shopkeeper.
Quarrel (झगड़ा) — I have no *quarrel* with him.

88. **Graceful** (सुंदर) — She has a *graceful* look.
Gracious (दयालु) — It is *gracious* of you to help me. God is *gracious* to all sinners who repent.

89. **Godlike** (ईश्वर या देवता जैसा) — Buddha was a *godlike* man.
Godly (पवित्र) — Gandhi led a *godly* life.

90. **Ghastly** (भयानक) — I cannot see a *ghastly* sight.
Ghostly (भूत-प्रेत जैसा) — She saw a *ghostly* sight.

91. **Gate** (फाटक) — Who is opening the *gate*?
Gait (चलने का ढंग) — I can recognize her by her *gait.*

92. **Human** (मानवीय) — *Human* life is very short.
Humane (दयालु) — He was a man of *humane* character.

93. **Hail** (स्वागत करना) — An old friend *hailed* me from the other side of the street.
Hale (स्वस्थ) — He is *hale* and hearty these days.

94. **Honorary** (अवैतनिक) — The post of President is *honorary.*
Honourable (आदरणीय) — My father is an *honourable* man.

95. **Informant** (सूचक) — The *informant* was rewarded.
Informer (भेदिया) — The *informer* was killed.

96. **Industrial** (व्यावसायिक) — Jamshedpur is an *industrial* place.
Industrious (परिश्रमी) — He is an *industrious* boy.

97. **Imaginary** (काल्पनिक) — He always tells *imaginary* tales.
Imaginative (कल्पनापूर्ण) — Wordsworth was an *imaginative* poet.

98. **Idle** (सुस्त, not working) — He is *idle* now.
Idol (मूर्ति) — Some people worship *idols.*
Lazy (सुस्त, disliking and avoiding work) — I spent a *lazy* afternoon yesterday.

99. **Judicial** (न्याय-संबंधी) — They are in the *judicial* service.
Judicious (विवेकशील) — Be *judicious* in taking decisions.

100. Key (चाभी) — Do you have a *key* to this lock?
Quay (जहाजी घाट) — The ship/boat touched the *quay* in the morning.

101. Lose (खो देना) — We must not *lose* time.
Loose (ढीला) — He likes a *loose* shirt.

102. Later (अधिक देर से) — He came home *later* than his brother.
Latter (बाद का) — Please answer the *latter* part of the question.

103. Luxuriant (अत्यधिक फैलनेवाला) — He has *luxuriant* hair.
Luxurious (विलासी) — Students should not be *luxurious.*

104. Liberty (आजादी, — गुलामी या जेल से) — The prisoner was set at *liberty.*
Freedom (व्यक्तिगत आजादी, आजादी) — India loves *freedom* all over the world.

105. Lovable (प्यारा, pleasant) — He is a man of *lovable* nature.
Lovely (सुंदर) — What a *lovely* flower!

106. Meat (मांस) — Some people do not eat *meat.*
Meet (मिलना) — Tell him my message if you *meet* him.

107. Memorable (याद रखने लायक) — 15th August is a *memorable* day.
Memorial (स्मारक) — The Taj Mahal is a *memorial.*

108. Momentary (क्षणिक) — Her feeling of fear was only *momentary;* it soon passed.
Momentous (महत्त्वपूर्ण) — It was a *momentous* event.

109. Might (शक्ति, past tense form of may) — *Might* is right. It *might* rain.
Mite (दमड़ी, a very small offering) — She is a poor woman, but she gives her *mite* to every beggar she passes on the street.

110. Negligent (असावधान) — He has been *negligent* in not locking the doors as he was told to do.
Negligible (नगण्य) — The damage to my car is *negligible.*

111. Notable (उल्लेखनीय, महत्त्वपूर्ण) — This is a *notable* event of my life. He was a *notable* lawyer.
Notorious (कुख्यात) — The police killed a *notorious* criminal last month.

112. Official (आफिस-संबंधी) — You should not read my *official* letters.
Officious (अनुचित हस्तक्षेप करनेवाला) — Don't be *officious* by nature.

113. Piece (टुकड़ा) — Please give me a *piece* of paper.
Peace (शांति) — We want *peace,* not war.

114. Pole (खंभा) — The ball hit the *pole* and went in.
Poll (मतदान) — I was not here during the last *poll.*

115. Practice (अभ्यास) — He has no *practice* of speaking English.
Practise (अभ्यास करना) — *Practise* hard to learn English.

116. Principal (प्राचार्य) — Mr K Sinha is our *Principal.*
Principle (सिद्धांत) — Be a man of *principle.*

117. People (लोग) — The *people* of my village are hard-working.

Pupil (शिष्य) — Teach good things to your *pupils.*

118. Populous (घनी आबादीवाला) — Calcutta is the most *populous* city in India.

Popular (जनप्रिय) — Mahatma Gandhi was a *popular* leader of our country.

119. Prescribe (निर्धारित करना, नुसखा लिखना) — This is the *prescribed* textbook on English grammar. The doctor *prescribed* a long rest.

Proscribe (गैरकानूनी करार देना) — 'In past history an intolerant ruler has often *proscribed* all religious beliefs other than his own.'

120. Plane (रन्दा, समतल, वायुयान) — He smoothed the wood with his *plane. Plane* the table smooth. He went to London by *plane.*

Plain (समतल भूमि, मैदान, सरल) — Please explain it in *plain* language. *Plain* living, high thinking. The *plains* of Bihar are very fertile.

121. Practical (व्यावहारिक) — He is a *practical* man.

Practicable (उपयोगी, साध्य) — Is it *practicable* to try to grow crops in deserts?

122. Prosecute (पर मुकदमा चलाना) — He was *prosecuted* for exceeding the speed limit.

Persecute (सताना) — Many people have been *persecuted* for their religious beliefs.

123. Precede (पहले आना) — Are you certain the minister's statement *preceded* that of the President?

Proceed (आगे बढ़ना) — Now that our plans are settled let us *proceed.*

124. Pair (जोड़ा) — I have a *pair* of black shoes.

Pare (बाहरी किनारा या चमड़ा काट देना) — You must *pare* your (finger-) nails.

125. Precedent (पूर्ववर्ती) — Is there a *precedent* for what you want me to do?

President (सभापति, राष्ट्रपति) — He is the *president* of the meeting. Who is the *President* of India?

126. Pray (प्रार्थना करना) — We *pray* to God for His mercy.

Prey (शिकार) — He fell a *prey* to disease.

127. Queen (रानी) — Have you ever seen *Queen* Elizabeth?

Quean (दुराचारी औरत) — Always avoid the company of a *quean.*

128. Quite (पूर्णत:) — I am *quite* well here.

Quiet (शांत) — She is *quiet* by nature.

129. Refuse (इनकार करना) — He *refused* to go there.

Refuge (आश्रय) — She took *refuge* in my house.

130. Right (अधिकार) — We have to fight for our *rights.*

Rite (धार्मिक रिवाज) — He died after receiving the *rites* of the church.

131. Roll (नामावली, लुढ़कना) — What is your *roll* number? The ball *rolled* under the table.

Role (भूमिका, पार्ट) — What *role* did he play in solving the problem?

132. **Root** (जड़) — These are the *roots* of a flower. The love of money is the *root* of all evil.

Route (रास्ता) — This is the shortest *route* from Muzaffarpur to Patna.

133. **Raise** (उठाना, बढ़ाना) — The price of paper has been *raised.*

Raze (पूरी तरह ध्वस्त करना) — An American city was *razed* by an earthquake.

134. **Sensible** (विवेकशील) — Hari is a *sensible* boy.

Sensitive (संवेदनशील) — Some people are very *sensitive* to criticism.

135. **Sensuous** (इंद्रियग्राह्य) — Keats's poetry is *sensuous.*

Sexual (कामुक) — A *sexual* life makes a man miserable.

Sensual (इंद्रियजन्य, of the body) — He led a *sensual* life (=a life of mere bodily pleasures).

136. **Soul** (आत्मा) — Our *soul* is immortal.

Sole (एकाकी) — Mr Rai is the *sole* agent of tea here.

137. **Story** (कहानी) — Martha told beautiful *stories.*

Storey (मंजिल) — We live on the second *storey* of the house.

138. **Sore** (दु:खी) — I feel *sore* about not being invited to the party.

Soar (उड़ना, हवा में ऊपर-नीचे जाना) — The plane was *soaring* like an eagle.

139. **Social** (सामाजिक) — Man is a *social* being.

Sociable (मिलनसार) — We are very *sociable* in our office.

140. **Stationary** (स्थिर, अचल) — A *stationary* object is easiest to aim at.

Stationery (लेखन-सामग्री) — He sells *stationery*. He deals in *stationery.*

141. **Spirituous** (मादक) — We should abstain from *spirituous* liquors.

Spiritual (आध्यात्मिक) — I am concerned about my *spiritual* welfare.

142. **Statue** (मूर्ति) — A new *statue* of Mahatma Gandhi was built there.

Statute (अध्यादेश, अधिनियम) — The new *statutes* are no longer in force.

143. **Stimulant** (उत्तेजक, प्रेरक) — Spirits and tonics are *stimulants.*

Stimulus (प्रोत्साहक) — Light is a *stimulus* to growth in plants.

144. **Stare** (गौर से देखना) — He is *staring* at me.

Stair (सीढ़ी) — These *stairs* are not very comfortable.

145. **Shoulder** (कंधा) — He carried the bag on his *shoulders.*

Soldier (सिपाही) — One Indian *soldier* killed five enemy soldiers in the last war.

146. **Tear** (आँसू, फाड़ना) — My wife burst into *tears* when she heard the bad news. Why did you *tear* your handkerchief?

Tier (टियर, पंक्ति, कतार) — Her wedding cake had three *tiers.*

147. **Temper** (मिजाज, क्रोध) — He is in a bad *temper* today. He is in a *temper* now.

Tamper (में हस्तक्षेप करना, दस्तंदाजी करना) — After the accident it was found that the car had been *tampered* with.

148. Temporal (सांसारिक, पार्थिव) — The lust for *temporal* power is the root of all evils.

Temporary (अस्थाई) — Many students find *temporary* jobs during their summer holidays.

149. Union (संघ) — There is a students' *union* in every university.

Unity (एकता) — We must work for Hindu-Muslim *unity.*

150. Vacant (रिक्त) — The post of a peon is *vacant.*

Empty (खाली) — The cup is *empty.*

151. Verbal (मौखिक) — He gave a *verbal* report.

Verbose (शब्दाडंबरपूर्ण) — A *verbose* speech has no effect.

152. Vanish (लुप्त हो जाना)—The thief ran into the crowd and *vanished* from sight.

Banish (वनवास देना) — Ram was *banished* for fourteen years.

153. Weak (कमजोर) — He is *weak* in English.

Week (सप्ताह) — How many *weeks* are there in a month?

154. Womanly (स्त्रियोचित) — She has all the *womanly* qualities.

Womanish [स्त्रियोचित (बुरे अर्थ में)]—This man's behaviour is *womanish.*

155. Wilful (जिद्दी, दुराग्रही) — I hate his *wilful* behaviour.

Willing (इच्छुक) — Are you *willing* to help him?

156. Zealous (उत्साही) — He is *zealous* to please his master.

Jealous (डाही) — Don't be *jealous* of Veena's success.

EXERCISE 1 (With Answer)

1. *Choose the most suitable word or phrase from the set given against each sentence:*

(a) The bread was so old that it was hardly ...... (*edible, tasteful, eatable*)

(b) He refused to ..... the machine. (*begin, start, drive*)

(c) What a good shirt he is ......! (*wearing, putting on, donning*)

(d) The baby ..... to eat the banana. (*refused, declined, denied*)

(e) Would you please .... the tap for me? (*open, switch on, turn on*)

(f) They would not ...... me in. (*permit, allow, enter*)

(g) I will....... you at exactly ten o'clock. (*wait for, hope for, expect*)

(h) .... I hope you haven't been waiting long. (*Sorry, Excuse me, Pardon*)

(i) Red and black are colours that ...... me very well. (*fit, match, suit*)

(j) He was not willing to accept the ..... (*wrong, blame, fault*)

Ans. 1. (a) *eatable*, (b) *start,* (c) *putting on,* (d) *refused*, (e) *turn on*, (f) *allow*, (g) *expect*, (h) *Excuse me*, (i) *suit*, (j) *fault*.

(ii) ANTONYMS (विपरीतार्थक शब्द)

Antonym का अर्थ होता है—विपरीतार्थक शब्द। Antonym is a word of opposite meaning to another.

अँगरेजी में Antonyms तीन प्रकार से बनाए जाते हैं :

(i) कुछ शब्दों के पहले negative prefixes (नकारात्मक उपसर्ग) जैसे : *im-, in-, ir-, dis-, un-, de-* का प्रयोग करके।

possible—impossible please—displease
decent—indecent wise—unwise
religious—irreligious control—decontrol

(ii) कुछ शब्दों के अंत में यदि-*ful* रहे तो उसे-*less* में बदल कर या *-less* रहे तो उसे-*ful* में बदलकर antonym बनाया जाता है। जैसे :

careful—careless hopeless—hopeful
cheerful—cheerless colourless—colourful

अपवाद : helpful—unhelpful; luckless—lucky आदि।

(iii) कुछ शब्दों के अनियमित रूप से, अर्थात नए शब्दों की रचना के द्वारा antonym बनाया जाता है। जैसे :

joy—sorrow good—bad

यहाँ इन antonyms को सावधानी से पढ़ें :

Words	*Antonyms*	*Words*	*Antonyms*
above	below	attractive	repulsive
absence	presence	advantage	disadvantage
accept	reject	allow	disallow
advance	retreat	always	never
adversity	prosperity	appear	disappear
agree	differ	bad	good
alive	dead	barbarous	civilized
all	none	different	similar
amateur	professional	difficult	easy
analysis	synthesis	diligent	lazy
ancient	modern	divide	multiply
arrival	departure	dwarf	giant
artificial	natural	dry	wet
assemble	disperse	deposit	withdraw
attack (v)	defend (v)	early	late
attack (n)	defence (n)	empty	full
attract	repel	entrance	exit
buy	sell	enemy	friend
best	worst	export	import
bottom	top	encourage	discourage

Words	*Antonyms*	*Words*	*Antonyms*
barren	fertile	extravagant	frugal, economical
beauty	ugliness	ever	never
beneficial	harmful	false	true
beautiful	ugly	far	near
beginning	end	fat	thin
belief	doubt	foolish	wise
bitter	sweet	freedom	slavery
blessing	curse	fail	pass
blunt	sharp	familiar	unfamiliar
bold	timid	fast	slow
bright	dull	famous	notorious
broad	narrow	fresh	stale
brave	coward	first	last
care	neglect	free	bound
cheap	dear	fortunate	unfortunate
clean	dirty	forget	remember
clever	stupid	gain	loss
cruel	kind	great	small
common	rare, uncommon	general	particular
creation	destruction	guilty	innocent
cold	hot	good	bad
create	destroy	grant	refuse
credit	cash	guest	host
crude	refined	haste	delay
day	night	heavy	light
death	birth	honest	dishonest
deep	shallow, light	hope	despair
deficit	surplus	maximum	minimum
hate	love	mighty	weak
happy	unhappy	moral	immoral
hard	soft	mortal	immortal
harm	benefit	new	old
head	tail	normal	abnormal
healthy	diseased, unhealthy	natural	unnatural
heaven	hell	nothing	everything
high	low	obey	defy, disobey
hollow	solid	offer	refuse
honour	shame	optimism	pessimism
hope	despair		
humble	proud		

Words	*Antonyms*	*Words*	*Antonyms*
interesting	dull, uninteresting	optional	compulsory
intentional	accidental	oral	written
inferior	superior	ordinary	unique, rare
include	exclude	old	young
ignorance	knowledge	open	shut
important	unimportant	peace	war
idle	busy	please	displease
ill	well	pleasant	unpleasant
improve	deteriorate	permanent	temporary
joy	sorrow	presence	absence
junior	senior	punctual	late, unpunctual
justice	injustice	profit	loss
kind	cruel	punish	reward
lend	borrow	praise	defame
long	short	pure	mixed, impure
light	darkness, heavy	public	private
living	dead	part	whole
leader	follower	persuade	dissuade
lenient	strict	present	absent
liquid	solid	pride	humility
loose	tight	prompt	slow
love	hatred	question	answer
make	mar	quick	slow
male	female	rare	common
major	minor	real	unreal, imaginary
majority	minority	rear	front
masculine	feminine	remember	forget
master	servant	unite	separate
rich	poor	use	misuse
right	left, wrong	union	separation
rise	fall	vague	exact, clear
rough	smooth	victory	defeat
slow	fast	virtue	vice
sin	virtue	wet	dry
timid	fearless	win	lose
trust	distrust	weak	strong
thick	thin	wisdom	folly
tragedy	comedy		

trust	doubt distrust, mistrust	wise wide	foolish, unwise narrow
truth	falsehood	young	old

EXERCISE 1 (With Answer)

Give the antonyms of the following:

1. (i) ascent; bravery; industrious; negative; retail; sober; urban; virtue.
(ii) acquit; low; light; increase; ascend; near; enemy; misfortune.
(iii) vast; despair; haughty; rash; immediate.
(iv) warm; differ; great; mortal; natural; virtue; increase; active.
(v) attract; compulsory; diligent; friendly; oral.
(vi) accept; exit; rough; wise; synthesis; praise; hope; creation; complex; drunk; civilization.

Ans. (i) descent; cowardice; lazy; positive; wholesale; rash/drunk, rural; vice.
(ii) convict; up; heavy/darkness; decrease; descend; far; friend; fortune.
(iii) tiny; hope; humble; sober; distant.
(iv) cool; agree; small; immortal; unnatural; vice; decrease; passive/inactive.
(v) repel; optional; lazy; unfriendly; written.
(vi) reject; entrance; smooth/fair; foolish; analysis; defame; despair; destruction; simple; sober; barbarism.

(iii) SINGLE WORD FOR A GROUP OF WORDS

(अनेक शब्दों के लिए एक शब्द)

भाषा को प्रभावशाली बनाने के लिए अनेक शब्दों के लिए एक शब्द का प्रयोग किया जाता है। साथ ही, इसका अत्यधिक उपयोग precis-writing में होता है। आगे दिए गए single word for a group of words को याद कर लें :

1. A minister representing a state in a foreign country=**ambassador** (राजदूत)
2. One who has no belief in the existence of God = **atheist** (नास्तिक)
3. The yearly return of a date=**anniversary** (वार्षिकोत्सव)
4. An assembly of listeners=**audience** (श्रोतागण)
4. The life history of a person written by himself=**autobiography** (आत्मकथा)
5. One who has power over everything=**almighty** (सर्वशक्तिमान)
7. One who plays for pleasure=**amateur** (शौकीन)
8. Without the name of the author=**anonymous** (गुमनाम)
9. Being unable to pay one's debts=**bankrupt** (दिवालिया)
10. The science of vegetable life=**botany** (वनस्पति-विज्ञान)
11. The life history of a person written by another=**biography** (जीवनी)
12. One who breaks out into a house to steal= **burglar** (चोर)
13. A plot of land that does not grow anything=**barren** (बंजर)

14. A person who lives at the same time as another=**contemporary** (समकालीन)
15. Of or from all parts of the world=**cosmopolitan** (सर्वदेशीय)
16. One who eats human flesh=**cannibal** (नरभक्षी)
17. A person who collects fares on a public vehicle=**conductor** (मार्गदर्शक)
18. A place for burial of dead bodies=**cemetery** (कब्रिस्तान)
19. List of books or other articles=**catalogue** (सूचीपत्र)
20. A play which ends in love and marriage=**comedy** (प्रहसन सुखांत)
21. A period of hundred years=**century** (शताब्दी)
22. A man who cures diseases=**doctor** (डाक्टर)
23. Government by the representatives of the people=**democracy** (लोकतंत्र)
24. Government carried on by an absolute ruler=**dictatorship** (तानाशाही)
25. A language that is no longer spoken= **dead** (मृतक)
26. The result of a match in which neither party wins=**draw** (बराबरी)
27. The conduct which cannot be excused=**inexcusable** (अक्षम्य)
28. Fit to be eaten=**eatable, edible** (खाद्य)
29. Fit to be chosen=**eligible** (उपयुक्त)
30. Done off hands without notes=**extempore** (तात्कालिक)
31. A man who wastes his money on luxury=**extravagant** (अपव्ययी)
32. One who believes in fate=**fatalist** (भाग्यवादी)
33. Resulting in death=**fatal** (घातक)
34. Inhabitants of France=**French** (फ्रांसीसी)
35. An agent between two parties=**go-between** (मध्यस्थ)
36. An unexpected stroke of good fortune=**godsend, windfall** (ईश्वरीय वरदान)
37. Given or done without payments=**gratis** (मुफ्त में)

A post for which no salary is paid
38. Performing work without pay } =**honorary** (सम्मानार्थ, अवैतनिक)
39. Conferred as an honour

40. A day of rest from labour=**holiday** (छुट्टी)
41. Contrary to law=**illegal** (गैरकानूनी)
42. That which cannot be read=**illegible** (अस्पष्ट)
43. One who can neither read nor write=**illiterate** (अनपढ़)
44. That which cannot be heard=**inaudible** (अश्रव्य)
45. Incapable of being seen=**invisible** (अदृश्य)
46. Incapable of being dissolved=**insoluble** (अविलेय)
47. The plan that cannot be put into practice=**impracticable** (अव्यावहारिक)
48. Not possible to express=**inexpressible** (अकथनीय)
49. Bad beyond correction or reform=**incorrigible** (सुधारातीत)
50. One who makes a scientific study of language=**linguist** (भाषाविज्ञानी)
51. The science of reasoning=**logic** (तर्कशास्त्र)
52. A place where scientific experiments are done=**laboratory** (प्रयोगशाला)
53. A room containing many books=**library** (पुस्तकालय)
54. Acquainted with alphabet=**literate** (शिक्षित)

55. A cinema-show which is held in the daytime=**matinee** (अपराह्न का खेल)
56. Animals which feed their young with milk from the breast=**mammals** (स्तनपायी)
57. Shopkeeper who sells food and general small household requirements=**grocer** (पंसारी)
58. One who does not want to do any work=**idler** (आलसी आदमी)
59. A paper written by hand=**manuscript** (हस्तलिपि)
60. Subject to death=**mortal** (मरणशील)
61. One who saves money by starving oneself=**miser** (कंजूस)
62. Government by a king=**monarchy** (राजतंत्र)
63. Having an evil reputation=**notorious** (कुख्यात)
64. A child whose parents are dead=**orphan** (अनाथ)
65. One who makes a powerful public speech=**orator** (वक्ता)
66. That which is no longer in use=**obsolete** (अप्रचलित)
67. Present everywhere at the same time=**omnipresent** (सर्वव्यापी)
68. One who takes a bright view of things=**optimist** (आशावादी)
69. A man who loves his country=**patriot** (देशभक्त)
70. A man who takes a dark view of things=**pessimist** (निराशावादी)
71. Practice of having more than one wife at a time=**polygamy** (बहुविवाह)
72. Practice of having more than one husband at a time=**polyandry** (बहुपतित्व)
73. One who knows many languages=**polyglot** (बहुभाषी)
74. A man who is liked by everybody=**popular** (लोकप्रिय)
75. A cure for all diseases=**panacea** (रामबाण)
76. A child born after the death of his father or a book published after the death of its author=**posthumous** (मरणोत्तर)
77. That which lives on another=**parasite** (पराश्रयी)
78. One who sets questions=**question-setter** (प्रश्न चुननेवाला)
79. A four-sided figure whose every angle is a right angle=**rectangle** (आयत), **square** (वर्ग)
80. Happening at the same time=**simultaneously** (समक्षणिक)
81. The taking of one's own life
82. The murder of one's ownself } =**suicide** (आत्महत्या)
83. One who is made to suffer for another=**scapegoat** (बलि का बकरा)
84. One who speaks for others=**spokesman** (प्रवक्ता)
85. A room where an artist or a photographer works=**studio** (स्टुडियो)
86. One who believes in the existence of God=**theist** (ईश्वरवादी)
87. A three-sided figure=**triangle** (त्रिभुज)
88. An instrument for measuring temperature=**thermometer** (तापमापी)
89. A play which ends in death and sorrow=**tragedy** (दु:खान्त नाटक)
90. Belonging to or done by all persons or things in the world=**universal** (सार्वभौम)
91. All of one mind=**unanimous** (सर्वसम्मत)

92. A man who lives on vegetables=**vegetarian** (निरामिष)
93. The style which is too full of words=**verbose** (शब्दबहुल)
94. A man whose wife is dead=**widower** (विधुर)
95. A woman whose husband is **dead=widow** (विधवा)
96. Method of sending messages without the help of wires=**wireless** (बेतार) or **radio** (रेडियो)
97. A place where clothes are kept=**wardrobe** (अलमारी)
98. Science of the life of animals=**zoology** (प्राणिविज्ञान)
99. A place where birds and beasts are kept for public to see=**zoo** (चिड़ियाखाना)

EXERCISE 1 (With Answer)

1. *Choose the correct answer:*

(i) 1. A hater of learning and knowledge:

(a) misologist (b) misogynist (c) philanthropist (d) misanthropist

2. A person who is very fond of sensuous enjoyments:

(a) hedonist (b) lusty (c) stoic (d) epicure

3. A decision on which one cannot go back:

(a) invulnerable (b) incorrigible (c) irrevocable (d) infallible

Ans. 1.—(a); 2.—(d) 3.—(c).

(iv) The Same Word Used As Different Parts of Speech

Air —Birds fly in the *air* (वायुमंडल, आसमान). (N.)
The *air* (हवा) has become hot. (N.)
He likes to *air* (दूसरों को दिखाना) his knowledge. (V.)

Arm —The old man was leaning on my *arm* (बाँह). (N.)
We must *arm* (हथियार से लैस होना/करना) the people living in the border areas. (V.)

Bank —The river is eroding its *bank* (किनारा). (N.)
I opened an account with a local *bank* (बैंक). (N.)
I *bank* (निर्भर करना) on your support. (V.)

Bark —The *bark* (छाल) of this tree is very useful. (N.)
His *bark* (भूँकना) is worse than his bite. (N.)
Dogs *bark* (भूँकना) at night. (V.)

Bat —In cricket the ball is hit with the *bat* (बल्ला). (N.)
Bats (चमगादड़) can see in the dark. (N.)
Kapil *batted* (बल्लेबाजी किया) well on a turning wicket. (V.)

Bear —The *bear* (भालू) is a hairy animal. (N.)
He could not *bear* (सहना) the pain. (V.)
This tree now *bears* (उत्पन्न करना) fruit. (V.)

Boil —In summer we usually have *boils* (घाव). (N.)
To prepare tea, you have to *boil* (उबालना) the water. (V.)

Box —He packed the books in a wooden *box* (बक्सा). (N.)
Do you *box* (मुक्का मारना, मुक्केबाजी करना) ? (V.)

Battle—A serious *battle* (लड़ाई) has taken place. (N.)
He *battled* (लड़ा) hard against the enemy. (V.)

Back —I lifted him on my *back* (पीठ) . (N.)
I will *back* (मदद करना) you in your plan. (V.)
He came in through the *back* (पिछला) door. (Adj.)
They will come *back* (लौटना) soon. (Adv.)

Bell —The *bell* (घंटी) is gone. (N.)
Who will *bell* (घंटी बाँधना) the cat? (V.)

Book —I have a new *book* (पुस्तक). (N.)
Please *book* (बुक करना) my luggage. (V.)

Bridge—He crossed the *bridge* (पुल). (N.)
Let us *bridge* (पुल बाँधना) the gap here. (V.)

Button—I have bought a costly *button* (बटन) . (N.)
Please *button* (बटन लगाना) up your shirt. (V.)

Capital—Delhi is the *capital* (राजधानी) of India. (N.)
I need more *capital* (पूँजी) to run my business. (N.)
It was a *capital* (बहुत अच्छा) joke. (Adj.)

Drink—We must avoid strong *drink* (मादक पेय पदार्थ). (N.)
We shall die without food and *drink* (पानी) . (N.)
I *drink* (पीना) a glass of milk in the morning. (V.)

Face —Wash your *face* (चेहरा) . (N.)
You have to *face* (झेलना, सामना करना) difficulty. (V.)

Fair —Sonepur *fair* (मेला) is one of the biggest fairs in Asia. (N.)
He is *fair* (न्यायपूर्ण) in his dealings. (Adj.)
She has a *fair* (साफ) complexion. (Adj.)
Make a *fair* (साफ) copy of this letter. (Adj.)
Be polite to the *fair* sex. (औरतें) . (Adj.)

Fan —I have a new ceiling *fan* (पंखा) . (N.)
I am a cricket *fan* (भक्त, शौकीन) . (N.)
Her rudeness *fanned* (उत्तेजित किया) our anger. (V.)
She was *fanning* (पंखा करना, हवा करना) her face with a newspaper. (V.)

Fast —We must observe *fast* (उपवास) once a week. (N.)
It is a *fast* (तेज) train. (Adj.)
The colour of this *sari* is *fast* (पक्का) . (Adj.)

Fine —The headmaster imposed a *fine* (जुरमाना) on the boy. (N.)
He was *fined* (जुरमाना किया गया) five rupees. (V.)
It was a *fine* (सुंदर) sight. (Adj.)

Head —He was hit on the *head* (सिर) . (N.)

Head (सिर से मारना) the ball. (V.)
He is the *head* (बड़ा) clerk. (Adj.)

House—He has no *house* (घर) to live in. (N.)
Our college is *housed* (आश्रय दिया) in a rented building. (V.)

Light —We get *light* (प्रकाश) from the sun. (N.)
Please *light* (जलाना) the lamp. (V.)
I want a *light* (हल्की) car. (Adj.)

Lock —She has lovely *locks* (गुच्छे) of hair. (N.)
I want a new *lock* (ताला). (N.)
Please *lock* (ताला बंद करना) the door. (V.)

Milk —*Milk* (दूध) is sweet. (N.)
Please *milk* (दुहना) the cow. (V.)

Ring —He has a gold *ring* (अंगूठी). (N.)
The bell *rings* (बजना) at 10 am. (V.)
Ring (टेलिफोन करना) me up tomorrow. (V.)

Rule —We must follow the *rules* (नियम) of the game. (N.)
Ashoka *ruled* (शासन किया) over a large empire. (V.)

Wrong—It is a *wrong* (गलत) answer. (Adj.)
He *wronged* (बेइंसाफी किया) me by saying I could never improve my work. (V.)
You have spelt the word *wrong* (गलत ढंग से). (Adv.)
He was in the *wrong* (गलती). (N).

(V) WORD-FORMATION

किसी शब्द के मूल रूप के पहले या बाद में एक small unit जोड़कर हम नया शब्द बनाते हैं जिसे word-formation (शब्द-निर्माण) कहते हैं। Word-formation के मुख्य सिद्धांत हैं :

(a) **Prefix:** Prefix (उपसर्ग) एक syllable है जिसे किसी शब्द के पहले लगाकर एक नया शब्द बनाते हैं। जैसे :

un+happy=unhappy   **Pre+historic=prehistoric**
im+possible=impossible   **in+decent=indecent**

(b) **Suffix:** Prefix की तरह suffix (प्रत्यय) भी एक syllable है जिसे शब्द के अंत में लगाकर एक नया शब्द बनाया जाता है। जैसे :

memory+ize =memorize   **capital+ism=capitalism**
kind+ness=kindness   **mile+age=mileage**

(c) **Conversion:** Conversion वह प्रक्रिया है जिसके द्वारा बिना prefix या suffix लगाए किसी शब्द के form-class या part of speech को बदल दिया जाता है। जैसे :

I *walk* to college every day. (verb)
I take a long *walk* every morning. (noun)

(d) **Compounding:** जब दो या दो से अधिक root form को मिलाकर एक word बनाया जाता है तब उसे compounding कहते हैं। Compounding में दो शब्दों के बीच कभी

hyphen (-) दिया जाता है, कभी दोनों को अलग-अलग लिखा जाता है, तो कभी उन्हें मिलाकर एक बना दिया जाता है। जैसे :

tax+free=*tax-free* (hyphen)
reading+room=*reading room* (no hyphen)
bed+room=*bedroom* (as one word)

(e) **Clipping:** कभी-कभी शब्दों के कुछ भाग को हटाकर नए शब्द बनाए जाते हैं। जैसे : telephone=*phone*
moving pictures=*movies or pictures*
microphone=*mike*

(f) **Blending:** कभी-कभी दो शब्दों को मिलाकर एक नया शब्द बनाया जाता है। जैसे :

breakfast and lunch=*brunch*
rural and urban=*rurban*
motorist's hotel=*motel*

अब और कुछ विस्तार से देखें कि अँगरेजी में word-formation prefix और suffix की सहायता से किस प्रकार होता है।

(a) Prefix + Words

1. **im** —im + pure = impure, im + possible = impossible, imperfect, impolite, improper.
2. **in** —in + decent = indecent, in + discipline = indiscipline, imcomplete, ineffective, invisible.
3. **ir** —ir + religious = irreligious, ir + responsible = irresponsible, irrelevant, irrespective, irregular.
4. **il** —il + logical = illogical, il + legible = illegible, illegitimate, illegal, illiterate.
5. **re** —re + build = rebuild, re + write = rewrite, recall, refund, renew, reclaim.
6. **em** —em + power = empower, em + bark = embark, embody, emplane.
7. **en** —en + danger = endanger, en + able = enable, enlist, enslave, enrich.
8. **de** —de + code = decode, de + value = devalue, deform, defame, demoralize.
9. **un** —un + happy = unhappy, un + expected = unexpected, untie, uncover, unable, unnatural, undo.
10. **dis** —dis + please = displease, dis + honest = dishonest, disrespect, dishonour, dislike, disappear.
11. **mis** —mis + lead = mislead, mis + trust = mistrust, misdeed, misjudge, misconduct.
12. **Pre** —pre+fix = prefix, pre + mature = premature, pre- school, pre-war, predict, prepaid.
13. **non** —non + sense = nonsense, non + gazetted = non-gazetted, non-vegetarian, non-co-operation non-violent.

14. **mini** —mini + car = mini-car, mini + skirt = mini-skirt, mini-computer, mini-house.

15. **semi** —semi + circle = semi-circle, semi + darkness = semi-darkness, semicolon.

16. **vice** —vice + president = vice-president, vice + principal = vice-principal, vice-chairman.

(b) Words + Suffix

1. **age** —leak + age = leakage, break + age = breakage, marriage, mileage, bondage.
2. **ar/er/or** —beg + ar = beggar, speak + er = speaker, sail + or = sailor, writer, orator, actor.
3. **ed** —hunt + ed = hunted, gift + ed = gifted, learned, talented.
4. **ist** —social + ist = socialist, loyal + ist = loyalist, Buddhist, communist, novelist, artist.
5. **ing** —Paint + ing = painting, swim + ing = swimming, gardening, speaking, reading.
6. **ism** —patriot + ism = patriotism, Hndu + ism = Hinduism, socialism.
7. **al** —arrive + al = arrival, propose + al = proposal, dismissal, denial.
8. **an/en** —India + an = Indian, America + an = American, wide + en = widen, broaden, quicken, golden.
9. **ic** —hero + ic = heroic, phonetic, cynic, logic, critic.
10. **ish** —fat + ish = fattish, boy + ish = boyish, selfish, greenish, girlish, reddish.
11. **less** —fear + less = fearless, hope + less = hopeless, senseless, childless.
12. **ful** —mouth + ful = mouthful, hand + ful = handful, hopeful, joyful, fruitful, fearful.
13. **ify** —beauty + fy = beautify, simple + fy = simplify, modify.
14. **ee** —pay + ee = payee, employee, nominee.
15. **ess** —lion + ess = lioness, actress.
16. **en** —maid + en = maiden, chicken.
17. **hood** —boy + hood = boyhood, childhood, manhood, girlhood.
18. **dom** —free + dom = freedom, kingdom, wisdom.
19. **ly** —easy + ly = easily, happily, greatly.
20. **ship** —friend + ship = friendship, headship, membership, hardship, lectureship.
21. **ness** —happy + ness = happiness, kindness, loveliness. darkness, boldness, goodness.
22. **ly, like** —man + ly = manly, child + like = childlike, brotherly, godly.

23. ion —act + ion = action, tension, expression, oration.

24. ment —pay + ment = payment, agreement, punishment, movement.

25. y —sand + y = sandy, hairy, creamy, wealthy, windy, dirty, needy, greedy.

अब देखें कि suffix या prefix की सहायता से एक प्रकार के शब्द दूसरे प्रकार में किस प्रकार बदल जाते हैं :

1. verb + er/or/ion/al/age/=noun

paint + er = painter, writer, learner, speaker
act + or = actor, dictator, narrator, supervisor
select + ion = selection, collection, completion, connection
arrive + al = arrival, approval, dismissal, refusal
marry + age = marriage, carriage, breakage, leakage

2. verb + tion/sion/ment/ance/ence/ure = noun

attract + ion = attraction, collection, connection, perfection
admit + sion = admission, decision
pay + ment = payment, agreement, appointment, achievement
assist + ance = assistance, acceptance, allowance, appearance
depend + ence = dependence, difference, existence, excellence
fail + ure = failure, departure, pleasure, procedure

3. Adjective + ness/ity/dom/cy/ty/ = noun

kind + ness = kindness, dullness, goodness, darkness
active + ity = activity, ability, reality, brutality
wise + dom = wisdom, freedom, martyrdom
accurate + cy = accuracy, privacy, urgency
cruel + ty = cruelty, royalty, safety

4. noun + al/ent/ful/less/ly = adjective

accident + al = accidental, cultural, natural, philosophical
gold + en = golden, wooden, woollen, earthen
beauty + ful = beautiful, hopeful, joyful, useful
care + less = careless, fearless, shameless, hopeless
brother + ly = brotherly, manly, cowardly

5. noun + ish/y/ic/some/like = adjective

boy + ish = boyish, childish, foolish, selfish
air + y = airy, wealthy, healthy, greeedy, dirty
artist + ic = artistic, heroic, scientific, dramatic
burden + some = burdensome, quarrelsome, troublesome
child + like = childlike, warlike, businesslike

6. noun + ify/en/ize = verb

beauty + ify = beautify, classify, electrify, personify
black + en = blacken, lighten, redden, frighten
capital + ize = capitalize, centralize, criticize, nationalize

7. adjective + en/ify/ize = verb

broad + en = broaden, deepen, darken, harden
false + ify = falsify, clarify, justify, purify
equal + ize = equalize, fertilize, generalize, familiarize

8. adjective + ly = adverb

bold + ly = boldly, easily, happily, quickly, slowly

9. be/em/en + noun/adjective = verb

befriend, becalm, empower, enrol, enable, enslave

□□□

18. SPELLING RULES

(I) Importance of Correct English

Correct writing के लिए सही spelling का ज्ञान अत्यावश्यक है। Bad spelling का प्रभाव परीक्षक पर बुरा पड़ता है और इससे छात्रों की निरक्षरता, अज्ञानता तथा असावधानी का बोध होता है। Correct spelling लिखने के लिए निम्नलिखित बातों का ध्यान रखें :

(i) आप dictionary हमेशा रखें तथा जब कभी किसी word के spelling में संदेह हो उसे dictionary में देख लें।

(ii) जिन शब्दों के spelling में आप अकसर भूल करते हैं उनका list बना लें तथा उन्हें सही लिखने का बार-बार अभ्यास करें।

(iii) Spelling के कुछ मुख्य नियमों को याद रखें तथा spelling लिखने में उनकी सहायता लें।

(iv) Formation of words की जानकारी रखें।

(v) शब्दों के pronunciation पर सावधानी बरतें, कभी-कभी गलत pronunciation से भी spelling गलत हो जाता है।

(vi) अपनी पुस्तकों को पढ़ते समय spelling को चिह्नित कर दें; ऐसा अभ्यास correct spelling लिखने में बड़ी मदद करेगा।

Spelling is a matter of sight, so train your eye to notice words carefully.

(II) Introduction

(i) **Vowels:** *a e i o u*

(ii) **Consonants:** *b c d f g h j k l m n p q r s t v w x y z*

(iii) **Suffix:** एक group of letters जो किसी word के अंत में जोड़ा जाता है, उसे suffix कहते हैं। जैसे : beauty, beautiful (ful यहाँ suffix है।)

(A) Spelling : dubling of 'l'

Rule 1. बहुत सारे words के अंत में *ll* रहता है जब उन्हें compound word बनाते हैं तब उनमें से एक *l* हट जाता है। जैसे :

a*l*most	doubtfu*l*	fulf*il*	we*l*fare
a*l*ways	usefu*l*	unt*il*	enr*ol*
a*l*ready	beautifu*l*	we*l*come	inst*il*
a*l*though	a*l*together	sk*il*ful	dist*il*

अपवाद : *all* right; *all* round; farewe*ll*; we*ll*-being; spe*ll*bound; unro*ll*

Rule 2. अगर किसी शब्द के अंत में l हो और उसके पहले कोई एक vowel हो तो उस 'l' को double कर दिया जाता है जब 'l' के बाद पुन: कोई vowel आए। जैसे :

quarrel	quarre*ll*ed / quarre*ll*ing	travel	trave*ll*ed / trave*ll*ing
equal	equa*ll*ed	level	leve*ll*ed / leve*ll*ing
expel	expe*ll*ed	cancel	cance*ll*ed / cance*ll*ing
jewel	jeweller	model	mode*ll*ed / mode*l(l)*ing

अपवाद : parallel paralleled peril perilous

(B) Spelling : Doubling Consonants

Rule 3. कुछ words एके syllable के होते हैं जिनके अंत में एक consonant रहता है और उस consonant के पहले एक vowel रहता है। अगर final consonant के बाद कोई vowel letter से suffix लगे तो उस consonant को double कर दिया जाता है। जैसे :

get	ge*tt*ing	put	pu*tt*ing
plan	pla*nn*ing / pla*nn*ed	drop	dro*pp*ing / dro*pp*ed
stop	sto*pp*ing / sto*pp*ed	commit	commi*tt*ing / commi*tt*ed
begin	begi*nn*ing	run	ru*nn*ing
transfer	transfe*rred* / transfe*rring*	war	wa*rr*ing
wool	woo*ll*en	worship	worshi*pp*ed / worshi*pp*er
prefer	prefe*rr*ed (but *preference*)	refer	refe*rr*ed / refe*rr*ing (but *reference*)

अपवाद :

suffer	suffe*r*ed	offer	offe*r*ed / offe*r*ing
benefit	benefi*t*ed	differ	diffe*r*ed

Note : *dine—dining—dinner*

picnic—picnic*k*ers—picnic*k*ing—picnic*k*ed

final—*c* is changed to *-ck* before—*ed, -ing, -er*

(C) Spelling : the final *y* and *i*

Rule 4. कभी-कभी किसी शब्द के अंत में 'y' रहता है। अगर 'y' के पहले कोई consonant रहे और 'y' के बाद कोई ending आए (-ing को छोड़कर) तो 'y' को 'i' में बदल दिया जाता है। जैसे :

cry	crying/cr*i*ed	try	trying/tr*i*ed
happy	happ*i*ness/happ*i*ly	apply	applying/appl*i*ed
study	stud*i*ed	marry	marrying/marr*i*ed/ marr*i*age

mercy	merc*i*ful	easy	eas*i*ly, eas*i*er
pity	pit*i*ful	carry	carr*y*ing/carr*i*ed
penny	penn*i*less	busy	bus*i*ness

अपवाद :

copy	cop*y*ing/cop*y*ist	baby	bab*yish*
try	try*ing*	study	study*ing*

Rule 5. अगर 'y' के पहले कोई vowel आए तो उसे प्राय: 'i' में नहीं बदल जाता। जैसे :

play	pla*y*ing/pla*y*ed	grey	gre*y*ing
buy	bu*y*ing/bu*y*er	stay	sta*y*ing/sta*y*ed
pay	pa*y*ment/pa*y*able	obey	obe*y*ed
pray	pra*y*ed/pra*y*ing	journey	journe*y*ed
betray	betra*y*ed	boy	bo*y*ish
grey	gre*y*ish	enjoy	enjo*y*ment

अपवाद :

say	sa*i*d/says	pay	pa*i*d/pays
day	da*i*ly	lay	la*i*d/lays

Rule 6. Plural बनाने या simple present tense में third person singular बनाने में—

(i) अगर 'y' के पहले कोई consonant रहे तो 'y' को 'i' में बदलकर उसमें 'es' जोड़ते हैं;

(ii) अगर 'y' के बाद पहले कोई vowel letter रहे तो 'y' के बाद केवल 's' जोड़ा जाता है। जैसे :

(i) study	stud*ies*	(ii) buy	buy*s*
spy	sp*ies*	ray	ray*s*
cry	cr*ies*	key	key*s*
baby	bab*ies*	monkey	monkey*s*
supply	suppl*ies*	day	day*s*
story	stor*ies*	joy	joy*s*
victory	victor*ies*	donkey	donkey*s*

(D) Spelling : word ending with *e*

Rule 7. कुछ शब्दों के अंत में 'e' रहता है। अगर ऐसे शब्दों के अंत में कोई vowel से शुरू होनेवाला ending जोड़ा जाए तो पहले वाला 'e' हट जाता है। जैसे :

live	living	bite	biting
move	moving/movable	love	loving/lovable
value	valuable	blame	blaming
issue	issuing	achieve	achieving
come	coming	hope	hoping
fame	famous	make	making
note	notable	refuse	refusing

Rule 8. अगर शब्द के अंत में '-ge' या '-ce' रहे तो 'e' को नहीं हटाया जाता जब उसके बाद कोई ending ('-e' या '-i' को छोड़कर) जोड़ा जाता हो। जैसे :

change	changing/chang*e*able	charge	charg*e*able
manage	manag*e*able	service	servic*e*able
marriage	marriag*e*able	notice	notic*e*able
advantage	advantag*e*ous	courage	courag*e*ous
replace	replac*e*able		

Rule 9. अगर किसी शब्द के अंत में '-ee', '-le' या '-ye' रहे और उसके बाद कोई ending (-ed) को छोड़कर) जोड़ा जाए तो final 'e' को नहीं हटाया जाता। जैसे :

see	se*e*ing	agree	agre*e*ing/agre*e*able
sale	sal*e*able	guarantee	guarante*e*ing
free	fre*e*ing	dye	dy*e*ing
eye	eye*i*ng		

Rule 10. कुछ शब्दों के अंत में आनेवाले 'e' को हटा दिया जाता है अगर उसके बाद कोई consonant ending (consonant से शुरू होनेवाला कोई suffix) लगे। जैसे :

argue	argument	simple	simply
true	truly	whole	wholly
awe	awful	nurse	nursing
due	duly		

अपवाद :

achieve	achiev*e*ment	hope	hop*e*ful
excite	excit*e*ment	nice	nic*e*ly

Note: (i) अगर कोई शब्द '-ie' से अंत हो और जब उसमें -ing जोड़ा जाए तो '-ie' को 'y' में बदल दिया जाता है। जैसे :

die	dying	tie	tying
lie	lying	vie	vying

(ii) निम्नलिखित शब्दों के final 'e' को रखा जा सकता है या हटा भी दिया जा सकता है। जैसे :

like	lik*a*ble	lik*e*able
mile	mil*a*ge	mil*e*age
judge	judgment	judg*e*ment
abridge	abridgment	abridg*e*ment
acknowledge	acknowledgment	acknowledg*e*ment

Rule 11. कुछ शब्दों के अंत में 'our' रहता है। English writers 'u' को रखते हैं किंतु American writers 'u' को हटा देते हैं। जैसे :

col*our*, favo*ur*, favo*u*rite, hono*ur*, humo*ur*,
labo*ur*, neighbo*ur*, rumo*ur*, behavio*ur*

Note: Laborious, honorary, vigorous, rigorous, vaporise में 'u' को British spelling में भी हटा दिया जाता है।

(E) Spelling: -ise and -ize

Rule 12. British English में अधिकांश शब्द जिनके अंत में -ise रहता है उन्हें -ize से भी लिखा जाता है। कुछ वैसे या उससे मिलते-जुलते शब्द देखें :

mechani*s*e	mechanize	reali*s*e	realize
computeri*s*e	computerize	analy*s*e	analyze

अपवाद : surprise, advertise

(F) Spelling: with suffix *ful*

Rule 13. (a) जब कभी 'full' किसी शब्द में जोड़ा जाता है तब दूसरा 'l' हटा दिया जाता है। जैसे : use + full = useful (लेकिन Adverb के रूप में usefully होता है।)

beauty + full = beaufiful (लेकिन Adverb form में beautifully होता है।)

(b) जब किसी शब्द के अंत में 'll' हो तो suffix लगाने के पहले दूसरा 'l' हटा दिया जाता है। जैसे :

skill + full = skilful

Note: full + fill = fulfil

(G) Spelling : some typical words

Rule 14. निम्नलिखित शब्दों के spelling पर ध्यान दें।

(a)	leave	live	piece	peace
	loose	lose	refuse	refuge
	new	knew	sole	soul
	no	know	steal	steel
	task	tusk	then	than
(b)	fifth	eighth	ninth	twelfth

(H) Spelling : British and American English

Rule 15.

(a) American English में final 'l' को double नहीं किया जाता। जैसे : traveler, leveling किंतु British English में—traveller, levelling लिखा जाता है।

(b) American English में कुछ शब्दों के अंत में -ter रहता है, किंतु British English में -tre रहता है। जैसे :

American: theater, center. *British*: theatre, centre.

(c) कुछ शब्दों के अंत में American English में -or रहता है, किंतु British English में -our रहता है। जैसे :

American: labor, honor, color. *British :* labour, honour, colour.

(d) American English में कुछ शब्दों के अंत में -og रहता है, किंतु British English में -ogue रहता है। जैसे :

American: catalog, dialog. *British*: catalogue, dialogue.

(e) बहुत सारे verbs के अंत में American English में -ize रहता है, किंतु British English में -ize या -ise रहता है। जैसे : *American:* realize. *British:* realize, realise.

(f) कुछ और American तथा British English में words के spelling की भिन्नता को देखें :

American	*British*	*American*	*British*
tire	tyre (*on a car*)	analyze	analyse
jail	jail, gaol	pajamas	pyjamas
program	programme	jewelry	jewellery
defense	defence	check	cheque (*from a bank*)
practice (verb)	practise	aluminum	aluminium

Note: India में हमलोग British English लिखते तथा बोलते हैं। अत:, आप British spelling ही लिखें।

EXERCISE 1

Write out the following forms correctly:

EXAMPLES : hit+ing=*hitting* compel+ing=*compelling*
fit+ed=*fitted* compel+ed=*compelled*

A. 1. *hit+ing* 2. *fit+ed* 3. *compel+ing* 4. *compel+ed*
5. *merry+er* 6. *cut+ing* 7. *journey+ing* 8. *visit+ed*
9. *company+s* 10. *valley+s* 11. *beauty+ful* 12. *knife+s*
13. *belief+s* 14. *busy+ness* 15. *craze+y* 16. *continue+ing*
17. *visit+or* 18. *come+ing* 19. *write+ing* 20. *propose+al*

EXERCISE 2

1. *Add—ing and—ed to the following:*

EXAMPLES: offer+ing=*offering* refer+ing=r*eferring*
offer+ed=*offered* refer+ed=*referred*

(a) offer, refer, conquer, bar, parallel, annual
(b) omit, commit, benefit, admit, regret, cry

2. *Add—ing to the following:*

(a) get, run, cut, shut, sit, dig
(b) begin, eat, sing, swim, forget, meet

3. *Add—ly to the following:*

(a) cruel, whole, true, happy, real, simple

EXERCISE 3

Add the endings given to the following words:

EXAMPLES : marry—age=*marriage* big—er=*bigger*
body—ly=*bodily* hot—est=*hottest*

(A) marry—age big—er hot—est fulfil—ed
body—ly win—er sun—y jewel—er

pay—ment	rub—er	begin—ing	fail—ure
study—ous	mud—y	omit—ed	travel—er

EXERCISE 4

Correctly spell each of the following words:

EXAMPLES :	totaly—*totally*	cought—*caught*	
	poltics—*politics*	faimly—*family*	
(A) totaly	cought	sugest	privious
thier	villeg	freind	profite
chife	maried	posible	mater
maney	colleg	realy	addmission

EXERCISE 5 (With Answer)

1. *Correctly spell the following words:*

Commitee; nursary; humerous, miscelanous; privilige; consious; occurance; maintainance.

Ans. 1. Committee; nursery; humorous; miscellaneous; privilege; conscious; occurrence; maintenance.

□□□

19. ADJECTIVES/DETERMINERS

(A) ADJECTIVES

1. *Look at these sentences:*

Rohan is a *smart* boy.	It is a *nice* house.
Priya is a *beautiful* girl.	Delhi is a *big* city.

(i) इन वाक्यों में आए शब्द *smart, beautiful, nice* तथा *big* Adjectives हैं।

(ii) ये शब्द अपने बाद आए Nouns क्रमश: boy, girl, house तथा city का वर्णन करते हैं।

(iii) Adjectives बताते हैं कि boy, girl, house तथा city किस प्रकार के हैं।

(iv) जो शब्द किसी व्यक्ति, चीज, घटना आदि का वर्णन करे, उसे Adjective कहते हैं।

An *adjective* is a word which describes people, things, events, etc.

'An adjective describes something (it tells us what something is like).'

—JOHN EASTWOOD: OXFORD PRACTICE GRAMMAR

(B) KINDS OF ADJECTIVES

Adjectives के आठ भेद होते हैं :

1. Adjectives of Quality

2. *Look at these sentences:*

Rahul is a *tall* boy.	He is an *old* man.
Lata is a *sweet* girl.	She has a *blue* car.

(i) इन वाक्यों में आए शब्द *tall, sweet, old* तथा *blue* Adjectives हैं।

(ii) इनका प्रयोग कर Nouns के गुण (quality), अवस्था (condition) तथा रंग (colour) का वर्णन करते हैं।

(iii) इन्हें Adjectives of Quality कहते हैं। इनका दूसरा नाम Descriptive Adjectives भी है।

(iv) वैसे Adjectives जो किसी व्यक्ति या वस्तु के आकार, गुण, अवस्था, रंग आदि का वर्णन करते हों, Adjectives of Quality कहलाते हैं।

(v) कुछ और Adjectives of Quality इस प्रकार हैं:

(a) **quality:** *true, untrue, false, difficult, interesting, etc.*

(b) **colour:** *blue, red, green, white, black, dark, light, etc.*

(c) **condition:** *good, bad, new, old, clean, dirty, fresh, strong, weak, happy, healthy, noisy, etc.*

(d) **taste:** *sweet, sour, bitter, etc.*

(e) **size:** *long, small, tall, high, short, wide, narrow, thick, thin, etc.*

(f) **shape:** *round, flat, square, circular, blunt, even, etc.*

(g) **feeling:** *hard, soft, dry, wet, hot, loud, etc.*

(h) **behaviour:** *kind, cruel, gentle, polite, rude, careful, naughty, clever, etc.*

(i) **general impression of a person or thing:** *nice, nasty, pretty, beautiful, smart, big, great, pleasant, little, etc.*

2. Adjectives of Quantity

3. *Look at these sentences:*

I want *some* sugar. He spent *all* the money.

I do not drink *much* tea. We have not *enough* food.

(i) इन वाक्यों में आए शब्द *some, much, all* तथा *enough* से किसी चीज या पदार्थ की मात्रा (quantity) का बोध होता है।

(ii) इन्हें Adjectives of Quantity कहते हैं।

(iii) Adjectives of Quantity का प्रयोग Uncountable Nouns के पहले होता है।

(iv) ऐसे Adjectives को जिनसे मात्रा (quantity) का बोध हो. Adjectives of Quantity कहते हैं।

(v) ये शब्द भी Adjectives of Quantity हैं : *any, little, less, more, most, no, whole, sufficient, a lot of, lots of, plenty of, a great deal of.*

3. Adjectives of Number

4. *Look at these sentences:*

I have *two* brothers. She got the *first* prize.

He has *many* books. He was the *second* man to go.

(i) इन वाक्यों में *two, many, first, second* से संख्या या क्रम का बोध होता है।

(ii) इन्हें Adjectives of Number कहते हैं या इन्हें Numeral Adjectives भी कहा जाता है।

(iii) *Two, many* से व्यक्ति या वस्तु की संख्या (number) का बोध होता है और *first, second* से उनके क्रम (order) का।

(iv) कुछ और Adjectives of Number इस प्रकार हैं :

all, any, both, enough, each, every, either, neither, few, fewer, more, most, several, some, no, one, two, etc., a lot of, lots of, plenty of, a number of, a large number of.

Note: (i) *all, some, enough* आदि के प्रयोग जब किसी Countable Nouns के साथ होते हैं, तब इन्हें Adjectives of Number कहा जाता है :

all/some/ enough/ any, etc. + countable noun = adj. of number

(ii) जब *all, some, enough* आदि का प्रयोग किसी Uncountable Nouns के साथ होता है, तब उन्हें Adjectives of Quantity कहा जाता है :

all/some/ enough/any, etc. + uncountable noun = adj. of quantity

Adjectives of Number	**Adjectives of Quantity**
All children like playing.	He lost **all** his **wealth.**
I saw **some people** I knew.	**Some money** will be needed.

4. Demonstrative Adjectives

5. *Look at these sentences:*

Demonstrative Adjectives	*Demonstrative Pronouns*
This book is mine.	*This* is a book.
That bird is small.	*That* is a bird.

(i) बायीं ओर के वाक्यों में *This, That* के बाद Nouns—(book, bird) आए हैं।

(ii) यहाँ *This, That* को Demonstrative Adjectives कहते हैं।

(iii) दाहिनी ओर के वाक्यों में *This, That* के तुरंत बाद Nouns नहीं है।

(iv) अत: *This, That* को Demonstrative Pronouns कहा जाता है।

(v) जब *this, that, these, those* के बाद कोई Noun रहे, तब *this, that, these, those* को Demonstrative Adjective कहते हैं :

this, that, these, those + noun = Demonstrative Adj.

(vi) ये हैं Demonstrative Adjectives:

this, that, these, those, such, same.

5. Interrogative Adjectives

6. *Look at these sentences:*

Interrogative Adjectives	*Interrogative Pronouns*
What name did you say?	*What* is your name?
Whose toys are here?	*Whose* is the toy?
Which way shall we go?	*Which* is your house?

(i) बायीं ओर के वाक्यों में *what, whose, which* के बाद Nouns (name, toys, way) आए हैं तथा इनसे प्रश्न पूछे गए हैं।

(ii) अत: what, whose, which को Interrogative Adjectives कहते हैं।

(iii) दाहिनी ओर के वाक्यों में what, whose, which के बाद Nouns नहीं हैं।

(iv) जिस Adjective के साथ Noun का प्रयोग कर प्रश्न पूछा जाए उसे Interrogative Adjectives कहते हैं :

what, whose, what + noun = Interrogative Adj.

6. Possessive Adjectives

7. *Look at these sentences:*

Possessive Adjectives	*Possessive Pronouns*
My coat is here.	This is *mine*.
Your shirt is there.	That is *yours*.

(i) बायीं ओर के वाक्यों में *my, your* के बाद Noun (*coat/shirt*) का प्रयोग किया गया है।

(ii) इस *my, your* से अधिकार या संबंध का भाव व्यक्त होता है—इनहें Possessive Adjectives कहते हैं।

(iii) किंतु *mine, yours* के बाद किसी Noun का प्रयोग नहीं किया जाता, अत: इन्हें Possessive Pronouns कहते हैं।

(iv) *My, your, our, his, her, its, their* से अधिकार या संबंध का भाव व्यक्त होता है, इन्हें Possessive Adjectives कहते हैं :

my, your, our, his, her, its, their + noun = Possessive Adj.

7. Distributive Adjectives

8. *Look at these sentences:*

Distributive Adjectives	*Distributive Pronouns*
Each man may try twice.	*Each* got a pen.
Every child is happy.	*Either* will do.
Neither statement is true.	*Neither* was present.

(i) बायीं ओर के वाक्यों में *Each, Every, Neither* के बाद Nouns (man, child, statement) आए हैं।

(ii) अत: each, every, neither को Distributive Adjectives कहते हैं।

(iii) किंतु दायीं ओर के वाक्यों में *Each, Either, Neither* के बाद कोई Noun नहीं आया है। अत: ये Distributive Pronouns हैं।

(iv) वैसे Adjectives जो दो या दो से अधिक व्यक्तियों या वस्तुओं में से 'प्रत्येक' (each one) का बोध कराते हैं, उन्हें Distributive Adjectives कहते हैं।

each, every, neither, either + noun = Distributive Adj.

8. Proper Adjectives

9. *Look at these sentences:*

Proper Nouns	*Proper Adjectives*
He lives in *India.*	He is an *Indian.*
He belongs to *Bihar.*	He is a *Bihari.*
Tom comes from *Britain.*	He has a *British passport.*

(i) *India, Bihar, Britain*—Proper Nouns हैं।

(ii) इन शब्दों से बने *Indian, Bihari, British*—Adjectives हैं। इनको Proper Adjectives कहते हैं :

(iii) Proper Noun से बने Adjective को Proper Adjective कहते हैं।

(iv) कुछ Proper Adjectives इस प्रकार हैं :

Africa-African (अफ्रीकी)	England-English (अँगरेजी)
America-American (अमरीकी)	China-Chinese (चीनी)
Bengal-Bengali (बंगाली)	Japan-Japanese (जापानी)
Britain-British (बर्तानी)	Pakistan-Pakistani (पाकिस्तानी)
France-French (फ्रांसीसी)	Nepal-Nepalese (नेपाली)

Note: Proper Noun की तरह Proper Adjective भी capital letter से ही प्रारंभ होते हैं।

(C) AGREEMENT

10. *Look at these sentences:*

I am a *good boy.*	I am a *good girl.*
We are *good boys.*	We are *good girls.*

(i) ऊपर *good* Adjective है जिसके रूप (form) में कोई परिवर्तन नहीं हुआ।

(ii) Singular और Plural, Masculine और Feminine Noun के पहले या बाद में प्रयुक्त Adjective के रूप में कोई परिवर्तन नहीं होता है।
(Adjectives in English have the same form for singular and plural, masculine and feminine nouns.)

Note: (i) इस नियम का एकमात्र अपवाद है—Demonstrative Adjectives: this और that.

(ii) *This* और *That* का प्रयोग Singular Nouns के पहले किया जाता है, किंतु *These* और *Those* का प्रयोग Plural Nouns के पहले होता है। जैसे :

I like { *this book/these books.* / *that book/those books.* }

(D) POSITION OF ADJECTIVES: ATTRIBUTIVE AND PREDICATIVE USE

Adjective का प्रयोग दो तरह से होता है :

(a) Adjective + Noun (b) Verb + Adjective

अर्थात Adjective का प्रयोग Noun के पहले होता है या Verb के बाद।

11. *Look at these sentences:*

adj. + noun	*adj.* + noun
Tom is a *rich man.*	This is a *beautiful song.*
They are *sick people.*	The girl has a *sweet voice.*

(i) इन वाक्यों में Adjectives + Noun का प्रयोग हुआ है।

(ii) Adjective + Noun को हम Attributive Use कहते हैं।

Adjective + Noun = Attributive Use.

12. *Look at these sentences:*

(i) *Verb (be-am/is/was) + adj.*	(ii) *Verb (look/seem/become...) + adj.*
I *am hungry.*	You *look ill.*
He *is tired.*	Raja seems *happy.*
The film *was boring.*	Tom *became rich.*
They *were careless.*	I *feel fresh.*

(i) इन वाक्यों में *verbs (am/is/was/were)* + adjectives और

(ii) *Verbs (look/seems/became/feel) + Adjectives* का प्रयोग हुआ है।

(iii) *Verb + Adjective* को हम Predicative Use कहते हैं।

(iv) ऐसे कुछ और verbs हैं जिनके बाद Adjective का प्रयोग होता है।

make *sound* *taste* *appear*

(verbs used in this way are called *linking verbs* or *copulas.*)

Verb + Adjective = Predicative Use

(E) ADJECTIVES USED IN ONE POSITION ONLY

अधिकांश Adjectives का प्रयोग दोनों तरह से हो सकता है। जैसे :

This is an *old* egg. The egg is *old*.

(i) कुछ Adjectives हैं जिनका प्रयोग या तो Attributive (adjective + noun) होता है या Predicative (verb + adjective).

(ii) किंतु वाक्य में एक के स्थान पर दूसरे का प्रयोग (उसी अर्थ में) नहीं हो सकता। जैसे ill (बीमार) का प्रयोग verb के बाद होता है, noun के पहले नहीं:

He is *ill*. किंतु He is an *ill man* नहीं होता।

(a) Adjectives + Nouns

13. *Look at these sentences:*

He is my *elder* brother. He is our *Chief* Minister.

Chess is an *indoor* game. This is the *main* building.

(i) कुछ Adjectives का प्रयोग Nouns के पहले होता है :

Adjective + Noun

elder, eldest, indoor, outdoor, chief, main, principal (=main) former, utter, only, upper.

(b) Verbs + Adjectives

14. *Look at these sentences:*

He *looks ill.* Your mother *is well.*

The baby *is asleep.* The man *is alive/awake.*

(i) कुछ Adjectives का प्रयोग Verbs के बाद होता है :

Verb + Adjective

ill, well, asleep, alive, awake, afraid, ashamed, alone, alike (similar), *pleased, glad, content* (= happy), *fine* (= in good health), *unwell.*

(F) ORDER FOR PLACING VARIOUS ADJECTIVES

कभी-कभी एक ही Noun को कई Adjectives qualify करते हैं। वैसी स्थिति में उन Adjectives को किस क्रम में लिखना चाहिए, उसका कोई fixed rule नहीं है।

फिर भी अगला Table आपके मार्गदर्शन (guidance) के लिए दिया जा रहा है :

Table

Examples: a high brick wall.
a valuable brown leather belt.

	Quality, etc.	Size, Length, Shape, etc.	Colour	Noun or Gerund	Noun
a	–	high	–	brick	wall
an	old	–	–	gold	watch
a	–	small	red	tin	box
–	new	–	black	–	shoes
a	valuable	–	brown	leather	belt
her	attractive	large	green	silk	dress

The Table is adapted from 'A Guide to Patterns and Usage in English'—A S Hornby

Note: (i) Possessive Adjective तथा Demonstrative Adjective एक साथ प्रयुक्त नहीं होते। जैसे :

This pen of mine ठीक है, न कि My this pen. These friends of his ठीक है, न कि His these friends.

(ii) किंतु वाक्य में All रहेगा तो Possessive या Demonstrative Adjective के पहले All आता है। जैसे :

All these boys — all my pens
all those birds — all his coats

all + this, these/my, your + noun

(G) ADJECTIVES USED AS NOUNS

The + Adjective With Plural Meaning

15. *Look at these sentences:*

The poor are homeless. *The hungry* need our help.
The rich live in good houses. *The old* are respected in Britain.

(i) इन वाक्यों में Adjectives—*the poor, the rich, the hungry, the old* का प्रयोग plural nouns के रूप में हुआ है।

(ii) the poor = the poor people — the old = the old people
the rich = the rich people — the hungry = the hungry people
the blind = the blind people — the young = the young people

(iii) आगे दिए गए Adjectives का प्रयोग Plural Nouns की तरह होता है।

Social/Economic: *the rich, the poor, the strong, the weak, the homeless, the hungry, the unemployed, the (under) privileged, the disadvantaged.*

Physical/Health: *the blind, the sick, the deaf, the dead, the living, the disabled, the handicapped.*

Age: *the young, the old, the elderly, the middle-aged.*

(iv) the sick का अर्थ है : the sick people किंतु एक व्यक्ति के अर्थ में a sick man कहा जाता है। जैसे:

The sick were in hospital.
The sick man was in hospital.
The blind are helpless.
The blind man is helpless.

(H) DEGREES OF COMPARISON

Amar, Sunil और Rahul की ऊँचाई (height) की तुलना करें :

Amar is a *tall* boy.
Sunil is *taller* than Amar.
Rahul is the *tallest* boy of the three.

(i) Tall शब्द Adjective है।

(ii) हम tall, taller और tallest से विभिन्न व्यक्तियों में समान गुण (height) की तुलना करते हैं।

(ii) इसे Degree of Comparison कहते हैं।

Degree तीन प्रकार का होता है :

(i) Positive (ii) Comparative (iii) Superlative

(i) Positive Degree

16. *Look at these sentences:*

You are a *brave* boy. This is a *fast* train.
I am a *happy* man. That is a *big* house.

(i) यहाँ *brave, happy, fast* और *big*—Adjectives हैं जो Positive Degree में हैं।

(ii) जब Adjective अपने मूल रूप में हो तथा किसी से तुलना का बोध नहीं हो या तुलना हो तो समानता का बोध हो तो उसे Positive Degree कहते हैं। जैसे :

He is a *brave* boy. He is *as brave as* a tiger.

(ii) Comparative Degree

17. *Look at these sentences:*

John is *stronger* than Hari. I am *younger* than my sister.
Priya is *bolder* than Rekha. Football is *more popular* than tennis.

(i) यहाँ *stronger, bolder, younger* तथा *more popular*—Adjectives है जो Comparative Degree में है।

(ii) जब दो व्यक्तियों या वस्तुओं के बीच तुलना करके यह बोध हो कि कोई गुण दूसरे से अधिक या कम है, तब उसे Comparative Degree कहते हैं।

(iii) Superlative Degree

18. *Look at these sentences:*

She is the *best* mother in the world.
It is the *oldest* building in the town.

(i) यहाँ *best* और *oldest*—Adjectives हैं जो Superlative Degree में हैं।

(ii) अगर तीन या तीन से अधिक व्यक्तियों या वस्तुओं की तुलना करके यह बोध हो कि एक में कोई गुण सबसे अधिक या सबसे कम है, तब उसे Superlative Degree कहते है।

(I) FORMATION OF COMPARATIVE AND SUPERLATIVE DEGREES

I.

Positive	*Comparative*	*Superlative*
old	older	oldest
tall	taller	tallest
cheap	cheaper	cheapest
high	higher	highest
great	greater	greatest
sweet	sweeter	sweetest

एक या दो syllables के Adjectives (जिनके अन्त में e नहीं होता) के Positive Degree में *-er* जोड़कर Comparative और *-est* जोड़कर Superlative बनाया जाता है :

positive + er = Comparative	positive + est = Superlative

II.

Positive	*Comparative*	*Superlative*
wise	wiser	wisest
fine	finer	finest
nice	nicer	nicest
brave	braver	bravest
wide	wider	widest
able	abler	ablest
sure	surer	surest

यदि Positive Degree के Adjective के अंत में पहले से ही *e* हो तो केवल *-r* जोड़कर comparative और *-st* जोड़कर Superlative बनाया जाता है :

positive + r = Comparative	positive + st = Superlative

III.

Positive	*Comparative*	*Superlative*
big	bigger	biggest
fat	fatter	fattest
hot	hotter	hottest
red	redder	reddest
sad	sadder	saddest
thin	thinner	thinnest

यदि Positive Degree के अंत में एक Consonant हो और उसके पहले एक Vowel हो तो अंतिम Consonant को Double करने के बाद *-er* लगाकर Comporative और *-est* लगाकर Superlative बनाया जाता है :

one Vowel + one Consonant = double Consonant

IV.	*Positive*	*Comparative*	*Superlative*
	easy	easier	easiest
	happy	happier	happiest
	dry	drier	driest
	heavy	heavier	heaviest
	lovely	lovelier	loveliest
	wealthy	wealtheir	wealthiest

यदि Positive Degree के अंत में y हो और पहले Consonant हो तो *y* को *i* में बदलने के बाद *-er* जोड़कर Comparative और *-est* जोड़कर Superlative बनाया जाता है :

change *y* to *i* + *er* = Comparative	change *y* to *i* + *est* = Superlative

V.	*Positive*	*Comparative*	*Superlative*
	gay	gayer	gayest
	gray	grayer	grayest

यदि Positive Degree के अंत में y हो और उसके पहले Vowel हो तो *y* को *i* में नहीं बदला जाता और सिर्फ *-er* जोड़कर Comparative और *-est* जोड़कर Superlative बनाया जाता है।

VI.	*Positive*	*Comparative*	*Superlative*
	beautiful	more beautiful	most beautiful
	useful	more useful	most useful
	difficult	more difficult	most difficult
	important	more important	most important
	intelligent	more intelligent	most intelligent
	interesting	more interesting	most interesting

(i) दो से अधिक syllables वाले Adjective के अंत में -er/-est नहीं जोड़े जाते।

(ii) बल्कि उनके पहले *more* का प्रयोग कर Comparative और *most* का प्रयोग कर Superlative बनाया जाता है :

more + positive = Comparative	most + positive = Superlative

VII.	*Positive*	*Comparative*	*Superlative*
	good	better	best
	bad	worse	worst
	little	less	least
	many / much	more	most
	far	farther / further	farthest / furthest
	old	older / elder	oldest / eldest

कुछ Adjectives के Comparative और Superlative अनियमित रूप से बनाए जाते हैं।

(J) CONSTRUCTIONS WITH COMPARISON

Comparison बनाने के नियम :

I. Use of *as … as/not as/so … as*

19. *Look at these sentences:*

Hari is *as tall as* his father. It is *not as cold as* ice.

This book is *as good as* that. Prema is *not so nice as* Richa.

(i) (a) समानता (equality) दिखाने के लिए *as* + positive form of the adjective + *as* का प्रयोग किया जाता है।

(b) *As … as* का प्रयोग positive sentences में होता है।

(ii) (a) असमानता (inferiority) दिखाने के लिए *not as/so* + positive form of the adjective + *as* का प्रयोग किया जाता है।

(b) *Not as/so … as* का प्रयोग negative sentences में होता है।

In negative comparisons, we can use *not as … as* or *not so … as*. Both are correct in Modern English.

She is *not so/as* nice *as* her sister.

—MICHAEL SWAN: PRACTICAL ENGLISH USAGE

II. With the comparative we use *than*:

20. *Look at these sentences:*

Kamala is *taller than* Usha. Mukul is *younger than* Rajeev.

This box is *heavier than* that. The weather is *better than* that of yesterday.

जब वाक्य में comparative degree रहे तब उसके बाद than का प्रयोग किया जाता है :

Comparative degree + than

III. (a) *Use of the + superlative*

21. *Look at these sentences:*

He is *the oldest* man in the village.

This is *the tallest* building in the town.

सामान्यत: superlative degree के पहले *the* का प्रयोग होता है।

Note: यदि Superlative Degree के पहले कोई Possessive Adjective (my, your, our, her) या Possessive Case (Noun + 's) आए तो Superlative के पहले *the* का प्रयोग नहीं हो सकता :

It is my *best* shirt. It is Raja's *best* coat.

(b) Use of *the … in/of*

22. *Look at these sentences:*

December is *the coldest* month *of* the year.

She is *the youngest of* all the sisters.

Anita is *the oldest* girl *in* the class.

Who is *the strongest* person *in* the world?

(i) सामान्यत: Superlative Degree के साथ of का प्रयोग होता है, पर

(ii) जब स्थान (place), देश, शहर आदि के प्रसंग में *of* की जगह *in* का प्रयोग होता है।

(c) Use of *most* + adjective

23. *Look at these sentences:*

You are *most* kind. (= You are very kind.)

It is a *most* amusing story. (= It is a very amusing story.)

कभी-कभी कुछ लोग a most का प्रयोग *very* के अर्थ में करते हैं। अत: most के पहले *the* का प्रयोग नहीं होता।

most + adjective, without *the*, means, *very*.

IV. Use of *the + comparative … the + comparative*

24. *Look at these sentences:*

The older I get, *the happier* I am.

The more you work, *the less* you learn?

The higher we go, *the colder* it gets.

इन वाक्यों से बोध होता है कि जब कोई गुण एक ओर बढ़ता है, तो उसी अनुपात में दूसरी ओर भी बढ़ता है। इसे parallel increase (ज्यों, ज्यों … त्यों त्यों) कहते हैं।

V. Use of *Comparative + and + Comparative*

25. *Look at these sentences:*

I am getting *fatter and fatter.*

He became *less and less* interested.

The day became *hotter and hotter.*

The weather is getting *colder and colder.*

Gradual increase (क्रमिक वृद्धि) या Gradual decrease (क्रमिक ह्रास) का भाव व्यक्त करने के लिए Comparative + and + Comparative का प्रयोग किया जाता है।

VI. Use of *the + Comparative degree + of the two*

26. *Look at these sentences:*

He is *the wiser of the two.*

Moti is *the taller of the two* boys.

यदि Comparative degree के पहले *the* आए तो उसके बाद सदा *of the two* आता है।

किंतु— Rajeev is *the tallest of the three.*

Madan is *the shortest of the three.*

अर्थात, the + superlative degree + of the three का प्रयोग करते हैं।

VII. Use of *one of + superlative*

27. *Look at these sentences:*

He is *one of the oldest* men.

She is *one of the tallest* girls.

One of के बाद सामान्यत: superlative degree का प्रयोग करते हैं।

VIII. *Latin Comparatives*

28. *Look at these sentences:*

He is *senior/junior* to me.

This pen is *superior/inferier* to that.

(i) कुछ ऐसे Latin भाषा से लिए गए adjectives हैं जो Latin में Comparative degree के adjectives हैं।

(ii) *Senior, junior, superior, inferior, prior* के बाद to का (than का नहीं) प्रयोग होता है।

(iii) इनके पहले *more / most* नहीं लगाया जाता है :

He is *more senior than* me. ×

He is *senior to* me. ✓

29. *Look at these sentences.*

She is a *perfect* wife.

Each person's fingerprints are *unique*.

(i) कुछ adjectives के comparison नहीं होते हैं, जैसे:

perfect, unique, round, square, flat, circular, Almighty, chief, common, complete, dead, empty, extreme, false, full, infinite, supreme, universal, excellent आदि।

(ii) इन सब शब्दों में *more* लगाकर comparative या *most* लगाकर superlative नहीं बनाया जाता। जैसे:

She is a *more perfect* wife. ×

She is *the most perfect* wife. ×

She is a *perfect* wife. ✓

(K) USE OF SOME ADJECTIVES/DETERMINERS

I. Much, Many

30. *Look at these sentences:*

I don't have *much money.* I don't have *many friends.*

Do you buy *much food?* Do you have *many books?*

(i) *Much* (अधिक) मात्रासूचक है। अत: इसका प्रयोग uncountable noun के पहले होता है :

much + uncountable noun

(ii) *Many* (अनेक) संख्यासूचक है। अत: इसका प्रयोग सदा plural noun के पहले होता है :

many + plural noun

(iii) *Much/Many* का प्रयोग सामान्यत: negative और interrogative sentences में ही होता है।

31. *Look at these sentences:*

Much milk is wasted. *Many boys* have come.

इन वाक्यों में *milk* और *boys* Subjects हैं। इसलिए इनके साथ *much/many* का प्रयोग हो सकता है।

32. *Look at these sentences:*

I bought *much milk.* I know *many boys.*

यहाँ *milk* और *boys* objects हैं। इनके साथ *much/many* का प्रयोग नहीं होगा। Affirmative sentences में *much/ many* की जगह *lots of, a lot of, a great deal of, plenty of* का प्रयोग होता है :

I bought *lots of/a lot of/ plenty of* milk. (much के बदले)

I know *lots of/a lot of/plenty of* boys. (many के बदले)

As a general rule, we use *a lot of* and *lots of* in positive statements and *many* and *much* in negatives and questions.

—John Eastwood: OXFORD PRACTICE GRAMMAR

1. *Adjectives* और *Determiners* में भेद :

(i) Traditional grammar में my, this, much, many, several, enough आदि को Adjectives कहते हैं। किंतु modern grammar में इन्हें Determiners के नाम से जाना जाता है।

(ii) Noun के पहले एक-से अधिक Adjectives का प्रयोग हो सकता है। जैसे—*my fat old* cat, *several tall young* students आदि।

(iii) किंतु Noun के पहले प्राय: दो Determiners का प्रयोग एक साथ नहीं होता। जैसे: *my* house या *this* house होता है, पर *this my* house नहीं होता। इसकी जगह *this* house of mine कहते हैं।

II. Each, Every

33. *Look at these sentences:*

Each man tries twice. *Every boy* has a book.

Look at *each side* of it. We want *every child* to be happy.

(i) *Each* (प्रत्येक) और *every* (प्रत्येक) के बाद singular countable noun का प्रयोग होता है :

each/every + singular countable noun

(ii) *Each* का प्रयोग दो या दो से अधिक countable noun के साथ होता है, पर *every* का प्रयोग तीन या तीन से अधिक countable noun के साथ होता है, केवल दो के साथ नहीं।

(iii) *Each* से अलग-अलग व्यक्तियों या वस्तुओं का बोध होता है, *every* से एक साथ व्यक्तियों या वस्तुओं का:

Each person in turn went to see the doctor.

Every country has a national flag.

We say *each* when we are thinking of people or things separately, one at a time. We say *every* when we are thinking of people or things together, in a group.

—Michael Swan: BASIC ENGLISH USAGE

(iv) *Each* से एक छोटे समूह का बोध होता है, *every* से एक बड़े समूह का। *Each* is more usual with smaller groups and can mean only two. *Every* means three or more, usually a large number.

—JOHN EASTWOOD: OXFORD PRACTICE GRAMMAR

Note: *Each/Every* के बाद plural noun या uncountable noun का प्रयोग नहीं होता:

Each/Every room has a number. ✓ *Each/Every rooms* has a number. ×

All the milk is white. ✓ *Each/Every milk* is white. ×

III. All, Both

34. *Look at these sentences:*

All cities are noisy.	I like *both cities.*
All the books are new.	*Both the boys* are tall.
All the milk is fresh.	*Both the books* are new.
All the food is hot.	*Both my sisters* are married.

(i) (a) *All* (सब, समूचा) से संख्या और मात्रा दोनो का बोध होता है।

(b) *All/All the* के बाद plural noun का प्रयोग किया जाता है।

(c) *All the* के बाद uncountable noun का भी प्रयोग होता है।

all(the) + plural noun/uncountable noun

(d) *All* के बाद *the, my, this* आदि का प्रयोग होता है।

(e) *All* के बाद singular countable noun का भी प्रयोग कर सकते हैं। तब All का अर्थ होगा—'संपूर्ण, पूरा' (the whole of):

She was here *all day*. (सुबह से रात तक)!

(ii) (a) *Both* (दोनों) का प्रयोग दो के अर्थ में होता है।

(b) *Both* के बाद *the, my, these, those* आदि का प्रयोग किया जाता है।

(c) *Both* या Both the के बाद plural noun का प्रयोग करते हैं:

both (the) + plural noun

Note: *Both* के बाद singular noun या uncountable noun का प्रयोग कभी नहीं होता:

Both the girls are clever. ✓ *Both the girl* is clever. ×

He lost *all the money.* ✓ He lost *both the money.* ×

IV. A lot of, Lots of, Plenty of, A great deal of, A number of

35. *Look at these sentences:*

I bought *a lot of sugar.*	I bought *a lot of* pens.
He drinks *lots of tea.*	He has *lots of friends.*
There is *plenty of milk.*	*Plenty of chairs* were there.
He has *a great deal of rice.*	He has *a number of friends.*

(i) (a) *A lot of, lots of, plenty of, a great deal of* का अर्थ होता है : 'बहुत'। इनसे मात्रा और संख्या दोनों का बोध होता है।

(b) *A lot of, lots of, plenty of, a great deal of* के बाद uncountable noun या plural noun का प्रयोग होता है :

a lot of, lots of, plenty of, a great deal of + uncountable noun/plural noun

(ii) (a) *A number of* का अर्थ होता है : बहुत। इससे केवल संख्या का बोध होता है।

(b) *A number of, a large number of, a great number of* के बाद plural noun का प्रयोग होता है :

a number of, a great number of, a large number of + plural noun

The room contained { *a(great)* / *a(large)* / *a(good)* } *number of* students.

V. Some, Any

36. *Look at these sentences:*

I have got *some friends*. I have not got *any friends.*

You have got *some money.* Have you got *any milk*?

(i) (a) Some (कुछ) का प्रयोग संख्या और मात्रा दोनों के लिए होता है।

(b) Some के बाद plural noun या uncountable noun को प्रयोग किया जाता है :

some + plural noun/ uncountable noun

(ii) (a) Any (कोई, कुछ) से संख्या और मात्रा दोनों का बोध होता है।

(b) Any का प्रयोग plural noun या uncountable noun के पहले होता है :

any + plural noun/ uncountable noun

(iii) *Some* का प्रयोग affirmative sentences में होता है, *any* का प्रयोग negative या question sentences में।

some in affirmative sentences	any in negative/question sentences

Note: *Any* का प्रयोग अगर affirmative sentences में हो, तो उसका अर्थ होता है—every:

Any children cān do this work. = *Every* child can do this work.

VI. Either, Neither

37. *Look at these sentences:*

Either book is good. *Neither road* is very good.

Either road will go to Patna. *Neither book* is satisfactory.

(i) *Either* (दोनों में से कोई एक) के पहले सदा singular noun का प्रयोग किया जाता है :

either + singular noun

(ii) *Neither* (दोनों में से कोई नहीं) के पहले भी singular noun आता है :

neither + singular noun

Note: कभी-कभी *either* का अर्थ—दोनों में से प्रत्येक होता है, खासकर *side* और *end* के पहले। *Either* के बाद आनेवाला noun हमेशा singular रहता है :

There are roses on *either side* of the door.

VII. Elder, Eldest, Older, Oldest

38. *Look at these sentences:*

My *elder brother* is an officer. Priya is *older than* Rohan.
My *elder sister* lives in Delhi. The tree is *older than* that tree.
Rajeev is my *eldest son.* My friend is the *oldest* in the class.
Sheela is your *eldest sister.* The school is the *oldest* school in Bihar.

(i) (a) *Elder* (अग्रज) और *Eldest* (आयु में सबसे बड़ा) का प्रयोग एक ही परिवार के निकटतम संबंधियों—भाई, बहन, बेटा, बेटी आदि के लिए होता है। इनका प्रयोग जानवरों या वस्तुओं के लिए नहीं होता।

(b) इनका प्रयोग noun के पहले होता है : *elder/eldest + noun*

(ii) (a) *older/oldest* (आयु में सबसे वृद्ध, सबसे बड़ा) का प्रयोग अन्य लोगों या वस्तुओं के लिए होता है।

(b) *older* के बाद *than* का प्रयोग अवश्य होता है, किंतु *elder* के बाद *than* का प्रयोग नहीं होता। (Note that before *than*-construction we always use *older*.)

(c) *oldest* के पहले *the* अवश्य लगाया जाता है।

Note: *Elders/Elderly:* Elders (गुरुजन) का प्रयोग सदा plural noun की तरह होता है। *Elderly* का अर्थ होता है : वयोवृद्ध:

Respect your *elders.*
Dr Mukul has specialised in the care of the *elderly.*

Some people consider *elderly* a more polite word than 'old'.

—COLLINS COBUILD: ENGLISH GUIDES

VIII. Such, Such a

39. *Look at these sentences:*

I do not like *such boys.* We do not like *such a boy.*
We had *such* rich *food.* It was *such an easy test.*

(i) Such (ऐसा) के बाद countable plural या uncountable noun का प्रयोग किया जाता है :

such + plural noun/uncountable noun

(ii) *Such a/an* के बाद singular noun का प्रयोग किया जाता है :

such a/an + singular noun

IX. A few, few, the few, A little, little, the little

(a) A few, A little

40. *Look at these sentences:*

I have *a few friends.* He drank *a little coffee.*

He bought a *few eggs*. He bought a *little milk*.

(i) (a) *A few* (some, though not many) संख्यावाचक है। इससे positive भाव प्रकट होता है।

(b) *A few* के बाद plural noun का प्रयोग किया जाता है :

a few + plural noun

(ii) (a) *A little* (some, a small amount) मात्रासूचक है।

(b) *A little* का प्रयोग uncountable noun के पहले होता है :

a little + uncountable noun

(b) few, little

41. *Look at these sentences:*

She had *few friends*. I have *little time* for reading.

Few students are in the class. An average MP has *little power*.

(i) (a) *few* (not many, नगण्य) संख्यावाचक है। इससे negative भाव प्रकट होता है।

(b) *few* के बाद plural noun का प्रयोग किया जाता है :

few + plural noun

(ii) (a) *little* (not much, बहुत कम, नहीं के बराबर) से मात्रा का बोध होता है।

(b) *little* के बाद uncountable noun का प्रयोग किया जाता है।

little + uncountable noun

(c) The few, The little

42. *Look at these sentences:*

The few friends I have are really helpful.

The little money he has will be spent soon.

(i) (a) *The few* (यद्यपि अनेक नहीं, फिर भी सब) संख्यावाचक है।

(b) The few के बाद plural noun का प्रयोग किया जाता है :

the few + plural noun

(ii) (a) *The little* (यद्यपि अधिक नहीं, फिर भी सब) मात्रासूचक है।

(b) *The little* के बाद uncountable noun का प्रयोग किया जाता है :

the little + uncountable noun

X. Fewer, Less

43. *Look at these sentences:*

Fewer workers are seen today. We have *less time* for our exam.

Fewer politicians are really honest. I have *less money* today.

(i) *Fewer* संख्यासूचक है। अत: इसका प्रयोग plural moun के पहले होता है :

fewer + plural noun

(ii) *Less* मात्रासूचक है। अत: इसका प्रयोग uncountable noun के पहले होता है :

less + uncountable noun

Note:

(i) Spoken English में बहुत सारे लोग fewer की जगह less का प्रयोग plural noun के पहले करते हैं, लेकिन कुछ लोग इसे गलत मानते हैं :

I have got *less friends* this year than ever before.

However, in modern English a lot of people use *less* instead of *fewer* before plural words, especially in an informal style. Some people consider this incorrect.

—MICHAEL SWAN: PRACTICAL ENGLISH USAGE

(ii) Price और number के साथ *less* का प्रयोग नहीं करना चाहिए।

a *less* price के बदले a *lower* price,

a *less* number के बदले a *smaller* number कहना चाहिए।

XI. Enough, Several

44. *Look at these sentences:*

Have you *enough milk?* *Several boys* are in the field.

He bought *enough chairs.* He sold *several houses.*

(i) (a) *Enough* (पर्याप्त, काफी) से मात्रा और संख्या दोनों का बोध होता है।

(b) *Enough* के बाद uncountable noun या plural noun का प्रयोग होता है :

enough + uncountable noun/ plural noun

(ii) (a) *Several* (अनेक, कई) से केवल संख्या का बोध होता है।

(b) *Several* के बाद plural noun का प्रयोग किया जाता है :

several + plural noun

XII. Farther, Further

45. *Look at these sentences:*

Let us not walk any *farther*. Don't make *further* delay.

Patna is *farther* from Sitamarhi than Hajipur is.

Have you any *further* questions?

(i) *Farther* का अर्थ है 'अधिक दूर' (= greater distance)

(ii) *Further* का अर्थ है 'अतिरिक्त' (= additional, in addition)

Note: आजकल *farther/further* या *farthest/furthest* का प्रयोग दूरी (distance) का बोध कराने के लिए होता है :

Mumbai is *farther/ further* away from Delhi.

What is the *farthest/furthest* place you have ever visited to.

When speaking of real places and distances you can use either **farther, farthest** *or* **further, furthest.**

—LONGMAN: DICTIONARY OF CONTEMPORARY ENGLISH

XIII. Later, Latter

46. *Look at these sentences:*

He came *later* than I. The *latter* part of the book is very impressive.

(i) (a) *Later* 'late' की Comparative Degree है।

(b) *Later* से समय (time) का बोध होता है।

(ii) (a) *Latter* 'former' का विपरीतार्थक शब्द है।

(b) *Latter* से क्रम या स्थान का बोध होता है।

XIV. Nearest, Next

47. *Look at these sentences:*

Vashi is our *nearest* station. Who will be the *next* PM of India.

Where is the *nearest* post office? I sat *next* to my friend.

(i) *Nearest* (सबसे नजदीक) से दूरी (distance) का बोध होता है।

(ii) *Next* (इसके बाद) से क्रम (order) का बोध होता है।

XV. Ill, Sick

48. *Look at these sentences:*

He looks *ill*. He is a *sick man*.

She suddenly fell *ill*. She is visiting her *sick uncle*.

Ill और *Sick* का अर्थ होता है : बीमार (having a disease).

(i) *Ill* का प्रयोग प्राय: verb के बाद होता है—यानी predicative use (after a subject and verb).

(ii) *Sick* का प्रयोग प्राय: noun के पहले होता है—यानी attributive use (before a noun).

In British English both *sick* and *ill* are used. *Sick* is used attributively (before a noun); *ill* is generally used predicatively (after a subject and verb)

—MICHAEL SWAN: PRACTICAL ENGLISH USAGE

Note: *Ill* का noun के पहले प्रयोग हो सकता है, पर उस अवस्था में *ill* का अर्थ हो जाता है—'बुरा' (bad), बीमार (unwell) नहीं :

I have no *ill will* against anybody.

XVI. Last, Latest

49. *Look at these sentences:*

Mr Sen was the *last speaker* today. Have you heard the *latest news?*

The *last letter* of the alphabet is z. This is the *latest edition* of the book.

(i) Last (अंतिम) से क्रम (order) या स्थान का बोध होता है।

(ii) Latest (सबसे हाल का) से समय (time) का बोध होता है।

Examples Worked Out

(A) *Fill in the blanks with suitable adjectives:*

1. Raja is a ... boy. Raja is a *tall* boy.

2. She is an … girl.	She is an *intelligent* girl.
3. Delhi is a … city.	Delhi is a *large* city.
4. The sky is … .	The sky is *blue*.
5. He is an … man.	He is an *honest* man.
6. She is a … girl.	She is a *foolish* girl.
7. He is an … sailor.	He is an *Indian* sailor.
8. Nehruji wore a … cap.	Nehruji wore a *white* cap.
9. He was … to see me.	He was *happy* to see me.
10. The Ganga is a … river.	The Ganga is a *holy* river.
11. Chess is an … game.	Chess is an *indoor* game.
12. Lata has a … voice.	Lata has a *sweet* voice.
13. The USA is a … country.	The USA is a *rich* country.
14. Tendulkar is a … cricketer.	Tendulkar is a *good* cricketor.
15. Kashmir is a … place.	Kashmir is a *beautiful* place.
16. Shakespeare was a … dramatist.	Shakespeare was a *great* dramatist.
17. He is very … .	He is very *fortunate*.
18. He gave me a … chance.	He gave me a *second* chance.
19. That girl has … eyes.	That girl has *lovely* eyes.
20. This is a … book.	This is a *new* book.
21. … toys are these?	*Whose* toys are these?
22. That is a … house.	That is a *big* house.
23. Snakes are … .	Snakes are *poisonous*.
24. Mr Bose is a … man.	Mr Bose is a *smart* man.
25. She has a … face.	She has a *smiling* face.
26. It is a … paper.	It is a *daily* paper.
27. He is a … man.	He is a *healthy* man.
28. The fox is a … animal.	The fox is a *clever* animal.

(B) *Fill in the blanks with suitable adjectives choosing from the brackets.*

29. … boys were there. (*Many/Much*)	*Many* boys were there.
30. How … money do you earn? (*much/many*)	How *much* money do you earn?
31. … member has a vote. (*All/Each*)	*Each* member has a vote.
32. He has … money. (*any/some*)	He has *some* money.
33. … my books are missing. (*All/Each*)	*All* my books are missing.
34. I have not got …milk. (*some/any*)	I have not got *any* milk.
35. … these books are mine. (*Every/Both*)	*Both* these books are mine.
36. He has … friends here. (*much/a lot of*)	He has *a lot of* friends here.
37. Tom is my … brother. (*older/elder*)	Tom is my *elder* brother.

38. She is … than me. (*elder/older*)	She is *older* than me.
39. Have … cup of tea? (*other/another*)	Have *another* cup of tea?
40. I have … money. (*not/no*)	I have *no* money.
41. There is … food for two. (*many/enough*)	There is *enough* food for two.
42. I am sitting … to him. (*nearest/next*)	I am sitting *next* to him.
43. … student admitted guilt. (*Either/Neither*)	*Neither* student admitted guilt.
44. This is the … railway station. (*nearest/next*)	This is the *nearest* railway station.
45. … country can stop the war. (*Either/Neither*)	*Either* country can stop the war.
46. He has a … money. (*little/few*)	He has a *little* money.
47. She has a … pens. (*little/few*)	She has a *few* pens.
48. He is … fool. (*such/such a*)	He is *such a* fool.
49. … pens are of no use. (*Such/Such* a)	*Such* pens are of no use.
50. He came here … than I. (*latter/later*)	He came here *later* than I.
51. … room is painted yellow. (*All/Every*)	*Every* room is painted yellow.
52. This is the … tree here. (*eldest/oldest*)	This is the *oldest* tree here.
53. What is the …news? (*last/latest*)	What is the *latest* news?
54. My aunt was…(*sick/ill*)	My aunt was *ill*.
55. The President is a …man. (*sick/ill*)	The President is a *sick* man.
56. I have got…flats. (*much/several*)	I have got *several* flats.
57. … students hate exams. (*Every/All*).	*All* students hate exams.
58. … guest in turn shook hands with the PM. (*Each/Every*)	*Each* guest in turn shook hands with the PM.
59. He gave … patient the same medicine. (*each/ every*)	He gave *every* patient the same medicine.

EXERCISE 1

Pick out all the adjectives in the following sentences:

EXAMPLE: She has bluish eyes. = *bluish*: adjective

1. She has bluish eyes.
2. Most birds can fly.
3. I ate some rice.
4. The egg is old.
5. She is a beautiful girl.
6. Ram is ill today.
7. Both doors are open.
8. He is a handsome boy.
9. Whose house is this?
10. Every word is false.
11. He gave me six apples.
12. He is a good salesman.
13. Which train did he catch?
14. Kolkata is a large city.
15. He is a senior teacher.
16. She is my elder sister.

17. I have no mangoes.
18. Either side may win.
19. All men are mortal.
20. Madan is better than Sohan.
21. Did you catch any biscuits?
22. What is the latest score?

EXERCISE 2

Fill in the blanks with suitable adjectives choosing from the ones given below:

(a) red, ripe, large, beautiful, dark, seven, rich, popular, lucky, happy, boring, hungry.

EXAMPLE: Thirteen is my … number.
= Thirteen is my *lucky* number.

1. Thirteen is my … number.
2. Radha is very … today.
3. Tom became a … man.
4. Cricket is a … game today.
5. The work was really … .
6. She is a … girl.
7. Hyderabad is a … city.
8. It was a … night.
9. Many mangoes are … .
10. Some roses are … .
11. I was very … on that day.
12. There are … days in a week.

(b) daily, ill, lovely, kind, full, Indian, wicked, hot, blind, sweet, strong, poisonous.

1. It is a very … day.
2. … boys are punished.
3. The old man is very … .
4. Her face is … .
5. Dara Singh is a … man.
6. Milton was a … poet.
7. That is a … snake.
8. The … cricket team has won.
9. The river is … of water.
10. It is a … paper.
11. Honey tastes … .
12. Ashoka was a … man.

EXERCISE 3 (With Answer)

Fill in the blanks with suitable adjectives:

EXAMPLE: This is … food.
= This is *fresh* food.

1. This is … food.
2. Jill has got … eyes.
3. She turned … .
4. The film was not very … .
5. It was a … and dark night.
6. This is the … road of Patna.
7. He is a … actor.
8. It was a cold, wet and … day.
9. The Ramayana is a … book.
10. Sometimes I feel … .
11. The manager looked … .
12. We have a … meeting.
13. The runner made a … start.
14. This is an … train.
15. The wall is ten feet … .
16. That dress is … .
17. He has bought a … coat.
18. I am … to see you.
19. … wood does not burn well.
20. He is a … man.

EXERCISE 4

Use each of the following adjectives in a sentence:

EXAMPLE: *fat:* He is a *fat* man.

Woollen: I have bought a *woollen* coat.

fat woollen tall poor small wise sad old healthy dark slow

ugly rich clever cruel strong young kind big lazy dull

long foolish handsome

EXERCISE 5

Fill in the blanks with *much* or *many:*

EXAMPLES: (i) I do not drink … coffee.

= I do not drink *much* coffee.

(ii) … people have been killed.

= *Many* people have been killed.

1. I do not drink … coffee.
2. … people have been killed.
3. Has he … money?
4. Do you need … books?
5. I did not go to … places.
6. Do you buy … food?
7. Do you get … rain here?
8. … men were not present there.
9. How … money do you want?
10. Have you got … friends?
11. Do you drink … tea?
12. How … times have you been there?

EXERCISE 6

Fill in the blanks with *some* or *any*:

EXAMPLES: (i) I want … razor-blades.

= I want *some* razor-blades.

(ii) I can't find … cigarettes.

= I can't find *any* cigarettes.

1. I want … razor-blades.
2. I can't find … cigarettes.
3. He has … pens.
4. Has he bought … bread?
5. I ate … rice.
6. He has not bought … oranges.
7. Please give me … milk.
8. Have you … sugar.
9. Give me … more.
10. Come … day you like.
11. There are … children outside.
12. Have you … further questions?

EXERCISE 7

Fill in the blanks with *all* or *every*:

EXAMPLES: (i) … plants need water.

= *All* plants need water.

(ii) … man had a gun.

= *Every* man had a gun.

1. … plants need water.
2. … man had a gun.
3. … boy ran a race.
4. … cities are noisy.
5. … Monday is horrible.
6. … student has to take the exam.
7. He ate … his food.
8. He comes here … evening.
9. … children need love.
10. Please switch off … the lights.
11. … shop in the street is sold.
12. … the houses are the same.

EXERCISE 8

Fill in the blanks with *a few or a little:*

EXAMPLES: (i) … labourers own cars.

= *A few* labourers own cars.

(ii) Give me … time to think.

= Give me *a little* time to think.

1. … labourers own cars.
2. Give me … time to think.
3. Last night I wrote … letters.
4. There was … water in the pot.
5. Have you got … envelopes?
6. Mix the powder with … water.
7. He has … very comfortable chairs.
8. … knowledge is a dangerous thing.
9. She has … friends.
10. Can you stay … days longer?
11. I am not ill, but I am … tired.
12. … boys were scattered about the room.

EXERCISE 9

Fill in the blanks with *elder or older:*

EXAMPLES: (i) He is my … brother.

= He is my *elder* brother.

(ii) The tree is … than that.

= The tree is *older* than that

1. He is my … brother.
2. The tree is … than that.
3. Hari is his … son.
4. He is … than his cousin.
5. My … brother lives in the UK.
6. Heera is … than his sister.
7. My nephew is … than his uncle.
8. I have an … sister.
9. Madan is … than his partner.
10. Ram is … than Sohan by two years.

EXERCISE 10

Supply the proper form (Comparative or Superlative) of the adjective:

EXAMPLE: *Clever:* This boy is the … of all.

= This boy is the *cleverest* of all.

1. *Clever:* This boy is the … of all.
2. *Easy:* This book is … than that.
3. *Tall:* He is the … of the two.
4. *Good:* Who is the … boy in the class?
5. *Rich:* My uncle is … than my father.
6. *Old:* He looks … than he is.
7. *Idle:* Madan is the … boy in school.
8. *Strong:* He is … than his friend.

9. *Cold:* December is the … month of the year.
10. *Large:* London is the … city in England.
11. *Bad:* It was the … film that we had ever seen.
12. *High:* Mt Everest is the … peak of the Himalayas.

EXERCISE 11

Fill in the blanks with suitable adjectives choosing from the brackets:

EXAMPLE: We … need chairs. (*little/several*)
= We need *several* chairs.

1. We need … chairs. (*little/several*)
2. … people think so. (*Many/Much*)
3. We did … exercises. (*any/some*)
4. I wrote … poems (*a little/ a few*)
5. You got … the letters (*every/all*)
6. … boxes are yours. (*Both/Each*)
7. Did you buy … food? (*many/much*)
8. … food makes me ill. (*Some/Any*)
9. Your brother looks … . (*young/younger*)
10. … shoe fits. (*Either/Neither*)
11. There are … books. (*some/any*)
12. I haven't met … twin. (*neither/either*)
13. She was … fool. (*such/such a*)
14. … children like toys. (*All/ Each*)
15. You are the … of all. (*nicer/nicest*)
16. He has … of books. (*lots/much*)
17. The PM is … (*ill/sickly*)
18. I earn … than she does. (*little/less*)
19. She drank a … water. (*little/few*)
20. You are my … uncle. (*older/elder*)
21. He looks … than you. (*taller/tall*)
22. … people love sweets.(*Much/Most*)

EXERCISE 12

Fill in the blanks with suitable adjectives choosing from the brackets:

EXAMPLE: Your house is … to mine. (nearest/next)
= Your house is *next* to mine.

1. Your house is … to mine. (*nearest/next*)
2. Do you need … advice? (*some/any*)
3. … men must die. (*All/Every*)
4. I have nothing … to say. (*farther/further*)
5. He did not eat … rice. (*any/some*)
6. I have … nice things. (*such a/such*)
7. This is the … news. (*last/latest*)
8. … man knows what to do. (*Each/All*)
9. She drank … the milk. (*whole/all*)
10. Where are the … players. (*another/other*)
11. That happened … time to me. (*many/many a*)
12. I can get off at the … stop. (*next/nearest*)
13. … aeroplane is 100% safe. (*None/No*)
14. There is … of food in the fridge. (*plenty/a number*)
15. I have never met … person. (*such/such a*)

16. We have ... seats for every one. (*enough/much*)

EXERCISE 13 (With Answer)

Fill in the blanks with suitable adjectives choosing from the brackets:

EXAMPLE: He drives as ... as he could. (*fast/faster*)

= He drives as *fast* as he could.

1. He drives as ... as he could. (*fast/faster*)
2. This is the ... boy in the class. (*latest/last*)
3. He never eats ... breakfast. (*many/much*)
4. He earns ... money than a postman. (*fewer/less*)
5. The baby cries the ... time. (*all/whole*)
6. I am getting fatter and ... (*fat/fatter*)
7. My ... daughter does all the house work. (*oldest/eldest*)
8. Please try to make ... noise. (*little/less*)
9. The older I get the ... I am. (*happy/happier*)
10. There were ... people at the party. (*a number of/much*)
11. Delhi is ... from Madras than Jaipur is. (*further/farther*)
12. My girl friend lives ... door. (*next/nearest*)
13. If you are busy now, I will meet you ... (*latter/later*)

EXERCISE 14 (With Answer)

Fill in the blanks with suitable adjectives:

EXAMPLE: Can you tell me ... road will take to the college?

= Can you tell me *which* road will take me to the college?

1. He is ... .
2. Prema is ... than Padma.
3. He made his wife ... .
4. They had ... of time.
5. He was as ... as a lion.
6. The traffic light turned ... .
7. The colour of my room is ... .
8. He takes ... milk everyday.
9. Ashoka is the man who is ... .
10. The teacher made the children ... .
11. India is rich but Indians are ... .
12. The Principal found the class ... .
13. We havent ... time at our disposal.
14. A ... beggar comes to my door everyday.
15. Some ... boys were swimming in the river.
16. A ... crowd gathered to hear the Chief Minister.

EXERCISE 15 (With Answer)

From the given alternatives select the most appropriate one to fill in the blanks in each of the following sentences:

1. Delhi is ... to Jaipur than Bombay.
   A. near B. nearer C. nearest D. more near
2. The king was a man of ... wisdom.
   A. great B. greater C. more great D. greatest
3. ... boys have taken biology than mathematics
   A. Much B. Many C. More D. Most
4. It became ... day by day, so we decided to go to Kashmir.
   A. hot B. very hot C. hotter D. the hottest
5. He is ... minister of the State Government.
   A. a best and honest B. the best and honest
   C. best and the most honest D. a good and honest

ANSWERS

Ex.3. 1. fresh 2. bluish 3. pale 4. good 5. cloudy 6. main 7. famous 8. windy 9. holy/sacred 10. lonely 11. nervous 12. regular 13. slow 14. early 15. high 16. new 17. blue 18. pleased 19. green 20. healthy.

Ex.13. 1. fast 2. last 3. much 4. less 5. whole 6. fatter 7. eldest 8. less 9. happier 10. a number of 11. farther 12. next 13. later.

Ex.14. 1. intelligent 2. taller 3. happy 4. a lot of 5. strong 6. red 7. yellow 8. fresh 9. great/kind 10. happy/fearful 11. poor 12. empty 13. much 14. blind 15. small 16. big.

Ex.15. 1. nearer 2. great 3. More 4. hotter 5. a good and honest.

□□□

20. MISCELLANEOUS TOPICS

1. Greetings and Salutations (Good morning, Good evening आदि के प्रयोग)

(A) Greetings (= नमस्कार, प्रणाम)

(i) Good morning (शुभ प्रभात)

(a) जब हम किसी व्यक्ति से सुबह में मिलते हैं तब हम उसे Good morning कहते हैं, Good morning के जवाब में अकसर Good morning ही कहा जाता है। जैसे :

Mr Joshi: *Good morning*, Doctor.
Dr Prasad: *Good morning*, Mr Joshi.

(b) सुबह में बिदा लेने के समय भी Good morning ही कहा जाता है।

(c) 'The first part of the day from the time the sun rises until noon' को morning माना जाता है।

(ii) Good afternoon (= शुभ अपराह्न)

(a) जब हम किसी व्यक्ति से afternoon (अपराह्न) में मिलने या विदा लेते हैं तब हम Good afternoon कहते हैं।

(b) Good afternoon के उत्तर में प्रायः Good afternoon ही कहा जाता है। जैसे :

Mrs Bose: *Good afternoon*, Mrs Verma.
Mrs Verma: *Good afternoon*.

(c) 'The period between midday and sunset' को afternoon कहा जाता है।

(iii) Good evening (= शुभ संध्या)

(a) जब शाम में किसी से मिलते हैं तब हम Good evening कहते हैं। जैसे:

(i) Mr Sinha: *Good evening*, Mr Sen.
Mr Sen: *Good evening*.

(ii) *Good evening*, Mr Bose. I'm sorry I'm so late.

(b) Good evening का प्रयोग शाम में मिलने पर होता है, परंतु (शाम में) विदा लेने के समय Good evening या Good night कहा जाता है।

'Common formal greetings are Good morning, Good afternoon, Good evening. These expressions can also be used when leaving people.'—MICHAEL SWAN

'On parting during the evening, people usually say Good night.'—F T WOOD

(c) 'The part of the day between about 6 pm and bedtime' को evening माना जाता है।

(iv) Good night (= शुभ रात्रि)

(a) जब रात में कोई घर जा रहा हो या सोने जा रहा हो तब वह Good night कहता है। जैसे :

Rahul: Good night, auntie.

(b) शाम में या रात में कोई किसी से विदा ले रहा हो तब वह Good night कहता है। जैसे :

I have to go now. Good night.
Good night, Mr Sinha, We will meet you tomorrow.

(c) 'Dark hours between sunset and sunrise' को night माना जाता है।

(v) Good day (= शुभ दिन)

(a) जब दिन में, खासकर सुबह या दोपहर में, कोई किसी से मिले या विदा ले तब हम Good day कहते हैं। जैसे :

Have a good day?
He said, "Good day to you."

(b) Good day को 'old-fashioned expression' माना जाता है। इसके बदले हम आजकल Hello या Goodbye का प्रयोग करते हैं।

(vi) Hello (= हेलो), Hi (= हाय)

(a) जब हम समान उम्र के परिचित व्यक्ति से मिलते हैं, तब Hello या Hi कहते हैं। किंतु इसका प्रयोग अपने से superior या unknown व्यक्ति के साथ नहीं करते। जैसे :

Rajeev: Hello, Mukul.
Mukul: Hello, Rajeev.

(b) फोन से बात करने के समय हम Hello का प्रयोग करते हैं। (Hello is also used in answering the phone) जैसे :

Hello, is Mr Sinha there?
Hello, who is speaking, please?
Hello, may I speak to the Principal, please?

(c) Hello तथा Hi का प्रयोग आश्चर्य या उत्सुकता व्यक्त करने के लिए भी होता है। जैसे :

Hello/Hi/,what's going on there?

(B) Parting (प्रस्थान, विदा)

(i) Goodbye (= विदाई के समय का नमस्कार)

(a) जब हम किसी से विदा लेते हैं तब हम Goodbye कहते हैं। जैसे :

Goodbye, John. See you tomorrow.

Goodbye is used between people on familiar terms when they are parting from each other: e.g., a man to his family or vice versa, as he leaves home to go to work; close friends or relatives after a visit, or after an outing together; one person seeing another off on a journey.—FT WOOD.

(b) Goodbye को hyphen के साथ या hyphen के बिना भी लिखा जाता है। जैसे :

Good-bye, Goodbye.

(ii) Bye-bye (=विदा, नमस्ते)

(a) अकसर बच्चों द्वारा इसका प्रयोग विदा होने के समय होता है। जैसे :

Bye-bye, Mukul.

(iii) Bye (= विदा, नमस्ते)

(a) Bye और Bye-bye, Goodbye कहने के अनौपचारिक तरीके हैं। जैसे :

Bye, Rahul

(iv) See you (= जल्दी मिलेंगे)

(a) यह Goodbye कहने का एक तरीका है जिससे हम उस व्यक्ति से पुनः जल्दी ही मिलने की संभावना व्यक्त करते हैं। जैसे :

See you shortly.

(C) Cheers के प्रयोग

(i) इसे लोग शराब या कोई अन्य मदिरा पीने के पहले एक-दूसरे को कहते हैं। जैसे :

Cheers! Let us celebrate the success.

(ii) इसका प्रयोग किसी टीम या खिलाड़ी का उत्साह बढ़ाने के लिए जोर से बोलकर किया जाता है। जैसे : Three *cheers* for Mohan Bagan!

(D) How are you? और How do you do? के प्रयोग

(i) **How are you?** का प्रयोग किसी व्यक्ति के health के विषय में जानने के लिए किया जाता है। 'How are you?' के उत्तर में प्राय: Very well, thank you या Fine, thank you या Very well/Fine, thanks कहा जाता है।

'How are you?' का उत्तर देने के बाद हम अकसर पूछते हैं—(And) how are you? या And you? या What about you?

(ii) **How do you do?** (आप कैसे हैं?) जब हमारा परिचय (introduction) किसी अनजान व्यक्ति के साथ होता है तब हम इसका प्रयोग करते हैं तथा इसके उत्तर में सामान्यत: How do you do? ही कहा जाता है।

2. The Courtesy Words *Please* and *Thank You* (Please तथा Thank you के प्रयोग)

(A) Thanks (धन्यवाद)

(i) लोगों को धन्यवाद देने के सामान्य तरीके इस प्रकार हैं : *Thanks* (धन्यवाद), *Thank you* (आपको धन्यवाद), *Thank you very much* (आपको बहुत-बहुत धन्यवाद), *Thanks a lot* (बहुत धन्यवाद), *Many thanks* (बहुत धन्यवाद), *Thank you, sir* (धन्यवाद महाशय)।

Note: *Thank you very much* is felt to be stronger than the plain *thank you.*

(ii) जब हमें कोई thanks दे तब उत्तर में हम कह सकते हैं :

Not at all. You are welcome. That's all right.

किंतु दुकान में जब हम कोई सामान खरीदते हैं तब दुकानदान को Thank you कहते हैं, तथा उसी तरह दुकानदार को जब पैसे मिल जाता है तब वह भी उसके उत्तर में Thank you ही कहता है।

(iii) जब कभी हम बिना request किए भी कोई चीज स्वीकार करते हैं तब एक जाने-माने formula की तरह thank you का प्रयोग किया जाता है। जैसे—जब कोई दुकानदार हमें खुदरा पैसा (change) लौटाता है, उसे हम thank you कहते हैं।

(iv) जब कोई हमें favour या kindness दिखाता है तब हम उस व्यक्ति की प्रशंसा करने के लिए लिखने या बोलने में thank you का प्रयोग करते हैं। जैसे :

Thank you for granting me two days' leave.

Thank you for giving us such an enjoyable holiday.

(v) Request (आग्रह) को और polite बनाने के लिए please का प्रयोग वाक्य के अंत में किया जाता है तथा जब आग्रह स्वीकार कर लिया जाता है तब कृतज्ञता (gratitude) व्यक्त करने के लिए thank you कहा जाता है। जैसे :

Would you pass me the newspaper, *please?* (*The newspaper is passed.*)

Thank you.

(vi) I thank you के बदले अकसर प्रयुक्त होनेवाला formula है Thank you. Thank you से स्वीकारात्मक भाव व्यक्त होता है और इसका अर्थ होता है— 'Yes, please'. Thank you से affirmative तथा negative दोनों भाव व्यक्त होते हैं।

Affirmative भाव व्यक्त करने के लिए Yes, thank you कहते हैं, किंतु negative भाव व्यक्त करने के लिए No, thank you कहते हैं जैसे—

Is your tea sweet enough?

Yes, *thank you.*

Would you like a cup of tea?

No, *thank you.* I have just had one.

(B) Please (= कृपया)

(i) बोलने में please का प्रयोग प्राय: वाक्य के अंत में किया जाता है, किंतु लिखने में या public notices में please का प्रयोग वाक्य के शुरू में किया जाता है तब जब request को imperative sentence में व्यक्त किया जाता है। जैसे—

Please close the door. *Please* open the window.

Please don't do that. *Please* be quiet.

Note: In speech, *please* is usually added at the end of a request. In writing and in public notices it is placed at the beginning if the request takes the form of an imperative. —FT WOOD: A REMEDIAL ENGLISH GRAMMAR FOR FOREIGN STUDENTS

Please का प्रयोग वाक्य के अंत में भी किया जाता है। जैसे—

A cup of tea, *please.* Two coffees, *please.*

(ii) अगर request की अभिव्यक्ति question form में हो तो please का प्रयोग प्राय: वाक्य के बीच में होता है। जैसे—

Will you *please* stop making a noise?

Will you *please* refrain from smoking?

Would you *please* pass the salt?

(iii) किसी प्रश्न को आग्रह में बदलने के लिए please का प्रयोग किया जाता है (used for turning a question into a request) जैसे—

Can you go now, *please*?
Can you go now? (=Is it possible?)
Will you pass the sugar, *please*?

(iv) कभी-कभी ध्यान खींचने के लिए आग्रह को और जोरदार बनाने के लिए please का प्रयोग किया जाता है (used to give force to or make polite a request for attention). जैसे—

Please, sir, I don't understand.

(v) किसी enquiry या invitation के स्वीकारात्मक उत्तर में Yes, please का प्रयोग किया जाता है। Yes, please से 'Yes, I accept and am grateful' का भाव व्यक्त होता है। जैसे—

Would you like a cup of coffee?
Yes, please.
Will you have another cup of tea?
Yes, please.

3. Apologies and Regrets
(क्षमा याचना तथा खेद प्रगट करने के तरीके)

(A) क्षमा याचना (apologies) हम कई तरह से व्यक्त करते हैं :

Excuse me, Sorry, I'm sorry, I am extremely sorry, Forgive me, Pardon me, I beg your pardon

(i) Excuse me (= क्षमा करें)

(a) अपने छोटे-मोटे impolite behaviour (अभद्र व्यवहार) जैसे छींकना, किसी के सामने कुछ ढकेलना आदि के लिए जब हम क्षमा माँगते हैं तब Excuse me कहते हैं।

(b) किसी से कुछ पूछने के लिए या टोकने के लिए Excuse me का प्रयोग किया जाता है। ज़ैसे :

Excuse me, could you tell me the way to the airport?
Excuse me, but I dont't think that statement is quite true.

(c) Excuse me के उत्तर में It's OK या That's OK कहा जाता है।

(ii) Sorry (= दु:खी)

(a) किसी चीज के लिए अफसोस, दु:ख या खेद प्रकट करने के लिए Sorry का प्रयोग होता है। जैसे :

Oh, sorry, did (I) step on your foot?

(b) Sorry के उत्तर में प्राय: That is all right या It's all right कहा जाता है।

(iii) I am sorry/I'm extremely sorry/Forgive me

(a) बड़ी गलती के लिए दु:ख प्रकट करने के लिए I am sorry या I'm sorry का प्रयोग होता है। जैसे—किसी के कपड़े पर चाय या कॉफी छलक जाने पर I am sorry कहते हैं।

(Oh) *I'm sorry.* { Are you all right? / I didn'tsee you sitting there.

I'm sorry I was unable to come to the meeting.

(b) I am extremely sorry .... जब हमें कुछ लंबे शब्दों में क्षमा माँगना होता है, तब हम कहते हैं :

I'm extremely sorry { *for forgetting to send that letter.* / *about that letter.*

Will you forgive me/excuse me if I have to leave early?

I hope you will *forgive me/excuse me* if I have to leave early.

(c) क्षमा याचना का उत्तर हम प्राय: दो तरह से देते हैं :

That's all right. Please don't worry.

(iv) Pardon me/I beg your pardon

(a) किसी अनिष्ट या दुर्घटना (mishap) जैसे—अनजाने में किसी के पैर को कुचल देना आदि के लिए जब हम क्षमा माँगते हैं तब हम Pardon me/I beg your pardon कहते हैं।

(b) We say *Pardon me* or *I beg your pardon*, politely, disagreeing with someone. जैसे : *Pardon me*, but I think in fact it starts tomorrow, not today.

(c) Pardon me/I beg your pardon के उत्तर में Don't worry/It's all right कहा जाता है।

(4) Good wishes, Congratulations, Condolences
(शुभ कामनाएँ, बधाइयाँ तथा शोक प्रकट करने की तरीके)

(A) (i) Good wishes—किसी के लिए good wishes (शुभ कामनाएँ) हम इस प्रकार व्यक्त करते हैं :

Good luck!
Best wishes for your vacation/holiday.
Have a good time at the theatre.
I wish you every success in your new career.

(ii) Good wishes sent to a third person—जब हम किसी अन्य व्यक्ति को शुभ कामना भेजते हैं तब हम कहते हैं :

Please give my best wishes to Mohan.
Please remember me to your father.
Please give my kindest regards to your wife.
Give my love to the children.
Say Hello to Ramu.

(iii) Seasonal greetings—

Merry Christmas.	Happy New Year.
Happy birthday (to you).	Many happy returns (of your birthday).
Happy Diwali.	Happy Id.

(B) Congratulations (बधाइयाँ) : किसी की सफलता, नौकरी, शादी आदि पर हम बधाइयाँ इस प्रकार देते हैं :

Well done (किसी की सफलता पर)

Congratulations on your engagement.
I was delighted to hear about...
May we congratulate you on your recent appointment?

(C) Condolences (शोक, संवेदनाएँ)—किसी दु:खांत घटना पर हम शोक या संवेदना इस प्रकार व्यक्त करते हैं :

Please accept my deepest sympathy on the death of your father.
I was extremely sorry to hear....

(D) (i) Offers (प्रस्ताव)—किसी व्यक्ति को किसी चीज के लिए हम इस प्रकार offer दे सकते हैं

offer (प्रस्ताव)	*acceptance* (स्वीकार)	*refusal* (इनकार)
Shall I get you a chair?	Yes, please.	No, thank you.
Can I open the door for you?	Yes, please.	No, thank you.

(ii) जब हम किसी offer को अधिक विनम्र ढंग से स्वीकार करते हैं, तब हम कहते हैं :

Yes, please. That's very kind of you.
Yes, thank you. I would love some more.

जब हम अधिक विनम्र ढंग से किसी offer को अस्वीकार करते हैं तब उसके संबंध में **refusal** का explanation भी देते हैं :

Shall I get you a chair?
No, thank you very much. I am just leaving.
Can I open the door for you?
No, please don't bother. I can manage, thank you.

5. Advice, Suggestions and Invitations (सलाह, सुझाव तथा निमंत्रण देने के तरीके)

(i) Advice—किसी व्यक्ति को हम इस प्रकार सलाह (advice) दे सकते हैं :

You ought to read this book.
You should stay in bed.
You would better take your medicine.
I would advise you to see a doctor.
If I were you, I would sell this car.

(ii) Suggestions—किसी व्यक्ति को हम इस प्रकार सुझाव (suggestions) दे सकते हैं :

I suggest we take the night train.
You might have a look at this book.
You can read this chapter before tomorrow.
Why don't you call on me tomorrow?
I suggest we go to bed.
Shall we listen to some music?
Let us enjoy ourselves.
Let us not waste time.
Why don't we have a party?
What about a game of football?
What about (having) a drink?

(iii) Invitations—निमंत्रण कई तरीके से दिया जा सकता है :

Come in and sit down.
Would you like to come with me?
May I invite you to dinner next Sunday?
Would you like to spend a week with us?

6. Warnings, Promises, Threats and Introductions (चेतावनी देने, वादा करने, धमकी तथा परिचय देने के तरीके)

(i) Warnings—किसी को चेतावनी (warning) हम इस प्रकार देते हैं

Mind! Look out!
Be careful (of your clothes). I warn you it's going to rain.
If you are not careful, that cloth will catch fire.

(ii) Promises—किसी व्यक्ति को हम वादा (promise) इस प्रकार करते हैं :

I will let you know tomorrow. I promise (you) I will be quick.
You won't lose money, I promise. You shall have the money tomorrow.

(iii) Threats—किसी को हम धमकी (threat) इस प्रकार देते हैं :

You dare touch me! I will report if you do that.
Don't you dare tell lies. Do that, and I'll tell your father.
Stop eating those sweets, or I'll take them away.

(iv) Introductions—किसी व्यक्ति को हम दूसरे व्यक्ति से परिचय (introduction) इस प्रकार कराते हैं :

May I introduce you to Mr Sinha? This is Mr Bose.
Meet my friend. I don't think you've met our neighbour, Mr Sen?

7. Dates and the Time (तिथि और समय लिखने और पढ़ने के तरीके)

(A) Dates—तिथि हम कई तरीके से लिखते हैं: 27 June, June 27, or June 27th, किंतु प्रथम तरीका को ही अधिक लोग पसंद करते हैं। इन तिथियों को इस प्रकार पढ़ा जाता है :

Written	*Read* (पढ़ा जाता है)
27 June	the twenty-seventh of June
June 27	June twenty-seven (or, *the twenty-seventh*)
June 27th	June the twenty-seventh
27th June	the twenty-seventh of June

कभी-कभी हम date इस प्रकार लिखते हैं : 7/6/88 इस तरह date लिखने में एक कठिनाई है। इस क्रम को Britain में day-month-year समझा जाएगा जब America में month-day-year, अर्थात 7/6/88 को Britain में June 7th, 1988 समझा जाएगा जबकि America में इसे July 6th, 1988 माना जाएगा। अतः, आप इस प्रकार date लिखना खासकर विदेशों में avoid करें।

(B) Years—साल के लिखने और पढ़ने के सही ढंग को सीख लें। 1700 को seventeen hundred पढ़ा जाता है, न कि one thousand, seven hundred.

1703 को seventeen hundred and three पढ़ा जाता है, न कि seventeen three.

कुछ और उदाहरण देखें :

Written	*Read* (पढ़ा जाता है)	*Written*	*Read* (पढ़ा जाता है)
1800	eighteen hundred	1512	fifteen twelve
1900	nineteen hundred	1662	sixteen sixty-two
1907	nineteen hundred and seven	1987	nineteen eighty-seven
1604	sixteen hundred and four		

(C) The Time—समय (time) बताने के दो तरीके हैं :

(a) **By figures**—Timetables तथा official notices में समय अंक (figures) में बताया जाता है। जैसे :

6.05, 5.30, 8.35, 6.23, 6.42, 6.57

(b) **The conversational method**—बातचीत (conversation) में शब्द का प्रयोग किया जाता है। जैसे :

half past ten, five past two, ten to three. In this method the minutes upto thirty are expressed in relation to the preceeding hour, as so many *past* that hour; those from thirty onwards are related to the next hour, and expressed as so many minutes *to* that hour (i.e., short of it). Thus in ordinary speech 1.50 would be *ten minutes to two*, and 5.43 *seventeen minutes to six*.—F. T. Wood

(i) **Quarter past, quarter to**—

घंटा (hour) के बाद अगर पंद्रह मिनट बीतता है तो quarter past कहते हैं, तीस मिनट बीतता है तो half past कहते हैं अगर पैंतालीस मिनट बीतता है तो अगले घंटा के साथ लगाकर *quarter* to (the next hour) कहते हैं। जैसे: *quarter past* five, *half past* six, *quarter to* ten

(ii) **Eleven five, six ten**—पाँच से विभाजित होनेवाले अंक जैसे five, ten, twenty, twenty-five आदि के साथ minutes शब्द का प्रयोग प्राय: नहीं किया जाता।

जैसे : 8.05=five past eight; 9.55=five to ten. किंतु अन्य figures के साथ minutes शब्द का प्रयोग किया जाता है। जैसे 8.11=eleven minutes past eight.

(iii) **O'clock**—Exact hour के साथ o'clock (=of the clock) का प्रयोग किया जाता है। जैसे :

nine o'clock, six o'clock, two o'clock.

किंतु जब hour के पहले minutes रहे तब o'clock का प्रयोग नहीं किया जाता। जैसे :

five past eleven (correct)

five past eleven o'clock (incorrect)

(iv) **Midnight**—Hour को सूचित करने के लिए midnight का प्रयोग किया जा सकता है। जैसे :

We did not get home until midnight.

किंतु ऐसे अर्थ में noon शब्द का प्रयोग नहीं किया जाता। जैसे :

I will meet you at twelve o'clock (correct)

I will meet you at noon. (incorrect)

(v) **A.M. and P.M.—**

(a) बारह बजे रात से लेकर बारह बजे दिन के समय को a. m. द्वारा सूचित किया जाता है। A.M. शब्द Latin words *ante meridiem=before midday* का लघु रूप है।

(b) फिर बारह बजे दिन से लेकर बारह बजे-रात तक के समय को p.m. द्वारा सूचित किया जाता है। P.M. शब्द *post meridiem=after midday* का लघु रूप है।

किंतु Spoken English में a.m. तथा p.m. नहीं बोला जाता। उसके बदले part of the day (morning, evening, night) का प्रयोग करते हैं। जैसे :

half past ten in the morning, half past ten at night, three o'clock in the afternoon. Midnight के बदले अकसर *twelve o'clock at night* बोला जाता है।

अब आप इस Table को ध्यान से देखें कि समय को अंकों में लिखने में उसे साधारणत: या बातचीत में कैसे पढ़ा जाता है :

Figures	*Read* (पढ़ा जाता है)	*Conversational Form* (बातचीत में)
11.0	eleven o'clock	eleven o'clock
11.03	eleven three	three minutes past eleven
11.05	eleven five	five (minutes) past eleven
11.15	eleven fifteen	quarter past eleven
11.25	eleven twenty-five	twenty-five (minutes) past eleven
11.30	eleven thirty	half past eleven
11.35	eleven thirty-five	twenty-five (minutes) to twelve
11.40	eleven forty	twenty (minutes) to twelve
11.45	eleven forty-five	quarter to twelve
11.55	eleven fifty-five	five (minutes) to twelve
11.57	eleven fifty-seven	three minutes to twelve
12.0	twelve o'clock	twelve o'clock

8. Days and Months

The days of the week	The month of the year	
Sunday (Sun.)	January (Jan.)	August (Aug.)
Monday (Mon.)	February (Feb.)	September (Sept.)
Tuesday (Tues.)	March (Mar.)	October (Oct.)
Wednesday (Wed.)	April (Apr.)	November (Nov.)
Thursday (Thurs.)	May	December (Dec.)
Friday (Fri.)	June	
Saturday (Sat.)	July	

Note: (i) कुछ महीनों के नाम जैसे May, June और July का short form नहीं होता है।

(ii) दिन और महीने का नाम हमेशा capital letters से शुरू होता है।

9. Telephone Numbers
(टेलिफोन नंबर पढ़ने के तरीके)

फोन के नंबर में प्रत्येक अंक को अलग-अलग बोला जाता है; zero (शून्य) को O (ओ) कहा जाता है।

307-4922 three o seven-four nine double two (किंतु USA में double two के बदले two two कहा जाता है।

52816 five two eight one six

Britain में 6622 को double six double two कहा जाता है; USA में six six two two कहा जाता है।

10. Numerals
(संख्या शब्द)

किसी भी संख्या को हम दो तरह से लिखते हैं :

(i) Cardinal number (ii) Ordinal number (any of the numbers 1, 2, 3, etc., that show quantity rather than number)

1 *one*	11 *eleven*	21 *twenty-one*	31 *thirty-one, etc.*
2 *two*	12 *twelve*	22 *twenty-two*	40 *forty*
3 *three*	13 *thirteen*	23 *twenty-three*	50 *fifty*
4 *four*	14 *fourteen*	24 *twenty-four*	60 *sixty*
5 *five*	15 *fifteen*	25 *twenty-five*	70 *seventy*
6 *six*	16 *sixteen*	26 *twenty-six*	80 *eighty*
7 *seven*	17 *seventeen*	27 *twenty-seven*	90 *ninety*
8 *eight*	18 *eighteen*	28 *twenty-eight*	100 *a hundred*
9 *nine*	19 *nineteen*	29 *twenty-nine*	1,000 *a thousand*
10 *ten*	20 *twenty*	30 *thirty*	1,000,000 *a million*

300 three hundred

160 a/one hundred and sixty

1,004 a/one thousand and four

6,000 six thousand

(ii) Ordinal numbers (showing position in a set of numbers)

first	*eleventh*	*twenty-first*	*thirty-first, etc.*
second	*twelfth*	*twenty-second*	*fortieth*
third	*thirteenth*	*twenty-third*	*fiftieth*
fourth	*fourteenth*	*twenty-fourth*	*sixtieth*
fifth	*fifteenth*	*twenty-fifth*	*seventieth*
sixth	*sixteenth*	*twenty-sixth*	*eightieth*
seventh	*seventeenth*	*twenty-seventh*	*ninetieth*
eighth	*eighteenth*	*twenty-eighth*	*hundredth*
ninth	*nineteenth*	*twenty-ninth*	*thousandth*
tenth	*twentieth*	*thirtieth*	*millionth*

(iii) जब ordinal numbers को अंकों में लिखा जाता है तब अंतिम दो letters को इसके साथ अवश्य जोड़ा जाता है। जैसे :

first = 1st
second = 2nd
third = 3rd
fourth = 4th

twenty-first = 21st
forty-second = 42nd
sixty-third = 63rd
eightieth = 80th

□ □ □